OXFORD MONOGRAPHS ON
LABOUR LAW

General Editors: Paul Davies,
Keith Ewing, Mark Freedland

THE PERSONAL EMPLOYMENT CONTRACT

1 0 APR 2006

General Editors: Paul Davies, Cassel Professor of Commercial Law at London School of Economics; Keith Ewing, Professor of Public Law at King's College, London; and Mark Freedland, Fellow of St John's College, and Professor of Employment Law in the University of Oxford.

This series is the first new development in the literature dealing with labour law for many years. The series recognizes the arrival not only of a renewed interest in labour law generally, but also the need for a fresh approach to the study of labour law following a decade of momentous change in the UK and Europe. The series is concerned with all aspects of labour law, including traditional subjects of study such as industrial relations law and individual employment law, but it will also include books which examine the law and economics of the labour market and the impact of social security law upon patterns of employment and the employment contract.

Titles already published in this series

The Right to Strike
K. D. EWING

Legislating for Conflict
SIMON AUERBACH

Justice in Dismissal
HUGH COLLINS

Pensions, Employment, and the Law
RICHARD NOBLES

Just Wages for Women
AILEEN MCCOLGAN

Women and the Law
SANDRA FREDMAN

Freedom of Speech and Employment
LUCY VICKERS

International and European Protection of the Right to Strike
TONIA NOVITZ

The Personal Employment Contract

MARK R. FREEDLAND FBA

OXFORD

UNIVERSITY PRESS

Preface to the Paperback Edition

The decision of Oxford University Press to publish a paperback edition of my work on the Personal Employment Contract, highly welcome to me though it is, nevertheless presents something of a dilemma. It offers the opportunity to make very minor corrections to the original text. The question which poses itself, more than two years after publication of the hardback edition, is whether or how far to attempt to deal with legal developments in the intervening period. The problem is that interim updating of this kind is necessarily superficial and cosmetic, perhaps even apt to create a disharmony between the original text and the updating citations. I am conscious that some predictions made more than two years ago as to precise directions of development have already been subtly if not directly invalidated. I nevertheless prefer to persevere with the original text rather than to engage in minor tinkerings with it. I hope for the opportunity for a full revisiting of this body of material after a further such period of years.

I hope it might be sufficient at this juncture to refer to one or two very significant areas of subsequent development since the book was first published, without attempting a systematic updating either so far as caselaw or legislation is concerned. The discussion of legality and the informal economy at pp 75ff is much affected by the decision of the Court of Appeal in *Vakante v Addey & Stanhope School* [2004] EWCA Civ 1065. The Court of Appeal in *Dacas v Brook Street Bureau (UK) Ltd* [2004] EWCA Civ 217, while very generously referring to my discussion of the organization of employment between employing entities at pp 40ff, nevertheless contrived to make that analysis slightly out-of-date. The discussion at pp 143ff of the employing entity's duty to take reasonable care of the worker's general psychological health and well-being and of the guidelines articulated by the Court of Appeal in *Sutherland v Hatton* [2002] EWCA 76, has been broadly endorsed by the House of Lords in *Barber v Somerset County Council* [2004] UKHL 13. The development of the implied obligation of mutual trust and confidence grows ever more complex and multifarious, and I shall not attempt to summarize its subsequent ramifications here. By way of exception, I remark that my anticipation (at pp 166–7, 344, 362 and 472) that the difficulty in delineation of the boundaries of the limiting doctrine of *Johnson v Unisys* would prove very intractable has been proved valid, and is only reinforced by the decision of the House of Lords in *Eastwood v Magnox Electric plc* [2004] UKHL 35. Finally, the secondary legislation further specifying the statutory dispute resolution provisions, which was anticipated at pp 344–5, was duly enacted in 2004 in the shape of the Employment Act 2002 (Dispute Resolution) Regulations 2004' SI 2004/752, which came into force on 1 October 2004.

Preface

The present work is an almost completely rewritten version of my book on the Contract of Employment which was published in 1976. Two years ago I embarked upon the writing of what was to be a very belated second edition of that book. Quite early on in that process I realized why I had been slow and reluctant to return to the re-editing of that book in the intervening years, for it quickly became clear that the subject needed to be fundamentally reconsidered. It was not only that there had been a very large number of judicial decisions, a great deal of relevant legislation, and extensive theoretical and practical writing about this subject. It was that this body of law no longer seemed to have even that degree of coherence which it had seemed to possess in 1976. Its scope and function, and the purpose and method of writing an account of it, had become very difficult to identify.

My response to the difficulties which I perceived has been to re-conceive the scope of the subject, and the method and purpose of writing about it. The scope has been enlarged; the work identifies and addresses a larger category of employment contracts, that of the personal employment contract, than the original book did. The method has been changed; instead of seeking to apply the general principles of the law of contract, the work now depicts this as a very autonomous body of contract law, intimately interlinked with a large body of employment legislation. The purpose also has undergone a certain shift; rather than that of pure exposition it has become one of trying to prepare the ground for a restatement of this body of law, in a way which the Introduction to the book will explain.

For these reasons I have come to regard this work as a very different one from the original book which was its starting point, and, for better or for worse, I present it as such. At the same time, I wish to retain and convey the sense that the present work has grown out of the earlier one. I therefore refer to my book on the Contract of Employment as 'the original work' or 'the original version' rather than as the first edition of the present work. The work deals with the law of England and Wales, and seeks to state the law as it stood on 31 December 2002; one or two subsequent developments have been included at proof stage.

In one respect I have found that the writing of this book requires, even more than the original book did, a particular way of addressing the reader which can best be achieved by speaking in the first person plural, the first person singular seeming too obtrusively personal, and the third person seeming too impersonal. In some of the works I have written, I have had the benefit of a co-author to sanction this usage. I hope that writing in this mode when I have no such excuse will not be regarded as regal or prime ministerial in tone.

    For help in the carrying out of the endeavour which this book represents, I have many people and some institutions to thank, though none of them has the slightest responsibility for its shortcomings. I have benefited greatly from discussions, general and particular, with the following friends and colleagues: Sue Ashtiany, Douglas Brodie, Hugh Collins, Colin Crouch, Anne Davies, Paul Davies, Simon Deakin, Keith Ewing, Sandra Fredman, Janet Gaymer, Nicola Lacey, Christopher McCrudden, Silvana Sciarra, Stephen Sedley, David Soskice, Alain Supiot, Katherine van Wezel Stone, Bill Wedderburn, and Simon Whittaker; and I am pleased to be able to add my daughter Emily Forrest to the list of those adept in the field of employment law with whom I have had such discussions. I have also had the advantage of research assistance from the following students or young researchers: James Ballance, Nicola Countouris, Jaswinder Kaur, Sarah-Jane King, Robert Linham, Nadia Motraghi, and Stephen Watterson. St John's College, Oxford and the University of Oxford have provided strong institutional support in various ways, and the editors and staff of Oxford University Press, particularly John Louth and Geraldine Mangley, have shown unlimited patience, faith, and forbearance, as a comparison of the date of this preface and the originally projected date of delivery of the manuscript would show. The greatest debt of all, however, is owed to my wife Geraldine, to whom this book is dedicated, and whose support through the *longueurs* of the writing process has been entirely indispensable.

MRF
Lagrasse, France
31 December 2002

Contents

Table of Cases

Tables of Legislation

STATUTES

STATUTORY INSTRUMENTS

DIRECTIVES AND OTHER INSTRUMENTS OF EC LAW

Abbreviations

AC	Appeal Cases
Ad & El	Adolphus & Ellis' Reports
All ER	All England Law Reports
B & Ald	Barnewall & Adolphus' Reports
BPCas	Brown's Parliamentary Cases
CA	Court of Appeal
Camp	Campbell's Law Reports
CB	Common Bench Reports
Ch.	Chancery
Ch.D.	Chancery Division
CLJ	Cambridge Law Journal
CMLR	Common Market Law Reports
CP	Common Pleas
CS	Court of Session
CSOH	Court of Session Outer House
De G M & G	De Gex, M 'Naghten & Gordon's Reports
DLR	Dominion Law Reports
E & B	Ellis & Blackburn's Reports
EA	Employment Act
EAT	Employment Appeal Tribunal
ECHR	European Convention of Human Rights
ECtHR	European Court of Human Rights
EPCA	Employment Protection (Consolidation) Act
ERA	Employment Rights Act
Esp	Espinasse's Reports
ET	Employment Tribunal
HL	House of Lords
ICR	Industrial Court Reports (1972–74)
	Industrial Cases Reports (1975–)
ILJ	Industrial Law Journal
ILO	International Labour Organisation
IRLR	Industrial Relations Law Reports
IT	Industrial Tribunal
ITR	Industrial Tribunal Reports
JP	Justice of the Peace
KIR	Knight's Industrial Reports
KB	Kings Bench
LQR	Law Quarterly Review
LT	Law Times

MLR	Modern Law Review
NZLR	New Zealand Law Reports
PL	Public Law
PLR	Pensions Law Reports
QB	Queen's Bench
QBD	Queen's Bench Divison
QBDCt	Queen's Bench Divisional Court
SCLR	Scottish Civil Law Reports
TLR	Times Law Reports
TR	Term Reports
TULRECA	Trade Union and Labour Relations (Consolidation) Act
TUPE	Transfer of Undertaking (Protection of Employment)
TURERA	Trade Union Reform and Employment Rights Act
WLR	Weekly Law Reports
WR	Weekly Reporter

Introduction: From the Contract of Employment to the Personal Employment Contract—Expansion and Restatement

The purpose of this Introduction is to describe the scope of the work which follows, and the method of analysis which is used in it. This will involve advocacy as well as description, because the choices which have been made about scope and methodology are controversial, perhaps even provocative. In fact one could say that the description of the scope and method of the work in a sense also sets out its central argument. As has been explained in the Preface, this present work is an almost completely rewritten version of the author's book on the Contract of Employment which was published in 1976. The original work[1] consisted of a detailed examination of the common law of the contract of employment. The Introduction to it began by acknowledging the limits and limitations of that subject.[2]

In this present work, some of those limits—and, it is hoped, some of those limitations—are outstripped, by extending the scope of the work to include other personal work or employment contracts. This ostensibly minor extension is in fact a radical one, which is also associated with a change of methodology, a shift into a mode of analysis which challenges some established orthodoxies, including certain ones which underpinned many of the arguments put forward in the original work. These changes from the original work contribute to a general view about the proper role and task of the law of personal employment contracts which it is the purpose of this Introduction, and indeed of this book as a whole, to develop and explain.

In the Introduction to the original work, there was set out a particular theoretical justification for writing a treatise about the common law of the contract of employment. Twenty-five years later, this writer is of the view

---

[1] Freedland 1976.

[2] The main points were made on page 1: 'This book consists of a detailed examination of the common law of the contract of employment—an area where, despite the marginal impact of many statutory provisions, the legal ground rules are still the judge-made ones. As will appear in later pages, writers on the law and sociology of employment have demonstrated extensively the social irrelevance of this "law of master and servant".'

that it is time to put down some different foundations and to build a rather different structure on the basis of them. Two sets of changes have necessitated this process of redesign. One is a set of changes in the role and functioning of the law of the contract of employment, and the other, at least indirectly linked to the first, is a set of changes in the shape and structure of the labour market. The ensuing paragraphs will seek firstly to recall the original theoretical justification, and secondly to show why those two sets of changes are now seen as requiring its modification.

In the original work, the law of the contract of employment was identified as a body of common law with two sharply distinct functions, both regulatory in nature. The first, a directly regulatory one, was that of constituting the apparatus for the legal enforcement of contracts of employment and the adjudication of disputes arising out of contracts of employment. The second was the more indirect and instrumental function of providing a body of legal theory which was necessary for the working of many other, generally statutory, parts of the system of employment law, which were constructed upon or around the contract of employment.[3]

It was accepted that, at least in the first of those two functions, the law of the contract of employment was largely obsolete, in two senses. It was obsolete in the sense that employers and workers only rarely used the legal enforcement of contracts of employment as a way of securing the adjudication of employment disputes. It was also obsolete in the different sense that, whether as the cause or the effect of the first kind of obsolescence, the law of the contract of employment reflected an outdated and outmoded set of approaches to the employment relationship, and to the role of the legal process *vis-à-vis* the employment relationship, as the then recent writings of Otto Kahn-Freund,[4] Roger Rideout,[5] and Alan Fox[6] had in different ways demonstrated.

All this was seen, in the original work, as casting the gravest doubt on the social utility or social adequacy of the law of the contract of employment, and upon its connectedness to the realities of the contemporary employment relationship. But that was not seen as inimical to the project of writing a treatise about the law of the contract of employment; it was felt that the duality of function of the law of the contract of employment ensured that it would retain a particular kind of practical as well as theoretical importance, which more than justified the enterprise of attempting a logical and coherent exposition of this body of law. It was thought especially important to analyse this body of law in its relationship with the general principles of contract law, and especially also with regard to what happened to contracts of employment after their initial formation, as this post-formation area of the law seemed

---

[3] Freedland 1976 at 1–3.   [4] See Kahn-Freund 1954 at 45.
[5] See Rideout 1966.   [6] See Fox 1974 at 81–90.

rather insufficiently analysed as compared with the law concerning the initial formation of the contract of employment.

If, in the present work, there is presented a rather different rationale for a rather different approach to scope and methodology, much of that change of position is attributable to the way in which employment law itself has evolved in the intervening years. This very complex evolution has a number of different aspects, each with major implications for the law of the contract of employment and indeed for the law of personal work contracts at large. There has been an enormous expansion during that period in the amount of litigation, and therefore of jurisprudence, concerning the contract of employment. This is true in respect both of litigation by way of direct enforcement of the contract of employment, and of litigation in which the law of the contract of employment is indirectly involved as part of the reasoning necessary to the application of some other aspect of the law.

In fact this whole distinction between direct and indirect involvement of the law of the contract of employment in litigation is a diminishing or disappearing one. For employment legislation has continued to interact with the common law of the contract of employment, in the sense both that legislation has invoked that body of common law and has had a major substantive impact upon it. A major example of such legislative impact is to be found, as will be seen in detail later, in the TUPE Regulations,[7] which profoundly modify the common law concerning the effect, upon the contract of employment, of changes in the ownership of the employing enterprise. Most recently, other very important changes have been made by the Fixed-term Employees Regulations[8] and by the provisions of the Employment Act 2002 imposing contractual duties of dispute resolution.[9]

We can also observe in recent years a certain degree of amalgamation of the common law of the contract of employment and statutory employment law in a jurisdictional sense as well as in a substantive sense. A milestone along this road was passed—after surprisingly long years of hesitation[10]— when, in 1994, a limited but nevertheless important jurisdiction to adjudicate upon certain claims for damages for breach of the contract of employment, and for sums due under such contracts upon their termination, was conferred[11] upon industrial tribunals, now restyled as employment tribunals.[12] This measure helped to dispel a perception that the direct enforcement of the

---

[7] SI 1981/1794 (as subsequently amended by the Trade Union Reform and Employment Rights Act 1993, s 33 and by SI 1995/2587).

[8] Fixed-term Employees (Prevention of Less Favourable Treatment) Regulations 2002, SI 2002/2034; see below, 317, 409.

[9] Employment Act 2002, ss 29–30 and Sched 2; see below 344.

[10] Authority for such a measure having first been conferred by the Industrial Relations Act 1971, s 133. The power to confer further jurisdiction is now contained in s 3 of the Employment Tribunals Act 1996.

[11] By the Industrial Tribunals Extension of Jurisdiction (England and Wales) Order (SI 1994/1623).   [12] By s 1 of the Employment Rights (Dispute Resolution) Act 1998.

contract of employment and its indirect development as a tool of interpretation of statutory employment law were quite separate processes occurring, at
first instance at least, in quite distinct judicial fora—the former in courts, the
latter in tribunals.

Indeed, this interaction between the common law of the contract of
employment and employment legislation has progressed so far as to produce significant areas of fusion between the two—a phenomenon which has
long existed, but which is now fairly central to this area of the law. For
example, a worker who claims that there has been an unlawful deduction
from his or her wages under the Wages Act 1986 is invoking what is technically, no doubt, a statutory cause of action, but the scope of which is
determined to quite an extent by the common law. So much is this the case
that the common law itself had to be developed in order to expound the
concept of 'deduction from wages'; and there results from this a body of
law about deduction from wages which should be regarded as truly an
aggregation of common law[13] and statute law. We should understand that
we are now talking about not so much the common law of employment
contracts, as the *common law based* law of employment contracts.

All this serves to alter the nature of the concerns about the obsolescence
of the law of the contract of employment which were expressed in the
Introduction to the original work. Since the time of that original work,
the outpouring of legislative measures affecting the law of employment
contracts, and of judicial decisions expounding it in all its aspects, has been
and continues to be such as to endow it with a considerable sense of vital-
ity and immediacy. There is no longer any sense, as there was in the 1970s,
that it is necessary to dredge up a few ancient cases in order to address
modern issues. On the contrary, those engaged in the expounding of this
part of the law often sink under the burden of analysis of its now huge
normative and technical apparatus.

However, this increase in the legal relevance of the law of the contract of
employment, that is to say its enhanced significance in legislation and
litigation, only served to heighten concern about its obsolescence in
another sense. For, even as the law of the contract of employment became
a matter for daily debate in courts and tribunals, one could doubt whether
its basic ideology, which caused such misgivings to Kahn-Freund, Rideout,
or Fox, had changed fundamentally. Moreover, even if that ideology was
undergoing changes, it might still be difficult for those changes to filter
through a discourse derived from the nineteenth- or early twentieth-
century law of master and servant, still drawing some of its case law, and
quite a lot of its idiom, from issues and disputes concerning valets, cooks

---

[13] For example, on the question of whether and when a failure to make a payment in lieu
of notice constitutes an unlawful deduction from wages, as considered in *Delaney v Staples*
[1992] ICR 483 (HL); see below, 210, 320.

and chambermaids, gardeners and agricultural labourers, millworkers, and black-coated clerks.

These new or renewed concerns were further concentrated by the considerable changes in the structure and functioning of the labour market which occurred, or at least accelerated, from the early 1980s onwards. Those were the changes whereby a greatly increased proportion of the workforce came to be employed in forms of employment, especially those of part-time, temporary, and casual work, which had come to be regarded as marginal ones during the period of the welfare state from 1945 onwards. As the law of the contract of employment was more and more intensely invoked as the foundation of a heightened legal regulation of the employment relationship, so it seemed less and less well adapted to providing categories and concepts which were suitable for the task.[14]

Writing in 1986, Bob Hepple addressed these concerns in an article on 'Restructuring Employment Rights' which must be regarded as one of the most significant contributions to the literature on this subject.[15] He argued most cogently that the whole programme of legislative construction of the positive legal rights of workers would be frustrated if statutory employment rights 'continued to be built on the traditional "cornerstone" of the common law contract of service',[16] and that a different concept of reference was needed as the basis for defining the personal scope of labour legislation, and constructing the design of statutory employment rights. His suggestion was that:

The contract of service should be replaced by a broad definition of an 'employment relationship' between the worker and the undertaking by which he is employed. That relationship would of course be based upon voluntary agreement between the worker and the undertaking to work in return for pay. The insistence on agreement makes it appropriate to describe this as a 'contract' rather than as a 'status', but it would be a contract of a new kind, one that encompassed both the intermittent exchange of work for remuneration and the single continuous contract.[17]

Hepple's arguments for breaking the mould of the contract of employment as the basis for the analysis and construction of rights and obligations between employers and workers, by basing them instead upon a directly relational conception, have great force and attractiveness. In this book, however, a different response is suggested to the problems and shortcomings of the law of the contract of employment as the basic apparatus of legal analysis of the individual employment relationship. Hepple in the passage cited above acknowledges rather reluctantly that the legal employment relationship, as he envisaged it, although broader than the contract of employment, and differently conceived from the contract of employment,

---

[14] Compare Wedderburn and Clark's notion of the 'crisis in fundamental concepts' as applied to the law of the contract of employment in Wedderburn & Clark 1983.
[15] Hepple 1986.   [16] Ibid at 69.   [17] Ibid at 74.

could still be regarded as contractual in nature. This book is written in the conviction that English employment law is deeply, perhaps even irrevocably, committed to a contractual analysis of the individual employment relationship, but that this analysis need not be and should not be confined to the contract of employment as such.

The programme of this work is therefore to conduct an analysis of a chosen category of contracts for personal work or employment which is wider than the category of contracts of employment, and which, we believe, corresponds quite closely to Hepple's notion of the contractual employment relationship. This wider category includes some though not all of the contracts known as contracts for services. It may well include, rather in the way that Hepple's 'contract of a new kind' does, arrangements for personal work or employment which lack the continuity of obligation judged necessary for them to qualify as contracts of employment. We refer to this extended category of contracts as that of the personal employment contract or the personal work contract. That explains the difference in title and core concept as between the present work and the original work on the contract of employment from which this book is derived.

Before, however, embarking upon the programme of analysis of the extended category of personal employment contracts, we feel that it is necessary to do more to establish a sound theoretical basis for this analysis. There is a problem to be addressed about the prescriptiveness of an analysis which takes this extension of category as its starting point. There are various forms in which the doubts about the theoretical integrity of this exercise might be expressed, but the main ways of putting them might be expected to be that this project was too strongly policy driven and prescriptive. That is to say, it might be objected that this work, being derived from a view of personal work relationships as essentially forming a unified family, was going to be an exercise in imposing a unificatory approach on the law of the contract of employment and of the contract for services. This fear might include a suspicion that the present author was likely to be in the business of seeking a 'levelling up' of all personal work contracts, that is to say maintaining that they should all conform to a model of the contract of employment which represented the 'best practice' of employers who accept the value of affording a high degree of social and economic security and protection to their employees.

That suspicion would probably be articulated as a view that it was both inappropriate and ultimately self-defeating to seek to deploy the law of employment contracts to interfere with the workings of the labour market. That proposition might weave together several strands of opinion. One such strand of opinion would be to the effect that to mould all personal employment contracts into this worker-protective shape would fly in the face of the pursuit of efficiency in the use of human resources. Another such strand of opinion would assert that the attempt to do so would rebound upon itself, and ultimately result in a 'levelling down' of contracts of employment to the less worker-protective form of other personal employment contracts. A third such strand of opinion might be the view that the law of personal employment contracts, like any other branch of the law of contracts, should be concerned with giving effect to voluntary agreements which are not unlawful, rather than with engineering them to produce a desired social and economic outcome.

One way to address such doubts is to consider in more detail the regulatory function or functions of the law of personal employment contracts. Hugh Collins, in his recent and highly significant treatise on the law of contract viewed from a regulatory perspective,[18] draws a distinction between two kinds of legal regulation of contracts; one kind of regulation was that of private law, the other was that of welfare regulation. In his view, by the close of the nineteenth century, modern legal systems had evolved a system of regulation of contracts involving both those types of regulation, each with its own separate legal discourse.[19] The role of private law was to provide a code of general principles, seen as fundamental to the legal order, which constituted a pre-political statement of rights and obligations in civil society. The role of welfare regulation, on the other hand, was to pursue specific instrumental purposes, such as those of 'fairness and distributive justice, alleviation of market failures, restrictions on the exercise of private power, and other welfare goals'.[20] Collins' argument goes on to assert that the private law of contract has since undergone a 'productive disintegration', so that it can readily be seen as playing both regulatory roles in particular contractual contexts.[21]

Collins' distinction between these two regulatory roles is very useful with regard to the law of personal employment contracts as we envisage it. Admittedly the specific instrumental regulatory purposes of the law of personal employment contracts cannot always satisfactorily be brought under the heading of 'welfare'. There is nevertheless a real distinction, between general private law regulatory functions and specific instrumental regulatory functions in the legal regulation of personal work contracts. Within the sphere of personal employment contracts, the private law of contract has for a very long time combined both kinds of regulatory function and continues to do so.

It is a sphere of contract law in which specific instrumental regulatory functions have been especially prominent, and this continues to be the case. The mixture and balance between these specific functions changes. In the nineteenth century, maintaining employers' discipline over workers was

---

[18] Hugh Collins, *Regulating Contracts* (Collins 1999).
[19] See Collins 1999 at 7–8; cf 31–52.   [20] Ibid at 7–8.
[21] Ibid, chapters 3–4.

predominant. It has remained important, but is now more mixed with protection of the welfare of workers. We shall see that these specific functions are exercised in many ways, but that the most important way in which they are exercised is by the construction of the implied terms of personal work contracts. Tracing these developments is highly informative about the way that employment law is being created and adapted in the courts—it is one of the best ways of obtaining insights into the jurisprudence of employment law as a whole. It certainly does not introduce a prescriptive element where none existed before.

It might be said that this provides a perfectly good rationale for a study which focuses on the contract law of employment, but that it does not justify extending that study beyond the law of the contract of employment as such. It might be asserted that the richly complicated and interesting interplay of regulatory functions, which has been identified above, occurs precisely within the law of the contract of employment, rather than in the larger sphere of personal work contracts as a whole. The wider screen might be felt to give a distorted image. It is hoped, however, to be able to show, in the course of this work, that this would represent too narrow a way of understanding how the regulatory functions of contract law have evolved in relation to personal work contracts. Quite a lot of the contractual doctrines and constructions which are particularly associated with the law of the contract of employment turn out, when considered with this dimension in mind, not to be necessarily limited to that particular contract type, but to be more generally applicable to personal employment contracts at large, perhaps in modified forms, but nevertheless still recognizably applicable. The regulatory functions of contract law *vis-à-vis* employment relations can be better understood in the context of personal employment contracts at large, than with reference to the contract of employment alone.

The discussion of regulatory functions may help to meet the concerns about the prescriptiveness or lack of objectivity of the analysis upon which this work embarks, but it does not altogether dispel those concerns. The analysis would still be open to the criticism of prescriptiveness if it seemed to impose some or all of the regulatory functions of the law of the contract of employment upon the whole range of personal employment contracts. It has been argued that some such spillover of regulatory functions does, quite authentically, occur; but that might still be perceived to be more of a prescriptive than a descriptive mode of analysis unless some more effective assurance of objectivity can be provided.

In the writing of this work, we have endeavoured to meet that need by an adaptation of method. A method of exposition is adopted which is that of restatement. This method of restatement is developed from the premise that the contractual analysis of the individual employment relationship has serious shortcomings in terms of its clarity, coherence, and ability to serve the regulatory functions of this area of contract law. A further premise is that those shortcomings might best be remedied by analysis of the whole category of personal employment contracts rather than the narrower category of contracts of employment.

However—and this is the crucial further premise upon which the method of restatement is constructed—it does not follow that, merely by extending from the narrower category of the contract of employment to the broader category of the personal employment contract, we can arrive at a clear, coherent, and functionally satisfactory analysis of the contract law of the individual employment relationship. It still must be recognized that, although some gains of clarity, coherence, and functionality may be made by carrying out a doctrinal analysis on a canvas which is broader than the traditional one, the full attainment of clarity, coherence, and functionality still involves important prescriptive or policy choices. Hence the ensuing chapters are envisaged as being a restatement of the existing law which seeks to provide a clear analysis where that is possible, and otherwise to identify ways in which clarity and functionality might be attained by a more prescriptive kind of reformulation, of the kind which could be accomplished only by the appellate courts or by legislation.

Inevitably those two situations shade into each other, and it is often difficult to know how much can be safely asserted as representing the existing law or coming within the interpretative space which the existing law affords. The method of restatement involves a commitment to recognize and identify instances where the analyses which are being put forward exceed those bounds. However, the analytical narrative would be stilted if it constantly insisted on that distinction at every point. So a conclusion is provided at the end of each chapter, which suggests how far reformulations canvassed in the course of the chapter fall within the scope of the existing law, and how far, on the other hand, they would have to be effected by deliberate and authoritative law reform.

It is hoped that sufficient assurance of objectivity will be provided by that method of analysis, and in particular by the way that it is proposed to handle the relationship between contract law as it applies to contracts of employment and as it applies to other personal employment contracts. It will be argued at length in the course of the first chapter that there is no sharp or deep distinction between two truly separate contract types here. Nevertheless, the supposed distinction is deeply embedded in the legislation, case law, and literature of employment law, so much so that an account of the contract law of employment, which purported simply to disregard it, would be likely to be viewed both as seriously over-prescriptive and, moreover, as unconvincing in this respect.

It is not intended to proceed in that way in the course of this work. Instead, it is proposed to indicate when a given doctrine or construction of contract law has been specifically associated with the contract of employment as such, and explicitly to consider how far it might be applicable to other personal work contracts. In the latter regard, care will be taken not to overstate the claim that some of the contract law which has been assumed to be limited to contracts of employment as such may nevertheless hold good for other personal employment contracts. Where that view would be a prescriptive one, requiring real reformulation rather than merely clarification, the method of restatement permits but requires that this is openly acknowledged.

One other aspect of the method of restatement used in this work should be explained. It concerns the connections between the law of personal employment contracts and the statute law, that is to say the parliamentary and governmental legislation, regulating the employment relation. This work is written in the belief that it is both feasible and useful to separate out and analyse a specifically contractual part of employment law. Nevertheless, the statute law of the employment relation has crucial connections into and with the law of personal employment contracts. These connections are of different kinds, and it is important to distinguish between those kinds of connection. Sometimes statutory provisions inform or transform the definition or content or operation of personal employment contracts. The Transfer of Undertakings (Protection of Employment) Regulations[22] provide a particularly good example,[23] but there are many others. The analysis which is conducted in this work treats such provisions as integral to the law of personal employment contracts—we do not wish or attempt to present the law of personal employment contracts as a topic of common law alone.

In many instances, however, statutory provisions regulating the employment relation have a different kind of connection with the law of personal employment contracts, in that they draw upon its definitions and conceptions in the formulations of their own normative content. Those formulations may refer unequivocally to the law of personal employment contracts, for example where the workers to whom statutory provisions are applied are defined as those working under contracts of employment. Sometimes the reference to the law of personal employment contracts is an equivocal one, and it becomes a difficult matter of interpretation and policy whether and how far to regard the statutory formulations as contractually based. That has been a major issue, for example, in the construction of the statutory conceptions of dismissal and of redundancy in the law of redundancy payments and of unfair dismissal.[24]

Where statutory formulations are construed as referring directly to the law of personal employment contracts, we can think of them as *statutory*

---

[22] SI 1981/1794 as subsequently amended.   [23] See below, 505–514.

[24] The leading account of this problem is provided by Steven Anderman's article on 'The Interpretation of Protective Employment Statutes and Contracts of Employment' (Anderman 2000).

contractual formulae. The discussion of them is important to our analysis of the law of personal employment contracts, not least because the law of personal employment contracts has itself developed partly through the construction of statutory contractual formulae. For example, the implied contractual obligation of trust and confidence has been developed largely in the course of interpretation of the statutory contractual formula of constructive dismissal.[25] Moreover, the use and testing of statutory contractual formulae indicates where contractual conceptions provide a workable technical apparatus for the statutory regulation of the employment relation.[26]

There is a further kind of connection between the statute law of the employment relation and the law of personal employment contracts, which is a looser one but still highly significant. The statute law of the employment relation contains a number of formulations which have contractual conceptions as their starting point but go beyond them or are different from them. Again, as with statutory contractual formulae, it may sometimes be very clear that a statutory formulation is of this kind, or it may be a difficult matter to decide whether this is the case or not. Thus, there is a statutory formulation of *continuity of employment* which takes a contractual conception as its starting point but clearly goes beyond it. The statutory formulation is contained in sections 210–218 of the Employment Rights Act 1996. On the other hand, as indicated above, it was difficult to decide whether the statutory formulation of conception of redundancy was intended to be a strictly contractual one, but it has been held to be a conception which is only partly contractual in character.[27]

There are many such statutory formulations, which have contractual starting points but go beyond them or are different from them. Sometimes they amount to the recognition of an employment relationship which is not a strictly contractual one. This is true, for example, of the statutory formulation of continuity of employment; it includes periods of time when no personal employment contract subsists but when a recognizable employment relationship is deemed to exist.[28] These statutory formulations can usefully be grouped together as *statutory variant formulae* or *statutory para-contractual formulae.* They create a statutory penumbra around the law of the personal employment contract. They are important in the analysis of the law of personal employment contracts but their importance is rather different from that of statutory contractual formulae. They demonstrate the shortcomings of contractual formulations and the perceived need to get away from contractual formulations, and sometimes they suggest ways in which the contractual formulations might themselves be differently constructed.

---

[25] See below, 154 et seq.   [26] Compare Anderman 2000.
[27] Compare Anderman 2000 at 227 et seq, and below at 241.   [28] See below, 98.

This brings us back to the method of restatement. We have argued that statutory contractual formulations and statutory para-contractual formulations are both in different ways important to our analysis of the law of personal employment contracts. But they are not absolutely integral to that analysis, and the analysis is apt to become cloudy if it constantly moves back and forth between analysis of the law of personal employment contracts as such, and discussion of statutory contractual and para-contractual formulae. The method of restatement allows us to refer to those formulae where it is helpful to the main analysis, without doing so comprehensively. So we shall discuss those formulae when it assists the clarification or reformulation of the law of personal employment contracts to do so.

This Introduction concludes by indicating why it has been treated as so important to establish a rationale for an extensive analysis of the private law or common law based law of personal work contracts. For this is at once to maintain a focus upon a body of basically judge-made law at a time when legislation, whether of the UK Parliament or of the European Union, seems overwhelmingly significant in employment law, and at the same time to presume to redraw the traditional boundaries of that body of law.

The hope is that, by so doing, it may be possible to show how the foundational jurisprudence of British employment law is capable of extending itself and adapting itself so that it is in harmony with the realities of the contemporary world of work, and can command respect as a coherent basis for the regulation of that world of work. If this involves abandoning some existing stereotypes, that need not result in, on the one hand, trying to pretend that the security of the welfare state model of employment could be extended to all types of workers in the modern labour market, nor, on the other hand, in having to accept that all workers are tending towards the state of being self-employed.

An exposition which accomplished those gains and avoided those pitfalls might have succeeded in identifying a body of employment jurisprudence with some important virtues. It might provide a basis for thinking, in a holistic way which was free of accumulated preconceptions, about the legal regulation of the personal work relationships of all sorts of workers—managers as well as manual workers, professional workers as well as those in commerce and industry, private sector workers as well as civil servants, casual and freelance workers as well as established staff. In this work it is hoped by means of the expansion of the area of contract law under consideration, and by the use of the method of restatement, to indicate some ways in which progress might be made in that direction. In the Conclusion we shall attempt an assessment of how far it has seemed possible to achieve this aim, and what remains to be done for the realization of the project upon which this work embarks.

1

Definition and Personal Structure

INTRODUCTION

Our analysis of the law of personal employment contracts begins with one of its most difficult parts; it is the part in which we seek to define the general concept of the personal employment contract and explain how the parties to it are identified and understood in the contract law of the employment relationship. The reason for this difficulty is that employment law has become extremely incoherent in the way that it defines the contracts which come within its scope, and even more so in the way in which it distinguishes between them. There is then a further set of difficulties in deciding whether and when employment relationships fall within any of the resulting contractual categories, and how the parties to each of those types of contracts are conceived of and defined.

In the first section of this chapter, we seek to explain how those difficulties have come about. We show how employment law came to be organized around the category of the contract of employment, to which a false unity was attributed. We explain that the contract of employment came to be systematically contrasted with another contract type, that of the contract for services, and we argue that this distinction has proved to be an equally false or unsatisfactory one. Employment law has expanded into that second category, but to an extent which is itself ill-defined and uncertain. We suggest that as a result it has become extremely difficult to decide whether certain employment relationships, or sets of arrangement for employment, fall into any of those contractual categories and if so which of them. This applies particularly to intermittent and to triangular employment relationships, and above all to those which are both intermittent and triangular, as an increasing number of employment relationships are in the contemporary labour market.

In the second section, we seek to suggest a set of definitions and distinctions which might provide a greater clarity and coherence in this foundational aspect of the law of employment contracts. In view of the depth of the difficulties which have been identified in the first section, this has to be an analysis which is partly prescriptive; it has to move from asserting what the law is towards a more controversial and less reliably objective statement of how it should be viewed, and ultimately how it would have to be authoritatively reformed in order to attain a coherent functional state. Using the broad notion of restatement which was articulated in the Introduction to this work, we seek to establish and identify the category of the personal employment contract. We recognize, not without some misgivings, that this has to be regarded as divisible into two broad types of contract, the contract of employment and the semi-dependent worker's contract, if our whole system of analysis is to be serviceable within the larger framework of contemporary employment law; but we begin to show that there are various types of work relationship which cut across that distinction in complex ways.

In the third section, we begin to demonstrate the gains in clarity of analysis which we argue are to be obtained by operating within the expanded category of personal employment contracts rather than within the traditional and narrower category which has dominated employment law, that of the contract of employment. Within that expanded frame, we seek to identify the way in which the law conceptualizes the parties to the personal employment contract in general, the worker and the employer. In the case of the worker, we have, again not without misgivings, to recognize that there are two subcategories corresponding to the contract of employment and the semi-dependent worker's contract, therefore respectively the employee and the semi-dependent worker. The concept of the employer is common to both of those subcategories, but we argue for a re-conceiving of the idea of the contractual employer and a restyling of it as the employing party or employing entity.

SECTION 1: THE PROBLEMS OF DEFINITION DISTINCTION AND INCLUSION IN THE LAW OF EMPLOYMENT CONTRACTS

In this section, we depict the basic theoretical and practical difficulties which result from the way in which the analysis of employment contracts has been almost exclusively concentrated upon a single contract type, the contract of employment, which is conceived of as a unitary or uniform type and as such is systematically contrasted with another supposedly unitary type, the contract for services. In the first subsection it is argued that this supposed unity of the contract of employment is an essentially false one, and in the second subsection it is further argued that the supposed systematic dichotomy between those two contract types is also a false one. In a third subsection we go on to argue that those practical and analytical problems have been aggravated by the use of further contractual categories in recent employment legislation, those of the contracts of 'employed persons', and the contracts of 'workers'.

A. THE FALSE UNITY OF THE LAW OF THE CONTRACT
   OF EMPLOYMENT

In the introduction to this chapter, we pointed to the existence of an acute set of problems in the way in which employment law defines the contracts which come within its scope, and in the way in which it distinguishes between them. The starting point for understanding that set of problems can be described in a phrase as the false unity of the contract of employment. That is to say, the law of employment contracts has come to embody a very strong central unifying proposition or implicit assumption. This is that the personal employment relationship can and should be understood in legal terms as a particular contract type, namely the contract of employment. To be more precise, the assumption has been that the *dependent* employment relationship should be understood in that way, for this unitary and unifying concept specifically contrasts itself with and excludes contracts for *independent* employment, or 'self-employment'. The latter contracts are also identified as a single contract type, that of the contract for services; and contracts of that type have generally been regarded as outside the scope and concerns of employment law, though as we shall see that view has begun to alter in a way which is reflected in recent employment legislation.

It has long been apparent to the theorists of labour law that there is a considerable artificiality in this imposition of the category of the contract of employment upon dependent employment relationships. Otto Kahn-Freund and Alan Fox, in the writings to which we referred earlier,[1] drew attention to the way in which this contractual analysis represented, for most workers, the disguising of a servile status in the form of an agreement between parties treated, as contract law does, as if there was a general equality of bargaining power between them. It is not, however, this kind of artificiality which is our present concern. In fact, the argument which will be pursued here is quite tangential to that of Kahn-Freund and Fox, and leads to conclusions with which they would by no means necessarily agree.

Some important steps in this argument are suggested by an extremely interesting analysis of the evolution of the law of the contract of employment in the first half of the twentieth century which has been carried out by Simon Deakin.[2] This highly perceptive exercise in employment law history begins, building on arguments earlier advanced by Kenneth Foster,[3] by showing that the re-conceptualizing of the master and servant relationship as the contract of employment was a product more of twentieth-century welfare legislation than of nineteenth-century common law jurisprudence as Kahn-Freund and Fox had suggested. Deakin, following on from Foster, shows how labour law maintained, right into the twentieth century, a sharp distinction between, on the one hand, the employment

---

[1] See above, 2.   [2] Deakin 1998.
[3] See Deakin 1998, footnote 8 and text at footnote 8.

relationship of higher status non-manual workers—which was, on the whole, viewed in contractual terms—and, on the other hand, the relationship of master and servant, or, as it tended to be styled after 1875,[4] of employer and workman, which was identified in terms of 'service' but not especially or typically in terms of the *contract* of service.

Deakin's argument goes on from this to show that, when in the early twentieth century the Workmen's Compensation legislation and National Insurance legislation did use the notion of the *contract of service* to define the scope of these new forms of social protection for workers, that concept was still very closely associated with the low status, primarily manual, work relationship of 'service', and that, when the courts used the 'control' test to identify the scope of the contract of service, the aim and effect of their so doing was to reinforce the continuing distinction between that group of workers and the higher status non-manual workers who were regarded as outside the purview of this social legislation. It was only in 1946, Deakin points out, that post-war social legislation adopted a common approach to both types of workers, following the recommendation of the Beveridge Report that distinctions between different categories of wage- and salary-earners should be abolished, and used the concept of *employment under a contract of service* to encapsulate this inclusive scope[5]—as the result of which, the terms 'contract of service' and the 'contract of employment' became synonymous with each other.

In many ways, and for quite a long period of time—at least for the succeeding twenty-five or thirty years—this unitary concept of the contract of employment, which was imported from welfare state social legislation into employment law, could be seen as socially progressive, factually accurate, and doctrinally coherent. The original work from which this book is derived was written with those as a conscious or unconscious set of assumptions. The unifying concept of the contract of employment was seen as socially progressive in the impetus which it gave to the reduction or elimination of differentiations between 'salary earners' and 'wage earners', or 'staff workers' and other workers, or 'white-collar workers' and 'blue-collar workers', especially as there seemed to be a political will to equalize upwards, that is to say to adjust the situation of the less-favoured category towards that of the more-favoured category; the provisions of the Contracts of Employment Act 1963 concerning minimum periods of paid notice of termination of employment provide an excellent example.[6]

---

[4] When the Master and Servant legislation, of which the latest version was the Master and Servant Act 1867, was replaced by the Employers and Workmen Act 1875.

[5] The crucial provisions were those of the National Insurance Act 1946 which established the broad category of 'employed earners' who are defined as 'any persons gainfully occupied in employment . . . under a contract of service'.

[6] The corresponding provisions now in force are those of ss 86–91 of the Employment Rights Act 1996 (ERA).

The unitary concept of the contract of employment also seemed factually accurate in that employment relationships did appear to be converging more and more systematically upon what we now tend to style the 'Fordist' model of secure 'permanent' full-time employment, such as was embodied in the 'typical' contract of employment. In those circumstances, it also seemed doctrinally coherent to expound the law of the contract of employment around that central model or paradigm, and to envisage the various differences in patterns of dependent employment relationships merely as different species of a single genus, which was the contract of employment as a contract type.

There is a temptation to question, in retrospect, the soundness of this position as at the time when the original work was written, and to suggest that this unitary concept of the law of the contract of employment represented a false unity by that stage, perhaps even from the outset. That suggestion would amount to the view that the postulated evolution of a single standard pattern for the dependent employment relationship was never fully realized, so that the expounding of the law of the contract of employment on that assumption amounted to papering over the cracks between different types of dependent employment relationship. With hindsight, we could see Alan Fox as having realized this when he described how, 'beyond the contract of employment', in his memorable phrase, there could be discerned in the practice of employment relations two competing dynamics towards, on the one hand, 'high trust relationships' and, on the other hand, 'low trust relationships'[7]—his fear being that the impetus towards the latter would be the more powerful and more destructive of the two unless that danger was appreciated.

However, rather than engaging in that retrospective argument, it is more to the point to observe that, however sustainable the unitary conception of the contract of employment might have been in the mid-1970s, it was certainly undermined by developments in the labour market in the succeeding twenty-five years, and in particular by the application, to employment relations, of the ideas or ideals of 'flexibility' and 'economic efficiency' which became dominant in the 1980s and 1990s. The pursuit of these ideals, and the evolution towards what are often now regarded as 'post-industrial' patterns of employment, have been, in varying degrees, a common phenomenon in Western European countries generally during this period, and Colin Crouch, in his recent magisterial survey of social trends in the Western European area, has characterized the vision of a standard stable employment relationship, around which our unitary concept of the contract of employment is constructed, as typifying a 'mid-century social compromise' which prevailed in that region—thus emphasizing how relatively transient

[7] See Fox 1974, especially chapters 2–3.

this apparently definitive construction of the labour market, as of the welfare state itself, was to prove to be.[8]

In those observations, Crouch is consciously seeking to identify large developments, and is painting on a broad canvas. With the present more microscopic focus upon the contract of employment in English law, we can observe how those large developments have falsified the unitary conception of the contract of employment, to an extent which has not always been apparent to those who have been operating within this discourse throughout the period concerned, and so perhaps have not noticed the ground shifting under our feet. The unitary concept of the contract of employment has been called upon to accommodate employment patterns of great and ever-growing diversity, as the process of 'flexibilization' generates increasingly ingenious and heterogeneous dispositions of power, responsibility, and economic risk within employment relationships—to the point where the unitary conception has burst under the strain thus imposed upon it. The nature and extent of that fracture is explored further in the next subsection.

B. The False Duality between the Contract of Employment and Other Personal Work or Employment Contracts

The false unity of the contract of employment is integrally linked to another major problem which the development of the labour market has posed for the analysis of the law of employment contracts. This problem—amounting to a fault line running through a whole section of common law based employment law—is that of the false duality of the law of personal work or employment contracts. This refers to the distinction between the contract of employment and the contract for services, or the dichotomy between the employee and the 'independent contractor'. We proceed to show why and how the 'false unity' which was expounded above is linked to the 'false duality' which is asserted in this subsection.

As has been shown earlier, there is an extremely interesting and important historical debate about the period at which, and the means by which, the unitary concept of the contract evolved. It has been shown how this has traditionally been regarded as largely the work of the common law judges in the nineteenth century, but that Deakin has persuasively argued that it should rather be considered as the result of twentieth-century social welfare legislation. On either view, though perhaps even more clearly on the latter view, the unitary concept of the contract of employment is not formed as a totally free-standing or isolated one. It developed—and this is the vital point—*in contrast to other work contracts*.

---

[8] See Crouch 1999, especially at 34–47, and chapter 3.

This was a process of formation which seems to have occurred through the first half of the twentieth century; it can probably, as Deakin argues,[9] be seen as having culminated in those provisions of the National Insurance Act 1946 which classified all workers, for social security purposes, as either 'employed earners' or 'those employed on their own account', those terms being treated as meaning respectively employed as an employee under a contract of service or employment, and, on the other hand, self-employed as an independent contractor under contracts for services. That dual classification embodied the aim of creating a general, uniform, social security system constructed around the full-time permanent workforce, while nevertheless allowing for the resistance of many professional workers and people in business to being fully absorbed into the state social security system. At least equal significance, in the creating and maintaining of this systematic binary division of the labour market, should be attached to the introduction, by the Income Tax (Employments) Act 1943, of the Pay-as-you-earn (PAYE) system whereby employers of 'employed earners', but not of independent contractors, were made responsible for deducting income tax at source from the earnings of those workers.

So completely did this dichotomy come to permeate the social security system and the income tax system that when, during the 1960s and 1970s, the major expansion of statutory individual employment rights took place, it was usually seen as obvious and uncontroversial to confer those rights on employees working under contracts of employment, but not upon other workers. The crucial pieces of legislation in this respect were the Contracts of Employment Act 1963, which introduced obligations to provide particulars of the terms of employment and to give minimum periods of paid notice of termination of employment, the Redundancy Payments Act 1965, and the provisions of the Industrial Relations Act 1971 by which the unfair dismissal jurisdiction was first introduced. There was an important exception in that the legislation of the 1970s concerning sex and race discrimination in employment applied to a much wider category of employed persons,[10] but that legislation came from a rather different institutional setting in which dichotomy between employees and the self-employed was much less strongly perceived and influential.[11]

Before considering the implications of that analysis, it is important to acknowledge the possibility of a very different historical view of this dichotomy. The above analysis stresses the contingent and circumstantial character of this development, asserting that it was a product of a particular set of social policies, imposed by legislation upon a specific labour market in a certain jurisdiction at a given moment in time. There is an alternative view

---

[9] See Deakin 1998 at 221–222.   [10] See below, 23.
[11] See Davies & Freedland 1993 at 152 161.

of the dichotomy as a much more universal and deeply embedded one which permeates the jurisprudence, as well as the legislation, of many legal systems over very long historical periods of time.[12] The dichotomy can, after all, be compared with the distinction made in Roman law between *locatio conductio operarum* and *locatio conductio operis*, literally the hire of services and of service, but corresponding respectively to the contract of service and for services. There is no doubt that most employment law systems reflect a strong intuition that there is a strong and clear distinction between dependent employment and independent working, and moreover that employment law is concerned with the former kind of work and not with the latter.

However, even if the two categories of 'employee' and 'independent contractor' have a degree of universality about them, the ease or difficulty of applying them to a particular labour market at a particular time nevertheless varies greatly. It is evident that the British courts have had a long struggle with this distinction, and that their task has seemed to become more arduous rather than less so as time has gone on. The accumulation of case law has added weight rather than wisdom. There follows a succinct account of how the employee/ independent contractor distinction has been drawn by the courts over the last thirty or forty years and is now drawn by them.

It is generally accepted that the courts have, during this period, taken their original starting point from a 'control test', which tests for the presence of a contract of employment by asking whether the employer controls, or at least has the right to control, not only what work the worker does but also the manner in which he or she carries out that work.[13] Throughout this period, however, the courts have acknowledged the insufficiency of this test as a complete one in itself. They have either supplanted it in favour of, or supplemented it with, a variety of other approaches. One such approach has been to ask whether the worker is or is not integrated into the organization of the employer.[14] Another such approach, which has been the predominant one in recent years, has been to ask whether the worker is 'in business on his or her own account'—treating a negative answer as demonstrating that the worker is an employee.[15] That has been coupled with an approach which asserts that the classification is to be made by reference to a multiplicity of factors, the list of which is usually regarded as open-ended but

[12] See Bruno Veneziani, 'The Evolution of the Contract of Employment' (Veneziani 1986) especially at 54–61.

[13] A recent example of its use is in *Lane v Shire Roofing (Oxford) Ltd* [1995] IRLR 493 by Henry LJ at 495.

[14] The classic citation for the integration or organization test is the judgment of Denning LJ in *Stevenson, Jordan & Harrison v MacDonald & Evans* [1952] 1 TLR 101, 111.

[15] Compare for instance Lord Griffiths in *Lee Ting-Sang v Chung Chi-Keung* [1990] ICR 409, 414.

as including the foregoing issues of control, integration, and business autonomy,[16] A recent trend has also been to insist upon continuing 'mutuality of obligation' as a requirement of the contract of employment.[17]

The foregoing summary would be quite misleading if it gave the impression of describing a well-defined, clearly articulated body of law which was certain and reliable in its application. Few impressions could be further from reality. The various tests which have been put forward turn out on examination to identify factors which are rarely totally present or totally absent in given employment situations. There is little agreement about how strongly a factor has to be present in order to characterize a work contract one way or the other. There is still less agreement about what relative weight to accord to particular factors, or about what combinations of factors are decisive. Hugh Collins, in an extremely important article on this topic,[18] set forth a highly sophisticated analytical solution to those problems in the form of a curve plotted around the two axes of risk distribution and bureaucratic control; but he rightly conceded that it would be difficult for the courts to use this as an instrument for practical reasoning. His simplification of that curve into a test using the two notions of, firstly, time performance versus task performance, and, secondly, the presence or absence of 'badges of membership' of the employing firm seems open to many of the above objections to the tests emerging from the case law.

The courts themselves have been well aware of the difficulty of applying the distinction. Hence we find not only a tendency to shift from one approach to another in expressing the test for the distinction, but also continuing doubt about how far to defer to the expressed intentions of the parties themselves, and also about whether the question is an issue of fact or of law, or in other words about how far decisions applying the distinction are open to appeal on points of law. In order to try to restrict endless appellate litigation, the apprehension of which is itself some indication of the uncertainty surrounding the distinction, the courts have tended to settle for a relatively non-interventionist view of the scope of the appellate jurisdiction, according to which the issue is generally seen as one of fact unless the tribunal of fact is to be regarded as having understood and applied the law perversely with regard to the evidence; thus, the courts in effect confine the appellate courts to judicial review of the legality of the first instance decision.[19] It was not surprising that when, in 1983,

---

[16] The approach is illustrated by *O'Kelly v Trusthouse Forte plc* [1983] ICR 728 (CA), especially by the judgment of Ackner LJ at 739–745.

[17] See, for an excellent analysis of this development, s 2.1.4 of Burchell Deakin & Honey 1999. [18] Collins 1990.

[19] Compare *Lee Ting-Sang v Chung Chi-Keung* [1990] ICR 409 (PC)—a decision on appeal from Hong Kong, but based on and contributing to English case law.

Bill Wedderburn and Jon Clark identified a 'crisis in fundamental concepts' within employment law, the distinction between employment and self-employment figured as their prime example.[20]

That, essentially, is the point about false unity and false duality. The creation of a strict legal dichotomy between the employed and the self-employed may have been, and may even have remained, a good legislative policy; but it is highly questionable whether this was ever really coherent as a distinction between two different types of contract. Under the pressure of the requirement to make sense of a dichotomy which was, in reality, imposed or maintained by legislation, the exponents of employment law arrived at a view of the contract of employment and the contract for services as being different from each other in their essential and structural nature, as a matter of common law. This was, for instance, an implicit assumption in the writing of the original work from which the present one is derived. But the search for a clear conceptual distinction showed that, ultimately, to be as elusive as the Philosopher's Stone.

There were, moreover, important developments in the structure of the labour market which were making the duality between employment and self-employment progressively harder to maintain as a boundary-defining category for employment law. Collins, in the article published in 1990 to which reference was made above, identified the 'challenge of vertical disintegration to employment protection laws'.[21] The thesis was that for much of the twentieth century the labour market had been subject to a process of integration into large enterprises combining more and more aspects of production and distribution of goods and services, within which workers were directly employed under contracts of employment. That phase was being succeeded by a period of reversal, of disaggregation of work organization, especially by various forms of subcontracting, which was moving large numbers of workers out of the pattern of permanent full-time employment in which they had been firmly integrated into stable employing organizations or enterprises. That development was fundamentally challenging to the construction of employment protection laws around the contract of employment and its contrast with the contract for services.

C. The Recent Growth of Multiple Categories of Contract in Employment Legislation

In this subsection it will be argued that the difficulties of the contract of employment/contract for services system have been complicated and aggravated by the use of new and diverse categories in employment legislation. The set of problems described in the previous subsection has, both predictably and appropriately, provoked a policy debate about whether and

---

[20] See Wedderburn & Clark 1983 at 144–145.   [21] Collins 1990.

how to redraw the boundaries of employment legislation. One possible policy response to the problem, persuasively advocated by Collins in 1990, was to adopt a more inclusive approach to the category of 'employees employed under contracts of employment', indeed to impose a presumption that work relationships came into this category unless it was demonstrably inappropriate to regard them as such. Another possible response, put forward by Bob Hepple in the mid-1980s, as described in the Introduction to this work,[22] was to extend at least some of the employment legislation, currently confined to workers with contracts of employment, to a new wider category of workers conceived of as being in an 'employment relationship' rather than as being employed under a contract of employment.

The actual response to the perceived need to redraw the boundaries of employment legislation has been a rather different one. It has consisted neither in expanding the concept of the contract of employment, nor in adopting the 'employment relationship' method of defining the boundary, but instead in using two contractual categories which are wider and more inclusive than that of the contract of employment, those of the 'employed person' and the 'worker'. These more inclusive legislative categories have not, however, consisted simply of an overriding of the distinction between the contract of employment and the contract for services, that is to say a direct extension of employment legislation to contracts for services as well as contracts of employment. These categories which have been increasingly used in recent employment legislation seem to be intermediate ones which include some but not all contracts for services. They are tending towards the identification of an intermediate category of semi-dependent employment contract; but their relationship to the contract for services and to each other is not yet fully clear.

The first of those two categories, that of the 'employed person' has been used in the successive measures against discrimination in the field of employment. This has been a long-standing exception to the confinement of individual employment legislation to workers with contracts of employment.[23] For the Equal Pay Act 1970 and the employment provisions of the Sex Discrimination Act 1975, the Race Relations Act 1976, and the Disability Discrimination Act 1995 are all applied to employment under a contract of service or apprenticeship *or any other contract personally to execute any work or labour* (or similar words).[24] This is therefore a contractually

---

[22] See above, 5.

[23] There is a long prehistory to the use of this formula in employment legislation; Simon Deakin suggests that this is explicable on the grounds that it is only in the recent era that the category of the contract of employment has come to comprise almost all workers in the standard or typical employment relationship—see Deakin, 'The Evolution of the Contract of Employment 1900–1950—The influence of the welfare state' (Deakin 1988) at 221.

[24] Equal Pay Act 1970, s 1(6)(a), Sex Discrimination Act 1975, s 82(1), definition of employment, Race Relations Act 1976, s 78(1) definition of employment, Disability Discrimination Act 1995, s 68(1) definition of employment ('or a contract personally to do any work').

defined category which by definition extends beyond contracts of employment. However, it does not extend to all contracts for services, but only those which are for the execution of work or labour *personally*. Not all contracts for services are for the personal execution of work in that statutory sense; some contracts for services fall outside that category because they do not essentially require or contemplate performance by the contractor himself or herself. This is a point of the utmost importance; the restriction to personal execution of work excludes many self-employed people from the category of persons employed.

That point was made and illustrated in the very important case of *Mirror Group Newspapers Ltd v Gunning*,[25] where the issue was whether an application to enter into an agency agreement for the wholesale distribution of newspapers to retailers related to a contract which came within the sex discrimination legislation as being one personally to execute any work or labour. It was a contract for services; but it was held to be one which was not personally to execute work or labour, in that it did not require or contemplate that the applicant would necessarily herself deliver the newspapers to the retailers. Balcombe LJ expressed the principle of the decision as being that the 'dominant purpose' of the agreement was simply the regular and efficient distribution of newspapers rather than the personal performance of that service by the contractor.[26] For some time the category of contract for personal employment as thus defined was the one which was used when it was wished to extend employment legislation beyond the contract of employment.

From the mid-1980s onwards, however, it became increasingly common for employment legislation to be applied to 'workers', which was a category of persons employed under a rather differently defined set of contracts. This was, like the category used in the discrimination legislation, primarily defined as 'contracts for the personal execution of any work or labour' (or similar words); but it was defined to extend only to contracts where the status of the party contracting to receive or purchase the services 'is not by virtue of the contract that of a client or customer of any profession or business undertaking carried on by the individual'.[27] It is convenient to think of this as the *profession or business to client or customer exception*. This formulation was used to identify the personal scope of Part I of the Wages Act 1986,[28] and of some of the employment law measures introduced after 1997, in particular the National Minimum Wage Act 1998[29] and the Working Time Regulations 1998.[30]

---

[25] [1986] ICR 145 (CA).   [26] Ibid at 156.
[27] The main statutory definition of the 'worker' is set out in s 230(3) of the Employment Rights Act 1996.
[28] Wages Act 1986, s 8(1) definition of 'worker', (2); provisions now contained in Employment Rights Act 1996 Part II and s 230(3).   [29] Section 54(3).
[30] SI 1998/1833, Reg 2(1) definition of 'worker'.

The aim of using this 'worker' formula seems to have been that of identifying a contractual category of semi-dependent workers more precisely than the 'persons employed' formula used in the discrimination legislation had done. The requirement of personal execution of work went some way towards this, excluding contractors who employed or subcontracted with other people to carry out the work in question, but it was evidently felt that some further or clearer confinement of the category was necessary before it could safely or appropriately be used to designate the personal scope of the new statutory employment rights which were being introduced. This explains the introduction of the customer or client to business or profession exception. The category of 'worker' is often referred to as excluding the 'genuinely self-employed', and those who describe it as such seem to regard the exception as accomplishing that exclusion.

That seems to be because the exception imports a restriction of *capacity*, in addition to a requirement of performance in person; it excludes the contractor who may carry out the work in question *in person*, but who does so in a business-person to customer capacity, or in a professional practitioner to client capacity. The piano tuner with whom I contract for the tuning of my piano or the accountant with whom I contract for the preparation of my annual tax return may work on his or her own, and may tune the piano or prepare the tax return himself or herself in person, but may nevertheless come within that exception because he or she is operating in a business or professional capacity. The exclusion of those working in what is perceived as an *independent* business or professional capacity thus further ensures that the 'worker' formula is confined to those with contracts for dependent or semi-dependent employment, and does not extend to all contracts for services.

There are thus now two different contractual categories in current legislative use which both extend beyond the contract of employment but do so in differently expressed ways. These developments have certainly expanded the personal scope of employment legislation, but the multiplication of contractual categories has brought its own increased uncertainties about that personal scope. Both the 'worker' category and the 'persons employed' category have now been held, as they rightly should, to include persons employed under contracts which are not contracts of employment.[31] However, the exact meaning of the requirement that the contracts

---

[31] In *Byrne Brothers (Formwork) Ltd v Baird* [2002] ICR 667 (EAT), building trade workers who contracted as self-employed labour-only subcontractors were held to be 'workers' within the meaning of the Working Time Regulations; in *Kelly v Northern Ireland Housing Executive* [1998] ICR 828 (HL), applications by a one-person firm of solicitors and by a designated solicitor in a small firm to provide legal services to a housing authority were held to relate to contracts of employed persons within the meaning of the Fair Employment (Northern Ireland) Act 1976 which in this respect is in the same terms as the discrimination legislation of the rest of the UK.

should be for the personal performance of work remains unclear in both contexts,[32] and it is not fully clear whether it has the same meaning in the two different contexts.

Moreover, it is most difficult to know whether and how far the 'worker' category and the 'persons employed' category differ from each other. They are expressed to do so; the client or customer to profession or business exception to the former means that it is logically narrower than the latter. However, it may well be that the client or customer to profession or business exception does no more than spell out or reiterate a notion of restriction as to capacity which is inherent in the notion of 'personal performance' anyway. That is to say, the requirement that the contractor should perform the work 'personally' may itself carry within it the idea that he or she should do so, not just in person, but also as a person operating in a working capacity rather than in the capacity of running a business or conducting a professional practice. If so, the two categories would be largely or entirely coincident. We cannot yet say whether that is the view of the courts; so far no decision has established a gap between the two concepts, but none has held them to be coincident.[33] This is a most serious and pressing uncertainty.

We therefore suggest that this is a situation in which the crisis in fundamental concepts has become if anything more serious, so far as employment contracts are concerned, than when Wedderburn and Clark identified it in 1983. In the next section we seek to establish a definitional category of personal employment contracts which may be helpful in responding to that set of theoretical and practical problems.

SECTION 2: THE PERSONAL EMPLOYMENT CONTRACT AS A DEFINITIONAL CATEGORY

In this section we put forward the initial basis for a response to the analytical problems which were identified in the previous section. This starts with a rather prescriptive kind of restatement; in the first subsection, a new definitional category is put forward as the basis for analysis of employment contracts as a whole, that of the personal employment contract. This new category is identified, explained, and related to the existing concepts and definitions of contract types in employment law.

In the second subsection, two subcategories, those of the contract of employment and the semi-dependent worker's contract, are also identified,

---

[32] There is, in particular, doubt as to the point at which a capacity for delegation or substitution deprives the contract of this attribute of being for personal performance. The question is not fully resolved in relation to sub-postmasters or sub-postmistresses, see *Sheehan v Post Office Counters Ltd* [1999] ICR 734 (EAT).

[33] An interesting test case would be whether those working under the contracts which were considered in *Kelly v Northern Ireland Housing Executive* (see n 31 above) would be regarded as 'workers' as well as being 'persons employed'.

explained, and related to the existing concepts and definitions of contract types in employment law. However, it is emphasized that splitting of the category of personal employment contracts into these subcategories, although necessary in order to give an accurate account of the law, is not very satisfactory in an analytical sense, and threatens the whole project of conducting a general integrated analysis of the law of the personal employment contract as a whole. Arguments are advanced to show that the method of restatement is helpful in tackling those difficulties.

In the third subsection it is acknowledged that the establishing of a composite category of personal employment contracts is no more than a starting point for the resolution of problems pointed out in the first section, and some indication is given of further issues requiring to be addressed in the basic analytical formulation of the law of personal employment contracts. A notion of complex personal employment relationships is invoked to assist in identifying those further issues.

A. The Personal Employment Contract Defined

In this subsection we put forward the notion or category of the personal employment contract (or personal work contract—the two terms will be used synonymously) as a general defining category for the analysis of employment contracts. We suggest that the concept of the personal employment contract, a wider one than that of the contract of employment, should be seen as encapsulating and expressing the set of contracts which constitute the concern and subject matter of employment law. That proposition is put forward as one which expresses a coherent view of the logic of contractual employment law as it currently stands. Nevertheless, we acknowledge it to be a reformulation in the sense that it is not directly or expressly authorized by the law as it currently stands; the terminology is not an existing term of art, and the conception is not directly equated to any one existing concept. So there is a task of justifying this reformulation and relating it to the existing law.

The justification for advancing the personal employment contract as a new definitional category consists in the fact that, in the course of the recent development of employment law, as explained in the previous section, the bounds of the contract of employment as a defining category have been fragmented and broken by the combination of changes in the functioning of the labour market and the corresponding changes in legislative and judicial thinking. It is those changes which tie our proposed definitional category into the existing law; we put forward the concept of the personal employment contract as an attempt to distil, out of the concepts of the employed person and the worker, as deployed in recent legislation, a coherent notion of the employment contracts of dependent and semi-dependent workers.

The concept which we thus put forward is that of the personal employment contract defined as comprising contracts for employment or work to be carried out normally in person and not in the conduct of an independent business or professional practice. We refer to or define the person who contracts to be employed in that sense as the worker. For reasons which will be given in a later section of this chapter, we generally refer to the human or legal person (or possibly the group of persons) who constitute the other party to the personal employment contract not as the employer but instead as the employing entity or employing party. So the concept which is advanced is that of the personal employment contract, as defined above, between the worker and the employing party or employing entity; this seeks to identify a combined category of dependent and semi-dependent workers which is advanced as the basic category of reference for the analysis of the employment relationship in contractual terms.

It will be helpful to relate this category to those which are currently used in employment law. Our concept of the personal employment contract is consciously and deliberately defined in such a way as to make our notion of the worker very close to that of the worker as defined in recent employment legislation. The defining notion which is put forward here of work normally in person and not in the conduct of an independent business or professional practice is close to that of the statutory conception of the worker, and to its definitional notions of personal performance and the profession or business to customer or client exception. We proceed to explain the two elements of our definition, those of 'normally in person' and 'not in the conduct of an independent business or professional practice'.

The concept of 'normally in person' is put forward as a way of avoiding the rather unsatisfactory notion of the 'dominant purpose of the contract' which has emerged in interpretation of the statutory concepts of the worker or employed person.[34] It is nevertheless intended to require the same or a very similar degree of performance in person as has been exacted by the case law interpreting the statutory notion of 'personally'. That means that the contract intends that the work or duties of the employment in question will be *predominantly* carried out or performed by the worker in person. It should be noted that current case law supports a tighter requirement of personal performance for contracts of employment than for semi-dependent workers' contracts, amounting to a requirement that the work or duties will be carried out or performed by the employee in person save in exceptional circumstances.[35] The conception of personal performance adopted in this work's definition of the personal employment contract is aligned with the looser one which has evolved for the statutory 'worker' definition.

---

[34] See above n 26.

[35] *Express & Echo Publications Ltd v Tanton* [1999] ICR 693 (CA); a slightly more relaxed view of that requirement was taken in *Macfarlane v Glasgow City Council* [2001] IRLR 7 (EAT).

The concept of 'in the conduct of an independent business or professional practice' is put forward as a clearer and less cumbersome rendering of the statutory profession or business to customer or client exception; it is intended to have a similar scope so far as the meaning of the statutory notion has become clear, though the use of the term 'independent' may make it a shade narrower. We offer the following explanatory fuller formulation of the concept we have put forward: 'in the course of a process or practice of production of goods including intellectual goods or provision of services of which process or practice the contractor is the primary and substantially autonomous organiser'. We suggest that this might be expected to be interpreted as a narrower concept than that of 'being in business on one's own account' as used in making the distinction between employees and self-employed persons.

This would mean, for example, that the freelance worker who was judged to be 'in business on his own account', and therefore not an employee in the income tax case of *Hall (Inspector of Taxes) v Lorimer*,[36] might nonetheless be held *not* to be working 'in the conduct of an independent business or professional practice', so that he could be classified as a semi-dependent worker entering into personal employment contracts with each of the many employers for which he worked. The same analysis would apply to the labour-only subcontractors in the construction industry who were held to be 'workers' in the statutory sense in *Byrne Brothers (Formwork) Ltd v Baird*.[37] However, we do not suggest that the two concepts can be easily or neatly separated, or that the case law can be sorted into a harmonious order.

Bringing those two elements together, we make it clear that our conception of the worker, although very close to the statutory conception of the 'worker', is not intended to be directly or necessarily coincident with it. Rather it is intended to fall within what the present writer sees as a very small gap between the statutory concept of the worker and that of the employed person; on the assumption that they are close to each other in meaning, our concept of the personal employment contract is intended to be neutral or non-committal between those two statutory notions, perhaps even a central definition upon which both the statutory concepts could in future be aligned. If, however, the gap between the statutory concept of worker and the statutory concept of employed person is held upon further interpretation to be a large one, our concept of the personal employment contract would approximate more to that of the statutory worker's contract than to that of the employed person's contract.

It is hoped in this way to have established a workable and meaningful general category of reference to encapsulate the set of contracts for

---

[36] [1994] ICR 218 (CA).   [37] [2002] ICR 667 (EAT).

dependent and semi-dependent work with which employment law is normally and properly concerned. However, there is a set of issues or difficulties about the divisions within that category which remain to be addressed, and which we seek to deal with in the next subsection.

B. The Two Subcategories of the Contract of Employment and the Semi-Dependent Worker's Contract

In this subsection, it is recognized that it is necessary for analytical purposes to divide workers working under personal employment contracts into two subcategories, those working under a contract of employment and other workers working under a contract other than a contract of employment. The first of those two subcategories is a familiar one, but the second is not, and there is an initial task of defining it, explaining it, and assigning an appropriate terminology to it. We begin with the question of terminology, explaining why the terminology of 'semi-dependent worker's contract' has been adopted for that second subcategory, and why it has been preferred to the other main alternative which presented itself, that of the 'non-employee worker's contract'. We then go on to identify some difficulties with this division into those two subcategories and explain how this difficult distinction will be carried through the further stages of this work.

In the previous subsection, the category of personal employment contracts was put forward and defined. In this subsection it is recognized that this is a category made up of two component parts, one of which is the contract of employment, and the other of which consists of the rest of the personal employment contracts which are left behind when the contract of employment is taken out. The second of those subcategories therefore has a definition which is partly positive and partly negative. It is positively defined as part of the category of personal employment contracts, but negatively defined as the residue of that category left behind by the contract of employment. That might be a reason for designating this subcategory partly negatively and partly positively as the non-employee worker's contract. This would reflect the way in which the statutory categories of employed persons and workers are technically constructed; each of them adds another element, composed of other contracts for personal performance of work, onto the basic element of the contract of employment. Our concept of the personal employment contract is in truth an aggregation of two such elements.

It is equally possible to approach the recognition and definition of these two subcategories in a functional or purposive way rather than a technical way. We could say that our general notion of the personal employment contract, like the statutory concepts of the employed person and the worker, seeks to combine two functionally identified types of worker, the dependent worker and the semi-dependent worker. The dependent worker is identified as the worker under a contract of employment; the other part of the overall category of personal employment contract, like the other part of the two statutory concepts, represents the semi-dependent worker. We could, in this second mode of definition, call the second category that of the semi-dependent worker, and we could call the contracts of such workers the semi-dependent worker's contract.

The choice between the two modes of definition is a difficult one. Either mode of definition strengthens the sense that these two subcategories have a true difference between them, implying that the two legal subcategories reflect truly and strongly different types of employment relationship. Our argument in the first section was against that view; that argument was that there was no really clear dividing line between the contract of employment and the contract for services, no real clear differentiation between two kinds of employment relationship upon which that legal distinction could be based. The use of either terminology threatens to renege upon that argument, but on balance it seems that the 'non-employee worker's contract' terminology does so to a greater extent by expressly tying itself to the technical legal concept of the 'employee'. For that reason, while recognizing that the two terminologies are synonymous, we have chosen that of the 'semi-dependent worker's contract' which does not as yet carry a weight of technical legal baggage.

Nevertheless, even if they are differentiated in that as far as possible non-technical way, by recognizing and working with those two subcategories, we still seem to undermine our general project of establishing and working with a composite category of personal employment contracts, and thereby arriving at an overall and integrated analysis of all the employment contracts which are within the proper scope of employment law. The present author does not conceal a hope that this may be a transitional problem, but for the time being at least it is a very real problem; we seek to address it first by indicating why it is necessary to accept and work with the division into two subcategories, and secondly by showing how the method of restatement may alleviate the difficulties of doing so.

It is necessary to conduct our analysis of the law of personal employment contracts in a way which recognizes and adverts to these two subcategories for two different reasons. The first is that the law of personal employment contracts in general has been very largely developed and formulated within the domain of contracts of employment; that was certainly the case during the crucial years of its rapid development from the 1960s onwards. So much is this the case that there is very little case law which deals directly with the law of the semi-dependent worker's contract. Much of that law has to be worked out by inference from the more fully developed case law of the contract of employment. An analysis which ignored that disparity would be a misleading one.

The second reason why we have to conduct our analysis of the law of personal employment contracts with the distinction between the two sub-categories kept quite firmly in mind is that much of the statute law of personal employment contracts makes and enforces that distinction. Many of the measures which impose mandatory terms upon personal employment contracts do so with respect only to contracts of employment and not with respect to semi-dependent workers' contracts. This is the case, for example, so far as the legislation concerning statutory minimum periods of notice is concerned, and with the TUPE Regulations providing for transfer of employment contracts upon the transfer of the employing undertaking. An accurate account of the law of personal employment contracts also has to recognize those disparities. That is why we have in part to reintroduce the very distinction between the contract of employment and the contract for services which was argued in the first section to be such an inherently unsatisfactory one.

This is where the method of restatement is of great utility. That is to say, it allows us to advance a reformulation of the law of personal employment contracts which, while recognizing and keeping in mind that it is a body of law evolving from two distinct elements, nevertheless presents it as a composite one and weaves the two strands together when it is analytically sound to do so. The method of restatement legitimates this exercise because it authorizes various degrees of extrapolation from and synthesis of the existing law as long as the extent or depth of reformulation is acknowledged and made explicit. On this basis, we proceed in the remainder of the work to present a single narrative analysis of the law of the personal employment contract as a whole, but one which where necessary indicates divergence between the two subcategories.

There are two particular reasons for regarding this kind of composite restatement of the law of personal employment as being workable and coherent. The first is that the area of semi-dependent workers' contracts which we have identified is a reasonably small and contained one, referring to employment relationships which are similar to those covered by the contract of employment in the legal and analytical issues which they present. That follows from our general argument that there is no sharp inherent difference between the two sets of employment relationships to which our two subcategories respectively refer.

The second and even stronger reason is that there is remarkably little existing law which has been articulated for the category of semi-dependent worker's contracts. We know that there is a good deal of legislation which applies to the contract of employment but not to the semi-dependent worker's contract. We know that there is another, largely recent body of legislation which applies to both types of contract alike. Beyond that, the law of the semi-dependent worker's contract is, to a striking and unexpected extent, an uncharted territory. An analysis of it as an entirely separate body of law would still have to be worked out very largely by extrapolation from the law of the contract of employment. So the idea of a composite analysis does not involve trampling upon a separate body of doctrine. In composing the law of personal employment contracts, we are writing on almost empty pages so far as semi-dependent workers' contracts are concerned.

The foregoing arguments are reasonably encouraging for our project of establishing the category of the personal employment contract and conducting a composite analysis of the law relating to contracts within that category, using the method of restatement. However, before embarking upon that analysis in detail, it is important to identify some further analytical difficulties, of great theoretical and practical importance, which have to be confronted, and which have not been resolved simply by establishing our basic category of reference.

C. The Personal Employment Contract and the Problems of Complex Employment Relationships

In this subsection we identify and try to be precise about some profound conceptual and practical difficulties which remain to be resolved once the personal employment contract has been established as our basic category of reference. These problems can usefully be identified as those of complex employment relationships. Particular ways in which employment relationships may be complex are by being triangular or multilateral, or by being intermittent, or by being both multilateral and intermittent. We advance this set of arguments because there is a danger of imagining that the problems of complex employment relationships are easily solved once we start working with the expanded concept of the worker under a personal employment contract rather than the narrower concept of the employee under a contract of employment. Matters are by no means as straightforward as that, and elaborate analysis of many aspects of the law of personal employment contracts will be necessary to attack those problems.

It is quite easy to see how there might be an illusion that many of the fundamental problems of contractual employment law disappear with the establishing of an overarching category of reference such as that of the personal employment contract. As we have seen earlier, there has for a long time, and rightly, been perceived to be a crisis in fundamental concepts in this area of law, and that crisis has for a long time, and equally rightly, been blamed on the narrowness and inflexibility of the law of the contract of employment. It is very tempting to think that this crisis can therefore be resolved by breaking the mould of the contract of employment and working with some larger more accommodating concept such as that of the 'employment relationship' or that of the 'worker' or the 'employed person', or of the personal employment contract as advanced in our own argument. It is easy to believe that various forms of work which do not fit easily into the category of the contract of employment will find a comfortable and well-designed legal niche waiting for them within one of these larger categories.

We have put forward the concept of the personal employment contract as the most useful overarching category of reference with which to attack the crisis in fundamental concepts. We have suggested that it is more effective to deploy a contractual concept than that of the 'employment relationship' because our system of employment law is so deeply committed to a contractual mode of analysis of employment relationships. However, although we put forward the personal contract of employment as our preferred basis of analysis, we do not suggest that it offers a panacea for the problems of legal definition, distinction, or inclusion of employment relationships.

The essential reason for these further problems is that the arrangements for employment which are made and operated in practice, and the employment relationships which exist on the basis of those arrangements, present complexities which have certainly proved difficult to accommodate within the framework of the contract of employment, but still present acute analytical difficulties even within a larger conceptual framework such as that of the personal employment contract. The main complexities, as we have indicated, are those of triangularity and intermittency. One or two examples will be helpful.

Many examples of the difficulties of triangularity are to be found in the sphere of agency employment, where extremely difficult issues arise as to whether the worker has an employment contract, if so of what kind and with whom. Such difficulties are illustrated by the recent case of *Montgomery v Johnson Underwood Ltd.*[38] Here an agency worker was held not to have a contract of employment with the employment agency, and seems to have been regarded as not having such a contract with the client business either; and it is far from clear whether the Court of Appeal would have regarded the agency worker as having a contract with either the agency or the client business such as to qualify him as a 'person employed' by either of them, or as a 'worker' employed by either of them.

The problems about continuity are equally well illustrated by decisions concerning casual or 'as required' workers, of which the most important to date has been the decision of the House of Lords in the case of *Carmichael v National Power plc*[39] that a tour guide who conducted tours round power stations when called upon to do so by the employing company was not employed under a continuing contract of employment because the set of arrangements did not involve a sufficient degree of continuing mutual obligation to amount to a continuing contract of employment. It is quite unclear whether the House of Lords regarded Mrs Carmichael as having a series of short-term contracts for the duration of each tour, and if so whether those contracts were contracts of employment or semi-dependent worker's contracts, or whether they regarded her as having a continuing semi-dependent worker's contract.

The way in which problems of triangularity may become compounded with problems of continuity is perfectly illustrated by the case of *Cheng Yuen v*

---

[38] [2001] ICR 819 (CA).   [39] [1999] ICR 1226 (HL).

Royal Hong Kong Golf Club[40] which concerned the question whether a caddie working at a golf course belonging to the Royal Hong Kong Golf Club was working under a contract of employment with the golf club. The golf caddie was a casual worker to the extent that he was free to choose when he wished to present himself for work; when he did so, which in fact occurred regularly over a period of nine years until he was made redundant by the Club, he was allocated to particular golfers for a particular round of golf, and paid by the Club for each such round, that payment being charged by the Club to the member concerned. The Hong Kong Labour Tribunal decided that the caddie did have a contract of employment with the Club, which decision was upheld on appeal to the High Court.

However, the Court of Appeal decided that the question was whether the caddie had a *continuing* contract of employment with the Club, and that he did not have the required continuing contract. So far, the case followed a somewhat similar course to that of the *Carmichael* case. However, the Privy Council decided the further appeal on the very different basis that the question was whether the caddie was employed by the Club or by the players. They held that as he was to be viewed as having a series of contracts for services with particular players, he could not be viewed as having a contract of employment with the Club, which was, in effect, licensing the caddie to work on its golf course for its members, rather than employing him. Comparison and contrast with other decisions shows that all kinds of problems are left unresolved as to how the issues of contract type, continuity, and triangularity should be seen as related to each other.

We return to all those issues in later sections or chapters; the point made at this stage is that no immediate solutions present themselves as a result simply of looking at these issues from the wider perspective of the personal employment contract rather than the narrower perspective of the contract of employment. There is still a great set of questions as to how far and in what way the contractual analysis can adapt to and accommodate the complexity of employment relationships which is encountered in practice, and which is tending to increase as the labour market itself evolves towards increasingly disaggregated and convoluted arrangements for employment. Within the more expansive framework of the personal employment contract it is still just as necessary as within the cramped confines of the contract of employment to attack those questions by painstaking analysis of the concepts and structures which make up the law of employment contracts. This dictates the agenda for the ensuing sections and chapters; we begin by considering how the parties to the personal employment contract are defined and conceptualized.

---

[40] [1998] ICR 131 (PC—on appeal from Hong Kong, but decided as if arising under English law).

SECTION 3: CONTRACTING PARTIES AND THE INSTITUTIONAL ORGANIZATION OF WORK

In the previous sections it has been argued that, by looking at the category of personal employment contracts as a composite whole, we can improve our understanding of the way in which personal work relationships are rendered into the form of contracts in our system of employment law. In this section we use that enlarged frame of reference to take a critical view of the way in which, in the law of personal work or employment contracts as a whole, the contracting parties are envisaged and conceptualized. In the first subsection we argue that a narrow focus on the contract of employment, coupled with a very stylized and artificial view of work organizations, has resulted in a seriously oversimplified and distorted way of identifying and conceptualizing the parties to personal employment contracts. In the second and third subsections we suggest the basis for an analysis of the contracting which corresponds better to the realities of the way in which work is institutionally organized at the present day, looking firstly at employing entities and links between them, and secondly at workers and the organization of the employing enterprise.

A. The Personal and Bilateral View of Contractual Employment Relations

In this subsection we shall argue that the legal analysis of employment contracts imposes a strongly defined and prescriptive view of the institutional organization of work which is outdated and artificial. The contracting parties are identified and conceptualized according to a set of assumptions that employment relations are organized on a particular personal and bilateral basis; it is a view which makes only very occasional contact with contemporary realities. We shall explore this view and point out its artificiality, and give some indication of the theoretical and practical problems which are posed by the fact that this view is such a dominant one. Those problems and possible alternative approaches are explored in the succeeding subsections.

As we shall find at most points in the course of our analysis of the law of personal employment contracts, that body of law is very largely concentrated upon or constructed around the contract of employment. That contract is essentially conceived of as a bilateral and personal one, a contractual relationship between one person who is the employer and another person who is the employee. This is a conception which reflects the smooth evolution of the law of the contract of employment from the pre-contractual law of master and servant, which was formulated over a long historical period during which employment relations could convincingly be analysed as being between an individual master and an individual servant, an example or extension of social and economic relations within the household. Otto Kahn-Freund demonstrated how the contract of employment had developed from this model of the law of master and servant as Blackstone had conceived of it in the eighteenth century.[41]

However, if the relation of marriage has remained a personal and bilateral one in the sense in which it was so in Blackstone's time, the relation of employment has not. It continues to be possible to think of the worker as an individual person (though this may understate various senses in which people work collectively or in conjunction with each other), and of the employment relation as a personal one in that sense. Indeed, our definition of the personal employment contract is constructed on that basis. However, it has become highly artificial to think of the worker as being in a bilateral relation with another individual person who is the employer. In order to understand that artificiality, it is important to consider the way in which the legal corporate entity has been equated to the individual human person in the conceptualization of the contractual employer.

As we pointed out above, the stereotype around which the conception of the contractual employer evolved was that of the master. Yet very few workers are today employed by an individual human person who owns the work enterprise, directly and personally conducts the employment relation, and trades in his own name rather than as an incorporated or partnership organization. (We would normally add 'or her' at this point, but omit to do so in order to make the point that the stereotype is not just of a human person but of a male human person.) So the understanding of the contractual employer as an individual human person in a simple bilateral relation with the worker is clearly artificial to that extent; it is factually untypical. A further and no less important kind of artificiality occurs when the stereotype of the employer, as an individual person in a simple bilateral relation with the worker, is imposed on the relation between the worker and the corporate work organization. That is now the predominant form of the employment relation, and the conceptualization of the contractual employer in that predominant form has an artificiality right at the heart of it.

The continued rationalization of contractual employment in bilateral and personal terms from the nineteenth century onwards has crucially depended upon regarding the legal corporate person, the incorporated company, as the direct equivalent of the individual human employer or master. In few corners of English law was the notion of legal corporate personality more fully internalized than with regard to the quintessentially human relationship which forms the subject matter of contracts of employment. It was not merely that the limited liability company was fully accepted as the employer in a legal contractual sense. It was also that the human personality of the master was attributed at a deeper level to the legal company in constructing the contractual conception of the corporate employer.

[41] See Kahn-Freund 1978.

The classic illustration is provided by the leading case of *Nokes v Doncaster Amalgamated Collieries Ltd.*[42] This, as students of employment law all quickly learn, was the case where a coal miner, charged under section 4 of the Employers and Workmen Act 1875 (under which it was still, at that period, a criminal offence for a workman to absent himself from work in breach of his contract of service) was held to have the defence that there was no contract of service in force between himself and Doncaster Amalgamated Collieries, the company asserting itself to be his employer. Doncaster Amalgamated Collieries claimed that role as the transferee of all the property rights and liabilities of the company by which the worker had originally been employed, and which had since been dissolved following this transfer of all its business under the company merger procedure provided by statute at that period.

The conclusion of the House of Lords, that the contract of service was too personal in nature to be assignable from one company to another without the knowledge and agreement of the worker concerned, still resounds today as an example of judicial concern with the rights and liberties of the worker as a citizen, even if, as will appear in a later chapter,[43] it is far from clear that the doctrine emerging from that case has a generally protective and beneficial operation so far as workers are concerned. The decision in *Nokes v Doncaster Amalgamated Collieries* thus marks the seamless transposition of the master and servant model into the twentieth century world of corporate structures and corporate restructuring. In their zeal to protect Mr Nokes from faceless oppression, the Law Lords who formed the majority in favour of the decision took a highly personified view both of the limited liability company by which he was originally employed, and of the limited liability company into which it had since been merged, viewing them much as if they were two different individual people.

We have to investigate that construction of the corporate contractual employer one stage further in order to understand the real nature of its artificiality. The underlying problem about the reasoning in *Nokes v Doncaster Amalgamated Collieries* is that it imposes a wholly oversimplified vision of the institutional organization of the employment relation. This may be illustrated in the following way. Lord Atkin cited in support of his reasoning the decision in *Griffith v Tower Publishing Co,*[44] where it was held that an author was justified in refusing to allow the contract for publication of his work to be transferred to another company; he quoted this key passage from Stirling J:

No doubt part of the inducement [for wishing the contract to remain with the original company] was also that the company had a very efficient manager. It was said that the company might have discharged him the next day without giving the

---

[42] [1940] AC 1014 (HL).   [43] See below, 493–494.
[44] [1897] 1 Ch 21 (ChD).

plaintiff cause to complain. That observation is well founded. The company might have discharged its manager the next day, and appointed new officers at any time; but still the plaintiff might well act on the assumption that the Tower Company and those who directed its affairs would select a manager who would maintain the reputation of the company.[45]

This makes a crucial point. The author's contract with the company did involve a personal and human relation with an individual, but that individual was not the company itself, it was the manager of the company, presumably himself an employee of the company. Stirling J assumed that 'those who directed the affairs of the company' would employ a similarly efficient manager even if they decided to dismiss that particular one. So the reality was that the company had a personal quality for the author because it was a work organization the character of which was maintained by the particular directors, managers, and workers who operated it, and by the hierarchy of relations between them. Yet the contractual relation is represented as a purely bilateral one between the legal entity of the company and the author. The work organization is reduced or simplified into a single individual; in the case of employment contracts, that individual is equated with a human employer. The complex multilateral relations within the work organization are represented as simple bilateral ones.

This difficulty is by no means confined to the doctrine in *Nokes v Doncaster Amalgamated Collieries*. The reasoning in that case was rather tendentious, and the set of issues about transfer of the contract of employment upon transfer of the business undertaking is now addressed by the radically different approach of the TUPE Regulations, which are discussed in a later chapter.[46] But this kind of oversimplification of the institutional organization of work is far more generally pervasive across the law of personal employment contracts. It causes many problems both of a theoretical and a practical kind in constructing a coherent analysis of the parties to the contractual employment relation. Those problems are examined in the following subsections, but two preliminary points are made before doing so.

Firstly, as an aid to the further analysis of those problems, we adopt a particular terminology to refer to the category of human or legal persons who may constitute the employing party. Because it is so important to keep it in mind that the employing party is not normally a single (male) human being trading as such, we shall use the terminology of the 'employing entity' instead of that of the 'employer' to refer to the human or corporate persons who may constitute the employing party. Secondly, we make the point that these problems cannot be neatly divided up into separate issues concerning the contractual definition and conceptualization of the employing entity on the one hand, and of the worker on the other. The definition and

[45] Ibid at 24.   [46] See Chapter 9, Section 4.

conceptualization of the one is entirely tied up with that of the other. This will emerge as we look first at the organization of employment between employing entities and then at the organization of work within employing entities.

B. THE CONTRACTING PARTIES AND THE ORGANIZATION OF EMPLOYMENT BETWEEN EMPLOYING ENTITIES

In this subsection it will be argued that the over-rigid construction of the contractual employment relation as a bilateral one between an individual employing entity and an individual worker is the cause of serious theoretical and practical problems in the analysis of situations where employment is organized between employing entities. In some such situations, especially those of agency employment and subcontracted employment, this individual and bilateral construction, particularly of the contract of employment, is not easily fitted to the organizational realities, and an acute form of the 'crisis in fundamental concepts' may occur, in which an employment relationship may fall right outside the contractual categories recognized by the courts. As Simon Deakin has very powerfully put it:

The need to establish a contractual nexus between employer and employee (or worker) can have the effect of completely dis-embedding the employment relationship from the organisational context in which the work is performed.[47]

We begin by explaining what is meant in this argument by the organization of employment. We use it to refer to the allocation or assignment of the main functions which are comprised in the notion of employing workers or acting as an employer. We can identify and distinguish four main functions: (1) engaging workers for employment and terminating their employment; (2) remunerating workers and providing them with other benefits of employment; (3) managing the employment relation and the process of work; and (4) using the worker's services in a process of production or service provision. Those functions may be exercised together by or within a single employing entity, or they may be exercised separately by different employing entities.

We use the concept of the organization of employment to mean the arranging of which employing entities or which persons within them are to exercise those functions. Thus employment might be organized *between employing entities* by arranging for a worker to be engaged for employment by an employment agency but remunerated by the client company which uses the worker's services. In this subsection we consider such situations in which those functions are shared or distributed between employing entities. Here we are concerned with the sharing or distribution of those functions from the inception of the employment relationship. In a later chapter we

---

[47] Deakin 2001 at 73.

consider situations in which those functions are redistributed in the course of an employment relationship.[48] We begin by illustrating the problems of analysis which may arise when employment is organized in complicated ways between employing entities. Next we consider how far in principle the individual and bilateral model of contractual employment may be stretched to accommodate the multilateral organization of work between employing entities. Finally we show how the courts are in fact failing to adapt the individual and bilateral model to situations of agency employment and labour-only subcontracting.

The problems of imposing the individual and bilateral model of employment contracts can be illustrated by returning to the decision in the *Hong Kong Golf Club* case, which was discussed earlier.[49] It was observed how the decision, as to whether the worker was an employee under a contract of employment with the golf club, was thrown into great confusion by the argument, which succeeded in the Privy Council, that the worker should be regarded as contracting with the individual club members for particular rounds of golf *rather than* with the golf club itself. So the worker was held not to have statutory employment rights in respect of the termination of his employment by the golf club.

This is a classic case where the law of the contract of employment imposed an over-rigid and oversimplified analysis. The employment of the golf caddie in question was organized in such a way that the functions of 'the employer' were distributed or shared between the golf club and the members for whom the caddie worked for particular rounds. The golf club could be seen as acting as the hirer, remunerator, manager, and user in a general sense. The members could be seen as acting in each of those roles in respect of each particular round of golf. Alternatively, one might see some of those roles as being taken solely by the golf club—the management role, for instance; or as being taken solely by the members—the role of user, for instance. But we cannot satisfactorily single out either the golf club or any member of it as the sole bearer of all the employment functions.

So the organizational framework within which this worker operated was sufficiently complex, and sufficiently multilateral, that no one bilateral relationship within it could give a complete picture as to who was acting as 'the employer': nor therefore could any one bilateral relationship form the basis for a satisfactory overall assessment of whether the worker was a dependent or an independent worker. Yet the law of the contract of employment seemed to require that the issue of the worker's entitlement to statutory employment rights was adjudicated on precisely that narrow basis. Because there was no complete bilateral employment relation between the golf club and the caddie, he was held not to be employed under a contract of employment.

---

[48] See Chapter 9, especially at 491–500.   [49] See above, 34–35.

So, in that decision, the bilateral and individual model of the contract of employment was applied in a rigid way. That raises questions about how much latitude the law of personal employment contracts allows for adaptation to the organization of employment between different employing entities. Such adaptation could take various different forms. It could consist of recognizing that the personal employment contract may exist between a worker and more than one employing entity, regarded either as several employing parties or as one joint employing party. It could consist, on the other hand, of establishing rules to attribute a bilateral contract to a primary or leading employing entity. On either basis, greater latitude might be allowed in recognizing semi-dependent workers' contracts than in recognizing contracts of employment.

We suggest there is a good deal of inconsistency and lack of clear resolution as to how much latitude the law of personal employment contracts does afford in these respects. At one extreme, there are situations in which, if employing entities formally contract as a joint employing party or as several employing parties, the arrangement is accepted as giving rise to a valid contract of employment; and there is every reason to suppose that it would equally easily be accepted as a semi-dependent worker's contract. That has long since been accepted where workers are employed jointly by a number of partners; in the law of personal employment contracts, there seems to be no problem about accepting the partnership firm[50] (and it seems the unincorporated association too) as a quasi-corporate employing entity or joint employing party.

The latitude for joint contracting between employing entities seems to extend beyond partnership firms. In *Harold Fielding Ltd v Mansi*,[51] the National Industrial Relations Court seemed to have no difficulty in accepting that a contract of employment existed between a worker and two companies which had formed an ad hoc partnership for the production of a musical entertainment; and there are various cases where two or more companies within an associated group of companies have sued in the same action upon employment contracts without encountering any objection to their appearing as multiple or joint employing parties.[52]

However, beyond those situations of formal joint or multiple contracting by employing entities, there seems to be no willingness or disposition on the part of the courts to accept or construct a multilateral employment with more than one employing entity, even in situations where employment functions are genuinely distributed between more than one distinct person

---

[50] As in *Briggs v Oates* [1990] ICR 473 (ChD). The same treatment is clearly appropriate for limited liability partnerships formed under the provisions of the Limited Liability Partnerships Act 2001. As to changes in the composition of employing partnerships, see below, 500–501.   [51] [1974] ICR 347 (NIRC); see below, 497.
[52] Compare, for instance, *Dawnay Day & Co Ltd v De Braconier D'Alphen* [1997] IRLR 285 (ChD) where there was an intricate structure of intra-group corporate employing entities.

or organization. Where there is a continuing distribution of employment functions between an intermediary employing entity such as an employment agency[53] or labour-only contracting enterprise and an end-user of the worker's services, the end-user is generally seen not only as having no direct employment contract with the worker as sole employer, but also as not being a party to a joint employment contract jointly with the intermediate employer.

This is illustrated by decisions such as *Morris v Breaveglen Ltd*[54] and *Bolwell v Redcliffe Homes Ltd*[55] which concerned labour-only subcontracting, and by decisions such as *MHC Consulting Services Ltd v Tansell*[56] and *Secretary of State for Education and Employment v Bearman*,[57] which concerned employment agencies or similar bodies with a continuing intermediary employment business role. It is not at all clear whether an employment contract for joint employment by the intermediary and the end-user could or would be more readily constructed on the footing that it was a semi-dependent worker's contract, but even if so that would have deprived the worker of the advantages of contractual employee status as the price of recognition of a contract which extended to both employing entities.

Moreover, the case law concerning labour-only subcontracting and agency employment indicates the presence of a further and more serious problem resulting from the rigidity of the individual and bilateral approach to contractual construction of the relation between worker and employing entity, at least so far as contracts of employment are concerned, though possibly not so far as semi-dependent workers' contracts are concerned. For, in the kind of complex organizational arrangements which we are considering, where employment functions are dispersed between different persons or organizations, it may well happen not merely that the courts will

---

[53] An expansion is necessary here. The Conduct of Employment Agencies and Employment Businesses Regulations 1976, SI 1976/715 distinguish between (1) employment agencies strictly so-called, which act as initial hiring agents in the making of contracts between workers and end-users, in which the end-user figures as the contractual employing party, and (2) employment agencies which have a continuing intermediary role in the employment relationship, in which case the agency is operating as an 'employment business', and the employment relationship is analysed as described in the main text above.

[54] [1993] ICR 766 (CA).   [55] [1999] IRLR 485 (CA).

[56] [2000] ICR 789 (CA). The decision was that the statutory relationship of principal and contract worker could be held to exist, for the purpose of the Disability Discrimination Act, even though there was a further intermediary employing entity in the form of a service company by which the worker was immediately employed. The issue could have been, but was not, resolved by treating the worker as being in the joint contractual employment of the end-user and the employment agency (which seems to have had a continuing employment business role).

[57] [1998] IRLR 431 (EAT). In this case the Employment Service figured in the role of end-user, and Royal British Legion Industries figured as an intermediary employment business for disabled workers. The point is that no attempt was made to construct a joint employment contract with both those organizations treated as employing parties, although the facts presented a compelling case for doing so.

contractual model is taken all too literally in the law of personal employment contracts. It should not be surprising that the results are sometimes quite hard to equate with the day-to-day realities of employment relations. Those day-to-day realities generally consist of complex horizontal or vertical or diagonal relations within patterns of organization of employment which are generally hierarchical in some degree. But, if we may take Thomas the Tank Engine as an example of the worker within a classical corporate employment hierarchy, the bilateral and individual contractual model of the employment relation tells us nothing about Thomas's relations with the other engines, or with the Fat Controller who, though presented as the railway company incarnate, is presumably himself also an employee of the company, an executive director or managing director with a contract of employment. To use another metaphor, not only does the bilateral and individual contractual model keep Coase's black box[63] firmly shut, but it also writes a fictitious description on the lid.

The strength with which the law of personal employment contracts adheres to this model produces various kinds of artificiality. The model ascribes a false uniformity to the structure of all contractual employment relations; all those relations are insisted upon as being equally individual and one dimensional; none of them is viewed as having a collective dimension or a hierarchical dimension in which the links with other workers, including managers, are revealed and accounted for. This may appear as a kind of egalitarian or democratic view in which senior managers of companies are treated as having personal employment contracts which are of the same nature as those of any other workers. There is indeed an importance, as will be argued in a later chapter, in taking a common view of the basic implied terms of all personal employment contracts. However, in various respects there seems to be a need for a greater accuracy and refinement of analysis of relations within the employing entity than the individual and bilateral model provides, and there are serious problems which result from a lack of accuracy or refinement.

One further element of theoretical explanation is necessary to indicate the general nature of the problems which arise. It concerns the sense in which the contractual relation of employment is regarded or should be regarded as one of subordination. The individual and bilateral approach to the contract of employment both depends upon and imposes a view of the employment relation as a one-step hierarchy between the employer or employing entity as hierarchically superior and the worker as hierarchically inferior. That is the sense in which it is a *legal* relation of subordination.

---

[63] Ronald Coase's classic article on 'The Nature of the Firm' (Coase 1937) was the starting point for a new genre of writing about institutional economics; it depicted the firm, in effect the employing entity as that notion is being used in this work, as an institution the very *raison d'être* of which was to minimize transaction costs by internalizing (into the 'black box') relations which would otherwise have to be the subject of formal and specific contracting.

During the evolution of the law of the contract of employment, that legal relation has been regarded as corresponding to a human or personal subordination of the worker to the employer. In the modern law of the contract of employment, that subordination may be a purely formal or structural one; it may but does not have to consist of or involve a real social and economic submission of one human being to the will or control of another or of a corporate organization.

In that sense, this is a model which applies to personal employment contracts at large, and not just to contracts of employment. They are all conceived of as one-step contractual relations of legal subordination of a worker to an employing entity in that formal or structural sense; but the degree of actual human social and economic subordination varies greatly within the whole category. Indeed, it is quite wrong to conceive of a spectrum of human social and economic subordination in which the contract of employment involves greater human or personal subordination while the semi-dependent worker's contract involves lesser subordination of that kind. The worker under a contract of employment may be a senior manager or executive in a position of great social and economic independence, and right at the top of a hierarchy of employment relations within a corporate or quasi-corporate employing entity. The worker under a semi-dependent worker's contract may be a casually employed person in a position of great social and economic subordination on the lowest periphery of such a hierarchy of relations. That is one demonstration of the way in which the separation of personal employment contracts into those two subcategories is such an unsatisfactory one.

This disjunction between legal subordination and factual subordination is a very significant feature of the individual and bilateral model of contractual employment. It gives rise to the first of the particular problems of operation of that model which we wish to single out. This is the difficulty of analysis which arises where a formal contract of employment exists between the legal corporate entity and a person who is its proprietor or controlling shareholder. Such an arrangement may satisfy the requirements of the individual and bilateral model of contractual employment although that person is not in any position of factual subordination at all. This means that even the managing director and sole or controlling shareholder of a company may validly enter as an employee into a contract of employment with that company, and may therefore acquire the statutory employment rights accorded to employees under contracts of employment, as the decision of the Court of Appeal in the case of *Secretary of State for Trade and Industry v Bottrill* [64] recently confirms.

The reasoning in this decision perfectly reveals the basic difficulty of operating with the formalized individual and bilateral model of contractual

[64] [1999] ICR 592 (CA).

employment in such situations. In order to control the abusive use of the contract of employment as a device whereby corporate proprietors may acquire statutory employment rights, the Court of Appeal relies upon the notion of 'sham' contracts, which will be held not to qualify the person concerned as an employee.[65] However, it proves rather difficult to distinguish between the sham contract and the 'real' contract, because the individual and bilateral model of the contract demands only a formal or structural subordination of the worker to a purely abstract legal person. It does not require factual subordination of the worker to any other person or group of persons within the employing entity.

So the notion of the sham contract is really no more than a control upon the opportunistic use of the employment contract to obtain particular advantages, for example where there is the likelihood of corporate insolvency. The individual and bilateral model of contractual employment, as it has developed in relation to the corporate employing entity, makes the application of such control very difficult because it is in its nature not a discriminating conception. In its subsequent decision in *Sellars Arenascene Ltd v Connolly*,[66] the Court of Appeal evokes the notion of 'behaving as an employee' as another way of limiting the availability of the contract of employment to corporate proprietors, but the notion is, for the reasons we have given, an essentially shadowy one, especially as it was emphasized that deep proprietary interest and entrepreneurial involvement in the corporate venture is not at all inconsistent with the status of employment under a contract of employment.[67]

The capacity of this model personal structure to degrade into a formalistic one has enabled the very widespread use of 'service companies', that is to say arrangements by which workers constitute themselves as employees under contracts of employment made with a company which the worker owns, and which has the sole function of acting as an employing entity for fiscal or similar purposes. Arrangements involving such 'one-person' service companies have been accepted as valid contracts of employment on the authority of the decision of the Privy Council in *Lee v Lee's Air Farming Ltd*.[68] To the extent that this practice has come to be regarded as an abusive adoption of an artificial technical form, that abuse has been addressed, in the governmental initiative known as IR35, as illegitimate tax avoidance, rather than by means of a general challenge to the validity of contracts of employment made with service companies of this kind.[69] Within the law

---

[65] See Lord Woolf MR at 604.   [66] [2001] IRLR 222 (CA).

[67] See Pill LJ at 225–226.

[68] [1961] AC 12 (PC). The continuing acceptance of such arrangements as valid contracts of employment is implicit in the decision in *MHC Consulting Services Ltd v Tansell* [2000] ICR 789 (CA).

[69] See Judith Freedman's discussion paper, Freedman 2001, at 97–104, referring to Finance Act 2000, s 60 and Sch 12.

of personal employment contracts, it is not necessarily inimical to the recognition of a valid contract that the arrangement involves no real employment relations within the corporate entity in any meaningful sense.

There is an even more general set of issues about the effects of the strength of the bilateral and individual model of the employment contract. One of the most significant ways in which this individualized, personalized model has imposed itself is by almost eliminating any construction of workers as making contracts of employment jointly or collectively. So effectively has that model entrenched itself that it has become uncontroversial, almost axiomatic, to regard collective agreements as juristically atomized into individual contracts between the employer or employers *and each individual worker.*

Thus there are many arguments about whether the collective agreement has been translated into the individual contract in the appropriate way or to the appropriate extent,[70] but we tend not to question the unstated assumption that the collective agreement cannot and does not operate as a collective contract of employment. When we speak of whether collective agreements can amount to legally enforceable contracts, we are not, even then, considering the possibility that they might amount to collectively made contracts of employment; we are merely canvassing the different possibility that they might be contracts between employers and trade unions or groups of workers, governing their collective dealings with each other rather than embodying directly any actual work relationships.

In fact we have become so accustomed to this particular kind of juridical atomization that we tend not to question the appropriateness of it even when it produces results greatly at variance with the organizational realities. In the late 1980s and early 1990s many employing enterprises de-collectivized their relations with their workers in the sense that they eliminated trade unions from their collective bargaining role in the establishing of terms and conditions of employment. This was a matter of profound consequence, and it was a matter of great controversy whether and when it involved a denial of workers' rights of freedom of association to place them under pressure to accept the so-called 'personal' contracts which were proposed. Yet from the perspective of the law of the contract of employment, those workers already had completely individuated personal contracts in the first place; all that seemed to be at stake, from that perspective, was the way in which the terms of the contract would be established rather than the very nature of the contract itself. This perception may have contributed to the view taken in *Associated Newspapers Ltd v Wilson*[71] that the collective bargaining of

---

[70] See the admirably full discussion in Deakin & Morris 2001 at 259–266.

[71] [1995] ICR 406 (HL). In *Wilson and NUJ v United Kingdom* [2002] IRLR 128, the European Court of Human Rights held that this decision and subsequent legislation represented a failure of compliance of UK law with Articles 10 and 11 of the European Convention of Human Rights.

terms and conditions is not of the very essence of trade union membership itself.[72]

However, it would not be realistic to see the choice of an individualized model of the contractual employment relation, rather than a fully collective one, as a matter of current controversy, especially in a period of decline in trade union membership and collective bargaining. More appropriate to be viewed as contentious at the present day is the difficulty, which the individualized model creates, in accepting that personal employment contracts of any kind, and contracts of employment in particular, may be entered into jointly, and therefore as multilateral rather than bilateral contracts, by more than one worker *in any sort of* combination with other workers. This poses real problems in a period when, as large-scale industrial collectivization of the workforce declines, so the incentives upon workers to present themselves for employment in small organizations or groupings of various sorts, such as pairs or teams of workers engaging in 'job-sharing' of various kinds, are tending to increase.

For the strength of the individualized and bilateral model of the personal employment contract in general and the contract of employment in particular is so great that almost any such combination between workers is apt to have the result that the arrangement concerned will be perceived as incompatible with the existence of a contract of employment, and may be treated as outside the whole realm of personal employment contracts. The point is well illustrated by the reluctance of the Law Lords in *Kelly v Northern Ireland Housing Executive*[73] to regard the solicitor in a small partnership firm as capable of being a 'person employed' in the statutory sense, and their clear conviction that she could not be regarded as working under a contract of employment, when working as the designated personal provider of legal services to the housing authority.[74]

The final argument which we advance about the analytical shortcomings of the bilateral and individual model of the contractual employment relation is the most general one of all. We argue that the rigid imposition of this model poses serious problems not only in defining and conceptualizing the parties to the personal employment contract but also in construing the nature of the obligations between them. The whole construction of the contractual parties and the contractual obligations is a continuous process of reasoning. Those obligations, like the parties themselves, can only be satisfactorily constructed in terms of the complex realities of relations within

---

[72] Compare, for instance, Lord Bridge at 416: 'it was plain that the employers were seeking by means of an attractive offer to induce their employees voluntarily to quit the union's collective bargaining umbrella and to deal in future directly with the employers over their terms and conditions of employment, but I can see nothing in the evidence recited in the industrial tribunal's decision to suggest that the employers were seeking to induce the employees to give up their union membership'.   [73] [1998] ICR 828 (HL).
[74] See, ibid, Lord Slynn at 836, Lord Griffith at 840.

the employing enterprise. Yet the bilateral and individual approach to the contractual employment relation shuts out those complex realities; it places them below the horizon of the legal conceptual reasoning which is used to construct both the parties to and the obligations of employment contracts.

Two illustrations of this argument will be given. They are cases which have not been specially regarded as concerning the definition or conceptualization of the parties to personal employment contracts, but rather as concerning their obligations. In fact they combine both sets of issues, and require an integrated analysis of both sets of issues. But the artificiality of the bilateral and individual approach to the contractual employment relation makes it very hard to provide that integrated analysis and still harder to reflect the complexities of workplace employment relations in that analysis. In *Laws v London Chronicle Ltd*[75] the issue was whether an employee had been properly dismissed for disobedience. Her offence was to have followed her immediate superior or manager out of the room when ordered not to do so by his superior or manager in the course of an altercation between the two managers. It was held that she had been wrongfully dismissed because she had not intended to repudiate her contractual obligations but had acted out of loyalty to her immediate superior.

The decision was a difficult one; it was a hard case. The real difficulty was that it was unclear to which manager this worker should have deferred, or how she should have resolved that question. This was partly a problem of deciding which manager represented the employing entity in that situation. The bilateral and individual construction of the contracts of employment of these workers gave no sense of that at all. It meant that each of them had a contract with the corporate employing entity, but which had failed clearly to locate her or him within a managerial structure. Hence it was hard to decide who had behaved in compliance with his or her contract of employment in giving or accepting instructions to stay in the room or leave the room. Ms Laws might have said she did not know who her employer was supposed to be. Her contract of employment conceived of as a simple bilateral relation with a legal corporation would not have given her the answer she needed.

This problem has come to assume very great proportions now that, as will be explained fully in a later chapter,[76] the implied obligation of trust and confidence has become central to the understanding of the contractual obligations of the contract of employment, perhaps also of the personal employment contract generally. The foundational decision for the implied obligation of trust and confidence is that of the House of Lords in *Malik v Bank of Credit and Commerce International*.[77] There it was held that the

---

[75] [1959] 1 WLR 698 (CA).   [76] See below, 154 et seq.   [77] [1997] ICR 606 (HL).

employing entity might in principle be regarded as having acted in breach of that obligation, and as being liable for damages to its middle managers, in that the business had been run in such a corrupt manner that when it collapsed its employees found it difficult to obtain other employment. This required a trial of whether the employing entity was actually in breach of that obligation and liable for such damages.

That proved an exceptionally difficult issue. The Court of Appeal has upheld the High Court's view that two employees who brought a test case could not recover such damages.[78] The matter was resolved as a question of causal connection between breach and difficulty in obtaining other employment. Behind that lurks a deeply unresolved question of how the employing entity and its culpability were to be conceptualized. The real problem was to know which employees were to be regarded as the perpetrators of the corrupt running of the enterprise, and which as the victims of it. A real resolution of the issues arising from *Malik v BCCI* would require a searching conceptual and practical analysis of the organization of employment within the employing entity concerned, and of the obligations of its workers, especially its managerial workers with regard to each other. As an instrument of that analysis, the law of personal employment contracts is blunted by its individual and bilateral approach to the employment relation.[79]

CONCLUSION

In this chapter it has been sought to establish the basic foundations of our analysis of the law of personal employment contracts. That argument has proceeded in two stages, in the first of which a definition of the personal employment contract was proposed, and its division into the subcategories of the contract of employment and the semi-dependent worker's contract was considered. In the second stage we analysed and criticized the way in which the parties to the personal employment contract are defined and conceptualized. In this conclusion it will be very briefly considered in what sense that argument has involved restatement of the existing law, and how far further restatement has been shown to be necessary or desirable.

The first stage of the argument, that of proposing a definition of the personal employment contract and its division into the subcategories of the contract of employment and the semi-dependent worker's contract, is a radical and prescriptive restatement of the existing law, for it seeks to redraw and enlarge the boundaries of a map of the law of employment

---

[78] *BCCI v Ali (No 2)* [2002] ICR 1258 (CA).

[79] Comparable issues arose with regard to organic or vicarious contractual liability for breach of the implied obligation of trust and confidence in *Moores v Bude-Stratton Town Council* [2001] ICR 271 (EAT).

contracts which has been centred on the contract of employment, and it proposes novel terminologies to describe the territory. We showed how this follows a path of analysis which the statute law of employment has already largely taken, by identifying and using the categories of the employed person and the worker, and by developing essentially contractual conceptions in order to do so.

That is one of the ways in which we suggest that the method of restatement may be able to improve the coherence and functionality of the law of employment contracts. In order to show this, we return to the idea of statutory variant or para-contractual formulae which we evoked in the Introduction. They were statutory formulations which take their starting point from a conception in the law of employment contracts but go beyond that conception and become something different. Often the evolution and use of such a formula demonstrates a functional shortcoming in the law of employment contracts. The legislators use the law of employment contracts to provide their categories of reference, or benchmarks; but they perceive a need for a particular conceptual mechanism which the law of employment contracts fails to provide so they produce a statutory variant formula.

In those situations, we suggested in the Introduction that it will often be desirable for the law of employment contracts to be restated, either by clarification or by authoritative reformulation, so that its own conceptual apparatus meets the functional need which the legislators encountered. That is subject to the proviso that the law of employment contracts would not thereby lose its general coherence, that is to say the sense of a logical and workable relation between its component principles and rules. In evolving and using the categories of employed person and worker, the legislators were producing variants on the fundamental definitional category of the law of employment contracts, that of the contract of employment. The argument of the first part of this chapter was that it would be useful and workable for the main definitional category of the law of employment contracts to be reformulated as that of the personal employment contract or personal work contract. Our argument acknowledges that this might require legislative restatement actually to make it work; if so we suggest that this would be desirable.

There are some respects in which the legislators have perceived the need for further statutory variants, that is to say extensions, upon the definitional categories of employed person or worker, and have acted upon that perception. One of them needs to be considered at this stage of our argument; it is that of 'home workers'. The terminology of 'home workers' is used to refer to persons working under a pattern of arrangements which has been historically very significant; it is the pattern whereby manufacturing enterprises engage persons to work on the production or processing of goods in their homes or domestic workshops, typically on the basis that the work may be performed either by them or by others brought in to assist, such as family members. Persons working under such arrangements are apt to fall outside not merely the definition of employees because the employing entity has insufficient control over their work, but also outside those of the employed person or the worker because they are not required to carry out the work personally.[80] It was wished to ensure the inclusion of such persons in the national minimum wage legislation. In order to do so, a specially extended formulation was used whereby home workers are included in the category of workers whether or not they contract to work personally.[81] The question for consideration is whether our general definitional category of the personal employment contract should embody a similar extension, but we suggest that to do so would excessively encroach upon the analytical coherence of the category as a whole.

Our argument went on to consider the division of the category of personal employment contract into the two subcategories of the contract of employment and the semi-dependent worker's contract. Our argument was in part descriptive and critical, in part prescriptive. It was descriptive and critical so far as it accepted the need for the division into categories but asserted the lack of a satisfactory basis for drawing that distinction. It was prescriptive to the extent that it argued for the new terminology of the semi-dependent worker's contract as a way of identifying and conceptualizing the 'other workers' notion which has emerged from the statute law of employment.

The method of restatement demands that we consider whether anything can be suggested to produce greater analytical clarity with regard to the division into subcategories. In principle when a distinction between two categories is so difficult to draw, it is a good idea to have a presumption which provides an initial allocation of particular fact situations to one category or the other. Hugh Collins has argued persuasively for such a presumption in favour of the contract of employment.[82] It does not seem that the present law supports such a presumption; it does not seem possible to assert such a presumption in either direction simply as a matter of clarification of the present law. It is, however, important to recall that our whole definitional category, the personal employment contract, is intended to exclude the genuinely self-employed person as opposed to the semi-dependent worker. We tentatively suggest that it would be coherent and workable to have an initial

---

[80] *Airfix Footwear Ltd v Cope* [1978] ICR 1210 (EAT) and *Nethermere (St Neots) Ltd v Gardiner* [1984] ICR 612 (CA) indicate that persons working under such arrangements may be regarded as employees, and *a fortiori* as employed persons or workers, but the framers of legislation have rightly regarded that categorization as open to doubt.

[81] National Minimum Wage Act 1998, s 35 (1), 'home workers' being defined by s 35(2) as individuals contracting with a person for the purpose of that person's business, for the execution of work to be done in a place not under the control or management of that person.

[82] This was the conclusion of his article on Vertical Disintegration (Collins 1990); see above, 22 23.

presumption that workers within that category were dependent ones coming within the legal category of employees under contracts of employment. However, we accept that this would require authoritative determination, and that important questions of policy are involved.

The second stage of the argument, which dealt with the way that the parties to the employment relation are defined and conceptualized in the law of personal employment contracts, was more critical than it was pre- scriptive. On the whole it described the present law and pointed out what were argued to be serious analytical shortcomings, rather than suggesting specific reformulations. At some points, areas of uncertainty were exposed where clarification is needed and would require authoritative determination such as the courts might provide, for example with regard to the question of when personal employment contracts may be made by multiplicities of employing entities and by multiplicities of workers. At some points, for example with regard to the treatment of employment via intermediary entit- ies such as employment agencies, questions of policy are clearly involved which would need to be addressed as such.[83]

However, there is also a set of issues about technical law reform too. Here again, as with the first stage of our argument, the method of restatement makes it appropriate to consider some important statutory variants, and decide whether they point to a case for reformulation of the existing con- tractual law. Our analysis of the current state of the law of personal employ- ment contracts showed that there was a complex of serious functional problems with regard to employment arrangements or relations involving an end-user of services and an intermediary entity such as an employment agency having some kind of employing role between that end-user and the worker. The problems were firstly, that there is great resistance to the con- struction of triangular personal employment contracts, secondly, that there may be great difficulty in deciding whether the worker's bilateral personal employment contract is with the end-user or the intermediary, but thirdly and most fundamentally that the triangular nature of the arrangement may have the effect that the worker fails to qualify as having a contract of employment or even as having a personal work or employment contract of any kind.

Two statutory variants have evolved to address those problems. One of those variants addresses the first two of those problems but probably does not address the third one. This is the *contract worker* variant, which is found in the legislation concerning discrimination in employment.[84] This variant

---

[83] The Contracts (Rights of Third Parties) Act 1999 was framed so as to avoid this area; see the exception for workers' contracts in s 6(3). This seems to have been in deference to a governmental consultation on changes to the legislative regime for agency employment which at the time of writing has still not given rise to any new legislation.

[84] Sex Discrimination Act 1975, s 9; Race Relations Act 1976, s 7; Disability Discrimination Act 1995, s 12.

operates so that, where an individual is employed by an intermediary[85] to work for an end-user,[86] the individual is deemed to be a contract worker to the effect that the legislation applies as between the worker and the end-user. It is not wholly clear whether in such a case the legislation also applies as between the intermediary and the worker, but it probably does. To that extent the legislation has constructed a statutory triangular employment relationship.

However, it is not clear whether that variant deals with the deeper problem that the triangularity of the arrangement may exclude the person working under the arrangement from the statutory categories of employee, employed person, or worker. Another statutory variant, that of the 'agency workers who are not otherwise "workers" ' was deployed in the National Minimum Wage Act and in the Working Time Regulations[87] in an effort to ensure that the triangularity of the arrangement does not rule the person working under that arrangement out of the category of worker. It includes such persons within the legislation concerned where they would not otherwise qualify as workers, and applies the legislation as between the working person and either the end-user or the intermediary, according to which of them is responsible for paying or does pay that person.

We suggest that it is deeply unsatisfactory that statutory variants of such complexity have to be constructed because of the lack of clarity of the approach of the law of personal employment contracts to the question of triangular or multilateral employment relations. The Employment Relations Act 1999 has created[88] free-ranging powers of secondary legislation to redeploy or refashion statutory categories to deal with problems of personal scope of employment legislation. It is, however, unlikely that the problems in this particular area can be satisfactorily resolved without some degree of authoritative reformulation of the underlying contractual law.

Outside those particular areas, the general criticism of the bilateral and individual approach to the construction of the contractual employment relation and the parties to it is advanced not so much as a suggestion for particular restatement, but instead as a preliminary argument to be used in considering more specific areas of contractual employment law in subsequent chapters. It is put forward as a way of indicating the continuity of

---

[85] The decision in *MHC Consulting Ltd v Tansell* [2000] ICR 789 (CA) was that this might include an arrangement through more than one intermediary.

[86] The important decision in *Harrods Ltd v Remick* [1998] ICR 156 (CA) held that this connection existed between the corporate proprietor of a department store and a person employed by a franchised stallholder within the store.

[87] National Minimum Wage Act 1998, s 34; Working Time Regulations 1998, SI 1998/1833 reg 36.

[88] Section 23—power to confer rights on individuals. At the time of writing the Department of Trade and Industry is engaged in a public consultation about the future use of these powers.

underlying issues and problems between the different aspects or areas of the law of personal employment contracts which are discussed in the ensuing chapters. The next chapter is concerned with an area with which that continuity of underlying issues and problems will become very apparent, that of the formation and internal structure of personal employment contracts.

2

Formation and Internal Structure

INTRODUCTION

The purpose of this chapter is to consider when, or in what conditions, the law will recognize that a personal employment contract has been validly made and has come into existence, and also to consider what internal structure the law accords to personal employment contracts. In this Introduction it will be explained briefly what is the scope and approach of this chapter and how it fits into the scheme of the work as a whole; and how the subject matter of this chapter, and the method of presenting it, relate to the headings under which contract law is normally expounded.

This chapter forms the second of a sequence of three chapters which are intended between them to create a picture of how the law conceives of and constructs the shape and content of personal employment contracts. In the previous chapter, the category of personal employment contracts was identified, the meaning of the term 'personal employment contract' was specified, and we considered how the parties to those contracts and the personal structure of those contracts are conceptualized. In the next chapter, we examine the way in which the express and implied terms of such contracts are construed.

The bridge between the subject matter of those two chapters consists of the law concerning the formation and internal structure of the personal employment contract. The first aspect, treated in the next section, consists of an analysis of some of the basic conditions for entering into a legally valid personal employment contract. In that section, we consider the application to personal employment relationships of certain of the doctrines of the general law of contract which govern or affect the formation of contracts in general, especially those concerning offer and acceptance, consideration, intention to create legal relations, and illegality. We also refer to the role of formal requirements in the making of personal employment contracts. This analysis focuses upon various ways in which the law distinguishes between those personal work relationships which do give rise to personal employment contracts and those which are deemed not to do so.

We then in the second section of the chapter embark upon a discussion, which forms a hinge upon which much of the rest of this work turns, in which it is considered what internal structure the law imputes to personal employment contracts. The idea of internal structure is used to explore the nature of personal employment contracts as relational contracts, and to address the crucial questions firstly of whether and when personal employment contracts should be regarded as having a two-level structure, and secondly how work and remuneration are related to each other within those contracts. That discussion discloses some further extremely difficult issues of internal structure, which concern the continuity of personal employment contracts; those problems are considered, and result in some possible suggestions for radical restatement which are put forward in the Conclusion to the chapter.

SECTION 1: THE CONDITIONS OF FORMATION OF PERSONAL EMPLOYMENT CONTRACTS

A. The Role or Function of the Conditions of Formation

The law which determines the basic conditions for the valid formation of contracts has a different role in the context of personal employment contracts from that which it has in relation to contracts in general. In the law of contracts in general, our concern with the basic conditions for the making of valid contracts is normally in order to know whether an enforceable contractual right or obligation has arisen. That may be our concern in the context of personal employment contracts; but more often the function of the basic conditions will be to determine whether a claimant has a gateway to statutory employment rights which depend upon the existence of a valid personal employment contract between the worker and the employing entity, or indeed upon the existence of one particular type of personal employment contract, the contract of employment.

So, in the cases which are discussed in expositions of the law of contract in general, the basic conditions for the making of valid contracts are usually applied to particular promises, undertakings, or courses of conduct, in order to determine whether they might support an action in contract to enforce them. In the employment context, the basic conditions are more often applied to know whether a personal work relationship, which would be recognized as a matter of factual description, has assumed the character of a legally valid personal employment contract and if so of which type. In that sense, the basic conditions for the making of valid contracts are often transposed into a different role or function when they fall to be applied in the employment context. We begin by examining how the requirement of contractual intention fulfils that role.

B. Contractual Intention and the Formation of Personal Employment Contracts

Within the law of personal employment contracts there is a particular body of law or doctrine which deploys ideas about contractual intention to distinguish between the personal work relationships which do and do not give rise to valid personal employment contracts. This body of law or doctrine corresponds to or covers the same ground as the general contract principles concerning intention to create legal relations and, to some extent, consideration; but it has become so specialized and functionally adapted to the demands of employment law that this is not a direct correspondence.

One important respect in which this specialized body of law fails to relate neatly to the general principles of contract law, is that, within the specialized body of law, the doctrines concerning contractual intention, on the one hand, and consideration, on the other hand, are interconnected in a particular, and more than normally complex, sense. This is mainly because of problems about the extent to which and the sense in which personal employment contracts consist of an *exchange* of work and remuneration. We address that set of problems later in this chapter, when we consider further the internal structure of personal employment contracts. Most of the issues concerning the requirement of consideration will be discussed under that heading; the present discussion is about contractual intention.

It will help to explain the relationship between contractual intention in general contract law, on the one hand, and in the law of personal employment contracts, on the other hand, if we identify it in the former context as 'intention to create legal relations' and in the latter context as 'intention to make a personal employment contract'. The former terminology, sanctioned by customary usage in the discourse of contract law, really refers to an intention that a given transaction or relationship shall give rise to a legally binding contract of whatever sort. The latter is put forward here as meaning an intention that a personal work relationship shall give rise to a legally binding personal employment contract in particular.

The best way of understanding this body of law, and the sense in which it is about the *intention* of the parties to a transaction or relationship, is to realize that neither the general doctrine of intention to create legal relations nor the law concerning intention to make a personal employment contract simply envisages the presence or absence of the requisite contractual intention. Instead, they envisage the parties as choosing between alternative modes of conducting their transaction or relationship, only one of which gives rise to a contract in general or to a personal employment contract in particular. It is this idea of choice between alternative modes of relationship which makes intention to create legal relations or intention to make a personal employment contract a distinct requirement for the making of valid contracts in general or personal employment contracts in particular. The requirement is that the parties to the transaction or relationship shall have intended to choose the contractual mode for the conduct of it.

In this sense, intention to make a personal employment contract is something more complex than simply a specialized version of intention to create legal relations. That is to say, the law concerning intention to make a personal

employment contract envisages a decidedly more complex series of alternative intentions than does the general law of intention to create legal
relations. In the general law of contracts, intention to create legal relations
is one of two alternative modes of transaction or relationship, the other
being the rather quaintly styled 'agreement binding in honour only'. This
evokes the notion of an agreement which does give rise to moral obligations
of a certain kind but not to legal or contractual obligations (legal and
contractual obligations being effectively equated for this purpose).

In the specific context of personal work relationships, the intention to
make a personal employment contract—that is to say, the choice to conduct
the personal work relationship in the mode of a personal employment
contract—is contrasted with quite an extensive set of alternatives. These
alternatives do not really come within the category of 'agreements binding
in honour only'. They are variants on a theme to the effect that personal
work relationships may be conducted on the footing of a set of obligations
which are essentially looser, more diffuse, and less reciprocally related to
each other than is the case with personal employment contracts. Such obligations may amount to legal obligations of some kind, they may even amount
to contractual obligations of some kind; but they are seen as not being sufficiently concrete and reciprocally related to ground an intention to enter
into a personal employment contract.

There are a number of groups of personal work relationships which have
at times been regarded as falling wholly or partly within that set of alternatives, and so not giving rise to personal employment contracts. These
groups include, in various different senses, the work relationships of voluntary workers, apprentices and trainees, holders of certain public or private
offices or appointments, and ministers of religion. It is informative to
survey the evolution of thinking about intention to make personal employment contracts in relation to those different groups. It will emerge that
there is a general tendency to presume in favour of an intention that any
given personal work relationship shall take the form of a personal employment contract, but that the application of that presumption is heavily
dependent upon the particular legal and remedial context in which the
question arises.

It is useful to begin that survey by thinking about voluntary workers.
Many arrangements for voluntary work do not involve payment of the
worker in any form at all, and such arrangements are regarded as not
amounting to or giving rise to personal employment contracts. In that situation, voluntary work, or volunteering as it is increasingly called, is seen
as an alternative mode of personal work relationship to the making of personal employment contracts. The intention to work as a volunteer is envisaged as being different from the contractual intention. In the doctrinal
terms of the general law of contract, there is neither intention to create legal
relations nor consideration. In the specialized context of the law of personal

employment contracts, it can be said that there is no intention to create such a contract.

However, it is becoming increasingly necessary, on the one hand, and difficult, on the other hand, for employment tribunals and courts to draw fine distinctions between volunteering arrangements where the parties are deemed to have chosen pure voluntary work and those where they are deemed to have chosen to make personal employment contracts. That necessity arises as statutory employment rights are extended from employees working under contracts of employment to workers in the statutory sense because those engaged in voluntary work may more readily be deemed to be workers than employees with contracts of employment. It has become more difficult as social and economic circumstances increasingly blur the line between those who are working within the labour market in economic personal work relationships, albeit on a very partial or casual basis, and those who are working similarly partially or casually, but on the different and non-economic basis of occupying their time for the benefit both of themselves and others.

One form which this line-blurring takes is the making of work arrangements described as voluntary work but involving the payment of the worker's expenses. The decision of the Employment Appeal Tribunal in the case of *Migrant Advisory Service v Chaudri*[1] indicates that, at least in the context of a concern to ensure an inclusive approach to the category of workers covered by the laws regulating discrimination in employment, the courts will treat such payments as consideration sustaining a personal employment contract where those payments are not strictly limited to actual out-of-pocket expenses. In the case of *Uttley v St John's Ambulance*,[2] where the payments of expenses to a volunteer first-aid worker were strictly limited to actual out-of-pocket expenses, the Employment Appeal Tribunal held that the worker was not an employed person within the meaning of the sex discrimination legislation. The reasoning provides a good example of the notion of absence of intention to enter into a personal employment contract.

For the Employment Tribunal had held that the payment of actual out-of-pocket expenses did not amount to consideration such as was necessary to the existence of a personal employment contract; but that even if, contrary to their view, there was consideration sustaining a contract, this was nevertheless to be viewed as a relationship of membership of a voluntary association rather than as a personal employment contract. The Employment Appeal Tribunal confirmed that the relationship of membership of a voluntary association is fundamentally distinct from the relationship of

---

[1] Appeal No EAT/1400/97 (28 July 1998), unreported; see Morris, D 1999 at 250–251.
[2] Appeal No EAT/635/98 (18 September 1998), unreported; see Morris, D 1999 at 251–252.

employment, and regarded it as clear that the claimant had no relationship with the organization other than one of membership. So the first-aid worker and the organization were deemed to have chosen to enter into a relationship of membership of a voluntary organization *rather than* a personal employment contract. It was this choice of an alternative mode of personal work relationship which negated the intention to enter into a personal employment contract. It is important to note that membership of a voluntary association may itself be contractual in character, but that is even so regarded as involving quite a different kind of intent from that which is required for a personal employment contract.

One of the elements in the relationship between the volunteer and the organization which was seen in that case to differentiate it from a contractual work relationship was the fact that it included the provision of training by the organization to the volunteer. The fact that a work relationship includes an element of training is in no way inconsistent with the work relationship constituting or being the subject of a personal employment contract. But when training of the worker is a central or dominant feature of a work relationship, highly difficult issues arise about whether the relationship gives rise to a personal employment contract, which may be viewed as issues of consideration, or of general intention to create legal relations, or of specific intention to make a personal employment contract.

An important part of the background to understanding these issues consists of the way that the relationship of master or employer and apprentice has been regarded in employment law. The relationship seems to have been regarded as a contractual one over a long period of time, whether or not remuneration moves from employer to the apprentice, in the form of wages or board and lodging, or from the apprentice to the master or employer in the form of a premium for acceptance into apprenticeship. It seems to have been assumed that the master or employer and the apprentice (perhaps via members of the apprentice's family where the apprentice is below the age of majority) intend to make a contract of apprenticeship, whereby the apprentice agrees to work for the master or employer, and the master or employer agrees to train the apprentice in the trade concerned, so that there is both intention to create legal relations and the mutual furnishing of consideration.[3] Moreover, contracts of apprenticeship are normally expressly included within statutory definitions of personal employment contracts, and are often even included within statutory definitions of contracts of employment—so that the contract of employment is often defined as a contract *of service or of apprenticeship*.[4]

---

[3] Compare for example the analyses of the master/apprentice relation in *Maw v Jones* (1890) 25 QBD 107 and *Dunk v George Waller & Son Ltd* [1970] 2 QB 163; see below, 357–358.

[4] As in the key definition for the purposes of the Employment Rights Act 1996 (ERA), contained in s 230(2) of that Act.

The issues concerning personal work relationships with a strong or predominant element of training all presented themselves in the case of *Edmonds v Lawson*[5] in which the Court of Appeal decided that a pupil barrister was not a 'worker' within the meaning of the National Minimum Wage Act 1998. In this case, those issues were further complicated by structural issues about the personal work relationships in question, about whether any contract to which this personal work relationship might give rise was with the pupil-master or with all the barristers comprising the set of the chambers into which the pupil had been accepted for pupillage. Despite those complications, the Court of Appeal decided that there was a general intention to create legal relations underlying this pupillage arrangement, and indeed that the arrangement did assume contractual form.

Nevertheless, it was held that the pupillage arrangement did not give rise to a personal employment contract such as would identify the pupil as a worker within the meaning of the Act. The pupil's relationship with the pupil-master was seen as not giving rise to a contract between them, because, since the pupil neither paid the pupil-master nor was subject to an obligation to work for the pupil-master, she did not furnish consideration for a contract with the pupil-master. The pupil was seen as being in a contractual arrangement with the set of chambers as a whole, for which she furnished consideration by undertaking an obligation (albeit probably not legally enforceable) to enter into and serve the pupillage, which was important to the set of chambers as well as to the pupil herself.

However, that contract with the set of chambers was seen as not being a personal employment contract of the kind that would identify the pupil as a worker within the statutory definition. It was held not to be a contract of service or apprenticeship because the pupil was under no obligation to work for the barristers in the set of chambers. It was further held that if the pupil did in fact undertake any work for any member of the set of chambers, that should be regarded as a contract for work for a client in the course of a professional practice, of the kind which falls within the profession or business exception, thus taking it outside the statutory definition of the worker's contract.[6]

The judges in the Court of Appeal in this case clearly felt that the pupil barrister did not come within the category of workers entitled to the National Minimum Wage because she was more in the nature of a trainee in the set of chambers under her pupil-master, rather than a worker for the set of chambers or for her pupil-master. Their vision of workers who are entitled to the National Minimum Wage was evidently closely confined to employees or apprentices working under contracts of service or apprenticeship. Their reasoning does not seem to have allowed for the possibility

[5] [2000] ICR 567 (CA).
[6] See above, 24–25, for explanation of the profession or business exception.

that there was, in the terminology of the present work, a semi-dependent worker's contract between the pupil barrister and the set of chambers as a whole. But the significance of the decision to the present discussion is that they were, on the one hand, prepared to accept that the pupillage arrangement was a contractual one, but, on the other hand, construed it as not amounting to a worker's contract. In the terms of the present discussion, they were prepared to find an intention to create legal relations but were not prepared to find an intention to make a personal employment contract. They perceived the relationship as contractual, but as representing the choice (following from the regime for pupillage maintained by the Bar Council) to make a contract for education and training rather than a personal employment contract.

There emerges from the foregoing discussion both of volunteers and trainees a disposition on the part of the courts to assume that, when employment law is constructed around personal employment contracts, and especially when it is constructed around contracts of employment as such, that is because employment law is concerned with and only with relationships which are about the exchange of work and remuneration, and that it is for the courts to define the nature and scope of personal employment contracts accordingly. We can see, in the rather special context of volunteers and trainees, that the courts may construct alternative models of relationships involving personal work but seen as not giving rise to personal employment contracts. There are a number of further such alternative models; we suggest that they can usefully be grouped together as models of office-holding rather than employment. We proceed to consider when and how far the courts are disposed to regard relationships involving personal work as in the nature of office-holding rather than employment.

We should begin by observing that office-holding is not usually viewed as actually being incompatible with the existence of a personal employment contract, and indeed that such notion of incompatibility as may have existed in the past seems to be fast diminishing. Nevertheless, office-holding still retains quite some importance as an alternative legal account of certain personal work relationships. The idea of office-holding as a non-contractual, or even at times a counter-contractual, way of conceptualizing some personal work relationships involves a number of factors, some or all of which are encountered in each of the particular personal work relationships in question, and which interact with each other. The most important of these factors seem to be: (1) that any payment which the office-holders receive is made by virtue of their holding the office in question rather than in respect of work done, so that there is not a contractual exchange of work and payment; (2) that office-holders are appointed to occupy positions within institutional structures rather than being employed by an employing entity in the contractual sense; and (3) that the office-holding is governed by a normative regime with some other basis or starting point than the contractual one.

The first of those three factors is nowadays the least potent of the three. Over a long historical period, we can observe how various terminologies were used to dissociate payment from work, and to set the recipients of such payment aside from (and often above) ordinary workers who were seen as receiving 'wages' which related directly to specific work. There were once some connotations of non-contractual office-holding in denoting workers as 'staff' who received a 'stipend' or a 'salary', though those terminologies have long since been fully absorbed into the vocabulary of personal employment contracts. A similar notion probably contributed to a historical, though long since abandoned, unwillingness to allow civil servants to sue for arrears of pay.[7] The idea survives in the form of an occasional (but probably diminishing) willingness on the part of the courts to view a part-time or occasional worker, for example in a voluntary association, as an office-holder in receipt of an honorarium *rather than* a worker under a personal employment contract, as in a test case in 1977 concerning those secretaries of working men's clubs who received more than negligible payments but had not been voted a full salary.[8]

The second factor identifies some people engaged in personal work as office-holders rather than workers under personal employment contracts because they do not have employing entities in the ordinary sense for whom they are to be regarded as working in a way that gives rise to a personal employment contract. For a long time, this factor contributed to a perception, which may still hold sway to some extent, that police officers and prison officers 'hold office of her Majesty as constables' *rather than* being employed under personal employment contracts. That this factor operated in relation to those engaged in those occupations was in part at least due to the fact that the functions of employing police officers and prison officers have historically been distributed in complex ways between the Crown (these days in the form of the Home Office) and various local bodies or authorities. Reasoning of this kind served to categorize a prison officer as the holder of the office of constable rather than as a person working under a private law contract in *R v Home Secretary, ex parte Benwell*;[9] but in *McClaren v Home Office*[10] the Court of Appeal has since held that a prison officer may be regarded as being employed under a private law contract, and the present position in this respect is somewhat unclear.[11]

---

[7] Compare *Reilly v R* [1934] AC 176 (PC).

[8] *102 Social Club and Institute Ltd v Bickerton* [1977] ICR 911 (EAT).

[9] [1984] ICR 723 (QBD).   [10] [1990] ICR 824 (CA).

[11] In particular it is unclear how far the current more contractually oriented approach to the relationship between civil servants and the Crown, as to which see below, 69–70, has impinged on the analysis of the situation of police and prison officers. The decision of the EAT in *Metropolitan Police Commissioner v Lowrey-Nesbit* [1999] ICR 401 suggests that constables in various special police forces will readily be regarded as employees under contracts of employment, and further erodes the notion of incompatibility between holding the office of constable and being employed under a contract of employment.

A somewhat comparable operation of the second factor occurs in relation to ministers of religion. One of the main ways in which the courts express a powerful reluctance to regard ministers of religion as workers working under personal employment contracts is by holding that their church or religious organization cannot be regarded as their employing entity in any contractual sense, and that they are therefore to be regarded as holding a spiritual office rather than as being a party to a personal employment contract. This was one of the factors which operated to produce or explain the recent decision of the Court of Appeal in the case of *Diocese of Southwark v Coker*[12] that a priest of the Anglican Church was the holder of an ecclesiastical office rather than an employee employed under a contract of employment and as such able to claim the right not to be unfairly dismissed. The Court regarded it as difficult to find within the church organization any one person or body who or which could satisfactorily be regarded as the entity employing the priest.

However, it is the third factor which has been much the most significant in promoting the perception that office-holding is a systemic alternative to contractual employment under a personal employment contract. That is to say, the most frequent reason for regarding a personal work relationship as constituting office-holding rather than contractual employment is that it is seen as falling under a different, non-contractual, legal and normative regime. The most obvious and significant such regime is that of public law, and almost all if not all of the situations in which the third factor operates could be thought about in terms of the relationship between public law and private law. Moreover, the generalization can be made that there is a marked trend towards viewing all or almost all personal work relationships, even in the public sector, as intended to be constituted as personal employment contracts under a private law regime rather than as office-holding under a public law regime.

Nevertheless, despite the validity of that generalization, the recent history of the choice between contractual employment regimes and non-contractual office-holding regimes is much more complex than that generalization might appear to suggest. In essence, the courts have been in the position of choosing, or imputing choices, not between two simple alternative regimes, but between various different employment regimes, some of which are (1) purely contractual private law regimes, others of which are (2) purely non-contractual public law regimes, and yet others of which are (3) mixed public and private law regimes. There have been various types and conceptions of office-holding, which have at different times been differently located in the second or third of those two categories. Without embarking upon an elaborate juridical history of public sector employment, we

---

[12] [1998] ICR 140 (CA).

propose briefly to analyse the recent development and current state of the law allocating personal work relationships between these categories.

The office-holding regimes which we would currently describe as coming within the scope of public law, as broadly defined, are of two contrasting types as to their duration and terminability; that is to say, they may either be (1) held at pleasure, so that the office-holding may be terminated at the will or discretion of the person, body, or authority of which the office is held, or (2) held under some kind of tenure which gives the office holding a fixed duration and/or restricts its terminability. The two types each contrast not only with the other, but with the basic model of the personal employment contract. That is to say, the holder of an office at pleasure systemically tends to have a less secure hold on the position in question than a worker under a personal employment contract, while the holder of a tenured office system-ically tends to enjoy a more secure hold on the position in question than a worker under a personal employment contract. We shall consider in slightly greater detail how each of those two types of office-holding has evolved in relation to personal employment contracts.

Much the most important occurrence of office-holding at pleasure is in the context of Crown service, where it established itself as the legal analysis of the relationship between the civil servant and the Crown. This analysis could be regarded as a proposition of Constitutional Law or of Public Law, in so far as it was derived from a notion of the unrestricted prerogative of the Crown to appoint and dismiss its servants. In practice, over a long historical period civil servants tended to enjoy greater security in their positions than those working in comparable occupations for private employing entities; but the Crown authorities attached much importance to maintaining their legal freedom of action, and in particular to asserting that the discretion of the Crown to dismiss at pleasure demonstrated the absence of contractual intention in the relationship between the Crown and its civil servants.[13]

However, from the mid-1960s onwards, the rapid positive development of the aspect of Public Law which concerns judicial review of administrat-ive action brought about an ironical reversal in the position of the Crown in its legal relationships with its civil servants. In the briefest summary, there were two aspects to this reversal of position. On the one hand, it became government policy from the early 1980s onwards to seek to increase the efficiency of the Civil Service, by means, *inter alia*, of a deliber-ate contractualization of the relationship between the Crown and its civil servants. On the other hand, the increased availability of judicial review to challenge dismissal from public offices generally, coupled with the erosion

---

[13] A more extended consideration of the subject matter of this and the ensuing two para-graphs is to be found in the present author's contribution (Freedland 1999a) to the symposium volume on *The Nature of the Crown* edited by Sunkin and Payne (Sunkin and Payne 1999).

of unrestricted Crown prerogative in the face of judicial review, meant that the Crown authorities now frequently found themselves wishing to assert that their relations with civil servants were essentially contractual and hence firmly in the sphere of private law, in order to resist claims for judicial review in respect of discipline or dismissal of civil servants.

The assertion of the private law character of the relationship between the Crown and its civil servants was made the more acceptable by the fact that unfair dismissal legislation had been applied to them since its inception in 1971, thus giving them legal protection against dismissal on what was viewed as an essentially private law basis. In the important case of *R v Lord Chancellor's Department, ex parte Nangle*,[14] the Crown successfully resisted judicial review of internal disciplinary proceedings against an executive officer in the Civil Service by means of this assertion, and in particular succeeded in arguing that the proposition, advanced by the Crown itself in the then current Code of Civil Service Pay and Conditions, that there was no contract of employment between the Crown and the civil servant did not represent the reality of the situation. The court held that the documents of appointment, objectively construed in context, did manifest an intention to enter into legal relations of the kind sufficient to locate the relationship in the private law sphere.[15]

If we turn to consider the development of the other main type of office-holding, that is to say tenured office-holding, we find that there is a rather similar, though not total, collapse of the non-contractual and public law notion of office-holding. However, because of the contrast between the two types of office-holding which has already been indicated, this development has taken a somewhat different route, and in order to follow that route it is necessary to describe briefly the trajectory which different types of clearly or arguably tenured public office-holding have followed. We shall refer to several types of personal work situation in relation to which such developments have occurred, namely, tenured public service offices, and tenure in academic, charitable, and ecclesiastical institutions.

The notion of tenured office-holding, which connects strongly but not entirely with the idea of property in a job, has a long history in British public service. In the general form of a claim to retain an appointment for life except in the case of grave misconduct, it underwent a general decline in the twentieth century; but in the particular form of a claim to an appointment

---

[14] [1991] ICR 743 (QBD).
[15] Despite that evolution in approach to civil servants employed (technically) 'at pleasure', the situation of other public or statutory office-holders 'at pleasure' continues to represent a possible exception to the increasingly contractualist approach, as is manifested for example in the decision of the EAT in *Lincolnshire County Council v Hopper* [2002] ICR 1301 that registrars of births, marriages and deaths (whose situation was considered but not resolved in *Miles v Wakefield Metropolitan District Council* [1987] ICR 368 (HL)) were not contractual employees.

which could be terminated only for good cause following a fair hearing, it experienced a dramatic judicial endorsement, in relation to a chief constable, in the leading case of *Ridge v Baldwin*[16] in 1963. In fact, when that decision initiated a revitalization of judicial review of administrative action and a concretization of English Public Law, it took as its starting point the affirmation of a sharp contrast between the 'purely' private law and contractual relationship of master and servant, and the situation of a 'pure' office-holder whose office was not terminable at pleasure, and who was entitled, if the office was of a sufficiently public character, to the application of the principles of natural justice before dismissal.

In the decade or so following *Ridge v Baldwin*, it began to appear as if the courts might recognize quite a wide category of mixed situations in which some public service workers, especially those whose employment had a statutory basis, might be regarded as employed under personal employment contracts, indeed under contracts of employment, but as also entitled to the application of public law principles before discipline or dismissal as if they were tenured office-holders. This development reached its high water mark in the decision of the House of Lords in 1971 in the case of *Malloch v Aberdeen Corporation*,[17] which concerned a schoolteacher whose employment was the subject of Scottish legislation which accorded it clear connotations of protected office-holding. There was even a rather surprising extension of this notion to a full-time official of trade union, perceived as the holder of a protected office, in the decision of the Court of Appeal in 1977 in *Stevenson v United Road Transport Union*.[18]

However, this development of a mixed model, which could combine the infrastructure of a personal employment contract with the superstructure of a tenured public office, was almost entirely halted after 1980. A crucial change in the legal environment occurred in the shape of the imposition of a new, or at least greatly strengthened, jurisdictional separation between private law and public law, ushered in by a new procedural regime for judicial review[19] to which those jurisdictional consequences were assigned by case law from the time of the decision of the House of Lords in 1982 in *O'Reilly v Mackman*.[20] In what must, perhaps rather regrettably, be regarded as the foundational case for the modern understanding of the public sector employment relationship, the Court of Appeal in its decision in 1985 in the case of *R v East Berkshire Health Authority, ex parte Walsh*[21] insisted that the public sector employment relationship must generally, unless there is a very strong particular reason to do otherwise, be regarded

---

[16] [1964] AC 40 (HL).   [17] [1971] 1 WLR 1578 (HL).
[18] [1977] ICR 893 (CA).
[19] Introduced in 1977 by the new Order 53 of the Rules of the Supreme Court, and accorded statutory force by s 31 of the Supreme Court Act 1981.
[20] [1983] 2 AC 237 (HL).   [21] [1985] QB 152 (CA).

as located squarely in the area of private law and as being of contractual character, so that the worker will not normally, and did not in this case, have recourse to judicial review to challenge disciplinary decisions relating to the employment, or decisions about dismissal from employment.[22]

It must be said that, as has already been suggested with reference to the employment of civil servants, this judicial preference for a private law and generally contractualist approach to public service personal work relationships has largely coincided with an increasing contractualism in the approach of successive governments to employment in the public services from the early 1980s onwards. Thus, it was clearly the policy of the government of the day, when promoting the provisions of the Education Reform Act 1988[23] which empowered Commissioners to change the employment statutes of universities and colleges of universities, to reduce or abolish the special protection of their tenure of their academic posts which university teachers had generally enjoyed before that. The fact that the Commissioners' statutes for universities and colleges, as eventually enacted under those powers, did not entirely succeed in achieving that result[24] should not be allowed to obscure the extent to which it had been the aim and object of the government to do so.

With the substantial, even though not complete, disappearance of public service office-holding, and of academic tenure, as viable and active non-contractual alternative models for personal work relationships, almost the sole surviving notion of office-holding under a non-contractual special regime occurs in relation to the holders of religious offices, especially though probably not solely in the Church of England. Here, as manifested in the decision in *Diocese of Southwark v Coker* as previously discussed, we can see still operating the conception of a special legal regime for employment within the statutes, or other particular internal code, of an ecclesiastical, charitable, or educational institution—of just the kind that was recognized, for academic tenure under visitatorial jurisdiction conferred by university or college statutes, in the decision of the House of Lords in *R v Hull University Visitor, ex parte Page*,[25] but which had already been abolished for future academic employment in universities and colleges by

---

[22] This tendency towards analysis of public or statutory office-holding as compatible with the existence of a personal employment contract was confirmed by the decision of the EAT in *Johnson v Ryan* [2000] ICR 236 that a statutory rent officer was an employee of the local authority. It should, however, be noted that, in *Perceval-Price v Department of Economic Development* [2000] IRLR 380, the Northern Ireland Court of Appeal held that it was only by an instrumental use of the EC Law Conception of the 'worker' that a tribunal chairman, as a statutory office-holder, could be held to be an employed person within the meaning of the domestic equal pay and treatment legislation. Moreover, the situation of the office-holder *at pleasure* may still continue to represent an exception to this tendency; see above, 70, n 15.

[23] Section 202–205.   [24] Compare Palfreyman and Warner 2001 at 201–204.

[25] [1993] ICR 114 (HL).

the time that case was decided by section 206 of the Education Reform Act 1988.

There has been a parallel rejection by the courts of the model of the public law tenured or protected office in that kind of public service relationship where the duties of the office are of such a nature as to ensure that, if the relationship is to be viewed as contractual, the contract in question will be regarded as a contract for services rather than a contract of employment. Here, however, the analysis has been rather complicated by the emergence of a third alternative, which is that the relationship is of an entirely statutory character, rather than of a contractual character, but that on the other hand it is a private law relationship rather than a public law one. The development of the case law has been intricate in this respect. In the case of *R v Derbyshire County Council, ex parte Noble*,[26] where a doctor, employed by a local authority to attend at the police station when necessary to act as a police surgeon, sought judicial review of the decision to terminate that employment, judicial review was held to be unavailable because the relationship was seen as an essentially private law relationship, and in fact as taking the form of a contract for services.[27]

In the case of *Roy v Kensington and Chelsea Family Practitioner Committee*,[28] the same issue arose, but the reverse way round; a general medical practitioner sought a declaration that the Family Practitioner Committee for his area, which was responsible for paying him for his work as a GP, was acting in breach of contract when they reduced his remuneration. It was argued for the Committee that this claim was inadmissible because this was a public law service relationship, so that any remedy the doctor might have should have been pursued by way of judicial review rather than by an action in private law. The Court of Appeal rejected that claim to strike out the action, holding that the doctor had, quite straightforwardly, a private law contract for services with the Family Practitioner Committee. The House of Lords, while equally rejecting the claim to strike out the action, and equally clear that this was a relationship justiciable in private law rather than in public law, nevertheless preferred to view the relationship as a private law statutory work relationship, rather than as a contract for services.[29]

[26] [1990] ICR 810 (CA).
[27] In this case it was not necessary to decide, and it was not decided, whether this amounted to a semi-dependent worker's contract (to use the terminology of the present work). We suggest that it represents a case just within the category, since the doctor was probably not to be regarded as operating in the course of his general professional practice, but rather as working personally for the police authority, when acting as a police surgeon.
[28] [1992] 1 AC 624 (HL).
[29] As in *Ex parte Noble*, above, it was not necessary to decide, and it was not decided, whether, if viewed as a contract of services, this amounted to a semi-dependent worker's contract (to use the terminology of the present work). We suggest that it represents a case outside the category, since, by contrast with the facts in *Ex parte Noble*, the contract in question related to the doctor's general professional practice.

Crucial to the present discussion is the fact that the House of Lords
administered what seems in retrospect to have been effectively the *coup de
grace* to any further development of the model of tenured public service
office-holding justiciable by means of judicial review and regarded as
coming within the sphere of public law.

The *Roy* case, however, marks the emergence of another possible alternative to the intention to enter into a personal employment contract, in the
shape of an intention to enter instead into a private law statutory work
relationship. In the *Roy* case, it made no difference to the outcome whether
the relationship was regarded in this light or as a contractual one. However,
it does make a crucial difference in relation to all those employment rights
which depend upon the existence of some kind of personal employment
contract. Thus, in the case of *Wadi v Cornwall Family Practitioner Committee*,[30]
upon which much reliance was placed when the *Roy* case was considered by
the House of Lords, and in the later case of *Ealing Family Health Services
Authority v Shukla*,[31] the fact, that general medical practitioners were judged
to have a purely statutory work relationship with the Family Practitioner
Committee for their area *rather than* personal employment contracts of any
kind, had the consequence that applicants for appointment as a GP fell outside the statutory provisions concerning race and sex discrimination in
employment.

It is suggested that this contrasting of private law statutory personal work
relationships with personal employment contracts is unwarranted, and may
serve to defeat the purposes of some employment legislation. It is unwarranted in the sense that there is generally no difficulty in accepting that personal employment contracts may be entirely in the nature of contracts of
adhesion where all the terms of the contract are prescribed for the parties
from wholly or partly external normative sources including legislation of all
kinds. That last proposition seems applicable both to contracts of employment and to other personal employment contracts. Legislators may in a real
sense be assumed to have factored this into their definitions of the personal
scope of employment legislation; they would have every right to assume
that personal work relationships will be regarded as contractual in character even if the terms are prescribed by legislation. So the intentions of
employment legislation may well be traduced by this particular line of
counter-contractual analysis.

In this discussion of the relationship between office-holding and personal
employment contracts, a number of bases have been identified for attributing intentions to the parties which are other than that of entering into a
personal employment contract. In deciding whether to attribute such other
intentions, the courts seem generally to presume in favour of an intention

[30] [1985] ICR 492 (EAT).   [31] [1993] ICR 710 (EAT).

to enter a personal employment contract. However, the decisions often deploy an overtly intuitive or impressionistic method of classification, in which it is debated whether the facts have the echoes of a contract, or create a broad sense that a contractual analysis is appropriate. The decisions, moreover, are often heavily dependent upon instrumental considerations, especially that of whether public law process or private law process is seen as more appropriate to the adjudication of the issue in question. The resulting state of affairs is one which in the requirement of intention to enter into a personal employment contract constitutes a significant constraint upon the category of the personal emolument contract, but one which is of regrettably uncertain scope. Our analysis continues by considering another such set of constraints which is, similarly, of considerable significance but less than clear in its scope.

C. LEGALITY AND THE INFORMAL ECONOMY

At the beginning of this section, it was asserted that, if the law of personal employment contracts is regarded as a species of the generic law of contract, it is often a very highly modified version of general contract law, not only because of the special features of employment relationships as compared with other economic relationships or transactions, but also because of the singular extent to which the law of personal employment contracts serves as an instrument or medium for the application of statutory regulation of personal work relationships, rather than as a body of law for determining when and how agreements may be enforced, which is the basic role of contract law.

In this subsection, it will be shown that this theme is very well illustrated by the use, in the employment context, of the idea of illegality as a factor which vitiates contracts. Broadly speaking, the doctrine of illegality of contracts is to the effect that the courts will not allow the enforcement of a contract which is vitiated by illegality, or by serious conflict with public policy, and, moreover, will not allow other kinds of legal claim to be based upon such a contract. In the employment context, this doctrine operates as a way of focusing discussion upon a set of issues about how far workers will be allowed to invoke employment rights against their employing entities when they are working, in one sense or another, wholly or partly in the 'informal' or illicit labour economy. The discussion of that set of issues will lead on to a discussion in the next subsection of a broader set of questions about the general role of ideas of public policy in the formation of personal employment contracts, which will be focused on the doctrine of restraint of trade.

We begin then with the question of constraints upon the formation of valid and enforceable personal employment contracts for work in the informal or illicit labour economy. This set of issues may arise in relation to work in suspect or unlawful occupations; it certainly used to be the case and may in some situations still be the case that prostitution would be regarded as raising such issues. The same issues in principle arise in relation to the employment of illegal immigrants or people working without the required work permit, or in relation to the employment of children below the permitted age. Thus, it is an offence, under section 8 of the Asylum and Immigration Act 1996, for an employer to employ under a contract of employment (but not, it should be noted, under any other sort of personal employment contract) a person subject to immigration control without valid and subsisting leave to be in the United Kingdom. This would be likely to have the effect that an immigrant, employed in such circumstances that this offence had been committed, would be held not to have a valid and enforceable contract of employment—though it might be held to the contrary if the employing entity and the employee both had a reasonable misapprehension that the employee was a legal immigrant with a valid work permit.

However, it is in the nature of those sectors of the informal labour economy where the employment involves direct and serious illegality that the workers concerned are unlikely to claim their employment rights. So we find that the effect of a personal employment contract being wholly or partly located in the informal economy has been considered, not in those contexts, but rather in relation to personal work relationships which involve arrangements for the evasion of tax or social security contribution. There have been a significant number of cases where such tax evasion arrangements have been invoked against workers seeking to enforce personal employment contracts, or seeking to invoke statutory employment rights which depend upon their being employed under valid and subsisting personal employment contracts.

In that situation, the employment tribunals and the appellate courts find themselves torn between two diametrically opposed sets of policy considerations. On the one hand, they wish to avoid condoning tax evasion by enforcing or treating as valid personal employment contracts which involve tax evasion. On the other hand, they wish to give effect, wherever it is reasonable to do so, to the employment rights of workers and to the policies of which those rights are the products; and they generally regard it as unmeritorious on the part of employing entities to invoke their own tax evasion arrangements as a ground for withholding those employment rights. The case law in which the courts are faced with this dilemma was reviewed and, as far as could be managed, reconciled, in the recent decision of the Court of Appeal in *Hall v Woolston Hall Leisure Ltd.*[32] Here, it was held that an employee should succeed in a claim for compensation, including compensation for loss of earnings, on the ground of unlawful sex discrimination in respect of her dismissal by reason of pregnancy, despite the objection, raised on behalf of the employing entity, that her contract of employment

[32] [2001] ICR 99 (CA).

was tainted by a tax fraud, in that the employing entity was concealing part of her earnings from the Inland Revenue.

In order to hold the balance between the opposing policy considerations, and to determine on which side it falls in each particular case, the courts have recognized two sets of variables, and have devised two techniques for responding to them. In a narrowly technical sense, one of these variables and one of these techniques come within the ambit of contract law, while the other variable and the other technique would be seen as falling outside that ambit and residing in the extra-contractual, mainly statutory, sector of employment law. However, both variables and both techniques come within and form part of the broad conception of the law of personal employment contracts which is being advanced in this work. That is because they form part of the area of intersection between personal employment contracts and the statute law affecting personal work relationships, which is seen as integral to the body of law which it is sought to identify and describe in these pages.

The first variable, and the corresponding responsive technique, which falls within the ambit of contract law in a strict sense, concerns the extent to which the claimant—the worker, in the scenario under discussion—is implicated in the illegality, in this case the tax evasion arrangement. The courts respond to this, as a matter of contract theory, by distinguishing between the impact of illegality as being, on the one hand, upon the contract 'as formed', and, on the other hand, upon the contract 'as performed'. According to this approach, where it is judged that an illegality has become integral to the whole set of contractual arrangements in question (whether by initial formation or subsequent variation), the illegality is said to reside in the contract 'as formed', and it follows that both parties are regarded as fully implicated in the illegality, and that the courts should not allow enforcement of the contract or of claims which depend upon the existence of a valid contract.[33] Where, on the other hand, it is judged that an illegality has not become integral to the whole set of contractual arrangements, the illegality is said to reside in the contract only 'as performed', and the courts view it as proper to allow enforcement of the contract or the making of claims assuming a valid contract, at the hands of a party who is not so deeply implicated in the illegality that his or her claim is necessarily to be viewed as tarnished by it.[34]

That approach gives the tribunals or courts a wide ambit of choice as to how to characterize the impact of the illegality. In making such choices,

---

[33] As in *Tomlinson v Dick Evans U Drive Ltd* [1978] IRLR 77(EAT), and *Salvesen v Simons* [1994] IRLR 52 (EAT).
[34] As in *Davidson v Pillay* [1979] IRLR 275 (EAT), *Coral Leisure Group Ltd v Barnett* [1981] IRLR 204 (EAT), *Newland v Simons & Willer (Hairdressers) Ltd* [1981] IRLR 359 (EAT), *Hewcastle Catering Ltd v Ahmed* [1991] IRLR 473 (CA).

the courts bring another variable into play, and have developed another responsive technique in relation to that second variable. The second variable consists in the nature of the claim against which the illegality is invoked, and how closely it is associated with the contract which is vitiated by that illegality. The courts seem increasingly, at least in the sphere of personal employment contracts, to envisage two contrasting types of claim, one of which consists of enforcing a contract or claiming rights which are very closely bound up with a contract, while the other of them consists of claiming rights which have some clear extra-contractual basis. Where the claim is of the first type, the effect of the illegality is decided largely or entirely by reference to the first variable, and according to the 'as formed/as performed' distinction. But where the claim is of the second type, the court has a greater latitude to allow the claim despite the illegality, on the basis that the illegality does not have to be seen as an obstacle to claims of that type. This was a method of reasoning developed particularly in the decision of the Court of Appeal in *Leighton v Michael*,[35] and further developed and applied in the *Hall v Woolston Hall Leisure* case.

It must be said that, even when armed with these sophisticated techniques, the courts have not found it at all easy to decide how to handle these tax evasion cases. The Court of Appeal in the *Hall v Woolston Hall Leisure* case seems to be edging towards a weak and rebuttable presumption that arrangements for tax evasion in personal work relationships are initiated or led by employing entities, and that workers are only secondarily implicated, so that the illegality can be seen to attach to the contract as performed rather than as formed. This seems to be combined with a perception that, while claims for statutory redundancy payments, and, most important and more controversially, unfair dismissal claims, are very closely bound up with personal employment contracts, claims in respect of unlawful discrimination in employment are not integrally linked to personal employment contracts and can be allowed despite the fact that the relevant personal employment contract is tainted with illegality as performed.

We thus find that the doctrine of illegality as known to the general law of contract, has to be tempered, in the context of personal work relationships, by reference to the policy and purposes of employment legislation. It is only in this form that the law of personal employment contracts can adequately address the set of issues about how far employing entities can locate their workers outside the formal labour economy and the employment rights possessed by those working within it. In a broad sense, we can discern a similar interaction between contract law and employment legislation when the courts have to decide whether workers who agree, in their personal

---

[35] [1995] ICR 1091 (EAT).

employment contracts, to be labelled as self-employed workers rather than as employees, have thereby deprived themselves of those employment rights which are confined to employees working under contracts of employment.

Where self-classification of that kind can be seen as verging upon 'sham self-employment', there is a somewhat comparable issue as to whether to treat the worker's statutory rights as bounded by contract and contract law, or whether to regard the statutory rights as free-standing and overriding ones attaching directly to the underlying factual employment relationship. In *Young & Woods Ltd v West*,[36] the Court of Appeal inclined strongly towards the latter view, but such an approach cannot be regarded as well established.

So far as the question of illegality and the informal economy is concerned, the courts increasingly seem to accept that this crucial regulatory function cannot be satisfactorily carried out by reference solely to the principles of contract law, conceived of in a narrow sense. The judges in the Court of Appeal who decided the *Hall v Woolston Hall Leisure* case were aware that both European Community Law, and European Human Rights Law as incorporated into English Law by the Human Rights Act 1998, might well[37] limit the extent to which illegalities in personal employment contracts could be invoked as giving rise to derogations from employment rights, especially from rights to equal treatment and against discrimination. By recognizing that, the court was quite rightly acknowledging a dimension to the law of personal employment contracts which is of real and growing importance, both with reference to the application of the doctrine of illegality and much more generally. In the next subsection we pursue that wider discussion by inquiring whether there exists in the law concerning the formation of personal employment contracts a general principle of public policy protecting the economic freedom of the worker.

D. RESTRAINT OF TRADE AND ECONOMIC FREEDOM IN THE
    FORMATION OF PERSONAL EMPLOYMENT CONTRACTS

It has been observed in the previous subsection how the doctrine of illegality, as applied in the context of personal employment contracts, results in a particular kind of interplay between general contract principles, general legal principles, and the special exigencies of the employment relationship. Moreover, that is an interplay which is becoming more elaborate as the impact grows, upon the law affecting personal work relationships, of EU law, public law, and human rights law. In this subsection we consider whether that

---

[36] [1980] IRLR 201 (CA).

[37] Each of the three judges in the Court of Appeal found it unnecessary to express a concluded view on this point, but was close to concluding that the Equal Treatment Directive would have that effect. See Peter Gibson LJ at para 26, Mance LJ at para 65, Moore-Bick J at para 84.

kind of evolution has progressed to the point where we can satisfactorily speak of a general principle of public policy protecting the economic freedom of the worker with regard to the formation of personal employment contracts.

There is one principle of English common law which provides a firm starting point for this rather speculative discussion. This is the principle of restraint of trade, which is to the effect that validity or enforceability should be denied to terms of contracts, or to contracts as a whole, which impose unreasonable restrictions upon the individual freedom to earn one's living as one chooses. It is clear that this principle of restraint of trade has an important role in controlling the enforceability of particular terms in personal employment contracts; that regulatory function is carried out under the heading of control of 'restrictive covenants'. Several important decisions also indicate that it can be deployed to challenge the validity or enforceability of personal employment contracts as a whole. The leading case of *Instone v Schroeder Music Publishing Co Ltd*[38] shows how that principle could be invoked to enable a popular music composer to assert the invalidity of a contract for the exclusive publication of his compositions on the ground of restraint of trade, in that 'the weak bargaining position of the composer had led to an unfair agreement under which the publisher undertook minimal obligations in return for total commitment by the composer'.[39] Although that case concerned a contract almost certainly not falling within the category of personal employment contracts,[40] we suggest that its principle should be regarded as fully applicable to those contracts.

Another very important case, this time concerning the arrangements for the professional engagements of a sports person, serves to reinforce the suggestion that the principle of restraint of trade may apply to deny validity or enforceability to a personal employment contract as a whole. It also shows how that principle imports a notion of freedom of access to employment. This is the case of *Watson v Prager*,[41] in which a professional boxer secured a declaration of unenforceability, on the ground of unreasonable restraint of trade, of the boxer-manager agreement between himself and his manager, who also acted as the promoter of the great majority of the contests in which the boxer took part. Because of the way those two roles were combined, the whole set of arrangements was akin to a personal employment contract in which the boxer worked for the manager-promoter. It was this conjunction of the two roles of manager and promoter, coupled with the fact that the British Boxing Board of Control, by supervising and

---

[38] [1974] 1 WLR 1308 (HL).   [39] Collins 1997 at 261.
[40] Because, in the terms of our definition of the personal employment contract, even if that agreement were regarded as a contract for work rather than a publishing contract, the composer would be likely to be regarded as doing that work in the conduct of an independent business.   [41] [1991] ICR 603 (ChD).

prescribing the terms of both management agreements and promotion agreements, regulated access to the occupation of professional boxing,[42] which identified the boxer–manager agreement as susceptible to review on the ground of restraint of trade in a way that a 'commonplace commercial contract' would not have been.[43]

There emerges from these cases a broad principle of restraint of trade which should be seen as governing the formation of personal employment contracts. According to that principle, there is a common law power in the courts to strike down agreements, arrangements, or contracts which seek unreasonably or unfairly to restrict workers' economic freedom or access to employment.[44] The view that such a principle may be applied to strike down agreements or arrangements which unreasonably or improperly restrict access to employment under a personal employment contract is supported by the leading case of *Nagle v Feilden*.[45] In that case, a woman working in the occupation of training horses and wishing to be granted a licence as a trainer by the Jockey Club was held to have an arguable case for a declaration that the arrangements made by the Jockey Club for allocating such licences were void as being in unlawful restraint of trade because they excluded women.

Thus, in *Nagle v Feilden*, the Court of Appeal was prepared to integrate into the notion of restraint of trade an inherent capacity to control practices regarded as placing arbitrary restrictions upon economic freedom; in that instance, sex discrimination in employment, though not at that time generally controlled by legislation, was seen as arbitrary in that sense. It is important to be cautious about the extent to which the courts will be prepared to apply principles, which they might see as belonging essentially to public law, to personal employment contracts which they see as existing in the sphere of private law, and the courts have generally been reluctant to articulate such a principle in terms of a 'right to work'.[46] Nevertheless it seems correct to regard a principle against arbitrary encroachment upon the worker's economic freedom as part of the law of formation of personal employment contracts.[47]

There is another reason for taking this view of the doctrine of restraint of trade as an aspect or manifestation of a broad principle of economic freedom which conditions the formation of personal employment contracts,

---

[42] The regulation of professional boxing by the British Boxing Board of Control had long been controversial and had undergone many changes; one such regime had been successfully challenged in *McInnes v Onslow-Fane* [1978] 1 WLR 1520 (ChD).

[43] See Scott J [1991] ICR 603 at 626.

[44] It has been debated how far that principle amounts to or gives rise to the recognition of a 'right to work', see Hepple 1981.   [45] [1966] 2 QB 633 (CA).

[46] Compare Megarry J in *McInnes v Onslow-Fane* [1978] 1 WLR 1520 at 1528.

[47] Judicial support, expressed extrajudicially, for this view is given by Sir John Laws's article, 'Public Law and Employment Law: Abuse of Power' (Laws 1997).

regulating not only particular terms but the whole basis upon which such contracts may be formed. The decision of the European Court of Justice in the *Bosman* case[48] made it clear that the EC Law principle of freedom of movement of workers within the Community applied to regulate systems of self-regulation of sporting activities which operate to constrain that freedom of movement—in this case, the rules of associations of football clubs which allowed the imposition of transfer fees upon the movement of professional football players between employment with different football clubs.[49] As with the doctrine of restraint of trade in English common law, that principle also seems applicable as a basis of the challenge to the validity or enforceability of personal employment contracts which violate the principle by replicating the restrictive features of self-regulatory arrangements between such associations of employing entities.[50] We suggest that there is now a clear continuity of principle between the English common law of restraint of trade and the EC law of freedom of movement in this respect.

This completes the discussion of the conditions of formation of personal employment contracts in a precise sense, but we proceed to consider the legislative requirements for the formal supplying of information about contract terms which arise upon the formation of certain personal employment contracts, because we suggest that those requirements should be seen as an integral and important part of the law concerning the formation of personal employment contracts.

E. FORMALITY AND INFORMATION IN THE MAKING OF PERSONAL EMPLOYMENT CONTRACTS

In this subsection we complete the discussion of the conditions of formation of personal employment contracts by referring to the legislative requirements upon the employing entity to supply formal particulars of specified terms of certain personal employment contracts, because we argue that, although those requirements do not strictly speaking impose conditions or restrictions of form or formality upon personal employment contracts, they are nevertheless centrally significant in the legal regulation of the formation of those contracts. It will be argued that they have that central significance for several reasons, but especially because of the way in which they maintain and reinforce the distinction between contracts of employment and other contractual employment relations so far as the formation of personal employment contracts is concerned.

---

[48] *ASBL Union Royale Belge des Sociétés de Football Association v Bosman* Case C–415/93 [1996] 1 CMLR 645.

[49] Thus operating in parallel with the principle of restraint of trade in English common law as applied in *Eastham v Newcastle United Football Club Ltd* [1964] Ch 413 (CA).

[50] Compare the very insightful study by John O'Leary and Andrew Caiger of 'The re-regulation of football and its impact on employment contracts', O'Leary and Caiger 2000.

The legislative requirements in question are primarily those which were originally imposed by the Contracts of Employment Act 1963 and are now contained in Part I of the Employment Rights Act 1996 (ERA), which confers upon employees employed under contracts of employment the right to a written statement of specified particulars of employment.[51] This requirement arises upon the beginning of employment;[52] particulars are to be given not later than two months after that beginning;[53] the requirement does not apply to employment which continues for less than one month.[54] Underlying those legislative requirements are the provisions of the EC Council Directive of 1991 concerning 'an employer's obligation to inform employees of the conditions applicable to the contract or employment relationship',[55] which has been held by the European Court of Justice to have direct effect in the national law of each member state.[56] The Directive was to a considerable extent based upon the British statutory provisions; the latter provisions were amended in 1993 to bring them into line with the Directive. There are, however, still certain respects in which it may be argued that the British provisions fail fully to implement the Directive, especially with regard to the scope of employment relationships covered, a matter to which we revert very shortly.

This body of legislation thus does not impose requirements of formality upon the actual making of personal employment contracts; the legislation does not require those contracts to be made in writing or in any prescribed form; instead, it is required that information about specified terms of those contracts be supplied in the conditions described above. This is intrinsic to the purpose and strategy of the legislation; the legislation has the purpose of ensuring that the process of contracting for personal employment is a transparent one and that those employed are informed of the terms of their employment; the strategy of the legislation is to achieve that protective purpose by enforcing the giving of information rather than by negating informally made employment contracts.

Although the legislation thus does not, strictly speaking, determine the conditions in which a personal employment contract may validly be made, it nevertheless regulates the process of formation in a real sense, because it determines the formalities and communication of information which are associated with that process. By controlling the extent to which and the form by which the worker is notified of the content of the personal employment

---

[51] The specification of what particulars have to be provided is contained in ERA, s 1(3)–(5).   [52] ERA, s 1(1).
[53] ERA, s 1(2).   [54] ERA, s 198.
[55] Council Directive 91/533/EEC of 14 October 1991, OJ L288, 18.10.1991, 32–35.
[56] *Kampelmann v Landschaftsverband Westfalen-Lippe (Joined Cases C–253/96–C–258/96)* [1998] IRLR 333 (ECJ). See Jeff Kenner, 'Statement or Contract?—Some Reflections on the EC Employee Information (Contract or Employment Relationship) Directive after *Kamplemann*' (Kenner 1999).

contract, the legislation informs not merely the process of formation, but even the shape and character of the contract itself. In practice, though not in theory, the list of particulars which are to be specified becomes the list of matters which the contract itself must specify; and the method of information giving becomes the method of contracting.

The first of those two points is illustrated by the fact that the insertion at one stage[57] and the partial alleviation at a later stage[58] of a requirement to give particulars of the grievance procedure to be followed by the worker seems to have been very important in determining whether the worker has a contractual entitlement to the provision of a grievance procedure.[59] The second of those two points is illustrated by the importance which the original provisions of the 1963 Act attached to allowing the particulars to be provided by reference to collective agreements, and the importance which was attached to requiring direct specification to each worker by amendment of the legislation in 1993. The framers of the original legislation had the intention of recognizing and facilitating the actual formation of employment contracts by collective bargaining, while the framers of the 1993 amendments had the contrary aim of encouraging the actual formation of employment contracts as a matter of individuated dealing with each particular worker.

For these reasons, the legislative requirements for the giving of information about the content of employment contracts have a crucial regulatory effect upon the formation of those contracts. That being so, it is a matter of the utmost importance that the legislation applies only to some and not to all personal employment contracts—we return very shortly to the question of which personal employment contracts are not included. This means that, while the formation of some personal employment contracts is a regulated process, the formation of others is not. It follows from the arguments which have been advanced that, in consequence of these two different levels of regulation of the process of formation, the legislation tends to impart a different shape and character to each of two different sets of personal employment contracts. Leaving aside the particular issue about individuation or collectivization, we may conclude that the legislation results in the evolution of two different types of employment contract, that is to say a formalized and an informal type.

The line between those two types is drawn in a way which is of great significance both in terms of the conceptual categories of the law of personal employment contracts and in the context of an increasingly casualized

---

[57] By the Employment Protection Act 1975.
[58] By the Trade Union Reform and Employment Rights Act 1993 (inserting ERA, s 3(2)–(4), which reduce the requirements for employing entities employing fewer than twenty employees).
[59] Compare *WA Goold (Pearmak) Ltd v McConnell* [1995] IRLR 516 (EAT).

labour market. The current legislation, by confining its requirements to employees under contracts of employment lasting for a month or more, strongly reinforces both the conceptual distinction between the two legal contract types of the contract of employment and the semi-dependent worker's contract, and the practical distinction between the permanent worker and the casual worker. The cumulative effect of those two distinctions would be hard to assess in statistical terms but the excluded type is presumably numerically significant, and the driving of this wedge between the two types is certainly of great analytical importance in understanding the formulation and impact of this part of the law of personal employment contracts.

In this respect, it is of particular importance to note that the framers of the EC Directive may have had a rather different approach and definitional strategy from that which informs the British legislative provisions. The Directive uses the narrower category of employee rather than the broader category of worker to designate its scope, thus appearing to have the same personal scope as the British legislation. However, by including the employment *relationship* as well as the employment contract,[60] the framers of the Directive probably intended to include a category of casual workers whose work relations would probably lack sufficient contractual continuity to qualify them as employees with contracts of employment as that category is understood in British law. Hence the definitional category of the Directive may be more inclusive of casual workers than is that of the British legislation. This would explain why the framers of the Directive accepted the need for a facility for national law to exclude employments 'of a casual and/or specific nature' provided that this non-application was justified by objective considerations,[61] and why the British legislators did not need to invoke that facility—the British 'contract of employment' category being narrow enough to exclude most such employments anyway.

If there is that divergence of starting points between the Directive and the British legislation, it points up the exclusiveness of the category used in the British legislation, and the way in which that legislation reinforces the stratification of employment relations into a superior, more regulated category and an inferior, less regulated one so far as the formation of contractual employment is concerned. The British legislation is probably in compliance with the Directive, to the extent that the Directive seems to defer to national laws sufficiently strongly to allow for the British position;[62] but the orientation of the two sets of rules may nevertheless be a somewhat different one. Recognizing that this is a matter of policy, we nevertheless suggest that this might be a matter which is appropriate for authoritative reformulation so far as British law is concerned. We suggest

---

[60] Article 1.1.   [61] Article 1.2 (b).   [62] Compare Kenner 1999 at 218–219.

that in such a reformulation it should be regarded as important to apply the requirement to provide contractual information across the whole range of personal employment contracts, even if the information to be provided was very limited with regard to short-term contracts.

In order to ensure the coherence and viability of such a reformulation, it would be important to have a clearer analysis than currently exists of a number of issues concerning the way in which personal employment contracts are structured, and especially of what is meant by the continuity of those contracts. In particular, such a reformulation would scarcely be operable if there were no clear resolution of the questions about whether the analysis of the structure and continuity of semi-dependent workers' contracts is the same as for contracts of employment. In the remaining sections of this chapter, the attempt is made to provide such an analysis.

SECTION 2: INTERNAL STRUCTURE AND CONTINUITY

In the first chapter of this work, we outlined the concept of the personal employment contract, and set out reasons for using it to address some of the shortcomings of a body of law cast in the dual mould of the contract of employment and the contract for services. In the second part of that chapter, we considered the ways in which the ideas of the employing entity and the worker are constructed in the law of personal employment contracts. We referred to that discussion as describing the personal structure of personal employment contracts. In the present chapter, we have so far considered the basic conditions for the formation of personal employment contracts. We now seek to complete the analysis of the identity, nature, and main attributes of personal employment contracts by considering how, in the law of personal employment contracts, the basic shape and duration of those contracts is conceived of and construed. In order to analyse the basic shape and duration of personal employment contracts, we evoke two central notions which will be used to organize the way that this discussion is presented. The first of these is the idea of the *internal structure* of personal employment contracts. This section firstly elaborates and discusses that idea. That discussion leads on to a consideration of the second of those two ideas, that of the *continuity* of personal employment contracts.

The first of these two ideas, therefore, is that every personal employment contract should be seen as having an internal structure which gives a shape to its detailed content. By this we mean as follows. The content of personal employment contracts, generally referred to as their terms and conditions, or their express and implied terms, can usefully be regarded as consisting of normative propositions, that is to say as rules or principles prescribing how the parties are to act or stating what rights and duties they have in relation to each other.[63] Most or all of the content of personal employment contracts can be expressed as normative propositions of one kind and another, and we improve our understanding of that content by articulating it in that way. However, it is equally important to think of those normative propositions, which make up the content of personal employment contracts, as standing in a structured relationship to each other. That is to say, we can think of personal employment contracts as not merely setting out normative propositions but also as saying how those propositions relate to each other.[64] We cannot fully understand the content of personal employment contracts unless we have a clear view of the *structures* by which the norms are linked together.

It will be argued that we can use this idea of structure to investigate the basic make-up of personal employment contracts, the way we apply the requirements of consideration and mutuality to those contracts, and the way we construe express and implied terms and regulate the relationship between them. In this chapter, that concept of structure is identified as 'internal' simply in order to distinguish it from the 'personal' structure of personal employment contracts, which was discussed in the previous chapter. The personal structure may be regarded as denoting the external shape of the personal employment contract, by identifying the persons between whom it is made and between which of them contractual links exist; the internal structure describes and interrelates the actual norms which make up the substance and inwardness of the contract.

There is a real need to analyse and understand the internal structure, in that sense, of personal employment contracts; some degree of success in doing that is crucial if the whole body of law concerning personal employment contracts is to possess coherence and functionality. In the absence of a clear analysis of that internal structure, we can expect to experience perpetual difficulty with questions about the *continuity* of personal employment contracts, and about the *relationship between work and remuneration*, as well as, more generally, between the whole range of workers' and employing entities' contractual rights and obligations. The idea of internal structure is developed by reference to the distinction between exchange transactions and relational contracts, and it is shown how that distinction gives rise to a two-level structure for personal employment contracts.

---

[63] Examples of such normative propositions would be 'the employing entity is to pay the worker a monthly salary of £2,000' or 'the worker is obliged to respect the confidentiality of the trade secrets of the employing entity'.

[64] To pursue the above examples, the personal employment contract might or might not make the employing entity's duty to pay a monthly salary contingent, in some way, upon the worker's respect for the confidentiality of the employing entity's trade secrets.

A. THE TWO-LEVEL STRUCTURE OF PERSONAL
   EMPLOYMENT CONTRACTS

We suggest that there is a state of structural uncertainty which character-
izes the law concerning the content of personal employment contracts. At
the heart of this structural uncertainty lies the dichotomy between
exchange transactions and relational contracts. Most of the problems about
the content and internal structure of personal employment contracts result
from doubt and ambiguity as to whether and when those contracts are to
be regarded more as exchange transactions than as relational contracts. In
this subsection, we shall offer an analysis of the internal structure of personal employment contracts which concentrates on locating those contracts as between exchange transactions and relational contracts. This is no
simple matter; it involves a challenge to a received set of understandings
about the make-up of personal employment contracts. It will be sought to
explain firstly what that received set of understandings is, and how it came
about, and secondly why a rather different analysis might be preferable.

We should begin by defining our terms. In this chapter, the term 'exchange
transaction' is used to mean the trading, at a particular moment in time, of
things, or acts, obligations, or promises against each other. The term 'relational contract', on the other hand, is used to mean the legal expression, in
contractual form, of a relationship which exists between human or legal
persons over a period of time.[65] If we define our terms in that way, it matters
a great deal whether we regard personal employment contracts as exchange
transactions or as relational contracts. This affects, and may even be determinative of, the way in which various kinds of statute law and statutory rights and
obligations apply to those contracts. It also greatly influences the way in
which the content of those contracts is construed and regulated.

There seems to be a fairly well-established understanding, which informs
the way that the law of the contract of employment has been expounded,
as to how to interpret contracts of employment as between exchange transactions and relational contracts. According to this understanding, contracts
of employment combine the qualities of exchange transactions with those
of relational contracts. They are exchange transactions wrapped up in relational contracts. We tend to assume, on the other hand, without analysing
them very carefully, that other personal employment contracts are bare
exchange transactions which are generally not embodied in relational contracts. That is one of the ways in which we try to differentiate systematically
between contracts of employment and contracts for services.

How does that understanding of personal employment contracts, and of
contracts of employment in particular, come about? We start with personal

---

[65] See, generally, Melvin Eisenberg, 'Relational Contracts' (Eisenberg 1995), a valuable
survey of the literature on this topic, and a useful corrective to the idea that there is a sharp
distinction between 'relational' and 'discrete' contracts.

employment contracts as exchange transactions. On the face of it, there seems to be nothing controversial or less than obvious in envisaging personal employment contracts as, quite simply, transactions by which work is exchanged for remuneration; indeed, it may seem perverse to suggest to the contrary. This assumption seems to be woven into the ordinary language with which we refer to work relationships; we speak about wages for work, or the wage/work bargain; we accept, in a general sense, that a worker has a claim to 'a fair day's pay for a fair day's work'. At the level of legal discourse, personal employment contracts seem to provide a clear illustration of the idea of contracts as generally and inherently consisting of exchange transactions. This is an idea which is integrated into the general law of contracts by the doctrine of consideration; the exchange of work for remuneration seems to be a particularly straightforward example of a transaction by which each party supplies functionally matching things or promises which are of value to the other, the doctrine of consideration being famously unconcerned with whether the *amounts* of such value correspond with each other.

However simple and straightforward that analysis seems, it does not suffice to provide a complete picture of the internal structure of personal employment contracts. We need to probe the analysis a bit more closely to reveal its incompleteness. When we envisage and describe personal employment contracts as being based upon simple exchange transactions in which work is traded for remuneration, we normally do so by thinking of work in terms of small units to which remuneration can be directly related. These small units are usually defined as amounts of time, such as a day or an hour. They might be defined as units of output, or as tasks, but, if so, those units will in themselves generally be associated with an approximate time span which is normally required for their performance. We find it easy and comprehensible to think of these small units of working time as items of value which can be traded for specific sums of money. The hour's work, or the day's work, for a stated wage seems to be the basic building block of the personal employment contract as an exchange transaction, from which larger contractual edifices may be constructed.

There are, however, real difficulties about constructing the personal employment contract as a simple exchange transaction, even if we can successfully break it down into small units of time such as a single hour. Are we to regard each hour of work as the subject of a simple promise by the employing entity to pay a stated wage for it, a promise which constitutes the whole extent of the contractual structure for the hour in question? If so, it corresponds to that curious and curiously named notion of the general law of contracts, the unilateral contract. As such, the contract would lack a time dimension; for until the work is complete, there is no contract yet in existence; and once the work is complete, the contract is fulfilled, no longer subsists, and gives way to the obligation to pay which arises from its fulfilment. It is this one-dimensionality of the unilateral contract, its lack of an existence over a period of time, which gives rise to the notion, in United States jurisprudence, of employment at will as not being contractual in any ordinary sense.[66]

On the whole, English contract lawyers, and even more so English employment lawyers, tend intuitively to see that approach as an unsatisfactory one, even in relation to a work arrangement of no more than an hour's duration. They tend to view such an arrangement as implicitly involving promises both to work and to employ for the hour in question, promises which subsist during the hour in question, thus giving a bilaterality and a temporal dimension to the contract which applies to that hour. It would also be accepted that, even during such a short reference period, there were further continuing contractual duties or obligations, relating, for instance, to the health, safety, and welfare of the workers, or to the worker's care for the employing entity's property, or for the safety of other workers. Yet all this serves to identify what is recognizably a *relational* contract, subsisting over an, admittedly short, period of time, rather than an exchange transaction which crystallizes into a contract of sorts, but one which is immediately completed and fulfilled at the very moment at which it arises.

There has in fact been a long-established recognition of personal employment contracts as relational contracts. Indeed, this had to occur if workers were to be accorded an action for wrongful dismissal, which involved the recognition that they had a contractually protected interest in the continuance of their employment. But this did not go uncontested as a matter of general principle; it was not until the decision of the House of Lords in 1853 in the leading case of *Emmens v Elderton*[67] that it was recognized that a personal employment contract for a specified time involved 'an engagement on the part of the employing entity to keep the employed in the relation in question during that time and not merely to pay him the wages for the services at the end'.[68] It is debatable to which categories of workers that analysis would have been regarded as applicable at that time,[69] but the decision certainly involves the rejection of the view that personal work relationships were to be regarded *in principle* as mere 'service and pay'

---

[66] See, for a very useful survey of the literature and re-examination of the legal doctrine, Andrew P Morriss, 'Exploding Myths: An Empirical and Economic Reassessment of the Rise of Employment At-Will' (Morriss 1994).   [67] (1853) 13 CB 495 (HL).

[68] See Crompton J, 13 CB 495 at 506.

[69] Crompton J saw this view as applicable 'wherever there is a contract for hiring or for employment on the one part and for wages or salary on the other' (at 506). That probably includes not only contracts of employment as now understood, but also at least some other personal employment contracts. The case concerned a retained attorney for a life assurance company who would not necessarily be regarded as an 'employee' as the law stands today.

relationships,[70] where the only contractual obligation upon the employing entity was to pay for service or services already rendered.

From such historical starting points, it has long since been recognized that there is more to the structure of the personal employment contract than a *simple* exchange of work and remuneration. It embodies various kinds of commitments, rights, and obligations which are about maintaining the work relationship over a period of time, and behaving according to a series of norms and standards during that continuance; to that extent, it clearly has the attributes of a relational contract. Those further elements can be seen as being constructed upon a base of exchange of work and remuneration. That is how we can reconcile the two ideas of the personal employment contract as, on the one hand, an exchange transaction, and, on the other hand, as a relational contract.

In the original work from which this one is derived, that view was expressed in terms of the idea of a two-level structure for contracts of employment:

The structural issue . . . is how far the contract protects each party's interest in the due occurrence of the exchange or series of exchanges which form the basis of the contract. In the case of the contract of employment, the exchange is of service against remuneration; but there is more to the contract than this simple exchange, because the employee undertakes an obligation to make himself available to render service, while the employer undertakes to enable the employee to earn his remuneration . . . Hence the contract has a two-tiered structure. At the first level there is an exchange of work and remuneration. At the second level there is an exchange of mutual obligations for future performance. The second level—the promises to employ and be employed—provides the arrangement with its stability and its continuity as a contract. The promises to employ and to be employed may be of short duration, or may be terminable at short notice; but they still form an integral and most important part of the structure of the contract. *They are the mutual undertakings to maintain the employment relationship in being which are inherent in any contract of employment properly so called.*[71]

That passage concluded with an implicit contrast between what was inherent in contracts of employment properly so called and what was not inherent in other personal employment contracts. It is now argued that such a contrast, implied though not strongly intended in the original work, would seem to be misconceived. The two-level analysis should be regarded as applying to personal employment contracts generally and not just to contracts of

[70] The 'service and pay' analysis had been accepted in *Aspdin v Austin* (1844) 5 QB 671 (where, very interestingly, it was applied to a manufacturing contract which had been presented as an employment contract), and in *Dunn v Sayles* (1844) 5 QB 685 (where it was applied to the employment of a surgeon-dentist for five years); it seems to have been emerging as a general analysis of a wide range of personal work relationships before *Emmens v Elderton*.   [71] Freedland 1976 at 20 (emphasis added).

employment strictly so called. Contracts of employment are rightly seen as having a relational dimension even if they are of very short duration. Semi-dependent workers' contracts are more likely to be of very short duration, but that is no reason to deny them a relational dimension.[72]

All this seems to suggest that the personal employment contract as an exchange transaction becomes merged or subsumed into the personal employment contract as a relational contract; and in terms of the technicalities of contract law that would indeed seem to be the case. Nevertheless, in a deeper sense the idea of the personal employment contract as an exchange transaction remains crucially distinct from the idea of the personal employment contract as a relational contract. The two ideas coexist as competing paradigms which exert pressures towards different approaches or solutions to issues of the construction or regulation of personal employment contracts. Because of this, there remain some problems about the internal structure of personal employment contracts which are not fully resolved simply by invoking the notion of a two-level structure. These problems are thrown into sharp relief when we come to consider the questions of what is meant by the exchange of work and remuneration, and by contractual continuity of employment.

B. Work and Remuneration in the Structure of Personal Employment Contracts

Among the key functions of the law of personal employment contracts, and at the heart of our analysis of the internal structure of personal employment contracts, is the identification of what is meant, in legal terms, by work, remuneration, and employment, and the specification of how they relate to each other. We have evoked the notion of the internal structure of personal employment contracts; that internal structure consists, basically, of the definition and interrelation of the three concepts of work, remuneration, and employment. Most of the rest of the law of personal employment contracts is in some sense or other based upon that internal structure. In the remainder of this section we seek to elucidate those crucial elements of the internal structure of personal employment contracts. In order to do so, we deploy the general theory about personal employment contracts as exchange transactions or relational contracts, introduced in the previous subsection.

We begin with the elements of work and remuneration. Given that work and remuneration are absolutely central concepts in employment law, and

---

[72] For a somewhat different, extremely well-articulated, view of the two-level structure, see Hugh Collins' reflections on the employment rights of casual workers in Collins 2000. His argument supports the idea that the two-level structure need not be confined to contracts of employment; but his argument does not necessarily involve the view that all personal employment contracts, or even all contracts of employment, have that two-level structure.

given also that we look in large measure to the law of personal employment contracts to give them legal meaning and substance, it is quite surprising how far those concepts, and even more so the relationship between them, are under-examined in the law of personal employment contracts. We tend to assume that the law of personal employment contracts contains and provides clear definitions of those concepts, and of the way they relate to each other. If we test that assumption, it turns out to be a largely false one. Both work and remuneration are revealed as deeply elusive notions, and no less elusive is the problem of how remuneration is related to work.

Within the law of personal employment contracts, we encounter many different ways of defining and conceptualizing work and its relationship to remuneration; we can use the contrast between exchange transactions and relational contracts to distinguish two broad approaches to the way in which this is done. We can make this distinction in relation to the idea of work itself. From an exchange-based perspective, work tends to be envisaged as the rendering of specific services, or the activity of expending effort on the performance of particular tasks, over a particular period of time. From an exchange-based perspective it is important to identify work in that way, because that produces a concept of work as measurable or quantifiable, and therefore easier to relate directly to remuneration. From a relational perspective, work tends to be envisaged in a different way. It is the implementation, over a period of time, of a set of arrangements whereby a worker functions in the service, or for the benefit, of another. On that view, work is identified as the activity of operating within a work relationship. That activity may be much less specifically defined, and much less closely assigned to particular periods of time, than would be required under the exchange-based approach.

These two approaches differ more deeply than in merely producing different dictionary definitions of the word 'work'. They give rise, ultimately, to different understandings of what work actually is or means. The relational approach tends to produce a more inclusive view of what counts as work or when a person can be said to be 'working'. The example can be given of a schoolteacher who, after the end of the school day, sits at home preparing her lessons for the next day or planning what to say at a staff meeting the next day. This would be more likely to be regarded as work from a relational perspective than from an exchange-based perspective. From an exchange-based approach, it is quite difficult to regard this activity as measurable in terms of time, both because of its intrinsic nature, and because it is taking place at home rather than in a place of work. From a relational approach, it presents less of a problem that it is difficult to measure the time assigned to this activity, and the fact that it occurs at home rather than at the place of work provides only a slight and fairly easily rebuttable indication that it is not occurring within the compass of the work relationship.

From that approach, the distinction between being 'on duty' and being 'off duty' tends to be a less sharp one, and the conception of work tends to be a looser and more expansive one. By evoking that distinction between being on duty and off duty, we touch on an even more profound set of conceptual and practical variables in the meaning attached to 'work'. Some forms of what might be regarded as 'work' fit more readily into the description of 'being at the disposal of an employer' than into that of 'engaging in an activity'. Many workers spend periods of time waiting to be called into action, or being 'on call'. Again, broadly speaking, this is more readily regarded as 'work' or as 'time spent at work' from a relational perspective than from an exchange perspective.

These choices between alternative understandings of work become very real when legislation regulates the amount of 'working time' for which workers may be required or allowed to be employed within stated periods of time, such as a day or a week or a month, and when the personal employment contract serves as the primary indicator of what counts as 'working time'—as is currently the case by virtue of the Working Time Regulations,[73] which were enacted by way of implementation of the EC Working Time Directive.[74] Not only do those Regulations impose different regulatory regimes as between workers who have 'measured working time' and workers who have 'unmeasured or only partly measured working time';[75] they also go to the heart of the ambiguity which we have identified in the contractual conception of work by defining working time as 'any period during which the worker is working, at the employer's disposal and carrying out his activity or duties'.[76] That mode of definition seems to have limited the notion of working time to time which would be counted *both* according to an exchange-based approach ('carrying out his activity or duties') *and* according to a relational approach ('at the employer's disposal').[77]

Those structural issues, already then complex enough even in the limited context of issues about the definition of work and working time, become much more so when we widen our focus to include the relationship between work and remuneration. This is one of the most interesting and yet difficult set of issues in the whole of the law of personal employment contracts. Once again, the contrast between the exchange transaction approach

[73] Working Time Regulations 1998, SI 1998/1833 as since amended by the Working Time Regulations 1999, SI 1999/3372.

[74] Council Directive 93/104/EC concerning certain aspects of the organization of working time, OJ L307/18, 13.12.93.

[75] Reg 20, as amended by the 1999 Regulations (see above, n 73).

[76] Reg 2(1), definition of 'working time'.

[77] If that view is correct, a question arises as to the consistency of this mode of definition with that of the Working Time Directive. The decision of the ECJ in the *SIMAP* case (*Sindicato de Médicos de Assistencia Pública (SIMAP) v Consellaria de Sanidad y Consumo de la Generalidad Valenciana*, C–303/98 [2001] ICR 1116) gives some indication of how such an argument might be approached, but the matter is a complex one.

and the relational contract approach provides a helpful analytical tool. It enables us to separate out various different ways in which the idea of work, which is itself, as we have seen, multifaceted and ambiguous, is interrelated with the, actually no less complex, notion of remuneration for, or from, employment.

The idea of 'remuneration' is not precisely defined in the law of personal employment contracts, but some observations about terminology may be made. We can think about 'pay', 'wages', and 'salary' either as synonymous with remuneration, or as imprecisely defined types of remuneration. These terms are now used more or less interchangeably in employment law, though they have slightly different social and economic nuances. Probably as a matter of general usage, and certainly in the law of personal employment contracts, 'remuneration' invokes the notion not merely of payment of one person by another or others, but, more specifically, of payment in the context of work or of employment. In other words, it is part of the meaning of remuneration that it has a connection with work or employment. It is this kind of connection which the framers of the legislation concerning protection of wages from deductions sought to capture when they defined 'wages' as, in relation to a worker, 'any sums payable to the worker in connection with his employment',[78] and when they excluded from wages, 'any payment to the worker otherwise than in his capacity as a worker'.[79] We need to examine the nature of that connection in order fully to understand both the meaning of remuneration and the internal structure of personal employment contracts.

Essentially, we can discern two main kinds of connection; they correspond to our distinction between the exchange-based approach and the relational approach. On the one hand, there is a direct and tight exchange-based kind of connectedness whereby remuneration is seen as being *for* or *in return for work*. On the other hand, there is a looser and more indirect kind of connection whereby remuneration is seen as being given *in respect of a period of employment*. This gives us two meanings or conceptions of remuneration, though it should be stressed at the outset that it is inherently difficult to allocate all the different arrangements for remuneration which are made in practice to one or other of those categories. There is a fairly strong tendency to use the term 'wages' to refer to the former kind of remuneration, and to use the term 'salary' to refer to the latter kind; but it follows from what has already been said that we cannot regard this as a firm and clear distinction.

That very brief discussion of the meaning of remuneration leaves many aspects of its definition unresolved, but it does give us enough of a working definition of remuneration to enable us to draw some conclusions about the relationship between work and remuneration. We have found that, by using

---

[78] A definition now contained in s 27(1) of the Employment Rights Act 1996.
[79] Ibid, s 27(2)(e).

a distinction between exchange-based approaches and relational approaches, we can identify, both in the arrangements that are in practice made, and in the legal analysis of those arrangements, various alternative ways of conceptualizing both work and remuneration and the interrelationships between them. Our use of the exchange/relational distinction has encouraged us to think about those alternatives as located on a spectrum, with a strongly exchange-based approach or character at one extreme, and a strongly relational approach or character at the other.

The main general point to be made, from those starting points, about the internal structure of personal employment contracts, is the following one. These various alternative forms of work and of remuneration combine with each other in a diverse way rather than in a systematic way. In any given personal employment contract, we might find, for instance, a strongly exchange-based approach to the element of work, but a strongly relational approach to the element of remuneration. No doubt there is some tendency for the different elements all to be grouped together towards one or other end of the spectrum in any one particular personal employment contract; but this is a much weaker tendency than would generally be supposed or assumed.

This kind of mixture is entirely predictable; it reflects the variety and sophistication of the arrangements for employment which are made, in theory by employing entities and workers jointly, but in practice usually by the enterprises which employ workers, and with the aim of optimizing the value of the workers' services to those enterprises in the labour and product market conditions which apply to the particular circumstances in question. When we draw on examples of employment arrangements from a long historical past, as we tend to do when drawing on the case law of personal employment contracts, it is not surprising that the picture becomes positively kaleidoscopic. Not only do social and economic circumstances change within these long time spans, but so also do styles of management and views about incentive systems.

Moreover, when such changes occur, they often create new, even more complex, variants, rather than reverting to earlier, simpler, patterns. For example, the recent fashion for applying various 'performance-related pay' systems to a very wide range of managerial and professional workers has made quite profound differences in the way that work and remuneration are interrelated for such workers. These systems are often regarded as an imposition upon such workers of older, narrowly exchange-based, systems of 'payment by results', even as approaching the sort of piece-rate payment systems which used to be widely applied to industrial manual workers in the nineteenth century and for quite a lot of the twentieth century. Yet many of today's 'performance-related pay' systems do not relate remuneration to output in any such direct way. Rather, they are elaborately constructed relational systems for management of the performance of workers by means of appraisals and the awarding of promotion or medium-term or even long-term supplements to remuneration.[80]

In just the same way as we saw that the contractual definition of working time became a real issue with the enactment of the Working Time Directive and the Working Time Regulations, so the contractual specification of the relation between work and remuneration has became a real issue with the enactment of National Minimum Wage legislation.[81] The imposition of a general minimum hourly wage has required not only a further exercise in the definition of working time, but a specification of the various ways in which personal employment contracts are regarded as interrelating working time and remuneration. Thus the legislation has drawn up a catalogue of different relations between working time and remuneration, using the conceptions of 'time work', 'salaried hours work', 'output work', 'unmeasured work', 'travelling payments', and the 'pay reference period'.[82]

The interpretation of those concepts invokes and turns upon the law of personal employment contracts in various complex ways. It raises the very questions of choice between a relational approach and an exchange approach to contractual interpretation which have been identified in this section. In the recent case of *British Nursing Association v Inland Revenue National Minimum Wage Compliance Team*,[83] the Court of Appeal was faced with just such a choice in deciding whether a worker was engaged in 'time work' when at home and available to carry out telephone answering duties; their decision that the whole of such time, and not merely the time spent on the telephone, counted as time work, reflected a relational approach.

However, this reliance upon a process of contractual construction to give meaning to the statutory concepts is no straightforward matter. Firstly, very difficult issues arise as to how far that process of construction should be one which is instrumental to the purposes of the particular legislation in question, and if so whether there should be divergences in construction of the same or similar concepts according to whether they occur in the context of working time regulation or minimum wage regulation. The Court of Appeal in the *British Nursing Association* case was clearly grateful to counsel for not taxing it with that particular problem;[84] but it cannot be evaded for long. Secondly, and most fundamentally to our present analysis, the matter is a deeply complex one because in the end it demands and presupposes

---

[80] See the very useful recent study by Geoff White and Janet Druker (eds), *Reward Management—A Critical Text* (White and Druker 2000).

[81] The National Minimum Wage Act 1998 and the National Minimum Wage Regulations 1999, SI 1999/584.   [82] See regs 3–10, as elaborated by regs 15–29A.

[83] [2002] IRLR 480 (CA).

[84] See Buxton LJ at para 20: 'The Employment Appeal Tribunal was asked to look at the Parliamentary debates in order to establish some sort of congruence between the present provisions and the Working Time Directive and Regulations. Mr Epstein showed good judgement in not pursuing that particular thread of his argument in this court.'

a precision of formulation in the personal employment contract as to the definition of work and remuneration and the relation between them which is quite simply not normally forthcoming.

Later in this section we revert to the issues about the need for and possibilities of contractual restatement to address those problems; but first we turn our attention to another and connected set of issues which has presented itself increasingly persistently in the course of this chapter, especially in the course of the present discussion of the internal structure of personal employment contracts, namely that of how the continuity of the personal employment contract is defined and conceptualized.

C. CONTRACTUAL CONTINUITY OF EMPLOYMENT

As one seeks to develop a sense of the definition and the structure, both personal and internal, of the personal employment contract, it becomes increasingly apparent that the notion of continuity of employment is central to the whole evolution of the law of these contracts. It is a key structural notion around which the whole idea of the personal employment contract is formed. For it is around this notion that the law recognizes or constructs contracts with a temporal existence, a time span during which an employing entity and a worker are seen as having a contractual work relationship which involves mutual contractual rights and obligations. It follows that there is a set of issues about contractual continuity of employment which, in some shape, manner, or form can be traced right back through the long history of the law of personal employment contracts.

It is, however, useful to think of the problem as being the subject of a distinctive current legal discourse, which is very much set in and related to the modern body of employment legislation. Modern British employment law has created a very specific set of such issues, by making many statutory employment rights dependent upon the existence and extent of the worker's period of continuous employment with a particular employer (or with 'associated employers') under a contract of employment or a series thereof.

This occurred when employment legislation, from the Contracts of Employment Act 1963 onwards, created a 'minimum floor' of statutory employment rights constructed around the termination of the contract of employment, and primarily contingent upon the worker's continuous employment under a contract of employment or an uninterrupted series of contracts of employment. There was a set of statutory variants; that is to say certain situations were designated as ones in which there was continuity of employment for statutory purposes although there was no contractual continuity.[85] But the basic approach to continuity was a contractual one.

---

[85] The current provisions are those of the Employment Rights Act 1996 Part XIV Chapter I on Continuity of Employment, in particular those of s 212(3) extending the definition of weeks which count in computing the period of continuous employment.

The introduction, from 1971 onwards, of unfair dismissal legislation, constructed in that particular way, greatly heightened the significance of contractual continuity of employment. As, from that time onwards, various forms and patterns of casual and 'atypical' employment assumed growing prominence in the labour market, it became inevitable that the law concerning this issue would be tested hard, and that there would be a new discourse about it.

The formulation of statutory employment rights in that particular way has evoked a notion of *contractual continuity of employment* which is a complex one. It requires both continuity of employment and continuity of contract, so that neither continuity of employment nor continuity of contract is sufficient in the absence of the other. This is significant, because there are various situations where we might well accept that a personal employment contract was subsisting though actual employment was not taking place, and various other situations where we could regard a person as currently in the employment of another in periods where there was no subsisting personal employment contract. Moreover, for certain key statutory employment rights such as those which arise in respect of redundancy and of unfair dismissal, it is required that contractual continuity of employment shall consist of employment not just under any kind of personal employment contract but under a contract of employment as such. These conditions interact with each other to produce a complex test of contractual continuity of employment.

This test, moreover, poses many problems about the internal structure of personal employment contracts in general and the contract of employment in particular. This is well illustrated by the difficulty which arises where a person is engaged for employment on a given date on the basis that he or she will start work at a specified later date, and where the engagement is cancelled before the date appointed for the start of work. Can the worker be said to be employed under a contract of employment before the date on which he or she is due to start work? Before that date, we might readily accept that a contract has come into being between the employing entity and the worker; but it is more difficult to accept that employment has commenced. If we take the view that employment has not commenced, can the contract be regarded, *at that stage*, as a contract of employment, or must it be regarded as a preliminary contract, a 'contract *for* employment', to enter into a contract *of* employment at the commencement of the employment itself? In a case in 1997,[86] it was held that in such a situation the worker in question had entered into a contract of employment, and that there had been a 'termination of the employee's employment' under that contract of employment; but the court was conscious that this was a difficult point, and that the law was being stretched in a purposive way to reach that conclusion. We return to that question in the conclusion to this chapter.[87]

---

[86] *Sarker v South Tess Acute Hospitals NHS Trust* [1997] ICR 673 (EAT).
[87] See 107, 'pre-employment mode'.

An even more difficult version of the same problem arises where a worker is not working for an employing entity in any active sense, and is not being remunerated, but has some prospect or expectation of working for a particular employing entity and being remunerated by that employing entity in the future. In such cases, especially where there have been previous periods of work and remuneration, it may not be clear, firstly, whether the worker is in the employment of the employing entity, secondly, whether if so there is a contract in force between them, and thirdly, whether, if both of those are so, that contract is a contract of employment. This is precisely the set of problems which has presented itself in relation to many workers with casual or intermittent patterns of employment.

The discussion of those issues can be regarded as having begun to concretize in its current form in the decision of the Court of Appeal in the case, in 1983, of *O'Kelly v Trusthouse Forte plc*.[88] This concerned a group of 'regular casual' staff working as waiters or wine butlers in the banqueting department of a large London hotel. The decision was, essentially, that the arrangements under which they worked could not be regarded as taking place under a continuous contract of employment which linked up their engagements for particular banqueting functions, although these workers did in fact work regularly over significant periods of time. In reaching that conclusion, the judges in the Court of Appeal drew on the notion of *mutuality of obligation*. As a broad concept in the general law of contract, mutuality of obligation can best be thought of as a way of expressing the requirement of consideration in the language of promissory obligations. In order for an exchange of promises to constitute a valid contract supported by consideration, each party must make promises which amount to the taking on of contractual obligations; there must be mutuality of obligation.

In the *O'Kelly* case, and in the almost exactly contemporary case of *Nethermere (St Neots) Ltd v Gardiner*[89] concerning part-time homeworkers without fixed hours of work, the idea of mutuality of obligation was applied as a specific concept in the law of personal employment contracts. In that specific context, it was concretized into the requirement that, in order for a pattern of, or set of arrangements for, working, employing, and remunerating to constitute a contract of employment with a continuing existence, there must exist continuous commitments, firm enough to be regarded as contractual in character, to present or future working on the part of the worker, and to present or future employing and remunerating on the part of the employing entity.

---

[88] [1983] ICR 728 (CA).
[89] [1984] ICR 612 (CA). The first presentation of this set of issues in terms of mutuality of obligation seems to have occurred before the EAT in the present case, where the appeal by the employing entity was argued in those terms by one ACL Blair, later to become very prominent in the political sphere.

Initially, in the *Nethermere* case, the imposition of this requirement did not seem inimical to the view that intermittent or casual workers might be regarded as working under continuous contracts of employment; the arrangements for home working which were under consideration in that case were held to comply with that requirement. However, subsequent case law, culminating in the decision of the House of Lords in the *Carmichael*[90] case concerning the part-time tour guides at power stations, which was discussed in the previous chapter,[91] has made it clear that the deployment of the requirement of mutuality of obligation has actually made it rather difficult to regard intermittent and casual workers as having continuous contracts of employment which exist between as well as during the periods in which they are actually working and being remunerated. An analysis of how this has come about throws light upon the way that the conjunction of the ideas of contractual continuity of employment and of mutuality of obligation operates as a major shaping force of the modern law of personal employment contracts.

The casting of the discussion about the contractual continuity of employment of casual or intermittent workers in terms of mutuality of obligation has fundamentally realigned the direction of that discussion. It has gradually shifted the discussion away from a primary concern with classifying the contracts in which arrangements for casual and intermittent work are embodied as contracts of employment or contracts for services. The discussion in terms of mutuality of obligation has increasingly been seen as posing a differently framed, and indeed logically prior, question; namely, do those arrangements give rise to a continuing contract, of any kind at all. Certainly so far as contracts of employment are concerned, the answer has been coming back as a more and more systematically negative one. This requires some further explanation.

The question about contractual continuity of employment, as cast in the form of a discussion of mutuality of obligation, brought with it what seemed at first to be a new way of *subdividing* contracts of employment, apparently carving out a new *subcategory* of contracts of employment referred to as 'global' or 'umbrella' contracts of employment. This new subcategory resulted from a certain particular way of applying the concept of mutuality of obligation to the work situations of casual and/or intermittent workers. According to this way of thinking, we start by envisaging those work situations, in the way that we described them earlier, as falling into two different types of periods of time; the first type is composed of those when the worker is at work for, or in the active employment of, a particular employing entity. These are interspersed, secondly, by intervals of time when the worker is not at work for or in the active employment of that

---

[90] *Carmichael v National Power plc* [1999] ICR 1226 (HL).
[91] See above, 34.

particular employing entity, but there is some prospect or expectation of resumption of work or active employment.

According to the theory of 'global' or 'umbrella' contracts of employment, these two types of period are seen as having quite different contractual connotations from each other. The first type of period is seen as one in which there is a *specific engagement*, which will in and of itself give rise to a short-term personal employment contract of some kind, quite possibly a contract of employment as such. Periods of the second type, on the other hand, are seen as probably not in themselves the subject of any kind of personal employment contract, and certainly not as in themselves the subject of contracts of employment. However, they may be regarded as periods where there is a *general engagement* by which specific engagements are linked up with each other. The requirement of mutuality of obligation is then applied to discover whether there is contractual continuity of employment throughout both types of period. If there is the required mutuality of obligation throughout the whole composite period, it will be regarded as the subject of a continuing (global or umbrella) contract of employment.

This way of applying the requirement of mutuality of obligation seems on the face of it to be neutral and uncontroversial. The approach really took root in the case of *Hellyer Bros Ltd v McLeod*,[92] where it was used to decide—negatively as it turned out—the question of whether trawlermen who worked for a given employing entity in a succession of fishing voyages with intervals of time between them had continuous contracts of employment over the whole succession of such voyages. It seemed a particularly obvious approach in that particular context, because the merchant shipping legislation which applied to these trawlermen created a sharp formal distinction between the status of these workers during voyages, when they were 'on articles' and clearly under written contracts of employment, and, on the other hand, between voyages when they were 'off articles' and not the subject of any formal or written arrangements for employment.

There seemed to be a similarly compelling logic to the drawing of a sharp differentiation between the 'general engagement' and the 'specific engagement' in the case of temporary agency workers. That approach was taken in *McMeechan v Secretary of State for Employment*,[93] which concerned the employment status of a temporary worker who was 'on the books' of an employment agency over a certain period of time, within which there were intermittent periods during which the worker worked on assignment to business enterprises which were clients of the employment agency. In the terms of our discussion of the personal structure of personal employment contracts in the previous chapter, this was seen as a case where the employing entity was the agency, functioning as an employment business, rather than the end-user. It was held that one of the periods spent working on

---

[92] [1987] ICR 526 (CA).   [93] [1997] ICR 549 (CA).

assignment could be regarded as a specific engagement during which the worker was employed by the agency under a contract of employment; but it was not decided whether there was a continuing contract of employment or general engagement of a contractual character which spanned the specific engagements.

However, this approach to contractual continuity of employment, which applies the requirement of mutuality of obligation over periods of time differentiated in that way, has turned out to be much more controversial than it initially appears. For this approach has made it very difficult to establish continuing mutuality of obligation over the whole, aggregate, period of time. The separation of the employment relationship into periods of specific and general engagement has turned out to identify prima facie gaps in contractual continuity of employment; that is to say intervals of time in which, almost by definition, there is no contractual continuity of employment in the normal sense. This has become apparent in the series of recent cases in which it has been held that workers under various forms of casual or 'zero-hours' or 'as required' arrangements do not have continuing contracts of employment, and in which the leading and determinative decision was that of the House of Lords in *Carmichael v National Power plc*.[94]

The method of restatement authorizes an inquiry into whether this approach to the continuity of personal employment contracts is a coherent one. It seems rather discordant with a good deal of older case law in which a largely unfettered power of lay-off on the part of the employing entity (that is to say suspension of employment on economic grounds) seems to have been treated as compatible with the existence of a continuing contract of employment. However, that might be attributable to a generally less exacting view of the obligations of the employing entity in earlier periods of the history of employment law; that case law and that issue are discussed later in this work.[95] The question for immediate consideration is whether the requirement of mutuality of obligation is being applied in a way which is analytically logical and functionally appropriate in the contemporary legal and factual context.

That question may be specified more precisely as one of whether the requirement of mutuality of obligation is being framed or applied too exactingly. It is appropriate to specify the question in that form, given that a series of hard cases have all had the outcome that no contractual continuity has been found to exist. This has been despite the fact that the courts in

---

[94] [1999] ICR 1226 (HL); also *Clark v Oxfordshire Health Authority* [1998] IRLR 125 (CA), and *Stevedoring & Haulage Services Ltd v Fuller* [2001] IRLR 627 (CA). The latest of those cases turned to some extent on the fact that the employing entity had expressly from the outset identified the arrangement as one for casual *ad hoc* employment—see, for discussion of that aspect, Patricia Leighton's note on the case (Leighton 2001).

[95] See below, 474–479.

question have been keenly aware that the effect of such decisions is to deprive the workers in question of entitlement to statutory employment rights, and it is no doubt for that reason that the courts have represented themselves as being in search of the 'irreducible minimum' of mutual obligation which would enable them to find a continuing contract of employment. We return to the question of whether there might be a smaller irreducible minimum of mutual obligation for contractual continuity under a semi-dependent worker's contract; our immediate question is whether the search for the irreducible minimum of mutual obligation to constitute a continuing contract of employment has been pursued to the appropriate degree.

We suggest that, although no doubt convinced that they are pursuing a minimalist approach to the requirement of mutuality of obligations, the courts, when deciding cases about contractual continuity of employment, have been operating within a particular vision of what constitutes an irreducible minimum of obligation when there might be other alternatives. We could see the judicial approach which has been taken in the recent case law on contractual continuity as tending towards a rather strict and symmetrical approach. While stressing that they are looking only for an irreducible minimum of mutuality of obligation, they have nevertheless conceived of that irreducible minimum as having to amount to a fixed and definite obligation, identifiable at any given moment, upon the employing entity to offer work in future, and, symmetrically, upon the worker to accept work as offered.[96]

There is a possible alternative view that there might be sufficient mutuality of obligation to sustain a continuing contract of employment where, if necessary over an extended period of time, it had become apparent that the parties were, from their different respective situations, genuinely committed to maintaining an intermittent or casual work relationship, so that it could not be said that either one of the parties had a totally unfettered discretion whether to continue the relationship or not. A possible formulation would be that the employing entity was subject to an obligation to give reasonable consideration to employing the worker, and the worker was under a corresponding obligation to give reasonable consideration to accepting employment when offered. A formulation of that kind would be consonant with the relational approach to the internal structure of personal employment contracts which was put forward at the beginning of this section.

---

[96] Thus for example the Court of Appeal in *Stevedoring Services v Fuller*: 'It is clear from the Employment Tribunal's reasoning that they were well aware that before they could find there was an overarching or global contract they had to find "an irreducible minimum of obligation on each side" necessary to create a contract of service. There could be no such mutuality if the position was simply that the appellants were under no obligation to offer work and the respondents were under no obligation to accept it.' [2001] IRLR 627 at para 6.

However, although formulations of that kind can be put forward as being compatible with the present law, in the sense of not having been decisively ruled out by the case law as it stands, they also point to serious gaps in the existing analysis of the internal structure and continuity of personal employment contracts. In particular it is very unclear whether the analysis of the internal structure and continuity of semi-dependent workers' contracts is the same as for contracts of employment. For example, might the looser formulation of the irreducible minimum of mutual obligation which was put forward above be regarded as inapplicable to contracts of employment but applicable to semi-dependent workers' contracts? In order for such formulations to be convincing and operable, they would need to form part of a more general restatement of the possible alternative forms of internal structure and continuity of personal employment contracts. We suggest that this is a need which has presented itself more and more acutely as this chapter has progressed; accordingly in the Conclusion we advance some suggestions towards a more general reformulation of that kind.

CONCLUSION

Analysis according to the method of restatement has seemed to produce rather different outcomes as between the different topics or aspects of formation and internal structure which have been considered in the course of this chapter. The law concerning the basic conditions of formation seemed analytically coherent and practically functional, with the exception of the law concerning provision of particulars of terms and conditions of employment. With regard to that topic, a prescriptive argument was advanced that the analytical coherence and practical functionality of the law of personal employment contracts would be significantly enhanced by extending the requirement to provide such particulars across the whole range of personal employment contracts.

That prescriptive argument is really a product or corollary of the underlying view, which was advanced in the first chapter, that there is no fundamental difference in nature between contracts of employment and semi-dependent workers' contracts. That underlying argument, however, and many of the detailed arguments which are consequent upon it, lack real force until we have established a clear analysis of the internal structure of personal employment contracts, which was the aim of the second section of the chapter. That turned out to present very considerable difficulties of analysis. There were considerable uncertainties about how employment, work, and remuneration are interrelated in personal employment contracts.

Arguments were presented for a two-level structure of analysis, which envisaged the internal structure of personal employment contracts in general as existing partly at a level of exchange of work and remuneration, and partly at a relational level in which mutual obligations are interrelated on a more diffuse basis. This reasoning seemed to establish a reasonably solid foundation of analysis which, we suggest, can satisfactorily be viewed as being common to semi-dependent workers' contracts as well as to contracts of employment. Indeed, this is advanced as a common analysis which helps to dispel the perception of fundamental difference in nature between the two types of contract.

However, significant areas of unclarity were strongly exposed, and these became extended as the discussion pursued the question of contractual continuity. It became apparent that these unclarities were problematical both at the level of practical policy and at the level of theoretical analysis. At the level of practical policy, there is a set of problems as to whether the working of the law of personal employment contracts is resulting in an excessive exclusion of casual workers from statutory employment rights predicated upon contractual continuity of employment. At the level of theoretical analysis, there is a major problem in identifying a clear notion of contractual continuity of employment, and in establishing how and in what precise terms the concept of an irreducible minimum of mutual obligation fits into that notion. The method of restatement prescribes that we should not presume to resolve the practical policy issues, but that we may advance suggestions for reformulation at the level of theoretical analysis.

For the latter purpose we put forward suggestions towards a scheme of analysis of the internal structure and continuity of personal employment contracts which, we argue, correctly follows or is supported by the present law; but it is more elaborated or highly specified than the present law, and we acknowledge that, as the specification becomes more detailed, so it becomes more speculative and debatable. This is, therefore, an argument for a clearer articulation of the models of internal structure and continuity which the law of personal employment contracts identifies and uses, and some tentative suggestions as to what those more clearly articulated models might be.

Our suggested analysis proceeds in three stages. Firstly, it distinguishes a number of different phases or modes of existence for personal employment contracts, the central one of which is the mode or phase of full contractual employment. Secondly, it proposes further distinctions between different ways of interrelating employment, work, and remuneration within the phase of full contractual employment. Thirdly, it distinguishes between different bases or types of personal employment contract according to the way in which those contracts combine different phases or modes; this establishes a set of different formulae for contractual continuity.

Firstly, then, we suggest a series of different phases or modes in which a personal employment contract may exist; they are four in number, namely

(1) the pre-employment phase,
(2) the full employment phase,

(3) the sub-employment phase,
(4) the post-employment phase.

We proceed to explain how the state or mode of the contract differs as between those phases, briefly identifying the areas in which this analysis is a difficult or controversial one.

(1) A personal employment contract may be held to exist in *pre-employment mode* when a contract has been made for employment to commence at a later date. This is controversial, to the extent that, when a contract has been made for employment to commence at a later date, it might be held that the personal employment contract had not yet come into existence, or that there was a special kind of contract for future employment in existence; but we suggest that it is appropriate to view the personal employment contract as having come into existence in pre-employment mode.[97] In that mode, the contract probably does not impose any current obligations on either party, other than those of, respectively, keeping the employment opportunity available on the appointed date and remaining available for employment on the appointed date. While the contract exists in that mode, the worker would probably not yet be described as being 'in the employment' of the employing entity.

(2) A personal employment contract exists in *full employment mode* during the time in which it imposes contractual obligations for current employment in the sense of mutual provision of work and remuneration. The worker would appropriately be described as being 'in the full contractual employment' of the employing entity, and we shall refer to periods in which personal employment contracts exist in this mode as periods of contractual employment. This, as we have indicated, is the central or core phase of the personal employment contract. The analysis of the internal structure of personal employment contracts concentrates mainly on this phase but is also much concerned with the relationship between this phase and the next one. Both of those matters are highly complex ones, particularly because of the variety of ways in which working time may be organized and specified within this phase. We return to that point shortly.

(3) A personal employment contract may be held to exist in *sub-employment mode* after a period of contractual employment has ended (that is to say after current obligations for the mutual provision of work and remuneration have ceased to obtain) but while there is still some degree of mutual obligation for the future resumption of employment, and/or while the wider obligations of the full employment phase other than those of actual work and remuneration continue to apply (such as those of mutual loyalty or confidence). In this phase, it is appropriate to regard the personal employment contract as being 'suspended'. In a later chapter,[98] we develop

---

[97] Compare above at 99.   [98] See below Chapter 9, 464–466.

the notion of contractual suspension, and consider fully how this phase is differentiated from the full employment and post-employment phases. During this phase we suggest it is appropriate to refer to the worker as not being in the full contractual employment of the employing entity, but as still enjoying *continuity of contract* under the personal employment contract which previously existed in full employment mode. This identifies a notion of contractual continuity under a personal employment contract which extends to those two phases.

(4) We also suggest that a personal employment contract should be regarded as continuing to exist, but in *post-employment mode*, after a period of contractual employment has ended and after there have ceased to be any mutual obligations regarding the resumption of employment. It would be more conventional to regard the personal employment contract as having ended or terminated or ceased to subsist at that point, but we shall argue in a later chapter that such a view does less than justice to certain very important obligations which may apply after the full employment phase and any sub-employment phase which may occur. During the post-employment phase, the worker would be regarded as no longer 'in the employment' of the employing entity. The concept of the post-employment phase, like that of the sub-employment phase, is examined more fully in that later chapter as part of a general theoretical treatment of the termination and transformation of the personal employment contract.[99]

The further stages of our suggested analysis of the internal structure and continuity of personal employment contracts therefore focus upon the second and third possible phases of existence of those contracts, and upon the ways in which personal employment contracts may combine those two phases. The second stage of the analysis focuses upon the internal structure of those contracts during the full employment phase. This stage of the analysis is in the nature of a call for reformulation with very preliminary suggestions as to the form that such a reformulation might take. We suggest that there is a real and quite pressing need for a much clearer formulation than currently exists of the internal structure of personal employment contracts during the full employment phase.

In particular, a clearer analysis and specification is needed of the various different ways in which personal employment contracts may identify, firstly, working time, and, secondly, the relation between working time and remuneration. It is important, moreover, to regard those as two distinct kinds of formulation, and to recognize the need to carry them out distinctly; doing the one task does not achieve the other. We have seen that the legislation regulating working time establishes some useful models and concepts for analysing the different ways in which and extents to which working time

---

[99] See below Chapter 8, Section 1, 405–407.

may be separated from non-working time. We have also seen that the minimum wage legislation establishes some equally useful models and concepts for understanding the different ways in which and extents to which working time may be related to remuneration.

But problems of reconciling and co-ordinating those systems have begun to present themselves, and we suggest that it will become increasingly important for the law of personal employment contracts to provide a common foundational analysis of the variety of internal structures which personal employment contracts exhibit. We suggest that the basis for such a common analysis may consist in the contrast which we have drawn between relational and exchange-based approaches both to the definition of working time and to the interrelating of working time to remuneration. However, further work would be required to develop analytical categories from those beginnings.

The development of that analysis, even to the preliminary level to which we have taken it, leads on to the third stage of reformulation of the internal structure of personal employment contracts. That is the stage which concentrates upon the continuity of those contracts, and the ways in which different modes or phases may be combined within a framework of contractual continuity. The second stage of the analysis indicated and sought to specify the variety of arrangements which may exist *within* the full employment phase of the personal employment contract. The third stage of the analysis indicates and seeks to specify a further set of different models which may exist *around* the full employment phase.

These are the different contractual patterns for combining the full employment phase with one or more sub-employment phases, that is to say phases of contractual suspension, while the continuity of the personal employment contract is still maintained. Identifying and clarifying the different patterns in which this may be done is crucial if the law of personal employment contracts is to provide a clear and functional analytical framework for the legal regulation of casual and intermittent employment relations. Our discussion of contractual continuity displayed a number of areas of obscurity where reformulation might be possible and helpful.

We suggest that it would be useful to regard the law of personal employment contracts as supporting three patterns of personal employment contract:

(1) the contract for continuous employment;
(2) the contract for intermittent employment;
(3) the contract for very short-term occasional employment.

We proceed to explain those contractual patterns, and to explore the conditions in which they may give rise to contractual continuity under personal employment contracts in general and contracts of employment or semi-dependent workers' contracts in particular.

(1) The contract for continuous employment. This refers to a pattern of employment contract which subsists over a significant period of time (which we may think of as being a week or more), normally and predominantly in full employment mode; it may include periods in which the contract functions in sub-employment mode or is suspended, but only in defined and exceptional circumstances (such as those of disciplinary suspension). This is a pattern of employment which by definition gives rise to or satisfies the requirements for contractual continuity; it seems clear that this pattern of employment may take the form either of a contract of employment or of a semi-dependent worker's contract, but there would be a tendency to regard it as taking the form of a contract of employment rather than a semi-dependent worker's contract.

(2) The contract for intermittent employment. This refers to a pattern of employment contract which subsists over a significant period of time as previously defined but during which periods in full employment mode may predictably rather than exceptionally be interspersed with periods in which the contract is suspended. This corresponds to the idea of the 'global' or 'umbrella' contract consisting of a general engagement with specific engagements within it. We suggest that it is both accurate and helpful to identify such contracts as being for intermittent employment rather than umbrella or global contracts, because it makes the point that this pattern, though not the typical one for the contract of employment, is nonetheless a normal form for personal employment contracts to take, rather than an esoteric and singular kind of employment contract. There may therefore be contractual continuity under a personal employment contract for intermittent employment, but doubt remains about the nature or degree of mutual obligation which is required, and particularly as to whether that requirement differs as between contracts of employment and semi-dependent workers' contracts.

(3) The contract for very short-term or occasional employment. This refers to a pattern of employment contract which subsists as a distinct engagement for a very short period of time, defined as being less than a week. Each such contract has contractual continuity within its short duration, but there is no contractual continuity to span intervals of time between such contracts. The case law has given rise to some doubt whether such contracts may be regarded as constituting contracts of employment as distinct from semi-dependent workers' contracts, but the prevailing view, which we suggest is the correct one, seems to be that such contracts may perfectly well take the form of contracts of employment.

There are some difficulties with this set of formulations, and particularly with the intermediate category of contracts for intermittent employment, to which we revert in a later chapter when the topic of contractual suspension is further analysed,[100] but we suggest that it nevertheless provides a reasonable starting point both for analysis of the contractual status of casual or intermittent workers, and for policy debate about the development of this aspect of the law of personal employment contracts. Thus it could form the basis of a discussion as to whether there should be *presumptions* in favour of regarding personal employment relationships as giving rise to one such contract pattern rather than another, and as doing so in the form of a contract of employment rather than a semi-dependent worker's contract or vice versa.

In particular, consideration might be given to instituting a presumption that any arrangement for personal employment, or personal employment relationship, recognizably continuing over a given period of time, gives rise to a contract of employment for continuous, or failing that for intermittent, employment over that period of time. That would place an onus of identification of the contract pattern upon the employing entity. This would also be a good starting point for discussion about whether and when it might be appropriate to *override* the express labelling of a casual employment relationship as one giving rise only to very short-term occasional contracts.[101]

Those latter points specifically open up a discussion, which has gradually presented itself in the course of this chapter and the previous one, about the appropriate approach to *adjudication* about the definition, formation, and structure of personal employment contracts; how far should that approach be an instrumental one, and to what ends? That is a set of questions which will be pursued throughout this work, but which will be a specially prominent one in relation to the topic of the next chapter, which deals with the content of personal employment contracts and concentrates on judicial construction of that content.

---

[100] See below, Chapter 9, Section 2, 464–467.
[101] This was the difficult problem which began to present itself in the case of *Stevedoring Services v Fuller*; see above, n 94.

3
Content and Construction

INTRODUCTION

In the first chapter of this work, we outlined the concept of the personal work or employment contract, and set out reasons for using it to address some of the shortcomings of a body of law cast in the dual mould of the contract of employment and the contract for services. In that chapter, we also considered the ways in which the ideas of the employer and the worker are constructed in the law of personal work or employment contracts. We referred to the latter part of that discussion as describing the personal structure of personal work or employment contracts. In the second chapter, we looked at the basic conditions for the formation of personal work or employment contracts, and at the internal structure of those contracts. In the present chapter, we seek to complete the analysis of the identity, nature, and main attributes of personal work or employment contracts by considering how, in the law of personal work or employment contracts, the content of those contracts is conceived of and construed.

In order to analyse the basic content of personal work or employment contracts, we evoke and rely upon a central notion which will be used to organize the way that this chapter is presented. This is the idea of the *guiding principles* for the interpretation and construction of personal work or employment contracts. We shall briefly introduce this idea, then develop it in greater detail. The content of personal work or employment contracts, generally referred to as their terms and conditions, or their express and implied terms, can usefully be regarded as consisting of normative propositions, that is to say as rules or principles prescribing how the parties are to act or stating what rights and duties they have in relation to each other.[1] Most or all of the content of personal work or employment contracts can be expressed as normative propositions of one kind and another, and we improve our understanding of that content by articulating it in that way. There is a real need for greater clarity in the exposition of the content of personal work or employment contracts. The content of personal work or employment contracts other than contracts of employment receives little or no attention. Much is written about the content of contracts of employment; but the account which is given of the law relating to that content is all too

---

[1] Examples of such normative propositions are given above at 67, n 63.

apt to seem like a juristic rag-bag of rules and doctrines enunciated over an extremely long historical period of time, and an impossibly over-extended range of social and economic contexts. The discussion of whether eighteenth-century merchant seamen had contracts for remuneration which were entire and indivisible over a long sea voyage[2] sits side by side with the current debate about the nature and extent of the implied obligation of mutual trust and confidence which has developed, in most recent times, around the plight of the middle managers of a corruptly run banking corporation.[3]

This diversity and longevity of the law of personal work or employment contracts is not in and of itself necessarily a defect. We demand of the law of personal work or employment contracts that it should be competent to address the whole range of personal work relationships which are encountered in the contemporary labour market. We might expect a body of doctrine to be enriched rather than impoverished by long historical accumulation. But the capacity of diversity and longevity to act as virtues rather than vices depends upon the existence of a strong doctrinal foundation to the body of law in question. Otherwise that which should be merely the example and illustration becomes the dominant paradigm and binding precedent.

The law concerning the content of personal work or employment contracts is somewhat in that latter condition; it is in a state of inherent uncertainty. This is still the case despite the ground-breaking work of Douglas Brodie on the implied obligation of mutual trust and confidence, in which he demonstrates its potential to turn the contract of employment into one which is subject to a general requirement of performance in good faith.[4] There are still too many crucial unresolved questions about the framework within which a general implied term of that kind might operate, and from which it would derive its precise meaning and significance in particular cases.

In this chapter, we advance the idea that the large and rather amorphous body of law which governs the content of personal work or employment contracts should be seen as being underpinned by a set of *guiding principles of interpretation*. We put these forward as the principles which emerge from the case law about the content of personal work or employment contracts. Sometimes they are articulated in the forms of general implied terms, or of doctrines of contract law which apply in particular ways to personal work or employment contracts. Sometimes they are simply a way of explaining the logic and the trends of the case law. We invoke them in an effort to further

---

[2] See *Cutter v Powell* (1795) 6 TR 320 (CCP).

[3] See *Malik v Bank of Credit and Commerce International SA* [1997] ICR 606 (HL).

[4] Douglas Brodie, 'The Heart of the Matter: Mutual Trust and Confidence' (Brodie 1996) and also, 'Beyond Exchange: the New Contract of Employment' (Brodie 1998), 'Legal Coherence and the Employment Revolution' (Brodie 2001a), 'Mutual Trust and the Values of the Employment Contract' (Brodie 2001b).

the construction of a coherent[5] jurisprudence of personal work or employment contracts. In the first section of this chapter the idea of guiding principles is explained in relation to the express and implied terms of personal work or employment contracts. In the succeeding sections which complete the chapter, we then articulate each of the guiding principles in more detail.

SECTION 1: IMPLIED TERMS AND GUIDING PRINCIPLES

In the previous chapter, we showed how the requirement of mutuality of obligation has been applied in order to test for contractual continuity of employment. In this section, we seek to place that particular doctrinal development in a larger context; we hope to do this by showing how mutuality of obligation is one of a set of guiding principles which shape the interpretation of the internal structure and content of personal work or employment contracts, and in particular the implying of terms into personal work or employment contracts. We can begin that investigation by considering, in slightly greater depth than we did in the previous chapter, the way in which ideas about mutuality of obligation have actually been deployed in adjudications about contractual continuity of employment. That will help to identify a more general paradigm for the way in which personal work or employment contracts are construed or constructed.

In the previous chapter, we were concerned with mutuality of obligation as a requirement for contractual continuity of employment, and were concentrating upon the way in which that requirement has been formulated. In fact, we were primarily concerned with the *formulation* of the requirement, and were inclining to treat the *application* of the requirement to particular sets of work arrangements as a secondary process which took place after the formulation of the requirement, and which was logically dictated by the prior formulation, so that it followed on more or less automatically from that formulation. However, when the operation of the mutuality requirement is explored further, we can start to recognize that the formulation of the requirement of mutuality, and its application to particular cases, are, in reality, integrally linked and interactive processes in the adjudication of any one particular case.

Moreover, that is true more broadly as a general description of the evolution of the law about the internal structure and content of personal work or employment contracts as a whole. That is to say, when the courts deploy a requirement of mutuality of obligation as a test of the continuity or validity of personal work or employment contracts, they are in effect constructing a basic model, or a set of basic models, of a valid personal

---

[5] Again the author acknowledges his indebtedness to Douglas Brodie's recent article on 'Legal Coherence and the Employment Revolution' (Brodie 2001a).

work or employment contract, and comparing actual work patterns or arrangements to that basic model to reach conclusions about the contractual standing of those actual work patterns or arrangements. This is an integrated and interactive process in the following double sense; firstly, that the model is to some extent or other derived from the actual work patterns or arrangements, and secondly, and even more importantly, that the actual work patterns or arrangements are interpreted by reference to the model.

In the previous chapter, we were, in effect, concerned with the first kind of interaction; we examined what kind of actual work arrangements or practices the courts incorporate into their model of a personal work or employment contract which displays an irreducible minimum of mutuality of obligation. This kind of incorporation occurs at a general level, in a way which passes unquestioned most of the time. When the courts formulate their notion of mutuality of obligation for contracts of employment, they are drawing on their knowledge and perception of the employment patterns and arrangements of 'typical' workers in order to devise an approach to those of 'atypical' workers. The same kind of incorporation of actual work arrangements into the mutuality model may occur at the level of the particular case in question. For example, in the *Nethermere* case,[6] there was evidence that the management of the employing company accepted a responsibility, or obligation, to share out available work opportunities evenly and fairly among its workforce of homeworkers. The Court of Appeal, in effect, built that obligation of sharing out work into its model of what might constitute a contract of employment displaying mutuality of obligation.

The reverse kind of interaction is even more interesting. For, on some occasions in the development of the case law about contractual continuity of employment, the courts have used the idea of mutuality of obligation as a guide to the interpretation of the work patterns or arrangements upon which they have to adjudicate, in order to decide what contractual obligations are to be found within those work patterns or arrangements. An excellent example is to be found in the judgment of Chadwick LJ in the Court of Appeal in the *Carmichael* case.[7] In his view, the exchange of letters whereby the claimants were engaged as tour guides on a 'casual as required basis' brought some kind of mutually binding contract into existence, at the very least because it obliged the employing company to provide training, and it obliged the claimants to undertake the training. He also took the view that the claimants were obliged to act as tour guides for particular tours when requested, with reasonable notice, to do so.

Drawing on the general notion of business efficacy (about which we shall have more to say later), but on a particular notion of *necessary reciprocity*, he

---

[6] *Nethermere (St Neots) Ltd v Gardiner* [1984] ICR 612 (CA).
[7] *Carmichael v National Power plc* [1998] ICR 1167 (CA) reversed by HL, [1999] ICR 1226.

reasoned that this obligation must be regarded as matched by an obligation on the part of the employer,

to ensure that work [as a tour guide] when available and in so far as it cannot be performed by full-time employees ... will be offered to those who have been recruited and trained as part-time station guides before being offered to anyone who has not been so trained.[8]

He also held that the employer was under a further ancillary obligation,

to deal with [the part-time tour guides] fairly inter se. That is to say, to share the available work amongst them on some basis, determined by [the employer] which can be seen to be fair.[9]

In the view of Chadwick LJ (not shared by the House of Lords on further appeal), these implied terms confirmed and completed the status of the whole set of arrangements as a continuing contract of employment.

There are certain problems about this kind of reasoning. If taken too far, it becomes a circular form of argument, in which the notion of mutuality of obligation in personal work or employment contracts is derived from the implied terms of those contracts, which are themselves derived from the notion of mutuality of obligation. Moreover, if taken too far in another respect, it becomes a circular way not just of implying terms into contracts, but of implying contracts as a whole, so that an obligation derived from a notion of mutuality of obligation as a necessary condition for a valid contract, confers contractual status upon a set of arrangements which would otherwise lack contractual status.[10]

Those problems may become acute if the notion of mutuality of obligation is used in an ill-defined or undifferentiated way. There may be instances in the case law concerning the continuity of personal work or employment contracts where the use of the idea of mutuality of obligation is open to that criticism. More often, however, the courts are deploying what is actually a fairly specific principle of mutuality of obligation, but which has not been fully articulated as such. We go on to argue that this is a useful way of understanding much of the law about the construction or interpretation of the content of personal work or employment contracts.

Thus far, we have been concerned with the concept of mutuality of obligation as a requirement for a valid personal work or employment contract, and therefore as a test for the continuing existence of such a contract. We saw in that connection how the idea of mutuality of obligation may influence the way that a pattern of or set of arrangements for employing and

---

[8] [1998] ICR 1167 at 1196.   [9] Ibid.
[10] This misgiving about circularity was felt and acted upon by the Court of Appeal in *Stevedoring & Haulage Services Ltd v Fuller* [2001] IRLR 627. Compare the approach to this difficulty which was suggested above at 104.

working is interpreted or construed as a personal work or employment contract. It became apparent how easily the discussion of whether there is a valid continuing personal work or employment contract slides into being a discussion about the interpretation of the terms of personal work or employment contracts, and, in particular, into being a discussion about implying terms into personal work or employment contracts. In this section, we seek to sketch out an overall conception of the construction and interpretation of the content of personal work or employment contracts according to a set of guiding principles, of which the principle of mutuality or reciprocity of obligations is a leading example.

In order to develop this conception, we should first indicate what is included within the notion which we have evoked of the construction and interpretation of the content of personal work or employment contracts. We intend this to refer to the whole process and discourse whereby the obligations, terms, and conditions of personal work or employment contracts, and the ways in which those obligations, terms, and conditions relate to each other, are expounded and specified in and by the courts in the course of legal decision making. It is a more specific conception than that of 'the content of personal work or employment contracts' as a whole, in that it refers particularly to the judicial exegesis of that content.

It is at once wider and narrower than the concept of 'the implied terms of personal work or employment contracts'; it is narrower, in so far as terms may be implied into personal work or employment contracts other than by or as the result of judicial interpretation or construction, for example by legislation. It is wider, in that judicial interpretation or construction of the content of personal work or employment contracts may consist of forms of specification other than by the 'implying of terms'—for example by defining liabilities to damages or to payment of sums due as contractual debts. Such adjudications may be, in the fullest sense, interpretations or constructions of the content of personal work or employment contracts, and yet not be satisfactorily or meaningfully regarded as the 'implying of terms'.

We single out this particular large conception of the interpretation or construction of the content of personal work or employment contracts because it identifies a body of doctrine and a process of adjudication which might be expected to possess an internal coherence, or a consistent and worked-out internal logic. Indeed, the cohesion and intellectual robustness of the law of personal work or employment contracts as a whole ultimately depends upon that expectation being fulfilled. The purpose of focusing on the interpretation and construction of the content of personal work or employment contracts as a holistic conception is both to test for that internal coherence, and to suggest ways of assessing and judging how it might best be achieved.

The discussion will initially focus on the implied terms of personal work or employment contracts but will not be confined to them. It will focus on them because they provide the best examples of attempts to respond to a perceived need for coherence of interpretation of the content of personal work or employment contracts; but it will not be confined to them because they are only one kind of interpretative mechanism, among several, through which overall coherence may be sought and may or may not be achieved.

The development of the law of implied terms of personal work or employment contracts is a fascinating and continuing story which amply illustrates the extensiveness and difficulty of the regulatory function of the law of personal work or employment contracts, and the extent to which that regulatory function is carried out by means of judicial interpretation or construction of the content of those contracts. Compared with that of many other types of contract, the content of personal work or employment contracts is to a very large extent dependent upon implied terms. It is not meaningful to compare proportions as between the different contract types, but it is clear that, in any account of the content, or terms and conditions, of personal work or employment contracts, implied terms of one kind or another are extremely prominent.

There are various reasons for that pre-eminence of implied terms in personal work or employment contracts. These reasons have to do with the procedural and substantive nature of personal work or employment contracts; they relate to the way in which personal work or employment contracts are made or constructed. We can group these reasons into those of indirect specification and those of incomplete specification. As we saw in the previous chapter, the law does not require a formal or written act of contract-making for personal work or employment contracts, and although, in the case of contracts of employment, the employer is required to issue statutory particulars of the main terms and conditions of employment, those particulars do not necessarily, or in and of themselves, represent the true terms and conditions of employment.[11] In this respect, the law creates or confirms a regime in which the content of personal work or employment contracts is usually not specified fully or directly as part of the initial act of contract making, that is to say at the point of engagement for work, or appointment to employment.

Thus, we shall consider the senses in which the specification of content is indirect and therefore produces implied terms rather than express terms in personal work or employment contracts. Firstly, much of the content of personal work or employment contracts is prescribed by legislation, and that legislative prescription often takes the form of, or gives rise to, implied terms inserted into those contracts. That implying of terms may take place in various different senses. Thus, a legislative norm affecting personal work or employment contracts may expressly take the form of a term implied

---

[11] Though they may be regarded as having acquired that character under the doctrine propounded in *Gascol Conversions Ltd v Mercer* [1974] ICR 142 (CA); cf above, 83.

into personal work or employment contracts, as with the right to equal pay between men and women which is conferred by the Equal Pay Act 1970 in the form of an 'equality clause', which is deemed to be a term of all personal work or employment contracts.[12]

In other instances, legislative provisions may expressly affect the contractual rights and obligations arising under personal work or employment contracts, and those provisions may in that sense give rise to implied terms in those contracts. For example, the National Minimum Wage Act 1998 confers upon the workers to whom it applies a specifically contractual entitlement to recover any shortfall between their actual remuneration and the remuneration they would have received if paid at the statutory minimum hourly rate.[13] This can be thought of as the subject of an implied term in the personal work or employment contract. So also might we sometimes regard a legislative norm which, although not expressly declaring itself to do so, in fact shaped or altered the content of the personal work or employment contract. (Note, however, that we are not asserting that every such legislative norm must be regarded as the subject of an implied term. Statutory rights and obligations may be associated with or attached to personal work or employment contracts without necessarily taking the form of implied terms of those contracts.)

There are also various other ways in which the specification of the content of personal work or employment contracts is indirect, in that it depends on the importation of norms from outside sources, and so consists of implied terms in the sense of incorporated terms. The personal work or employment contract may in various respects be or consist of an individual version or counterpart of collective norms, whether formed by collective agreement or by the exercise of managerial rule-making power, for example in the form of 'works rules'. Note that this is different from saying that the personal work or employment contract may be a standard form contract or contract of adhesion. That makes the different point that the worker, when engaged for employment, may have no choice but to accept the employing entity's standard terms of engagement, which may nevertheless be presented expressly, directly, and in full to the worker for his or her individual acceptance. The point about indirect specification is the rather different one that the content of the personal work or employment contract may be constructed of norms (which may apply to a group of workers collectively) which have not been expressly articulated in full in the terms of engagement of the individual worker.

The need for the implying of terms where the content of the personal work or employment contract is not directly specified shades off into the need for terms to be implied because that content is *incompletely* specified.

---

[12] Equal Pay Act 1970, s 1(2).
[13] Section 17(1): 'the worker shall be taken to be entitled *under his contract* to be paid as an additional remuneration an amount...' (emphasis added).

That is to say, we can envisage a spectrum of situations in which terms need to be implied; at one extreme are those where it can be said that the content of the contract is fully clear, but has to be derived from sources other than a specification of them which has been expressly and directly agreed between the parties. At the other extreme are situations where some of the norms governing aspects of a personal work relationship simply have not been specified at all in any meaningful sense, either directly or indirectly, and yet where we demand of the personal work or employment contract which pertains to that relationship that it shall have normative content governing those aspects. A good example is that of sick pay. We shall see that there are situations where there has been no meaningful specifying of whether or to what extent a worker is to be paid during absence due to sickness, but where we nevertheless insist that the personal work or employment contract must, properly construed, provide a specification as to that point.

It is important to notice how the nature of the need for implied terms, and in consequence the nature of the implied terms themselves, seems to change as one moves along that spectrum. At the extreme of clear but indirect specification, the need is simply to recognize and follow a well laid out paper trail to the sources in which the norms in question are contained, such as a company handbook for its workers, or a collective agreement; and the implied or incorporated terms consist simply of the norms which are spelt out in those sources. In general contract law, this is viewed as a requirement for a purely factual inquiry, and the terms which are ascertained as the result of that inquiry are conceived of as 'terms implied in fact'.

As we move along the spectrum towards incomplete specification, so the requirement for ascertainment of terms becomes a more extensive and complex one. In the absence of paper trails leading straight to norms which are clearly applicable to the particular personal work or employment contract, the requirement becomes that of a more wide-ranging inquiry into the normative context in which the particular personal work or employment contract was made and in which it actually operates. Reference has to be made to more general normative sources, such as 'the custom of the trade' or 'good employment practice' in the occupation or industry concerned. The implied terms which are ascertained in that way will tend to consist of larger, more general, propositions than those arrived at in the manner described in the previous paragraph. It becomes debatable whether they should be regarded as 'terms implied in fact' or 'terms implied in law'.[14]

---

[14] That is not least because of the inherent difficulty and unsatisfactoriness of the distinction between terms implied in fact and in law. The argument advanced here follows and seeks to build upon Lord Wilberforce's view of the various categories of implied term as 'shades on a continuous spectrum'—*Liverpool City Council v Irwin* [1977] AC 239 at 254. For a very useful exploration of the case law of that distinction in the employment context, see Gaymer 2001 paras 5–010 to 5–030.

At the extreme of incomplete specification, the requirement for ascertainment of terms becomes such as to involve an inquiry, often at a profound level, about the very nature of the work relationship which is embodied in the personal work or employment contract in question. The implied terms which result from such inquiries may become so fundamental as to amount to general norms for a wide range of personal work or employment contracts, or even for the totality of personal work or employment contracts. Good examples, to which we shall need to revert, are the implied term as to co-operation, and that as to mutual trust and confidence, which now seem to be regarded as applicable to all contracts of employment. (We consider later whether they might be regarded as applying to semi-dependent workers' contracts.) Such implied terms would certainly be regarded as 'implied in law' rather than 'implied in fact'.

There is even a sense in which the requirement to ascertain the content of the personal work or employment contract may operate beyond the scope of 'implied terms', so that it can be met only by formulating and applying a structural principle for personal work or employment contracts, or a rule or doctrine of the law of personal work or employment contracts. For example, we shall see later that this has proved necessary in order to determine whether and in what sense a contract which is terminable by notice may be terminated by payment in lieu of notice. We shall return to consider further the significance of these structural principles which may transcend 'implied terms'; but for the moment it is useful to pursue our argument with reference to implied terms.

Having discussed when and in what sense the need to imply terms into personal work or employment contracts arises, and how the nature of that requirement varies, and so gives rise to different types of implied terms, we now need to consider the implying of terms into personal work or employment contracts as a matter of the interpretation or construction of those contracts. It is crucial to the present argument to observe that the implying of terms into personal work or employment contracts normally both requires and consists of interpretation or construction of those contracts *as a matter of judicial adjudication*. That is to say, the presence and content of implied terms, and their impact upon the contract in question, depends upon a process of normative determination which is entrusted to the courts and tribunals which administer employment law.

This kind of normative determination, or process of construction, is required even in those instances where the implication of a term, and its content and impact upon the contract, seem to have been so comprehensively spelt out in a statutory provision that the implication of the term appears to be automatic, and its content and impact appear to be self-evident. A good example is the equality clause which is deemed to be included in all personal work or employment contracts by virtue of section 1 of the Equal Pay Act 1970.[15] Section 1(1) provides that:

If the terms of a contract under which a woman is employed at an establishment in Great Britain do not include (directly or by reference to a collective agreement or otherwise) an equality clause they shall be deemed to include one.

There are many questions of ordinary statutory construction involved here, in identifying what is 'a contract under which a woman is employed at an establishment in Great Britain'. For example, this turns out to apply to all personal work or employment contracts, not just contracts of employment;[16] it also applies to men's contracts as well as to women's contracts; a significant body of case law exists to determine whether a person's employment is located, on the one hand, at an establishment within the country or, on the other hand, abroad.

There are also, however, deeper questions about the presence of the statutory equality clause within the contract, and about its impact upon the contract. The statutory equality clause is deemed to be included only if the terms of the contract do not otherwise include an equality clause. An equality clause is defined as a provision which *has the effect that* the statutory equal pay requirement is implemented. So the question of whether a statutory equality clause is included in a given contract depends, in theory at least, upon an adjudication as to whether the statutory equal pay requirement is already in substance built into the personal work or employment contract. In practice, it is rarely if ever disputed that a statutory equality clause is automatically included in all the personal work or employment contracts which are within the ambit of the Act, but the potential need for adjudication is clearly present.

If that particular need for adjudication is more theoretical than practical, an entirely real and practical need for adjudication presents itself when we consider how the equality clause fits into the personal work or employment contract, or what impact it has on the contract as a whole. For the equality clause operates to modify existing terms, or to add new terms, until the statutory equal pay requirement is fulfilled. The equality clause is a modifier of terms and conditions, rather than a substantive term or condition in itself. A vast body of domestic British and European Union law exists to expound the statutory equal pay requirement and how it applies to particular cases. The fact that the equal pay requirement is implemented by means of a modifier clause has the consequence that we have, in effect, to draw on the whole of that body of law in order to ascertain the content of any given personal work or employment contract.

If that amount of interpretation and construction is necessary even for a contract term which appears on first impression to be automatically

---

[15] See also above at 120.   [16] Equal Pay Act 1970, s 1(6)(a).

implied and fully self-executing, we should expect that a great deal of interpretation and construction, often of a truly creative kind, is involved in the ascertainment of the whole range of terms which may be implied 'in fact' or, even more especially, for the reasons previously given, of terms which may be implied 'in law'. In other words, identifying the content and effect of the implied terms of personal work or employment contracts involves a series of complex and difficult evaluations both at the technical legal level and at the level of policy and value judgements.

In those circumstances, we should also expect that there is a *theory* of interpretation and construction which the courts and tribunals develop and draw upon in order to carry out the process of articulating the implied terms of personal work or employment contracts in a coherent and consistent way. We shall argue that such a theory can be advanced to explain the decisions which courts and tribunals take in the course of that process. However, that will involve, rather boldly, going behind many of the declared rationales for implying terms into personal work or employment contracts, and identifying a kind of reasoning which is often not fully acknowledged in those declared rationales.

It is necessary to go behind the judicially declared rationales for implying terms into personal work or employment contracts for a set of reasons, which has to do with the particular way in which common law judges are accustomed to explain and to legitimate the process by which implied terms are ascertained. That is to say, they are usually at pains to portray that process as a purely reflexive one of discovering and implementing the intentions of the contracting parties themselves—as, therefore, a process which respects freedom of contract and defers to the results of the exercise of that freedom. It is a deep irony that courts and tribunals claim to expound the implied terms of personal work or employment contracts without making law, and without making terms either. They present themselves, ultimately, as drawing upon law that already exists to ascertain terms which have already been agreed by the contracting parties.

In this way, the courts and tribunals assert the neutrality and objectivity of the process in which they are engaged when ascertaining the implied terms of contracts, and also engage themselves to maintain those virtues as fully as they can in their adjudications about implied terms. However, when the process of ascertainment of implied terms actually involves creative law-making, the real difficulty presents itself that the courts and tribunals are reluctant to evolve positive rationales for that creative law-making because they are committed to disclaiming the creative law-making role. Taken to extremes, that reluctance produces a paradox; the theory for the creative implying of terms into contracts is that there is no such thing as the creative implying of terms into contracts.

The tendency towards that paradox is quite a real one in relation to personal work or employment contracts, where, for the reasons which we have previously explained, the creative law-making role in the ascertainment of implied terms is actually an extensive one. Courts and tribunals have had to resolve deep and intricate controversies about the content of personal work or employment contracts with analytical tools which they declare to be the bluntest of blunt instruments, capable of fashioning only the simplest and most self-evident of solutions. This is a common theme throughout the discourse of implied terms; it is said that terms can be implied only where either there is strong evidence that the parties did in fact agree that the term in question should be incorporated in their contract, or can be treated as having so agreed because its inclusion is so obvious as to pass the 'officious bystander' test,[17] or is 'necessary to give business efficacy to the contract',[18] or 'reflects the inherent nature of the type of contract', or is simply giving effect to general legal obligations imposed by statute or under the law of tort or of restitution.[19] Occasional assertions that a more creative process of construction is actually involved tend to be marginalized or rejected over a period of time.

In the context of personal work or employment contracts, if not more widely, courts and tribunals can and do make significantly creative use of the powers of interpretation and construction which these ostensibly restrictive formulations confer upon them. In fact, the minimalism and simplicity of these formulae actually enlarges the creative space within which the courts and tribunals can operate. For example, it is generally agreed that the single most important development in the law of the contract of employment in recent years has been the recognition of a generally implied term as to mutual trust and confidence. This generally implied term seems to originate in a judgment of Arnold J in 1978 in which he asserted that the task of the Employment Appeal Tribunal was to:

imply into a contract of this sort [ie one consisting partly of expressed and partly of implied terms] such additional terms as are necessary to give it commercial and industrial validity.[20]

Relying upon that mandate, the Employment Appeal Tribunal adopted a formulation which had been put forward by the lawyers acting for the employee that:

it was an implied term of the contract that the employers would not, without reasonable and proper cause, conduct themselves in a manner calculated or likely

[17] As put forward by Mackinnon LJ in *Shirlaw v Southern Foundries (1926) Ltd* [1939] 2 KB 206 (CA) at 227.

[18] This formulation is derived from the well-known passage in the judgment of Bowen LJ in *The Moorcock* (1889) 14 PD 64 (CA) at 68.

[19] These formulations seek to express the approach taken in *Liverpool City Council v Irwin* [1977] AC 239 (HL), and to reproduce the notion of 'importation of general legal obligations' which forms part of Hugh Collins' analysis of the grounds on which implied terms in contracts are recognized—see Collins (1997) at 223–224.

[20] *Courtaulds Northern Textiles Ltd v Andrew* [1979] IRLR 84 at 85.

to destroy or seriously damage the relationship of confidence and trust between the parties.

Those lawyers were therefore, without realizing it, drafting what has since come to be regarded as a defining doctrine of the modern law of the contract of employment,[21] perhaps even for the law of personal work or employment contracts at large. We shall hope to show that this, on the face of it surprising, piece of forensic law-making did not take place in a theoretical vacuum. Nevertheless, it was, in a real sense, the very exiguousness of the declared rationale for implying general terms into personal work or employment contracts which allowed it to occur.

However, it is that paucity and minimalism of the declared rationales for implying terms which also leaves it extremely open to debate as to what is the underlying justification for implied terms, or, to put it in another way, as to what is the real nature of the process in which courts and tribunals engage when they ascertain those implied terms. Hugh Collins has advanced for consideration two such kinds of justification as possible general explanations or underlying rationales for implied terms in the law of contract as a whole. He has also argued for a particular rationale for the regulation of the employment relation.[22] We shall argue for an explanation or underlying rationale for implied terms in the law of personal work or employment contracts which falls somewhere between those two general rationales, and is somewhat different from the particular rationale advanced by Collins.

The first of the two alternative general justifications which Collins canvasses is that the courts are willing to recognize implied terms because they accept a responsibility to provide default rules so that contracting parties can be confident that they do not need to specify all the terms of their contracts every time they engage in a fresh transaction.[23] This justification appeals to economists because it represents the courts as contributing to the efficiency of the contracting process by reducing the transaction costs involved. However, Collins concludes that this will not serve as a full justification for all that the courts do with regard to implied terms in the general law of contract; and this leads him to prefer an alternative general justification, which is that the courts are in his view ultimately concerned to incorporate a fair and practical allocation of risks between the parties, and so to give effect to their view of the reasonable expectations of the parties to the transaction.[24]

In his more recent reflections which are specifically concerned with employment law, Collins advocates a rationale for the regulation of the

---

[21] Compare Brodie 1996 and The Hon Mr Justice Lindsay, 'The Implied Term of Trust and Confidence' (Lindsay 2001) especially at 15–16.   [22] See Collins 2001.
[23] Collins 1997 at 227–228.   [24] Ibid at 228.

employment relation, and for the formulation of the implied terms of employment contracts, which is that of maximizing the competitiveness of business by pursuing a model of flexible employment. His argument contrasts that model of flexible employment with a traditional model of good faith employment; he represents employment law as embarked upon a trajectory from the good faith employment model to the flexible employment model, along which he believes that it is likely to be projected with greater velocity. He identifies the model of flexible employment as 'both a predictive and an explanatory device'. While not denying the predictive power of this model, we would argue that, as an explanatory device, it depends upon a rather exaggerated contrast with a supposedly traditional model of good faith employment.

In our suggestion, we can best arrive at a general explanatory rationale for the ascertainment of the implied terms of personal work or employment contracts in the following way. The process of ascertainment of the implied terms of personal work or employment contracts is part of a larger process of interpretation and construction of the content of personal work or employment contracts. That larger process sometimes has the character of fact finding as to what the parties agreed. Sometimes, on the other hand, it assumes the character of regulation, in the sense that the interpretation and construction is directed towards achieving goals or implementing policies. Even if it is at the fact-finding end of that spectrum, but especially as it tends towards the regulatory end of the spectrum, the whole process of interpretation and construction of personal work or employment contracts is informed by a set of approaches or principles. These can be regarded as the *structural principles* or *guiding principles* which are provided by the law of personal work or employment contracts for the interpretation and construction of the content of personal work or employment contracts.

These structural or guiding principles have evolved in the course of adjudication which is mainly about the content of those personal work or employment contracts which are today regarded as contracts of employment strictly so called. We shall argue, however, that they should not be seen as necessarily confined to such contracts, and we shall consider how far they can be regarded as extending to all types of personal work or employment contracts. There is a core group of three such principles which tend slightly more towards the purely interpretative, derive mainly from adjudication rather than legislation, and which can be seen as quite closely tied to a broad organizing notion of mutuality of obligation. These are the principles of:

(1) mutuality and reciprocity,
(2) care and co-operation, and
(3) trust and confidence.

We can then see in the course of emergence two further, and rather more obviously regulatory, principles, which are in the course of being internalized into the adjudicative process. These are the principles of:

(4) loyalty and freedom of economic activity, and
(5) fair management and performance.

We proceed to seek to demonstrate the operation of these principles in the interpretation and construction of the content of personal work or employment contracts.

The argument which we advance is that the five principles serve to identify the main goals or values which courts and tribunals pursue when interpreting and construing the content of personal work or employment contracts, and when, therefore, declaring and developing the common law concerning the content of those contracts. As the common law courts have not themselves articulated those goals or values as a set of governing principles, there is a large element of attribution in the analysis which follows. It is an attempt at synthesis of a body of doctrine. So this analysis is bound to be controversial; we cannot count upon established reasoning to support it. In the end it will be for the reader to decide how far the argument is sustainable, and how far, on the other hand, it is merely tendentious.

The nature and functioning of these principles is best explored by taking them one by one; but one preliminary general comment may be useful. There are various dimensions in which their functioning varies. The most important such dimension is that of their strength or coerciveness; they vary in the forcefulness with which they shape and inform the content of personal work or employment contracts. At one extreme, they may override the express terms of personal contracts, though this will normally occur only if they can be seen as embodying public policy—as with principle 4—or if they are clothed with legislative force—as with principle 5. At the other extreme, they may provide no more than a tentative guide to the resolution of genuine ambiguity in the express content of personal work or employment contracts. In between those extremes, they may give rise to general implied terms—as, often, with principles 2 or 3—or they may point to the presence of particular implied terms—as, quite widely, with principle 1.

From this it will be apparent that these structural or guiding principles are proposed as a conceptual device which links together a wide range of rules and doctrines about the content of personal work or employment contracts. It is hoped to show that this device has real explanatory force. Firstly, it provides a framework within which we can see courts and tribunals making choices between the different approaches to the structure of personal work or employment contracts which we identified in an earlier section of this chapter. Secondly, it helps to explain the reasoning by which courts and tribunals integrate their own interpretative and regulatory approaches with the other normative sources which bear upon the content of personal work or employment contracts, such as legislation or collective bargaining. All this can be made out more fully in relation to each particular proposed structural principle.

The structural or guiding principles are identified very largely from case law which relates to contracts of employment. We shall note at various particular points how far their application extends to other personal work or employment contracts; and we shall consider that as a general issue at the conclusion of our discussion of the particular principles. Similarly, we shall consider at various particular points how far the guiding principles, or the rules and the implied terms which are derived from them, are derogable or mandatory in some or all personal work or employment contracts; and we shall also return to that as a general issue by way of conclusion to this chapter.

SECTION 2: THE PRINCIPLE OF MUTUALITY OR RECIPROCITY

A. MUTUALITY OR RECIPROCITY AS A GUIDING PRINCIPLE

We suggest that, at the core of the common law of personal work or employment contracts, evolved largely in the context of contracts of employment but not strictly limited to such contracts, there is to be found a guiding principle that the specification of the obligations of employment shall be such as to ensure an adequate and reasonable degree of mutuality or reciprocity between the rights and obligations of the worker and those of the employing entity.

The principle exists in a relatively general form; it is not, for example, maintained specifically enough yet to have given rise to an implied term as to mutuality or reciprocity. It is applied in a way which is quite deferential to the express and specific terms of personal work or employment contracts. Its application also displays a wide diversity of view and approach as to what is meant by mutuality and reciprocity. Nevertheless, it does not seem contrived or artificial to explain quite a large and significant body of the case law about the content of personal work or employment contracts in terms of this principle. That is to say, when issues arise within the law of personal work or employment contracts, especially about the specification of obligations as to work, and as to remuneration, the courts and tribunals can be seen as adjudicating, and as rationalizing their adjudications, in such a way as to express and give effect to the principle we have identified above. In the course of doing that, courts and tribunals make and express the kind of choices which we identified in the previous chapter between different models of the internal structure of personal work or employment contracts, and between different approaches to those models.

In fact, if we pick up and take further arguments which were developed in that earlier chapter, we could see the courts and tribunals as being in the course of a continuing fluctuation between two versions of the principle of mutuality and reciprocity. There is one version of the principle which is typified both by a particular vision of personal work or employment contracts and a particular approach to the law of personal work or employment contracts; and there is an emergent newer version of the principle, typified both by a different vision of personal work or employment contracts and a different approach to the technicalities of the law of personal work or employment contracts. We proceed to describe those two versions more fully, and then to show how they compete in the working of the case law.

The first version of the principle is one in which there are several sharply defined and sharply differentiated models of the personal work or employment contract, and in particular of the relationship between work and remuneration. These models, which now seem somewhat archaic, are those of: (1) the managerial, commercial, or clerical employee receiving a monthly or annual 'salary' not calculated by reference to hours actually worked; (2) the domestic or agricultural servant receiving a monthly or annual 'wage' not so calculated and often partly consisting of provision of board and lodging; (3) the manual worker receiving 'wages' which are calculated by reference to hours actually worked, or to actual output in the form of 'piece-work rates'; (4) the professional practitioner, commission agent, or freelance worker whose 'fees' or 'charges' or 'pay' are related to task completion.

Some caveats must be entered about this set of models. Firstly, it appears to correspond to a general division between 'contracts of employment'—categories (1) to (3)—and 'contracts for services'—category (4). However, it follows from the arguments which were developed in the first chapter of this work that no such simple binary classification would be remotely satisfactory, either now or at any earlier period. Secondly, this system of models asserts a neatly ordered set of social and economic work categories which, equally, cannot be perfectly mapped on to the labour market at any given historical moment. All one can say is that this system of models evolved in legal thinking about personal work or employment contracts during the nineteenth century and was highly influential for quite a lot of the twentieth century, especially the first half of it.

Keeping those caveats in mind, we can nevertheless see how this set of models gives rise to several different relationships between work and remuneration, and therefore to several possible ways of perceiving what might constitute adequate and reasonable reciprocity between work and remuneration. We suggest that there is a version of the reciprocity principle in which this rather strongly developed set of models is combined with a particular doctrinal approach to the law of personal work or employment contracts. According to this approach, rules are formulated, and are assigned, in effect, the status of general rules of law, for the ways in which work and remuneration are interrelated in each of the main models of the personal work or employment contract.

This is an approach associated with a set of technicalities about the pleading of contractual claims, which concentrates on the formal matching of obligations between employer and worker. It is expressed in a notion of correspondence of 'consideration' as between the two parties to a personal work or employment contract, of which the simplest and most direct expression is the idea that 'the consideration for work is wages, and the consideration for wages is work'.[25] That idea is easier to apply to some of the four models of personal work or employment contracts than to others; it fits types (3) and (4) better than it fits types (1) and (2), because, in the latter two models, remuneration is less directly related to actual work than in the former two. So, within this approach, an alternative notion of reciprocity emerges which fits types (1) and (2), whereby the consideration for remuneration is seen as being 'readiness and willingness to work' rather than actual work. This is an approach which comes from the technicalities of pleading, rather than from the realities of personal work relationships. It rapidly leads to artificiality; it suggests that a salaried employee is notionally available for work at any time. In fact, the difference between working time and non-working time for such workers may be very precisely specified, although their remuneration is not directly related to that specification.

We suggest that this whole approach to the notion of reciprocity can be contrasted with an approach which has been in some sense present over a very long period, but which has tended to assert itself more strongly in the recent era of the law of personal work or employment contracts. According to this approach, there is a recognition that personal work or employment contracts cannot satisfactorily be fitted into a set of sharply distinguished models, or made the subject of a set of rules for each such model. Moreover, there is an idea of reciprocity which is less dependent on a formal correspondence of consideration. This idea is one which pays more attention to a wider range of substantive issues; these issues include the extent to which one party to the personal work or employment contract has created, over a period of time, reasonable expectations in the other party which are based on reliance; they also include questions about the remedial context in which the relationship between work and remuneration is being tested.

We shall seek to demonstrate how this divergence of approach to the principle of reciprocity may explain the way in which certain particular questions about the relationship between work and remuneration are handled in the law of personal work or employment contracts. It should be stressed from the outset that the evolution in approach which is being

[25] That famous, deliberately blunt, assertion is that of Greer LJ in *Browning v Crumlin Valley Collieries Ltd* [1926] 1 KB 522 at 528.

depicted does not amount to a systematic or purposive shift towards a law of personal work or employment contracts designed to be specially protective of workers.

B. PROVISION OF WORK

In this part of this section, we address the question of whether and to what extent the principle of mutuality and reciprocity gives rise to contractual duties upon employing entities to provide workers with work. We may think of duties upon employers to provide workers with work as being of two kinds: on the one hand, they may be (1) duties to provide opportunities to earn remuneration by working or being at the employing entity's disposal for work; on the other hand, they may be (2) duties to provide work *as well as* remuneration so that the worker may acquire or maintain skills, experience, or reputation. In the first form, such duties are closely bound up with duties to guarantee minimum levels of remuneration, and we begin by considering those linked kinds of contractual obligation.

We argued in an earlier section that the idea or principle of mutuality of obligation applies negatively so that a personal work arrangement which is completely non-obligational will be viewed as inadmissible to the category of personal work or employment contracts. The question now is whether and how far the principle of mutuality, reciprocity, and stability of work and remuneration will fasten on a slight or limited evidence of continuing obligations and concretize them within continuing personal work or employment contracts. How far, in other words, when employing entities build into personal work or employment contracts wide discretions about the provision of opportunities to earn remuneration, will those discretions be construed as bounded or limited by the reciprocity principle?

According to the traditional way of expounding the law of personal work or employment contracts (or, to be precise, the law of contract of employment as the only type of personal work or employment contract which is normally the subject of systematic exposition) we might try to answer that question by distilling a rule or set of rules from the whole accumulated body of common law jurisprudence, which, in relation to personal work or employment contracts, extends over more than two centuries of case law. We suggest that a better understanding of the current law is to be obtained by asking how far and in what ways the law of personal work or employment contracts is given a certain shape and form by the primary normative sources, that is to say legislation, and collective and individual agreements, as supplemented by case law principles.

Thus, for example, there is a body of case law from the mid-nineteenth to the mid-twentieth century which can be regarded as giving rise to implied terms for the provision of a reasonable amount of work, or enough work to allow a reasonable amount of remuneration to be earned, for workers under particular types of personal work or employment contracts whereby remuneration was wholly dependent upon output or task completion, such as workers paid entirely by piece-rates[26] or by commission.[27] However, rather than regarding these as rules of construction for the modern personal work or employment contract, we should regard the general rules as the statutory ones established, for contracts of employment, by the legislation on guaranteed pay,[28] and for personal work or employment contracts generally by the minimum wage legislation.[29] The minimum wage provisions, by way of establishing minimum hourly rates of pay, take significant steps towards stabilizing the relationship between output and pay, for workers paid by piece-rates or on a commission basis, across the whole of the hours of the worker's 'pay reference period'—typically a day, or a week, or a month.[30]

We should then consider whether and to what extent those statutory rules are supplemented by the application of guiding principles of interpretation such as that of mutuality or reciprocity. The basic issue of principle about the provision of work and the guaranteeing of minimum remuneration is one that we have encountered earlier as a question of mutuality and continuity, and one that we shall encounter again later in the context of the suspension and termination of personal work or employment contracts. It is the question of what, if any, are the minimum constraints placed by the law of personal work or employment contracts upon the capacity of the employing entity to acquire and exercise, within the personal work or employment contract, a complete discretion as to whether to provide the worker with work in the sense of the opportunity to earn remuneration. We have seen that, if a set of arrangements for personal work is regarded as totally casual or non-obligational, those arrangements may be held to lack the character of a continuing personal work or employment contract, or at least of a continuing contract of employment.

That distinction between a casual non-obligational work relationship, on the one hand, and a continuing personal work or employment contract, on the other, would, however, be undermined if the law of personal work or employment contracts recognized a continuing personal work or employment contract, while nevertheless accepting that the employing entity might have an unfettered discretion, within that contract, to 'lay off' the worker—that is to say, to refuse to provide the worker with work and the

---

[26] Compare *R v Welch* (1853) 2 E & B 357; *Re Bailey, Re Collier* (1854) 3 E & B 607; *Whittle v Frankland* (1862) 2 B & S 49; *Thomas v Vivian* (1872) 37 JP 228.

[27] *Turner v Goldsmith* [1891] 1 QB 544, where Lindley LJ said, at 548, 'The company would not be employing the Plaintiff within the meaning of the agreement unless they supplied him with samples to a reasonable extent.'   [28] See below, 134, 474, 485–486.

[29] Compare above, 65–66.

[30] This is the effect of s 1(1) of the National Minimum Wage Act 1998 coupled with regs 24–29 of the National Minimum Wage Regulations 1999, SI 1999/584—see especially regs 25 on 'Fair estimate' agreements for output work, and compare also reg 28 on 'Daily average' agreements for unmeasured work.

opportunity to earn remuneration, doing so on a supposedly temporary basis, but so that it is entirely for the employing entity to say when or even whether work will be resumed. We began to consider this question in an earlier chapter[31] and return to it in greater detail in a later chapter,[32] but make the point at this stage that the case law does indicate some degree of *principled* resistance on the part of tribunals and courts to that kind of unfettered unilateral discretion with an apparent contract. That resistance can best be explained by reference to a principle of mutuality or reciprocity of obligations.

One of the strongest affirmations of that principle occurred in the case, in 1906, of *Devonald v Rosser & Sons*.[33] The issue in the case was whether workmen paid on piece-rates in the tinplate trade in South Wales could be deprived of work and remuneration during a twenty-eight day period of notice to terminate their employment by reason of a downturn in trade experienced by their employing entity. Both at first instance and on appeal to the Court of Appeal it was held that the employing entity was bound by the contract of employment to find the worker a reasonable amount of work, enough to enable the worker to reach his average earnings. The particular question of guaranteed remuneration during the period of notice is now partly at least the subject of statutory regulation, in the form both of the guaranteed pay provisions[34] and the provisions for pay during statutory notice periods for workers under contracts of employment.[35] It is the reasoning at the level of general principle in this decision which remains of great importance.

For, both at first instance and on appeal, the courts deployed a notion of mutuality or reciprocity to uphold the argument for the workmen. Jelf J at first instance put it thus:

The first question, then, is whether the plaintiff on the above facts shews an implied right on his part by the contract, unless there is a custom to the contrary, to be provided, while the contract lasts with a reasonable amount of work. *Apart from authority, it would be very strange if such a right is not implied; for otherwise the bargain is of a very one-sided character.* The workman must be at the beck and call of the master whenever required to do so, and yet he cannot, though ready and willing to work and earn his pay, earn a single penny unless the master chooses...[36]

In the Court of Appeal, Farwell LJ made the same point in the terms that:

Whatever the kind of work on which the workman is employed, the rights and obligations of the respective parties are treated as standing on the same footing.[37]

It is important to note how this principle operated; it produced the result that the contract was construed as fundamentally corresponding to

---

[31] See above, 100–101   [32] See below, 474–479.   [33] [1906] 2 KB 728 (CA).

[34] Employment Rights Act 1996 (ERA), ss 28–35.   [35] Ibid, s 87.

[36] [1906] 2 KB 728 (CA) at 731 (emphasis added).   [37] Ibid at 744.

the version put forward on behalf of the worker, rather than to the employing entity's version. The onus was therefore upon the employing entity to establish that a custom to the contrary effect formed part of the contract. The requirement of mutuality or reciprocity is then reasserted in the form of a tough application of the limits on the incorporation of customs as contractual terms. As Farwell LJ put it:

A custom to be good must be reasonable, certain, and notorious. Jelf J has found as a fact that it was not notorious, and I certainly do not disagree with that finding. Further, in my opinion it is neither reasonable nor certain, because it is precarious, depending on the will of the master.[38]

Central to this mode of reasoning is therefore an idea that contracts must be construed so that they display a *reasonable* degree of mutuality or reciprocity. We shall, in the next subsection, pursue the general issue of how that notion of reasonable mutuality or reciprocity is conceptually defined; but we shall first consider the specific question of how far the tribunals and courts regard it as giving rise to a duty on the employing entity to provide actual work, above and beyond the opportunity to earn remuneration.

It would seem that, despite occasional instances to the contrary, the courts and tribunals do not in general regard the provision of actual work as part of the inherent mutuality or reciprocity of the personal work or employment contract, or even of the contract of employment strictly so called. In 1940, it was asserted by Asquith J that there was, in effect, a general presumption against an obligation upon the employer to provide actual work:

The contract of employment does not necessarily, or perhaps normally, oblige the master to provide the servant with work. Provided I pay my cook her wages regularly, she cannot complain if I choose to take any or all of my meals out. In some exceptional cases, there is an obligation to provide work.[39]

By 1974, Lord Denning could take the view that '[t]hings have altered much since then'[40] and that the employer's duty to enable the employee to maintain the employment relationship had the social dimension of ensuring the employee a function within the enterprise. But, when the point was argued before the National Industrial Relations Court in the same case, Sir John Donaldson indicated the Court's more cautious view that there was not normally a contractual right to work solely for the sake of the employee's job satisfaction.[41]

There may today be scope for building on the specific exceptions which have from time to time been recognized to that generally negative position. Some cases, concerning personal work or employment contracts which are

[38] Ibid at 743.
[39] In *Collier v Sunday Referee Publishing Co Ltd* [1940] 2 KB 647 (QB) at 651; see further below, 488.
[40] In *Langston v AUEW* [1974] ICR 180 (CA) at 190.
[41] In *Langston v AUEW (No 2)* [1974] 510 (NIRC) at 522.

not necessarily contracts of employment, have recognized the interest of entertainment workers such as actors in actually carrying out an engagement so as to gain publicity and experience.[42] A small number of other older cases, concerning appointments to managerial jobs or offices, seem to recognize the worker's particular interest in being allowed to carry out the duties of such a post.[43] We shall see later that there is some increase in judicial readiness to generalize this kind of recognition in workers' interests in the standing and reputation which their work confers upon them.[44] That could be regarded as an aspect of the development of a sense of the inherent mutuality or reciprocity of personal work or employment contracts. We turn to consider how that development fits into theories about allocation of risk and control of discretion in the modern law of personal work or employment contracts.

C. Mutuality—Allocation of Risk and Control of Discretion

In this subsection, we consider how far the principle of mutuality or reciprocity can be regarded either as a method of allocation of risk between employing entity and worker, or as a method of control of discretion. We begin with the question of allocation of risk. In one sense, it is straightforward to see the principle of mutuality or reciprocity as one which is concerned with the allocation of risk; the application of the principle brings about allocations of risk which would or might not have occurred had the principle not been applied. However, this is to use the idea of allocation of risk in so general a sense as to reduce it to insignificance. A more pointed question is one which we can identify from the literature of the law and economics, namely, does the principle of mutuality or reciprocity give rise to a set of default rules aimed at allocating risks, as between employing entity and worker, to the party best able to bear the risk?[45]

There are instances where the principle of mutuality or reciprocity has been applied in exactly that way. Perhaps the best illustration of all occurs in the case of *Devonald v Rosser & Sons*,[46] where Farwell LJ proposed the

---

[42] *Marbé v George Edwardes (Daly's Theatre) Ltd* [1928] 1 KB 269—£3,000 damages recovered for loss of reputation in not being allowed to act; *Herbert Clayton & Jack Waller Ltd v Oliver* [1930] AC 209—£1,000 damages recovered by an actor under the same head; but a more limited view was taken in *Withers v General Theatre Corpn* [1933] 2 KB 536.

[43] *Collier v Sunday Referee Publishing Co Ltd* [1940] 2 KB 647; *Hall v British Essence Co Ltd* (1946) 62 TLR 542. Compare now *William Hill Organisation Ltd v Tucker* [1999] ICR 291 (CA), in which it was held that the entity employing a senior dealer in the expert business of spread betting was not free to place him on 'garden leave' in the absence of express contractual provision for doing so—see below, 487–488.   [44] See below, 488–489.

[45] This formulation is suggested by Paul Skidmore's very perceptive essay on the allocation of entrepreneurial risk in employment contracts; see Skidmore 1997 at 221.

[46] [1906] 2 KB 728 (CA).

following justification for ruling in favour of the worker's implied contractual right to be provided with a reasonable opportunity to earn remuneration:

We must bear in mind that we have to regard the matter from the point of view not only of the master, but of the workman. Both master and workman have to make their living. The master makes his living by realising a profit; the workman makes his by his wages. The master's profits are ascertained as an ordinary rule de anno in annum. But the workman has to live de die in diem, and his wages presumably do not leave a large scope for saving for a future day when no employment is forthcoming.[47]

It should not, however, be thought that whenever this kind of deliberate risk allocation occurs, that necessarily consists in allocation of risk from the worker to the employing entity. It did so in that case; but, as we shall see in a later chapter, the contrary allocation occurred in *Browning v Crumlin Valley Collieries Ltd*,[48] where the risk of loss of earnings due to the closure of a coal mine because of its dangerous condition, not being the fault of the employing entity, was viewed as one which it was not intended the employing entity should bear.[49] Such allocations are fully as capable of being regarded as within the principle of mutuality or reciprocity as are those in favour of the worker. No one *particular* allocation of risk is dictated by that principle. The principle can be regarded as in full force and effect at the present day although neither of those two particular risk allocations is directly applicable.

The development of the case law treatment of sick pay, which again we consider in more detail in a later chapter,[50] provides further illustration of the way in which the principle of mutuality produces risk allocations which are highly specific to their particular contexts, so that the particular allocations have to be viewed as highly circumstantial rather than as being of general application. Thus, one reason advanced for the decision in favour of continuation of wages during sickness in 1939 in *Marrison v Bell*[51] was that:

[T]he great majority of employed persons in this country are employed on terms of a week's or, at any rate, a month's notice—mostly a week's notice; and consequently there is no social need for protecting the employer from the liability of having to go on paying wages which he is always able to terminate after a short time.[52]

But by 1983, in *Howman & Son v Blyth*,[53] Browne-Wilkinson J saw the practical position as being completely different because unfair dismissal protection prevented employers from terminating the employment of sick employees at short notice;[54] this was seen as a reason for implying a limited

---

[47] Ibid at 743.   [48] [1926] 1 KB 522 (KB).   [49] See below, 475–477.
[50] See below, 216–218.   [51] [1939] 2 KB 187 (CA).   [52] Ibid, Scott LJ at 204.
[53] [1983] ICR 416 (EAT).   [54] Ibid at 420.

duration to sick pay in the particular case because:

It would be unfair to saddle employers in modern circumstances with an obligation to pay full wages until they could properly dismiss the employee.[55]

These instances might encourage us to think that the principle of mutuality or reciprocity operates systematically as an instrument of risk allocation. However, this would be true only in a rather limited or indirect sense. It is actually quite rare for courts and tribunals to use risk allocation reasoning when construing personal work or employment contracts. A good example of their preference for other modes of reasoning is to be found in the area of apportionment of remuneration, that is to say deciding how much if any remuneration is earned and payable in respect of periods of work which are foreshortened or incomplete for whatever reason. We consider this area in detail in a later chapter;[56] at this stage we draw attention to the fact that, although apportionment of remuneration could be regarded as a classic form of risk allocation, courts and tribunals have much preferred to approach issues of apportionment with techniques of reasoning which make no open concession to ideas of risk allocation, such as those of the doctrines of 'entire contracts' and 'substantial performance'. Sometimes issues of apportionment will be determined by the use of a principle of mutuality or reciprocity, but, even when that occurs, the principle is not normally invoked in terms of risk allocation but in other and more general terms.

This is very well illustrated by the decisions of successive tribunals or courts in the case of *Ali v Christian Salvesen Ltd*,[57] which raised a special and complex issue of apportionment arising from the now widespread practice of making personal work or employment contracts on the basis of 'annualized hours'. This is a practice whereby the worker's hours of work are defined on an annual basis, so that the worker will receive overtime or premium payments for hours worked in excess of the stated level *over a complete year*. In this case the issue was whether a worker made redundant in the middle of the calculation year should receive overtime payment for hours worked in excess of the weekly average though below the annual threshold. The set of arrangements for the annualized hours was contained in a collective agreement which made no provision for apportionment within the calculation year.

---

[55] [1983] ICR 416 (EAT). Compare, as recent instances of allocation of risk of sickness according to broad notions of reciprocity and mutuality, *Beveridge v KLM (UK) Ltd* [2000] IRLR 765 (EAT)—worker held entitled to pay when willing to return to work after sickness and certified as fit by her own doctor though not by the employing entity's medical adviser; *Manchester City Council v Thurston* [2002] IRLR 319 (EAT)—worker entitled to continuation of sick pay during depressive illness associated with disciplinary hearing, sickness absence regarded as not 'attributable to his own misconduct'.   [56] See below, 201–208.
[57] [1996] ICR 1 (EAT); [1997] ICR 25 (CA); see below, 283–284.

This was a prime issue for risk allocation. The Employment Appeal Tribunal held that an apportionment provision should be implied as a matter of mutuality or reciprocity, Mummery J including among the reasons the view that:

it cannot have been the intention of the parties to the agreement that an employee should be expected to perform hours of work (for which there are hourly rates) but not be entitled to be paid for them.[58]

The Court of Appeal took a more formalistic view that, as the parties to the collective agreement had not made explicit arrangements for apportionment, no such arrangements should be implied. The current position would therefore seem to be that courts and tribunals do draw upon a principle of mutuality or reciprocity when interpreting personal work or employment contracts; that this principle has the theoretical potential to operate as the basis for systematic risk allocation, but that there is only rather slight evidence of judicial willingness to use the principle in that way. In the course of this chapter we consider how and to what extent a systematic approach to risk allocation has developed through other principles of interpretation, particularly those concerned with care and co-operation and trust and confidence.

Another way in which the principle of mutuality or reciprocity might be deployed is that it might be used as a systematic way of preventing either party to the personal work or employment contract from acquiring unlimited arbitrary or discretionary power in relation to the other party. That is to say, it could be the basis for construing personal work or employment contracts so as to exclude unlimited arbitrary or discretionary power. How far could we view this as actually being the case? We have already observed some instances where that has occurred, in relation for example to the employing entity's power of lay-off.[59] It also occurs when, as will be shown in a later chapter, courts and tribunals interpret personal work or employment contracts so as to place heavy restrictions upon workers' powers to take industrial action. It was very significant that, as we have seen,[60] Chadwick LJ in the Court of Appeal in the *Carmichael*[61] case invoked a notion of 'necessary reciprocity' to sustain a finding that the employing entity did not have an unfettered discretion whether or not to offer any work to its part-time tour guides, though, as we have also seen, that approach to construction did not prevail in the House of Lords in that case.

However, we could not yet assert that the principle of mutuality or reciprocity has become generally applicable as a control upon unlimited arbitrary or discretionary power. There are several reasons to be cautious about taking that view, some more negative and others more positive in

[58] [1996] ICR 1 at 12.   [59] See above, 132–136.   [60] See above, 116–117.
[61] *Carmichael v National Power plc* [2000] ICR 1226 (HL).

their implications for the development of the law of personal work or employment contracts. Firstly, on the more negative side, as we saw in the *Clark*[62] and *Carmichael* cases, courts and tribunals will tend to take a restrictive view of how far the principle of mutuality or reciprocity authorizes or requires them to construe casual or intermittent personal work arrangements as continuing personal work or employment contracts.

Secondly, but on the more positive side, there are a number of instances where courts and tribunals do in fact construe personal work or employment contracts so as to control unlimited arbitrary or discretionary power, but have not yet rationalized those controls into a general principle of mutuality or reciprocity. Sometimes that is because a control of that kind has remained isolated, not integrated into a general framework of principled reasoning. For example, the employee's implied obligation of 'obedience to lawful orders' has been subjected to the limitation that those orders must be 'reasonable' ones; but that limitation has remained shadowy and ill-defined because it has not been located in a larger body of principles of interpretation.[63]

In other instances, the courts and tribunals do seem to be developing controls upon arbitrary or discretionary powers, especially those of employing entities, and do seem to be placing those controls within a general framework of principled reasoning; but they prefer to invoke principles other than that of mutuality or reciprocity. There is, as we shall see in a later section of this chapter, a strong current preference for invoking a general principle of trust and confidence, at least in relation to contracts of employment. That principle, usually cast as it is in terms of *mutual* trust and confidence, can itself be traced back to an underlying notion of mutuality or reciprocity. However, although one might predict that the principle of mutuality or reciprocity may eventually emerge as the basic norm for the interpretation or construction of personal work or employment contracts as a whole, that position has not yet been reached. It is appropriate at this stage to see the other guiding principles as discrete and free-standing ones, and we go on to consider them in that light.

SECTION 3: CARE AND CO-OPERATION

The second guiding principle which emerges from the case law of personal work or employment contracts is that personal work or employment contracts will be construed so as to oblige each of the parties to take

---

[62] *Clark v Oxfordshire Health Authority* [1998] IRLR 125 (CA)—see above, 103.

[63] *Laws v London Chronicle Ltd* [1959] 1 WLR 698 (CA) and *Pepper v Webb* [1969] 1 WLR 514 are the latest decisions significantly to address the question of the reasonableness of orders in a purely contractual context, but the question frequently arises in the unfair dismissal context, where, however, it tends to be subsumed into a more general issue of the overall reasonableness of the decision to dismiss, as in *Haddon v Van den Bergh Foods Ltd* [1999] ICR 1150 (EAT) (which must itself be read subject to *Foley v Post Office* [2000] ICR 1283 (CA)).

reasonable care of the other's physical and economic interests, and to co-operate with each other in realizing the objectives of the personal work or employment contract in question. This principle applies somewhat differently as between employing entities and workers; the main weight of the obligation of care falls upon the employing entity, while the obligation of co-operation has been primarily applied to workers. It is debatable how far this principle applies beyond the scope of the contract of employment strictly so called to other personal work or employment contracts. We consider the evolution and application of this principle first as between employing entities and employees, and then as between employing entities and semi-dependent workers.

A. AS BETWEEN EMPLOYING ENTITIES AND EMPLOYEES

We begin with the application of the reasonable care principle to employing entities. It is not controversial that entities employing employees under contracts of employment owe them implied contractual obligations, corresponding to obligations imposed under tort law, to take reasonable care of their health and safety by providing them with a reasonably safe system of work; and that employing entities also owe their employees or former employees an implied contractual duty, again corresponding to a duty in tort, to avoid deliberate or negligent misstatement when writing references for them. It is controversial how far the reasonable care principle extends beyond that, both in the obligations which it imposes and in the personal work or employment contracts to which it applies.

We can distinguish between two different versions of the reasonable care principle as it applies to employing entities; these represent two different views about how far the reasonable care principle extends, and how far it is likely to extend in the future. One version of the reasonable care principle, as applying to employing entities, identifies it as a direct and simple and limited application of the general law of the tort of negligence. The other version identifies it as a more specialized, and particular development of responsibilities on the part of the employing entity to care for the welfare and well-being of the worker, as an intrinsic feature or property of the employment relationship. The current case law generally supports the former version of the reasonable care principle better than it supports the latter version, but there are areas of case law where the latter version can be seen as applying.

The tort-based version of the employer's reasonable care principle is the result of a long incremental common law development, in which two very important staging posts are the affirmation in the 1930s of an employer's general duty to take reasonable care for the safety of those in its employment,[64] and the recognition in the 1950s that this duty could equally well be regarded

---

[64] *Wilson & Clyde Coal Co v English* [1938] AC 57 (HL).

as a duty in tort or as an implied obligation of the contract of employment.[65] Although the Health and Safety at Work etc Act 1974 imposed general statutory health and safety duties upon employers in respect of employees,[66] and upon those conducting work undertakings or occupying work premises in respect of persons at work more generally,[67] those duties do not seem to have been integrated as implied obligations into personal work or employment contracts, in the way that one might otherwise have expected, presumably because of the provision that the general statutory duties shall not give rise to civil actions.[68]

The more specifically employment-law based version of the employer's reasonable care principle emerges mainly from recent case law about constructive dismissal, in which the implied obligations of the employing entity arising under contracts of employment are spelt out in order to determine whether the conduct of the employing entity has amounted to a repudiatory breach of contract. As we shall shortly see, most of the development of the implied obligations of the employing entity which is occurring in the context of constructive dismissal is focused upon the principle of mutual trust and confidence, but some of it is seen as a matter of reasonable care for the employee's health, safety, and welfare.

There is a crucially important area in which the two versions of the reasonable care principle vie with each other, and tend towards divergent outcomes; this area is that of the obligations of the employing entity of care for the mental or psychological health, safety, and welfare of the worker. The issue is the extent of the responsibility of the employing entity for stress experienced by the worker at work or in connection with work which is severe enough to make the worker wholly or partly incapacitated for work, or to make the worker perceive himself or herself as unable to continue to work in the situation or environment in question. In recent years, there has been a mounting consciousness that this is a major social, economic, and legal question, especially, though not solely, for workers with managerial roles or duties who have been expected to operate with increasingly scarce resources, particularly in the public sector.

A very far-reaching development of the tort-based version of the employer's reasonable care principle occurred in the leading case of *Johnstone v Bloomsbury Health Authority*,[69] which concerned the claims of junior hospital doctors to restrain their employers from imposing excessive working hours such as to cause stress, anxiety, and depression associated with inadequate sleep. Here the principle was successfully invoked as an implied limitation on the contractual entitlement of the health authority

---

[65] See *Lister v Romford Ice Co* [1957] AC 555 (HL), *Matthews v Kuwait Bechtel Corpn* [1959] 2 QB 57 (CA).   [66] Section 2(1).   [67] See s 3(1).

[68] See s 47. In *Waltons & Morse v Dorrington* [1997] IRLR 488 (EAT), Morison P at 490 spoke of s 2 as a 'good starting point' for a broader implied term (as to which, see below, text at n 73), but this was different from directly founding a contractual obligation on the statutory provision.   [69] [1991] ICR 269 (CA).

employer to require its junior hospital doctors to work in excess of 72 hours a week. The two judges who formed the majority in the Court of Appeal resolved the problem of conflict between the *implied* term as to reasonable care for health and safety and the *express* term as to overtime working by regarding the implied obligation as controlling the exercise of a discretion to fix hours of work which was conferred by the express term.[70]

In that case, the willingness to allow the reasonable care principle to cover the worker's general psychological health and well-being was heightened by the evident link to the doctor's capacity to care for the health and safety of his or her patients.[71] In other contexts, this key issue of employer's liability has been approached mainly by tort-based reasoning in which the emphasis is on identifying a specific injury to the worker's health, and in which an essentially cautious approach is taken to questions of causation and foreseeability where mental or psychological, as opposed to physical, injury is concerned. That approach is well illustrated by a decision of the Court of Appeal in 1993 in which it was found that there had been no breach of the employer's duty of care where a senior civil servant suffered a mental breakdown associated with work stress.[72] From a similar conceptual approach, and on not strikingly different facts, a decision that there had been a breach of the duty of care was given in 1994 in the now very well-known case of *Walker v Northumberland County Council.*[73]

This case seemed to offer the prospect that the tort-based approach might give rise to a general duty on employing entities to manage work situations and to allocate organizational resources with a higher level of care than had previously been exacted for the mental health of workers. That prospect was somewhat diminished by the decision in the House of Lords in the leading case of *White v Chief Constable of South Yorkshire,*[74] where it was held that the Chief Constable was not liable for a breach of the employer's duty of care in respect of the psychiatric injuries suffered by police constables who in the course of their duties had witnessed the deaths and injuries which had occurred at the Hillsborough football stadium in 1989. Although one could view this decision as in some sense confined to the particular sorts of damage to mental health which are caused by witnessing specific major traumatic events, it does nevertheless have negative implications for the scope of the employer's duty of care more generally.

---

[70] See ibid Stuart-Smith LJ at 275, and Sir Nicholas Browne-Wilkinson VC at 283–284. Sir Nicholas Browne-Wilkinson VC expresses his ruling as confined to the case where the contract confers a power to fix hours rather than itself fixing the hours; and he expressly distances himself from what he perceives to be the view of Stuart-Smith LJ that the implied obligation would restrict the express term of the contract *even in the latter case.*

[71] Compare Stuart-Smith LJ at 279–280: 'I have no doubt that it is a matter of grave public concern that junior doctors should be required to work such long hours without proper rest that not only their own health may be put at risk but that of their patients as well.'

[72] *Petch v Customs and Excise Commissioners* [1993] ICR 789 (CA).

[73] [1995] ICR 702 (QBD).   [74] [1999] ICR 216 (HL).

This is the case in two respects. Firstly, the decision strongly reinforces the notion that the duty of care should be viewed as essentially more limited with respect to psychiatric injury than with respect to physical injury; the duty is seen as grounded in an obligation of care to avoid damage to physical health which should only very cautiously be extended to damage to mental health. Secondly, the decision indicates that the employment relationship should not be viewed as one giving rise to a specially heightened set of duties of care for health and safety as compared with other relationships to which the general duty in negligence applies. These implications seemed to be confirmed by the way that the Court of Session in Scotland approached a subsequent case[75] which was concerned with work-related stress symptoms which were not post-traumatic in the Hillsborough sense.

On the other hand, a much more positive and developmental view of the employing entity's duty of care for its workers' health, safety, and mental and physical welfare was taken by the House of Lords in the very important recent case of *Waters v Metropolitan Police Commissioner*.[76] In this case, it was decided that a police officer might in principle have a cause of action in negligence, breach of statutory duty, or contract against her chief constable, regarded as in effect her employer, in respect of failure to protect her from harassment or bullying by fellow officers, following her complaint of a sexual assault upon her by a fellow officer, causing her psychiatric injury. Perhaps the House of Lords was more prepared to hold the employing entity liable in principle for psychiatric injury attributable to systemic managerial failure where, firstly, this involved no *pressing* contrast with the liability owed to members of the public as in the *White* case, and where, secondly, it involved no *immediate* challenge to managerial resource allocation as in the *Walker* or *Rorrison* cases.

Moreover, we can also discern the emergence of a broader, less constrained, version of the obligation of the employing entity of care for the health, safety, and welfare of the worker in the context of adjudications about unfair dismissal, and of the question whether an employee has been constructively dismissed. This is well illustrated by the recent decision of the Employment Appeal Tribunal in the case of *Waltons & Morse v Dorrington*[77] where that court recognized an implied term in the contract of employment to the effect that:

The employer will provide and monitor for his employees, so far as is reasonably practicable, a working environment which is reasonably suitable for the performance by them of their contractual duties,[78]

and held that there was a breach of that obligation where a non-smoking employee was forced to work in a smoke-filled atmosphere. When the

---

[75] *Rorrison v West Lothian Council* 2000 SCLR 245 (CSOH).
[76] [2000] ICR 1064 (HL).   [77] [1997] IRLR 488 (EAT).   [78] Ibid at 491.

employing entity's obligation of care is framed in those broad terms, especially when it refers to responsibility for the working environment, it includes a notion of *careful managerial supervision*. That notion has actually been more fully developed under the principle of mutual trust and confidence, and we shall consider it further in that context.

The approach in such cases is somewhat to be contrasted with the rather more restrictive tort-based approach pursued in the recent general reformulation of the employing entity's duty (whether regarded as an implied contractual duty or as a duty imposed by the tort law of negligence) to protect employees against psychiatric[79] illness caused by stress at work. This reformulation was undertaken by the Court of Appeal in a group of decisions reported under the name of *Hatton v Sutherland*.[80] The reformulation asserted a series of tort-based principles or requirements, of which the most important are: (1) foreseeability of such stress as to endanger health; (2) where there was such foreseeability, breach of the duty thereby arising; (3) demonstration that the breach of duty has caused or materially contributed to the harm suffered; and (4) apportionment so that the employing entity is liable only for that proportion of the harm suffered which is attributable to its wrongdoing.

The application of these principles to the four particular cases which were under appeal resulted in the allowing of the employing entity's appeal in three cases and a dismissal of the appeal 'with hesitation' in the fourth. As an indication of the approach to the allocation of the risk of work-related stress illness as between the employing entity and the employee which this reformulation involves, it is highly significant that the Court of Appeal endorsed the sentiment of Devlin J expressed in *Withers v Perry Chain Co Ltd*[81] that:

The relationship between employer and employee is not that of schoolmaster and pupil. The employee is free to decide for herself what risks she will run.

It has been pointed out[82] that this approach may be at variance with the general requirement of risk assessment with regard to health and safety in the workplace which is now imposed under domestic and EC legislation.[83]

If the employing entity's general obligation to care for the safety, health, and welfare of its employees is developing partly in the context of tort law and partly in the context of the law of unfair dismissal, that presents

---

[79] The use of the term 'psychiatric illness' to mean 'mental illness' is now firmly entrenched in the case law.

[80] [2002] ICR 613 (CA). See also now *Coxall v Goodyear Great Britain Ltd* [2003] ICR 152 in which the Court of Appeal explores the extent of the employing entity's responsibility to dissuade or prevent a worker from continuing to work on health and safety grounds.

[81] [1961] 1 WLR 1314 at 1320.

[82] See Brenda Barrett, 'Clarification of Employers' Liability for Work-related Stress' (Barrett 2002) at 294.

[83] See Management of Health and Safety at Work Regulations 1999, SI 1999/3242.

something of a contrast with the development of the employing entity's duty of care to the employee in respect of references, where the development of the obligation, although vigorous, has been more narrowly tort-based. Both the vigour and the ultimate limitedness of development of that kind are indicated in the most recent decision to date in this area, that in the case of *Kidd v AXA Assurance*.[84] The obligation had been decisively recognized in the key decision of the House of Lords in the case of *Spring v Guardian Assurance plc*.[85] The Court of Appeal had built upon that foundation in the case of *Bartholomew v London Borough of Hackney*.[86] In the *Spring* case, Lord Woolf had even gone so far beyond a narrowly tort-based approach as to declare that:

just as in the earlier authorities the courts were prepared to imply by necessary implication a term imposing a duty on an employer to exercise due care for the physical well-being of his employees, so in the appropriate circumstances would the court imply a like duty as to his [sic] economic well-being, the duty as to his economic well-being giving rise to an action for damages if it is breached.[87]

However, in *Kidd v AXA Equity & Law Life Assurance Society plc*[88] Burton J reverted to a more restrictive mode of analysis, holding that, although the obligation included not merely a duty to take reasonable care not to give false information about the subject of the reference but also a duty to take reasonable care not to give *misleading* information, it nevertheless did not extend so far as to include a duty to take reasonable care to give a reference that was full and comprehensive or full, fair, and comprehensive.[89] The reasons given for caution in any extension of the duty—the limitation on the duty to disclose or speak, the fact that the liability would be for economic loss, and the reluctance of the courts to expand liability for omissions[90]—all come very directly from the discourse of the tort of negligence.[91]

The general duty of care also applies in the reverse direction, that is to say such a duty is owed by employees to their employing entities; however, in this case the duty has a very different and essentially more limited or marginal role. The duty of care owed by employees to their employing entity derives its place in the modern law of the contract of employment

---

[84] *Kidd v AXA Equity & Law Life Assurance Society plc* [2000] IRLR 301 (QBD).
[85] [1994] ICR 596 (HL).   [86] [1999] IRLR 246 (CA).
[87] [1994] ICR 596 at 647.   [88] [2000] IRLR 301 (QBD).
[89] Compare, however, *Cox v Sun Alliance Life Ltd* [2001] IRLR 448 (CA), in which it was indicated, by Mummery LJ in particular at 469, paras 105–106, that the employing entity would be in breach of its obligation if it made unfavourable assertions without having taken reasonable care to ensure that the factual basis for them had been investigated and that the investigation had provided reasonable grounds for them.
[90] See Burton J [2000] IRLR 301 at 307.
[91] So did the decision in *Legal & General Assurance Ltd v Kirk* [2002] IRLR 124 (CA) that a financial consultant could not claim damages for negligent misstatement in respect of an assertion by the employing entity that he had left his employment owing an 'industry debt', because there had been no misstatement directly to a third party.

largely from the decision of the House of Lords in *Lister v Romford Ice & Cold Storage Co*,[92] where it was invoked nominally by the employing entity but in reality by the employing entity's insurers to establish the employee's liability to indemnify the employing entity in respect of its vicarious liability to a third party for injury caused by the negligent driving of a motor vehicle in the course of his employment. The House of Lords traced the duty back to the early case of *Harmer v Cornelius*,[93] though that case really concerns competence rather than care,[94] and also seems to concern what we would now regard as semi-dependent workers rather than employees.[95] Although still the source of a theoretical capacity for employing entities to sue their employees for damages, as was demonstrated in the early 1980s case of *Janata Bank v Ahmed*,[96] this duty is rarely invoked as such by employing entities for the obvious prudential reasons spelt out by Ackner LJ in that case.[97] Moreover, this duty as owed by employees has been quite marginal to the recent evolution of the general principles of construction of contracts of employment.

At the time of the original work from which this one is derived, there seemed to be some prospect that the underlying mutual obligations of care arising between employees and employing entities, especially those owed by employees to their employing entities, were coming to be rationalized in terms of a general principle or duty of co-operation.[98] This notion was much encouraged by the then recent decision of the Court of Appeal in the famous *ASLEF (No 2)* case,[99] in which industrial action in the form of 'working to rule' (that is to say deliberately over-zealous insistence on observing the minutiae of the rules of work) on the part of railway workers was held to involve breach of their contracts of employment. Lord Denning MR spoke of a prohibition upon wilful disruption by the employee;[100] Buckley LJ envisaged an implied term to perform the contract in such a way as not to frustrate its commercial objective;[101] Roskill LJ defined the obligation as 'an implied term that each employee will not, in obeying his lawful instructions, seek to obey them in a wholly unreasonable way which has the effect of disrupting the system, the efficient running of which he is employed to ensure'.[102] Although none of these judges used the terminology of co-operation, their decision has generally been regarded as connoting the acceptance of a duty of co-operation as an intrinsic feature of the contract of employment.[103]

---

[92] [1957] AC 555 (HL).   [93] (1858) 5 CB (NS) 236.
[94] See below, 153.   [95] See below, 151–154.
[96] [1981] ICR 457 (CA).
[97] Ibid at 810, describing how it had subsequently been found necessary to make arrangements to prevent the *Lister* liability from being invoked by motor insurers.
[98] See Freedland 1976 at 27–32.
[99] *Secretary of State for Employment v ASLEF* [1972] ICR 19 (CA).
[100] Ibid at 56.   [101] Ibid at 62.   [102] Ibid at 72.
[103] See Deakin & Morris (2001) 328 333, 'The reciprocal duty of co-operation'.

Thus far, however, the obligation or principle of contractual co-operation has not really taken root as a significant aid to the interpretation or construction of contracts of employment. That may be due to its evident ambiguity as to whether it involves purely negative obligations or both positive and negative obligations. The negative obligations generally regarded as implicit in the idea of contractual co-operation can be seen as amounting to a duty not to prevent or hinder the occurrence of an express condition precedent upon which the performance by the promisor depends. The positive obligations sometimes asserted to be part of the notion of contractual co-operation can be framed as a duty to take all such necessary or additional steps in the performance of the contract as will either materially assist the other party or will generally contribute to the full realization of the bargain.[104] Not only is that ambiguity unresolved within the general law of contract,[105] but, one may surmise, tribunals and courts would find it a peculiarly difficult question to resolve in the employment context because it evokes ideological differences of approach to employment relationships.

Thus, although those ideological differences were well to the fore in the *ASLEF (No 2)* case itself, that central ambiguity did not present itself very strongly on the particular facts, because the case could be and was decided on the basis of a negative obligation to refrain from wilful disruption of the employing entity's productive activity. However, that ambiguity becomes more difficult to avoid in relation to questions such as whether employees are in breach of contract where they refuse to adapt to changes in working methods which the employing entity seeks to introduce,[106] or refuse to undertake work which is not clearly and specifically within their contractual duties but which it is judged necessary for them to do if the employing entity is to function effectively,[107] or where they take or threaten industrial action involving 'withdrawal of goodwill'.[108] Perhaps because of that ambiguity and the provocative effects of using the vocabulary of co-operation to resolve it, that vocabulary has in fact been little used in those very cases where one might have expected it.

So, although, in the three leading cases after the decision in *ASLEF (No 2)* in which those particular issues were addressed, an expansive or positive view of the employee's obligations was taken, in none of them was the language of co-operation much used. In the *Cresswell* case, where it was held that the clerical staff of the Inland Revenue were obliged to accept the

---

[104] See Stoljar 1953; compare Burrows 1968.

[105] Compare Collins 1997 at 306–309 for an account of co-operation in the general law of contracts which avoids the positive/negative distinction.

[106] Compare *Cresswell v Board of Inland Revenue* [1984] ICR 508 (QBD).

[107] Compare *Sim v Rotherham Corporation* [1986] ICR 897 (ChD).

[108] Compare *British Telecommunications plc v Ticehurst* [1992] ICR 383 (CA).

computerization of their tasks and working methods, it was simply said that:

there really can be no doubt as to the fact that an employee is expected to adapt himself to new methods and techniques introduced in the course of his employment.[109]

In the *Sim* case, where it was held that teachers were contractually obliged to provide cover for absent colleagues, it was said that:

It is ... a professional obligation of each teacher to co-operate in running the school during school hours in accordance with the timetable and other administrative regulations or directions from time to time made or given.[110]

However, in that case the discourse of the judgment was much more cast in terms of the professional obligations of teachers to comply with the reasonable instructions of the head teacher than in terms of a general obligation of co-operation.

Even in the *Ticehurst* case, which comes as close as any of the cases in this group to a concept of positive co-operation by treating managerial employees as being in breach of their contracts of employment when they refused formally to resile from a collective 'withdrawal of goodwill', the underlying obligation of the employees was not described in terms of co-operation as such, and the judges in the Court of Appeal clearly preferred to regard the *ASLEF (No 2)* case as identifying an obligation of fidelity rather than an obligation of co-operation:

The analysis which I respectfully find most apt to define the relevant duties of Mrs Ticehurst under her contract of employment as a manager by BT, is that stated by Buckley LJ, namely, 'an implied term to serve the employer faithfully within the requirements of the contract'.[111]

There are corresponding difficulties in regarding a principle of co-operation as a general or even frequent mode of construction of the employing entity's obligations under the contract of employment. Such a principle is quite often invoked to explain the decision of the House of Lords in *Southern Foundries v Shirlaw*,[112] where it was held that a company bore towards its managing director an obligation to maintain the contractual relationship for the whole of the term of his service agreement which was not limited by the making of a provision in the articles of the company for the removal of directors from office by another company which had acquired a controlling interest. This could be viewed as involving a (negative) obligation of co-operation in the sense that the employing entity was treated as liable in contractual damages for preventing the employee director from performing his part of the contract. However, the decision is

---

[109] Walton J [1984] ICR 508 at 518.   [110] Scott J [1986] ICR 897 at 929.
[111] Ralph Gibson LJ [1992] ICR 383 at 398.
[112] *Southern Foundries (1926) Ltd v Shirlaw* [1940] AC 701.

probably better explained as one where the court *resisted* an implied *exception* to a fixed-term contract, than as one where it imposed an obligtion of co-operation.

Moreover, although, more recently, in the leading case of *Scally v Southern Health Board*,[113] the House of Lords reached a result which would have been explained very naturally in terms of a principle of co-operation, there was no disposition at all to account for the decision in those terms. It was decided that the employing health authority had been in breach of an implied term in the contract of employment of doctors in failing to alert them to opportunities to increase their eventual pension entitlements, under the occupational scheme which formed part of their contracts of employment, by making additional voluntary contributions in the form of purchase of added years. Rather than locating this decision within a notion of contractual co-operation, the House of Lords articulated an entirely circumstantial proposition to the effect that where a contract of employment negotiated between employers and a representative body contained a particular term conferring on the employee a valuable right contingent upon his acting as required to obtain the benefit, of which he could not be expected to be aware unless the term was brought to his attention, there was an implied obligation on the employer to take reasonable steps to publicize that term.[114]

An even more marked reluctance to cast the employing entity's underlying obligations to its employees in terms of a principle of co-operation, this time with a negative impact on the outcome of a dispute about contractual construction, occurred in a very important decision concerning the impact of a change of ownership in a company upon employee share options in the 1987 case of *Thompson v ASDA*.[115] The issue, which was somewhat analogous to the issue in the *Shirlaw* case, was whether the ASDA Group could rely on a rule in its group share option scheme which would cause employees of a subsidiary company of the group to lose their employee share options when that company ceased to be part of the group because ASDA sold its shareholding in that company. The claim of the employees of the subsidiary, that the ASDA Group could not in those circumstances rely on the rule to defeat the share options, was rejected.

The claim could be regarded as invoking either an implied term as to co-operation, or a principle of co-operation whereby a party to a contract will not be allowed to take advantage of his own acts to avoid his obligations under the contract or to defeat the rights of the other party under it. It was held that this claim could only possibly succeed in the form of an implied term in the share option scheme, and that it could not in fact succeed in that form, because it was not possible to frame a commercially viable implied term. Although it was acknowledged that existing judicial

---

[113] [1991] ICR 771 (HL).   [114] Compare Lord Bridge [1991] ICR 771 at 781–782.
[115] *Thompson v ASDA MFI Group plc* [1988] IRLR 340 (ChD).

authority in favour of the employees' claim pointed towards an implied term as to co-operation,[116] the court was clearly unwilling to accept a general implied term or principle of construction to that effect.[117] Many subsequent case law developments concerning the underlying obligations of employing entities which might conceivably have taken place in the form of the development of a principle of co-operation have in fact been articulated in the form of a principle of mutual trust and confidence.

B. As Between Employing Entities and Semi-Dependent Workers

As was remarked earlier, it is debatable how far the principle of care and co-operation extends beyond employing entities and employees so as to apply as between employing entities and other personal workers. On the face of it, the applications of the principle are framed so that they appear to apply only between employing entities and employees. However, behind that façade of specificity to the contract of employment, tendencies can be discerned which may point to a wider application to other personal work or employment contracts.

Thus, if we take the employing entity's duty of care for the health, safety, and welfare of workers, we find that this is generally framed in a highly employee-specific way. This is true of the tort-based duty, even when transformed into an implied contractual term. For example, the willingness of the House of Lords in the *Waters* case[118] to take the wide view of the employing entity's duty to protect a police officer from bullying or harassment at work seems to have depended crucially upon being able to regard her as an employee or quasi-employee, and this is tied into the fact the employing entity's duty, regarded as one of supervision of the police officer's fellow officers, was envisaged as essentially applying to the activities of employees acting in the course of their employment, almost as if it were a *vicarious* liability.[119] This highly employee-specific formulation seems to be even more intrinsic to the duty to provide a non-damaging or non-hostile working

---

[116] Compare Scott J [1988] IRLR 340 at 345: 'That language [of Lord Blackburn in *Mackay v Dick* (1881) 6 AC 251 at 263] I take to be the language of an implied term approach to the problem. If co-operation is necessary, it is implied that co-operation will be forthcoming.'

[117] Compare *Mallone v BPB Industries* [2002] ICR 1045 (CA) where the Court of Appeal, although imposing quite rigorous control upon the discretion of the employing entity to cancel the mature share options of a senior executive dismissed for poor performance, preferred to base that control upon a requirement of rationality rather than of co-operation.

[118] *Waters v Metropolitan Police Commissioner* [2000] ICR 1064 (HL); see above, 144.

[119] Compare Lord Slynn [2000] ICR 1064 at 1068: 'If an employer knows that acts being done by employees during their employment may cause physical or mental harm to a particular fellow employee and he does nothing to supervise or prevent such acts, when it is in his power to do so, it is clearly arguable that he may be in breach of his duty to that employee.'

environment which emerges from the constructive dismissal cases such as that of *Waltons & Morse v Dorrington*[120] which were considered earlier.

On the other hand, the employing entity's general duty to avoid negligently injuring the health and safety of those working within its enterprise is not, as a matter of the general structure of the law of the tort of negligence, confined to those workers who are in a direct contractual relationship with the enterprise,[121] so there seems in that sense no reason why, even in the form of a contractual implied term, it should be confined to those working under a contract of employment strictly so called. That view is supported by the fact that the distinction between the contract of employment and other personal work or employment contracts is extremely difficult to draw at the margins anyway. It would therefore be more satisfactory to view the duty as one which becomes less demanding as the worker moves along the classificatory spectrum from full dependence towards full independence, than to view it as one which cuts off abruptly and completely at some notional, but in practice elusive, point along that spectrum.

The same argument can be made out with regard to the employing entity's duty of care with regard to references. Indeed, in this instance, that argument is strikingly well supported by existing case law. For the two key decisions concerning this duty relate to people in the occupation of marketing financial instruments: in one case, that of *Spring v Guardian Assurance*,[122] the person was quite possibly a semi-dependent worker and, in the other case, that of *Kidd v AXA Assurance*,[123] the person was undoubtedly a semi-dependent worker; yet in both cases, despite this acknowledged extension beyond the employee category, the duty of care is expounded exactly as if it related solely to employees in the strict sense. In the latter case the judge goes so far as to declare that:

no distinction is drawn which is dependent upon whether the relationship is one of employer and employee, which expressions I shall hereafter use, even though in *Spring*, and in the instant case, such was not the relationship.[124]

So far as the semi-dependent worker's obligation of care to the employing entity is concerned, the argument is a finely balanced one. So far as this obligation is seen as one of applying reasonable skill and competence, and

---

[120] [1977] IRLR 488 (EAT); see above, 142.

[121] The general statutory duty in respect of health and safety at work is extended in a similar way by s 3 of the Health and Safety at Work etc Act 1974. The possibility of the application of that section to create a duty *to a self-employed worker* is indicated by Lord Hoffmann's disapproval, in *R v Associated Octel Ltd* [1996] ICR 972 (HL) at 979, of *RMC Roadstone Products Ltd v Jester* [1994] ICR 456 (QBD).

[122] [1994] ICR 596 (HL); compare Lord Slynn at 633: 'There was undoubtedly a contract [between the plaintiff worker and the second defendant company] as the judge found. Whether that was a contract of service or for services for present purposes in my view does not matter.'

[123] *Kidd v AXA Equity & Law Life Assurance Society plc* [2000] IRLR 301 (QBD).

[124] Burton J [2000] IRLR 301 at 305.

as such derived from the old case of *Harmer v Cornelius*,[125] it can be seen as extending to the modern equivalents of the semi-dependent workers who were cited as examples of the bearers of the obligation in that case.[126] On the other hand, so far as the obligation is regarded as one of indemnifying the employing entity for liability negligently incurred to third parties, as in the *Lister v Romford* case,[127] that might be regarded as entirely bound up with, and hence limited by reference to, the employing entity's vicarious liability for the negligence of its employees acting in the course of their employment.[128]

A rather larger and more fundamental question is how far the duty or principle of co-operation extends beyond the fully dependent employment relationship to the semi-dependent employment relationship. As we have seen, the principle has not developed very actively in the context of the fully dependent employment relationship in recent years; but, in so far as it has developed, two versions of it can be discerned with contrasting implications for its extension to semi-dependent employment. The first version identifies the principle of co-operation as specially applicable to contracts which embody personal relationships involving a high degree of mutual trust between the parties. The second version, by contrast, envisages the principle of co-operation as a matter of commercial rationality which may apply as between business people, or business organizations dealing with each other as such. The first version would tend to confine the principle to fully dependent employment relationships while the second would identify it as more readily extensible to semi-dependent employment.

There seems to be a widespread assumption that it is the first version of the principle which applies to employment relationships; but in fact the, admittedly thin, stream of case law about the application of the principle to employment relationships is quite equivocal between the two versions. We should not be surprised to discover that the reasoning in the *Shirlaw* case or in the *ASDA* case fits the second version more than the first; these are, after all, cases about the impact of corporate transactions upon the obligations of the employing entity under a director's service agreement and a share option scheme. Somewhat more surprising is the discovery that the reasoning of the judges in the Court of Appeal in the *ASLEF No 2* case, regarded as the archetypal application of the principle of co-operation to the obligations of employees, also inclines towards the second version rather than the first. Thus Buckley LJ emphasized that:

With regard to the direction to the men to work strictly in accordance with the rules, the contracts of employment between the board and the railwaymen are

---

[125] (1858) 5 CB (NS) 236.   [126] See above, 147, n 95.   [127] [1957] AC 555 (HL).
[128] Compare *Janata Bank v Ahmed* [1981] ICR 457 (CA), where the duty is firmly couched in these 'master and servant' terms.

entered into as part of the board's commercial activity. Such contracts have commercial objectives and are based on commercial considerations.[129]

Lord Denning, equally, drew upon commercial contract cases to support the notion of a duty to refrain from wilful disruption of the achievement of the (commercial) objectives of the transaction.[130]

This points towards a view that the principle of co-operation, so far as it applies to personal work or employment contracts as a whole, need not be envisaged as confined to contracts of employment. It is quite significant that, in the *ASLEF No 2* case, Lord Denning's 'homely instance', of a situation where a worker would be in breach of a duty of non-disruption, seems to relate to a very short-term personal work or employment contract with a semi-dependent or fully independent worker:

Suppose I employ a man to drive me to the station. I know there is sufficient time, so that I do not tell him to hurry. He drives me at a slower speed than he need, with the deliberate object of making me lose the train, and I do lose it. He may say that he has performed the letter of the contract; he has driven me to the station; but he has wilfully made me lose the train, and that is a breach of contract beyond all doubt. And what is more, he is not entitled to be paid for the journey.[131]

What remains unresolved is whether, if and to the extent that a more expansive and positive version of the principle of co-operation applies to contracts of employment, that version might also be applicable to contracts with semi-dependent workers. It can be asserted that there is no intrinsic reason why that should not be the case; but beyond that point the answer is very speculative because of the absence of case law. The very absence of case law is itself testimony to the fact that the courts have tended in recent years to address those issues in terms of different principles, to which we now turn our attention.

SECTION 4: TRUST AND CONFIDENCE

As the result of very extensive and significant case law development since the original work was written, the construction of personal work or employment contracts has been transformed by the rapid evolution of a principle to the effect that contracts of employment, and possibly also other personal work or employment contracts, will be interpreted and applied so as to give effect to a mutual obligation, as between employing entities and workers, upon each contractual party to retain the trust and confidence of the other party. The nature, content, and scope of this principle are not yet fully defined; indeed, in some respects they are still keenly controversial.

---

[129] [1972] ICR 19 at 72.   [130] See ibid Lord Denning MR at 55–56.
[131] [1972] ICR 19 at 55.

Those controversies can best be understood by reference to the short but eventful historical development of this principle since the mid-1970s.

A. As Between Employing Entities and Employees

That historical development, down to the time of the writing of the present edition of this work, both begins with and culminates in a crucial and highly complex interaction between the common law of the contract of employment and the law of unfair dismissal. The status and definition of the principle have to be viewed in the context of that interaction. This is a highly context-specific and instrumental body of case law.

The principle was initially articulated in the form of an implied term in contracts of employment, the function of which was to give shape to a contractual definition of the concept of constructive dismissal for the purposes of the law of unfair dismissal. Although the unfair dismissal legislation did not, when first introduced in 1971, expressly extend beyond outright dismissal, it was amended in 1974 so as to include termination of the contract by the employee 'in circumstances in which he is entitled to terminate it by reason of the employer's conduct'.[132] There was controversy in the tribunals and the courts as to whether that entitlement was to be tested according to a broad concept of the reasonableness of the employer's conduct or by reference to a stricter notion of repudiatory breach of contract. The adoption by the Court of Appeal in 1977[133] of the latter, contractual, test necessitated, in the ensuing years, extensive refinement of the rather exiguous body of law defining what constituted repudiatory breach on the part of the employing entity.

There was therefore a process of formulation of implied terms, which were in effect back-formations, in the sense that they were terms the breach of which would amount to expulsive or repudiatory conduct sufficient to constitute constructive dismissal by the employer. It was in this particular crucible that the implied term as to mutual trust and confidence was formed. Before the ruling insisting upon a specifically contractual test for constructive dismissal, the tribunals and courts had begun to formulate the test in terms of conduct by the employer rupturing the employee's confidence or trust in the employment relationship. This emerged as a common theme both in cases which envisaged the test in contractual terms,[134] and also in cases where the test was regarded as a broader one.[135]

After the ruling in the *Western Excavating* case, it became clear not only that the test for constructive dismissal had to be contractual, but also that

---

[132] Originally para 5(2)(c) of Schedule 1 to the Trade Union and Labour Relations Act 1974, now s 95(1)(c) of the Employment Rights Act 1996.

[133] In *Western Excavating (ECC) Ltd v Sharp* [1978] ICR 221.

[134] A very good illustration is *Robinson v Crompton Parkinson Ltd* [1978] ICR 401 (EAT).

[135] Compare *Isle of Wight Tourist Board v Coombes* [1976] IRLR 413 (CA); *Fyfe & McGrouther Ltd v Byrne* [1977] IRLR 29 (EAT).

this meant identifying in each case a fundamental express or implied term which the employer could be regarded as having broken. The mutual trust and confidence test for repudiation was neatly embodied in a contractual formulation as the breach of an implied term as to mutual trust and confidence in the case of *Courtaulds Northern Textiles Ltd v Andrew*.[136] This formula was readily taken up in the Employment Appeal Tribunal, probably because it usefully replicated the pre-*Western Excavating* law of constructive dismissal, while avoiding the extreme of simply pronouncing an implied term that the employer must behave fairly and reasonably, which would have involved open defiance of the controls upon constructive dismissal which the Court of Appeal had imposed in that case.[137] By the mid-1980s, the implied term had become an orthodox tenet of the law of constructive unfair dismissal.[138]

This implied term would go on to assume a central role in the common law of the contract of employment; but it reflected its origins in the law of constructive unfair dismissal in several crucial respects. In some ways, those origins gave the implied term great actual or potential width. Firstly, it stressed the importance of mutuality as between employer and employee because it was, essentially, extending to employers an obligation as to trust and confidence which was well recognized as applying to the employee.[139] Secondly, it represented a formulation of a general behavioural standard for judging whether the conduct of one of the parties had left an employment relationship in a condition of viable continuance or placed it in a state of breakdown. Thirdly, it identified an obligation which could be represented as an implied term, but, as its pre-history had shown, could equally well be formulated in non-contractual terms. On the other hand, the origins of the term also imported a certain confinement of its purpose; it was formulated as a term the breach of which would amount to repudiation, rather than as a term the breach of which would give rise to a claim in damages. All these features would be important in shaping its subsequent history.

For the most part, that subsequent history has consisted of developing the potential of the implied term and transcending its limitations. By the late 1980s, the decision in *United Bank v Akhtar* demonstrated the capacity of this implied term to operate as an overarching term, which would control the exercise of powers conferred on either party by the express

---

[136] [1979] IRLR 84 (EAT) at 85 (Arnold J); see above, 125.
[137] Compare *Post Office v Roberts* [1980] IRLR 347 (EAT); *Woods v WM Car Services (Peterborough) Ltd* [1981] ICR 667 (affirmed [1982] ICR 693 (CA)).
[138] Compare *Lewis v Motorworld Garages Ltd* [1986] ICR 157 (CA).
[139] The point was well taken by Kilner Brown J in *Robinson v Crompton Parkinson Ltd* [1978] ICR 401 at 403: 'Although most of the decided cases deal with the master seeking remedy against a servant or former servant for acting in breach of confidence or in breach of trust, that action can only be on the basis that trust and confidence is mutual'; compare Lord Denning MR in *Woods v WM Car Services (Peterborough) Ltd* [1981] ICR 693 at 698: 'Just as a servant must be good and faithful, so an employer must be good and considerate.'

terms and other implied terms of the contract, and indeed would even control the whole manner in which the parties conducted and developed the employment relationship. In the *Imperial Tobacco* case,[140] Sir Nicholas Browne-Wilkinson VC took the immensely significant step of treating the implied term of mutual trust and confidence as giving rise to or consisting of an obligation upon the employer which:

applies as much to the exercise of his rights and powers under a pension scheme as [it does] to the other rights and powers of an employer.[141]

Subsequent pension scheme cases have built upon that idea.[142]

In a seminal commentary piece written in 1996, Douglas Brodie built upon these notions of mutual trust and confidence as an overarching obligation which applied to the conduct of the employment relationship in all its aspects.[143] In particular, he suggested that the obligation of mutual trust and confidence could and should serve as a rationalizing notion for a number of earlier cases which, without necessarily employing the terminology of mutual trust and confidence, had nevertheless constituted the sort of interpretation in depth of the implicit content of the contract of employment which the idea of mutual trust and confidence invokes. A central illustration of that thesis was the decision of the House of Lords in the case of *Scally v Southern Health and Social Services Board*[144] that a public authority employer had been in breach of an implied obligation to keep its workers informed of valuable opportunities, offered under the occupational pension scheme which applied to their employment, to make additional pension contributions which would enhance their ultimate pension benefits.

In the leading case of *Malik v BCCI*,[145] the House of Lords decisively endorsed Brodie's arguments and recognized the existence of a general implied obligation of mutual trust and confidence attaching to contracts of employment at large. Lord Nicholls referred to:

the portmanteau, general obligation not to engage in conduct likely to undermine the trust and confidence required if the employment relationship is to continue in the manner the employment contract implicitly envisages.[146]

---

[140] *Imperial Group Pension Trust Ltd v Imperial Tobacco Ltd* [1991] ICR 524 (ChD).

[141] Ibid at 533.

[142] The most important such case is that of *Hillsdown Holdings plc v Pensions Ombudsman* [1997] 1 All ER 862 (ChD) (see below, 232); compare also *South West Trains Ltd v Wightman* [1998] PLR 113 (ChD). See David Pollard, 'Employers' powers in pension schemes: the implied duty of trust and confidence' (Pollard 1997).

[143] Brodie 1996.   [144] [1991] ICR 771.

[145] *Malik v Bank of Credit and Commerce International SA* [1997] ICR 606.

[146] Ibid at 610. It remains unclear whether this is to be preferred as the precise formulation, or whether, for example, the prescribed conduct is that *calculated* to undermine rather than *likely* to undermine; compare the Hon Mr Justice Lindsay, 'The Implied Term of Trust and Confidence' (Lindsay 2001); see below, 158.

Lord Steyn pronounced that:

The evolution of the implied term of trust and confidence is a fact.... I regard the emergence of the implied obligation of mutual trust and confidence as a sound development.[147]

That decision undoubtedly entrenched the idea of the implied obligation of mutual trust and confidence in the common law of the contract of employment, as has been made clear by a plethora of subsequent decisions. However, it failed to resolve, it even perhaps intensified, a whole set of unresolved questions about the nature and the content of this general implied obligation. In the ensuing paragraphs, it will be sought to identify and address some of the most pressing of those questions.

As to the content of the implied obligation, there seems to be general, if tacit, agreement among both judges and commentators that this is not self-evident; it is seen to require further expounding before it can be applied directly to the facts of particular cases. There seem to be three main ways of doing this. One way has been to specify the implied obligation as a precise and detailed verbal formulation. Another has been to develop it as a grouping or family of more particular and concrete implied terms or implied obligations. A third way has been to expound it as a broad set of approaches or behavioural standards. These three methods have been employed both successively and cumulatively; it will be useful to consider them each in turn.

Initially, the implied obligation of mutual trust and confidence developed in the first of those three modes. In the very first case in which the obligation is concretized in its present form, it was identified in the form of an adoption of a formula advanced by lawyers pleading the case for the employee which was then amplified by the court:

It was an implied term of the contract that the employers would not, without reasonable and proper cause conduct themselves in a manner calculated or likely to destroy or seriously damage the relationship of confidence and trust between the parties... We think that, thus phrased, the implied term (as regards 'calculated') extends only to an obligation not to conduct themselves in such a manner as is intended, although not intended by itself, to destroy or seriously damage the relationship in question.[148]

This process of the honing of a forensic formulation has continued apace in the form of arguments about the 'small print' of the implied obligation.[149] However, it is not surprising that the debate about whether 'calculated and likely' is a better formulation than 'calculated or likely' has

---

[147] *Malik v Bank of Credit and Commerce International SA* [1997] ICR 606 at 622.
[148] Arnold J in *Courtaulds Northen Textiles Ltd v Andrew* [1979] IRLR 84 at 86; see above, 125, 156.
[149] See Lindsay 2001 at 7–9.

not provided a real key to understanding what the concept of mutual trust and confidence really involves.

One other way of enlarging upon the general implied obligation has been to envisage it as issuing forth into a number of more specific and circumstantial implied terms. In fact, as we have indicated, this reasoning was applied retrospectively in the *Malik* case, so that the specific implied term which formed the ratio decidendi of the *Scally* case, namely that all employees in a certain category had to be notified by their employer of their entitlement to certain benefits, was seen as a part or aspect of the evolving general implied obligation.[150] In the *Malik* case itself, the employing bank was held to be 'under an implied obligation to its employees not to conduct a dishonest or corrupt business', this being 'no more than one particular aspect of the portmanteau, general obligation' of mutual trust and confidence.[151] On this approach, the implied obligation is accorded the status of a framework within which more precisely targeted implied terms can be formulated.[152] Almost any particular implied term of the contract of employment could in theory be placed under that umbrella; it remains to be seen how far this framework approach will lead to the swallowing up of existing, hitherto distinct, implied terms.

A third approach to the expounding of the content of the implied obligation of mutual trust and confidence can also be discerned. On this approach, the implied obligation constitutes a general standard of behaviour for employing entities and employees, which is elaborated in particular contexts or aspects of employment relations. This is a process of normative elaboration which comes between the general formulation of the implied obligation of mutual trust and confidence and its specific application to any given set of facts. For example, in the important case of *Moores v Bude-Stratton Town Council*,[153] Lindsay J provided an analysis of verbal abuse 'as an occasion of breach of the implied term as to trust and confidence' which contained guidance on such questions as whether and when a single incident of verbal abuse might constitute a breach of the implied obligation which was repudiatory of the contract of employment as a whole.[154]

Another very important example of this kind of normative elaboration occurred in the case of *Gogay v Hertfordshire County Council*,[155] where it was held that the employing entity had acted in breach of the implied obligation of trust and confidence by suspending a residential care worker from

---

[150] See Lord Steyn [1997] ICR 606 at 621.

[151] Per Lord Nicholls [1997] ICR 606 at 610.

[152] Compare, for example, the way in which, in Deakin and Morris 1998 at 333–334, it is argued that the implied obligation of mutual trust and confidence provides 'the most appropriate basis' for the decision of the EAT in *WA Goold (Pearmak) Ltd v McConnell* [1995] IRLR 516 that a contract of employment contains an implied term requiring the employer to provide a grievance procedure.   [153] [2001] ICR 271 (EAT).

[154] Ibid at 277–278 (minority view).   [155] [2000] IRLR 703 (CA).

her work in a children's home following an allegation that she had abused one of the children in her care. In the Court of Appeal, the question was seen as turning upon whether there was 'reasonable and proper cause' for the employing entity's action, and a distinction was drawn between proper investigation of whether children were at risk, and automatic or 'knee-jerk' suspension of the employee in the face of the allegation. The use of this third approach, which seems to be emerging as the prevailing one, raises a set of key questions as to what is the conceptual basis, or what are the conceptual bases, for this kind of normative elaboration of the implied obligation of trust and confidence.

The courts have consistently rejected a direct equation between trust and confidence and the idea of reasonableness. From the outset of the development of the implied obligation of trust and confidence, as we have seen, the courts felt that they would betray the whole notion of an authentically contractual test for constructive dismissal if they accepted that there was an implied term which resulted in a general test of whether the employing entity had acted reasonably in all the circumstances.[156] That position was recently reasserted in *Clark v Nomura Ltd*[157] where Burton J stated that:

I do not consider it right that there be simply a contractual obligation on the employer to act reasonably in the exercise of his discretion, which would suggest that the court can simply substitute its own view for that of the employer.[158]

Continuing to make outstanding contributions to the literature on the implied obligation of mutual trust and confidence, Douglas Brodie has written two further articles about the conceptual basis for the normative content of the implied obligation.[159] In those two articles, he argues that there are two main conceptual bases for this normative development, and that from these two conceptual bases we could expect a convergent evolution. The two bases are, firstly, the essentially private law notion of a requirement of good faith in the performance of certain classes of contract, and, secondly, the notion, which has received its main development in the context of public law, of control of the exercise of certain powers or discretions by reference to the ideas of legality, rationality, procedural regularity, and the realization of legitimate expectations. The convergent evolution which he envisages is towards a single and overarching conception of the obligation of mutual trust and confidence which will combine both those notions in an expression of the core values of the common law. In that respect, he expressly draws upon arguments advanced by Dawn Oliver in a recent treatise which proposes the thesis of a set of common values which straddle the 'public/private divide' in English law.[160]

---

[156] See above at 156.   [157] [2000] IRLR 766 (QBD).   [158] Ibid at 774.
[159] Brodie 1998 and Brodie 2001b.   [160] Oliver 1999.

Brodie makes it clear that his arguments are, in part at least, aspirational; they represent his views of the way in which it would be desirable and coherent for the implied obligation of mutual trust and confidence to develop in relation to the contract of employment.[161] How accurate an assessment or prediction do they represent of the actual evolution of that implied obligation? There is much that can be said in support of his assessment. As to the role of the idea of good faith in contractual performance, in the *Imperial Tobacco* case, Sir Nicolas Browne-Wilkinson VC made a very direct equation between the employer's obligation of mutual trust and confidence and the obligation to exercise fiduciary powers in good faith; he said, referring to the implied term of mutual trust and confidence: 'I will call this implied term "the implied obligation of good faith".'[162] This equation, fraught with dynamic potential, fits in well with what Jack Beatson and Daniel Friedman have depicted as the role of the idea of good faith in a general movement 'from "classical" to modern contract law',[163] and with what Hugh Collins has described as 'the productive disintegration of private law'.[164]

As to the role of public law principles or modes of reasoning, there is, equally, much which can be adduced in favour of the view that these exert a great influence on the way that the implied obligation of trust and confidence is expounded. The impulse to regulate the arbitrary or capricious use of discretionary power is an identifying attribute of public law reasoning; the case law of mutual trust and confidence is infused with that mode of reasoning. Again, the *Imperial Tobacco* case provides a precise example.[165] The judgment of the Court of Appeal in the *Gogay* case, delivered by Hale LJ, reads exactly as if the court were engaged in judicial review of the way in which the employing local authority had exercised its power of suspension and had interrelated the exercise of that power with its use of the quite distinct power to initiate an investigation of an allegation of abuse on the part of the worker in question.[166] This is all in line with the depiction of the proper place of public law principles in the law of the contract of employment in the recent extrajudicial writings of some leading common law judges.[167]

Moreover, it emerges, from those judgments and from those writings about the implied obligation of mutual trust and confidence, how strong the arguments are for regarding that obligation as the subject of a mutually reinforcing interaction between private-law based notions of good faith in

---

[161] See, for instance, Brodie 2001a at 90–91 on 'Legal Coherence'.
[162] [1991] ICR 524 at 533.   [163] See Beatson and Friedmann 1995 at 1–17.
[164] See Collins 1999 at 53–55.
[165] See Sir Nicolas Browne-Wilkinson VC: 'Say, in purported exercise of its right to give or withhold consent, the company were to say, capriciously, that it would consent to an increase in the pension benefits of members of union A but not of the members of union B. In my judgment, the members of union B would have a good claim in contract for breach of the implied obligation of good faith.' [1991] ICR 524 at 533.
[166] See [2000] IRLR 703 especially at 707–710.
[167] See Sedley 1996, Laws 1997, Steyn 2000.

contractual performance and public law based notions of non-arbitrary, and rational use of conferred powers. That sense of mutual reinforcement can only be strengthened as human rights and rights against discrimination are accorded an increasing role in the expounding of the implied obligation of mutual trust and confidence. Examples of that increasing role are to be found in Bob Hepple's argument for the systematic inclusion, in that obligation, of respect for the fundamental rights incorporated into English law by the Human Rights Act 1998,[168] and in the development of the notion of sexual harassment as a breach of the implied obligation by Morison J in the recent case of *Reed v Stedman*.[169]

How far will this essentially developmental and dynamic approach to the implied obligation of mutual trust and confidence be taken in practice? We may expect that it will continue to be the predominant basis for the application of the implied obligation; but it will probably come up against a set of constraints which will express a judicial anxiety not to allow the implied obligation to tip the balance of interpretation of contracts of employment too far against employing entities or in favour of employees. One such constraint has recently been imposed by the House of Lords in the leading case of *Johnson v Unisys Ltd*,[170] where it was held that an employee director of a computer software company did not have a cause of action for damages based upon breach of the implied obligation of mutual trust and confidence in respect of a mental breakdown which he alleged had been caused by his summary dismissal without a fair hearing and in breach of the company's disciplinary procedure. Four of the five Law Lords who decided this appeal held that the implied obligation of mutual trust and confidence was not in principle available to sustain the kind of claim arising out of his dismissal which this employee was making.[171] They took the view that to hold otherwise would be to allow an inappropriate alternative to the statutory claim to remedies for unfair dismissal.

It is easy to identify that policy concern, but much more difficult to understand how it could give rise to a logically coherent limit or constraint upon the implied obligation as to mutual trust and confidence. The fact that four Law Lords took the view that the implied obligation could satisfactorily be limited in that way tells us some important things about their perception both of the *source* and the *juridical nature* of the implied obligation. There are important unresolved issues in relation to both of those questions. By understanding the directions of judicial thinking in those two respects, we may hope to refine our understanding of the likely course of

---

[168] See Hepple 1998.   [169] [1999] IRLR 299 (EAT).   [170] [2001] ICR 480.
[171] The other Law Lord deciding this appeal, Lord Steyn, took the view that the claim was in principle sustainable, but that the claimant would be unable to show a sufficiently clear link of causation between the employing entity's breach of the implied obligation and the claimant's subsequent mental breakdown.

future development of the implied obligation as a whole. In each of those two respects, two alternative analyses present themselves.

So far as the source of the implied obligation is concerned, the two alternative analyses which seem possible are, either, on the one hand, that the implied obligation is derived from the assumed or attributed intentions of the parties to the contract, or, on the other hand, that it derives from norms imposed by the common law upon the parties to the contract as a direct consequence of their being engaged in an employment relationship. The distinction may seem a meaningless one to those who find the theory that implied terms reproduce the intentions of the parties an artificial one in the first place. But for those who accept that implied terms may to a greater or lesser degree be satisfactorily regarded as capturing the implicit agreement between the employing entity and the worker, there will be a significant difference between obligations which have that source, and obligations imposed *ab extra* upon the contractual relationship in question.

In the case of mutual trust and confidence, the increasing use of the terminology of 'implied obligation' rather than 'implied term' suggests a growing preference for the second, *ab extra,* analysis. The preferability of that analysis is greatly reinforced by the arguments which were used in the *Johnson v Unisys* case, especially in the key judgment of Lord Hoffmann. That judgment sticks firmly to the terminology of implied terms; it puts the issue as one of whether an implied term limiting the mode of exercise of the employer's power of dismissal can be superimposed upon, or set against, the ostensibly unlimited express power of dismissal which was accorded to the employer by this particular contract of employment. However, the decision whether to imply such a term is presented as being entirely a question for the judges to answer by reference to their perception of the dictates and policies of the common law.

Thus, Lord Hoffmann states the view that, in the employment context, the common law is no longer so constrained by deference to the employer's freedom to impose terms upon the employee as it used to be. It may proceed 'by analogy with statutory rights'. It could, in this case, have recognized that an implied term of mutual trust and confidence limited the employer's power of dismissal, or could have implied an obligation to exercise the power of dismissal in good faith. (The latter, for Lord Hoffmann, would have been a 'more elegant solution' to the same substantive effect.) Nevertheless, such a term or obligation should not in fact be implied, because that would conflict with Parliament's intention, when enacting the unfair dismissal legislation, that the latter should provide the sole channel of complaint about the manner of exercise of contractually unlimited powers or rights of dismissal. The deference was thus to the intention of Parliament (no matter how fancifully that was understood) rather than to the intention of the parties; the normative formulation was unmistakably a proposition of the common law itself.

This distinction between the possible sources for the implied obligation of mutual trust and confidence is an important one, if only because of its bearing upon the difficult question of whether and how far it is possible to derogate from, or contract out of, the implied obligation. To the extent that the implied obligation is regarded simply as an implied term of the contract of employment, it should in principle give way to express terms which are inconsistent with it. It is debatable at what point express terms of the contract are to be seen as inconsistent with this implied term. A coherent approach might be to say that only those express terms which directly limit or exclude the implied obligation are inconsistent with it; but the case law may support a wider notion of inconsistency.[172] At all events, a minimalist conception of inconsistency would give effect to a term which expressly excluded the implied obligation if that implied obligation is regarded as an implied term arising from the unstated but shared intentions of the parties.

However, let us suppose, on the other hand, that the implied obligation is to be regarded as the expression of a norm of the common law which identifies this obligation as an inherent attribute of the contract of employment, an ingrained feature of the employment relationship which underlies that contract. In that case it might well be inappropriate to treat the implied obligation as giving way to an express term of the contract, even perhaps to a term which expressly purported to exclude or limit the obligation. This is probably emerging as the preferable analysis of the *source* of the implied obligation; but even if we know what the source of the implied obligation is, there are still some crucial questions to be resolved about the *juridical nature* of the implied obligation.

At this point it is important to recall our theoretical starting point for this chapter as a whole, namely that the law of personal work or employment contracts embodies principles of interpretation or construction, some of which may consist of or give rise to implied terms or implied obligations in personal work or employment contracts generally or in some particular categories of personal work or employment contracts. These principles, and these implied terms or implied obligations, may exist at a number of different levels of generality. They vary as to how far their scope and effects are precisely defined. Sometimes their existence is established and accepted although their scope and effect remains very unclear. The implied obligation of mutual trust and confidence is just such a principle. It was recognized, in the *Malik* case, at a very high level of generality. It is not surprising that pressing needs have emerged for more precise specification of its scope and effects. Doubts have thus arisen about the juridical nature of the implied obligation. How far is it a normative principle, or how far, on the other hand, is it simply a rule or group of rules?

---

[172] Compare Lindsay 2001 at 9–10.

The most urgent of those needs for specification was created by the *Malik* case itself. For not only did the House of Lords in that case endorse the implied obligation of mutual trust and confidence as a very general principle for the interpretation or construction of contracts of employment, but they also assigned a very particular effect to it: they held that breach of the implied obligation on the part of the employing entity gave rise to a cause of action, or liability, in damages. Moreover, they held that this cause of action, or liability, was not, at least in the circumstances of the particular case before them, subject to the damage-limiting rule associated with the decision of the House of Lords in *Addis v Gramophone Company Ltd.*[173] We shall see in a later chapter[174] that the precise formulation of that damage-limiting rule is highly controversial; suffice it at this point that it has to do with damages for wrongful dismissal where the manner of dismissal causes injury to the feelings, mental health, well-being, reputation, and/or subsequent employability of the employee concerned.[175]

The question therefore arose, and was addressed in the *Johnson v Unisys* case, whether the evolution of the implied obligation of mutual trust and confidence had created a widely applicable contractual cause of action or liability in damages, not limited by the rule in the *Addis* case, upon which employees would frequently be able to claim in respect of their dismissal from employment, thus giving them a common law contractual claim which might reduplicate a claim they might have under the statutory provisions relating to unfair dismissal, and give rise to larger awards of compensation than were available under those provisions. The House of Lords in the *Johnson v Unisys* case was clearly of the view that this outcome was undesirable and inappropriate as a matter of policy. Judging that the *Malik* case had placed it beyond doubt that the implied obligation of mutual trust and confidence had the *effect* of circumventing the damage-limiting rule in the *Addis* case, they avoided that undesirable outcome by assigning a limited *scope* to the implied obligation, namely that it did not apply to limit the manner of exercise of a power of dismissal.

There is a real policy debate about whether or not this was an appropriate *rule* for the House of Lords to have made; but even those who accept the suitability of such a rule might agree that it is quite difficult to reconcile with the previously held view of the implied obligation of mutual trust and confidence as an emergent *principle* of the law of the contract of employment. (Lord Millett opined in the *Johnson v Unisys* case that the implied obligation was not, in its very nature, appropriate for application to

---

[173] [1909] AC 488.   [174] See below 358–359.

[175] This damage-limiting rule should be distinguished from another damage-limiting rule which frequently interacts with it, namely the doctrine that it must be assumed the employing entity would have performed in the manner least unfavourable to itself; compare Elias J in *Hagen v ICI Chemicals and Polymers Ltd* [2002] IRLR 31 (QBD) at paras 150–155.

the termination of employment relationships, because it was 'concerned with preserving the continuing relationship which should subsist between employer and employee';[176] but that seems to be an argument more based in expediency than in pure principle.) In order to make sense of the case law, we probably now have to accept that the implied obligation does not have quite such a strong hold upon the common law of the contract of employment as appeared in the immediate aftermath of the *Malik* case. At that time it appeared that it could be directly invoked as a principle of universal application; now it appears to be mediated through distinct judge-made policy rules.

While such a view might seem regrettable to those who, like the present author, had regarded the development of the implied obligation into a general and direct principle as an ameliorative one, it does at least reinforce the argument against regarding the implied obligation as a derogable one, that is to say one from which the parties, and in particular the employing entity, can contract out. For we might concede that the contract might exclude the application of some of the particular rules to which the implied obligation gives rise, while maintaining that the general principle involved, and some other particular rules emerging from it, were so inherent to the core concept of the contract of employment as to be incapable of exclusion from that contract. It must be admitted that this argument is only a speculative one in the present state of the case law.

We conclude this subsection by attempting to summarize the main trends in a very rapidly developing body of case law concerning the implied obligation of mutual trust and confidence in the contract of employment. It is undoubtedly the most powerful engine of movement in the modern law of employment contracts. The courts sometimes apply the accelerator and sometimes the brake. Since and as the result of the decision of the House of Lords in *Johnson v Unisys*, it has become necessary, in assessing the extent of this implied obligation, to distinguish between the two areas of (1) discipline and dismissal, and (2) other managerial decision making. In the former area, that decision has had a seriously restrictive effect.[177] In *King v University of St Andrews*,[178] the Scottish Court of Session was prepared to regard the negative effect of *Johnson v Unisys* as narrowly confined to decisions to dismiss and the manner of effecting and communicating them, and hence treated the implied obligation as regulating the conduct of the prior disciplinary investigation. However, the Court of Appeal has since taken a very different approach in *Eastwood v Magnox Electric plc*,[179] and

---

[176] [2001] IRLR 279 at 287.

[177] See a very useful casenote by Douglas Brodie, 'Fair Dealing and the Disciplinary Process' (Brodie 2002).   [178] [2002] IRLR 252 (Ct Sess).

[179] [2002] IRLR 447 (CA). Compare *McCabe v Cornwall County Council* [2003] IRLR 87 (CA): the Court of Appeal distinguished the *Eastwood* case to the extent of refusing to strike out the claimant's action.

treated the implied obligation as inapplicable to provide the basis for a claim of breach of contract, or as the basis of a similar claim in tort, in respect of the whole of a managerial course of conduct which culminated in the dismissal of the employee concerned. In a later chapter it is considered whether an implied obligation of dispute resolution may be asserted to fill the gap which has thus been opened up.[180]

In the wider area of managerial decision making where that restriction does not apply,[181] the approach to the implied obligation generally continues to be an expansive one. There is admittedly some reluctance to allow the implied obligation, like the underlying notion of mutuality or reciprocity from which it is derived,[182] to become a catch-all concept for all arguments about the implied content of the contract of employment, as was manifested in *Hagen v ICI Chemicals and Polymers Ltd*[183] where Elias J preferred an analysis in terms of the tort of negligent misstatement to determine the employing entity's liability for misleading advice about the pensions and benefits which employees would receive if they agreed to go with a transfer of the part of the undertaking in which they worked to another company.[184] It has also remained very debatable what the relationship is between breach of the implied obligation and repudiatory breach; in *Morrow v Safeway Stores plc*,[185] the Employment Appeal Tribunal took the view that a breach of the implied obligation is *ipso facto* a repudiation of the contract of employment, but we suggest that the contrary view that conduct must amount to repudiation before it can be held to be a breach of the implied obligation[186] may yet be held to be correct.

However, despite those remaining uncertainties, there can be little doubt that there is evolving under the umbrella of the implied obligation of trust and confidence an increasingly stringent regulation of managerial decision making, particularly with regard to pay, pensions, and benefits, to ensure that it is not arbitrary or capricious, especially as between different workers employed in a comparable situation within the employing entity concerned.

---

[180] See below, 393–395.

[181] On the difficulty of drawing that boundary, see a casenote on *Johnson v Unisys* by the present author, Freedland 2001. Compare now *McCabe v Cornwall County Council* [2003] IRLR 87 (CA)—see n 179 above.

[182] See above, 139–140.

[183] [2002] IRLR 31 (QBD).

[184] Compare also *Mallone v BPB Industries plc* [2002] ICR 1045 (CA), where the contractual discretion to cancel a senior executive's mature share options was controlled in terms of irrationality, but not in terms of breach of the implied obligation of trust and confidence although that might have seemed an obvious basis. The share option scheme may have been regarded as wholly separate from the contract of employment, which was with an Italian subsidiary company; we suggest that such a separation would itself be questionable. See below, 228–229.   [185] [2002] IRLR 9 (EAT).

[186] Compare Elias J in *Hagen v ICI Chemical and Polymers Ltd* [2002] IRLR 31 at para 55, recalling Lord Steyn's emphasis in *Malik v BCCI* upon the seriousness of the undermining of trust and confidence which was necessary to constitute a breach of the implied obligation—see [1997] ICR 606 at 624, 628.

Building in this respect upon the decision in *Clark v Nomura International plc*[187] (though not referring to the earlier case), the Court of Appeal in *Transco plc v O'Brien*[188] held that the employing entity had been in breach of the implied obligation in omitting to offer to one particular employee a revised contract with enhanced benefits which was offered to a group of employees from whom, it was held, the claimant could not properly be differentiated. The closeness of the reasoning to that with which the requirement of rationality is applied in judicial review was very noticeable.

We suggest that reasoning of this kind reinforces the view of the implied obligation, which derives from the decision in *Imperial Group Pension Trust Ltd v Imperial Tobacco Ltd*,[189] as a very significant determinant of the employing entity's implied obligations under the contract of employment with regard to pension provision[190] as well as with regard to other aspects of pay and benefits. The implied obligation appears increasingly, despite some remaining judicial reluctance to be formally committed to such a view,[191] to amount to an obligation of fair dealing with respect at least to pay and benefits.[192] In a later section we suggest that this set of developments can be placed within the framework of an overarching principle of fair performance and management; in the next subsection we turn to consider the crucial question of how far this implied obligation extends to semi-dependent workers.

B. As Between Employing Entities and Semi-Dependent Workers

There is an extremely important question of whether and if so in what form the implied obligation of mutual trust and confidence applies as between employing entities and semi-dependent workers. Despite the importance of the question, the discussion of it must perforce be a brief one, because there is hardly any relevant case law, so that the answer is almost entirely a matter of speculation. All the case law in which there has been positive recognition or development of the implied obligation has been in the context of contracts of employment; the cases have uniformly been those in which it has been uncontroversial that the worker is an employee in the strict sense. Moreover, in that case law, the courts and tribunals clearly regard themselves as developing a body of doctrine which is in a substantive

---

[187] [2000] IRLR 766 (QBD)—see above, 160.   [188] [2002] ICR 721.

[189] [1991] ICR 524 (ChD).   [190] See above, 157.

[191] Compare Pill LJ in *Transco plc v O'Brien* [2002] ICR 721 at 727, paras 23–24, expressing reservations about the use in the EAT of the expression 'fair and even-handed manner' to characterize the standard of behaviour exacted by the implied obligation.

[192] Compare *Cantor Fitzgerald International v Bird* [2002] IRLR 867 (QBD), where it was held that the employing entity had acted in breach of the obligation of mutual trust and confidence by aggressively seeking to impose a change in the remuneration arrangements of a group of very highly paid brokers.

sense specific to the contract of employment; the implied obligation is not seen as being derived from the general law of the contract, but, rather, from the general law of employment. In one recent case in which it was argued that the implied obligation should be regarded as applicable, by analogy or extension, to a contract other than a contract of employment, that of *Bedfordshire County Council v Fitzpatrick Contractors Ltd*,[193] that claim was emphatically rejected, on the basis that the implied obligation was quite specific to the contract of employment.

All this might seem to point strongly to the view that this obligation is not to be implied into semi-dependent workers' contracts. However, there may be more room for argument about this than there appears to be on first impression. The *Bedfordshire County Council* case concerned a contract for highway maintenance between a local authority and a construction company which was not in the remotest sense a contract for personal employment of any kind. The judgment of Dyson J identified the implied obligation of trust and confidence as a doctrine which was peculiar to the statutory unfair dismissal regime;[194] yet in fact, as we have seen, that is only one of the contexts in which the implied obligation has developed. He took the view that:

There is no relevant analogy to be made between a complex commercial contract and a contract of employment.[195]

Both that decision, and the body of case law concerning the implied obligation as it attaches to contracts of employment, could be regarded as leaving open the possibility that the implied obligation might extend to contracts where there is a relevant analogy to the contract of employment. This takes us back to the argument advanced in the first chapter of this work that the borderline between the contract of employment and the semi-dependent worker's contract is at best an imprecise one, and that the similarities between the two contract types are much more significant than the ultimately elusive differences between them. How far does that argument support the extension of the implied obligation to semi-dependent workers' contracts?

It might be said that, imperfect though the distinction is between the two types of contracts, the distinction is nevertheless at its most cogent in relation to this implied obligation, because this implied obligation derives so obviously from the quality of the contract of employment as the embodiment of a personal and high-trust relationship, to be contrasted as such with the semi-dependent work relationship. To that argument, it might be countered that, as was argued in the first chapter, the semi-dependent work relationship may actually be a personal one and a high-trust one to the

[193] (1999) 62 Construction Law Reports 64 (QBD—Technology and Construction Court).   [194] Ibid at 72.
[195] Ibid.

same extent as the fully dependent work relationship. Indeed, some semi-dependent workers' contracts may embody more personal and even, in a sense, higher-trust relationships than some contracts of employment. The freelance management consultant hired to conduct a problem-solving audit of a company's management system and practice may well be entrusted with more responsibility for the conduct of the enterprise and subjected to greater personal demands and risks than many of the employees who have long-term contracts of employment with the employing entity.

That argument can be pursued by considering the particular interests which are being protected by the development of the implied obligation of mutual trust and confidence. The description of the obligation as a mutual one is more meaningful in a historical dimension than in relation to its present function. The implied obligation has its origins in a set of concerns for employers; but its modern development has been concerned with the protection of the dignity, autonomy, and personal security and integrity of employees.[196] In the modern law, the interests of employing entities are reflected more by the placing of limits on the assertion of the implied obligation by employees—as in the *Johnson v Unisys* case—than by positive claims based upon the implied obligation made by employing entities. Having identified the main interests which are currently being vindicated by resort to the implied obligation, we can observe that these are interests which semi-dependent workers also invest in their employment relationships. Courts and tribunals have some reluctance to accept this at a descriptive level or respond to it at a prescriptive level; but the implied obligation has developed, both formally and substantively, as an instrument for the precise balancing of competing or conflicting interests in particular employment conditions, which could be adjusted to the circumstances of semi-dependent work relationships.

So the application of the implied obligation of mutual trust and confidence to the contracts of semi-dependent workers should not be regarded as a closed question. Courts and tribunals might be expected to find the foregoing argument a difficult and counter-intuitive one. However, particular cases might present themselves where, on further examination, the argument became a compelling one. In order to be able to make a more rounded assessment of that argument, and indeed of the status of this implied obligation more generally, it is necessary to relate this implied obligation to the remaining two principles of interpretation and construction which are proposed in this chapter, to the first of which, that of loyalty and freedom of economic activity, we now turn our attention.

---

[196] This is the shift reflected in Lord Denning's judgment in *Woods v WM Car Services Ltd* [1982] ICR 692 at 698.

SECTION 5: LOYALTY AND FREEDOM OF ECONOMIC ACTIVITY

A. THE GENERAL PRINCIPLE

In this section we consider a dimension of the content and interpretation of personal work or employment contracts which is somewhat different from those discussed in previous sections of this chapter. Our concern in this section is with the extent to which the law of personal work or employment contracts, on the one hand, requires workers to identify their personal economic interests with the employing entities by which they are employed, and, on the other hand, asserts the freedom of workers to pursue their own personal interests as separate ones in a competitive market economy. We have placed our discussion of that dimension under the heading of 'loyalty and freedom of economic activity'. The initial premise of this section is that it is useful to bring together, into a composite discussion under that title, a particular group of common law doctrines, rules, and positions about the relationship between express and implied terms. It will be hoped to show that we can maximize our understanding of this group of normative positions or propositions by analysing them in this way and under this heading.

In order to give a coherent structure to this analysis, we propose the hypothesis that there can be asserted to be a general principle of loyalty and freedom of economic activity in the law of personal work or employment contracts. It is to the following effect: that workers are required to display that degree of loyalty to their employing entity which is appropriate to the particular circumstances of their employment and their personal work or employment contract; but employing entities are required to display a corresponding degree of respect for their workers' freedom to engage in competitive economic activity. This section consists of an exploration of the question of whether and if so how far such a principle is maintained through those aspects or parts of the law of personal work or employment contracts which, we argue, are directed to that set of concerns.

The suggested principle which is the subject of this section is therefore made up of two distinct elements, that of loyalty and that of freedom of economic activity; and it is important to note that these are two opposed or conflicting concerns. The former concern is primarily with the interests of the employing entity, while the latter is primarily with those of its workers. If they are both to form part of a single principle, that principle has to consist of a balance or reconciliation between them. It is precisely that character which we assign to the principle into which we suggest that these two elements should be regarded as amalgamated. So in order to describe our suggested principle, we have to see in what way the balancing operation, upon which it is premised, does in fact take place; and, in order to know whether the principle is a viable one in theory and in practice, we need to evaluate the coherence of the rules by which that balancing operation is conducted.

172 Content and Construction

That description and that evaluation are, of necessity, complex ones. That is partly because the assertion of the principle of loyalty and freedom of economic activity deliberately seeks to unify, into a single body of law, two broad areas of case law which generally are considered in isolation from each other and regarded as having little functional connection with each other. The first of those two areas to which we shall refer is itself a rather ill-defined one, which we shall group under the heading of 'fidelity'. Succinctly described, it is the area of case law which concerns the worker's implied obligations of confidentiality, disclosure, and accounting to the employing entity, and general protection of the economic interests of the employing entity. The second of these two areas appears on the face of it to be rather more clearly delineated; it is the area of 'restraint of trade' which concerns the control of contractual terms and contractual practices on the basis that they unduly restrict the economic freedom of the worker, that is to say the worker's freedom to 'trade', or to engage in productive or market activity.

When identified in that way, the law about 'fidelity' and the law about 'restraint of trade' sound as if they are two sides of the same coin, corresponding respectively to the 'loyalty' and 'freedom of economic activity' of our suggested composite principle. That is to say, it sounds as if the law of fidelity is about the protection of the economic interests of the employing entity from improper competition or adverse economic action by the worker, while the law of restraint of trade is about the vindication of the worker's capacity for proper competition or adverse economic action. That description, however, does not correctly identify the relationship between these two bodies of law. It is important to understand why that is the case. Each body of law, properly understood, has both of those two concerns, and represents some kind of balance between those two concerns. However, because each body of law operates differently from the other, as a different piece of legal technology, the two concerns are differently expressed in each body of law, and perhaps as a consequence are accorded different relative priority. In short, the legal technology for implying obligations into contracts is very different from the legal technology for controlling express obligations already in contracts.

That is the case even where the two processes are clearly understood to have the same objectives, or to be carried out with the same underlying approach. That cannot be taken for granted in this instance. Within this body of law as a whole, two divergent or competing approaches can be discerned; we can contrast a unitarist with a pluralist approach. (At the time when the original work was written, it was conventional to make such a contrast with regard to the interests of workers perceived as essentially *collective* interests;[197] in the current body of law, the interests of workers are

---

[197] That analysis was raised to a high level of sophistication in Eric Batstone's treatise, *Working Order: Workplace Industrial Relations over Two Decades* (Batstone 1980); see especially 3–32 and 296–316.

perceived as essentially individual ones, particular to each worker.) The unitarist approach asserts, normatively, a strong identity of the worker's economic interests with those of the employer, and therefore tends to insist that the worker's economic interests are pursued through those of the employing entity; the pluralist approach, by contrast, asserts that the worker has a legitimately separate set of economic interests, and while accepting that these may be required to be pursued in conjunction with those of the employing entity, does not treat them as merging into the latter set of interests.

Again, these two approaches may appear on the face of it to be simply two sides of the coin, a simple according of positive or negative value to loyalty, on the one hand, or, on the other hand, to freedom of economic activity. It will be argued that the two approaches, and the contrast between them, are more complex and nuanced than that. In any event, it is quite clear that the two approaches do not match up neatly with the two bodies of law about fidelity and restraint. It is not the case that the law about fidelity is the subject of a blatantly unitarist approach while the law about restraint of trade pursues a simple pluralist approach. In each body of law we find a shifting interplay between the two approaches. Partly for technical reasons, the interplay is different in each body of law. In the ensuing subsections, we consider this theme in detail.

B. FIDELITY

In this subsection it will be suggested that within the body of law which deals with workers' implied obligations of fidelity, the current direction of development seems to incline towards a unitaristic approach. In order to substantiate that suggestion, it is necessary first to identify this body of law and establish its main starting points. As was indicated above, the limits and structure of this body of law are rather ill-defined. There are endless references in the case law to implied terms, duties or obligations owed by employees to employing entities and having to do with adherence to the employing entity and its interests. However, the terminology used varies enormously as between 'fidelity', 'loyalty', 'good faith', 'faithfulness', and 'confidence' or 'confidentiality'. These terms are sometimes regarded as synonymous, but at other times as distinct. It is often unclear whether other related terminologies, such as that of accounting or of disclosure, represent distinct implied obligations, or subsets of those other concepts.

Behind that fog of terminologies, the shadowy outline of a normative structure can be discerned. So far as employees are concerned—we revert to the situation of semi-dependent workers later—a central and crucial distinction is made between the implied obligations which apply during employment and those which apply after employment. During employment, two sets of implied obligations operate cumulatively and in conjunction with each other—in fact, they often become indistinguishable from each other. One set of implied obligations is quasi-proprietary in character;

it applies to protect the intangible assets of the employing entity, in particular its intellectual property in a wide sense including its commercial know-how and goodwill. This set of obligations is focused upon the notion of the employing entity's 'trade secrets' and other confidential information analogous to trade secrets. It can be seen as part of a generic set of obligations to refrain from breach of confidence which is not special to the employment relationship, and which exists independently of the contract of employment rather than being derived from it.

While the employment relationship continues, that set of obligations is overlaid with a set of broader implied obligations upon employees, more directly derived from the contract of employment, to advert to the interests of the employing entity, and not to compete with those interests or act negatively in relation to them. At this stage, therefore, the larger vocabulary of 'fidelity', 'loyalty', or 'good faith' is frequently deployed. However, once the employment relationship has ended, the employing entity's claim to that broader kind of adherence is seen to fall away, and the second set of implied obligations ceases to apply, leaving just the first set in place. So within the law of implied obligations associated with the contract of employment, a balance is struck between loyalty and freedom of economic activity which hinges upon the termination of employment. A unitarist approach is taken to the implied obligations which apply during the continuance of employment, while a pluralist approach is taken to those which apply after the termination of employment.

Within that structure, an assessment can be attempted of the broad direction in which the case law is moving. There is a great danger of being too ready to derive trends from the outcomes of small numbers of cases. However, with that caveat one can point to a slightly pluralist inclination in judicial approaches in the last twenty years. The decision in *Faccenda Chicken Ltd v Fowler*[198] was a landmark one in this respect. This was a case where the sales manager of a company which sold poultry from refrigerated vans left his employment and established a competing company conducting the same activity; a number of former employees of the first company were taken into that second company, and drew upon their knowledge of the selling activity of the first company. The first company sought injunctions to restrain this competing activity and damages for loss caused by it. Both at first instance and in the Court of Appeal, there was a concern not to apply to the former employees the implied obligations of fidelity to which they had been subject during their employment, and therefore to take an appropriately restrictive view of what constituted protected confidential information after they had left that employment.

This pluralist inclination was maintained in a number of subsequent cases concerning implied obligations of fidelity operating after employment

---

[198] [1986] ICR 297 (CA).

has ended. Thus in *Lock International plc v Beswick*,[199] Hoffmann J took a narrow approach, substantively, to the concepts of trade secrets and confidential information, and, procedurally, to the granting of interlocutory injunctions and Anton Piller orders. In *Wallace Bogan & Co v Cove*,[200] the Court of Appeal held that the general freedom of ex-employees, in the absence of a valid express covenant to the contrary, to canvass or do business with customers or clients of the former employers applied to solicitors as much as to any other trade or profession. In *Brooks v Olyslager Oms (UK) Ltd*,[201] the Court of Appeal firmly reasserted the notion, derived from the *Faccenda Chicken* case, that the implied duty of good faith or fidelity imposes a much more restricted obligation upon employees after employment has ended than during its continuance.

For a long time, on the other hand, there has seemed to be a contemporary countervailing trend, bespeaking a unitarist approach, to intensify the rigour of implied obligations of fidelity during the continuance of the employment relationship. Thus, in *Thomas Marshall (Exports) Ltd v Guinle*,[202] it was held that an express covenant on the part of an employee not to 'disclose' confidential information relating to the employer's business was supplemented by an implied obligation not to 'use' such information, which derived from the employee's underlying duty of fidelity and good faith towards his employer. In *Sybron Corporation v Rochem Ltd*,[203] the Court of Appeal confirmed that a specially stringent set of positive requirements to disclose the misconduct of fellow employees might attach to senior employees in positions of high responsibility within the management of an enterprise. In *Lancashire Fires Ltd v Lyons & Co*,[204] the Court of Appeal took an expansive view of the implied obligations of fidelity, both during and after employment, of an employee who had, after his employment ended, set up a rival business to that of his former employing entity; it was clear that the 'springboard' preparatory activities of the employee during his employment had not merely left him open to the claim of breach of his obligations of fidelity during employment, but had coloured the construction of his implied obligations in the subsequent, post-employment, period.

In very recent years, this trend has seemed to accelerate, to the point where the employee's duty of fidelity during the continuance of employment appeared to match the employer's implied obligation of trust and confidence. It seemed that employees might be held to be in breach of that implied obligation where they engaged in a very widely defined category of opportunistic self-interested economic activity during the continuance of their employment. Thus, in the admittedly rather esoteric circumstances of the case of *Neary v Dean of Westminster*,[205] Lord Jauncey, exercising the

---

[199] [1989] 1 WLR 268 (ChD).   [200] [1997] IRLR 453.   [201] [1998] IRLR 590.
[202] [1978] ICR 905 (ChD).   [203] [1985] Ch 209.   [204] [1997] IRLR 113.
[205] [1999] IRLR 288; see also below, 327.

visitatorial jurisdiction over disputes concerning those working in Westminster Abbey, treated an employee of that institution as owing duties which placed him in the position of a fiduciary towards his employing entity. It began to seem as if there might be generally implied in contracts of employment the broad obligation upon the employee to do nothing to impair his or her ability to act at all times in the best interests of the company, which may be imposed by an express trust and confidence provision as recently construed by the Court of Appeal in *Ward Evans Financial Services Ltd v Fox*.[206]

However, in what seems likely to prove a decision of equal moment to that in the *Faccenda Chicken* case, Elias J in *University of Nottingham v Fishel*[207] seems to have put effective limits upon the construction of the employee as a fiduciary by virtue of the implied obligations of fidelity which the employee owes to the employing entity. His view was that the employment relationship is not, in general terms, a fiduciary relationship, because it does not, in those general terms, require an employee to pursue the employer's interests at the expense of his or her own; it stops short of that, so that the default position is that the employee must act with regard to the employer's interests rather than systematically placing those interests above his or her own.[208] Therefore, the employee is not under an obligation to account for profits, on a restitutionary basis, in respect of every breach of his or her implied obligations of fidelity, but only for those arising out of specific contractual obligations the undertaking of which has placed him or her in the position of a fiduciary with respect to those obligations.

This is of profound importance; it asserted, both in the particular case and generally, that employees may maintain an entrepreneurial perspective upon their employment relationship during its continuance without necessarily being treated as fiduciaries acting in conflict with their duties. This approach was of special significance given the character of the particular employment relationship in the present case. The employee, a medical scientist working in the field of clinical embryology, was working as the scientific director of the employing university's infertility unit, called 'Nurture', which he was running as a profitable concern. Much of his work therefore consisted of carrying out employment functions, that is to say acting as employer of those working in that unit. It is no coincidence that this decision holds that the part of this employment relationship in which the employee's fiduciary duties were engaged was the part in which he was discharging employment functions, namely when exercising his power to make arrangements for the work of those working under his supervision.

This case thus represents a particularly interesting example of the way in which the implied obligations of fidelity are applied so as to hold a balance

---

[206] [2002] IRLR 120 (CA).   [207] [2000] ICR 1462 (QBD).
[208] Compare ibid Elias J at 1492–1493.

between the obligations of the worker as adherent to an employing entity and the freedom of the worker to function as an autonomous economic actor. The way in which that balance is struck, within the law of personal work or employment contracts as a whole, will become clearer when we describe how the law concerning restraint of trade bears upon that question. However, there is one more element of the discussion of implied obligations of fidelity which requires discussion at this stage. Thus far, the analysis has been effectively confined to the situation of employees with contracts of employment; it needs to be related to the situation of semi-dependent workers.

So far as those workers are concerned, the answer, as so often in relation to those workers, is a matter of speculation and reasoning from general principles in the absence of decided cases.[209] The result of reasoning from general principles might appear on the face of it to be that the implied obligations of fidelity are an identifying feature of the contract of employment which are, almost by definition, inapplicable as such to other personal work or employment contracts. However, it is suggested that the analysis which we have put forward gives rise to a more nuanced result in which the implied obligations of fidelity are partly or to some extent applicable to other personal work or employment contracts.

There are two features of our analysis which point to this result. The first is that it identifies the implied obligations not in absolute or uni-directional terms, but rather as involving a balancing process between competing values or expectations. The second is that it envisages a core or foundational set of obligations of a quasi-proprietary nature coupled with a superstructural set of obligations of a more simply contractual nature, such that the former subsist both during and after employment while the latter cease to apply when employment ends. It would seem coherent to accept that the implied, quasi-proprietary obligations of fidelity might attach to semi-dependent workers' contracts, given that this would result in a balancing process between competing economic claims or interests rather than a simple equating of obligations as between employees and semi-dependent workers.

It would be not merely consistent with that analysis, but positively predicted by that analysis, that, although semi-dependent workers would be subject to some implied obligations of fidelity, they would in general be less exacting than those of employees with contracts of employment. In

---

[209] Though the following analysis derives some incidental support from the recent decision of the Court of Appeal in *Campbell v Frisbee* [2003] ICR 141 (CA) which concerned the construction of an express confidentiality agreement associated with a 'contract for services' between a well-known fashion model and her personal assistant. The decision is, however, only preliminary in character, consisting of the allowing of an appeal against a summary judgement; it does not conclusively determine the case or the issues of law which it raises.

particular, one might expect that the core set of quasi-proprietary implied obligations would be broadly applicable to semi-dependent workers while the penumbral set of obligations of a more simply contractual nature would not. On this view, there would be a much less sharp distinction between the employment phase and the post-employment phase for the implied fidelity obligations of semi-dependent workers than for those of employees. This is a coherent outcome, in so far as the underlying distinction between the two types of workers, fragile and elusive as it is, rests upon the notion of degrees of intensity of absorption of the worker into the employing organization. Semi-dependent workers are by definition less fully absorbed than employees while their employment subsists, so the contrast between the employment phase and the post-employment phase is often for them a less sharp one.

C. Restraint of Trade

In this subsection it will be argued that the law of restraint of trade has, from very different conceptual starting points from those of the law of implied obligations of fidelity, converged on a very similar set of positions. An attempt will be made to offer a critique of the way in which, as a result of that convergence, the balance between loyalty and freedom of economic activity is struck within the law of personal work or employment contracts as a whole. For once, it will be found that there is a significant amount of case law relating to semi-dependent workers, and indeed that this case law provides important insights into the case law concerning employees with contracts of employment.

The conceptual starting points of the law of restraint of trade in the employment context are, in terms of a distinction made earlier, decidedly pluralist in character. The common law has embodied, over a very long period, the perception that it is both contrary to the public interest, and oppressive of workers, for their freedom to engage in economic activity, whether as workers or entrepreneurs, to be unreasonably restricted by their personal work or employment contract after the ending of the employment which is the subject of that work contract. This has been the basis for treating terms in personal work or employment contracts which consist of such restrictions as prima facie unenforceable. Within the compass of the common law of personal work or employment contracts, this is an unusually strong theoretical basis for controlling the express terms of contracts.

Within the context of the law of the contract of employment, the process of vindication of the public interest in freedom of personal economic activity, which that theoretical framework seems to promise, has in fact resolved itself into a process of balancing the interests of particular workers and their employing entities in respectively maximizing and minimizing that freedom in the post-employment phase. This resolution into a balancing process has occurred through a recognition that a post-employment restriction on the employee's economic activity will fall outside the category of unreasonable restraint of trade if, but only if, it is reasonably necessary to protect a legitimate interest of the employing entity. By that recognition, the law of restraint of trade is organized, in the context of the employment relationship, as a confrontation between, on the one hand, the employee's freedom to engage in economic activity, or 'trade', the very freedom upon which the doctrine of restraint of trade is posited, and, on the other hand, a set of employers' countervailing interests perceived as legitimate ones.

Coming from a diametrically opposed set of starting points, the law of restraint of trade is thus brought into an alignment towards contracts of employment which is basically not dissimilar from that of the law of implied obligations of fidelity. Indeed, that similarity of alignment is greatly heightened by two very significant features of the law of restraint of trade in the context of contracts of employment. Firstly, the law of restraint of trade in the employment context is almost exclusively focused upon post-employment restrictions of economic activity, thus leaving the default position concerning restrictions on external economic activity during employment to be set, in practice, almost entirely by the law of implied obligations of fidelity.

Secondly, when the law of restraint of trade comes into play to control post-employment restrictions, the set of interests of the employing entity which are deemed to be legitimate in this connection are, in effect, the same set of quasi-proprietary interests in intangible assets, in the nature of intellectual property, trade secrets, specific commercial 'know-how', and goodwill, as we saw were protected by that core part of the law of implied obligations of fidelity which applies in the post-employment phase as well as during employment. At this point, the link between the law of implied obligations of fidelity and the law of restraint of trade has become formal and systemic. From the *Faccenda Chicken*[210] case onwards, the concept of protected confidential information has developed as one which is common to both bodies of law.

All this supports a view of the restraint of trade doctrine as operating, within the employment context, as part of a larger apparatus, provided by the common law of personal work or employment contracts as a whole, for interpreting and controlling contractual provisions in order to minimize deviation from a notional equilibrium between the claims of employing entities on the adherence of their workers and those of the workers to retain an economic autonomy. That view is borne out by the cases where the restraint of trade doctrine has been invoked by those whose situation is ambiguous as between those of dependent, semi-dependent, and fully independent workers. As we move beyond the field of fully dependent employment, into areas of more ambiguous employment status, we find

---

[210] *Faccenda Chicken Ltd v Fowler* [1986] ICR 297 (CA), see above, 174.

cases where the restraint of trade doctrine gives rise to a broad scrutiny, not just of direct post-employment restrictions on economic activity by workers, but also of the restrictiveness, with regard to the workers' economic autonomy, of their personal work or employment contracts taken as a whole.

In that context, the doctrine of restraint of trade combines and interacts, sometimes in very complex ways, with other aspects or rules of common law or of equity which control the terms and functioning of contracts, such as those concerning undue influence and inequality of bargaining power,[211] or those limiting the grant of equitable remedies which would have the effect of compelling a person to work.[212] Various examples of such applications and interactions are to be found in the relations between professional sports persons or entertainers and their employers, managers, or agents. Particularly interesting groups of cases where this kind of interest balancing has occurred in recent times have been those concerning professional footballers[213] (where the litigation has actually been focused on transfer arrangements between employing entities,[214] now also the subject of regulation under EC law[215]), professional boxers,[216] and performers and writers of popular music.[217]

By extending, in this way, the range of our examination of restraint of trade cases from those concerning employees to those concerning semi-dependent workers, we eventually encounter cases, on the very outer edge of our category of personal work or employment contracts, where it is unclear whether the restraint of trade issues are to be regarded as arising between workers and employers or as between parties to commercial or business contracts. This is highly important because the doctrine of restraint of trade is more protective of the post-employment economic freedom of employees than it is of the economic freedom of persons who are parties to purely business contracts. The point is very well illustrated by the singularly interesting case of *Allied Dunbar (Frank Weisinger) Ltd v Weisinger*.[218] Mr Weisinger was a very successful salesman of financial services and products who worked for more than ten years as a 'sales associate' of the Allied Dunbar group of insurance companies, selling their

---

[211] *Instone v A Schroeder Music Publishing Co Ltd* [1974] 1 WLR 1308 (HL).

[212] See *Warner Brother Pictures Inc v Nelson* [1937] 1 KB 709.

[213] As to when professional footballers are to be regarded as employed under contracts of employment or as semi-dependent workers, compare O'Leary and Caiger, 'The Re-regulation of football and its impact on employment contracts' (O'Leary and Caiger 2000) at 323–327.

[214] *Eastham v Newcastle United FC Ltd* [1964] Ch 413. (There are interesting analogies with the restraint of trade control exerted in *Greig v Insole* [1978] 1 WLR 302 over the placing of restrictions on the employment of professional cricketers by the body controlling the sport.)

[215] Particularly as the result of the *Bosman* case in the ECJ (*ASBL Union Royale Belge des Sociétés de Football Association v Bosman* Case C–415/93 [1996] 1 CMLR 645 (ECJ)), see above, 82.

[216] *Warren v Mendy* [1989] ICR 525 (CA); *Watson v Prager* [1991] ICR 603 (CA).

[217] *Page One Records v Britton* [1968] 1 WLR 157 (CA); *Instone v A Schroeder Music Publishing Co Ltd* [1974] 1 WLR 1308 (HL).   [218] [1988] IRLR 60 (ChD).

financial products such as insurance policies on a commission basis. His success resulted from his ability to build up and maintain a strong personal clientele. He was treated as self-employed, and during that period he fits squarely within the category of semi-dependent worker which is being used in the present work.

This period of work was ended by an agreement between him and Allied Dunbar whereby his sales practice was bought out by Allied Dunbar, to be run thereafter as a notionally distinct business by the wholly owned subsidiary of Allied Dunbar which figured as the defendant in this action. Mr Weisinger was to act as a consultant in the running of that business, but was subject to a constraint on dealing with clients of his former practice, and to a prohibition from engaging in the business of selling financial services for two years after the ending of his consultancy. Those two constraints were held not to be unenforceable covenants in restraint of trade; one important factor in the decision was that it was decided that the validity of the covenants should be judged by the principles applicable between the vendor and purchaser of a business 'rather than by the stricter principles applicable between employer and employee'.[219]

It is important not to overgeneralize from those rather special facts; if we are fitting the covenants in question into the context of personal work or employment contracts, they really figure more as part of an agreement for the *ending* of employment as a sales associate, than as part of an agreement for *entering into* employment as a consultant. This case, special as it is, is nevertheless quite paradigmatic of many modern personal work relationships; and it is as such a good point of departure for a general critique of the working of the restraint of trade doctrine as an interest-balancing mechanism between loyalty and freedom of economic activity with regard to personal work or employment contracts. That critique will be concentrated upon two related sets of issues; firstly, the coherence or suitability of the overall criterion of assessment, and, secondly, the capacity of the restraint of trade doctrine to achieve appropriate outcomes or to offer appropriate remedial responses.

As to the first of those two sets of issues, it is suggested here that the overall criterion of assessment is a coherent and suitable one. For the courts seem generally committed to an inquiry as to whether a particular contractual constraint or set of constraints upon a worker's economic autonomy is reasonably required to protect the legitimate interests of the employing entity, those being assessed, in effect, by reference to the worker's implied or underlying obligations of adherence to the interests of the employing entity, especially to those core intangible interests to which a quasi-proprietary status is accorded by the law of breach of confidence.

---

[219] Ibid per Millett J at para 21.

This, despite a fairly recent major judicial assertion to the contrary to which we shall return in a moment, amounts to a kind of proportionality test; and as such it constitutes the basis for the sort of interest balancing which, we have argued, this part of the law of personal work or employment contracts properly involves. In a number of recent cases, the courts take a searching look at whether the employing entity has demonstrated a legitimate interest sufficiently concrete to sustain a post-employment restraint on economic activity competing with that of the employing entity; that becomes a more and more prominent and difficult question as the economy activity in question, whether in the manufacturing or service sector, becomes more and more heavily invested in highly specific knowledge and information technology. In each case, the legitimacy of the employing entity's interest in the restraint is, in effect, weighed against the extent of the negative impact of the restraint upon the worker. Examples of that kind of adjudication about proportionality are to be found in *Lansing Linde Ltd v Kerr*,[220] *FSS Travel and Leisure Systems Ltd v Johnson*,[221] *Scully UK Ltd v Lee*,[222] and *SBJ Stephenson Ltd v Mandy*.[223]

However, the impression that this might give, of a really coherent and smoothly functioning process of interest balancing according to a well worked out notion of proportionality, would be illusory. There are many major problems, even dysfunctionalities, in the working of this body of law. The judgment of Millett J in the *Allied Dunbar* case points to one such problem. Millett J vehemently rejected what he saw as the argument advanced on behalf of Mr Weisinger, as the vendor of his 'sales practice', that the reasonableness or otherwise of the contractual restraints should be determined by the use of 'the now fashionable concept of proportionality'. However, he does not appear to have been rejecting the criterion which we have identified above as amounting to a proportionality criterion; on the contrary, he seems to have espoused it. His rejection seems to have been of the suggestion that the restraints should be subjected to a precise financial cost-benefit analysis from the point of view both of the covenantor and the covenantee. His view was that to allow such an inquiry would be to embark, to an inappropriate extent, upon an assessment of the adequacy of the consideration for the contractual constraints. In this case, the value of those constraints to the two parties had been determined by negotiations in which the worker/vendor had been at no obvious disadvantage.

In the more usual case where employing entity and worker have not in any meaningful sense negotiated a separate price for the constraint in question, that problem does not seem to present itself in such a difficult form. Nevertheless, the problem is inherently present to a greater or lesser

---

[220] [1991] IRLR 80 (CA).   [221] [1998] IRLR 382 (CA).
[222] [1998] IRLR 259 (CA).   [223] [2000] IRLR 233 (QBD).

extent whenever such an adjudication takes place. In order to apply a searching proportionality test, the adjudicator must conduct a rigorous comparison of the comparative costs and benefits of the constraints in question for each party. This may be couched in terms of an inquiry of the extent of the comparative *rights and legitimate expectations* of each party, rather than in terms of the adequacy of consideration, and the adjudicators may be able to rest upon a strongly perceived sense of the public interest in the economic autonomy of workers. However, as soon as they have to move beyond the fairly well worked out rules for determining the validity of conventional restrictive covenants into a deeper set of questions about whether particular personal work or employment contracts are functioning, *by their very structure*, in undue restraint of trade, the doctrinal underpinnings seem less stable, and the very basis of the balancing process becomes more contested.

Moreover, even to the extent that the restraint of trade doctrine can be regarded as applying a reasonably coherent proportionality criterion in employment cases, a concern remains as to whether that doctrine functions to ensure appropriate outcomes, or to provide appropriate remedial responses, in particular cases in the employment context. There are two, interrelated, factors which seem to militate against its capacity to do so. The first factor is the 'all or nothing' notion of unenforceability of covenants in restraint of trade. The second factor is the complexity of the interaction between the restraint of trade doctrine and other aspects of the law of personal work or employment contracts. We refer in turn, in the following paragraphs, to each of these two sets of factors.

The first factor which reduces the capacity of the restraint of trade doctrine to hold the balance between loyalty and freedom of economic activity with clarity and precision is, then, the fact that it offers no halfway house of partial application; in effect, either a given contractual provision, or 'covenant', is held to be completely valid, or it is held to be completely unenforceable. Sometimes this produces outcomes so perverse as to be offensive to any conception of efficient regulation. Thus, in *Wyatt v Kreglinger & Fernau*[224] a textile dealer had a contractual pension entitlement from his employing entity which was conditional upon his observing a set of constraints upon his economic activity in that occupation; the employing entity was able to rely on the fact that those constraints were so wide as to be in unlawful restraint of trade as a basis for refusing to make the pension payments in question.

Even in the more ordinary case where the worker claims to treat a constraint imposed by an employing entity as unenforceable because of its excessive width, it may be unsatisfactory that the courts have little or no scope for effecting a partial application of an excessively wide constraint.

---

[224] [1937] 1 KB 793 (CA). Compare also *Bull v Pitney Bowes Ltd* [1967] 1 WLR 273. (This particular outcome might now be precluded by ss 91–94 of the Pensions Act 1995.)

As the result of the decision in *D v M*,[225] it appeared that this rigidity might be so complete as to enable the worker to claim to treat a constraint as unenforceable merely because it purported to apply even where the employing entity had unlawfully terminated the employment;[226] but the Court of Appeal in *Rock Refrigeration Ltd v Jones*[227] came out against so dogmatic an application of the doctrine. The Court of Appeal had also appeared, in its decision in *Provident Financial Group Ltd v Hayward*,[228] to have devised a wider basis for achieving such partial application, by granting an interim injunction enforcing a more restricted version of the constraint in question; but in the more recent decision in *Mont (UK) Ltd v Mills*,[229] it seems to have veered away from such adjustments, fearing that the prospect of adjustment would create incentives for employing entities to exact very wide constraints, knowing that even successful litigation by workers would merely result in a cutting back of those constraints rather than in their being held to be totally unenforceable. No doubt that is a serious point, but it still seems questionable whether so draconian a method of control is appropriate.[230]

This leads on to the second area of concern; it is questionable whether a blunt instrument of regulation can function satisfactorily when it is has to operate in very complex and often uncertain conjunctions with other aspects of the law of personal work or employment contracts. Thus, as we have seen, the doctrine of restraint of trade applies overwhelmingly to post-employment constraints on the worker's economic autonomy, leaving the situation during employment to be regulated by the law of implied obligations of fidelity, and, it should be added, of mutual trust and confidence. Yet those implied obligations are, as we have seen, evolving and transmuting quite rapidly; and so, as we shall see in later chapters, is the whole body of law determining when employment is deemed to have terminated under a personal work or employment contract, when the personal work or employment contract itself is deemed to have terminated, and with what remedial consequences. So the legal context within which the law of restraint of trade has to operate, in relation to personal work or employment contracts, is itself a decidedly fluid and interactive one, sufficiently so to make the boundaries of the law of restraint of trade decidedly contested and at times unstable.

---

[225] [1996] IRLR 192 (QBD).
[226] Thus purporting to defy the principle enunciated in *General Billposting Co Ltd v Atkinson* [1909] AC 118 (HL); see below, 391–392.   [227] [1997] ICR 938.
[228] [1989] ICR 160 (CA).   [229] [1993] IRLR 172.
[230] Compare the comment of the Court of Appeal in *Campbell v Frisbee* [2003] ICR 141: 'We do not believe that the effect on duties of confidence assumed under contract when the contract in question is wrongfully repudiated is clearly established' (Lord Phillips MR, para 22). See Notes on the decision by Linda Clarke and the present author (Clarke 2003, Freedland 2003).

This set of difficulties may be illustrated from various cases which have revolved around the practice known as 'garden leave' whereby employing entities seek to minimize the effects of post-employment competition by their workers by interposing, between the worker's period of active employment and the ending of the employment, a period in which the worker is still employed and in receipt of remuneration and is therefore subject to very high constraints on autonomous economic activity, but is not actually working. One might imagine that the doctrine of restraint of trade could be brought to bear directly on such a practice, in order to hold the balance between the employee's obligations of loyalty and his or her claims to economic autonomy; but in fact the legal effect of an employing entity's imposition of garden leave is determined by an enormously complicated interplay of a number of not yet fully resolved legal debates.

Thus, it is far from clear whether or in what precise circumstances an employing entity will act in breach of a personal work or employment contract by imposing garden leave. The decision of the Court of Appeal in the case of *William Hill Organisation Ltd v Tucker*[231] suggests that an employing entity which is not expressly empowered by a contract of employment to impose garden leave may well, by so doing, place itself in breach of an implied obligation to provide work as well as remuneration, itself amounting to a breach of the implied obligation of trust and confidence. If so, it is likely, though not totally certain, that the employing entity has wrongfully repudiated the contract of employment, and thereby rendered all contractual constraints upon the employee inapplicable under the doctrine in *General Billposting Co Ltd v Atkinson.*[232] The point was argued in the recent case of *SBJ Stephenson v Mandy*,[233] but was not decided because it was judged on the facts that the employing entity had not actually imposed garden leave, but had, instead, agreed to the employee remaining away from work.[234]

If, on the other hand, an imposition of garden leave upon an employee is regarded as within the employing entity's contractual powers, is the full set of implied obligations of fidelity which attach during the period of employment still in force, or is the lesser set of post-employment implied obligations applicable during garden leave? This depends on the ever obscure set of rules for determining when employment subsists or is at an end under a personal work or employment contract. In the very recent case of *Symbian Ltd v Christiansen*,[235] it was held that an express constraint prohibiting the worker from working in any employment 'during the term of this agreement' did remain applicable during a period of garden leave, the imposition of which was in accordance with the contract. This constraint was held to be *partially* enforceable to the extent of an injunction prohibiting the

---

[231] [1999] ICR 291; see below, 487.   [232] [1909] AC 118 (HL); see below, 390–392.
[233] [2000] IRLR 233 (QBD).   [234] See ibid at para 63.   [235] [2001] IRLR 77 (CA).

employee from working for the particular competitor organization, Microsoft, for which he wished to work during the period of garden leave.

That remedial approach in turn opens up some further complex questions about the interplay between different relevant legal rules or doctrines. Does it mean that the doctrine of restraint of trade may be the subject of partial application to arrangements for garden leave, although it has to be applied in an 'all or nothing' fashion to post-employment constraints? Does it, on the other hand, mean that the rule against negative injunctions, to enforce constraints operating during employment which would have the effect of forcing the employee to work, does not apply to garden leave arrangements because they do not oblige the employee to *work*, but, on the contrary, to remain idle? The *Symbian* case does imply a positive answer to both those questions, but neither of them is directly addressed in the course of the decision in the Court of Appeal.

These complexities have been explored at some length not solely because of their immediate importance to an understanding of the working of the law of restraint of trade in the context of employment, nor even just because they contribute to an understanding of how the overall balance between loyalty and freedom of economic activity is maintained in the law of personal work or employment contracts taken as a whole. They have an even larger significance to this work as a whole. They indicate the need, acute in this instance, for a holistic as opposed to a fragmented understanding of the way in which the law of personal work or employment contracts functions. This demands, at the very least, an interrelating of the different doctrines and rules which determine the content of personal work or employment contracts. Ultimately, it demands a further synthesis of those rules and doctrines with that still larger set of rules and doctrines which deals with the formation, evolution, and termination of personal work or employment contracts. This is a theme which we shall now pursue into the next section of this chapter.

SECTION 6: FAIR MANAGEMENT AND PERFORMANCE

A. An Overarching Principle

In this section, it is suggested that the principles of interpretation and construction of personal work or employment contracts which we have so far identified can all usefully be synthesized into an overarching general principle of contractual fair management and performance. This principle is that personal work or employment contracts will be interpreted and construed so that the parties to the contract are subject to obligations of management and performance which are fair and reasonable with regard to the nature and provisions of the personal work or employment contract in question and the general normative framework within which it exists. This section is devoted to an argument as to why that might be a useful analysis.

Firstly, we should offer some explanation of what this suggested principle means and how it is derived from the existing law. The principle envisages a *process of interpretation and construction* of personal work or employment contracts so as to give effect to a *set of implied obligations* which consist of the application of a *set of standards*—those of fairness and reasonableness with regard to the nature and provisions of the personal work or employment contract in question—to a set of *actions or activities*—those of management and performance. We hope to have explained, in the first section of this chapter, what is meant by a process of interpretation which gives effect to implied obligations; but we should expand upon what are meant by the standards and the set of activities.

The set of activities—management and performance—could be seen as very loosely corresponding to, respectively, the functions of the employing entity and of the worker under a personal work or employment contract. That is to say, management broadly refers to the employing activity or function of the employing entity, while performance broadly refers to the work activity or function of the worker. Using the idea of 'management' accords a positive identification to the employing function, while using the idea of 'performance' makes the point that the worker's activity or function is not totally confined to working, as it typically includes adhering to the employing enterprise in a wider sense, for example by refraining from certain competitive activity during and, to a lesser extent, after employment. However, these terms are not simply the equivalent of 'employing' and 'working'; they are to some extent interchangeable between employing entities and workers. Thus some of the actions or activities of employment are better described as 'performance' than as 'management', particularly the payment of remuneration. On the other hand, some workers have management functions and activities; this re-emphasizes the argument about the complex internal personal structure of employing entities which was developed in the previous chapter.

The set of standards which our suggested principle applies to these activities—that of contractual fairness or fairness in accordance with the nature and provisions of the personal work or employment contract in question—is meant to represent a synthesis of the various particular standards or implied obligations which were identified and described in earlier sections of this chapter.[236] The suggestion is, therefore, that the notions of mutuality

---

[236] This argument therefore transcends the more particular issue, lately explored in the decision of the Court of Appeal in *Transco plc v O'Brien* [2002] ICR 721 (CA)—see above, 168, as to whether or how far the implied obligation of mutual trust and confidence has itself come to represent a generalized obligation of fair dealing or reasonable decision making.

or reciprocity, care and co-operation, mutual trust and confidence, and loyalty and freedom of economic activity, can all be gathered into an overarching idea or standard of contractual fairness. This represents a fusion of those particular obligations, or standards, into a composite notion of fairness; but this notion of fairness is a specific one in two senses. Firstly, it is specific to the law of personal work or employment contracts. Secondly, it is specific to the nature and provisions of the particular personal work or employment contract or group of personal work or employment contracts to which the standard is being applied.

What we are therefore putting forward is a framework principle, one which sits at a still higher level of generality above the various particular principles which we have identified, some of which themselves had the quality of being framework principles. At this very high level of generality, one might expect that the principle as a whole would amount to more than the sum of its particular parts. That is indeed the case in this instance, in at least two respects, to both of which we shall now refer. The first has to do with the creative interaction between the particular principles. The second has to do with a larger interaction between those principles and the general normative framework with which personal work or employment contracts exist and function.

The point about creative interaction between particular principles is this one. In the previous sections, we encountered various situations where approaches to the implied obligations of employing entities and workers were evolving in ways which were quite difficult to assign methodically to one particular principle rather than another. A given development might occur partly under the banner of mutuality or reciprocity and partly under that of mutual trust and confidence or of care and co-operation. These different concepts constitute a melting pot in which new concepts and configurations are formed. The recognition of an overarching general principle may enable us to observe and track such interactive developments more easily and effectively because we have a framework with which to locate them.

This links up with the second point about the general normative framework. It will be recalled that we referred to that general normative framework in our definition of our suggested general principle; we designated it as one of the determinants of the standard of fairness and reasonableness. By this we intended to refer to the way in which norms and normative ideas from sources outside the common law of personal work or employment contracts are fed into the process of local interpretation and construction of personal work or employment contracts. We have referred in the previous chapter to such influences from the public law of judicial review, and from various kinds of statutory regulation which bear upon personal work or employment contracts. We can understand these impacts upon the process of interpretation and construction of personal work or employment contracts better from the perspective of an overarching framework principle than from the standpoint of particular principles viewed in isolation from each other.

B. The Principle Located with Regard to Other Fairness Principles

It might be felt that, by generalizing our suggested principles of interpretation and construction of personal work or employment contracts into one overarching principle, and by expressing that principle in terms of fairness, we have deprived this body of principles of its distinctiveness, and have casually conflated it with other principles of fairness which are established by public law and by relevant areas of statute law. In this subsection it will be argued that the overarching principle, even if it interacts with other principles of fairness, is nevertheless distinct from them.

It is certainly the case that our argument about the guiding principles of interpretation and construction, as regards the several principles and over arching general one, admits and asserts the influences upon them of other relevant legal principles or groups of rules which assert notions of fairness. Thus our argument invokes and refers to the influence of public law principles, not least those now conventionally grouped together under the heading of fairness[237] (though our argument does not go to the lengths of necessarily endorsing Dawn Oliver's thesis of convergence of public and private law on a set of common values[238]). We also stress at a number of points, including at the level of the overarching general principle, the interaction between our suggested common law guiding principles and many statutory provisions explicitly and implicitly directed towards securing fairness between employing entities and workers. In this respect, we boldly reject the 'oil and water' approach to the relationship between common law and statute which Jack Beatson has recently strongly attacked[239] as an inappropriate and outmoded orthodoxy still entertained by the judges and some academic commentators. In the law of personal work or employment contracts that approach is in our view already quite untenable as an account of the way the common law is expounded in substance, and even in terms of the rhetoric in which that substance is couched.[240]

However, all this is far from suggesting that the common law principles of construction of personal work or employment contracts have simply merged into notions of fairness coming from those other sources. We have referred to the distinctiveness of the common law principles, as we advanced here, from those of public law; we need, however, to identify their distinctiveness from two relevant bodies of statute law, those concerning

---

[237] Compare above, 161, and see Davies and Freedland 1997 at 323–327.

[238] See Oliver 1999.

[239] See Beatson 'The Role of Statute in the Development of Common Law Doctrine' (Beatson 2001) at 251 et seq.

[240] Compare the discussion, above at 162–164, of the reasoning of HL in *Johnson v Unisys Ltd.*

unfair contract terms and those concerning unfair dismissal. The less relevant of the two bodies of statute law is that which concerns unfair terms in
consumer contracts, that is to say the Unfair Contract Terms Act 1977 and
the Unfair Terms in Consumer Contract Regulations 1999 which were
enacted in order to implement the EC Directive on that topic.[241] This body
of regulation is of marginal application to personal work or employment
contracts, both as to its scope and its substance. So far as the 1977 Act is
concerned, we address that comment to the provisions of section 3 concerning the control of unreasonable terms in consumer and standard form
contracts, rather than to the provisions of section 2 preventing the exclusion or restriction of liability for death or personal injury resulting from
negligence. The latter provisions would seem to be fully applicable in favour
of workers[242] *vis-à-vis* provisions purporting to restrict or exclude such liability under personal work or employment contracts, and are fully relevant,
as a matter of substance, to such contracts.[243]

We would argue that the regulation of fairness of contract terms by
section 3 of the 1977 Act is largely irrelevant to personal work or employment contracts because it is not primarily directed at personal work or
employment contracts and is not particularly appropriate to them. It is true
that, in *Brigden v American Express Bank Ltd*,[244] it was recently held at High
Court level that section 3(1) of the 1977 Act was in principle applicable to
a contract of employment, so that a provision for the dismissal of the
employee by notice came under the scrutiny of consumer contracts which
that section provides. However, despite the persuasiveness of eloquent
arguments advanced in a powerful article by Loraine Watson,[245] personal
work or employment contracts do not really fit naturally into the categories
of consumer contracts or standard form contracts to which section 3
applies. Although, technically, workers may be argued into either category,
if the provisions of section 3 are invoked in favour of workers this involves
regarding them as, essentially, the users or recipients of goods or services,
whereas it is the nature of personal work or employment contracts that
workers figure as the providers of services. That is why there is an
artificiality about applying section 3 for the protection of either workers or
employing entities under personal work or employment contracts.

---

[241] EC Directive 93/13, OJ L95/29; Regulations SI 1999/2083.

[242] Paragraph 4 of Sch 1 to the Act provides s 2(1) and (2) shall not extend to a contract
of employment, except in favour of the employee. It is suggested that the section does extend
to other personal work or employment contracts, in principle in favour of either employing
entity or worker, though in practice that will normally be in favour of the worker.

[243] Compare *Johnstone v Bloomsbury Health Authority* [1991] ICR 269 where the CA held
that the contractual requirement of availability for overtime upon a junior hospital doctor was
arguably void under s 2(1).   [244] [2000] IRLR 94 (QBD).

[245] Watson 1995.

Thus it may be convincing to say that workers, and employees in particular, are not 'contracting in the course of a business' when they enter into personal employment contracts, but that is more because of their dependency (total or partial) upon the employing enterprise then because they are contracting in the non-business capacity of private consumers. This artificiality also explains why the better view seems to be that the 1999 Regulations do not apply to those contracts.[246] This is not to say that workers will not as such need any kind of protection as consumers. Such protection might be substantially appropriate in respect, for example, of some aspects of provision of employee benefits such as share option schemes. However, and this is the crucial point for the purposes of the present discussion, the sort of consumer-oriented conception of fairness control which emerges from these pieces of legislation is not obviously well adapted to the exigencies of personal work relationships or contracts. It is no accident or surprise that, in the *Brigden* case, although Marland J accepted that the claimant's contract of employment fell within the ambit of section 3(1) of the 1977 Act, he regarded the provision for termination by notice as in no way falling foul of section 3(1) (as being an exclusion clause or one permitting non-performance or substantially different performance from that reasonably expected), and also regarded that provision for termination as able to pass the 'reasonableness' test of section 3(2) had that been applicable. The conception of fairness of consumer contracts which emerges from all this legislation is one very much directed at terms which purport to permit, or to restrict or exclude liability for, unsatisfactory provision of goods or services, whereas issues about the formulation or functioning of personal work or employment contracts do not normally present themselves in those terms.

There is a very different relationship between the unfairness principle which we are putting forward in this section and the notion of unfairness which is embodied in the unfair dismissal legislation. This time, there can be no doubt of the relevance and applicability of that notion of unfairness; it applies precisely to contracts of employment (though not to other personal work or employment contracts). So the relationship between that notion of unfairness and our suggested fairness principle is, to that extent, a much more immediate one. It is not necessary or appropriate, within the compass of the present work, to embark upon a detailed discussion of the notion of unfairness which is embodied in the unfair dismissal legislation. In any event, that task has been carried out to the highest of standards by Hugh Collins in his treatise on 'Justice in Dismissal'.[247] It suffices for the present purpose to remark that this concept, at the other extreme in this

---

[246] Compare *Chitty on Contracts*, 28th edn (1999), vol I, para 15-018.
[247] Collins 1992—see particularly 70–139.

respect from the notion of fairness embodied in the unfair contract terms legislation, is entirely specific to the employment situation, being formed around a conception of broad justifications for dismissal,[248] upon which is superimposed an undefined and open-ended test of whether an employer acted reasonably in actually effecting the dismissal in question.[249] It should be added that various items of employment legislation have engrafted, onto this broad conception, particular grounds upon which dismissals are deemed to be, or are treated as automatically being, unfair because they violate what are seen as being specific employment rights.[250]

Almost the only feature of the legislative intentions for the basic definition or conception of unfairness about which one can feel at all confident is that it was formulated in contradistinction to the implied norms and perceived approaches of the law of the contract of employment. That is to say, the perception was that the law of the contract of employment had done less than was now seen as necessary to regulate employers' contractual powers of dismissal, and particularly to control their exercise in an arbitrary or abusive way whether in a procedural or substantive sense. Judicial interpretation and development of this conception has served in various ways to bring it back into some degree of alignment with the common law of the contract of employment, but the conceptual basis for the law of unfair dismissal has remained stoutly non-contractual, if not counter-contractual.

That non-contractual character of the law of unfair dismissal is still strong enough to ensure that it may seem surprising, even counter-intuitive, for us to have suggested that we can identify, in terms of fairness, an overarching principle of the common law of personal work or employment contracts, when, in the domain of employment law, the notion of fairness is so strongly associated with this consciously non-contractual statutory jurisdiction. We therefore still need to justify the assertion that there can be a guiding principle of interpretation of personal work or employment contracts which is not only distinct from the statutory notion of unfairness as found in the law of unfair dismissal but also deserving of the terminology of 'fairness' and yet at the same time authentically contractual in the sense of truly belonging to and being rooted in the law of personal work or employment contracts. We shall try to establish that claim in the remainder of this section.

C. FAIR MANAGEMENT AND PERFORMANCE IN THE LAW OF PERSONAL WORK OR EMPLOYMENT CONTRACTS

In this subsection it will be argued that the overarching principle of fair management and performance, which we are putting forward, is genuinely embedded in the law of personal work or employment contract in such a way as to make it distinctive from other, statutory, formulations of fairness which

---

[248] Employment Rights Act 1996 (ERA), s 98(1)–(2).   [249] ERA, s 98(3).
[250] See ERA, ss 99–105.

impact upon the law of personal work or employment contracts, in particular that of the law of unfair dismissal. We advance this argument from two perspectives; the first looks back to the material about the nature, structure, and interpretative principles of personal work or employment contracts which has been presented thus far in this work, while the second looks forward to the material about the evolution and formation of personal work relationships or contracts with which the remainder of the work will be concerned.

First looking back, then, at the areas surveyed so far in this work, we suggest that it will be readily apparent that the guiding principles of interpretation which we have put forward, although we have associated them with broadly expressed values such as those of care, co-operation, loyalty, or freedom of economic activity, are nevertheless contractual in character, in the sense that they are derived from and rooted in the principles, rules, and technicalities of the law of personal work or employment contracts. This is true in at least two senses. Firstly, the standards or values which these principles embody have to be articulated and effectuated through the technical rules about the implying of terms or obligations into personal work or employment contracts, and about the construction or interpretation of those contracts more generally. The standards or values are not free-standing; they have to be understood as mediated through a context of contractual rules and techniques. Thus, since it has been argued that the rules and techniques for implying terms or obligations into personal work or employment contracts create an essentially complex and subtle relationship between the express terms and the implied terms, the derogable and inderogable content of personal work or employment contracts, it follows that the guiding principles which we have identified express their respective values or standards in a particularly contractually technical form, and in a form, moreover, which is specific to the law of personal work or employment contracts.

Secondly, it is argued that the guiding principles, and therefore the overarching notion of fair management and performance, are also embedded in the law of personal work or employment contracts at a more profound level; they reflect not merely the rules and technicalities of the law of personal work or employment contracts but also fundamental ideas, which are themselves part of the body of general principles of contract law, albeit often in a specially adapted form. Thus, the notion of mutuality of obligation which underpins many of the guiding principles which we have identified probably deserves to be regarded as a general principle of contract law in and of itself; and it is certainly connected to the general contractual notions of consideration and intention to create legal relations.

All this may seem to identify a conception of a set of guiding principles, and of an overarching guiding principle, which is so essentially contractual in character as to make the rather extra-contractual notion of fairness an inappropriate one by which to identify this body of principle. That would be to press the contractualist point of view too far. Even in this context of contractual rules and principles, we have observed the emergence, in the interpretation and construction of personal work or employment contracts, of a set of commitments to broad ideas of balance, proportionality, and non-abuse of power which are sufficiently concrete as to link this body of law into the set of legal values evoked by the notion of fairness, albeit in a specific-ally contractual fashion. Moreover, it may seem as if we are idealizing the law of personal work or employment contracts by imagining it as giving rise to a set of guiding principles and an overarching principle which manage to find and give effect to a perfectly equilibrated body of underlying norms for personal work relationships. That is by no means the case, as will appear more clearly when we relate the guiding principles to the law concerning the evolution and termination of personal work relationships and contracts, which forms the subject matter of the remainder of this work.

One of the central arguments which will be advanced in the succeeding chapters is that there is an essential and profound continuity of issues as between the law concerning the nature, formation, and content of personal work or employment contracts and the law concerning their evolution and termination. This has already manifested itself at a number of points; it is, for example, already apparent how closely the principles concerning mutual trust and confidence, and loyalty and freedom of economic activity, are related to and tied up with the law concerned with actual and constructive dismissal or termination of the work contract. This will appear repeatedly in subsequent chapters when our focus is precisely upon the evolution and term-ination of personal work or employment contracts. So much is that the case that it will be argued that the guiding principles and the suggested overarching principle can be regarded as themes which inform and explain that body of law about the evolution and termination of personal work or employment contracts; they form a conceptual framework for that body of law in much the same way as they do for the law concerning the structure and content of the personal work or employment contract.

However, the proposed application of this framework of guiding prin-ciples to the law concerning the evolution and termination of personal work or employment contracts will not be an uncritical one. For it will appear that the implementation of those guiding principles often becomes con-founded and convoluted in the face of various technical, and sometimes outmoded or dysfunctional, rules or doctrines of contract law which come into play in relation to the evolution and termination of personal work or employment contracts. Indeed, this may be even more apparent from the perspective of the law of personal work or employment contracts as a whole than it would be from the narrower perspective of the law of the contract of employment alone. So the framework of guiding principles and the sug-gested overarching principle of contractual management and performance will be used not just as an explanatory apparatus with which to approach the law concerning the evolution and termination of personal work rela-tionships, but also as a critical apparatus with which to assess the coherence of the actual law. Even so, however, the guiding principles and the suggested overarching principle are not put forward as an abstract ideal, but rather as normative principles which can satisfactorily be discerned in the texture of the basic law of personal work or employment contracts as we have described and analysed it thus far.

CONCLUSION

This chapter has involved an ambitious combination of the project of expansion of the law of the contract of employment with the method of restatement. The result has consisted of an avowedly creative articulation of a set of guiding principles which are put forward as accounting for or rationalizing the construction of the express and implied content of personal work or employment contracts. This exercise in analysis and reformulation culminated in the proposal of an overarching or general principle of fair management and performance, which was advanced as the basis of a synthesis of the more specific guiding principles which had thus far been identified. As at a number of stages in the present work, it is readily acknowledged that there is a prescriptive edge to this analysis, and that authoritative determination would be required to place it beyond doubt that the proposed guiding principles accurately represent the law of construction of the content of personal work or employment contracts. That is not least because the foregoing analysis has challenged a number of received assumptions or orthodox views about that content and construction.

In particular, we have asserted a number of continuities which override distinctions often perceived as sharp or decisive ones. Thus, this chapter maintains and reinforces the general challenge to the division of the world of employment contracts between the contract of employment and other personal work or employment contracts. It has been argued that a number of principles which have been perceived as specially characteristic of the contract of employment, such as those of mutual trust and confidence, and of loyalty and freedom of economic activity, should be regarded as applicable to semi-dependent workers' contracts, even if in a different or less intensive form. The chapter has also sought to elide, at a number of points, the discussion of contractual content into that of contractual formation (via the concept of mutuality or reciprocity), and to establish a continuity between the construction of the express and the implied content of personal work or employment contracts. In the course of so doing, we have signalled further kinds of thematic or analytical continuity with other areas of the law of personal work or employment contracts, namely those which are concerned with the evolution and termination of such contracts. In succeeding chapters, the body of restated doctrine which it has been sought to establish in the first three chapters will be used as an apparatus of analysis or criticism with which to scrutinize the existing law in those areas, beginning with the topic of performance and breach.

4
Performance and Breach

INTRODUCTION

In the previous chapters of this work, the law of personal work or employment contracts has been examined in terms of the nature, formation, and content of those contracts. That is to say, we have been concerned with the way in which the personal work relationships are translated into the legal form of personal work or employment contracts, and how those contracts are formulated in or by the law of personal work or employment contracts. This provides an initial view of what personal work or employment contracts consist of and how they are envisaged. In the remainder of the work, we seek to present the law of personal work or employment contracts as providing a framework for the evolution of personal work relationships from that formation onwards.

Much of that exposition will in fact be concerned with the termination of personal work relationships and personal work or employment contracts. That is because, in ways which will become more and more apparent in later chapters, the law of personal work or employment contracts is very heavily focused upon the termination of the work relationship and the contract. This in turn is partly because, for obvious practical reasons, most of the situations in which or in relation to which the law of personal work or employment contracts is involved occur at or in consequence of the termination of personal work relationships. Litigation about personal work relationships tends mainly to occur at or about the ending of those relationships rather than during their continuance.

However, that is only part of the reason for this high concentration of the law of personal work or employment contracts upon the termination of those contracts or the relationships which underlie them. There is a further reason, which consists in the fact that termination is a central, one might almost say the central, conceptual focus of the law of personal work or employment contracts. As will become apparent in later chapters, much of the law of personal work or employment contracts is constructed around the notions of termination by notice, summary dismissal, and wrongful dismissal. Between them, those notions represent, in ways which will be explained in full detail, the basic rights and wrongs upon which the law of personal work or employment contracts is largely premised.

This focus of the law of personal work or employment contracts upon termination is so powerful that much of the discussion in the previous chapters, although we have organized that discussion in terms of the initial formulation of personal work or employment contracts and their structure and content, is actually closely related to the termination of those contracts. An obvious example is the way in which much of the modern law concerning the implied terms or obligations of personal work or employment contracts has been formulated around the notion of constructive dismissal;[1] but, although that is a very prominent example, it is actually only one among many.

This sense that the law of personal work or employment contracts is largely built around the ending of those contracts becomes even stronger when we turn from the discussion of their general nature and initial formation to discussion of their subsequent evolution. Our mode of discussion of that subsequent evolution is to begin with events or phenomena which occur or appear to occur during the continuance of the employment relationship rather than at its conclusion—performance and breach, variation and suspension. However, it will appear that all these topics are actually to a high degree related to the termination of personal work or employment contracts, especially the topic of suspension.

For that set of reasons, this chapter and the next two between them can be seen as forming a second stage on the way towards an overall account of the law of personal work or employment contracts which culminates in a third and critical stage of discussion of the termination of those contracts (or, as will be explained, their transfer between employing entities). For the same set of reasons, the general legal analysis of personal work or employment contracts should be regarded as one which is cumulative and continuous as between all three of its stages. In fact, we shall very often be examining the same phenomena or issues, from different angles or perspectives, at one or more of the three successive stages.

Crucial in the view of the present writer to establishing that continuity between the different stages of this work is the part of the law of personal work or employment contracts which is identified and considered in the present chapter under the heading of 'performance and breach'. Under that heading, we consider some aspects of the law of personal work or employment contracts which deal with questions of whether the worker and the employing entity have carried out or have broken their respective obligations under the personal work or employment contract, and what consequences attach to their having done so. These are mainly questions about whether workers have sufficiently performed their work obligations to entitle them to remuneration but they include questions of liability to damages or to other remedies for non-performance of work or non-payment of remuneration.

[1] See above, 155; below, 339–340.

Although the law concerning those questions forms only quite a small part of the law of personal work or employment contracts, it has a significance which exceeds its size. This is true for several reasons. Firstly, it forms the bridge between the law of formation of personal work or employment contracts and the law concerning the effect of occurrences in the personal work relationship after its particular formation. That is to say, it makes the link between, on the one hand, the principles of interpretation and construction and the doctrines concerning the original structure of the contract which were considered in earlier chapters, and, on the other hand, the law which recognizes and deals with changes in the state or status of the contract.

The second reason for regarding this small section of the law of personal work or employment contracts as a hinge upon which much of the whole body of law turns is that it demonstrates, even more clearly than the discussion of structure in the second chapter of this work, the essential interrelatedness of the obligations on the two sides of the personal work or employment contract, that of the worker and of the employing entity. Each set of obligations of performance is essentially conditioned upon the other, so that the notions of performance and breach emerge as, generally speaking, relational ones rather than absolute or free-standing ones. This perception enables us to develop some central notions about the structure of the personal work or employment contract in operation as well as in its notional or original state of formation.

A third and final factor which makes this part of the law of personal work or employment contracts very significant to the understanding of that body of law as a whole has to do with the way that rights and remedies come together at this point in our exposition. For most of the time, in the present work, we are concerned with the law of personal work or employment contracts as a theoretical construct which is used in a wide variety of interpretative contexts. Yet that theoretical construct is, ultimately, formed around the recognition of contractual claims and remedies. In this chapter, it becomes more apparent how some of the key conceptions which are foundational to the law of personal work or employment contracts are inseparably bound up with or conditioned by rules and doctrines about remedies such as claims for debt or damages.

In fact, in this chapter, we shall be basically concerned with contractual doctrines which deal with the worker's claims to remuneration or remedies for non-payment of remuneration, and with the claims or remedies of the employing entity in respect of failure of performance, but we shall postpone until later chapters the treatment of those topics in terms of variation, suspension, or termination of personal work or employment contracts. We begin by returning to a question touched upon in our earlier discussion of the structure of the personal work or employment contract, namely the divisibility of performance of contractual obligations into units.

SECTION 1: PERFORMANCE, DIVISIBILITY, AND DEDUCTION

In this section, we begin to consider the doctrines, approaches, or techniques of reasoning which have evolved within the law of personal work or employment contracts in order to determine how the performance of the obligations of each of the parties to the personal work or employment contracts is interrelated to that of the other; basically, therefore, how the performance of the worker's obligation to work or render service is interrelated to the performance of the employing entity's obligation to employ and, in particular, to remunerate. These doctrines, approaches, or techniques have evolved over a long historical period, and in many different contexts. Their development has come together, in the modern law, in case law on the effects of industrial action short of outright strike action upon the worker's entitlement to remuneration, and our discussion in this chapter will converge on that relevant recent case law. It begins with some early history of thinking about entire and divisible contracts.

It seems a fairly safe general proposition, and one which follows from our observations about the structure of personal work or employment contracts in an earlier chapter,[2] that among the many principles or rules which interrelate the rights and obligations of workers and their employing entities is one to the effect that the employing entity's obligation to remunerate, or the worker's right to remuneration, is, in some sense or another, conditional upon the worker's performance of his or her work obligations under the personal work or employment contract. That generalization covers a very broad spectrum of possibilities; it was observed in the earlier discussion that this might, at one extreme, connote a very tightly specific exchange of remuneration for performance of work measured in precise units of time or output, or that this might, at the opposite extreme, represent an obligation to pay remuneration because the worker had simply performed his or her obligation to maintain the employment relationship and contract according to its terms over a particular period of time. We could refer to this as the *principle of interdependence of remuneration and performance*, as long as we bear in mind that the notion of performance, in that context, is a very broad one, variously defined in specific or diffuse terms.

In whatever way that principle of interdependence is formulated for any given personal work or employment contract, there will be complex issues as to how, precisely, performance is defined, and what are the rules which deal with failures of or deviations from performance as thus defined. We shall see that the doctrines or rules or approaches which have evolved to address those issues have interacted with each other, to produce a set of very intricate legal mechanisms. It is difficult to give a simple clear account

---

[2] See above, 92–98.

of the workings of this set of mechanisms, but some general lines of development can be identified. In general terms, the law of personal work or employment contracts has evolved away from an approach which was based upon two stereotypes of contrasting personal work relationships towards an approach which involves much more finely tuned interpretation or construction of the effects of incomplete or defective contractual performance in particular fact situations.

The two stereotypes which form the starting point for this evolution can be identified by reference to our earlier discussion of the internal structure of personal work or employment contracts, and in particular by reference to the spectrum of structures from relational ones to exchange-based ones. The law concerning performance and breach evolves, historically, around a relational stereotype of salaried employment, and a more exchange-based stereotype of employment for wages. The relational stereotype of salaried employment is characterized by a diffuse or loosely defined set of links between performance and remuneration over relatively long periods of time, such as a year, quarter year, or month. The more exchange-based stereotype of employment for wages, by contrast, is characterized by a specific or tightly defined set of links between performance and remuneration over relatively short periods of time such as a week or a day or an hour. Before what we can usefully regard as the modern period of the law of personal work or employment contracts from about 1965 onwards, the contrast between those two stereotypes was strongly present in employment in practice and heavily influential upon legal analysis. Since then, the force of that contrast has diminished rapidly, and the legal analysis has become more closely responsive to the particular employment context.

A. Entire and Divisible Contracts and Substantial Performance

This shift of approach can be discerned in relation to the first of the doctrines or sets of legal rules which evolved to address issues of performance and breach of personal work or employment contracts, namely the doctrine which distinguishes between entire and divisible obligations or contracts, and which originally seemed to create a rule or presumption in favour of interpretation of obligations or contracts as entire rather than divisible.[3] This doctrine is strongly associated with the early case of *Cutter v Powell*[4] which concerned a sailor, employed as second mate for a voyage from Jamaica to England for the lump sum of 30 guineas payable ten days after the arrival of the ship in Liverpool, who died when the ship was about ten days short

---

[3] It should be noted that this usage of the terminology of 'entire contract' is quite different from that in which it means that all the terms of a contract are contained in a particular document or set of documents, which therefore constitute the 'entire agreement'; an 'entire agreement' clause in that sense was recently construed in *White v Bristol Rugby Ltd* [2002] IRLR 204 (QBD).　　　　　　　　　　　　　　　　　[4] (1795) 6 TR 320.

of home after six weeks of the voyage. It was held that, the contract being an entire one, no part of the agreed remuneration was recoverable by his estate.

The event of death in the course of employment would, in the present-day law of personal work or employment contracts, be regarded and handled as a matter of termination of the contract under the law of termination by frustration or operation of law;[5] but the case remains very important to the understanding of how the law of personal work or employment contracts evolved with regard to the entirety or divisibility of performance and obligations of performance. The decision has historically been regarded as creating a presumption that personal work or employment contracts were to be regarded as entire ones, in the sense that the obligation to remunerate was to be presumed to be dependent upon complete performance of the contract by the worker over the whole period in respect of which remuneration is calculated and contractually payable—in the particular case, the voyage as a whole.

It is unnecessary to specify exactly how such a presumption would have operated because it is highly doubtful whether such a presumption actually existed. It has been convincingly argued[6] that *Cutter v Powell* was a very special case where the outcome reflected a view that this contract was for specially high remuneration because it was made in a tight labour market, so that it would be against public policy to place the risk of non-completion on the employer. Moreover the judges emphasized that their decision was based upon the terms of this particular contract rather than upon general usage.[7] Furthermore, Laurence J expressly contrasted the particular case with 'the common case of a hired servant' said to be

hired with reference to the general understanding upon the subject that the servant shall be entitled to his wages for the time he serves though he do not continue in service during the whole year.[8]

In the original work from which the present work is derived, it was argued[9] that the nineteenth-century case law which could be regarded as supporting a general presumption against apportionment of yearly or quarterly wages[10] is actually better understood as a presumption of forfeiture of unpaid wages upon dismissal for misconduct, which would no longer apply.

By the early to middle years of the twentieth century, a position would seem to have been reached in which there was no presumption of entirety for personal work or employment contracts as a whole, but, instead, a difference of approach to the situation of salaried workers, on the one hand, and workers for wages, on the other. The important case of *Moriarty v*

---

[5] See below, 451.   [6] Stoljar 1956.
[7] Compare Lord Kenyon CJ, 6 TR 320 at 324, Ashurst J 324–325, Laurence J, 326.
[8] Ibid.   [9] See Freedland 1976 at 128–130.
[10] Cases such as *Spain v Arnott* (1817) 2 Stark 256, *Turner v Robinson* (1833) 5 B & Ad 789, *Ridgway v Hungerford Market Co* (1835) 3 Ad & El 171, *Lilley v Elwin* (1848) 11 QB 742.

Regents Garage Co Ltd[11] indicated that, like the annual remuneration of company directors, the monthly remuneration of salaried workers would normally be presumed, as a matter of common law, to be entire by the year in the former case and by the month in the latter case. However, such salaries were regarded as subject to daily apportionment under section 2 of the Apportionment Act 1870[12] though the wages of 'inferior servants' were not regarded as subject to that statutory provision.

By the period at which that case was decided, a rather different approach had evolved towards the divisibility of performance and remuneration in the case of workers for weekly, daily, hourly, or piece-rate wages. For such workers, although they were typically paid at weekly intervals, the courts had become readier to accept that remuneration accrued due as smaller units of performance were completed, that is to say days or hours or piece-rated units of output. That this was the approach at least to piece-rates is evidenced by the important case of *Parkin v South Hetton Coal Co Ltd* (1907),[13] though Darling J implied the survival of an earlier tendency to regard wages as entire by the week or fortnight when he said of the contract of employment of an underground mine-worker who was paid at piece-rates, wages being ascertained and paid at fortnightly intervals:

I do not think he was hired by the week or the fortnight to be paid wages at the end of the week or fortnight calculated for the week or fortnight, as in the case as that of a man hired to drive a cart at £1 per week, who if he drives for a day or two and then goes away has not carried out his contract. I come to the conclusion that this man really was working on piece-work.[14]

Since that period, there would seem to have been, both in the practice of personal work relationships and contracts, and in the approach to the interpretation of them in courts and tribunals, an erosion of the distinction between salaried workers and workers for wages, and an evolution towards arrangements which link remuneration and performance, in ways which are often highly complex, and which cut across the earlier stereotypes. The courts and tribunals seem to be tending towards a general presumption that performance and all kinds of time-related remuneration and benefits are divisible so that such remuneration and benefits accrue due by the day. This has recently taken the form of general application to all contracts of employment of section 2 of the Apportionment Act 1870,[15] but contractual interpretation as a matter of common law would seem to point in the same direction.[16]

---

[11] [1921] 1 KB 423.   [12] See ibid Lush J at 429–430, McCardie J at 444.
[13] (1907) LT 98 (QB), (1907) LT 162 (CA).   [14] (1907) LT 98 at 99.
[15] Compare Scott J in *Sim v Rotherham Metropolitan Borough Council* [1986] ICR 817 at 935.
[16] Thus, in the recent cases of *Thames Water Utilities v Reynolds* [1996] IRLR 186 (EAT) and *Taylor v East Midlands Offender Employment* [2000] IRLR 760 (EAT), the Act was regarded as applying to establish that the quantum of accumulated entitlement to holiday pay on the termination of employment should be based on the notion of a day's pay as 1/365th of the annual salary; and the particular contracts were interpreted to decide whether the worker should be credited with days of holiday pay in respect of weekend days between days of work.

The effect of this evolution is that the doctrine of entire contracts is now unlikely to be successfully invoked to negate accrual due, of remuneration, in daily units. The result is that the doctrine of substantial performance has become, as Scott J indicated in the case of *Sim v Rotherham Metropolitan Borough Council*,[17] largely irrelevant to adjudication about the right to remuneration under personal work or employment contracts. That doctrine mitigates the rigour of the doctrine of entire contracts; it is to the effect that failure of performance cannot be invoked as a reason for withdrawing remuneration in respect of an entire contract or contractual obligation where the contract or obligation has been substantially performed, in the sense that there has been no substantial failure of performance.[18] The doctrine has been significant in relation to those building contracts which are deemed to be lump sum contracts rather than contracts for payment by instalments. It is unlikely to come into play in relation to personal work or employment contracts in so far as the obligations of work and remuneration are regarded as divisible into daily units. To the extent that semi-dependent workers' contracts are more likely to be regarded as lump sum contracts than contracts of employment are, the doctrine of substantial performance may have a more significant role in relation to them. For personal work or employment contracts more generally, other techniques for determining the effects of failure of performance upon entitlement to remuneration have a greater role, and we now turn our attention to another set of such techniques.

B. FINES, FORFEITURES, DAMAGES, AND DEDUCTIONS

The law of personal work or employment contracts seems to be in the course of a transformation from an approach which used to turn on the distinction between salaried workers and workers for wages. The transformation is towards an approach which, in effect, applies a general principle of fair management and performance without that earlier social and economic stratification. This is well demonstrated by the development of rules of interpretation with regard to fines, forfeitures, damages, and deductions. In some contexts, that change of approach has been favourable to employing entities; in others, it has favoured workers. Notions of relative fault and relative merit as between workers and employing entities now seem to override the earlier social and economic stratifications which used to limit or moderate those notions.

At some risk of bold or sweeping generalization, it may be said that, in the law of personal work or employment contracts during the nineteenth century and the first half of the twentieth century, workers for wages were considerably more likely than salaried workers to be regarded as having

[17] [1986] ICR 897 (ChD) at 935.
[18] Compare *Bolton v Mahadeva* [1972] 1 WLR 1009 (CA).

contractual arrangements whereby their remuneration was subject to fines, forfeitures, damages, or deductions in respect of incomplete or defective performance of their work obligations. The general trend of interpretation in this direction no doubt reflected the fact that wage-earning workers, being in a weaker social and economic situation than salaried workers, were more likely as such to be subjected to express contractual arrangements which placed the risk of incomplete or defective performance upon them. Their contracts were more likely to be judged to incorporate trade customs of deduction for defective work, as in the highly significant case of *Sagar v Ridehalgh & Son Ltd*.[19] In this case, not only was a custom of deduction for defective work from weavers' wages in Lancashire recognized as having contractual force, but one at least of the judges in the Court of Appeal seemed willing to regard the employing entity as entitled so to deduct as a matter of common law, that is to say as a result of the inherent effect or characteristic of the personal work or employment contract in question.[20]

The approach which underlies that decision may be contrasted with a very different approach towards salaried employees, such as is illustrated by the decision in *Healey v Société Anonyme Française Rubastic*,[21] where a managing director justifiably dismissed in view of dishonest conduct was held entitled to claim arrears of salary in respect of a period during which he had been concealing that earlier dishonest conduct. Avery J observed that the effect of permitting the doctrine of conditions precedent to negate this claim would be to backdate the dismissal to the time of the original misconduct.[22] The much earlier and very significant decision in *Button v Thompson*[23] had taken a similar approach to the effect of continuing misconduct on the claim to monthly wages of a merchant marine engaged for a voyage of up to twelve months, thus treating this worker as if employed on a salaried basis.

Although it would be unsatisfactory to attempt to reduce a large body of case law and employment practice over a long period of time to simple generalizations, it can be pointed out that, throughout the period under consideration, manual workers for wages also tended to be regarded as being liable to pay *damages* or *fines* for incomplete or defective work. The two notions of damages and fines were closely interconnected under the Master and Servant, or later the Employers and Workmen, legislation under which the magistrates' courts supported and enforced a treatment of breach of contract on the part of manual workers as both civil and criminal offences.[24] This system and this approach were confined to 'servants' or 'workmen', categories which, it has now been shown, were historically *contrasted* with that of the 'employee' under a contract of employment.[25]

---

[19] [1931] 1 Ch 310 (CA).   [20] See ibid Lord Harmsworth MR at 323–326.
[21] [1917] 1 KB 946.   [22] Ibid at 947.   [23] (1869) LR 4 CP 330.
[24] See Freedland 1976 at 136–141; Deakin & Morris 2001 at 22–25.
[25] See Foster 1983 and Deakin 2000.

This replicates the historical wage/salary contrast which underlies and explains much contractual practice and some case law about fines and deductions for incomplete or defective work.

An important aspect of that body of law and practice was that it constituted an apparatus for controlling and sanctioning collective industrial action. Thus there was a well-developed practice of county court actions against individual mine-workers which had this purpose. It gave rise to some case law about the liability of individual workers in damages for their participation in collective stoppages of work. In *National Coal Board v Galley*[26] the Court of Appeal adjudicated upon a claim of this type, where the, by then, nationalized, employing entity for the mining industry sought to hold individual colliery deputies liable for the whole loss of production caused by their collective refusal to work Saturday morning shifts and consequential shutdown of the pits for those shifts. In holding the deputies liable not for the whole loss of output but for the notional cost of employing a personal substitute for each missed Saturday morning shift, the court was, in effect, maintaining a system whereby workers for wages might be fined for industrial action by loss of wages, though not treated as contractually assuming the whole risk of financial loss to the employing entity caused by the industrial action.[27]

The contractual approach or regime which that decision confirmed would almost certainly have been regarded as confined to workers for wages, at that mid-twentieth-century period. In the succeeding period, during the 1960s and 1970s, there seemed to be a very general trend, both in contractual practice and in the law of personal work or employment contracts, towards an upward approximation of the regime of employment, of workers for wages, so that it merged into the regime for salaried workers. The emerging body of employment protection legislation reinforced or even led that trend in various respects. However, in a group of decisions in the 1980s which forms a watershed in the modern development of the law of personal work or employment contracts, the courts seemed to have moved in a very different direction in determining the liability of salaried workers to deduction from remuneration in respect of industrial action. The result has been an extension of the approach, earlier confined to workers for wages, to workers of most or all types.

That extension took place in the context of various occurrences of industrial action on the part of salaried and professional workers which were the subject of litigation in the later 1970s and 1980s. Often, that industrial action consisted of refusal to carry out part of the duties assigned to those workers by the entities which employed them, usually in fact the very

---

[26] [1958] 1 WLR 16.
[27] In this respect the Court of Appeal followed the earlier decision in *Ebbw Vale Steel Iron & Coal Co v Tew* (1935) 1 Law Journal Notes County Court Appeals 284.

assignments which were in dispute. Where employing entities withheld remuneration in respect of such industrial action, there might well be a double issue of whether the worker's refusal of assigned duties was in breach of contract and, if so, with what effect upon the entitlement to remuneration. The landmark case of this kind was that of *Sim v Rotherham Council*.[28] This concerned teachers' refusal to provide cover, that is to say to take classes, for absent colleagues, and the contractual legality of the deductions made by the education authorities from their salaries in respect of those refused duties.

Scott J held that the refusal of duties had been in breach of contract— that is to say, that the contractual duties of these teachers did include providing cover for absent colleagues—and that the deductions which had been made from their remuneration were justifiable, and indeed contractually lawful, as an exercise by the employing entities of their equitable right of set-off of damages for breach of contract from the remuneration paid to these workers. He was of the view that this could perhaps equally have been treated as an exercise of a common law right of abatement which had been, in effect, subsumed into the equitable right of set-off.[29] It was that common law right to abate contractual payments by reference to rights to damages which Lord Harmsworth MR had invoked in obiter dicta in the case of *Sagar v Ridehalgh & Co Ltd*,[30] to which reference was made above.[31]

The result of this development is that personal work or employment contracts generally now appear to be presumed, as a matter of common law (including the law of equity), to confer upon the employing entity the sort of power to impose fines or deductions in respect of deliberate partial refusal to carry out assigned duties which was formerly well recognized in relation to workers for wages but much less clearly established in relation to salaried workers. (We shall revert later to the question whether that presumed power has been restricted by the statutory controls on deductions from wages which were introduced by the Wages Act 1986.[32])

We could regard this presumed power as demonstrating the emergent vision of a principle of fair management and performance, such as has been identified in earlier chapters. Typically of that vision, it confers extensive but controlled discretion upon the management of employing entities. The employment managers are accorded a discretion to withhold remuneration in respect of refusal to carry out assigned duties, which is to be exercised by reference to factors such as the amount of pecuniary loss attributable to the refusal, the wilfulness or contumacy of the refusal, and the proportion which the refused duties bear to the totality of the worker's duties, assessed by time or by any other appropriate measure. The courts have a free-ranging power

---

[28] [1986] ICR 897 (ChD).   [29] Ibid at 940–943.
[30] [1931] 1 Ch 310 at 323–326.   [31] See above, 205.
[32] See below, 209–219.

to substitute their own view of the appropriate deduction for that of the employing entity; they could be regarded as exercising that supervisory power in accordance with a principle of fair management and performance, though they have not clearly articulated the basis of its exercise.

All this is well illustrated by the decisions in the *Sim v Rotherham MBC* case, and in the slightly earlier case of *Royle v Trafford BC*.[33] In the former case, Scott J lightly scrutinized the small deductions which had been made by the various education authorities involved (as this was actually a conjoined trial of four separate cases) and noted that they had been accepted as representing not more than the amount of damages to which the defendants were entitled for the breach of contract committed by the relevant plaintiff.[34] In the latter case, the refusal of duties consisted of refusing to accept an enlargement of the number of pupils the teacher was required to accept into his class. Remuneration was withheld on the basis of the proportion of the time spent teaching non-enlarged classes to the teacher's total required teaching time. Park J decided that this represented an inequitably large deduction, and substituted a much smaller deduction reflecting the ratio of the size of the classes actually taught to the demanded class size. This according of primary discretion to the employing entity but of secondary discretion to the court is of great significance. It forms one part of a set of doctrinal developments in the relationship between remuneration and performance. We now turn our attention to other such developments.

C. EQUITABLE CONTROL UPON PENALTIES

In this subsection we remark upon the significant absence, in the history of the law of personal work or employment contracts, of use of the highly important and relevant control upon penalty provisions exerted by the law of equity, and we draw attention to its recent entry into the field, hitherto only on a very limited scale.

The equitable control upon penalties consists of a doctrine which treats as illegal and unenforceable any contractual provision for liquidated damages which purports to be a genuine pre-estimate of damages in the event of breach or wrongful repudiation but amounts to the imposition of a penalty upon the contract breaker. The control was articulated most clearly in *Dunlop Pneumatic Tyre Co Ltd v New Garage & Motor Co Ltd*[35] in the context of a contract for the sale of tyres from the manufacturer to distributors which stipulated fixed payments to the manufacturer for sales to consumers below the list price which it was at that time lawful for the manufacturer to impose. The stipulation was held to be a legitimate pre-estimating of damages rather than the exacting of an intimidating penalty, according to an approach identified by Hugh Collins as one of 'risk averaging'.[36]

---

[33] [1984] IRLR 184.   [34] [1986] ICR 897 at 936.   [35] [1915] AC 79 (HL).
[36] Collins 1997 at 348.

Given the extent to which personal work or employment contracts have been a prime location for provisions for deductions from remuneration in respect of poor or incomplete performance, and given also the extent to which the language of 'fines' or 'forfeitures' for 'offences' has been used in stipulating for such deductions, it is very striking that this equitable control upon penalties has been so little invoked in relation to those contracts. A recent exception which proves this rule was provided by the decision of the Employment Appeal Tribunal in *Giraud UK Ltd v Smith*,[37] where a provision in a driver's contract of employment that his failure to give the required four weeks' notice of termination of employment would 'result in a deduction from your final payment equivalent to the number of days short' was held to be an illegal and unenforceable penalty provision. It weighed with the court that the employing entity was free to claim greater damages as an alternative to invoking this provision, so this was regarded as a 'heads I win, tails you lose' stipulation, that is to say as one lacking in mutuality. We proceed to consider whether the statutory system of control of deduction from wages now provides a basis for active development of this kind of judicial regulation.

D. The Statutory Control of Deduction from Wages—
   A Trigger for Contractual Development?

The question arises whether the contractual treatment of the relationship between performance and remuneration, as thus far analysed, has been affected or even altered by the introduction in 1986 of a new set of statutory controls on deductions from wages, and by the subsequent case law applying those new statutory provisions. It is arguable that those provisions did give rise to a slightly more critical or rigorous contractual regulation of that relationship than had previously been applied.

In 1986, the Wages Act replaced the still extant Truck Acts 1831 to 1940 with a new and very differently conceived set of provisions for the protection of wages, now contained in Part II of the Employment Rights Act 1996 (ERA). Where the Truck Acts had placed certain significant substantive and inderogable controls upon deductions from the remuneration of certain categories of workers, the Wages Act largely dispensed with those substantive and inderogable controls, except for some special provisions relating to deductions for cash shortages and stock deficiencies in retail employment.[38] Apart from those special provisions, the protective provisions of the Wages Act were of a much more limited and essentially derogable kind, concerned with ensuring that deductions were 'authorized' either by statutory provision or by a written provision of the worker's contract or by the worker's written agreement to the making of the deduction.[39]

---

[37] [2000] IRLR 763 (EAT).   [38] See now ERA, ss 17–22.
[39] See ERA, s 13.

So after 1986 there ceased to be statutory evaluative standards for fines and deductions, such as those imposed by the Truck Act 1896 requiring that the fine or payment by the 'workman' should not exceed the loss which the workman had caused to the employer and should be fair and reasonable in all the circumstances of the case.[40] The new provisions also left workers susceptible, as they had been under the Truck Acts, to withholding of remuneration by employers without the worker's specific agreement, under common law rules or doctrines which operated to reduce the primary obligation to remunerate, and so did not give rise to 'deductions' within the meaning of the Act.[41] Moreover, the framers of the Wages Act were careful not to enable workers to challenge the employer's entitlement to withhold remuneration in respect of industrial action even where that withholding did amount to 'deduction' in the statutory sense.[42]

However, the new statutory scheme, although much more deferential to contractual agreement or ad hoc agreement than the Truck Acts had been, nevertheless turned out to have entitled workers to quite a wide-ranging inquiry into whether their contractual employers had complied with their obligations in respect of remuneration and its relation to performance on the workers' part. That was mainly by reason of the provision that:

Where the total amount of wages paid on any occasion by an employer to a worker employed by him is less than the total amount of the wages properly payable by him to the worker on that occasion (after deductions), the amount of the deficiency shall be treated . . . as a deduction made by the employer from the worker's wages on that occasion.[43]

This provision, probably intended to be purely supplementary to the main requirement of authorization for deductions, in fact created a new statutory claim in respect of underpayment of 'wages properly payable'.

Since the case law has treated any partial or complete non-payment of remuneration as coming within this notion of underpayment, and since the primary standard for the 'proper payability' of wages has been assumed to be a contractual one,[44] the worker may use this provision to invoke, before an employment tribunal, any sense in which the contractual employing entity's provision of remuneration is in less than complete compliance with its contractual obligations. It became clear, from decisions such as that of the Employment Appeal Tribunal in *Bruce v Wiggins Teape (Stationery) Ltd*,[45] that this process might be used successfully to challenge a contractual

[40] See Truck Act 1896, ss 1–2, the subject of a detailed exposition at the moment of their repeal in *Bristow v City Petroleum Ltd* [1988] ICR 165 (HL).

[41] Compare Deakin 1992 at 856.

[42] See the provision now contained in ERA, s 13(5) which disapplies s 13 from deductions on account of the worker's having taken part in a strike or other industrial action.

[43] Now ERA 1996, s 13(3).

[44] All this is implicit in the reasoning of the House of Lords in *Delaney v Staples* [1992] ICR 483, the leading case on this provision.   [45] [1994] IRLR 536.

employing entity's unilateral reduction of the rate of remuneration as being not in compliance with the personal work or employment contract.

The existence of this particular facility to claim for unauthorized deduction from wages is thus giving rise to a body of case law which addresses, in this very concrete form, the larger question of what implied freedom the contractual employing entity has to modify those terms and conditions of employment or employment arrangements which determine or affect the worker's remuneration. It seemed from the *Bruce v Wiggins Teape* case as if the Employment Appeal Tribunal was in the course of recognizing a rather robust notion of the worker's implied entitlement to resist unilateral variation of terms and conditions or arrangements having the effect of reducing remuneration. Later case law has been less encouraging in this respect. In *Hussman Manufacturing Ltd v Weir*,[46] the Appeal Tribunal was very ready to treat the employing entity as having an implied prerogative to alter the worker's pattern of shift working, and unwilling to view that prerogative as limited by the worker's claim to stability of earnings—the point being that the alteration of work pattern deprived the worker of a bonus previously received for working unsocial hours.

It may well be that the court in that case was taking an unduly limited view of the impact of the employing entity's implied obligation of mutual trust and confidence. The same tendency was evidenced in the decision of the Court of Appeal in the slightly unusual but significant case of *New Century Cleaning Co Ltd v Church*,[47] which concerned window-cleaners employed in teams.[48] The issue was whether the employing entity had made an unauthorized deduction from wages by imposing a 10 per cent reduction on the sums allocated to the teams for jobs of work assigned to the whole team, which were then shared out by the team leader in order to calculate the wages of each worker in the team. The Court of Appeal held by a majority that the worker had no claim to treat this as an unauthorized deduction from 'wages properly payable', because the worker's claim to wages, derived from the previously prevailing job rates, had never amounted to a concrete entitlement to an ascertained amount of remuneration.

This probably amounted to the conclusion that the worker had no contractual right to stability of the rate of remuneration. It may be that the worker would have been regarded as having that protection if it had not been for the intervening discretionary share-out between the members of the team. However, even the dissenting judge, Sedley LJ, who was prepared to regard the worker as having suffered a deduction from the 'wages properly payable' to him, did not see that claim as based upon a *contractual* entitlement to calculation of wages on the basis of the full, unreduced, rates for the jobs allocated to the teams as a whole. He felt that, if account was taken not just of the contract alone but of the payment system in a larger sense, it

---

[46] [1998] IRLR 288.   [47] [2000] IRLR 27.   [48] See Freedland 1999b.

could be said that the worker had suffered a reduction in and therefore a deduction from his agreed wages.[49]

In the view of the present author, that conclusion could have been, and would more satisfactorily have been, regarded as identifying a contractually based entitlement on the part of the claimant. The contractual employing entity could have been regarded as having given an implied contractual undertaking to maintain the job prices at their full existing rates, or some such requirement could have been derived from the employing entity's implied obligation of trust and confidence. This would have been preferable to resorting to some ill-defined para-contractual notion of 'wages properly payable'. If that conclusion was judged appropriate, the conceptual apparatus of the personal work or employment contract could easily have sustained it. That view of the potential for such constructive contractual interpretation is supported by recent case law developments in the general treatment of the relationship between remuneration and performance and breach to which we now turn our attention.

SECTION 2: PERFORMANCE, WORK, AND SERVICE

In order to identify and understand the doctrinal developments which started to emerge in the preceding section, we have to investigate even more deeply the way in which the relationship between performance and remuneration is envisaged in the law of personal work or employment contracts. This involves a further development of a discussion about the structure of personal work or employment contracts upon which we embarked in an earlier chapter. The essential point is that the law of personal work or employment contracts recognizes not one but many ways of interrelating performance and remuneration, and attributes different models of that relationship according to the context in which that relationship is being ascertained. The main key to that highly complex legal relationship is the realization that there are a number of conceptually different ways of understanding what constitutes sufficient performance of the worker's obligations under the personal work or employment contract to create the entitlement to remuneration. We shall first consider this in the context of payment during absence due to sickness, and then in the very different context of payment during (partial) industrial action on the part of the worker.

A. PERFORMANCE AND REMUNERATION DURING SICKNESS

It very frequently used to occur, and still in the post-1960s era of employment law sometimes occurs, that the express terms of personal work or employment contracts leave it quite unclear whether or how far a worker is

---

[49] [2000] IRLR 27 at 31.

entitled to a continuation of remuneration during absence due to sickness or incapacity. The post-1960s era is different from the previous era to the extent that, since 1963, most employees under contracts of employment have a statutory entitlement to particulars of their terms and conditions of employment as to sick pay.[50] Moreover, since 1982 employees under contracts of employment have had an entitlement to statutory sick pay from their employing entities in respect of short-term sickness absence, that entitlement being the subject of a detailed and precise statutory specification.[51]

Before that development of statutory sick pay, and especially before the imposition of the obligation to particularize sick pay, it was, therefore, often necessary for personal work or employment contracts to be interpreted or construed as to their implicit treatment of the issue of security of income during absence due to sickness. This interpretation or analysis could take and has taken various different forms, and hence is considered at a number of different stages in the course of the present work. It could be regarded as a question of the structure of the personal work or employment contract, or of its implied terms, or it could be considered as a question of whether the personal work or employment contract is suspended during absence due to sickness, or, if the absence is a prolonged one, terminated by frustration as a result of it.

However, probably the most interesting and revealing of all the conceptual forms which the analysis of payment during sickness has taken is that of a discussion of the relationship between remuneration and performance. Much of the case law about payment during sickness addresses that issue not in terms of whether there is special implicit provision for sick pay, but rather in terms of whether the normal entitlement to remuneration continues during absence due to sickness. That case law may have been largely displaced by the introduction of statutory sick pay as the default entitlement for employees under contracts of employment, but it still tells us an immense amount about how the relationship between performance and remuneration has been understood or fashioned by the law of personal work or employment contracts.

This older case law about payment during absence due to sickness[52] is so particularly informative because it involves the formulation of a notion of what constitutes sufficient performance of the worker's obligations under the personal work or employment contract to enable the worker to claim contractual remuneration. This is not to say that there is or could satisfactorily be a simple uniform notion of remuneration-entitling performance which pervades all personal work or employment contracts. That is far from being the case, if only because employing entities can and do create, agree,

---

[50] Currently contained in ERA 1996, s 1(4)(d)(ii).

[51] See now Social Security Contributions and Benefits Act 1992, Part XI and Regulations thereunder.

[52] This older case law is fully described in the original work—see Freedland 1976 at 108–114—and is analysed further below, 216–218.

or impose immensely complex and highly crafted remuneration and benefit provisions. Indeed, it may be argued that the law of personal work or
employment contracts has failed fully to recognize or respond to the complexities of the remuneration and benefit systems which are encountered in
practice. But, even if it has not admitted to the full intricacies of contractual practice, the law of personal work or employment contracts has not
envisaged a single, simple relationship between remuneration and performance. Instead, it has evolved its own approach to that relationship with its
own intricacies and technicalities.

Those legal intricacies have come about, as is often the case, in the
course of development of contractual remedies. In this case, they have
come about in order to answer the question, what does a worker have to
plead or prove in order to make good a contractual action for remuneration? There is, in a real sense, a body of remedial law which addresses that
question, and which constitutes legal doctrine about remuneration-
entitling performance. The key to understanding this body of remedial law
consists in the contrast between 'work' and 'readiness and willingness
to work'. The notion of readiness and willingness to perform contractual
obligations comes about, or comes into play, as an alternative to actual
performance, upon the basis of which a party to a contract may in certain
circumstances claim to have satisfied the conditions for enforcing the obligations of the other party where those latter obligations are contingent upon
the performance of correlative obligations by the former party.

So readiness and willingness to perform represents a notion of *constructive*
performance, that is to say something which is deemed to amount to performance in certain circumstances. The basic circumstance in which that will
take place is that in which the latter party has prevented the former party
from actually performing his, her, or its obligations; it is a notion of constructive performance which ensures that one party cannot defeat the other's
contractual claims by obstruction. In the employment context, it may mean
that the employing entity cannot prevent the worker from acquiring an entitlement to remuneration simply by wrongfully preventing the worker from
working (though there is a difficult question whether the entitlement is
thereby reduced to one of damages rather than remuneration as such).

In the context of personal work or employment contracts, this doctrine
of constructive performance, originally a rule or doctrine of the law of
pleadings or remedies, has come to assume a central substantive importance in shaping, at a profound level, the way that the relationship between
remuneration and performance is understood and interpreted. It means
that the right to remuneration can be regarded as tied to or conditional
upon either 'work' or 'readiness and willingness to work'. A reverse formation occurs from the legal processing of claims arising from the personal
work or employment contract back into the analysis of the personal work
or employment contract itself. We come to envisage personal work or

employment contracts in which workers are paid either for 'working' or for 'being ready and willing to work'. This is in one sense a highly artificial construct, almost a legal fiction; the vocabulary of 'readiness and willingness to work' is not to be found in the actual terms and conditions of employment under which workers are employed.

However, the reasons why this particular legal construct is so well accepted and so influential in the law of personal work or employment contracts, despite its apparent artificiality, are highly interesting. It gives tribunals and courts considerable interpretative latitude in construing personal work or employment contracts and in adjudicating upon the circumstances in which claims to remuneration will be regarded as valid ones. But this is not an interpretative discretion claimed and asserted in a void, or perversely against the facts. It arises within a space which is created by the complexity, the diversity, and the incompleteness of the arrangements which are made in practice for the interrelating of work and remuneration. A worker would not often be able to say, convincingly, that he or she is paid for being ready and willing to work; but he or she would often be able to say that it is not precisely clear what is his or her entitlement to remuneration or benefits in the circumstances which have arisen, and which have in some way disrupted the ordinary performance of his or her work obligations.

In fact, many of those inherent uncertainties can be traced back to the varieties in the structure of personal work or employment contracts which we identified in Chapter two, and in particular to the broad contrast between diffuse relational structures and tight exchange-based structures. The contrast between performance as 'actual work' and performance as 'readiness and willingness to work' can be and frequently has been used to capture and express that structural contrast. In tight exchange-based structures, remuneration is seen as conditional upon 'actual work', while, in looser relational structures, remuneration is regarded as conditional upon 'readiness and willingness to work'. This equation is not absolutely precise, nor are any of the elements which make it up; but it is nevertheless highly persuasive and influential.

That persuasiveness and influence is enhanced by the fact that it roughly matches up with the historical distinction between salaried workers and workers for wages. It was possible to regard the latter category as remunerated for 'actual work' and the former category as remunerated for 'readiness and willingness to work'. The effect of making this set of equations has been, conceptually and practically speaking, less than totally coherent or satisfactory. Ultimately, it produces a confusion as to whether 'readiness and willingness to work' represents, on the one hand, a notion of *constructive* performance, or, on the other hand, a notion of *actual* performance, albeit of a diffuse, loosely conceived, kind. Moreover, it is a concept which is open to quite a large degree of interpretative manipulation, as becomes apparent when we consider the different contexts in which it has been invoked.

The first such context to be considered here is that of remuneration during absence due to sickness. In the decision which is really the foundation of common law thinking in this area, that of *Cuckson v Stones*,[53] the notion of readiness and willingness to work was used to justify the conclusion that remuneration continued to be payable during absence due to sickness in the case of a person employed for a fixed term of ten years as a master brewer responsible for the management of a brewery. The ruling was that:

> Looking to the nature of the contract sued upon in this action, we think that want of ability to serve for a week would not of necessity be an answer to a claim for a week's wages, *if in truth the plaintiff was ready and willing to serve had he been able to do so*, and was only prevented from serving during the week by the visitation of God, the contract to serve never having been determined.[54]

This involves an idea of constructive performance in a double sense, firstly in treating readiness and willingness to perform as the functional equivalent of actual performance, and secondly in treating the worker as ready and willing to perform though he was not able to work.

The later treatment of the ratio of that case as if it were applicable to all contracts of employment caused the common law concerning payment during sickness to become remote from the practice of employment in this respect. Schwarzer argued, in a learned article upon remuneration during sickness,[55] that the decision represents a judicial reaction to the pressing social problem of the impact of sickness upon the wage earner, and a limited encouragement of paternalism on the part of the employer—a harking back to an earlier period in which the judges had at times approached the relationship of master and servant as one in which the servant was part of the master's household, and as such was entitled to his protection in sickness and in health.[56] But this view neglects the evidence of the judgment of the court in the decision itself; for the court was at pains to stress that this was 'an agreement of a very peculiar nature',[57] and the peculiarity consisted in the fact that the employee was a senior employee entitled to a particular security of tenure, and was able, moreover, to discharge a part of his managerial and organizational functions from the distance of his sickbed.

This was a case far removed from that of the manual industrial employee, who would have been most unlikely to succeed in such a claim at that date. For a long time, the doctrine in the case was applied only to employees of a comparable seniority and occupational level. Thus, the rule was applied in 1878 to a mercantile clerk employed at a salary of £120 per annum[58]

---

[53] (1858) 1 E & E 248.   [54] Ibid at 256 per Lord Campbell CJ (emphasis added).

[55] Schwarzer, 'Wages during Temporary Disability-Partial Impossibility in Employment Contracts' (1952) 5 Stanford LR 30—republished in (1952) 8 Industrial Law Review.

[56] Schwarzer 1952 at 33–36.   [57] E & E 248 at 256 (Lord Campbell CJ).

[58] *K v Raschen* (1878) 38 LT 38. It was held that the employee was not disentitled to continuance of remuneration by reason of the attributability of his illness (VD) to his own conduct, because that conduct had occurred before he entered into the employment and was not connected with the employment.

and in 1902 to an executive employed in the business of a piano manufacturer, the employee being also the holder of a share in the business as a condition of his obtaining the employment.[59] But in 1939, the rule was applied in *Marrison v Bell*[60] to a shop assistant, employed at a weekly wage, and the general proposition was asserted that:

[U]nder a contract of service, irrespective of the question of the length of notice provided by that contract, wages continue through sickness and incapacity from sickness to do the work contracted for until the contract is terminated by a notice by the employer in accordance with the terms of the contract.[61]

This was an overgeneralization in terms of the employment practice of the period. Lord Denning (as he was later to become) published a casenote in the Law Quarterly Review proposing a method whereby the rule could be harmonized with the social distinctions between different types of employment.[62] He suggested that the question of whether remuneration was payable for readiness and willingness to work if of ability to do so, or whether, by contrast, wages were payable only for actual work, must depend upon the type of employment concerned. Hence, he said, payment during sickness was progressively less likely as one went from cases of service agreements for terms of years, to other cases of payment by the month or at longer intervals, to payment calculated by the week, to payment calculated by the day, and finally to piece-rate wages.[63]

This casenote perfectly captures the idea that the common law of personal work or employment contracts had, from the time of *Cuckson v Stones* onwards, really recognized two different kinds of relationship between remuneration and performance, and had articulated them in terms of the difference between remuneration for 'actual work' and for 'readiness and willingness' to work. In the following key passage, he set out an idea of how this could be rationalized in terms of the general common law of contracts:

In some cases the consideration for wages is *actual performance* of the work, so that if it is not performed, the servant is entitled to nothing. In other cases the consideration for work is *faithful service* which a man performs when in health by doing his work and when sick by trying to get well so as to do his work, in which case he is entitled to wages both when he is at work and when he is sick.[64]

We shall see in the course of this chapter that Lord Denning's conceptual system was to be profoundly influential in the development of the legal understanding of the relationship between performance and remuneration in other areas; but his idea of an essentially dual system did not take root in the area of payment during sickness. Here, the conceptual and practical

---

[59] *Warren v Whittingham* (1902) 18 TLR 508.   [60] [1939] 2 KB 187.
[61] See ibid, Scott LJ at 198.
[62] In a note on the decision in *Marrison v Bell* (above) at (1939) 55 LQR 353.
[63] Ibid at 354–355.   [64] Ibid at 354 (emphasis added).

development proceeded along different lines which will be briefly described.

For a time, Lord Denning's dual system was adopted as a way of deflecting a spate of actions for arrears of payment during sickness brought by manual employees. In *O'Grady v M Saper Ltd*,[65] the Court of Appeal denied that there was any such general rule in favour of continuation of remuneration during sickness as had been suggested in *Marrison v Bell*; instead, MacKinnon LJ formulated the following test:

What were the terms of the employment? Were they an agreement that the man should be paid when ready and willing to work, or that he should only be paid when he was actually working?[66]

He concluded 'without hesitation' that the worker in question, who received weekly wages, was employed on the latter basis.[67]

However, in *Orman v Saville Sportswear Ltd* (1960),[68] Pilcher J ruled that the default position for contracts of employment generally was that:

Where the written terms of the contract of employment are silent as to what is to happen in regard to the employee's rights to be paid whilst he is absent from work due to sickness, the employer remains liable to continue paying so long as the contract is not determined by proper notice, except where a condition to the contrary can properly be inferred from all the facts and the evidence in the case.[69]

This ruling probably reflected the partial dissolution, by that period, of the sharp distinction between salaried workers and workers for wages; thus the worker in question was a production manager in a factory employed on what was described as a 'weekly salary' (plus a piece-rate bonus based on the output of the factory, the continuation of which during sickness absence was the particular issue in dispute). Previously, weekly remuneration would generally have been described as wages rather than salary.

The reality of that case, and of the subsequent development of the law concerning remuneration during absence due to sickness, was that this issue could not satisfactorily be approached as a general question of whether ordinary remuneration continued during sickness, but rather as a particular question of whether and how much special provision for maintenance of income during sickness was to be read into the personal work or employment contract. As will be shown in a later chapter,[70] both case law and statute law shaped the law in that form from the 1960s onwards. This meant that the contrast between 'actual work' and 'readiness and willingness to work' has become much less central to the ascertainment of entitlement to sick pay. However, the way that these two concepts are handled has remained crucial to the question of continuation of remuneration during industrial action, to which we now turn our attention.

---

[65] [1940] 2 KB 469.   [66] Ibid at 473.   [67] Ibid at 474.
[68] [1960] 1 WLR 1055 (QBD).   [69] Ibid at 1065.   [70] See below, 482–484.

B. PERFORMANCE, REMUNERATION, AND INDUSTRIAL ACTION

In the previous subsection, we observed how the deployment of the two concepts of 'actual work' and 'readiness and willingness to work' created an interpretative space within which different answers could be assigned to questions about the entitlement to remuneration during absence due to sickness—within which, therefore, different relationships could be sketched out between remuneration and performance of work obligations. We concluded with the observation that entitlement to sick pay has largely ceased to be worked out within that interpretative space. However, in the period between 1970 and 1990, a number of crucial decisions were taken about the effect of partial industrial action upon entitlement to remuneration which were located precisely within that interpretative space, and which considerably affected the way in which the relationship between performance and remuneration was understood in the law of personal work or employment contracts.

In order to make it clear what the issues were in these decisions, we need to identify a concept of 'partial industrial action', and also to explain what the approach to such industrial action seems to have been before these decisions were taken. It will be helpful to adopt a working definition of 'partial industrial action' which contrasts such industrial action to total or outright industrial action, known as 'strike action'. We may think of strike action as complete withdrawal of labour or outright refusal to work, concerted between a group of workers, in respect of a period of time which is a unit of calculation of remuneration. So workers paid hourly rates of remuneration take strike action by concertedly refusing to work for particular hours. Partial industrial action occurs, by contrast, where workers refuse to work for part of such a period of time, or refuse to carry out the part of the duties assigned to them for such a period of time.

During the long historical period in which industrial action, whether total or partial, was largely confined to manual industrial workers, the practical and legal treatment of the effect of such industrial action seems to have been along the following lines. There was some doubt whether such industrial action was necessarily in breach of the personal work or employment contract, but in any event total industrial action disentitled workers to remuneration during the calculation periods in question, whether those were hours or days or weeks. Partial industrial action, if it was in breach of the personal work or employment contract, entitled the employing entity to refuse to allow the workers in question to work, and therefore to refuse remuneration. However, if workers were allowed to continue to work despite their partial industrial action, that action probably did not disentitle workers from their normal remuneration during the calculation periods in question, except to the extent that the employing entity could make deductions from remuneration reflecting the degree of incompleteness (which could be but were not necessarily conceived of as damages for breach of contract).

Two decisions in the modern period manifested a tendency towards a strict view of the entitlement of such workers to remuneration during partial industrial action. They both concerned the form of partial industrial action known as 'working to rule' which consists of a deliberately uncooperative or overzealous application of rules of working such as to disrupt the operation of the activity of the employing entity. It is very well known how, in *Secretary of State for Employment v ASLEF (No 2)*,[71] such 'working to rule' was held to be in breach of the contracts of employment of the workers in question. Less widely remarked is the fact that Lord Denning MR also maintained that this breach of contract also disentitled the workers to remuneration while they were working to rule:

I ask: Is a man to be entitled to wages for his work when he, with others, is doing his best to make it useless? Surely not. Wages are to be paid for services rendered, not for producing deliberate chaos. The breach goes to the whole of the consideration...[72]

That position, though not necessary to the decision, has generally been regarded as an intrinsic part of the doctrine emerging from the case; it is, in fact, a very important step beyond the analysis of the work-to-rule as breach of contract, crucial as that is in itself.

Another very significant step in the same direction was taken in the rather esoteric but actually very important decision in the case of *Henthorn and Taylor v Central Electricity Generating Board*.[73] The case concerned manual workers at a power station who engaged in an unofficial (that is to say, not trade union endorsed) 'work-to-rule' consisting of refusal to undertake overtime or to be transferred to different duties, which refusal they regarded as within their contracts of employment, but the employing entity regarded as in breach of those contracts. During this 'work-to-rule' the workers attended for work; it is unclear whether they were permitted to carry out actual work.[74] Remuneration was withheld in respect of the period in which the 'work-to-rule' was taking place; two workers sued to recover remuneration.

The issue on appeal was what burden of proof lay on each party. The Court of Appeal held that the workers bore the burden of proving that they were 'ready and willing to work'. This meant they would have to prove that their work to rule did not involve any breach of contract. In the light of the *ASLEF* decision, that was clearly going to be a heavy burden. The notion of 'readiness and willingness to work' was effectively transformed, in the context of partial industrial action, from being a doctrine of constructive performance entitling some workers to claim remuneration in circumstances where full actual performance was not possible, its function in the case of absence due to sickness. It became an exacting requirement that workers,

---

[71] [1972] ICR 19 (CA).   [72] Ibid at 56.   [73] [1980] ICR 361 (CA).
[74] It appears from the statements of claim that one claimant was allowed to work but that the other was not. The Court of Appeal did not distinguish between those two situations.

in order to be entitled to remuneration, must not be, and must be able to show that they are not, maintaining a refusal of assigned duties in breach of contract.

All this became more problematical in the 1980s when the practice of taking industrial action spread so that it more often extended to non-manual, sometimes 'professional' workers employed on monthly or yearly salaries, that is to say with much longer calculation periods for their remuneration. We have previously observed how the power of deduction from the remuneration of such workers in respect of partial industrial action was recognized or confirmed in the *Royle* and *Sim* cases.[75] Significant further steps in the same conceptual and practical direction were taken by the House of Lords in the leading case of *Miles v Wakefield MDC*.[76] The issue was whether the local authority under which a superintendent registrar of births, marriages and deaths held office was entitled to make deductions from his remuneration, in respect of his refusal, by way of partial industrial action, to conduct weddings on Saturdays. It was argued unsuccessfully on behalf of the registrar that he held an office the incidents of which were unlike those of a contract of employment, and that, even if he was employed under a contract of employment or on analogous terms, his remuneration was not susceptible to deductions in respect of his refusal of Saturday morning duties.

All the Law Lords who decided the case were agreed that the registrar held an office the incidents of which were analogous with the employment of a salaried employee, and that accordingly his right to remuneration was dependent upon his carrying out actual work or being ready and willing to work, and could not be regarded as dependent merely upon his continuing in office for the period in question. They also all, in effect, adopted the strict approach to the proof of actual work or readiness and willingness to work which had been taken in the *Henthorn and Taylor* case. They all, in effect, agreed with a proposition articulated most clearly by Lord Oliver that the registrar could not claim remuneration for Saturday mornings because he had not worked or been ready and willing to work on Saturday mornings:

[W]here the employee declines to work at all for a particular period—and...this case has to be approached on the basis that the plaintiff was simply withholding his services on Saturdays—then, subject to the question whether the wages or salary are apportionable on a periodic basis, I can see no ground upon which the employee who declines to perform that condition upon which payment depends can successfully sue for the remuneration which is dependent upon its performance.[77]

That was enough to decide the case, because the employing entity was not claiming to withhold the whole monthly remuneration, just the part of it attributable to Saturday mornings, thus conceding that the salary was

[75] See above 207–208.   [76] [1987] ICR 368.   [77] Ibid at 400.

apportionable on a daily or half-daily basis. However, Lords Brightman and Templeman seemed willing to pursue this logic more fully. They seem to have taken the view that on these facts, and *a fortiori* had this been employment under a contract of employment, the claimant was to be regarded as not having performed the obligations of his office such as to entitle him to remuneration *for the whole monthly payment period* in question. Their view seems to have been that in such circumstances a worker has no *contractual* claim for remuneration for the time actually worked, but only, at best, a *quantum meruit* claim, therefore a restitutionary claim, for the amount and value of the reduced work performed and accepted.[78]

It has not, in the view of the present writer, since been resolved whether, when reduced or qualified working is deemed to have been accepted by the employing entity, the claim for remuneration which results is to be regarded as being apportioned contractual remuneration or as *quantum meruit* payment; in the view of this writer, the former view is within the legitimate scope of contractual construction, and would be an appropriate application of a broad principle of fair management and performance. Be that as it may, in other respects the strict logic of the *Henthorn and Taylor* case and of *Miles v Wakefield MDC* has since been vigorously applied in such a way as to bring the remuneration/performance relationship for salaried workers into line with that which has long been applied to workers for hourly wages.

Thus in *Wiluszynski v Tower Hamlets LBC*,[79] where a salaried estate officer employed by a local authority had taken part in partial industrial action by refusing to carrying out a particular small part of his contractual duties, namely the answering of queries from councillors, it was held that the council was entitled to withhold the whole remuneration for the period of days during which the estate officer had engaged in that refusal, although he had carried out his other duties during those days. This was on the basis that the worker, by refusing that duty, had shown himself unwilling to perform his work obligations as a whole, and had accordingly given the employing entity an option whether to accept or reject reduced work; furthermore, the employing entity had effectively rejected reduced work as contractual work by continually reminding the employee that, if he chose to continue with reduced work, he was doing so on a voluntary rather than a contractual basis, and by refraining from requesting or directing that work.

Perhaps, however, the most exacting application of this logic was to be reserved for the case of *British Telecommunications plc v Ticehurst*,[80] which concerned members of the managerial staff of BT who had engaged in partial industrial action consisting of occasional days or half days of strike action, and a 'withdrawal of goodwill', akin to a 'work-to-rule'. It was held that these workers could properly be excluded from work, and were not entitled to

---

[78] [1987] ICR 368 at 383 (Lord Brightman), 391–392 (Lord Templeman).
[79] [1989] ICR 493 (CA).   [80] [1992] ICR 383 (CA).

remuneration while so excluded, on the ground of their refusal to enter into a positive undertaking to abandon their partial industrial action and work in accordance with the terms of their contracts of employment. This strict application of the notion of 'readiness and willingness' to work perfectly demonstrates the way in which it has come to amount to a requirement, at least upon senior or managerial workers, to abjure prospective industrial action and profess positive loyalty to the interests of the employing enterprise over a period of time. That seems to be the prevailing version, in the context of partial industrial action, of the principle of fair management and performance against which, we assert, the legal treatment of the relationship between remuneration and performance can usefully be assessed. We turn to consider other actual or possible developments in that legal discourse.

C. TOWARDS A PRINCIPLE OF FAIR MANAGEMENT AND PERFORMANCE WITH REGARD TO REMUNERATION AND BENEFITS

While these various evolutions take place in the particular doctrines relating to fines, deductions, damages, apportionment, and readiness and willingness to perform, the whole treatment of the relationship between performance, remuneration, and breach of contract is at the same time undergoing a process of more fundamental and general change. This seems to amount to a progression towards the sort of principle of fair management and performance for which we argued in the previous chapter. In fact, the treatment of that relationship could be regarded as the area in which that principle has developed most fully. In this subsection, we suggest that the case law supports the notion that there is a particular principle of fair management and performance with regard to remuneration and benefits.

This development is manifested in several recent decisions where employees have successfully claimed damages for breach of their employing entity's obligations relating, in some sense, to their remuneration and benefits (using those terms in a wide inclusive sense). These were the cases of *Clark v BET plc*,[81] *Clark v Nomura Ltd*,[82] *Transco plc v O'Brien*,[83] and *Mallone v BPB Industries plc*.[84] It will be useful to consider the implications of each of these decisions in turn. In each case, the claimant was able to invoke an implied obligation of the contractual employing entity to comply with a standard of behaviour involving respect for the interests and expectations of the worker, such as that of mutual trust and confidence. The significance of the cases for the present purpose lies in the way that these standards of behaviour were formulated, and were held to apply to the employing entity's decisions concerning the allocation of remuneration to the worker. It is not without importance that the first two cases concerned employees with a central and very high-status role within the organizations by which

---

[81] [1997] IRLR 348 (QBD).   [82] [2000] IRLR 766 (QBD).
[83] [2002] ICR 721 (CA).   [84] [2002] ICR 1045 (CA).

they were employed, and that the disputes related to extremely large claims in respect of the remuneration to which they alleged that they were entitled.

In each of these cases, we can observe a mounting willingness on the part of the courts to recognize a novel kind of contractual entitlement on the part of the employees concerned. This amounts to an obligation on the part of their contractual employing entities to exercise powers or discretions, with regard to their remuneration and its relation to their performance, in such a way as to avoid arbitrary disregard of reasonable expectations as to how that relation will operate. The case of *Clark v BET* concerned the chief executive and managing director of the BET company, who was dismissed, following a takeover of that company, without the three years' notice to which he was entitled. The case concerned the amount of damages for wrongful dismissal to which he was entitled. Two key questions were how far the damages should reflect the prospect that the employee would, firstly, have received salary increases under a contractual provision for the employee's salary to be 'reviewed annually and increased by such amount if any as the board shall in its absolute discretion decide', and would, secondly, have received bonuses under a contractual provision for the employee to 'participate in a bonus arrangement providing a maximum of 60 per cent basic salary in any year'.

A very similar set of issues had arisen thirty years previously in the case of *Lavarack v Woods of Colchester Ltd*,[85] which concerned the wrongful dismissal of the claimant from his employment as the European sales manager of the defendant company at a salary of 'not less than £4,000 per annum' plus 'such bonus (if any) as the directors . . . shall from time to time determine'. The wrongful dismissal had deprived the claimant of over two years of promised employment. During that time, employees of the company in similar positions had continued to receive bonuses until the bonus had been commuted into a salary increase of £1,000 per year. The issue was whether the damages should reflect the expectation of bonus or salary increase. The majority of the Court of Appeal held that they should not, because the claimant's loss must be assessed on the assumption that the company would do no more than comply with its strict legal obligations, and the payment of a bonus or salary increase was not within those obligations. Lord Denning dissented, on the basis that the employee was entitled to be compensated for the full amount of the emoluments which he would have earned but for the wrongful dismissal, and that it had been found as a fact that he would have received that amount of salary increase.

By contrast with the position of the majority of the court in that case, the approach of Timothy Walker J in the *Clark v BET* case displayed a much greater willingness to view the factual prediction that the claimant employee would have enjoyed salary increases and bonus payments as

[85] [1967] 1 QB 278 (CA).

grounded in contractual obligations on the part of the defendant company. As to salary increases, he judged that:

there was here a contractual obligation on BET to provide, and a contractual right in Mr Clark to receive, an annual upward adjustment in salary. It is only the amount (if any) that is in the absolute discretion of the board.[86]

Moreover, he decided that there was a further obligation on the board, in assessing the amount, to consider figures from a comparative group of companies, and that there would be a breach of contract 'if the board had *capriciously or in bad faith* exercised its discretion so as to determine the increase at nil and therefore to pay no increase at all'.[87] This sustained the view that it should be assumed that the claimant would have received salary increases of 10 per cent per year. The reasoning concerning the bonus was similar. It was decided that the claimant had the right to participate in a bonus scheme, and, in an even more significant step, that the scheme must be such that the maximum bonus could in practice be achieved because 'it would defeat the purpose of the contract to set targets which were incapable of performance'.[88] This gave rise to an assessment of bonus as 50 per cent of salary during the period under consideration.

This concretization of the implicit content of the contract by reference to the underlying purpose, or supposedly shared reasonable assumptions of the parties about how the contract is to work, was taken further in the *Clark v Nomura* case. The issue in that case was whether and how far the claimant, a senior proprietary trader in equities employed by the defendant finance house, was entitled to damages for breach of contract in that the defendant company had refused to allocate him any bonus during the year in which he was dismissed. The evidence as to the terms of the claimant's employment was conflicting as to how far the letter of appointment had been overridden by subsequent oral agreement, but it was found that the claimant was entitled to participate in 'a discretionary bonus scheme which is not guaranteed in any way and is dependent upon individual performance'. Burton J decided that the employing company had acted in breach of contract in not paying a bonus, and awarded damages of £1.35 m, which reflected the levels of annual bonus which the claimant had hitherto received and the profits which he had made for the company during the year concerned.

The precise basis for this finding of breach of contract and for the way of assessing the damages is extremely interesting. Burton J held that the defendant company had 'two contractual obligations, to assess the bonus dependent upon individual performance by the claimant, and not to do so irrationally or perversely (or capriciously)'.[89] Properly understood, these

---

[86] [1997] IRLR 348 at 349.   [87] Ibid (emphasis added).   [88] Ibid at 350.
[89] [2000] IRLR 766 at 775.

two contractual obligations are completely interdependent. In combination with each other, they perfectly illustrate the way in which the courts now seem willing to recognize an obligation upon the contractual employing entity to exercise its powers in a non-arbitrary way with regard to the reasonable expectations of the parties as to how the contractual relationship will operate.

As with all assessments of reasonable or legitimate expectations, the application of this obligation to the history of the contractual relationship in question involved a partly descriptive and a partly normative process of adjudication. That is to say, it required the court both to form a picture of the expectations which had been formed and to articulate and apply rules or principles to decide which of those expectations were reasonable ones. The descriptive, expectation-finding, approach revealed two competing outlooks upon this employment relationship. The employee claimed that his entitlement to be assessed and awarded a bonus upon his individual performance substantially entitled him to a commission upon the profits of the funds which he identifiably managed for the company. This tended towards a picture of the relationship as a franchise within the company.

The employing company, on the other hand, asserted that the assessment of the employee's individual performance entitled it to evaluate the extent of his commitment to its corporate goals and culture, and, in that connection, to consider the employee's 'longevity', that is to say to reward the employee for prospective continuing commitment and to penalize him for the absence of that commitment. The decision was made on the basis of a normative view that the employing entity could not be allowed to make abusive use of a criterion of assessment which lent itself to abuse because the employing entity could control or even manipulate the way in which it applied. The longevity criterion was strongly open to that objection. The employing entity could discriminate arbitrarily between employees by deciding that one employee, whose performance was otherwise equal to that of other employees, lacked 'longevity' because he or she did not fit into the corporate culture and so was unlikely to be retained for as long as the others. In the extreme case, which was precisely the one which had occurred here, the employing company could decide that the employee had demonstrated his total absence of 'longevity' in that the company had decided to dismiss him.[90]

This case was also a clear or egregious one in the sense that not only had the employing company adopted a non-objective criterion for the exercise of its discretion concerning the award of bonus, but that it had also applied that criterion in an extreme way by deciding to pay the employee no bonus at all for his final year. If a moderate sum had been awarded—let us say £250,000 (no more than ten times the national average annual salary)—it is unlikely that the court would have interfered with the quantification.

---

[90] [2000] IRLR 766 at 774 775.

Nevertheless, an extremely important precedent was set for the scrutiny of
the exercise of employing entities' powers to relate remuneration to performance. A particularly significant aspect of the decision was its insistence
that employees in the same situation had a contractual entitlement to be
treated equally in the assessment of their individual performance and its
impact on their bonus awards.[91]

The third of the recent cases, that of *Transco plc v O'Brien*, in a sense goes
even further down the track of requiring employing entities to abide by a
principle of fair management and performance in their decision making
about remuneration and benefits and their relation to the reasonable expectations of the worker in the whole context of the particular employment
relationship in question. In that case, it was held that the implied obligation
of trust and confidence applied so as to render it a breach of the claimant's
contract of employment that he was denied eligibility to an incentive
scheme providing for, among other things, enhanced benefits in the event
of redundancy. Here again, the decision is of great interest not only for
what it says about the general standards of conduct of employing entities
which are now contractually required of employing entities in the exercise
of powers and discretions, but also in the way those standards were applied
to the particular employment relationship in question.

So far as the general standard of conduct is concerned, the decision represents a significant further step in the progress towards formulating a
notion of the implied obligation of trust and confidence which will enable
that obligation to be applied without appearing to subject employing
entities to a universal standard of reasonableness, which continues to be
regarded as an inappropriate view of the role of the law of personal work or
employment contracts. Two main ideas are being deployed in order to do
this; the first is that, once the employing entity has engaged in conduct
which is objectively likely to damage the relationship of trust and confidence with the worker, the employing entity must show sufficient cause for
that conduct to demonstrate that it was not perverse or capricious conduct.
That is essentially the doctrine emerging from the *Malik v BCCI* case. The
second idea, building upon the notion of the implied obligation of mutual
trust and confidence as a requirement of *fair dealing* as expounded by Lord
Steyn in the *Johnson v Unisys Ltd* case,[92] identifies, as a leading instance of
confidence-damaging conduct, decisions which differentiate between workers
who are in like case, without obvious justification for doing so.[93]

This amounts to an extremely important contractual principle of
equality of treatment between workers. Its application to the facts of the
case was also particularly interesting, because it involved making and
applying a normative analysis of the precise character and complexion of

[91] Ibid.   [92] [2001] ICR 480 at 492E–G.
[93] Compare Mr Recorder Langstaff QC in *BG plc v O'Brien* [2001] IRLR 496 at 500–501.

the claimant's employment relationship in order to identify the appropriate comparator workers and to decide whether that comparison had been appropriately pursued. The claimant's complaint was that he had been refused eligibility to a particular financial incentive scheme which was offered to 'permanent employees'. His complaint was upheld by an employment tribunal on the basis that he was entitled to be treated as a permanent employee, and the company's appeal to the Employment Appeal Tribunal and the Court of Appeal was rejected on the ground that there was evidence from which that conclusion could properly be drawn.

Behind this apparently straightforward factual assessment lies a complex process of evaluation. The real point was that the incentive package was designed to enable the employing company to make a particular group of managerial workers redundant over a five-year period and yet retain individuals for as long as they were needed within that period. The real question was whether this employee, a finance and administration manager for the company who had joined the company as a temporary agency worker, had become sufficiently integrated as to merit treatment as a permanent employee. In an extended sense, this involved an evaluation of how this worker's performance should be related to his remuneration package by comparison with other workers employed by the company.

It is also noteworthy that the employing company's breach of contract, its failure to give effect to a contractual principle of fair dealing or fair management and performance, consisted in failing or refusing to offer to vary the contract of employment, indeed to offer such a significant variation in the terms and conditions of employment as to amount in the eyes of the parties to a revised contract of employment, and perhaps in the eyes of the law a new and different contract of employment. The Employment Appeal Tribunal and the Court of Appeal held that the implied obligation of mutual trust and confidence could and did extend to holding the employing entity to a requirement to take positive action of that kind, because that positive action had been taken in favour of other workers in like case.

The recent case law evolution towards a principle of fair management and performance with regard to remuneration and benefits is not mediated solely through the implied obligation of trust and confidence. In *Mallone v BPB Industries*,[94] the Court of Appeal upheld the control exerted by the High Court upon the discretion of the employing entity to cancel the mature share options of a senior executive dismissed for poor performance. The control was based upon a notion of irrationality, the working out of which has strong overtones of reliance and legitimate expectation:

[The fact that an employee might retain valuable share options despite poor performance] is not a valid reason for treating the whole scheme as a sort of mirage: whereby

---

[94] [2002] ICR 1045 (CA).

the executive is welcomed as a participant, encouraged to perform well in return for reward, granted options in recognition of his good performance, led on to further acts of good performance and loyalty, only to learn at the end of his possibly many years of employment, when perhaps the tide has turned and his powers are waning, that his options, matured and vested as they may have become, are removed from him without explanation.[95]

This form of reasoning may have been preferred to that of the implied obligation of trust and confidence because the latter obligation may be seen as that of the employing entity in a strict technical sense, whereas in this case the share option scheme was provided by the head company in the BP group while the employing entity was the Italian subsidiary company.

From that group of very recent cases,[96] and from a number of other relatively recent decisions which have been discussed in this and the previous chapter, there begins to emerge a new approach to the construction in personal work or employment contracts of arrangements which provide for remuneration and benefits and relate those provisions to the performance of the worker. It is an approach which it is useful to encapsulate in the notion of a principle of fair management and performance, but which could also be regarded as an integrative or holistic approach, and which could as such be contrasted with an atomistic approach to the construction of arrangements for remuneration and benefits. We suggest that these two approaches at the moment vie with each other for primacy; the integrative approach, though predominant, is far from universal.

The integrative approach manifests itself in a willingness or disposition to regard arrangements for remuneration and benefits as interdependent or interlocked, to be construed as a whole even where that involves putting together arrangements from different sources or made between a number of different parties. For example, the decision of the House of Lords in *Scally v Southern Health Board*[97] treated the employing entity as responsible for keeping its workers informed about advantageous opportunities for additional voluntary contributions to their retirement pensions although the superannuation scheme for the making of those contributions was quite distinct from their general remuneration arrangements and was maintained by a distinct entity.[98] In *Aspden v Webbs Poultry & Meat Group (Holding) Ltd*[99] it was held that the employing entity's contractual right of dismissal must not be exercised so as to frustrate the employee's entitlement to income replacement under the company's permanent health insurance

---

[95] Rix LJ at 1060 para 44.

[96] To which may be added the decision to similar effect in *Cantor Fitzgerald International v Bird* [2002] IRLR 867 (QBD).   [97] [1991] ICR 771 (HL).

[98] The doctors in question were employed by regional health boards, but the superannuation scheme was maintained by the Department of Health and Social Security as a whole.

[99] [1996] IRLR 521 (QBD)—see below, 484.

scheme. In the *Mallone* case, the head company of the group within which the senior executive in question was employed was required to exercise its discretion under its share option scheme in such a way as to give effect to legitimate expectations arising from the contract of employment with the subsidiary company.

The contrary, atomistic, approach consists in regarding and construing the elements which make up the worker's set of arrangements for remuneration and benefits as essentially independent both of each other and of other aspects of the employment relationship (such as arrangements for job security) to be accorded or denied contractual effect on a free-standing basis. A good illustration is afforded by the decision of the High Court in *Grant v South-West Trains Ltd*,[100] where contractual effect was denied to the employing entity's equal opportunity policy, so defeating a claim that contractual travel concessions in respect of opposite-sex partners of the workers in question should extend to same-sex partners. Equally significantly, the Privy Council, in its recent decision in *Reda v Flag Ltd*,[101] decided that the employing entity's contractual entitlement to terminate the contracts of employment of senior executives without cause (on payment of the lesser of salary for the remainder of a three-year fixed term or twelve months' salary) had been lawfully exercised even though the purpose was to avoid according them stock options under a stock option plan which was about to be introduced and was introduced for remaining employees.

That latter decision particularly highlights a feature of the whole of the foregoing discussion of the contractual relationship between performance and remuneration. It has been notable to what an extent that relationship is an evolutionary one; that is to say, it is integrally linked up with the evolution and termination of the particular employment relationship in question. Thus it connects into that aspect of the law of personal work or employment contracts which is concerned with the events which alter the terms and the character, status, or situation of the contractual relationship between its formation and its termination. In the next chapter we consider a large group of those events, under the heading of the variation of personal work or employment contracts. Before doing so, we first relate our discussion of the principle of fair management and performance to one particular aspect of remuneration and benefits which requires special discussion, that of pension provision; and we draw some conclusions from this chapter as a whole.

D. FAIR MANAGEMENT AND PERFORMANCE WITH
REGARD TO PENSION PROVISION

In this subsection it is argued that the principle of fair management and performance which we have articulated with regard to remuneration and benefits generally is precisely applicable to pension provision by the

---

[100] [1998] IRLR 188 (QBD).   [101] [2002] IRLR 747 (PC).

employing entity. So exactly is this the case that it would be suitable to regard the employing entity's contractual pension promise or pension obligation to its workers as a general promise or obligation of fair management and performance in respect of pension provision, which shapes and determines the construction of the employing entity's particular contractual pension obligations. In the application of that general pension promise or obligation, we can observe or predict the same tension between integrative approaches and atomistic approaches as was encountered in relation to remuneration and benefits generally. This subsection proceeds to justify the assertion of a contractual principle of fair management and performance with regard to pension provision, and to indicate how that tension between integrative and atomistic approaches might be expected to manifest itself.

The assertion that a contractual obligation of fair management and performance is equally applicable to pension provision by the employing entity as to the provision of other forms of remuneration seems on the face of it a surprising one, because it runs counter to an intuition that pensions law is quite distinct from the law of personal work or employment contracts. It is indeed the case that the main institutional apparatus of occupational pension provision is the pension scheme trust, and that pension scheme trustees are the subject of a specialized regulatory regime which is substantially separate from that which applies to the employing entity; it is the regime of trusts law administered by courts with an equity jurisdiction, overlaid with Inland Revenue regulation which is concerned with the fiscal implications of occupational pension provision, with statutory regulation of the administration of pension funds, and with the regulatory jurisdiction of the Pensions Ombudsman.[102] However, it is consistent with that to say that the obligations of the employing entity itself are construed and regulated from a set of starting points essentially derived from the personal work or employment contract.

These contractual foundations of the analysis of the pension obligations of the employing entity were laid by the remarkable decision of Sir Nicolas Browne-Wilkinson as Vice-Chancellor in the *Imperial Tobacco* case.[103] That decision, treating the employing entity as subject to the implied obligation of trust and confidence to its employees when exercising its rights and powers under the trust deed which governs its occupational pensions scheme, served not merely to establish the primacy of the contractual analysis of the employing entity's obligations with regard to pension provision, but also to sketch out a highly integrative approach to that contractual analysis. That is to say, the employing entity was held to a standard of decision making which required it to take an overall view of the impact of its

---

[102] See, for an excellent general account, Nobles, *Pensions and the Employment Relation* (Nobles 1995).

[103] *Imperial Group Pension Trust v Imperial Tobacco Ltd* [1991] ICR 66 (ChD).

decisions upon the legitimate expectations of its workforce as to the way in which their pension entitlements would be managed both during and after their employment. That implied contractual standard was held to permeate the employing entity's dealings with the pension fund trustees over dealings with the pension fund surplus in the later decision in *Hillsdown Holdings plc v Pensions Ombudsman*.[104]

That same integrative contractual approach has, over a succession of cases starting with *Scally v Southern Health Board*[105] and continuing through *Outram v Academy Plastics Ltd*,[106] and *Hagen v ICI Polymers & Chemicals Ltd*,[107] produced quite a well-developed obligation of communication and the provision of accurate information and advice upon the employing entity towards its workers with regard to decisions on their part which are concerned with or affect their pension entitlements.[108] However, those are more in the nature of procedural rather than substantive obligations. It is much less clear whether that integrative approach would or will be taken in relation to the currently very pressing set of substantive questions about the extent of the freedom of the employing entity to use powers of amendment and discontinuance in existing pension schemes, to move from the traditional final salary basis of occupational pension scheme benefits to the very different money purchase basis which is typically less advantageous from the worker's point of view. The approach of the Privy Council in *Reda v Flag Ltd*[109] may presage an approach in which powers of amendment and termination of pension schemes, like powers of dismissal, are perceived and analysed in more atomistic, free-standing, and therefore less circumscribed terms than the *Imperial Tobacco* decision suggests.

CONCLUSION

As in the previous chapters, the argument of this chapter has been a prescriptive one. It has involved, in particular, the argument that distinctions between entire and divisible contracts, and between performance of work and readiness and willingness to work, provide a rather unsatisfactory set of techniques for the analysis and development of the relationship between performance, breach, and entitlement to remuneration and benefits in the modern practice of employment relations. The shortcomings of those

---

[104] [1997] 1 All ER 862 (ChD).   [105] [1991] ICR 771 (HL).
[106] [2000] PLR 283 (CA).   [107] [2002] IRLR 31 (QBD).
[108] Though a somewhat more cautious approach was taken in *University of Nottingham v Eyett* [1999] ICR 721 (ChD), where it was held that the implied duty of mutual trust and confidence in a contract of employment does not include a positive obligation on the employing entity to warn an employee who is proposing to exercise important rights in connection with the contract of employment that the way he is proposing to exercise them may not be the most financially advantageous.   [109] [2002] IRLR 747 (PC)—see above, 230.

techniques have been considered with special reference to the areas of entitlement to remuneration during absence due to sickness, and during periods when partial industrial action is being taken. The outlines were sketched, on the basis of recent case law, of an application of the proposed general principle of fair management and performance to construction of the relationship between performance, remuneration, and benefits. It was suggested that this analysis was fully applicable to the apparently rather separate area of the employing entity's obligations with regard to pension provision.

Two supplementary points are emphasized in conclusion; again, they are consonant with arguments which have emerged from earlier chapters. Firstly, although the ideas which have been put forward in this chapter are derived from the case law of the contract of employment, they seem to apply equally well to semi-dependent workers' contracts. The notion of a presumption in favour of the continuation of remuneration during absence due to sickness would seem scarcely applicable to semi-dependent workers' contracts, but in any event it has been argued that such a presumption should today be regarded as extremely dubious even with regard to contracts of employment. It was argued that the development of statutory protection from unlawful deduction from wages should be seen as a significant trigger for development in thinking about the permissibility of deductions as a matter of common law, and it is highly important that this statutory protection was provided for the whole category of 'workers' rather than being confined to employees under contracts of employment as many post-1960s statutory employment rights had been. Finally, the point is reiterated that the construction of the relationship between performance and breach turns out to be very largely a matter of the regulation of the evolution of contractual employment relations over periods of time, and of the conditions in which changes in the terms of those relations may be effected. There is therefore an essential continuity between the subject matter of this chapter and the question of variation which is considered in the next.

5

Variation

INTRODUCTION

In this chapter, we continue an analysis, embarked upon in the previous chapter, of the way in which the law of personal work or employment contracts engages with or handles the evolution of the personal work relationship between its formation and its termination. The main developments which occur in the course of that evolution are categorized, in the law of personal work or employment contracts, as variation or as suspension. In this chapter, we consider the way in which the idea of variation is formulated and treated within that body of law, and how the treatment of variation fits into our analysis of the way that the law of personal work or employment contracts functions and fulfils its task.

We begin by identifying, in outline at least, the way that the terminology of 'variation' is used in the law of personal work or employment contracts. There are in fact various kinds of ambiguity in the way that this terminology is used; these ambiguities reflect deep unresolved issues about the descriptive and normative functions of the law of personal work or employment contracts. Firstly, it is useful to address a relatively superficial technical ambiguity; when we speak of contractual variation, we may refer either to variation of the terms of a contract, or to variation of the contract as a whole. Within the law of personal work or employment contracts, that seems to be a distinction without a difference; where the terms are varied, the contract as a whole is thereby varied, and where a personal work or employment contract as a whole is varied, that must mean that one or more of its terms has been varied.

Secondly, on the other hand, we need to consider a far deeper and more significant ambiguity in the usage of the terminology of variation. When we discuss 'variation' in the law of personal work or employment contracts, we are in reality talking about a large set of changes or developments in the dispositions of the personal work relationship, that is to say in the arrangements for and surrounding work and remuneration, which may or may not involve variation of terms or variation of the contract in a narrow technical sense. We are apt to use the terminology of 'variation' to describe such changes or developments in arrangements without having resolved, perhaps even without having considered, some profound ambiguities. Firstly, there may be issues as to whether they represent changes merely in the practice of the employment relationship, or, on the other hand, in the obligations or normative provisions of the employment relationship. Secondly, there may be questions whether, even if there are changes of the latter kind, they amount to changes in the terms of the personal work or employment contract as such.

These ambiguities, and these issues and questions, are raised in very many of the disputes which arise in the course of operation of personal work relationships, or upon the termination of those relationships. Most such disputes occur because managers, on the one hand, and workers, on the other, disagree about whether the other is or are in compliance with the obligations which each believes to attach to the work relationship. Those disagreements are comprised of two interlinked elements; one element is the question of what the obligations of the relationship were at its outset, and the other is the question of whether the obligations have changed or been modified since the inception of the work relationship.

When seeking to address such disputes, and in particular when subjecting them to legal analysis, we find it convenient, indeed logical and natural, to think about those two elements or questions as separate ones, and to discuss the latter question as one of 'variation' of the obligations of the work relationship. In practice, the two questions are usually inseparable. If a personal work relationship has been in existence and in operation for a significant period of time, it is generally very difficult to recreate a clear snapshot of its profile of obligations at the outset, which is not shaped by perceptions of obligation derived from the subsequent history of the relationship.

Thus issues frequently arise, after a worker has been in the employment of a particular contractual employing entity for some period of time, as to what is the worker's job specification, what is his or her place of work, what are his or her hours or time of work, and what are the arrangements for his or her remuneration. When those become legal issues, they are generally issues as to what were the *obligations* of workers and employing entities in those various respects. The normal starting point for such inquiries is the question of what are the relevant *contractual* obligations. The answer to that question constitutes the primary legal specification of the worker's job, place of work, working time, and remuneration arrangements. In other words English employment law, when confronted with the need to define the terms and conditions of a personal work relationship at any given moment, normally deals with the problem by constructing, by means of backwards projection, an original personal work or employment contract, and by then considering how subsequent developments have related to that original contract—in particular, whether they come within the scope of the original contract or have resulted in a variation of the original contract or of its terms.

That mode of thinking represents much more than a casual or superficial feature of English employment law; it is a deeply embedded position. It is the point at which English employment law most strongly embraces a classical contractual analysis of the employment relationship. This, as the present writer and Paul Davies argued in 1984,[1] involved the imposition of an essentially static contractual model upon an essentially dynamic or evolutionary personal work relationship. The complex normative fabric of the employment relationship is systematically reduced to an initial treaty which remains in force until its termination unless it is modified by another equally decisive and definitive agreement. As a narrative of the history of the generality of personal work relationships, this has much the same artificiality as the theoretical insistence that they are entered into as contracts negotiated between individuals, and that those individuals are freely exercising equal bargaining power.

In fact, the two theoretical positions—the individual bargain model and the static contract model—complement and reinforce each other. They combine to produce a composite position which is even more artificial than its constituent parts. It is the static contract model which makes the individual bargain model a particularly contrived or counter-factual one. Most employment relationships are formed on the basis of standardized terms, which have been set by the employing enterprise, whether as the result of collective bargaining or, more commonly, simply as the result of unilateral norm-formation by the enterprise itself. Most of the formal revisions of the terms of employment will be equally standardized, either by employing entities' norm-making or by collective bargaining. Within that formal framework, there may occur much more fragmented or individualized formation of obligations, expectations, or perceived entitlements; but this normally takes place in the course of the employment relationship. Often, the detailed norm-making which really defines the employment relationship does not take place at its inception, nor does it fall neatly into subsequent identifiable episodes or transactions. Much of the real norm-making therefore disappears from view when the employment relationship is viewed through the filter of the static contract model. This deprives the individual bargain model of the slight factual accuracy which it might otherwise possess when applied to the generality of employment relationships.

This particular kind of disjunction between the factual narrative and the contractual analysis of the employment relationship has been the subject of some very powerful critiques of the workings of the law of the contract of employment and of its role in employment law in general. The problem, and indeed the fundamental nature of that problem, was clearly identified in Hugh Collins' seminal piece of writing about 'market power, bureaucratic power, and the contract of employment' where he commented that:

The orthodox analysis holds that the contract of employment consists of an agreement between the parties which defines at the outset their reciprocal obligations. The contract's terms exhaust their obligations and can only be varied by agreement

---

[1] Davies & Freedland 1984 at 289–294.

between the parties.... This analysis creates a number of problems for matching doctrinal results with normal employment practices... Before considering these problems, however, we should notice a more fundamental difficulty for the orthodox analysis... The simple characterisation of employment as a contract fails to grasp the nature of the social relations involved... Plainly, the ordinary relations of authority found in employment cannot be reduced to a simple contractual formulation.[2]

For Hugh Colllins, the traditional contractual analysis gave rise to deep anomalies which flowed from its 'failure to recognise that the employment relation combines both market and bureaucratic dimensions'.[3] He clearly believed that this failure was endemic to the contractual analysis of the employment relation, mainly because of the commitment of the contractual analysis to reduce the employment relation to one or a succession of static agreements. In a somewhat similar vein, Steve Anderman has more recently argued that the tribunals and courts have been excessively ready to interpret statutory provisions having the function of protecting workers by reference to the law of the contract of employment.[4] One of his particular concerns is that statutory notions such as the worker's job specification or place of work have often been treated as essentially contractual ones despite the fact that the contractual specifications may be at variance with the factual description of the worker's job or place of work.[5]

It is useful to question why these writers regard this dysfunctionality of the law of the contract of employment as a matter of such concern, and why it seems to them to be irremediable within the approaches of the techniques of reasoning of that body of law. Anderman's concern is that the deference to contract in the interpretation of statutory protections for workers operates to enable employing entities too easily to 'contract out' of those statutory protections by shaping the terms and conditions of employment contracts so as to render the statutory provisions inapplicable or nugatory. He believes, in other words, that judicial interpretation too readily reduces some statutory protections to the status of *jus dispositivum* or derogable law when they should be maintained as *jus cogens* or mandatory, that is to say overriding, law. He is right to remind us how easily the contractual perspective upon the individual employment relationship may lead to results of that kind.

Collins' concerns were, in a sense, even more fundamental ones. He believed that, whether in the context of statutory interpretation or in the context of the direct application of the common law of the employment relationship, the contractual mindset stood in the way of the regulation of the fairness with which employing entities acquired and exercised discretionary powers—whether regarded as market power or bureaucratic power—over their workers. He contrasted that mentality with the very different

[2] Collins 1986 at 3. [3] Ibid. [4] Anderman 2000. [5] Ibid at 229–233.

approach which was taken towards those discretionary powers when they could be regarded as public powers amenable to the principles of public law. He, equally with Anderman, was right to point out the instrumental potency of the contractual approach in enabling employing entities, or employing organizations, to treat the contract of employment as a source of or vehicle for extremely wide directive authority, while equally enabling them to resist subsequent encroachment upon that authority whether from collective bargaining or from the developing custom and practice of the individual employment relationship in question.

Both Collins and Anderman may validly have identified features of the law of personal work or employment contracts which are absolutely inherent to that body of law. On that view, we would have to see it as virtually impossible that this body of law could develop in such a way as to provide the kind of regulatory interpretation of the employment relationship which those writers, and the present writer too, would see as desirable. That is to say, one which is genuinely responsive to or reflexive of the respective claims and needs of people in work relationships and of the enterprises by which they are employed. However, in the course of this chapter it will be suggested that this view may slightly underestimate the potential for positive development in that direction which has been demonstrated by the evolution of the case law concerning the variation of personal work or employment contracts in recent years.

In short, it will be argued that the courts and tribunals have tended, in their approach to the variation of personal work or employment contracts, towards a greater understanding than had previously been displayed of the personal work or employment contract as a relational contract. This tendency challenges the analysis of the contract of employment according to classical contract theory. It is that latter classical analysis, and its consequences for the interpretation of employment legislation, against which Collins' and Anderman's strictures are really directed. In the following three sections of this chapter, the law of variation of personal work or employment contracts will be discussed within a framework which follows that of classical contract theory. Clear and sharp distinctions will be made between the original formation of the contract, its variation, and its ultimate termination. Some recent changes of approach will be noted, but will still be presented as falling within that classical conceptual framework.

In a final section of the chapter, on the other hand, it will be argued that those recent changes of approach may signal the emergence of a fundamentally different framework of thinking about the way in which personal work or employment contracts should be understood or interpreted. The same body of case law will be re-examined and regrouped according to a set of tentative hypotheses about a relational contract approach. This will evoke, and explore more fully than we have hitherto done, notions of fair dealing and the protection of reasonable expectations. A set of questions will be raised about whether this forms the basis for an analysis of all aspects of the evolution and termination of personal work or employment contracts, which questions will be pursued in the following chapters of this work.

SECTION 1: VARIATION WITHIN THE ORIGINAL CONTRACT

A. VARIATION AND CONTRACTUAL FLEXIBILITY

In this subsection, we are not concerned with variation of the terms of personal work or employment contracts in a strict sense. For we are concerned with a logically prior question, which is that of how far the terms of personal work or employment contracts will be construed as having their own inbuilt elasticity or flexibility, so that working conditions or the arrangements for work can be changed within the original terms of the contract without the need for variation of the contractual terms themselves. This is a question of the extent of the legal recognition of managerial prerogative. For even when the processes of negotiation and consultation are well developed, the rules of work are essentially the employer's rules, and the right to vary the terms and conditions of employment is normally reserved to the employing entity rather than the worker.[6] In considering the extent to which this type of managerial prerogative operates in practice, and is protected in law, it is useful to distinguish between the different main types of terms and conditions of employment which may be in issue. The main terms of employment to be discussed in this connection are:

   (1) the place of work;
   (2) the job specification;
   (3) the hours and times of work.

1. The Place of Work

The scope of the employing entity's prerogative to vary the place of work has been the subject of many difficult disputes in the administration of the redundancy payments and unfair dismissal legislation. The disputes arise where, for example, employing entities, unable to provide further employment for a given worker in the place where he has been working, have offered employment elsewhere and have sought to deny liability for

---

[6] The various ways in which employees assert their own control over working conditions do not normally seek to alter the rules of work themselves—see William Brown, 'A Consideration of "Custom and Practice"' (Brown 1972); compare also Deakin 1999, especially section 2—'The employment contract as a mechanism of governance: economic and legal conceptions'.

a redundancy payment on the basis of such an offer. The drafting of the legislation is such that a series of distinct issues may be raised where the employee refuses that offer and claims a payment. The problem may be treated as one of whether the situation comes within the definition of 'redundancy'[7]—whether in particular the place in which the employee is offered further work can be regarded as within the geographical scope of his original job.[8] The same matter can, on the other hand, be treated in terms of the question of whether there has been a dismissal in the statutory sense.[9]

If the employing entity was offering the employee work at a place which was within the geographical area contemplated by his contract of employment, it can be said that a termination of employment resulting from the unwillingness of the employee to move is neither an outright nor a constructive dismissal within the meaning of the unfair dismissal or redundancy payments legislation. If, however, it is held that there has been a dismissal by reason of redundancy, then a particular issue about mobility arises under the redundancy payments legislation as to whether the employee has unreasonably refused an offer of employment suitable in relation to him or her.[10] A discretion is thereby conferred upon the adjudicating tribunal as to how far it will, as a matter of policy, insist that the employee must be prepared to be geographically mobile, and will hold that an employee who does not show the required mobility cannot claim a redundancy payment.

It is therefore clear that the question of definition of the place of work and of geographical mobility is important in a number of contexts in the application of employment protection legislation. The usual starting point for that definition or specification is the personal work or employment contract itself. The courts may on occasion break out of the contractual mode of definition of the place of work, perhaps because that mode of definition seems insufficiently sensitive to do justice in particular cases.[11] However, the normal point of departure for the inquiry is the construction of the express or implied terms of the personal work or employment contract. The courts were thus called upon, from the mid-1960s onwards, to develop a set of approaches or default rules for that process of contractual definition.

---

[7] The current provision defining redundancy is s 139 of the Employment Rights Act 1996 (ERA).

[8] *McCulloch Ltd v Moore* [1968] 1 QB 360; *Sutcliffe v Hawker Siddeley Aviation Ltd* [1973] ICR 560; *UK Atomic Energy Authority v Claydon* [1974] ICR 128.

[9] Dismissal is currently defined for the purposes of unfair dismissal legislation by s 95 of the Employment Rights Act 1996, and for the purposes of redundancy payments legislation by ss 136–137 of that Act.

[10] The provision under which that issue arises is currently that of s 141 of the Employment Rights Act 1996, in particular s 141 (1), (2), and (3)(b).

[11] As, notably, in the recent case of *High Table Ltd v Horst* [1999] IRLR 513 (CA). See, generally, on this point, Anderman 2000 at 229–233.

In *O'Brien v Associated Fire Alarms Limited* (1968),[12] the Court of Appeal
made it clear that there was no question of any presumption of mobility in
favour of the employing entity. The Industrial Tribunal had found that two
electricians and their mate were obliged to be mobile within a radius of at
least 120 miles despite some seven years in the employment concerned
during which they had worked within commuting distance of their homes.
The Divisional Court abdicated any responsibility for laying down guiding
principles, by treating the matter as one of fact alone in which they could
not interfere with the Tribunal decision. The Court of Appeal, holding the
implication of a term into a contract to be a question of law for the Court,[13]
took notice of the absence of any positive evidence of any term entitling the
employing entity to call upon the employee to move, and held that there
was no ground upon which they could make an implication to that effect.[14]

O'Brien's case effectively destroyed the idea of any presumption in favour
of mobility beyond the area within which the employee can commute to
work. A group of cases concerning steel erectors helped to identify more
precisely the factors which will be treated as determining the employee's
obligations of mobility. It was clear that the practice between the employing entity and the particular employee—the extent to which the employee
had been continually given work in one area near his home or had been
moved throughout the country—would be the critical factor. In *Ingham v
Bristol Piping Co Limited* (1970)[15] and in *Mumford v Boulton and Paul (Steel
Construction) Limited* (1970)[16] the Divisional Court and the Court of
Appeal held against an implied term requiring the employee to be mobile
throughout Britain; in *Stevenson v Tees-side Engineering Limited* (1970)[17] the
Divisional Court held in favour of such a term. In the former two cases,
the existence of any indications that the employee knew from the outset
that he would be expected to be mobile was a matter of speculation only.
In the latter case there were positive indications to that effect, in that evidence was given that the employee had been specifically asked whether he
was prepared to work away from home and had answered affirmatively.
Moreover, the court attached significance to the fact that the employee was,

[12] [1968] 1 WLR 1916.
[13] Lord Denning MR at 1923B; Salmon LJ at 1925B; Edmund Davies LJ at 1927E–F; cf
Abernethy v Mott Hay & Anderson (1973) 8 ITR 228, where Sir John Donaldson said on a
point of the same kind, 'In our judgment the tribunal's conclusion [against a term obliging the
employee to do site work] was a mixed finding of fact and law. In so far as it was a matter of
fact it was amply supported by the evidence and in so far as it was a matter of law it was correct.' (At 231C. Decision affirmed [1974] ICR 323.)
[14] Lord Denning MR at 1923D–G; Salmon LJ at 1925F–1926; Edmund Davies LJ at
1927E. But contrast Sir John Donaldson, 'It is without doubt the law that there is no dismissal
where both parties to a contract of employment freely and voluntarily agree to vary its terms.
This happens whenever there is an increase in rates of pay or a promotion'—*Sheet Metal
Components Ltd v Plumridge* [1974] ICR 373 at 376E–F.   [15] (1970) 5 ITR 218.
[16] (1971) 6 ITR 76.   [17] [1971] 1 All ER 296.

by the statutory particulars of his terms of employment, referred to the Memorandum of Agreement for the steel-erecting industry which at various points contemplated and made arrangements appropriate to 'away contracts'. (This was not, however, one of those relatively straightforward cases where the relevant and applicable collective agreement differentiated between mobile and static employees by providing an extra allowance for the 'travelling men' (*sic*), not merely for expenses attributable to actual travelling, but in respect of their being liable to be instructed to travel at the will of the employing entity.[18])

The decisive contrast between these cases seems to lie in the fact that in the *Ingham* case there was only very slight evidence that the employee had ever during the period of the relevant employment worked outside his commuting area, and that there had been no such outside working in the *Mumford* case, whereas in the *Stevenson* case it appeared that the employee had spent a considerable part of his time working away from home at various points during his employment. In the *Stevenson* case, the court was readier than in the two earlier cases to find that an implied term requiring mobility of the employee was necessary to the business efficacy of the contract of employment given the way the steel-erecting industry was organized. In the *Ingham* case, by contrast, the court had been disposed to regard occasional employment outside the commuting area as 'the kind of helpfulness one is entitled to expect from employees' rather than evidence of an original obligation of mobility.[19] But this contrast must be read very much in the light of the different history of the employment in the two cases as far as actual past mobility was concerned. It was this latter distinction on the facts which was decisive and conditioned the court's reasoning on the other issues.[20]

Since those early cases under the redundancy payments and unfair dismissal legislation, the courts have developed a number of techniques of reasoning, in relation to variation of the place of work, which between them confer considerable latitude to respond to the circumstances of the particular work relationship in question. In *Jones v Associated Tunnelling Co Ltd*,[21] Browne-Wilkinson J in the Employment Tribunal sketched out an approach whereby every contract of employment was to be regarded as containing an express or implicit statement of the employee's place of work

---

[18] For example *Bounds v WH Smith & Co Electrical Engineers* (1966) 1 ITR 53; *McCaffrey v Jeavons & Co Ltd* (1967) 2 ITR 636.   [19] (1970) 5 ITR 218 at 221 (Lord Parker CJ).
[20] In *Sutcliffe v Hawker Siddeley Aviation Ltd* [1973] ICR 560, the NIRC applied the *Stevenson* case despite the fact that the employee—an aircraft electrician—had acquired a base during two years' employment. The trend appeared to be against allowing the employee to set up a custom localizing his employment. In *Litster v Fram Gerrard Ltd* [1973] IRLR 302, it was established that a term permitting transfer from one contract site to another will not justify transfer from one permanent depot to another.
[21] [1981] IRLR 477; see also below, 274–275.

and of the employing entity's power, if any, to vary the place of work, that is to say, a mobility clause.[22] Hence it was appropriate for a tribunal or court to infer that statement from the express terms of the contract and the circumstances of the case; the implied statement to be inferred in the present case was that the employee could be required to move to a different work site as long as that was within reasonable commuting distance of home.

A case which appears, on first impression, to take a radically different line in fact comes within the same broad approach to the construction of the contractual place of work and mobility obligation. In *Little v Charterhouse Magna Assurance Co Ltd*,[23] the Employment Appeal Tribunal ruled that there was no warrant to make any restriction, whether within commuting distance of home or to any other location, of the area within which the employee could be called upon to work. The contrast in approach between the two cases is much more apparent than real. In the first case, the employee was claiming to be entitled, under his contract of employment, to resist a move to a site of work which was still within commuting distance of his home. In the second case, the employee was the general manager of the employing entity, indeed, its managing director in all but name, and was regarded as having committed himself to moving with the employing entity during the five-year fixed term of his contract. In both cases, the assessment of the place of work and of the mobility obligation was a circumstantial one within a single interpretative approach.

It should be noted that the courts in developing such an approach confront a doctrinal objection, namely that, by assessing the contractual specification of the place of work and the mobility obligation in the circumstances of the work relationship as those have evolved during the continuance of employment, the courts are, in effect, allowing for a gradual or creeping variation of the content of the personal work or employment contract. This view, asserted for instance by the Court of Appeal in *Janata Bank v Ahmed*,[24] may be offset by the growth of methods of construction of personal work or employment contracts which succeed in evaluating the implicit content of the personal work or employment contract as dynamic in nature, but which do so in a subtle and indirect way.

The courts seem to be in the course of developing a new set of techniques for adjudicating upon the appropriateness of the contractual specification of the place of work and extent of geographical mobility which can be demanded of the worker. This seems to consist in their assuming a capacity to imply, with such a contractual specification, the requirement that

---

[22] In *Aparau v Iceland Frozen Foods plc* [1996] IRLR 119, the EAT rejected the notion that every contract of employment must, logically, contain a specification of mobility which is distinct from its specification of the place of work.   [23] [1980] IRLR 19.

[24] [1981] ICR 791 at 808; see below, 273.

the managerial prerogative which that specification creates must be exercised fairly and reasonably. An important pointer in that direction was the decision in *United Bank Ltd v Akhtar*,[25] where it was held that the power of recreation conferred upon the employment by a mobility clause was subject to an implied requirement of reasonable notice. Although the existence of a general test of reasonableness was denied by the Employment Appeal Tribunal in *White v Reflecting Roadstuds Ltd*,[26] that was before the full concretization of the implied obligation of mutual trust and confidence, which, as we have seen earlier, has moved matters a long way further in that direction.[27] A rather unusual but extremely interesting imposition of such a requirement upon a power of relocation occurred more recently in the case of *Curling v Securicor Ltd*,[28] where it was held that, where the management of an employing entity wishing to relocate a worker perceived themselves as having the choice between invoking a contractual mobility clause or expressing the relocation as an offer of suitable alternative employment, they would not be allowed to dodge between the two approaches and hope to be able to adopt the most profitable at the end of the day. We turn to consider whether parallel developments are occurring with regard to the contractual specification of the content of work.

2. The Content of Work: The Job Specification

At the time of the original work upon which the present one is based, the main tendency to be observed with regard to the employing entity's prerogative of requiring the employee to be occupationally mobile is that the contractual scope of the prerogative could be enlarged as the result of the practices of collective bargaining, and in particular of productivity bargaining. It was common for collective agreements, especially those covering a wider area than a single plant, such as area or national agreements, to define job categories and to specify occupations in fairly broad terms, perhaps in order to allow further differentials and narrower categories to be established in more localized negotiations. If such collective agreements were incorporated into individual contracts of employment, for example by reason of reference to them in written particulars issued in accordance with the statutory requirements,[29] the result might be that the individual contract might be seen as having reserved to the employing entity a right to vary the job specification within fairly generous limits.[30]

It can thus be said that the incorporation of collective agreements into individual contracts sometimes operated to widen managerial rights to vary the terms of these contracts. Productivity agreements were especially likely to have such an effect. For it was a particular feature of productivity

[25] [1989] IRLR 507 (EAT).   [26] [1991] ICR 733 at 741G.
[27] See above, 167–168.   [28] [1992] IRLR 549 (EAT).   [29] See above, 82–85.
[30] Compare *Callison v Ford Motor Co Ltd* (1969) 4 ITR 74 (IT).

agreements that they frequently imposed extensive obligations of occupational mobility upon the employee, with corresponding obligations upon the employing entity in respect of retraining and offering suitable work where the agreement is a well-balanced one. This is, indeed, one of the central objectives of productivity bargaining, since the worker is thereby being paid an advantageous wage in return for the surrender of counter-productive limitations upon the scope of his or her job.

In the subsequent period since the original work was written, there have continued to be many initiatives by which the managers of employing entities seek to secure enhancements of workers' occupational mobility; but these have tended to be pursued more by means of unilateral development of schemes for flexible and efficient management than by collective productivity bargaining. This emerges clearly from the recent work of Duncan Gallie and others on the restructuring of the employment relationship.[31] In one respect, the courts have built this kind of development into the implicit content of personal work or employment contracts; from the time of the leading case of *Cresswell v Board of Inland Revenue*,[32] workers have readily been regarded as subject to an implied obligation to adapt to the computerization of their work function. The subsequent case of *McPherson v London Borough of Lambeth*[33] provides a good instance. However, this could be regarded as an implicit requirement of adaptability of skills rather than of occupational mobility in the wider sense of flexibility as to job definition or function.

In that wider sense, the approach of the courts to the evolution of contractual job definitions and obligations of occupational mobility is less clear than it might be by reason of a tendency, even more marked than in relation to the issues of place of work, to prefer an extra-contractual approach to job definition for statutory purposes, particularly in the context of the statutory concept of redundancy. It may well be that the courts are assuming that the contractual definition will be a more static and formalistic one than is appropriate for the purpose of adjudications about redundancy; this seems to emerge from the recent decision of the House of Lords in the case of *Murray v Foyle Meats Ltd*.[34]

3. Times and Hours of Work

With regard to times and hours of work, a similar set of issues arises as for the place and content of work, namely (1) how far are personal work or employment contracts construed so as to confer upon the parties, and in particular upon employing entities, a power to vary the times and hours of

---

[31] See Gallie, White, Cheng and Tomlinson 2000, especially chapter 3—'Discretion and Control'. [32] [1984] ICR 508 (QBD).
[33] [1988] IRLR 470 (ChD).   [34] [1999] ICR 827.

work, and (2) how far and in what sense does employment protection legislation adopt a contractual definition of the times and hours of work?

So far as the first question is concerned, there does not seem to be a general rule, or even a general presumption, as to whether personal work or employment contracts are to be construed as having fixed working time or working time which is variable either by the employing entity or by the worker. The Working Time Regulations[35] expressly contemplate that working time may either be 'measured', 'partly measured', or 'unmeasured', and it will probably now become necessary to distinguish more sharply between contracts with fixed working time and those with variable working time in order to apply the distinction between the degrees to which working time is to be regarded as measured. This is not to say that working time may not be both measured and variable; that is precisely the nature of many arrangements for the working of 'overtime' (though not of all arrangements for 'overtime', for 'overtime' may be obligatory at a certain fixed level upon both employing entities and workers, in which case, in the form of 'guaranteed overtime', it usually signifies simply a part of working time for which the worker is paid at an enhanced rate).

There is, on the other hand, some very significant case law on the question of how far contractual effect will be accorded to arrangements which confer very wide latitude upon workers, and more particularly upon employing entities, to vary the times and hours of work. There may be a tendency towards a more restrictive construction of apparently very wide powers. A wide power was treated as effective in the case of *National Coal Board v Galley*.[36] Colliery deputies were there employed under contracts of employment which expressly incorporated the terms of national and local collective agreements currently in force. The relevant national agreement provided that the deputies should be paid an upstanding weekly wage— a wage, that is, which did not vary according to the time worked during each week. It also contained an agreement that deputies should work 'such days or part days of each week as may reasonably be required by the management in order to promote the safety and efficient working of the pit and to comply with statutory requirements'.

Upon the issue whether this provision entitled the employing entity to require the employees to work Saturday shifts, one argument of the employees was that they could not be regarded as having subjected themselves individually to so large a discretion on the part of the management. Both at first instance and in the Court of Appeal, that argument was rejected and it was held that the workers were individually bound by this clause in the national agreement. The reasons given were applications of general contractual principles. Finnemore J at first instance held that since

[35] 1998, SI 1998/1833, reg 20 (as amended by SI 1999/3372); see above, 94.
[36] [1958] 1 WLR 16. See the annotation by Kahn-Freund at (1958) 21 MLR 194.

the part of the agreement fixing wages was indubitably incorporated into the individual contracts by reference, the rest of the agreement was also incorporated, because the employee could not accept the national agreement in part and not in whole.[37] This type of argument is liable to ignore the distinction between the normative and the procedural aspects of collective agreements, as well as the distinction between the parts expressing understandings and intentions and those imposing obligations. In the Court of Appeal that decision was upheld, on the ground that, as the courts will where necessary imply a condition of reasonableness into contracts and treat them as workable on that basis,[38] it followed that, where a contractual obligation was itself cast in terms of reasonableness, it was sufficiently precise to be enforceable.[39]

One should not overgeneralize that decision as a systematic endorsement of very wide managerial prerogative to vary the hours of work. On these particular facts there were probably good reasons for holding that the deputies were individually bound by the clause in the collective agreement.[40] It is true also that the main argument on behalf of the deputies was not so much that they were not bound to work such reasonable hours as might be required of them, as that the hours actually required of them were not reasonable. Their main aim was to secure a judicial arbitration as to what were reasonable hours, rather than to deny the legal effect of the agreement. In the event, the requirement upon the workers concerned to work for a twelfth consecutive day was held not to be unreasonable.[41]

However, it may be that a more critical approach to such provisions is supported by later case law, and in particular that their potential to produce outcomes amounting to abuse of power would be more closely scrutinized. That prospect is offered partly by the decision in *Johnstone v Bloomsbury Health Authority*,[42] where the Court of Appeal held that, as regards a contractual term purporting to enable the employing health authority to require a junior hospital doctor to work for up to 88 hours per week on average, either the term itself[43] or the exercise of the power which it conferred[44] was subject to an overriding duty of care for the health and safety of the worker. The same prospect is offered, more generally, by the development of the

---

[37] Compare the reasoning of the Industrial Tribunal in *Joel v Cammell Laird Ltd* (1969) 4 ITR 206.

[38] Pearce LJ [1958] 1 WLR 16 at 24 citing *Hillas & Co Ltd v Arcos Ltd* (1932) 147 LT 503 and *Foley v Classique Coaches Ltd* [1934] 2 KB 1; cf also *British Bank for Foreign Trade Ltd v Novinex Ltd* [1949] 1 KB 623, *Powell v Braun* [1954] 1 WLR 401; contrast *May & Butcher v R* (1934) 2 KB 17n. [39] Pearce LJ [1958] 1 WLR 16 at 24.

[40] This was, for example, the view taken by Kahn-Freund in his contemporary note at (1958) 21 MLR 194.

[41] It would now amount to a breach of reg 11 (Weekly Rest Period) of the Working Time Regulations 1998, SI 1998/1833. [42] [1991] ICR 269—see above, 142–143.

[43] Compare Stuart-Smith LJ at 276–277.

[44] Compare Sir Nicolas Browne-Wilkinson VC at 283–284.

implied obligation of mutual trust and confidence, of which that decision is sometimes regarded as an example.[45]

As to the question of how far and in what sense employment protection legislation adopts a contractual definition of the times and hours of work, the situation is a complicated one. There is a statutory definition of 'normal working hours'[46] (chiefly important for calculating redundancy payments)[47] which distinguishes between different types of overtime arrangement. The statutory scheme proceeds in two stages. The first stage is to exclude hours paid at overtime rates from 'normal working hours'.[48] The second stage is to admit as an exception those hours which are paid at overtime rates but are within the 'number or minimum number of hours fixed by the contract of employment in the week'.[49]

If this scheme is applied to the different types of arrangement for overtime, it becomes clear that the problematical case is that where the employee is bound to work overtime at the instance of the employing entity but the employing entity is not bound to provide overtime. In the case where the employing entity is bound to provide overtime and the employee is bound to work it, it is clear that the hours of overtime count as 'normal working hours' and that overtime here represents merely an enhanced rate of payment for certain hours.[50] In the opposite case where overtime is voluntary for both employing entity and employee, it is equally clear that the hours concerned are not 'normal working hours'; they are not contractually fixed hours.[51]

The intermediate case is that where overtime is compulsory for the employee but not for the employing entity;[52] the effect of that situation is that the employing entity has the prerogative as a matter of contract to vary the number of hours worked (paying at overtime rates for the excess over a fixed number of hours). The view of the courts appeared at first to be that such hours could be part of 'normal working hours' (and they were decidedly reluctant to conclude that overtime was in any given case contractually obligatory upon the employing entity).[53] In *Tarmac Roadstone*

[45] See above, 155 et seq.

[46] Now contained in s 234 of the Employment Rights Act 1996.

[47] It is used in the calculation of the 'week's pay' as stipulated by the provisions of ss 220–229 of the Employment Rights Act 1996. Those sections are used for the employment rights provided by that Act; they are modified in their application for the purpose of calculating the week's pay for the purposes of reg 16 (Payments in respect of periods of leave) of the Working Time Regulations 1998, SI 1998/1833.   [48] 1996 Act, s 234 (1)–(2).

[49] Ibid, s 234 (3).

[50] *Armstrong Whitworth Rolls Ltd v Mustard* [1971] 1 All ER 598.

[51] *Redpath Dorman Long (Contracting) Ltd v Sutton* [1972] ICR 477.

[52] There is a further theoretical possibility of a situation where provision of overtime is compulsory upon the employing entity but overtime working is voluntary for the employee. But this situation appears not to arise in practice.

[53] Cf *Pearson v William Jones Ltd* [1967] 1 WLR 1140; *The Darlington Forge Ltd v Sutton* (1968) 3 ITR 196; *Loman and Henderson v Merseyside Transport Services Ltd* (1967) 3 KIR 726; *Turriff Construction Co Ltd v Bryant* (1967) 2 ITR 292; *Byrne v Lakers (Sanitation & Heating) Ltd* (1968) 3 ITR 105; *Lynch v Dartmouth Auto Casings Ltd* (1969) 4 ITR 273.

Holdings Ltd v Peacock,[54] however, the Court of Appeal ruled that in this intermediate situation the overtime cannot be part of 'normal working hours' because its amount is fixed ad hoc by the employing entity rather than being 'fixed by the contract' in the sense that the statute requires. This was despite the fact that contract law generally treats as contractually fixed and certain any quantity for which the contract provides a fixing method though it does not fix a quantum from the outset.[55] So in that context at least the legislation has adopted a particular contractual conception of 'normal working hours' and the courts have taken a restrictive view of the way in which that conception applies to overtime arrangements.[56]

B. AN IMPLIED PROVISION FOR VARIATION BY PROPER NOTICE

In this subsection we turn to consider another possible form of variation which might be regarded as being within the scope and inherent elasticity of the personal work or employment contract as originally formed. There seems once to have been a view that these contracts have implied within them a provision for agreed variation upon notice of the length required to terminate the contract; or in other words, that a right to vary by notice can be implied into the contract where there is a right to terminate by notice. This represents an analysis of the law concerning variation of contracts which is probably no longer correct. A more accurate result is reached by considering what is involved in a right to vary the terms of a contract. That right has two aspects; it involves both a right to demand the continuance of the contract on the new terms and conditions, and also the absence of liability for refusing to continue it on the old terms.

It seems that the latter result, the absence of liability for termination, used to be thought to follow from a notice to vary the terms of a contract which is as long as the notice required to terminate the contract. The courts seemed prepared to treat a notice of the requisite length, which says that employment will be available only on changed terms and conditions, as having the same effect, where the party receiving the notice is unwilling to accept the change, as an unconditional notice to terminate the contract.[57] We can see this view in operation in the analysis of a strike notice which was offered by Davies LJ in *Morgan v Fry*.[58] He suggested that such a notice

---

[54] [1973] ICR 273; cf *Gascol Conversions v Mercer* [1974] ICR 420.

[55] Eg *Hillas & Co Ltd v Arcos Ltd* (1932) 147 LT 503.

[56] The statutory provisions for ascertaining the continuity of employment formerly (before the revocation by SI 1995/31 of the thresholds which excluded part-time work) evoked the notion of a contract of employment 'normally involving' employment for a stated number of hours weekly. For the comparable difficulties of construction which that notion created, compare *Secretary of State for Employment v Deary* [1984] IRLR 180 (EAT).

[57] Cf *Santen v Busnach* (1913) 29 TLR 214; *White v Riley* [1921] 1 Ch 1 (strike notices); and see below, 480.

[58] [1968] 2 QB 710. On strike notices and s 147 of the Industrial Relations Act 1971 see Foster (1971) 34 MLR 275 and (1973) 2 ILJ 28; O'Higgins (1973) 2 ILJ 152; Hepple & O'Higgins, *Individual Employment Law* (London, 1971) at 110–113. As to the possibility of suspension, see below, 480–481.

amounted to an offer to continue the employment on different terms, and a notice to terminate the employment if those terms were not acceptable to the employing entity; and it was his view that there was no illegality in such a notice if it was of the proper length.[59]

There even used to be some authority for the view that the worker is in such a case bound by the new terms where he continues in the employment, for this was at issue in *Rowsell v Metropolitan Water Board* (1915).[60] The plaintiff was employed upon seven days' notice and seven days' notice was given to discontinue overtime pay and the payment of travelling expenses. Having acquiesced in this change for seven years, the employee claimed arrears of those payments for that period. This claim was rejected, and Lord Reading CJ laid it down that 'if he continues to serve, as he has continued to serve, the Metropolitan Water Board after they have given him a proper notice to alter the terms of the contract of employment which they had taken over, he cannot afterwards bring an action for the wages he has lost'.[61] That reference to 'a proper notice to alter the terms of the contract of employment' represents probably the clearest articulation of the notion of an implied right to vary by notice, the notice being 'proper' in the sense that it is of the length required to terminate the contract, rather than in the sense that it is specifically authorized by the contract.

However, it would seem that, in such a case, the inability of the worker to claim his former terms and conditions is caused by a waiver of them by him, or by what is deemed to be a distinct agreement to a contract on changed terms, rather than by the original contract of employment entitling the employing entity to vary its terms by notice. The extent to which a variation of terms and conditions of employment may acquire effect by reason of waiver or estoppel or deemed agreement is considered later in the present chapter.[62]

Moreover, even if the employing entity has a right to rely in that special sense upon his notice to vary the terms of the contract, it seems clear that it cannot and does not have the further right to demand the continuance of the contract on the new terms, in the sense of treating it as a breach of contract in the worker to refuse to continue upon the new terms; nor can the employing entity deny that it has dismissed the worker where the latter refuses to continue the employment at all (assuming that the variation concerned has been a major one).[63] Indeed, there has been a clear and strengthening trend, throughout the present era of interpretation of employment protection legislation from the late 1960s onwards, to regard an employing entity's purported or attempted imposition of significant

---

[59] [1968] 2 QB 710 at 733F–G; in *Horizon Holidays Ltd v ASTMS* [1973] IRLR 22, a strike notice was expressly conditional upon failure to reinstate certain employees. No objection was taken on this ground.   [60] (1915) 84 LJ(NS)KB (pt 2) 1869.
[61] Ibid at 1874.   [62] See below, 255–261.
[63] *Sutcliffe v Hawker Siddeley Aviation Ltd* [1973] ICR 560 (NIRC).

changes in the terms and conditions of employment, which are adverse ones from the point of view of the worker, as repudiatory breach of contract in the absence of clear express authority in the personal work or employment contract for such variation.

This view emerged from the decision of the Court of Appeal in *Marriott v Oxford & District Co-operative Society Ltd (No 2)* [64] and has been effectively maintained since that time. In the case of *Alexander v Standard Telephones & Cables Ltd (No 2)*,[65] Hobhouse J seems to revert to the recognition of a right to vary as the result of the right to terminate, but the supposed right turns out on examination to be only a partial one, susceptible to resistance by the worker:

it is always open to an employer, as a matter of contract, to say to his employee that after the expiry of the contractual notice period the employer will only continue the contract of employment on different terms. Such a notice is equivalent to giving notice to terminate the existing contract and offering a revised contract in continuation of and substitution for the existing contract. The period of notice has to be the notice that is required to terminate the existing contract. It is then up to the employee to decide whether he is willing to accept the revised terms. If he chooses not to, his employment is ended at the expiry of the notice period; if he does accept, then it continues on the varied terms. *If the employee declines to accept the new terms and the employer nevertheless continues to employ him, then it is the former terms, the terms of the existing contract, which continue to apply.*[66]

For these reasons the right, which it is often believed that the employing entity has, of varying the contract by a notice as long as that required to terminate the contract, is apparent rather than real, in the absence of a special provision in the original contract creating such a right.

SECTION 2: VARIATION BY SUBSEQUENT AGREEMENT

Very many disputes about the operation of personal work or employment contracts arise from situations where employing entities provide work or remuneration on a changed basis from that which the workers in question assert as the previously agreed and accepted one. Hence such disputes turn upon the question of whether and at what point there has been a valid and binding variation of the arrangements for work and remuneration. In order to process such disputes in contractual terms, courts and tribunals in effect formulate that question in two stages. At the first stage the question is what latitude for variation was built into the personal work or employment

---

[64] [1970] 1 QB 186. Followed on this point in *Shields Furniture Ltd v Goff* [1973] ICR 187 (NIRC); *Maher v Fram Gerrard Ltd* [1974] ICR 31. Compare also *Rigby v Ferodo Ltd* [1988] ICR 29 (HL).
[65] [1991] IRLR 286 (QBD).   [66] Ibid at 296, para 60 (emphasis added).

contract from the outset. At the second stage, it is considered whether variation not within that latitude is nevertheless valid and effective by reason of subsequent agreement or the equivalent of such agreement. In the first section of this chapter, we considered the first question, and observed that courts and tribunals were on the whole tending to an increasing caution towards assertion of wide-ranging or open-ended variability in personal work or employment contracts as formed. In this section it is considered whether a comparable approach is taken to subsequent agreement or its equivalent.

At this second stage, courts and tribunals are, in effect, considering the evolution of personal work relationships as itself being a continuing process of contracting; the question is whether the parties to the personal work or employment contract have remade their original contract. So the rules and requirements for formation of personal work or employment contracts, which were considered in the second chapter, present themselves again in a different context; not at the outset of a personal work relationship, but during its subsequent evolution. The interesting set of issues is how the technical rules and doctrines which apply to original formation are applied in this different context, and according to what views of the legitimate mutual expectations which have arisen during the development of the personal work relationship.

A. The Requirement of Consideration

The first such issue is that of whether and when an alleged variation will be deemed invalid for want of consideration to support it. Where an employing entity asserts a variation which is adverse to the worker, it does not seem to have been regarded as arguable that the employing entity has not given consideration for that variation. The question has arisen where an employing entity has asserted that an alleged variation in favour of a worker is unsupported by consideration. In fact, the general contractual principle that consideration is required to support a subsequent variation, or that a promise does not support a contractual variation where that promise is to do what one is already bound by contract with the promisee to do, itself originates in certain early cases concerning the contracts of employment of seamen, where the seamen were unable to recover wage increases promised in the course of voyages. Such a case was *Stilk v Myrick*,[67] where a seaman who had entered into a contract for a voyage (out and return) was held unable to recover additional wages promised for the return voyage. The report of Espinasse shows the decision to be based on the ground of public policy which had been applied in *Harris v Watson*,[68] namely that it was

[67] (1809) 6 Esp 129; 2 Camp 317. See Treitel, *Law of Contract* (10th edn, 1999) at 88–89.
[68] (1791) Peake 102.

against the general interest for seamen to be able to extort wage increases in mid-voyage by threats of refusal to proceed with the return voyage. But the report in Campbell shows the decision to be based upon the lack of consideration for the promise to pay additional wages. And in *Harris v Carter*,[69] where a promise to pay additional wages to a seaman was similarly held to be unenforceable, the result was expressly based upon both grounds in the alternative.

The fact that these cases undoubtedly contributed to the formulation of the doctrine of the general law of contract, and in that sense form part of the modern law, should not lead us to overlook the special features of the historical context within which the personal work relationships in question were set. That should also give rise to caution about the relevance to the modern law of the decision in *Price v Rhondda* UDC,[70] a decision concerning the security of tenure of married women teachers employed by a local authority, originally on the terms that their employment was terminable by one month's notice by the employing authority. A subsequent undertaking on the part of the employing authority to grant a minimum security of tenure to these teachers was treated as lacking in legal effect because the teachers had given no corresponding promise to remain in their employment for that length of time, and thus had given no consideration for this variation of the original contract.[71] The application in this type of case of a requirement of consideration for contractual variation was open to fundamental criticism in terms of the fairness of the dealings of local education authority employing entities with married women teachers at that period.

The reasoning of the court in that case was quite inappropriate, because the promise by the employing authority to extend the minimum period of service no doubt represented a response to political pressures and opinions concerning the rights which should be accorded to married women teachers, and it was really beside the point to look for some additional undertaking by the teachers which could be balanced against this promise. In the recent case of *Lee v GEC Plessey Telecommunications plc*,[72] an employing entity purported to withdraw in 1990 an enhancement offered in 1985 of the severance payments which it undertook to make to its production workers in the event of their being made redundant. One argument advanced on behalf of the employing entity to justify that withdrawal of the enhanced redundancy terms was that those enhanced terms had never become binding upon the employing entity in the first place, because the workers in question had given no consideration for the enhancement.

---

[69] (1854) 3 E & B 559. So also *Hopkins v McBride* (1901) 50 WR 255; *Harrison v Dodd* (1914) 111 LT 47.   [70] [1923] 2 Ch 372 (ChD).
[71] See Eve J, ibid at 385.   [72] [1993] IRLR 383 (QBD). See also below, 281.

That argument was rejected on the ground that where employees continue to work following a renegotiation of their terms and conditions of employment as to, for example, pay or, as here, severance pay, the employing entity has secured a benefit and avoided a detriment by reason of the resolution of the dispute which led to the renegotiation; so the workers have in that sense provided the required consideration. Connell J was content to distinguish the case of *Price v Rhondda Urban District Council* as one where the concession made by the employing entity had not been made in the context of a negotiation of terms and conditions of employment. It is suggested that a higher court might be prepared to go further, and find that an improvement of workers' terms and conditions of employment can generally be presumed to have been effected because it is judged by the employing entity that there is sufficient advantage to itself to justify doing so. Such a view would be subject to the possibility of the kind of argument about duress which succeeded in the *Universe Tankships* case.[73] This would seem to represent a satisfactory overall approach to the requirement of consideration for variation of personal work or employment contracts by subsequent agreement.

B. WAIVER OR ESTOPPEL

We suggest that there is a comparable need for a balanced and reflexive approach to the deployment, in the context of personal work relationships, of technical doctrines of contract law concerning waiver and estoppel, in order to decide whether there has been a valid and effective subsequent variation of terms and conditions of employment. Sometimes, and particularly where employing entities allege a subsequent variation of terms and conditions which is in their favour, it has been argued that a variation is effective because the other party has waived the right to object to the variation or is estopped in the circumstances of the case from denying its validity. This is, in effect, an invoking of the doctrine of equitable promissory estoppel, or at least one of the variants upon it, whereby a variation acquires a binding effect upon the party on whose part it represents a concession. This is not the place in which to attempt to state the results of all the discussion of that doctrine which has taken place in recent years. It will be sufficient to cite the statement of the principle in the Privy Council in *Ajayi v RT Briscoe (Nigeria) Ltd*:

The principle, which has been described as quasi-estoppel, and perhaps more aptly as promissory estoppel, is that when one party to a contract in the absence of consideration agrees not to enforce his rights, an equity will be raised in favour of the other party. This equity is, however, subject to the qualifications,

---

[73] *Universe Tankships Inc of Monrovia v International Transport Workers' Federation* [1982] ICR 262 (HL).

(a) that the other party has altered his position,
(b) that the promisor can resile from his promise on giving reasonable notice, which need not be a formal notice, giving the promisee reasonable opportunity of resuming his position,
(c) the promise only becomes final and irrevocable if the promisee cannot resume his position.[74]

There are difficulties of both a technical and a fundamental nature in applying this doctrine to the variation of contracts of employment. For example, the doctrine of equitable promissory estoppel is generally expressed in terms which suggest that it may apply only where the variation consists in a forbearance to enforce existing rights, and not where it consists in the granting of new rights.[75] If that is indeed the case, then it would result in a distinction which would be wholly artificial in the context of the personal work relationship. If strictly applied, it could mean that the doctrine might apply to an undertaking by the employing entity to reduce the length of the basic working week, but not to an undertaking to raise the basic hourly rate of pay. Yet both these types of variation may have the same purpose and the same effect of raising the total weekly remuneration; and the choice of mode in which to express that increase may be dictated by the contingencies of managerial practice or of collective bargaining.

A more fundamental question about the use of the doctrine of waiver or estoppel to regulate the validity of variations of contracts of employment is whether it is too technically legal in character. The doctrine is itself subject to a test of whether it is equitable for it to be applied in any given case.[76] However, it is suggested that the application of this rather formalized notion of equity in the variation of personal work or employment contracts is likely to be exceedingly difficult in view of the various kinds and degrees of pressure exerted by employing entities and employees upon each other in the course of settling and varying the terms and conditions of employment. It is suggested that the doctrine of equitable promissory estoppel is not the right tool for the job of deciding when it is proper to give binding effect to changes in terms and conditions of employment. Arguments by which employing entities sought to raise an estoppel against a worker in respect of an alleged variation of terms and conditions which was adverse to the worker were rejected by the Employment Appeal Tribunal in the cases of *Waine v Oliver Plant Hire Ltd* (1977)[77] and *Jones v Associated Tunnelling Co Ltd* (1981),[78] so that this technique or argument does not seem to be in active current use.

---

[74] [1964] 1 WLR 1326 at 1330 (Lord Hodson).
[75] See, on this point and more generally, Treitel 1999 at 97 et seq. The rule in *Combe v Combe* [1951] 2 KB 215 relates to the rather different point that the doctrine cannot be invoked to enforce a promise which does not take place in the context of, and as a modification of, an existing contractual relationship.
[76] Compare *D & C Builders Ltd v Rees* [1966] 2 QB 617 (CA).
[77] [1977] IRLR 434 (EAT).   [78] [1981] IRLR 473 (EAT).

C. THE REQUIREMENT OF CONSENT AND VARIATION
   BY CONDUCT

The requirements for a valid variation of the personal work or employment
contract which have been discussed above lead to two general questions:
(1) what evidence of consent will be required to validate a variation of
terms and conditions which is deemed to be subsequent to the original
contract and beyond the latitude for change which the original contract
confers, and (2) how far, therefore, may the contract be effectively varied
by conduct, in the sense that evidence of consent is derived from conduct
rather than from express and unequivocal agreement? A number of different approaches to these questions are to be found in the cases. Between
them, they affirm a judicial concern with the genuineness of consent on the
part of workers to variations of arrangements for work and remuneration
which employing entities propose or claim to propose. This has been a
growing feature of the development of the law of personal work or employment contracts during the current era of interpretation and application of
employment protection legislation.

   Examples of such approaches are to be found in earlier case law. Thus the
Divisional Court in *Dorman Long & Co Ltd v Carroll* (1945)[79] treated a
variation in the actual conduct of the parties as not affecting their mutual
contractual obligations by distinguishing between the substance of those
obligations and the mere manner of their being carried out. Colliery workers
employed as fillers agreed, in 1943, to a scheme of reorganized working
whereby they were to work an extra shift on Saturdays. After eighteen
months and the passing of the most acute phase of the wartime emergency,
the employees gave eight days' notice to terminate the extra shift (their
employment itself being terminable upon fourteen days' notice). Their
employing entity's claim for damages for breach of contract under the
Employers and Workmen Act 1875 was rejected on the ground that there
had never been a variation of the obligations of the employees in the first
place, but merely 'an alteration of the method of carrying out the original
agreement',[80] with the result that it was no breach of contract for them to
revert to the original terms. It was also held that the agreement to work the
extra shift was in any event terminable by reasonable notice and had been
so terminated. This seems to have reflected an underlying feeling, both
before the magistrates and on appeal to the High Court, that the employees should not be penalized for their willingness to shoulder extra burdens
in a time of emergency.

   Similar approaches began to assert themselves, as ways of dealing with
cases where the merits seemed strongly on the side of the worker, from the
late 1960s onwards. Thus, there have been instances where the conduct of

[79] [1945] 2 All ER 567.   [80] Ibid at 599A–B (Humphreys J).

workers has been held to have no concessionary effect upon their contractual rights by reason of a lack of intention to affect legal rights. That approach can be observed in the case of *Saxton v National Coal Board*[81] where a mine-worker, who had for many years worked as a continuous shift worker on a seven-day week, worked for five days each week during the last few months of his employment because the colliery had ceased production work. The Board contended that there had been a consensual variation of his contract of employment, such that his redundancy should be assessed on the footing that his contract of employment obliged him to work only for a five-day week at the time of its termination. That argument was rejected, and the assessment was based upon the seven-day week. The merits of the case were clear; thus Lord Parker CJ said:

I dislike, I confess, that attitude of the Board in this case where...they are really making use of the employee's willingness to work, and to work for a lower wage, as a means of avoiding making a redundancy payment.[82]

The court accordingly took the view that:

Here was a man who was being called upon to co-operate to help his employers to run down this colliery, and one would think that in those circumstances it was difficult to say that he was working as he did otherwise than without prejudice.[83]

A similar analysis was envisaged in the reasoning of the Divisional Court in *Parkes Classic Confectionery Ltd v Ashcroft*,[84] where an Industrial Tribunal was directed to consider the possibility that a *de facto* reduction in the working hours of an employee did not reduce the 'normal working hours' of the worker concerned because the parties had gone on with an effective contract specifying the original normal working week which was 'still legally in existence though not meticulously observed'.[85]

A more fundamental revision of judicial thinking about variation and consent occurred in the context of judicial construction of the statutory concept of dismissal for the purposes first of the redundancy payments legislation, and then, from 1971 onwards, for the purposes of the unfair dismissal legislation too. A strong requirement of consent to contractual variation was affirmed in the landmark decision of the Court of Appeal in *Marriott v Oxford & District Co-operative Society Ltd (No 2)*,[86] where it was held that the action of an employee in remaining at work for a period of

---

[81] (1970) 5 ITR 196.   [82] Ibid at 200.   [83] Ibid at 200 (Lord Parker CJ).
[84] (1973) 8 ITR 43.   [85] Ibid at 46.
[86] [1970] 1 QB 186 (annotated by the present writer at 33 MLR 93). Cf *Scott v Executors of AE Marchant* (1969) 4 ITR 319 at 324, where the Tribunal pointed out that 'voluntary acceptance of new terms must be distinguished from taking Hobson's choice'. The 'Hobson's choice' point was reiterated in *Sheet Metal Components Ltd v Plumridge* [1974] ICR 373 at 377E.

a couple of weeks following the imposition by the employing entity of reduced remuneration and a lower status did not constitute a consent to a variation of the contractual terms and conditions. This was a matter of critical importance in defining the statutory concept of dismissal because it meant that the attempt to impose the variation assumed the character either of wrongful repudiation which entitled the injured party to treat the contract as terminated, or of a wrongful outright dismissal.

The principle concerning consent to variation in the *Marriott* case was quickly accepted and acted upon by the National Industrial Relations Court. This was in *GKN (Cwmbran) Ltd v Lloyd*,[87] where the employee, a camshaft straightener in a foundry, remained at work for about four weeks after the termination of his original job. During that four-week period he was employed in a different foundry from previously, in an unskilled capacity as opposed to the previous semi-skilled capacity, with a reduction in wages of at least £7 per week. The Court treated this merely as further employment taken in mitigation of his loss rather than continuation of the previous employment. In *Shields Furniture Ltd v Goff*,[88] the Court similarly held that three weeks' work and two weeks' paid holiday occurring after the employing entity had imposed changed conditions of employment was not 'so long an elapsed period of time that one ought to assume an agreed variation or replacement of the previous contract'.[89]

Although the decision in the *Marriott (No 2)* case[90] represented a rule that a variation would be regarded as consensual only where the consent is a genuine one, it did not deal with the question whether the employing entity could be sued upon an obligation to continue the employment on the old terms in respect of the period following the imposed variations during which the employee remained at work. The earlier law, as represented by *Rowsell v Metropolitan Water Board* (1915)[91] seemed to be to the effect that, if an employment relationship continues for a substantial period following the imposition of varied terms and conditions, it would be held that the party upon whom the variation was imposed had waived his right to insist upon the former terms and conditions. The element of consent would, in effect, be supplied by conduct, and this would debar a worker from asserting a right to the continuation of the previous terms and conditions of employment.

However, in two key cases in the 1980s, a negative approach to consent by conduct, similar to that of the *Marriott (No 2)* case, was taken in common law actions for recovery of wages. In *Burdett-Coutts v Hertfordshire*

---

[87] [1972] ICR 214.
[88] [1973] ICR 787 (NIRC); statutory provisions now contained in ERA s 141 have since accorded a 'trial period'; compare above, 241.
[89] [1973] ICR 187, Sir John Brightman at 190G–H.
[90] [1970] 1 QB 186 (above, 258).   [91] (1915) 84 LJ (NS) KB (pt 2) 1869.

County Council,[92] the 'dinner ladies' case,[93] it was held in the High Court that the workers in question could recover arrears of wages following a change of terms and conditions imposed unilaterally by the employing entity, although they had remained in employment, *de facto* on the new terms, after those changes had been made, and had instituted their action while still in employment de facto on the new terms. To like effect was the decision, to be discussed in a later chapter,[94] of the House of Lords in *Rigby v Ferodo Ltd*,[95] where the worker's continuing in employment on the worsened terms and conditions of employment was held not to have involved his implied acceptance of them even after the several years which elapsed between their imposition and the trial of the action at first instance.

That represents the current state of the law on implied acceptance of variation of personal work or employment contracts, except that there has been another line of development of interpretation of the statutory concept of dismissal which has had results that relate in a very complex way with the law as thus described. This is the development associated with the case of *Hogg v Dover College* (1988),[96] in which it was held, where a teacher's terms and conditions of employment were unilaterally downgraded by the employing college, that he could be regarded as having been actually or constructively dismissed for the purposes of the unfair dismissal legislation although he continued to work on the new and downgraded conditions, not just for a short period of time which could be regarded as a tentative and non-committal trial period, as in the *Marriott* case, but on a lasting basis as in the *Burdett-Coutts* or *Rigby* cases. This raises an apparent inconsistency: does not the doctrine in *Hogg v Dover College* involve the conclusion that the worker has, however unwillingly, accepted the ending of his or her former personal work or employment contract, and the making of a new and different contract on inferior terms? Does that mean that the worker has been deemed to consent by conduct to a variation of the terms and conditions of employment, a variation, moreover, which is sufficiently fundamental as to amount to a termination of the contract and its replacement by a different contract?

This apparent inconsistency can be resolved up to a certain point. In one sense, the doctrine in *Hogg v Dover College* does not involve any notion of deemed consent to variation. On the contrary, it assumes that the variation is imposed on the worker, and treats that imposition as amounting to a dismissal for statutory purposes. This involves the very controversial idea that an imposition of this kind can be said to have terminated the existing personal work or employment contract; we shall consider that problematical view in a later chapter.[97] But it does not depend upon deemed consent to

---

[92] [1984] IRLR 91.   [93] See Friedmann 1984.   [94] See below, 386–387.
[95] [1988] ICR 29 (HL).   [96] [1990] ICR 39 (EAT).   [97] See below, 386–387.

a variation; properly understood, it actually reinforces the notion that a worker is not to be treated as accepting a variation merely by remaining in employment on the new terms which have been imposed.

On the other hand, a difficulty nevertheless remains. The doctrine in *Hogg v Dover College* concerns cases where, *ex hypothesi*, the personal work relationship has continued after and despite the *de facto* imposition of changed terms and conditions of employment. The doctrine asserts that the existing personal work or employment contract can be regarded as terminated. Yet we have to accept that the personal work relationship has not merely continued but has continued in the form of a personal work or employment contract. It would be analytically and practically unacceptable to contend that the relationship continued in a non-contractual form. For that reason, a new personal work or employment contract must be deemed to have been formed, and the worker must be deemed to have agreed to its formation by continuing with the personal work relationship after and despite the *de facto* imposition of new and inferior terms and conditions of employment. So in that special sense there has been both an imposed variation and a deemed consent to it. This analytical point will be carried forward into the next section, in which we develop the distinction between those variations which do involve contractual termination and replacement and those which do not.

SECTION 3: VARIATION DISTINGUISHED FROM TERMINATION AND REPLACEMENT

In the previous section we considered the conditions for an effective variation of the terms of a contract of employment by subsequent agreement. Towards the end of the section, two major points emerged from the discussion of some difficulties or inconsistencies which presented themselves. Firstly, we saw that there was, after all, a certain sense in which variation might take effect by imposition as well as by agreement. Secondly, we saw that variation by imposition was being accorded a certain degree at least of contractual effect or effectiveness. This was in the particular case where it was deemed to amount to the termination of the existing personal work or employment contract, and its replacement by a new and different personal work or employment contract. It may well be that an imposed variation acquires contractual effectiveness *only* if it amounts to the termination of the existing personal work or employment contract and its replacement by a different contract.

This introduces and demonstrates the importance of the fact that, if a change in the terms of employment fulfils certain conditions, it will be regarded in law as being more than a simple variation; as being, in fact, a termination of the existing contract and its replacement by a new contract upon different terms. In this way there arises a method of terminating the contract of employment—namely, a termination by a change in content—as part of a process of substituting a new contract for the old. Termination by agreed change of content has long since been recognized in contract law under the name of rescission and replacement. There now emerges in the context of the law of personal work or employment contracts, albeit in a rather uncertain and controversial way, a parallel notion of termination by imposed change of content. It will be useful to consider more precisely the conditions upon which these kinds of termination by variation will be held to take place.

A. Consensual Variation as Termination and Replacement

The distinction between variation, and rescission coupled with replacement, is one of the more esoteric aspects of the law of termination of contracts, both as to contracts generally and as to personal work or employment contracts in particular. The distinction was an important one for the purposes of applying the requirements of evidence in writing imposed on certain types of contract by section 4 of the Statute of Frauds 1677 and by section 4 of the Sale of Goods Act 1893. It was partly because these provisions became enmeshed in a web of technicalities that they lost their usefulness and were amended and ultimately repealed.[98] It is useful to consider the treatment of the issue in general contract law and in relation to the contract of employment in particular.

The general principle of contract law, thereby to decide whether there has been rescission and replacement, has to be derived from two decisions of the House of Lords which applied the distinction to contracts for the sale of goods, in order to decide whether there was a contract worth over £10 requiring to be evidenced in writing. *Morris v Baron & Co*[99] concerned a large commercial contract for the sale of cloth. Disputes having arisen concerning delivery and payment, and legal proceedings having been commenced, a later agreement was reached by which the parties were to withdraw their action and cross-action, and certain concessions and allowances were to be made to the buyers. Upon the question whether this amounted to a rescission and replacement of the original contract, it was ruled that this depended upon the intention of the parties, and it was found that there had been the requisite intention to rescind the old contracts, and to replace them by an entirely new agreement. Lord Dunedin proposed the specific test that:

In the case [of variation] there are no such executory clauses in the second arrangement as would enable you to sue upon that alone if the first did not exist; in the

---

[98] The scope of s 4 of the Statute of Frauds 1677 was greatly reduced by s 1 of the Law Reform (Enforcement of Contracts) Act 1954, and s 4 of the Sale of Goods Act 1893 was repealed by s 2 of the 1954 Act.

[99] [1918] AC 1; cf *Tallerman & Co v Nathan's Merchandise Prop Ltd* (1957) 98 CLR 93; *Don Lodge Motel v Invercargill Licensing Trust* [1970] NZLR 1105.

[case of rescission] you could sue on the second arrangement alone, and the first contract is got rid of either by express words to that effect, or because, the second dealing with the same subject matter as the first but in a different way, it is impossible that the two should be both performed.[100]

A similar treatment of the distinction between variation and rescission plus replacement by a new contract occurred in the later case of *British & Beningtons Ltd v NW Cachar Tea Co.*[101] The case concerned a group of contracts for the sale of tea to be delivered at the Port of London. Delays having occurred in delivery as a result of congestion in the port, it was agreed that the buyers would accept delivery at provincial ports instead of London with an allowance per pound in return. It was held, following the earlier case, that the test for deciding whether this latter agreement had rescinded and replaced the earlier contract, or merely varied it, was one of the intention of the parties, but that here the intention was merely to vary and not to rescind and replace it by a new contract. Lord Sumner ruled upon the distinction between variation and rescission that:

The question is whether the common intention of the parties [when making the later agreement] was to 'abrogate', 'rescind', 'supersede', or 'extinguish' the old contracts by a 'substitution' of a 'completely new' and 'self-contained' or 'self-subsisting' agreement 'containing as an entirety the old terms together with, and as modified by, the new terms incorporated'.[102]

In the context of the personal employment contract, various different applications of the distinction between variation and rescission plus replacement have appeared from time to time. The case law suggests that the general contractual principle should be regarded as modified by a concept of the identity of the particular employment itself, so that a change in terms of employment should be seen as involving the termination of one contract and its replacement by another where, but only where, there is a change of job involved.

The view was at one time taken that any and every change in the terms of a personal employment contract resulted in its rescission and replacement by a new contract. However, this view was taken in the context of the application of the requirement formerly imposed by section 4 of the Statute of Frauds that contracts not to be performed within a year of the making must be evidenced in writing. In *Williams v Moss Empires Ltd*,[103] the intentions of the parties in varying their contract could be fully implemented by the court if, but only if, the agreement to vary was seen as the formation of a new contract. In that case, the employee was a music hall artiste employed under a written contract for a term of three and a half years at a yearly salary. Upon the outbreak of war, and in consequence of wartime conditions, an agreement was made between theatre proprietors and the Variety Artists Federation to distribute the risks of a falling-off in audiences

---

[100] [1918] AC 1 at 26.   [101] [1923] AC 48.   [102] Ibid at 67; cf Treitel 1999 at 172.
[103] [1915] 3 KB 242.

between owners and artistes, and to distribute the same risks evenly as between artistes by substituting for existing salaries a scheme whereby the receipts of the halls were to be pooled for a twelve-week period, and 50 per cent of them were to be divided among the artistes in proportion to their existing salaries. The plaintiff, not a member of the Federation, agreed verbally to his employers applying the scheme, but then sought to recover his originally agreed salary in reliance upon the Statute of Frauds. It was held that he was now bound by a new contract, Sankey J ruling that 'The result of varying the terms of an existing contract is to produce, not the original contract with a variation, but a new and different contract'.[104]

Clearly, upon the merits of the case the judge was under an incentive to take a wide view of the circumstances in which there could be said to be a rescission and replacement of the original contract. In that case it was necessary, in order to achieve the desired result, to treat any and every modification of contractual terms as resulting in a new contract. The workings of the Statute of Frauds were, however, such that it could be necessary to take entirely the opposite view in order to prevent a fraudulent reliance upon the statute. Such a case was *Adams v Union Cinemas Ltd.*[105] A cinema manager had been employed since 1934 under an oral contract of employment which was not required to be evidenced in writing.[106] In 1937 he was promoted to the position of controller of a large number of cinemas and was told that he could make his arrangements for two years, this being qualified by the statement 'You will see how you get on with the work'. When this employment was terminated by the defendants upon one month's notice and the plaintiff sued for damages for wrongful dismissal, the defendants argued *inter alia* that the 1937 promotion had resulted in the termination of the existing contract, and its replacement by a new contract which could not be enforced because it was for a fixed term of two years, and was therefore required to be evidenced in writing. This argument was rejected on the ground that this was not a contract for two years, but was a mere variation of the previous contract which could be enforced though not evidenced in writing. Stable J indicated that variations of this kind should not be regarded as resulting in the formation of a new contract: 'I think that everyone would be astonished if they were told that, when an employee is put to more responsible work, or given a rise of salary, that constitutes an entirely new contract.'[107] However, it cannot satisfactorily be said as a general rule that a promotion does not involve the formation of

---

[104] [1915] 3 KB 242 at 247–248.
[105] [1939] 1 All ER 169 (affirmed by CA [1939] 3 All ER 136 on other grounds).
[106] Because it was for an indefinite period. Such contracts were treated as falling outside s 4 of the Statute of Frauds in that they might be performed within a year.
[107] [1939] 1 All ER 167 at 171C–D.

a new contract. That would be too sweeping a view.[108] Hence it is clear that the cases which depend upon the Statute of Frauds generally resulted in a distortion of the law upon this point.

In some employment cases the distinction between variation and rescission has been a material one for the purpose of deciding whether a given term of the old agreement continued to apply after the making of the modifying agreement. The courts have wavered between the different tests of whether the new agreement represents a major departure from the pattern of the old contract in terms of content, or whether, on the other hand, it is inconsistent with the continued existence of the old contract in a structural or drafting sense. Thus in *Meek v Port of London Authority*[109] the plaintiffs were employed by the defendants from 1908 onwards, on contracts of which it was a custom, and assumed by the Court of Appeal to be a legally binding term, that the defendants would meet the income tax liability of those employees who were sufficiently well paid to incur such taxation. By the time, in 1912, that the plaintiffs had been promoted to a grade such that their incomes incurred tax, the employing authority had already given notice of the discontinuance of this practice. By virtue of the terms of the earlier statutory transfer of employment from private port employing entities, these plaintiffs were, it was held, entitled to claim that the terms of their original contracts of employment should not be changed. The question whether they had therefore become entitled to have their tax paid depended upon whether the old contracts had continued in force, in which case they were so entitled, or whether on the other hand they had been rescinded and replaced by a new contract upon the promotion. It was held by the Court of Appeal that the promotion did result in a change of contract. In their view it was not as if there had been an automatic increment in salary and improvement in conditions growing out of the original contract; it was rather that the position of the employees had been changed by the employing entities' voluntarily promoting them to a higher grade.

By contrast, a similar issue was handled in *SW Strange Ltd v Mann*[110] by considering whether the employing entity had replaced the original contract as a document and whether they had in a formal sense terminated one contract and replace it by another. The plaintiffs, a firm of bookmakers, sought to enforce against the former manager of one of their betting shops a restrictive covenant which had been contained in his original contract of employment. One issue was whether that covenant had survived an agreement between the parties, following earlier differences between them, that the defendant should be appointed manager of the credit department.

---

[108] Cf Pennycuick J in *Re Mack Trucks (Great Britain) Ltd* [1967] 1 WLR 780 at 780: 'It must frequently happen in the case of a long period of service with a single employer that employer and employee enter into a whole succession of new contracts, eg on promotion or for other reasons.   [109] [1918] 2 Ch 96 (ChD).
[110] [1965] 1 WLR 629.

It was held that this agreement, recorded in a company minute, represented the cancellation of the old contract and the formation of a new agreement of which the restrictive covenant no longer formed a part. The reason given was that a second agreement which is inconsistent with an earlier agreement abrogates the whole of the earlier agreement and not merely the inconsistent terms.[111] This was a point of construction of documents; the matter could as well have been based upon the fact that one appointment had been terminated and replaced by an inferior post.

It was at one stage thought that the distinction between variation and rescission plus replacement might be material for the purposes of the concept of dismissal in employment protection legislation in that a rescission and replacement might constitute a dismissal where a mere variation would not.[112] In *Marriott v Oxford & District Co-operative Society Ltd (No 2)* the Divisional Court,[113] regarding the distinction as relevant to their decision, took a very narrow view of the circumstances in which there could be said to be a rescission and a new contract rather than a variation. Lord Parker CJ indicated that a change in terms amounted to a rescission and replacement of the contract only if it constituted so fundamental a variation that nobody could claim that the original contract was still in being.[114] The Tribunal could not be said to have erred in law in holding that the demotion from foreman to supervisor and the reduction of £1 per week was not so fundamental a change. This reasoning was potentially dangerous to many claims based upon the statutory concept of dismissal; we proceed to consider how the problems which it left behind were subsequently addressed.

First, the decided cases signally failed to agree upon a test for rescission and replacement of the contract of employment, and, furthermore, failed to indicate whether the courts should take a wide or a narrow view of the application of that concept. There is neither a ruling principle nor a guiding presumption. This difficulty can best be resolved if it is once realized that the real problem is the identification of the job. The Court of Appeal in *Meek v Port of London* held, in effect, that if a promotion constituted a change from one job to a better job, then, but only then, it represented the cancellation and replacement of the contract of employment. The Divisional Court in *Marriott v Oxford & District Co-operative Society Ltd (No 2)* was arguably wrong in holding that the demotion and consequential reduction in wages did not amount to the withdrawal of one job and its replacement by a different and inferior post.

There was, moreover, a still greater problem about that decision, namely that it was taken on the assumption that the variation could be regarded as a consensual one, and that it could as such be regarded as a dismissal

---

[111] [1965] 1 WLR, Stamp J, at 636G–637B.   [112] See Freedland 1976 at 67–68.
[113] [1969] 1 WLR 254 (reversed on other grounds by CA [1970] 1 QB 186).
[114] Ibid at 259C–D.

provided only that it amounted to a consensual rescission and replacement. However, Lord Denning MR in the Court of Appeal,[115] with the agreement of his fellow judges, held that the distinction was quite immaterial to the real issue. The question was whether the change in terms and conditions was consensual or not. If not, there was a dismissal by the employing entity for the purposes of the Act. But if the change had been agreed between the parties, then it would not have constituted a dismissal even if it had been a rescission and replacement of the contract, because, in the words of Lord Denning MR, 'If the parties agree consensually to vary the terms of the contract of employment, or to rescind it and substitute a new contract of employment, the plain fact is that the contract is not terminated by the employers but by consent.'[116] So the distinction between variation and consensual rescission plus replacement was held not to be an important one for the purposes of the application of the statutory definitions of dismissal contained in the redundancy payments and unfair dismissal legislation. The relevant distinction was between consensual variation and imposed variation. This does, however, mean that there is a further distinction between imposed variation and imposed termination plus replacement, which we proceed to consider below.

B. Imposed Variation as Termination and Replacement

The development of the doctrine of dismissal by imposed variation, from its beginnings in the *Marriott* case and its confirmation in *Hogg v Dover College*, raises the question, how fundamental or extensive must an imposed variation be in order to constitute a dismissal by termination and replacement? Two main alternatives seem to present themselves, and the case law does not seem fully decisive between them, though it seems to incline towards the former alternative. The first alternative possibility would seem to be that the test is the same as or parallel with the test for consensual rescission plus replacement. This would suggest a relatively restrictive test, such as seemed to emerge from the foregoing discussion; was the imposed variation such as to change the whole identity and character of the job in question? The second alternative possibility would be that of a different approach whereby the question was whether the imposed variation was sufficient to amount to a (wrongful) repudiation of the personal work or employment contract.

We shall consider the concept of wrongful repudiation more fully in Chapter seven. It suffices at this juncture to say that, although the test for wrongful repudiation could in principle be regarded as the same as the test for consensual rescission, it is in practice rather wider, if only because the very nature of the variation as an imposed one tends to characterize it as a repudiation even if it is not so fundamental as to change the whole identity

---

[115] [1970] 1 QB 186.   [116] Ibid at 191H–192A.

and character of the employment in question. The *Marriott* case itself illustrates this point. Regarding the question as one of consensual variation, the Divisional Court held that it did not amount to rescission and replacement. Regarding the question as one of imposed variation, the Court of Appeal held that it did amount to termination of the existing contract. This seemed to signify that they regarded it as sufficient that the imposed variation did amount to a repudiation of the contract, that being a looser, more inclusive, notion than the notion of rescission in the consensual context. But there was no explicit reasoning on this point.[117]

Subsequent case law is less than clear on this point. In *Hogg v Dover College*, it was emphasized that the variation which had been imposed in the particular case in question was a fundamental one.[118] In the case of *Alcan Extrusions Ltd v Yates*,[119] the Employment Appeal Tribunal applied the principle of *Hogg v Dover College* in a case concerning production workers in a factory where the employment had imposed a change from a system of fixed shifts to a system of continuous rolling shifts; this represented a deterioration of terms and conditions of employment for the workers in question. It was held that the industrial tribunal had been entitled to conclude that there had been a dismissal because the new terms were 'so radically different from the old as to pass beyond mere repudiatory variation of the old contract, so that they could properly be characterized as the removal of the old contract and the offer, by way of substitution, of a new and substantially inferior contract'.[120] This clearly implies that the doctrine in *Hogg v Dover College* does not come into play whenever there is a 'repudiatory variation' of terms and conditions of employment, but only where that repudiatory variation is so radical as to amount, in and of itself, to the removal of the old contract. The acknowledgement of that distinction is very important, but we do not yet have a clear sense of how it is to be drawn in relation to particular facts.

SECTION 4: A RELATIONAL APPROACH TO VARIATION

A. A Relational Approach and Implicit Contracts

In this section it will be argued that we can view or interpret the law concerning the variation of personal work or employment contracts or the terms of those contracts according to a different theoretical analysis or framework of understanding from that which has informed the previous

---

[117] Indeed, Winn LJ issued a warning against over-elaborate academic theorizing around issues of this kind, which we are presuming to disregard! See [1970] 1 QB 186 at 193.
[118] [1990] ICR 39 at 42 per Garland J.   [119] [1996] IRLR 327.
[120] Ibid at 330 para 27 per Judge Smith QC.

sections of this chapter. The previous sections have proceeded according to the classical framework of contract theory, which views the formation of the contract and of its terms as a single event occurring at a single moment in time. That contract and those terms endure unless and until the contract comes to an end, or the terms are changed by means of a subsequent transaction which can be identified as a valid act of redrawing of those terms, essentially therefore an agreement to change the terms.

At the time when the original work, from which this one is derived, was written, the law of variation of contracts of employment seemed to fit very squarely into that framework of analysis. Since that time, there are many decisions which can be explained equally well, if not better, if we view the courts and tribunals as taking a certain kind of relational approach to the variation of personal work or employment contracts. In order to explain this argument, it will be helpful to say something about relational approaches in general, and about the notion, which we can loosely associate with them, of recognizing and giving effect to implicit contracts.

In proposing this argument, we are using the terminology of relational approaches, we hope in a way which is faithful to the literature about 'relational contracts',[121] to mean approaches to contractual issues which display a readiness to recognize certain contracts as relational ones and to shape the regulatory interpretation of them accordingly. Recognizing certain contracts as relational ones means accepting that they express and give effect to continuing, perhaps even long-term, relationships rather than just to discrete or 'spot' transactions which can satisfactorily be viewed in isolation from each other. Shaping the regulatory interpretation of them accordingly means accepting that the existence of the continuing relationship has normative implications which affect the content of the legal contract and the way in which the law should handle disputes about that content.

Understood in that way, relational approaches have aims or methods or outcomes which are very similar to those embodied in the notion of recognizing and giving effect to implicit contracts. That, equally, is essentially an idea that those associated in continuing relationships invest expectations in those relationships and derive expectations from those relationships, which are inappropriately downgraded when those relationships are reduced to a series of formal discrete transactions. Relational approaches generally seek to redress that downgrading by imputing obligations of good faith, co-operation, mutuality, loyalty, or partnership. The literature about 'relational contracts' or about 'implicit contracts' generally cites employment contracts as a prime example of a contract type which should be regarded as relational, and which should be construed so as to recognise and to give effect to the implicit contracts which emanate from the underlying relationship.

---

[121] A very good succinct account of this literature is given by Melvin Eisenberg; see Eisenberg 1995.

These are arguments, or examples, of relational approaches which we have drawn upon in earlier chapters of the present work.

In this chapter, however, we concentrate upon one particular kind of relational approach. Eisenberg, illuminatingly, depicts[122] the writers of the literature on relational contracts as proposing a number of 'rules' which are better suited to the regulation of those types of contracts than are the 'rules' generated by the classical theory of contract law. Among a number of such 'rules' which are about good faith and partnership, he also cites 'rules that would soften or reverse the bite of the rigid offer and acceptance format of classical contract law, and the corresponding intolerance of classical contract law for indefiniteness, agreements to agree, and agreements to negotiate in good faith, in the case of relational contracts'.[123] In this section, we argue that the emergence can be observed, and observed increasingly clearly, of an approach to the variation of personal work or employment contracts which proposes principles, if not precisely 'rules', which are very much to that effect.

This argument, if it can be successfully made out and sustained, might have a transformative effect upon the way in which we understand and regard quite a lot of the law of personal work or employment contracts. However, before seeking to instantiate or substantiate that argument from the case law, it is important for us to be candid, and indeed self-critical, about the method of interpretation of the case law which is being used here. We are engaged upon a task of interpretation which is, in a much more limited sphere, not entirely unlike that undertaken by Hugh Collins in his work on 'Justice in Dismissal'.[124] In the Introduction to that work, Collins depicts himself as 'examin[ing] both the legislation and the decided cases with a view to discovering the underlying principles which best explain the political and legal decisions behind them'.[125]

For him, this is a two-stage process; the first of which involves 'seeking general principles which are broadly consistent with the legal materials'. There is then a further stage at which 'a further choice must be made between the range of principles which might account for the law', which choice 'necessarily involves a moral decision'. That is the stage at which, in this writer's understanding of Collins' methodology, an avowedly moral evaluation is made as to which, among alternatives which have presented themselves at the first stage, is the conception of 'justice of dismissal' that is the 'best' in the sense not only of being the one which is most powerfully explanatory of the existing law, but also the one which is the most philosophically rational and coherent.

This is not the place in which to examine how successfully Collins has managed to combine the descriptive and the prescriptive elements in his

---

[122] See Eisenberg 1995 at 298–299.   [123] Ibid at 298.   [124] Collins 1992.
[125] Ibid at 3.

interpretative discourse. All would agree that he has, one way or another, enormously enhanced our understanding of and capacity intelligently to criticize the law of termination of employment in the United Kingdom. Nevertheless, despite the overall success of the use of that methodology, in the present chapter of the present work we will proceed differently at the second stage of the analysis. The first stage will, as Collins did on a larger canvas, identify an alternative conception, from that of classical contract law, of the flexibility of the personal work or employment contract. At the second stage, however, rather than attempting to engage in a critical moral evaluation between the alternatives which have been identified, we shall, instead, limit ourselves to such prediction as seems feasible about which of the alternative approaches is, as a matter of practical reality in the courts and tribunals, more likely to prevail.

Reverting to the first of those two stages, we shall depict the emergence of a possible alternative relational approach to the variation, or the flexibility, of the personal work or employment contract, on the basis of two interconnected elements in post-1960s case law. The first of those two elements consists of an evolutionary approach to specific terms, and the second consists of a requirement of fair dealing in the formulation of specific terms.

B. An Evolutionary and Evaluative Approach to Specific Terms

In this subsection, the argument is advanced that there has been a significant shift in recent case law away from the essentially static understanding of the formation of the terms of the personal work or employment contract, and towards an evolutionary approach to the formulation of specific terms. This shift is fraught with significance, because it has the potential to re-balance the personal work or employment contract, so that its basic premises or default rules are somewhat changed. Instead of being primarily directed towards the creation and maintenance of strong managerial prerogative, those basic premises or default rules become more concerned with identifying and vindicating the reasonable mutual expectations of both or all the parties to the personal work or employment contract.

The understanding of the formation of the terms of the personal work or employment contract which is imposed by classical legal contract theory is essentially static, in that it envisages that the whole process of the formation of terms takes place at the single moment at which the contract is made. This sets up a logic in which any given contractual term or provision which has validity at any given moment in the life of the personal work relationship in question has to be regarded either as the result of that initial and momentary act of term formation, or as the result of a subsequent discrete transaction whereby the initial contract or its terms were varied. It has long been recognized that this construct is an essentially artificial one, in the sense that the terms of the contract are not usually all settled upon or even communicated at the moment when the contractual work relationship is created. What has been perhaps slightly less obvious or remarked upon is the way in which this construct in and of itself supported the strong view of unfettered managerial prerogative which, historically at least, was at the heart of the law of the contract of employment.

Perhaps in a sense this is what Alan Fox identified when, writing as a sociologist rather than as an exponent of legal doctrine, he nevertheless offered a profound insight into the development and character of the law of the contract of employment.[126] He commented upon the facility and effectiveness with which the values and norms of the master and servant relationship were, in the course of the nineteenth century, translated into the apparently very different conceptions of classical legal contract theory. In fact, it was the insistence on instant overall term formation at the outset of the contract which made this possible. If the blank canvas of the contract had to be painted in straight away, it was natural and logical to view this as having been done with the broad brushstrokes which accorded general managerial control to the master and imposed submission to that control upon the servant.

The main catalyst for change away from that classical approach was the wave of employee protection legislation of the 1960s and 1970s which in various ways required exact articulation of the terms of contracts of employment in a way that had previously been only sporadically necessary. Two particular aspects of that legislation can be seen in retrospect to have brought about real change of approach. It is now a commonplace, as we have seen earlier in this work, that the fact that this body of legislation invoked a notion of constructive dismissal, which was expounded by the courts as a contractual one, required a wholesale re-evaluation of the content of the continuing contract of employment. Less remarked upon is the way in which the statutory requirement upon the employing entity to supply the employee with particulars of the main terms of employment, originally introduced by the Contracts of Employment Act 1963, also changed the very way in which the courts approach the ascertainment of those terms, as was shown in Chapter two of this work.

The fact that this particular legislation pursued its aim of requiring clarification to employees of the main terms of their employment, not by obliging employing entities to issue written contracts of employment from the outset, but rather by making them supply particulars at a later time, has tended to be seen as denoting the weakness of this measure of formalization of contracts of employment. However, this fact, coupled with the duty which this legislation imposed upon employing entities continually to keep the particulars up to date, actually greatly increased the normative significance of these statutory provisions. It meant that the employee could demand an accurate articulation of the main terms and conditions of

---

[126] Fox 1974 at 181–190.

employment as they stood at the moment at which he or she chose to apply to the employing entity for them, or to a tribunal to complain of the employing entity's default in supplying them.

This in turn had the consequence that the tribunals and courts, in the exercise or supervision of the statutory jurisdiction of ensuring that correct particulars had been supplied, had to recognize that the formulation of terms and conditions could only really be satisfactorily understood as a dynamic or evolutionary process. The orthodoxy, according to classical legal contract theory, might still be, as it was put in *Janata Bank Ltd v Ahmed*,[127] that the notion of the 'creeping variation' of the contract of employment was 'an impossible concept', so that 'the continuously changing contract is unknown to the law'.[128] However, matters were, in practice, being handled differently where applications in respect of missing or defective particulars of terms and conditions were concerned. A key case in this respect is that of *Mears v Safecar Security Ltd*,[129] where an employee sought but failed to use that procedure to establish an implied term entitling him to continuation of remuneration during absence due to sickness. There was no evidence of any arrangement with the employee or notification to the employee at the outset of his employment as to whether he would or would not receive sick pay; but there was clear evidence that, during subsequent absences due to sicknesses, he had not received sick pay, and that other employees in a similar situation had not done so.

On behalf of the employee it was argued that he was in these circumstances entitled to benefit from a rule or presumption in favour of continuation of remuneration during sickness absence, and that the terms of the contract had to be ascertained without reference to 'subsequent actings' following the initial making of the contract and therefore of its terms, unless those actings amounted to a formal variation of the contract. The Court of Appeal ruled that reference could and should be had to subsequent actings, as they provided the best evidence of what the original agreement should be taken to have been. They therefore held that to give effect to 'what was left' of the presumption in favour of sick pay derived from the decision in *Marison v Bell*[130] would be inappropriate because, as Stephenson LJ put it:

To apply it, as if there were 'nothing more', would be manifestly unjust, for it would require the industrial tribunal to compel an employer, who, though in breach of his statutory duty to give the required particulars, would never have agreed to pay any employee wages when absent sick, to pay them to an employee who never expected to get them. The appeal tribunal were right in holding that they were not driven by law to uphold a conclusion so repugnant to common sense and the justice of the case.[131]

---

[127] [1981] ICR 791 (CA).   [128] Ibid at 808 per Donaldson LJ.
[129] [1982] ICR 626 (CA).   [130] [1939] 2 KB 187 (CA)—see above, 217.
[131] [1982] ICR 626 at 651–652.

This therefore amounted to the treating of the formulation of the contract term as to sick pay as having, in the absence of evidence of a concrete term at the outset, an evolutionary quality or dimension which had to be considered in order to arrive at the right answer as to the particulars which should have been supplied. It is notable, indeed it is of crucial importance, that the acceptance of this evolutionary dimension to the process of ascertainment of the terms of the contract transforms that whole process into one which is much less formalistic, and much more evaluative of the substantive merits of the case. That is because the tribunals are now, in effect, invited to consider what are the reasonable expectations of the parties to the contract in light of evidence as to the way the employment relationship has in fact been conducted and has in fact evolved.

The Court of Appeal was later to retrench somewhat upon the position which Stephenson LJ had taken up. In *Eagland v British Telecommunications plc*,[132] the judges declared that they could not agree with the guidance given to industrial tribunals in the *Mears* case in so far as it suggested that they were, in the last resort, to *invent* the terms which were to be implied. However, even in the *Eagland* case the Court of Appeal accepted that it was permissible for the tribunal to find a mandatory term (in the sense of a term of which particulars must be given) to have been agreed upon 'expressly or by implication *or by inference from all the circumstances including in particular the general conduct of the parties*'.[133] This seems to have included conduct occurring during the course of the employment as well as at its inception, so the evolutionary aspect of term formulation continued to be recognized even on the more cautious view, which was taken in that case, of the latitude which was conferred by the written particulars jurisdiction.

In fact, by the time of the *Eagland* decision, matters had developed to a point where tribunals and courts did not need to admit that they were 'inventing' or imputing terms in the absence of any evidence of a formulated term at the outset of the relationship; the techniques for 'discovering' terms already enabled them to make an evaluative assessment of the obligations which had concretized during the course of the contractual relationship. This is well illustrated by the approach taken in the case of *Jones v Associated Tunnelling Ltd*,[134] where the main issue was whether the employing entity could require the employee to transfer from one place of work to another which was equally near to his home, and it was held that the applicable term as to place of work and mobility was that the employee could be required to work at any place within reasonable daily reach of his home.

---

[132] [1993] ICR 644.   [133] Ibid at 654 per Leggatt LJ (emphasis added).
[134] [1981] IRLR 477 (EAT); see above, 243–244.

The way in which that term was found to be applicable is extremely interesting. There was no evidence on which to base a view that a term as to place of work had actually been agreed or notified at the outset of the employment; statements of particulars which had subsequently been issued asserted a mobility obligation in different terms, and there was no evidence that the employee had adverted to the mobility provisions in those particulars. The Employment Appeal Tribunal held that it was appropriate to ascribe a term as to place of work which represented the 'lowest common denominator' of what both parties would have accepted as the mobility obligation to which the employee was subject. This was judged to be an obligation to be mobile within reasonable commuting distance of home, because the evidence suggested that the employee would, at a hypothetical moment of testing by an 'officious bystander', have objected to any transfer beyond that distance.

This method of ascertaining the term which was to be ascribed appears on the face of it to be purely descriptive of the arrangement about place of work and mobility which had been built into the contractual work relationship from its inception. However, closer examination reveals that the formulation of the term was actually treated as an evolutionary process, and that its ascertainment actually involved an evaluation of the expectations which the parties had reasonably formed during that evolutionary process. The formulation is evolutionary, in that the hypothetical officious bystander puts his or her question to the parties not at the outset of the employment, but at some later time when the actual history of the employment relationship can be taken into account.

Furthermore, the ascertainment of the normative outcome of this evolutionary process is an evaluative or prescriptive one, involving a judgment of what the parties *ought* to accept as the specification of their mutual obligations in the light of the dealings that have taken place. There was no meaningful evidence as to whether the employee *in fact* maintained that his contract of employment was or had resolved itself into one which involved no mobility obligation at all. The real question was whether he could *reasonably* maintain that. Managers had sent the worker particulars which asserted that he was subject to a wide mobility obligation. The question was whether they could fairly maintain that this was from the outset or had become a norm of the contractual relationship. This involved judgements about whether there could *fairly* be said to be an implied variation of the contract, or whether it was fair to treat the worker as estopped from denying such a variation.[135]

---

[135] Compare Browne-Wilkinson J, ibid at 481: 'it would be unrealistic of the law to require him to risk a confrontation with his employer on a matter which has no immediate practical impact on the employee'.

Both these aspects of the process of term ascertainment in the *Mears* case and the *Associated Tunnelling* case—the evolutionary aspect and the evaluative aspect—combine to produce an approach to the variation of personal work or employment contracts which is very different from that which is derived from classical legal contract theory. Both elements intertwine with each other to produce a method of term ascertainment in which the question of whether the contract has been varied becomes inseparable from the question of what its terms were in the first place, that is to say at the inception of the contractual work relationship. Term formation and term variation have, in truth, become merely facets of a single issue as to what reasonable expectations should be regarded as identifying the contractual norms of the personal work relationship in question. The huge importance of this development will become more apparent when, in the following subsection, we locate it alongside the parallel development of obligations of fair management and performance in the conduct of the employment relationship.

C. An Obligation of Fair Management and Performance with Regard to Variation

In the previous subsection, we depicted the development of an approach to term formulation which is both evolutionary and evaluative, and which elides the formal distinction between initial formation and subsequent variation. In this subsection, it is argued that development assumes a transformative significance when it is combined with the recent enhancement of behavioural standards in the implied content of the personal work or employment contract. The foremost example of that enhancement, upon which we shall initially concentrate, is the emergence of the implied obligation of trust and confidence as attaching at least to all contracts of employment, if not, as has been contended earlier in this work, in great measure to all personal work or employment contracts.

That latter development interacts with the former one in the following crucial way. It seems to be generally accepted that the newly emergent implied obligation of mutual trust and confidence, like other behavioural standards which form part of the implied content of personal work or employment contracts such as obligations of care for health and safety, applies from the very inception of the contractual employment relationship. (In the view of the present writer, it might convincingly be argued that it applies from the formation of the contract even if that antedates the commencement of the working part of the employment relationship.)

This means that the behavioural standard of mutual trust and confidence, in place right from the commencement of employment, applies to the whole conduct of the contractual employment relationship. As the formulation of specific terms is more and more clearly understood as an evolutionary process, taking place over a time continuum which has its beginning in the formation of the contractual employment relationship, so it becomes more and more clear that specific term formulation is itself an integral part of the conduct of the relationship, part of a course of dealings the whole of which is subject to the behavioural obligation as to mutual trust and confidence, implied during and from the first day of the subsistence of the contract.

On the face of it, this may appear to be a very radical view of the way in which the law of personal work or employment contracts approaches both the making and the variation of the terms of those contracts. It seems to subject both term making and term variation to substantive behavioural standards in a way which is resolutely denied by classical legal contract theory. However, this kind of reasoning has actually long been embedded in the way that we approach some aspects of the ascertainment of the terms and conditions of personal work or employment contracts. We shall argue that recent developments represent the extension of that mode of thinking to different dimensions of that process. It will be useful to distinguish between behavioural standards applying to workers, and those applying to employing entities, that is to say to the conduct of work relationships by employing enterprises.

In the law of the contract of employment, we have become so familiar with, as to take for granted, a mind-set in which the specific obligations of workers are shaped and defined by the general behavioural standards which are imposed upon them as part of the implied content of their contracts. The specific terms of employment are often judged by reference to those standards, and this often dissolves the distinction between the initial formation and the subsequent variation of those specific terms. For example, in the case of *Cresswell v Board of Inland Revenue*,[136] the central issue was whether the Board of Inland Revenue was acting within the bounds of the contracts of employment[137] of its staff when requiring them to operate or utilize computer systems to perform their tasks, or whether, on the other hand, this was to seek to impose new and different contracts of employment.

Crucial to the court's conclusion that the former view was the correct one was what Walton J regarded as the undoubted fact that:

An employee is expected to adapt himself[138] to new methods and techniques introduced in the course of his employment.[139]

This meant that the behavioural standard of adaptability or flexibility was built into the employee's contractual obligations, so that the specific terms

---

[136] [1984] ICR 508 (ChD).

[137] It was, rather surprisingly, not seriously contested in this case that these workers, although clearly civil servants, were employed under contracts of employment as such, although the question of whether civil servants were so employed had for long been and still remained a question of keen controversy; compare above, 69–70.

[138] Walton J referred to the employees throughout his judgment as if they were all men despite the fact that four of the eight plaintiffs were women, which was probably a representative proportion of all the staff in the categories concerned.

[139] [1984] ICR 508 (ChD) at 518.

and conditions which made up his or her job content were defined accordingly. Moreover, that was equally the case whether that definition was regarded as the result of initial formation or subsequent variation of those terms and conditions.

It is not, however, being argued here that Walton J's decision was a one-sided one which imposed behavioural standards upon the employees alone and not upon the enterprise or its managers. It was equally obvious, in his view, that:

in a proper case the employer must provide any necessary training or re-training;

and that it would:

in all cases be a question of pure fact as to whether the re-training involves the acquisition of such esoteric skills *that it would not be reasonable to expect the employee to acquire them.*[140]

He judged that events (consisting of the actual smooth introduction of computerization of the PAYE system) had shown that it was perfectly reasonable to expect these workers so to adapt their working methods. So the ascertainment of specific terms and conditions—the conclusion that these workers' job specifications at the time in issue included working with computers—was based on an evolutionary and qualitative evaluation of the basis on which the contractual employment relationship had both been formed and conducted.

The use of reasoning of this kind has been very greatly intensified by the emergence of the implied obligation of mutual trust and obligation as a behavioural standard for the conduct of the contractual employment relationship by all those involved in it, the employing enterprise and its managers as well as its workers; and that has become increasingly applicable both to the formulation and the variation of terms and conditions of employment, and has bridged the distinction between the initial formation and the subsequent variation of those terms and conditions. A good illustration of this trend, already discussed in an earlier chapter,[141] is the decision in the case of *Transco plc v O'Brien*[142] that the employing enterprise had been in breach of the implied obligation of trust and confidence in refusing the claimant the favourable redundancy terms which they offered to other employees in relation to whom the claimant was held to be entitled to expect the same treatment.[143]

---

[140] [1984] ICR 508 (ChD) at 519 (emphasis added).
[141] See above, 223–228.   [142] [2002] ICR 721 (CA).
[143] A somewhat comparable application of the implied obligation of trust and confidence to the variation of terms of personal employment contracts occurred in *Cantor Fitzgerald International v Bird* [2002] IRLR 867 (CA), where it was held that the employing entity had acted in breach of that obligation in making an aggressive attempt to impose a variation of remuneration arrangements upon a group of employees; see also above, 229.

This decision involves, very clearly, the full elision of issues about variation of the terms and conditions of employment with issues about their formation and content, and the subjection of the whole unified set of issues to a qualitative evaluation of the conduct of the contractual employment relationship from and including its inception. For, in one sense, the issue was about whether the employing entity had acted contractually properly in relation to a *variation* of the contract of employment, that is to say in deciding whether to offer this employee what in the judgment of the Employment Appeal Tribunal is referred to as 'a revised contract of employment with enhanced redundancy terms'.[144] In another sense, however, the issue was about the continuing content of the original contract of employment and about whether the employing enterprise was giving effect to the reasonable expectations of the employee arising out of the contractual relationship as it had actually evolved and been conducted. This was held to require a recognition that, as matters had developed, it would be arbitrary and destructive of trust and confidence to treat this worker other than in the way that other 'permanent employees' had been treated.

The same point is made even more clearly by the equally recent decision of the Court of Appeal in the case of *French v Barclays Bank plc*,[145] where it was held that the employing entity had acted in breach of its contractual obligation of trust and confidence in changing to the employee's detriment the terms of a bridging loan which had been granted to the employee to assist him in moving house when he was relocated at its request. The decision or actions of the employing entity were variously referred to as a change of policy, or a change in the terms on which loans were made to employees, and the Court of Appeal did not make it clear whether they regarded this as, on the one hand, an attempt by the employing entity to impose a variation of the terms of the contract of employment (or of an associated contractual loan scheme), or, on the other hand, as the inappropriate exercise of a discretion conferred by the terms of the contract of employment.

The Court of Appeal did not need to make such a distinction because they took the view that there was a central composite set of issues with a central composite answer. The central composite issue was:

What the terms of the contract of employment of Mr French were as at January 1989 [the time at which the employing entity required the employee to relocate] *and what Mr French's legitimate expectations from those terms would be*.[146]

The central composite answer was that:

First, he was subject to the mobility clause ... Second, if he was asked to relocate he would not expect to be asked to do so at a loss ... Third, there would be implied

---

[144] *BG Plc v O'Brien* [2001] IRLR 496 (CA) at 500 per Mr Recorder Langstaff QC.
[145] [1998] IRLR 646.   [146] Ibid at 649 per Waller LJ (emphasis added).

into the contract a term that the bank would not act so as to destroy the confidence and trust existing between the bank and its employee... There would be some overlap between the obligations and duties imposed by the express terms and those imposed by such an implied term. But it would... clearly be a breach of this implied term for the bank to insist on a relocation, offer a bridging loan... and then seek to alter those terms to the detriment of Mr French.[147]

Further analysis of the facts confirmed that these had indeed been the claimant's legitimate expectations, and that the employing entity had acted in breach of contract by failing to give effect to them. The behavioural standard of trust and confidence had controlled the conduct of the contractual relationship from its inception, both helping to shape the legitimate expectations which the parties acquired over time and determining whether they had acted reasonably in relation to those expectations. The (apparently unconscious) similarity between this mode of reasoning and that of judicial review of administrative action on the ground of irrationality is a striking one. Yet this reasoning was deployed strictly and purely in the factual and conceptual context of the law of personal work or employment contracts. All this could be seen as tending towards the general imposition by the courts and tribunals of mutual obligations of fair dealing in the formation, implementation, and variation of the terms and conditions of personal work or employment contracts. There are indications that such an approach is being taken in order to ascertain the effect of collective bargaining upon individual personal work or employment contracts. We proceed to consider the extent and impact of that development in the next subsection.

D. FAIR MANAGEMENT AND PERFORMANCE, VARIATION, AND COLLECTIVE BARGAINING

Rather as with the law of performance, breach, and remuneration as discussed in the previous chapter, we suggest that the law concerning the effect of collective bargaining upon the identification and evolution of terms and conditions of employment can usefully be understood by reference to an overarching principle of fair management and performance. However, the development of that overarching principle, with regard to the effect of collective bargaining upon personal work or employment contracts, is no simple or straightforward matter; there is a continuing tension between relatively formalistic and relatively creative approaches to the application of such a principle. We proceed to illustrate the development of the general principle and the tensions which are attendant upon that development.

Until relatively recently, the questions both of initial incorporation of collective agreements into personal work or employment contracts and

---

[147] [1998] IRLR at 649 (Waller J).

of subsequent variation of those contracts by collective agreement have been treated almost entirely as issues of individual contracting with each particular worker. This insistence on the individuation of the collective bargaining process as the condition and determinant of its legal effect has imparted an artificiality and constrictedness to the reasoning and decisions of courts and tribunals in this area. That approach was still very much the dominant one in *Alexander v Standard Telephones & Cables Ltd (No 2)*,[148] where it was held that the seniority provision of the redundancy procedure which formed part of the collective agreement between the employing entity and the recognized trade union was not incorporated into the employment contracts of individual workers so as to give them a personal contractual entitlement to the application of a 'last in, first out' order of selection for redundancy. The individuated approach was strongly emphasized by Hobhouse J:

The relevant contract is that between the individual employee and his employer; it is the contractual intention of those two parties which must be ascertained. In so far as that intention is to be found in a written document, that document must be construed on ordinary contractual principles. In so far as there is no such document or that document is not complete or conclusive, their contractual intention has to be ascertained by inference from the other available material including collective agreements.[149]

That approach is one which militates against the contractual effectiveness of the normative provisions of collective agreements, especially those which are in their nature not immediately implemented in practice, such as those which deal with the handling of redundancies which may occur in the future.

A shift in approach and methodology with regard to the normative impact of collective bargaining seems to have occurred since that time. Something of a turning point occurred in the decision in *Lee v GEC Plessey Telecommunications Ltd*.[150] Here it was held that a group of workers were entitled to a declaration that their contracts of employment included a term derived from a collective agreement entitling them to enhanced severance payments in the event of termination of their employment on the ground of redundancy, and that this entitlement had not been removed by a subsequent collective agreement involving a pay increase for those workers coupled with an agreement that the enhanced severance payments would not apply to certain subsequent redundancies. That decision was rationalized in the traditional terms of the normative impact of the collective agreements upon the individual contracts; thus it was held that the workers had provided consideration for the original introduction of the enhanced redundancy payments, that the union had not been acting as their agents

---

[148] [1991] IRLR 286 (QBD).   [149] Ibid at 292, para 31.
[150] [1993] IRLR 383 (QBD).

in making the subsequent collective agreement, and so forth. However, that rationalization was preceded by and based upon a primary analysis of the collective bargaining process itself, from which the crucial conclusion was that the subsequent agreement should not, as a matter of substance, be regarded as a composite package involving the abandonment of the enhanced redundancy terms for this group of workers.

Another milestone along that road towards a more holistic substantive view of the impact of collective bargaining upon the contractual rights of individual workers was the decision of the Court of Appeal in *Adams v British Airways plc*.[151] Here the issue was whether, upon the takeover of one airline by another, the provision in the collective agreement between the airline and the pilots' union, whereby pilots took their seniority from the date of first joining the service of the employing entity, operated to bring in the pilots of the airline which had been taken over as new entrants or with the benefit of their existing seniority. The Court of Appeal arrived at the latter view by means of a searching analysis of the substance of the collective seniority arrangements in their overall factual and commercial context.[152] Of key significance in the conducting of that analysis was the recognition by the Court of Appeal that this was an adjudication between the conflicting interests of two groups of workers[153]—the pilots of the airline which was being taken over and the pilots of the acquiring airline—and that the employing entity owed a duty to both groups of workers to act fairly and reasonably with proper regard for the mutual trust and confidence which should be inherent in the relationship with them.[154]

A further illustration of this approach of genuinely collective evaluation of claims to rights deriving from collective agreements is provided by the case of *Edinburgh Council v Brown*,[155] where the Employment Appeal Tribunal had to decide whether the employing entity was acting in accordance with contracts of employment when it did away with a previous policy and practice of treating regrading decisions as retrospective to the date on which the application for regrading had been made. The policy of retrospection had been adopted by the employing entity as a result of a recommendation from its joint consultative committee following deliberation with union representatives. The abandonment of the policy resulted from a recommendation made by its personnel committee in which the unions had

---

[151] [1996] IRLR 574 (CA).

[152] A somewhat comparable protectiveness of the rights of workers acquired from collective agreements upon a transfer of employment is manifested in *Whent v Cartledge Ltd* [1997] IRLR 153 (EAT). Compare the general discussion of the operation of the TUPE Regulations upon acquired rights under contracts of employment, below, 505 et seq.

[153] The action was brought by the pilots of the acquiring airline claiming that the recognition of the acquired seniority of the pilots of the taken-over airline constituted a breach of the contracts of employment of the pilots of the acquiring airline.

[154] Sir Thomas Bingham MR at 578, para 29.   [155] [1999] IRLR 208.

not been involved except that, at its own request, one of them was allowed to be heard by the committee.

In order to ascertain whether the employee was to be deemed to have agreed to the withdrawal of retrospection, the Employment Appeal Tribunal in effect evaluated whether it had been the subject of an adequate and meaningful collective bargaining process. It was held that, whereas the retrospection arrangement had been introduced by a process which could be so regarded, its withdrawal had not been the subject of an equivalent process involving genuine participation on the part of representatives of the employees. The withdrawal was therefore regarded as a purported but ineffective unilateral variation of the contract of employment by the employing entity to the detriment of the employee. We proceed to consider how far this kind of partly substantive and partly procedural direct evaluation of the collective bargaining process has become the typical method of construction of the impact of that process upon individual employment contracts.

It would seem a reasonable assessment to say that, although this has indeed become the predominant method of construction, there is a degree of tension between a relatively formalistic and a relatively creative approach to its application. In two recent decisions, that tension appears between the reasoning in the Employment Appeal Tribunal and in the Court of Appeal. In the case of *Ali v Christian Salvesen Food Services Ltd*,[156] the issue was whether, when a collective agreement had varied existing employment contracts by replacing a payment system based upon weekly hours with one based upon annualized hours, it had impliedly provided for workers whose employment was terminated before the end of the payment year to be credited for hours of overtime worked although the annual threshold for overtime payment had not yet been reached. At both levels of appeal the collective bargaining process was scrutinized for the answer, but different approaches produced different answers. The Employment Appeal Tribunal took the relatively creative approach that this was an obvious gap which the collective bargainers would have recognized and which the court should fill by implying a term for prorating.

The Court of Appeal took the opposite view; its reasoning was that:

It is in the nature of such an agreement that it should be concise and clear—so as to be readily understood by all who are concerned to operate it. One would expect the parties to such an agreement to set their face against any attempt to legislate for every possible contingency. Should there be any topic left uncovered by an agreement of that kind, the natural inference . . . is not that there has been an omission so obvious as to require judicial correction, but rather that the topic was omitted advisedly from the terms of the agreement on the ground that it was seen as too controversial or too

---

[156] [1996] ICR 1 (EAT); [1997] ICR 25 (CA); see above, 138.

complicated to justify any variation of the main terms of the agreement to take account of it.[157]

There seems so little reason to accept this as an explanation for the omission to deal with this overwhelmingly likely contingency that this must be regarded as a rationalization for a rather literal or formalistic approach on the part of the Court.

In the very recent case of *Henry v London General Transport Services Ltd*[158] there was a comparable difference in approach at the two appellate levels, although in this instance it produced no difference in outcome. Here the issue was whether individual employees were bound by a so-called 'framework agreement' between the managers of the enterprise in which they were employed, and the sole recognized trade union for bargaining purposes, which provided for a set of changes to terms and conditions, which were adverse ones so far as the workers were concerned, and which were to apply in the event of a proposed management buyout which did in the event take place. The evidence was that a significant majority of the workforce had voted in favour of the adoption of the framework agreement at workplace meetings, but that, when it was put into operation, it was accepted only under protest by staff at some of the bus garages from which the enterprise was operated. Both the Employment Appeal Tribunal and the Court of Appeal concluded that the framework agreement might have been incorporated into individual employment contracts, and remitted the case back to the employment tribunal for further inquiry as to the facts.

However, the styles of reasoning were divergent. That of the Employment Appeal Tribunal was cast in a mould radically different from that of orthodox contract theory, and involved an overt substantive and procedural evaluation of the dealings through which the terms of the contractual employment relationships in question had evolved. That element of evaluation was introduced by the use of the notion of custom, or custom and practice, as a source of contractual norms. This evokes the fact that custom has sometimes been treated as a source of specific terms and conditions of employment, and that Otto Kahn-Freund famously deployed this idea to suggest that specific terms derived from collective agreements could be regarded as incorporated into individual contracts on the basis that the collective agreements represented the 'crystallized custom' of the employment relationships in question.[159]

In the judgment of the Employment Appeal Tribunal, a subtle but significant transformation of that approach took place. The idea of custom was applied not, as in Kahn-Freund's theory, to the specific terms which were the outcome of the collective bargaining process, but to the actual or notional norm by which collective agreements were incorporated into individual

---

[157] Waite LJ [1997] ICR 25 at 31B–D.   [158] [2001] IRLR 132.
[159] See Kahn–Freund 1954 at 56–57.

contracts of employment. In other words, the so-called 'bridging term' which links the collective agreement to the individual contract was itself subjected to the test of whether it complied with the conditions upon which customs are accepted as forming part of the content of individual contracts of employment. As such, it was therefore scrutinized for the three required qualities of 'reasonableness, certainty, and notoriety'.

In this case, the practice of regarding the outcomes of collective agreements as automatically or directly incorporated into individual contracts of employment, deemed to have the agreement of individual employees, was regarded as displaying those qualities in sufficient measure as to qualify it as a contractually binding custom. The requirement of reasonableness was regarded as satisfied:

given the large number of staff concerned, the occasional commercial need for a speedy decision on changes in employment rights and the consequential difficulty in conducting individual negotiations and given also the settled history of the union's negotiating role over a number of years.[160]

This is a style of reasoning which encapsulates the kind of substantive and procedural evaluation of the collective bargaining process which has been presented as a radical recent development in the present subsection.

The Court of Appeal, by contrast, had little time for this careful analysis of the reasonableness of the custom of incorporation of the outcomes of collective agreements into individual employment contracts.[161] That Court was far more disposed simply to regard the workers as having accepted the reduction in pay by working under the new terms and conditions for a significant period of time, this amounting to an individual affirmation of the contract according to the analysis in *Cox Toner International Ltd v Crook*.[162] In the equally recent decision in *Harris v Richard Lawson Autologistics Ltd*,[163] the Court of Appeal took a rather similar approach when they treated the workers' *de facto* continuation in employment, following a reduction in remuneration agreed with the workers' shop steward, as confirming the employing entity's entitlement to rely upon the ostensible authority of the shop steward to negotiate terms of employment on the workers' behalf. There is some risk that these rather formalistic and individuated approaches may result in a lack of attention to the *representativeness* of the collective bargaining process, which is a matter of special importance with regard to collective agreements *in peius*, that is to say involving a deterioration in terms and conditions of employment for the workers concerned, such as were under consideration in these very recent cases.

---

[160] [2001] IRLR 132 at 136 per Waller LJ.

[161] See Pill LJ at [2002] IRLR 474, para 30: 'I have to say that [apart from certain specific points] I find the EAT's reasoning on the custom and practice issue difficult to understand and accept.'   [162] [1981] ICR 823 (EAT).

[163] [2002] IRLR 476 (CA).

We turn from the immediate questions about the incorporation of original terms from collective agreements and the effecting of variation of terms by collective agreements, to a consideration of the general issue of whether a change is occurring in the wider approach to the variation and evolution of personal work or employment contracts.

E. Variation, Flexibility, and Competitiveness

We have argued that there is in the course of emergence, albeit somewhat intermittently, a style of reasoning about the variation of personal work or employment contracts, in which, instead of being judged according to classical formal notions in which initial formation is sharply distinguished from subsequent variation, the question of variation is subsumed in a general evaluation of the normative development of the contractual employment relationship. The recent case law both supports the idea of such a development and affords some important insights into the evaluative criteria or instruments of adjudication which the courts and tribunals are using for this purpose. We have seen that, in general terms, courts and tribunals now draw heavily upon the idea of mutual obligations of trust and confidence, and we have argued that this contributes to a broad notion of fair management and performance within contractual employment relationships. That argument poses the question of how we might expect such a notion to be expounded and worked out in detail.

The judgment of the Employment Appeal Tribunal in the *Henry* case provides some useful pointers, even if, as we have seen,[164] the Court of Appeal later reverted to a more traditional style of reasoning. The Employment Appeal Tribunal was unusually willing to articulate the background considerations which it felt should be borne in mind in making these assessments in cases such as the one it was now called upon to consider. These background considerations were concerned with the interrelating of notions of fairness, flexibility, and competitiveness. The judgment of Lindsay J begins by placing the particular issue in the case in question in a larger context in which managers of enterprises operating in an environment of competitive tendering and management or management and employee buyouts need to have the assurance that they can make binding deals with their workforce to effect labour economies which will ensure their commercial survival.

In such situations, the court opined that:

In our view the law, if it is possible to do so consistently with principle, should recognise the exigencies of commercial life and do nothing to discourage collective bargaining. Moreover, where a majority of employees have approved new and less advantageous terms of employment and have thus made sacrifices so that their employer could obtain work or stay in business and keep up the employment of existing staff, there can be an unattractive moral dimension where some only,

---

[164] See above, 285.

a minority, of the workforce later claim that they are still entitled to be paid at the former and higher rate.[165]

On the other hand:

Against such practical need for a speedy and reliable practical response, there is a need also to ensure that individuals are adequately informed and adequately consulted and that the less attractive terms are not imposed unfairly or without a real opportunity to protest against or reform or refuse them. As in so many areas of the law, a balance needs to be struck.[166]

Hugh Collins' recent article on 'Regulating the Employment Relation for Competitiveness'[167] shows how this kind of analysis has become embedded in the policy discourse of the most recent governments with regard to employment law. It is still quite striking to find that reasoning being deployed in the hitherto normally austerely classical process of ascertainment of whether there has been a valid variation of the terms of the contract of employment. At the beginning of this section, the undertaking was to try to predict whether this style of reasoning would become predominant in the law of personal work or employment contracts.

There are some strong reasons for anticipating that it may do so. The most important of these is that this kind of reasoning seems to enable courts and tribunals engaged in the adjudication of issues arising under the law of personal work or employment contracts to define their own functions in ways that seem to them to be coherent and convincing. The ideal of discovering and effectuating a notion of fair management and performance in the conduct of contractual employment relationships, having regard to considerations of flexibility and competitiveness, is one which those courts and tribunals can convincingly address to themselves as well as to the parties to those relationships. It is likely to have enduring appeal as a recipe for deploying value judgments without being partisan as between employing entities and workers. The decisions which have been cited as displaying this approach are as much inclined in favour of employing entities as of workers.

Current developments in both the law and the practice of employment contracting focus attention upon the development of control over the variation of terms and conditions of employment in the interests of flexibility and competitiveness. An important paper by Simon Deakin published in 1999 on 'Organisational Change, Labour Flexibility and the Contract of Employment'[168] reported and analysed the findings of an empirical study upon employment contracts of organizational change at enterprise level in the early and middle 1990s. It showed that the main effect of the so-called 'individualization' of employment contracting during that period had been

---

[165] [2001] IRLR 132 at 133.   [166] Ibid.   [167] Collins 2001.
[168] Deakin 1999.

not so much a transfer of bargaining from collective to individual level, but rather a strengthening and formalization of the discretionary powers of employing enterprises to vary the terms and conditions of employment and arrangements for employment of their workers. This flexibilization from the point of view of the employing entity, which Deakin's study showed might result from collective bargaining as well as from unilateral rule formulation by the employing entity, does much to heighten the continuity between variation *within* contractual terms and variation *of* contractual terms which has been remarked upon in the course of this chapter.

In those circumstances, a continuous set of issues is identified as to how the law of personal work or employment contracts regulates, in the interests of flexibility and competitiveness, the exercise by employing entities of discretions with respect to the variation of contractual arrangements for employment. We have sought to show how the common law of personal work or employment contracts is beginning to develop a body of jurisprudence which addresses this question. A highly significant statutory model for further development is offered by the provisions of the Employment Act 2002 with regard to flexible working. These provisions[169] essentially confer upon employees who are parents of young children a right to apply for flexible working, which means, more specifically, a right to request variation of their contract of employment so as to provide for a flexible working pattern (to enable them to combine work and parental responsibilities more effectively).

Their significance to the present discussion consists in the way in which they formulate the sole grounds on which the employing entity may refuse such a request:

(1) An employer to whom an application [for flexible working] is made— ...
   (b) shall only refuse the application because he considers that one or more of the following grounds applies—

      (i) the burden of additional costs,
      (ii) detrimental effect on ability to meet customer demand,
      (iii) inability to re-organise work among existing staff,
      (iv) inability to recruit additional staff,
      (v) detrimental impact on quality,
      (vi) detrimental impact on performance,
      (vii) insufficiency of work during the periods the employee proposes to work,
      (viii) planned structural changes, and
      (ix) such other grounds as the Secretary of State may specify by regulations.[170]

Provision is made to ensure that the employing entity will be required to follow a prescribed procedure of discussion of the application, explanation

---

[169] Employment Act 2002, s 47, inserting new Part 8A on Flexible Working into the Employment Rights Act 1996. At the time of writing these provisions are due to come into force on 6 April 2003.   [170] New s 80G of the Employment Rights Act 1996.

of grounds of refusal to the employee, and offer of opportunity to appeal against refusal.[171]

We suggest that the future development of the common law notion of fair management and performance, as it applies to the exercise of contractual discretions to vary arrangements for employment, might very usefully be modelled upon this approach to the making out of a sound business case, in the interests of flexibility and competitiveness, for the exercise of such discretions by the employing entity in its own interest, or for the refusal to exercise such discretions in the interests of workers. It is not suggested that the implied contractual obligations could or would amount to the kind of concrete duty to exercise a discretion in favour of the worker, in the absence of justification for refusal, which the statute imposes in this particular context, but rather that this set of criteria might be used in a looser sense to guide a decision whether the employing entity had complied with the broad behavioural standard which the implied contractual term requires. We proceed from that argument to offer brief conclusions which summarize and evaluate the argument of the chapter as a whole.

CONCLUSION

In this chapter, the method of restatement has been used to concentrate attention upon the potential for development of the law concerning variation of arrangements for work and remuneration under personal work or employment contracts in a particular direction. That direction is away from the classical view of variation as a matter of formal re-contracting, according to which view the key determinants of the contractual effect of purported variations are factors such as consideration, contractual intention, waiver or estoppel, and the distinction between variation of contract and the rescission of one contract and its replacement by another. That direction is towards an analysis of the law of variation which emphasizes the continuity of issues between the treatment of variation and the construction of the express and implied content of the contract itself. In this chapter, that continuity of issues has been depicted as crucial towards the understanding of personal work or employment contracts as the legal expression of continuing relationships in which the administration and adjustment of arrangements for work and remuneration is largely under the control of the employing entity; and it has been argued that the task of the law of personal work or employment contracts is to achieve a consistent and balanced construction and regulation of that set of discretionary powers.

The suggestion has been that there are real tendencies towards that achievement, so that in this area the method of restatement can be applied

---

[171]   See new s 80G(2) of the Employment Rights Act 1996.

more in a descriptive than in a prescriptive sense. Two caveats must, however, be recorded. One is that the application of these arguments to semi-dependent workers' contracts remains, as throughout most of this work, highly speculative. On the one hand, there is no single point in the argumentation of this chapter at which there seems any positive need, in terms either of theoretical coherence or judicial authority, to draw a distinction between contracts of employment and semi-dependent workers' contracts. On the other hand, the central notion of fair management and performance, which has been invoked as an instrument of reasoning and of positive development of the law, may yet, despite the arguments which have been advanced to the contrary in this work, be treated as uniquely applicable to contracts of employment rather than to semi-dependent workers' contracts.

The second caveat is one which embarks upon a line of argument which will be pursued at length in the succeeding chapters. It has appeared in the course of this chapter that a significant strand in the reasoning about variation of employment contracts consists of the idea that the employing entity has an underlying power of variation which is derived from its power of termination. Although not strongly proclaimed in the modern law, this notion still has a latent influence on the law of variation. It has the potential to undermine the notion of fair management and performance. In the next two chapters, it will be shown that the notion of the employing entity's right of termination as an unfettered one is a pervasive and persistent theme in the common law of employment contracts. The inconsistency and tension between that perception and the growth of common law regulation of other contractual discretions of the employing entity will emerge as a fault line running through the law of personal work and employment contracts. So the arguments which have been advanced in this chapter must be considered in a particular practical and theoretical context created by the law about the termination of those contracts as considered in the succeeding chapters.

6

Lawful Termination by the Employing Entity

INTRODUCTION

Having in previous chapters considered the formation and the evolution of personal work or employment contracts, in this and the succeeding chapters we turn to consider their termination. In treating that large and highly complex subject, we shall make use of, and seek further to develop, an apparatus of explanation and criticism which has been devised in the course of the earlier chapters. The main features of that apparatus which have so far emerged are:

(1) that it is useful to work within a composite category of personal work or employment contracts rather than with a basic distinction between contracts of employment and contracts for services;

(2) that we should recognize that the exposition of the law of personal work or employment contracts by courts and tribunals is crucially conditioned by the different adjudicative contexts in which it takes place;

(3) that we can think about much of the law of personal work or employment contracts as explicable in terms of a principle or set of principles of fair dealing; and

(4) that we should recognize that many of the apparently clear and well understood core concepts of the law of personal work or employment contracts are actually deeply contested or indeterminate.

This explanatory and critical apparatus is tested to the utmost, and placed under the maximum degree of tension, when it is applied to the analysis of the law of termination of personal work or employment contracts. The composite category of personal work or employment contracts becomes especially hard to maintain in the face of the perception that the very concept of 'dismissal' is special to contracts of employment and does not apply to other personal work or employment contracts. The case law displays very different features according to whether it is laid down in the remedial context of awarding damages or injunctions, or, on the other hand, in the interpretative context of interpreting statutory notions of dismissal or termination of the contract of employment. A set of principles of fair dealing is discernible, but unusually difficult to trace through a forest of technical doctrines and rules about remedies. Finally, it becomes apparent that many key concepts, such as that of the termination itself of the personal work or employment contract, have no single clear meaning. In this chapter, we start to seek ways of organizing and thinking about the subject of termination which may recognize and respond to those difficulties.

SECTION 1: TERMINATION, DISMISSAL, AND LEGALITY

A. TERMINATION, LEGALITY, REMEDIAL LAW, AND REGULATORY INTERPRETATION

We begin that exercise of organizing our analysis of the law concerning the termination of personal work or employment contracts by questioning whether we should regard an overall or general analysis of that topic as feasible and useful. The answers to those questions will then suggest particular ways in which to construct that analysis. Essentially, it will be argued that the feasibility and utility of a general analysis of the termination of contracts of employment has been assumed or taken for granted by writers on employment law, not least by the author of the present work. This assumption should not lightly have been made, because it has been and remains extremely difficult to arrive at such an analysis in a coherent way, and the perception that there must logically be a cohesive story of the termination of personal work or employment contracts which is out there waiting to be discerned may be a misleading one. It will be suggested that we nevertheless need to seek the nearest available approach to a cohesive story, and that the best way to do so is by considering the interplay between remedial law and regulatory interpretation in the making of this body of law.

There have been two main reasons for assuming that a general analysis of the termination of personal work or employment contracts is both feasible and useful. Firstly, the making of such an analysis has seemed to be a satisfactory way of establishing the doctrinal foundations of the contract law of employment, by analogy with the way in which we postulate an analysis of the termination of contracts of all kinds as part of the doctrinal base for the general law of contracts. Secondly, the body of employment legislation enacted from the time of the Contracts of Employment Act 1963 onwards has assumed and depended upon such an analysis, by linking many rights of employees to the termination of their contracts of employment, and more especially to the termination of those contracts by the employing entity, which is the essence of the concept of 'dismissal' as widely used in that legislation. For that perfectly good set of reasons, expositions of the law of the contract of employment or of employment law as a whole normally contain a set of chapters which between them amount to a comprehensive and categorical treatment of the termination of contracts of employment.

This mode of exposition is apt to create an illusion about the way in which the law concerning the termination of contracts of employment, or of personal work or employment contracts in general, has evolved in the courts or tribunals in which its case law has been decided. In the terms of the distinction, introduced earlier in this chapter, between remedial law and regulatory interpretation, the present law about the termination of personal work or employment contracts has most of its historical origins in remedial law, especially in the case law concerning the action for damages for wrongful dismissal—even if, as will appear, that case law was later heavily overlaid with regulatory interpretation of statutory deployment of contractual concepts such as that of dismissal. So we should regard the action for wrongful dismissal as the starting point for the historical construction of the law of termination of personal work or employment contracts.

Although the case law of the action for damages for wrongful dismissal is quite foundational to the law concerning the termination of personal work or employment contracts, that case law was not, before the current era of individual employment law, greatly concerned with the issue of how and when the personal work or employment contract is terminated. The action was, historically, based on dismissal in the sense of de facto ending of the employment relationship by the employer, even before it was clearly established that the relationship was generally to be understood in terms of a continuing relational contract or series of contracts.[1] The central issues were the wrongfulness of the dismissal and availability of damages in respect of it, rather than the contract-terminating character or effect of the dismissal. The issue of wrongfulness came to be expounded more and more firmly in contractual language in the course of the nineteenth century; but it would still be inappropriate to think of that legal discourse as being actually derived from, or part of, a theory about the termination of contracts in general or contracts of employment in particular.

From that central starting point in the law of wrongful dismissal, a body of case law developed which could, by the time of the original version of the present work in 1976, be represented as a general schematic treatment of the whole subject of the termination of the contract of employment. Indeed, by that time, the framers of employment legislation were both demanding and presupposing such a scheme as a necessary tool for the interpretation of their enactments. Meeting that demand was an important task, but the achievement of it, as with much of the law of the contract of employment, was at the cost of a certain loss of awareness of the historical dimension and evolutionary character of this body of law. We can recover some of that awareness, it is to be hoped without becoming too antiquarian in our approach, by concentrating on the two notions of wrongful dismissal and lawful dismissal.

---

[1] Compare, generally, the analysis of this evolution offered in Deakin 2001.

Those two notions of wrongful and lawful dismissal evolved in counter-point to each other. Since at no time in the history of the law of the employment relationship or contract was the idea entertained that *all* dismissals were wrongful, or even presumptively wrongful—quite the contrary, in fact—it follows that the notion of wrongful dismissal had to evolve by distinction from, or by contrast with, some kind of notion of rightful dismissal. There can be no doubt that such a notion developed vigorously, in the form of a concept of *lawful* dismissal; the only doubt is when and how far that concept took shape in specifically *contractual* terms, rather than as the product of customary or statutory norms (as established, for example, by the Master and Servant Acts[2]). The very terminology of 'lawfulness' hints at a notion which is based more on general norms forming part of 'the law of the land', than upon the private norms of contract.

Anyway, by whatever historical steps—a question which is fascinating but should not take up further space here—a conception of lawful dismissal has evolved in the form of a series of default terms or interpretative models of the contract of employment. We can even discern, more widely, the outlines of a conception of the lawful termination, by the employing entity, of personal work or employment contracts in general. However, that conception is in great need of re-examination and modern re-evaluation; that must be the necessary preliminary or key to a real understanding of the law of termination of personal work or employment contracts as a whole. The remainder of this chapter is accordingly devoted to such an analysis. It will lead on to a corresponding reconsideration, in the next chapter, of the notion of wrongful termination by the employing entity.

B. Lawful Termination by the Employing Entity, Duration, and Job Security

In the previous subsection, it was argued that we should understand the law of termination of personal work or employment contracts as being not really derived from a general theory or notion of contractual termination, but rather as being constructed around a central antithesis between the ideas of wrongful dismissal and lawful dismissal from employment under a contract of employment. In this subsection, we seek to develop the notion of lawful termination of personal work or employment contracts by the employing entity, and to argue that it should be regarded as a deeply complex and multifaceted notion which is at the core of the conceptions of the *duration* of personal work or employment contracts, and of the kind and degree of *job security* which the law of personal work or employment contracts provide for the workers who are party to them. This might seem a rather obvious set of propositions; but it seeks to present a challenge to an often-encountered understanding of the law of termination of personal

---

[2] Compare Freedland 1976 at 144–145, Deakin 1998 at 214.

work or employment contracts which is apt to be oversimplified, or over-fragmented, both in a descriptive and in a normative sense.

At the heart of this widely-held perception of the termination of personal work or employment contracts are two quite distinct bases for the termination of contracts of employment by the employing entity; one is that of dismissal by or upon notice of a certain length which is specified as an express or implied term of the contract or by statute, while the other is that of summary dismissal for or in response to serious misconduct or repudiatory breach of contract on the part of the employee. The first of those two pillars of the edifice of termination of the contract of employment would be seen as defining our main notion of the duration of the contract of employment, whereas the second one, that of summary dismissal, would be seen as rather more incidental or peripheral to our conception of the duration of the contract. Here it will be argued that these are part of a larger set of interlocking powers of contractually lawful termination of personal work or employment contracts by the employing entity, which between them give a more complete picture of the duration of personal work or employment contracts. That picture has in its turn to be set in the frame of the law of wrongful termination and other forms of termination of personal work or employment contracts to establish an overall notion of the job security which those contracts provide in greater or lesser—sometimes much lesser—measure.

The first stage of that construction of a holistic account of contractual job security consists, therefore, in a bringing together of a number of elements all of which, it will be argued, are essential to an understanding of the duration of the personal work or employment contract and its contractually lawful termination by the employing entity. This is a structure which cannot satisfactorily be rested entirely on the two pillars of dismissal by notice and summary dismissal. It should be seen as having a more complex architecture based upon the elements of:

(1) termination by notice,
(2) termination by non-renewal,
(3) termination by payment in lieu of notice, and
(4) summary termination.

These are the main methods by which the personal work or employment contract may be terminated by the employing entity on a contractually lawful basis.

Before this analysis is pursued further, it will be important to make some explanatory points about the terminology which has been used in composing that framework, and to acknowledge some difficulties about that terminology. That is necessary because so much of the terminology of the law of termination of personal work or employment contracts has been overstretched and overstressed in the effort to capture ambiguous and contested conceptions in a variety of very different adjudicative contexts. The explanatory points which we make at this stage are as follows. Firstly, 'termination' is used here to refer to *contractual* termination; this is not self-evident, and is worth stressing, because in the discourse of employment law that word is variously used to refer to termination of the employment contract or the employment relationship, or is used ambiguously between the two.

Secondly, the terminology of 'termination' has been preferred to that of 'dismissal', because the latter term is often regarded as applicable only to contracts of employment rather than to personal work or employment contracts at large. We argue that the terminology of 'dismissal' should not be viewed as confined in that way, but this usage is strong enough to dictate a preference for a terminology which is neutral in that sense. Thirdly, the terminology of 'termination by non-renewal' is an elliptical and rather suspect one; it is shorthand for 'the invoking of the expiry of a fixed term as a basis for contractual termination', and it makes a questionable assertion that we should understand that happening not merely as an action or decision on the part of the employing entity, but also as an action or decision 'not to renew the contract'. We shall seek to defend this usage, but it is right to acknowledge that it does have that particular significance. Finally, and crucially, the use of this whole set of four terminologies does not assert or assume that each or any of them could refer only to contractually lawful termination of personal work or employment contracts. The possibility is left open at this stage that any of them might include *wrongful* termination of personal work or employment contracts; but within this chapter, those terminologies are used to refer to lawful termination.

Those terminological points having been made, our main argument continues as follows. This set of elements in a composite notion of lawful termination of the personal work or employment contract by the employing entity can usefully be thought of, indeed we suggest can best be thought of, not just as a set of methods by which the contract may be terminated by the employing entity but, by extension of the same logic, as a set of actions or decisions by the employing entity and even as the exercise of a set of powers accorded to the employing entity by or within the law of personal work or employment contracts. This argument is by no means self-evidently sound, especially with regard to termination by or upon the expiry of a contractual fixed term; however, we put it forward as nevertheless an appropriate analysis, both in a descriptive and a prescriptive sense, even of that particular kind of termination.

We return later to the particular problem of applying that analysis to 'termination by non-renewal'; it suffices to assert at this stage that this analysis is descriptively and prescriptively appropriate in a general sense. It is descriptively appropriate in the sense that we provide an apt factual account of terminations of personal work or employment contracts by the employing entity if we think of them as the product of actions or decisions taken by managers as or on behalf of the employing entity. More important still, it is normatively appropriate because it makes the point that the law of personal work or employment contracts has the task and function both of assigning powers of contractual termination, and of regulating their exercise whether in a tight or in a loose sense.

This last point is a central one to our whole treatment of the termination of personal work or employment contracts. For (returning in a different way to a point made earlier) it is by the assignment and regulation of powers of contractual termination that the law of personal work or employment contracts creates and shapes its own particular conceptions both of the duration of personal work or employment contracts and of the job security which they confer. Our argument continues by depicting, in a very brief outline, how those conceptions are constructed within the law of personal work or employment contracts, as a preliminary to analysing those constructs in detail and in depth. In drawing in that brief outline, we presume to advance our own view of that outline against what we shall depict as a received but incomplete view of it. As we have indicated, the received view seems to be constructed around the notions that the contract of employment normally, or even archetypally, confers upon the employer a right of dismissal upon notice (for which there is sometimes substituted the specification of a fixed term), and a separate right of summary dismissal for serious misconduct or repudiatory breach of contract on the part of the employee.

According to this view, the duration of the contract and its provision of job security are essentially defined by the right of dismissal upon notice or by the alternative specification of a fixed term. On that received view the contract may, and is indeed in many cases presumed to, provide for termination on short notice (time-limited only by statutory minimum periods imposed by legislation from 1963 onwards) or for the termination on the expiry of a very short fixed term (again time-limited only by that same legislation). Equally on that received view, those provisions for termination need not be and are presumed not to be limited as to the grounds of termination or the procedure for termination. As a result of these dispositions, the law of the contract of employment gives great, indeed almost complete, latitude to employing entities to limit the duration of contracts of employment and therefore to limit the job security which those contracts confer.

It must be admitted that this received view informs and goes a long way to account for much of the law of the termination of the personal work or employment contract. However, real tendencies and real potentialities are revealed by challenging that received set of perceptions and subjecting the current law to an analysis premised upon different starting points. We shall argue that two different starting points might usefully be taken. Firstly, we should recognize that the practice of arranging and contracting for the duration and termination of personal work relationships is much more complex than the received perception suggests, and needs a set of models which are different from the received ones in order to account for it satisfactorily. Secondly, we should recognize that the basis of judicial regulation of and adjudication upon the duration and termination of personal work or employment contracts is, again, different from and more complex than the received view of it. Both those starting points will be briefly explained, then more fully developed in later sections or subsections of this chapter.

The first of these two suggested new starting points could, therefore, be styled *the complex model of contracting for duration and termination*. There are various dimensions of complexity to be explored, which are not acknowledged in the received account of the law of the contract of employment. It will suffice at this stage to draw attention to two of them. One of these consists in the fact that, whereas the received wisdom is that arrangements for duration and termination of employment consist of a simple choice between, on the one hand, the specification of a fixed term, and, on the other hand, the conferring of powers of termination by notice, in reality arrangements are often made which consist of combinations of fixed periods and notice provisions.

Another equally important dimension of complexity consists in the fact that arrangements for duration and termination may not be specified solely in terms of time—in terms, therefore, of periods of employment or of periods of notice—but may also be specified in terms of the *grounds* of termination and/or the *procedure* for termination. This is a crucial point. For example, the actual duration of a personal work or employment contract may be more effectively controlled by a provision that the contract is terminable only for gross misconduct following a disciplinary hearing than by a provision that it is terminable only upon three months' notice. As an empirical observation this may appear to be reasonably uncontroversial; yet it has not been properly factored into the received account of the way in which the law of personal work or employment contracts regards the duration and termination of those contracts.

The set of arguments about the complex model of contracting for duration and termination will be developed further in the next section of this chapter, with regard to the powers of termination by notice or by non-renewal. The second suggested new starting point concerns a different dimension of complexity in the law of termination of personal work or employment contracts, again not fully acknowledged in the received body of doctrine, but this time relating to the basis or mode of adjudication by which this body of law is applied and shaped. This may therefore be referred to as *complex adjudication about duration and termination*. It is expounded more fully in the next subsection.

C. Lawfulness in Termination—A Theory of Adjudication

Just as there seems to be a received body of doctrine which imposes a rather simple analysis upon contracting for duration and termination of personal work or employment contracts, so also does there seem to be a rather straightforward received view of the basis on which courts and tribunals adjudicate upon those issues. This view, perfectly reasonable in a sense and certainly the one upon which the original version of the present work was premised, was that there was a single discourse and mode of adjudication for all issues concerning the termination of contracts of employment, in whatever legal context those issues arose, whether it was in an action for damages for wrongful dismissal or for an injunction to enforce a covenant against competition, or in the course of interpreting a statutory provision about income tax or social security benefits. It was assumed, in short, that there was one common way of expounding the law of contracts of employment. (As for other personal work or employment contracts, there was and still is scarcely anything amounting to a connected discourse about the law relating to them.)

For much of the period between the two versions of the present work, the discourse of the law of termination of contracts of employment has appeared, superficially, to become more unified rather than less so. There seemed to be an incipient tendency at the earlier time for the contract of employment to fragment into two genres, one whose termination was the subject of the common law and equity and their set of remedies, and the other whose termination was regulated by judicial review and the principles of public law. The decision of the House of Lords on appeal from the Scottish Court of Session in the great case of *Malloch v Aberdeen Corporation* in 1971[3] seemed to mark out the growing extent and significance of the latter genre. However, the primacy of the former discourse, that of private law, was firmly and successfully reasserted by the Court of Appeal in the no less important case of *R v East Berkshire Health Authority, ex parte Walsh* in 1984.[4]

Nevertheless, if the direct invasion of public law was repelled, the law of termination of personal work or employment contracts was undergoing a more subtle and complex diversification of its discourse and its mode of adjudication, which incidentally, as we shall see, brought about an indirect (though very partial) readmission of public law thinking. This new, more insidious, diversification came about largely as the result of the introduction of unfair dismissal legislation in 1971, and its cumulative consequences with those of the redundancy payments legislation enacted in 1965. For the purposes of our argument, those two sets of measures will be regarded as constituting a body of statute law which we shall refer to as 'job security legislation'. This is not a very rigorous terminology, for we can debate whether redundancy payments legislation in particular should be regarded as being truly concerned with job security, and we can also debate whether other legislation should also be regarded as coming within that category, for

---

[3] [1971] 1 WLR 1578.   [4] [1984] ICR 743; see above, 71–72.

example the legislation about transfer of employment which is considered in a later chapter. However, the terminology is sufficiently accurate and useful to justify its adoption for the purposes of the present argument.

That argument proceeds as follows. We have remarked in earlier chapters upon the variety of interpretative contexts in which the law of personal work or employment contracts is invoked, and upon the variety of instrumental purposes which may accordingly shape and incline its development. When we come to the body of law about the termination of personal work or employment contracts, we find that this diversity of interpretative contexts and instrumental purposes has become so significant as to create, in effect, distinct modes or genres of adjudication which are applied or used in its exposition. In the period between the two versions of the present work, there has been time for two such genres to emerge. The original genre is that of adjudication upon the termination of personal work or employment contracts in the context of litigation about common law and equitable remedies. We can now discern a distinct genre of adjudication upon the termination of personal work or employment contracts which has subsequently formed itself in the significantly different context of litigation about rights conferred by job security legislation. It will be convenient to refer to these two genres as respectively the 'common law remedial genre' and the 'statutory job security genre' of adjudication about the termination of personal work or employment contracts. Again it is emphasized that these are suggestive terminologies, used for the purpose of exploring a set of arguments, rather than fully rigorous ones.

Our understanding of the statutory job security genre of adjudication has been very greatly enhanced by Steve Anderman's authoritative survey of much of the case law concerned, under the title of 'The Interpretation of Protective Employment Statutes and Contracts of Employment'.[5] He is writing, however, from a different critical stance from the one which is taken here. His concern is with the over-use by judges of contractual concepts in the interpretation of what he styles 'protective employment legislation', a notion largely though by no means entirely according with that of 'job security legislation' which we have invoked for the purposes of the present argument. His argument is that, by choosing a primarily or solely contractual approach to the definition and articulation of certain key concepts in protective employment legislation when an extra-contractual mode of definition could have been adopted, tribunals and courts have often caused this legislation to function less effectively than it should have done in vindicating the rights and expectations of workers which it was enacted to protect.

Our present concern is not so much to contribute directly to that very important discussion, but rather to draw attention to the effects upon the

---

[5] Anderman 2000.

law of personal work or employment contracts itself of its being harnessed in this way to the expounding of protective employment legislation or job security legislation. Those effects, in a sense the reverse effects from those in which Anderman is interested, are fully as profound as the ones which most interest him. Our assertion here is that they have brought about nothing less than the emergence of the distinctive genre of exegesis of the law of termination of personal work or employment contracts which we have identified as the statutory job security genre.

This genre of adjudication is distinctive from the previously existing genre in its capacity to generate both its own technicalities of contract law, and its own particular combination of technical and policy discourse. It has its main institutional base in the Employment Tribunals, and even more especially in the Employment Appeal Tribunal, an appellate tribunal the primary task of which is to apply employment legislation, but which is sufficiently senior in the judicial hierarchy to be significantly authoritative in its exposition of the law of personal work or employment contracts. However, the genre is not distinctive to those tribunals; it is also developed, perhaps in a slightly less distinctive form, further up the hierarchy of appeals from Employment Tribunals, in the Court of Appeal and the House of Lords.

This genre of adjudication is well illustrated by some exceedingly intricate case law concerning the definition and dimensions of the 'fixed-term contract' in the context of job security legislation. There have been two particularly difficult issues in this regard; the first concerns the question of whether the statutory conception of the 'fixed-term contract' includes a contract which is for a fixed term but is terminable by notice within the term. The second, and more complex, issue is as to whether and when the expiry without renewal of a series of fixed-term engagements which between them have lasted for x years or more, but the last one of which is for a period of less than x years, can be regarded as the expiry of a fixed-term contract for x years or more. The way in which these questions have arisen and have been answered perfectly instantiates the notion we advance of a distinctive genre of statutory job security adjudication of issues in or touching upon the law of personal work or employment contracts.

The first question was the subject of an abrupt reversal of technical reasoning on the part of Lord Denning on policy grounds. In *BBC v Ioannou*,[6] anxious to ensure that the rights to redundancy payment or to compensation for unfair dismissal should not easily be able to be waived by the employee, the Court interpreted the notion of the fixed-term contract narrowly when it defined the contracts in relation to which such waivers were possible. However, faced with the fact that this narrow view would also confine the range of fixed period contracts the non-renewal of which could

[6] [1975] ICR 267 (CA).

count as a 'dismissal' by the employing entity, in *Dixon v BBC*[7] he simply declared the earlier view to have been a mistaken one.[8] The second question is the subject of much more difficult case law. The legislation originally (that is to say in 1965 for redundancy payments and in 1971 for unfair dismissal rights) set x at two, providing that the rights in question could be waived in, but only in, the case of employment under a fixed-term contract for two years or more; x was later reduced to one for unfair dismissal; and eventually the possibility of waiver of unfair dismissal rights was completely abolished.[9]

This raised the problem of how far successive engagements could be aggregated into a single contract of employment for one year or more. In *BBC v Kelly-Phillips*,[10] the Court of Appeal has held that they generally can be aggregated in that way (though the judges seem not to have agreed upon the question of whether there must be at least one earlier engagement for x years or more where the final engagement is for less than x years[11]). The interesting point is that the tribunals and courts were called upon to devise a technical analysis of the notion of the extendable single contract or 'renewal under the same contract' in a specifically *statutory* context; it was an issue upon which remedial common law provides no clear answer. That is to say, when adjudicating upon common law or equitable remedies for breach or termination of personal work or employment contracts, tribunals and courts have not really faced the need to distinguish between extending the duration of one contract and making a new contract for a further period.[12]

The result was that a general theoretical issue in the common law of personal work or employment contracts had to be addressed against a background of highly context-specific statutory policy considerations; namely, how broad a capacity should there be for derogation from statutory job security rights. In the *Kelly-Phillips* case the court prioritized the value of legal certainty in job security legislation; it was seen as desirable that these statutory provisions for waiver should have a single clear meaning, even if that permitted the employing entity, in an opportunistic way, to obtain and maintain a waiver from the employee of his or her statutory job security rights in relation to the expiry of a set of very short-term engagements.

---

[7] [1979] ICR 281 (CA).   [8] Ibid at 285.

[9] See Employment Rights Act 1996, s 197, of which subsections (1)–(2) were repealed by the Employment Relations Act 1999.   [10] [1998] ICR 587.

[11] Peter Gibson and Thorpe LJJ seem not to have regarded that as necessary, while Evans LJ does seem so to have regarded it.

[12] Another way in which to put this point is that the problem underlying cases such as *Dixon*, *Ioannou* and *Kelly-Phillips* is that the notions of extension and renewal of personal employment contracts, although the subject of some degree of statutory definition—thus, s 235(1) of the Employment Rights Act 1996 defines 'renewal' as including 'extension'—are not in any meaningful sense defined or distinguished in the common law of personal employment contracts. Compare below, 434, n 53.

(That opportunistic behaviour may now be subject to legislative control in the form of the Fixed-term Employees (Prevention of Less Favourable Treatment) Regulations 2002.[13])

As this genre of statutory job security adjudication upon contractual issues has developed, the potential has increased for tension or conflict between, on the one hand, the results which it produces in particular statutory contexts, and, on the other hand, the outcomes of the rather different mode of adjudication which seems to be followed in deciding issues of remedial common law. This tension is now being experienced right at the very core of the law of termination of personal work or employment contracts in the following way. The most important single development in the law of personal work or employment contracts in the present era of employment law has been the recognition and detailed articulation of the implied obligation of mutual trust and confidence as it applies to the employing entity as well as to employee or worker in general. That development was initially a manifestation—in fact much the most important single manifestation—of the emerging genre of statutory job security adjudication. It was a product of the need to identify a coherent concept of constructive dismissal for the purposes of the job security legislation. It was a contractual conception which evolved from and was shaped by the technical demands and policy considerations of the statute law of unfair dismissal.

It was inevitable, and indeed perfectly appropriate, that this contractual conception, formed in the mould of statutory job security adjudication, should be used and tested in the arena of the remedial common law of personal work or employment contracts. It was brought decisively into that arena by the decision of the House of Lords in *Malik v BCCI*,[14] which not only accorded recognition to the implied obligation at the highest level of authority, but also declared it to be the theoretical basis of a claim for breach of contract arising upon the termination of the employment of the claimant workers, thus locating it squarely within the sphere of the remedial common law of the termination of personal work or employment contracts. We could almost regard the *Malik* case as having effected or completed a kind of transplant of the implied obligation of mutual trust and confidence from the genre of statutory job security adjudication into the genre of remedial common law adjudication.

As with many pioneering operations, the initial result was a decisive rejection of the new body part. In its equally momentous decision in the case of *Johnson v Unisys Ltd*,[15] the House of Lords in effect decided that the implied obligation of mutual trust and confidence was inapplicable to or within the remedial common law which related to dismissal of employees by employing entities, with the result that the claimant employee was held

---

[13] SI 2002/2034; see below, 317–318.   [14] [1997] ICR 606; scc above, 157–158.
[15] [2001] ICR 480; see above, 162–163.

not to have a common law cause of action in breach of contract arising from the manner in which he had been dismissed or the way in which his dismissal in that manner had adversely affected him and his subsequent employability. That decision restored to active operation a very much older doctrine coming from the decision of the House of Lords in the case of *Addis v Gramophone Company*,[16] which imposed those restrictions upon the damages which could be awarded in a common law action for wrongful dismissal.

The House of Lords in the *Johnson v Unisys* case rationalized the restriction which they were placing upon the scope of the implied obligation of trust and confidence as a deference on their part to an intention, which they said was embodied in the unfair dismissal legislation, that the remedial capacity of the common law of wrongful dismissal should remain limited in the way that it had been when that legislation was introduced. As an account of the intention of Parliament, or as a statement of deference to such an intention, that was more than slightly artificial. It was really an assertion of *their own underlying view* that the law concerning the termination of personal work or employment contracts now had two distinct context-specific aspects, one in the sphere of adjudication about job security legislation, the other in the sphere of the common law of contractual remedies—and that developments in one sphere should not necessarily be replicated in the other sphere.

When the House of Lords, rather unconvincingly it must be said, attributed that view to the framers of the unfair dismissal legislation, that was probably because it was doctrinally difficult for them to express it as their own internal perception as to how the law of the termination of personal work or employment contracts should be developed. For to express this as their own view would have involved the open acceptance that there were now two distinct bodies of doctrine, to be chosen according to the type of litigation which was involved. That would have implied the abandonment of a sort of gold standard of a single universal body of contract law about the termination of personal work or employment contracts or relationships, of which there would be a great and understandable reluctance to let go.

As a result, there is now a real unresolved tension, within that ostensibly unified body of contract law, between two genres of adjudication clearly capable of producing divergent outcomes. That is not to say that the two genres can or should be systematically separated, either in the primary judicial discourse or in the secondary academic discourse. But we do need to examine this tension in order to be able to assess whether and when it is a productive one or a destructive one. The best way to do that will be to construct a clearer picture of the underlying remedial common law approach to the termination of personal work or employment contracts, both as to lawful termination and as to wrongful termination. The next

[16] [1909] AC 488.

step towards that construction will consist in analysis of the way that the particular powers of termination by notice and non-renewal are constructed, and how they are interrelated with the further powers of summary termination and termination by payment in lieu of notice.

SECTION 2: LAWFUL TERMINATION BY NOTICE, NON-RENEWAL, OR PAYMENT IN LIEU OF NOTICE

In this section, we seek to develop our analysis of the powers or methods of lawful termination of personal work or employment contracts by employing entities, and to do so by concentrating on what is often regarded as the single most important power of termination, that of the giving of notice to terminate. However, we contend that this power must be considered in very close association with an equally important method of termination, that of the invoking of the expiry of a fixed contractual term of employment; and we have argued earlier that termination by this method can also normally be regarded as the exercise of a power of termination by the employing entity, and so can be thought of as the exercise of a power of non-renewal. In the first subsection, we consider when and why the law of personal work or employment contracts confers those powers upon employing entities, and how by doing so it gives an outline specification of the duration of personal work or employment contracts. In the second subsection, we seek to set that outline contractual specification in an explanatory framework which refers to implicit contracts as well as to explicit ones. In the third subsection we consider whether and when there is a distinct mode of lawful termination by payment in lieu of notice, and where the law about payment in lieu of notice fits into the structural picture which has been built up in the first two subsections.

A. Notice, Non-Renewal, and Contractual Duration

In this subsection, we shall seek to describe and analyse the basic patterns of duration and termination which are recognized, assumed, or implied by the law of personal work or employment contracts. In the matter of termination of personal work or employment contracts, both the legislation and the case law are effectively confined to contracts of employment as such; the legislation is expressly confined to those contracts, and the case law relates almost entirely to those contracts, so we shall have to consider the situation of other personal work or employment contracts as a distinct issue. Contracts of employment are generally regarded as falling into two very different types so far as their duration and termination is concerned, that is to say the contract of indefinite duration and the fixed-term contract.

By considering the role which the powers of termination by notice and of non-renewal have played in the law of personal work or employment contracts, we shall begin to suggest some ways in which that basic analysis needs to be modified if the legal theory is to be internally coherent and is to accord with the social and economic realities of employment relationships as they currently exist. The main argument will be that the dual typology of (1) contracts of indefinite duration and (2) fixed-term contracts both asserts too rigid a separation of contracts of employment into two types and exaggerates the functional contrast between those two types.

Within that generally accepted dual typology, our argument focuses initially on the first of those two duration types, the contract of indefinite duration. The generally accepted dual typology includes the view that this is the primary or predominant type of contract of employment, or the default model for the contract of employment. There is a very interesting and important discussion as to how this typology and that view evolved over a long historical period; however, rather than pursuing that discussion from, for example, the early nineteenth century as is frequently done, we suggest that it is more helpful towards an understanding of the present-day law to trace it from the beginning of the present era of employment law, which we have located in the early 1960s and identified with the wave of employment rights legislation the enactment of which began with the Contracts of Employment Act 1963.

Two decisions of that period provide an invaluable starting point, that of the Court of Appeal in the case of *Richardson v Koefod*[17] and that of the House of Lords in the case, decided some years earlier, of *McClelland v Northern Ireland General Health Services Board*.[18] They both make the point that the primary type or default model for the contract of employment was by then clearly recognized as being the contract of indefinite duration; but this was not in the sense of a contract which was not terminable, it was in the sense that it was terminable upon reasonable notice. In the *Richardson v Koefod* case, it was held that a contract of employment which did not clearly specify its date or mode of termination (therefore, in the old terminology, a 'general hiring') should be regarded as terminable by reasonable notice rather than as being for a period or minimum period of a year according to a doctrine, held in that case to be by then defunct, known as the 'presumption of an annual hiring'. In the *McClelland* case, it was held by a narrow majority that the reasonable notice default model, although undoubtedly the predominant one, nevertheless could not be imposed upon a contract of employment which was described as being for 'permanent employment' and which contained express provision for termination by notice but only on certain specified grounds.[19] (We return shortly to the

---

[17] [1969] 1 WLR 1812.   [18] [1957] 1 WLR 594.

[19] A minority of the Law Lords judged that the reasonable notice default model should be held applicable even to such a contract.

vitally important question of how that contract of employment therefore differed from the reasonable notice default model.)

This is crucial to an understanding of the modern law of the termination of personal work or employment contracts; by the time these cases were decided, the common law default model for the contract of employment was one which was constructed around the power of the employing entity to terminate upon reasonable notice. It may be that, at some much earlier historical time, we could say that there was an original position in which a contract of employment to which no fixed period had been attached was truly regarded as being of indeterminate duration, perhaps therefore for the life of the worker if the worker so wished, and that the employer's power of dismissal by notice was subsequently grafted on. This writer is disposed to doubt that view, and to think that the 'notice rule' importing a power of termination upon reasonable notice was always integral to the very conception of a contract of employment of indefinite duration. At all events, these decisions show that this was clearly the case by the 1960s, indeed that the notice rule had become *the central identifying feature* of the default model of the contract of employment.

Once this is understood, it starts to undermine the contrast between the two contract types. In particular, it dispels any sense that the contract of indefinite duration is inherently more susceptible or less susceptible to being lawfully terminated than the contract for a fixed period. The 'notice rule', even as underpinned by the statutory minimum length provisions, creates a power of termination which may be exercisable on quite short notice because the length of notice regarded as 'reasonable' for the type of employment in question may not be great. On the other hand, the contract of indefinite duration may be subject to termination by notice which is expressly required to be of long duration, while a fixed-term contract may be made for a short period only. (We are leaving aside for the moment the question whether the Fixed-term Employees (Prevention of Less Favourable Treatment) Regulations 2002 also or further undermine the contrast between the two contract types.)

Moreover, it seems to be an inherent feature of the 'notice rule' that it provides for, that is to say treats as a default model, notice which not only may be quite short *but may be given on any grounds, and the giving of which is not subject to any procedural conditions*. If we need an authoritative modern starting point for this view, we could regard all the Law Lords who decided the *McClelland* case, both those in the majority and in the minority, as having affirmed it. It is an inherent feature of the 'notice rule', because the common law view was that all the job security protection which should be implied was embodied in the requirement that the notice be of *reasonable length* and that no further control upon the notice power was appropriate. This is of the utmost significance, because it means that, when the default model applies, the employing entity is just as free, in contractual terms, to exercise the power of termination by notice as it would be to exercise a power of non-renewal of a fixed-term contract, that is to say to invoke the expiry of the fixed term as a basis for treating the contract and the employment itself as being at an end.

The vital importance of this point is that it actually forms or transforms the duration of the contract itself, at a conceptual as well as at a practical level. We might put the matter thus: that if a substantively or procedurally limited power of termination, by the giving of a period of notice, is conferred by a personal work or employment contract, that contract may nevertheless be regarded as having an identifiable duration which is independent of the power of termination. Thus we might say there was a contract for five years but terminable by notice, or even a contract until retirement age but terminable by notice. However, if the power to terminate by notice is a completely unfettered one, defined only by the length of notice to be given, then the contract has little or no meaningful period of duration other than the period of notice. It becomes, in effect, a *rolling term contract* in which the term is defined by the period of notice to which the worker is entitled. As such, it is much more like a fixed term contract than is acknowledged when a strong conceptual contrast is asserted between 'fixed-term contracts' and 'contracts of indefinite duration'. Our argument is that this is precisely the paradigm which the common law of personal work or employment contracts imposes in the form of the so-called 'notice rule'. We return to this point later in the next subsection when we discuss the impact of the EC Directive on Fixed-term Work[20] on the English law of personal work or employment contracts.

Additional factors operate further to undermine the contrast between these two supposedly contrasting contract types. According to their respective default models, both contract types equally confer upon the employing entity a further distinct power of summary termination upon a wide set of grounds relating to the worker's conduct and performance, the details and general significance of which are considered in a later section of this chapter. Moreover, when we consider the issue of termination by payment in lieu of notice later in this chapter, we shall see that it is arguable that the employing entity may have a similar power of termination of the fixed-term contract by means of payment in respect of the unexpired term.

Furthermore, and this of extreme importance, the two contract types often overlap in practice, in the sense that personal work or employment contracts, or contracts of employment at least, often consist of hybrids between the notice contract and the fixed-term contract. Thus, the case law, which was discussed earlier, which decided that the statutory concept of the 'fixed-term contract' included a contract for a fixed term but also terminable by notice, indicates that this hybrid had to be recognized and

[20] Council Directive 99/70/EC of 28 June 1999, OJ L175, 10.07.1990, 43–48.

accommodated within the scope of the job security legislation. Some personal work or employment contracts may even take that particular hybrid form which used to be known as the 'periodic contract' whereby the contract automatically renews itself for a succession of fixed periods unless notice of non-renewal is given.

There is even an argument that we should regard the normal form of the contract supposedly of indefinite duration as in truth a form of hybrid, because, as well as being terminable by notice, it often, perhaps even typically, has a kind of fixed term, because it is a contract *until retirement*, which may be a clearly fixed date, and otherwise will normally be within a fixed band of time (such as between the ages of 60 and 65). We shall return later to that difficult question of the contractual analysis of employment until retirement; we should note at this point that the Fixed-term Employees (Prevention of Less Favourable Treatment) Regulations 2002[21] make special provision to ensure that a contract automatically terminating upon retirement will, for the purposes of those Regulations, be regarded as a contract of indeterminate duration rather than a fixed-term contract.[22]

Thus it has begun to appear in various senses that the division of personal work or employment contracts in general and contracts of employment in particular into the two categories of contracts of indeterminate duration and fixed-term contracts is not a straightforward one; and that classification is further blurred or complicated by the above-mentioned Fixed-Term Employees Regulations. In order to analyse the root causes of these difficulties of classification, and to understand the purpose and the likely impact of those Regulations, it will be useful to consider how the two contract types relate, or fail to relate, to the patterns of duration and expectations of job security which attach to actual labour market practice of personal work relationships. We attempt to do that in the next subsection.

B. NOTICE, NON-RENEWAL, AND IMPLICIT CONTRACTS

In this subsection, it will be argued that the difficulties and complexities which attend the dual typology of contracts of employment, as they emerged in the previous subsection, may be attributable to a degree of mismatch between the two contract types—the fixed-term contract, and the contract of indeterminate duration—and the rather different patterns which personal work relationships assume in the labour market, not just in terms of their factual duration, but also in terms of the expectations as to duration which are associated with them. The notion of a contrast between legal contracts and implicit contracts will be used to investigate that kind of mismatch. It will be suggested that the Fixed-Term Employees Regulations have in a certain sense tried to address that mismatch, but may not have

---

[21] SI 2002/2034.   [22] Reg 1(2), definition of 'fixed-term contract' (b)(i).

succeeded in doing so because of some of the inherent features of the dual typology system, which stand in the way of improving the match between the legal contract and the implicit contract. Identifying those inherent features will lead on to an inquiry, in later subsections, about the conditions which attach to the exercise of the legal powers of termination by notice or non-renewal.

In this subsection, we shall use the terminology of the implicit contract to describe the set of expectations which workers and employing entities might reasonably share as to the obligations attaching to their personal work relationships. The concept of the implicit contract focuses attention upon the divergences which may exist between that set of expectations and the set of legally binding obligations which may be recognized and embodied in the corresponding personal work or employment contracts. From the perspective of analysis of legally binding personal work or employment contracts, the identification of implicit contracts often seems to be a subjective or partisan exercise, one which is designed to demonstrate that the respective expectations of employing entities, or, perhaps more typically, of their workers, are not as fully recognized as they should be in the legally binding contract. Nevertheless, the concept of the implicit contract is a useful one in elucidating some problems about the way in which the dual classification between contracts of indeterminate duration and fixed-term contracts operates.

Having asserted the usefulness of examining the relationship between the implicit contract and the legal contract so far as the duration and termination of personal work or employment contracts is concerned, we need to be rather more precise about the way in which we shall conduct that inquiry. Having tried to define what we mean by the implicit contract for the purposes of this discussion, we should also identify the concept of the legal contract which is being placed in contradistinction to it. We mean by that the express agreements in which employing entities and workers embody their personal work relationships, those agreements being shaped and formulated by the law of personal work or employment contracts, therefore both by legislation and through judicial adjudication.

We could if we wished account for the law concerning the termination of personal work or employment contracts in terms of a long history— perhaps over a period of three centuries or more—of tension and adjustment between legal contracts and implicit contracts. We might even wish to see the original adoption of the contractual model of the personal work relationship as coming out of a tension between the legal forms and the implicit or societal understandings of the personal work relationship. However, in order to understand the state of the law of personal work or employment contracts at the present day, it is more useful to take a modern perspective by continuing to concentrate on the development from the early 1960s onwards.

During the 1960s, the law of termination of personal work or employment contracts began to emerge from a phase in the history of employment law, known as the period of 'collective *laissez-faire*', during which the employment relationship was not highly juridified in two senses. Firstly, it was not the subject of statutory regulation in any fundamental sense. Secondly, there was a practice of industrial relations and employment relations which did not rely heavily upon the mechanisms of the legal system to pursue claims and resolve disputes, and so there was a general absence of litigation generating case law which would define and develop an actively contemporary formulation of the law concerning the termination of the contract of employment or the personal work or employment contract more generally. The few decisions of the higher courts in this area of law from that period present themselves as isolated, esoteric, and backward-looking in their vocabulary and their approach. The decision, discussed earlier, in *Richardson v Koefod*[23] provides a good example.

That state of affairs was a self-reinforcing one; because the social and economic issues concerning job security were not fully or intensively addressed within the law of personal work or employment contracts, that body of law tended to atrophy and so tended to become remote from the pressures and practice of the labour market. This was a kind of vicious circle which it was increasingly sought to break by the enactment of job security legislation, and we shall revert to the question of what impact that job security legislation had upon the law concerning the termination of personal work or employment contracts itself. The point made at this stage of the argument is that, at the beginning of the modern era of employment law, all these factors had combined to produce a state of affairs in which the legal personal work or employment contract and the implicit personal work or employment contract could be and frequently were decidedly remote from each other.

In some areas of the labour market or the world of work, there might be an acknowledged and tolerated discrepancy between the implicit personal work or employment contract and the legally recognized one so far as job security was concerned. The extreme and striking instance of this was employment in the civil service, where established civil servants had the greatest institutionally recognized expectations of job security of any major group of workers, yet where their employment was regarded as so readily terminable in legal terms that, as we have seen in Chapter two, it was strongly doubted whether that employment had contractual status at all. In other words, there was the utmost discrepancy between the implicit contract and the legal version of that contract.

At the beginning of the modern period of employment law, that particular discrepancy was generally viewed as a benign or non-problematical one,

---

[23] [1969] WLR 1812; see above, 306.

largely because of a prevailing confidence that the implicit contract of established civil servants would be systematically implemented in practice, and that this observance would be underpinned by effective collective bargaining and representation of the workforce by trade unions or professional associations. After a long period of what would now be regarded as a period of 'full employment' or very low unemployment, somewhat similar assumptions were pervasive throughout the public sector of the labour market and indeed through much of the private manufacturing sector. In this situation, it was easy for the implicit personal work or employment contract and the legal personal work or employment contract to become progressively more remote from each other. When adverse economic conditions increasingly challenged the expectations embodied in the implicit contract, it would become apparent and indeed obtrusive that the judicial conception of the personal work contract had, for the most part, failed to recognize those increased expectations. In fact, judicial insistence upon the strong presumption of terminability upon reasonable notice of any contract of employment not of clearly fixed duration could work strongly against that recognition. That is what happened in the case of *Richardson v Koefod*. The employee contended that she had been implicitly promised a secure job of at least a year's duration; the alleged presumption of an annual hiring, which would have recognized that expectation, was rejected as archaic in favour of an interpretation of the contract as terminable upon a few weeks' notice. In the *McClelland* case,[24] it was only by a narrow majority that the House of Lords refrained from imposing the 'notice rule' upon a contract of employment which provided for termination only in specifically defined circumstances, and which thus expressly gave effect to an implicit expectation of high job security. Even the Law Lords in the majority regarded this as a very special and atypical kind of employment contract.

In fact we can see from such cases not merely reasons why the common law concerning the termination of personal work or employment contracts *sometimes* failed to recognize or give effect to the implicit contract as to job security but reasons why it was *systemically likely* to fail to do so. We can understand this more clearly by constructing a set of typical patterns of expected duration of employment and job security in the recent and contemporary labour market, and assessing how those patterns relate to the legal patterns which are constructed by and within the law of personal work or employment contracts. It will be helpful to begin with the question of duration and to move on to the closely related but more complex question of job security.

It will also be useful to invoke a concept of an 'engagements for employment', to describe an arrangement for employment over a period of time, in a way which is neutral as to whether that engagement coincides with

---

[24] *McClelland v Northern Ireland General Health Services Board* [1957] 1 WLR 594 (HL).

a personal work or employment contract, or any particular type of personal work or employment contract, for that period of time. We suggest that engagements for employment can be meaningfully divided into three broad types as to their expected duration. Here, we use the notion of expected duration not to refer merely to factual predictions as to duration but rather to identify the expectations which workers and employing entities might regard as obligations or entitlements, though not necessarily contractually enforceable ones—in fact, therefore, the expectations embodied in the idea of the implicit contract.

We suggest that there are four broad duration types of engagements for employment in the recent and contemporary practice of employment relations. These are:

(1) long-term or career engagements;
(2) medium-term or part-career engagements;
(3) temporary engagements; and
(4) very short-term or occasional engagements.

This typology does seem to identify four quite significantly different schemes or modes by which employment relations are organized, in terms of the ways in which employing entities arrange to meet their perceived demands for services from workers, and in terms of the ways in which workers arrange their working lives.

Obviously the designation of engagements for employment as being of long, medium, short, or very short duration is to some extent arbitrary, and that arbitrariness may appear to be increased if we attempt to assign specific periods of time to those notions. Nevertheless, we suggest that the above four-part typology might be robust enough to support the following time specifications, as long as those are regarded as loose or approximate ones:

(1) a long-term or career engagement is for employment either until retirement age, which according to current convention and practice is normally between 60 and 65, or for a period of more than ten years;
(2) a medium-term or part-career engagement is for a period of between one year and ten years;
(3) a temporary engagement is for a period of less than one year, which may be measured in months or weeks; and
(4) a very short-term or occasional engagement is for a period of less than a week.

In order to establish a full explanatory account of the development of the law of personal work or employment contracts, it would be important to assess what the corresponding duration types were in earlier historical periods, and which were the predominant types, and how those duration types were mirrored or expressed in the law of personal work or employment contracts at those earlier historical periods. We suggest that such an assessment might well reveal that the law of personal work or employment contracts has, through many historical periods, tended to have a built-in time lag, so that it has often carried forward an earlier vision of the duration types which are predominant in the labour market. In the present work, for reasons earlier presented, we confine ourselves to making that assessment in respect of the recent evolution and contemporary state of this body of law.

Within the last forty years, that assessment seems to produce the following results. By the beginning of the 1960s, the practice of employment relations was in the course of an upward evolution between and within the four duration types which we have identified. That is to say, where engagements for employment of types (2), (3), and (4) had earlier been predominant, engagements of type (1) were becoming the dominant type, and engagements of types (2) and, even more particularly, (3) were tending towards the longer end of their respective time bands. This was a trend which was confirmed and slightly reinforced by the introduction of statutory minimum periods of notice in 1963. From the early 1980s onwards, that trend has been more than somewhat reversed by changes in the practice of employment relations aimed at creating a more 'flexible' labour market, so that there has been quite a marked downgrading of engagements for employment between and within the four duration types.

It has proved quite difficult to reflect and express these trends in the law of personal work or employment contracts. As we have seen, the modern law of personal work or employment contracts is constructed upon the dual typology of (A) contracts of indefinite duration terminable upon reasonable notice, and (B) fixed-term contracts. There has been a general tendency to equate engagements of type (1) with contracts in mode (A), and engagements of types (2), (3), and (4) with contracts in mode (B). This has been apt to produce a distorted relationship, that is to say a mismatch, between, on the one hand, the duration types of actual engagements or implicit contracts and, on the other hand, the duration types of legal personal work or employment contracts. There are various ways in which this mismatch may occur, which we shall now seek to explain.

The first of those kinds of distortion is apt to occur simply because the law of personal work or employment contracts does not constrain the choices which may be made between types (A) and (B), nor, apart from certain legislative interventions, the duration of fixed periods or notice periods which may be specified within types (A) and (B) or within hybrids combining both types. Putting the point simply, notice may be long or short, and fixed periods may be long or short. Therefore, to categorize a personal work or employment contract as being either of type (A) or of type (B) in and of itself says nothing about whether it expresses an engagement of type (1), (2), (3), or (4). Each of the types of engagement (1), (2), (3), or (4) could be couched in a legal contract either in mode (A) or in mode (B) or in a combination of the two modes.

The point, then, about the relationship between duration types and legal modes, is that a great deal (though not everything, as we shall shortly see) depends upon the *length* of termination time which is specified in any of these modes of contracting. A career-length engagement need not be expressed by a contract of indefinite duration; it can be embodied in a legal contract for a fixed period of twenty years. A temporary engagement need not take the form of a short, fixed-term contract; it may equally well be embodied in a contract of indefinite duration but terminable upon short notice. This indicates a sense in which there is an absence of systematic positive matching between the duration type of the engagement and the legal mode of contracting for it.

There is a further sense, however, in which there could be said to be not merely an absence of matching but a systemic mismatch between the implicit contract and the legal contract. The legal mode (A), the contract of indefinite duration, cannot be said to give effect to an engagement of type (1), ie career-length, or type (2), ie part-career length, unless it is not terminable by notice, or the notice is of very long duration, or is tightly constrained in some other way. Yet, as we have seen, the law of personal work or employment contracts imposes, in the form of the 'notice rule', a strong presumption or default model that the contract of employment of indefinite length is terminable by reasonable notice, which is normally within the range of a few weeks to a few months, and which is not constrained by any other conditions. That is the essence of the 'notice rule'.

There thus results from the 'notice rule' a marked or almost paradoxical mismatch between the legal contract and the implicit contract. At the outset of the modern era of employment law, which we have located in the early 1960s, the career-length engagement seemed to be the predominant, or typical, duration type for dependent employment. The legal contractual vehicle for this 'typical' form of employment was the contract of employment of indefinite duration. Yet the application of the 'notice rule' had the result that the legal contract was, in effect, a short-term or temporary one because of the unconstrained power of the employing entity to terminate the contract upon very short notice or relatively short notice—since neither the common law notion of 'reasonable length', nor the statutory minima, secured a right to long notice for the great majority of the members of the workforce at that time or even subsequently.

In fact, the existence of the 'notice rule' and its dominance in the shaping of the common law conception of the duration of personal work or employment contracts has made the whole relationship between the legal contract and the implicit contract a difficult one. These difficulties are now coming to affect the way in which the law of personal work or employment contracts handles the fixed-term contract as well as the contract of indeterminate duration. As we have seen, just as there may be a disparity or mismatch between the indeterminate duration notice contract and an implicit contract for part-career or full-career employment which underlies it, so there may be a similar mismatch between a fixed-term legal contract and an implicit contract for longer-term employment which underlies it. That is to say, there may be an implicit contract for extension or renewal of the legal contract, which is not recognized in the legal contract itself. This requires some further explanation.

In a sense we recognize that implicit contract by thinking about the expiry of a fixed-term contract as a non-renewal by the employing entity. We are making the point that the ending of the employment relationship in that way may represent a decision on the part of the employing entity not to implement an expectation of extension or renewal of the engagement for employment. This is precisely why, in the main areas of job security legislation, it has been regarded as necessary and appropriate to include within the statutory conception of 'dismissal' the expiry of a fixed-term contract without renewal. That was regarded as *appropriate* because it would bring that kind of ending of the employment relationship within the scope of the legislation in question, by treating it as a terminatory action taken by the employing entity.

The treatment of the expiry of the contract of employment without renewal as a 'dismissal by the employer' in job security legislation was also, and quite correctly, regarded as *necessary* because, in the common law of personal work or employment contracts, the expiry of a fixed-term contract without renewal would not be regarded in that way at all. If the job security legislation had simply defined dismissal as the termination of the contract of employment by the employer, it is most unlikely that the expiry of a fixed-term contract of employment without renewal would have been regarded as dismissal by the tribunals or courts applying that legislation. They would almost certainly have taken the view that the expiry of the contract without renewal did not count as a dismissal, because it was not an act of termination by the employer, but simply the automatic ending of the contract according to its own self-executing provisions. From the standpoint of the classical theory of the law of the contract of employment, it is positively counter-intuitive to regard the expiry of a fixed-term contract of employment as a dismissal by the employer.

This was one of the great partings of the ways between the common law of the contract of employment and the statute law of job security. It did much to ensure that an implicit contract for medium-term or long-term employment would not be defeated when it was embodied in the form of a succession of short, fixed-term legal contracts, which would be taken at face value as wholly free-standing, short-term engagements so far as the common law was concerned. This meant, in fact, that statute law of job security could pierce the veil of the short, fixed-term legal contract of employment, and look behind it to see whether there was an implicit contract for long-term or open-ended employment.

This divergence between the treatment of the fixed-term contract of employment in the statute law of job security and the common law of personal work or employment contracts has continued to exist. However, the EC Directive on Fixed-term Work of 1999[25] required member states to give effect to a principle of equally favourable treatment for fixed-term workers as compared with permanent workers, who were understood to be and defined as being workers with employment contracts or relationships of indefinite duration. In particular, the Directive required member states to take one or more of a specified set of measures 'to prevent abuse arising from the use of successive fixed-term employment contracts or relationships'.

In the United Kingdom, the measure taken in implementation of that Directive was the enactment of the Fixed-term Employees (Prevention of Less Favourable Treatment) Regulations 2002.[26] The measure which responded to the particular requirement to prevent abusive use of successive fixed-term contracts was regulation 8, which actually in certain specified conditions transforms fixed-term contracts of employment into (apparently) contracts of indefinite duration terminable by reasonable, or at least minimum statutory, notice. The specified conditions are essentially that the worker is employed under a succession of two or more fixed-term contracts for a total period of four years or more where the use of the fixed-term format for the last such contract 'was not justified on objective grounds'.

It is possible that the worker-protective intentions of this provision, that is to say the intentions to ensure that the fixed-term format may not be used by the employer to evade the implicit contract of employment in an abusive way, may in part be defeated because of the particular regime for the termination of contracts of employment which the common law of personal work or employment contracts provides. The key function of ensuring that the termination of the fixed-term contract would come within the control of the job security legislation had already been substantially fulfilled by the job security legislation itself. The transformation, by regulation 8, of the underlying contract of employment from a fixed-term contract into a contract apparently of indeterminate duration may have the ironical effect of rendering the contract terminable by notice of a much shorter duration than that of the fixed term of the original contract.

There is an underlying problem here which explains these anomalies, and these difficulties in matching the legal contracts to the implicit contracts. In order to understand that problem, we have to remind ourselves that the attaching of job security to an employment relationship, whether by contract or by legislation, does not consist solely in specifying its duration; it is a more complex specification which crucially includes defining the conditions upon which the powers of termination accorded to the employing entity may

---

[25] Council Directive 99/70/EC of 28 June 1999, OS L175, 10.07.1990, 43–48.
[26] SI 2002/2034; see above, 303, and below, 409.

be exercised, both in a substantive and a procedural sense. The Fixed-term Work Directive is constructed around a model, which actually obtains in many continental European employment law systems, whereby the employment contract or relationship of indefinite duration is inherently subject to close controls upon its termination. In the employment law of the United Kingdom, substantially equivalent controls have been superimposed by job security legislation, especially by the law of unfair dismissal.

However, and this is the crucial point, in the underlying common law conception of the employment contract described as being 'of indefinite duration', the 'notice rule' has largely continued to provide a power of termination which is not only of relatively short duration but has also, which is even more important, remained basically unfettered as to the conditions upon which it may be exercised. As was argued in the previous subsection, this means that the typical or archetypal contract of employment, as basically conceived of in the common law of personal work or employment contracts, is really, to all intents and purposes, nothing more than a rolling term contract for the duration of the notice period. As such, it fails to give effect to implicit contracts for career-length or even part-career length employment. That is why the transformation of fixed-term contracts into 'contracts of indefinite duration' *as basically envisaged by the English law of personal work or employment contracts* could not reliably achieve the objectives of the Fixed-term Work Directive.

In a later section of this chapter, we shall examine in detail the way in which that set of issues about the controls upon powers of termination has been approached in the law of personal work or employment contracts, but before doing that we need to bring into the picture some further very important powers of termination which may be conferred or recognized by the law of personal work or employment contracts, those of termination by payment in lieu of notice, and of summary termination in response to serious misconduct or other major breach of contract on the part of the worker.

C. Payment in Lieu of Notice as a Power of Lawful Termination

At this point in our analysis of the termination of personal work or employment contracts, we introduce the topic of payment in lieu of notice. The role of payment in lieu of notice in the law of termination of personal work or employment contracts is a surprisingly difficult one. The analysis of termination of employment where payment in lieu of notice was given by the employing entity, or where it might have been expected but was not given, reveals a bewildering variety of conceptual and practical possibilities, and a continuing set of uncertainties about how to choose between those alternatives. Nor are these complexities merely superficial ones; they reflect tensions at the heart of the law of personal work or employment contracts. It will be necessary to touch upon the topic of payment in lieu of notice at many points in the course of our account of the law of termination of personal work or employment contracts.

It is appropriate to begin by relating it to the powers of lawful termination by non-renewal, or, more particularly, by notice. The first point to be made in working out that relationship is that the set of issues which we are accustomed to consider under the heading of 'payment in lieu of notice' should in truth be regarded as concerning both payment in lieu of notice and payment in lieu of unexpired fixed term. It quite often occurs, as for instance in the case of *Abrahams v Performing Rights Society Ltd*,[27] that what is referred to as payment in lieu of notice could, on the facts of the case, equally well be regarded as payment in lieu of unexpired fixed term. Indeed, it follows, from what has been said earlier in this section about the essential functional similarity between termination by notice and termination by the non-renewal of a fixed term, that payment in lieu might, as a general or conceptual proposition, be regarded as an equivalent alternative to the latter mode of termination just as well as to the former mode of termination. So we should think of 'payment in lieu of notice' as including payment in lieu of unexpired fixed term unless the context specifically indicates to the contrary.

The following issues seem to arise, and to be of genuine theoretical and practical importance, with regard to payment in lieu of notice considered as the basis for lawful termination of personal work or employment contracts:

(1) When will employing entities be regarded as having the contractual right to effect termination of personal work or employment contracts by payment in lieu of notice?

(2) Where there is such a right, will the termination be viewed as taking effect immediately upon the date upon which the payment in lieu was made or was due, or upon the later date at which the notice would have expired?

(3) Upon either view, will the payment in lieu be viewed as remuneration for employment, or as compensation for the loss of or ending of employment?

The short answer to all three questions is that the outcome depends upon the interpretation of the particular contract and the particular surrounding facts of any given case. However, some tendencies can be detected, which both emerge from and contribute to the general approach of the law of personal work or employment contracts towards the lawful termination of those contracts.

Firstly, courts and tribunals do not seem to regard employing entities as having a general right to terminate personal work or employment contracts

---

[27] [1995] ICR 1028 (CA).

by payment in lieu of notice as an automatically implied alternative to their rights to terminate by notice (or non-renewal). In other words, such a right or power will not be implied in the absence of express provision for it; the default interpretation of personal work or employment contracts seems to be that they do not confer such a right upon the employing entity. It is hard to point to cases where this point is directly in issue, but it would seem to follow from Lord Browne-Wilkinson's authoritative legal analysis of payment in lieu of notice in the case of *Delaney v Staples*.[28] Lord Browne-Wilkinson portrays payment in lieu of notice as falling into four principal categories, of which the fourth and 'by far the most common' type is as payment of compensation for the employer's breach of contract in dismissing without notice. If there were a general right in the employing entity to terminate the personal work or employment contract by payment in lieu of notice, that fourth category of situation would scarcely occur, and would certainly not be the most common analysis of payment in lieu of notice.

The statutory provisions imposing a minimum duration upon notice to terminate the contract of employment,[29] calculated by reference to the employee's period of continuous employment, in a sense confirm that position, since those provisions do not offer an alternative of payment in lieu of that minimum period of notice. Indeed, it is arguable that the provisions actually negate the implication of a power to terminate by payment in lieu of the minimum period of notice, and override express provisions conferring such a power upon the employing entity. That view is supported by the presence of a proviso to the statutory provisions which expressly enables either party to *accept* a payment in lieu of notice, since that proviso might be regarded as superfluous if the statutory provisions did not negate express or implied powers of termination by payment in lieu of the minimum period of notice.[30]

However, the resolution of that question, and indeed the whole question of the extent and nature of express or implied powers of termination by payment in lieu of notice, turn upon our second issue of whether such a power is regarded as effecting immediate termination or termination at the date of the expiry of the notice in lieu of which the payment is made. It seems that where powers of termination are expressly conferred, they will normally be understood as powers of immediate termination; and when it is debated whether a power of termination by payment in lieu of notice can

---

[28] See [1992] ICR 483 (HL) at 488–489. Compare also below, 388.

[29] Currently contained in s 86 of the Employment Rights Act 1996.

[30] The President of the Industrial Tribunals for England and Wales, Sir Diarmaid Conroy QC, took that view soon after this legislation was first introduced in *Chapman, Blair & Atchinson v Executors of WG Leadley* (1966) 1 ITR 84 at 85; and the President of the Employment Appeal Tribunal, Morison J, seemed to share that view in *Cerberus Software Ltd v Rowley* [2000] ICR 35 at 40H–41E, though he felt that it would require the authority of the Court of Appeal to determine the point.

be implied, or is negated by the statutory provisions, that debate normally refers to powers of immediate termination.[31] When the issue is whether there is an implied power of immediate termination, the general answer seems to be that no such power will be implied.

When, on the other hand, the issue is whether there is a power to terminate by payment in lieu of notice in the different sense of a power to terminate the contract at the date at which due notice would have expired, but to insist that the worker does not work during the period of notice, different considerations apply. In this case, the question would now be identified as one of whether the employing entity can insist upon placing the worker upon 'garden leave' during the period of notice in the absence of an express provision entitling it to do so. The answer seems to be that no positive entitlement to do so will be implied as an automatic corollary to the right to terminate by notice; however, the worker may be unable to treat the imposition of 'garden leave' during notice as constituting breach of the personal work or employment contract unless he or she can point to a contractual claim to be allowed to work as well as to be remunerated during the period of notice. We discuss in a later chapter[32] how far and in what circumstances such claims, amounting to claims of a specific 'right to work' will be recognized; it appeared from that discussion that some particular basis for such a claim must be shown, such as that the worker's future employability will be impaired if he or she is not allowed to work during the period of notice.

That distinction between a power of termination by payment in lieu of notice as, on the one hand, a power of immediate termination, and, on the other hand, as a power of termination when notice would have expired, gives part of the key to the answer to the third question of whether the payment in lieu of notice will be regarded as remuneration in respect of the period of notice. In the latter case, the payment in lieu would generally be regarded as remuneration, and the decision in the income tax case of *Richardson (Inspector of Taxes) v Delaney*[33] seems to sustain that view. Where there is a power of immediate termination by payment in lieu of notice (which will not readily be implied but may be expressly conferred), there is some conflict of authority as to whether the payment is to be regarded as remuneration. Lord Browne-Wilkinson in *Delaney v Staples* suggests that in this case 'the payment in lieu is not a payment of wages in the ordinary sense since it is not a payment for work to be done under the contract of employment'[34]—so that failure to make such a payment would not constitute a 'deduction from wages' in the statutory sense.

---

[31] As Morison J put it, in practical terms, in the *Cerberus* case, 'employers want the option of a lawful summary dismissal so that the restrictive covenants apply without the employee being on the premises, or on garden leave, whilst under notice' [2000] ICR 35 at 40G.
[32] See below, 487–489.   [33] [2001] IRLR 663 (ChD).
[34] [1992] ICR 483 at 489.

On the other hand, it has recently been held by the Court of Appeal in the income tax case of *EMI Group Electronics Ltd v Coldicott (Inspector of Taxes)*[35] that payments in lieu of notice made in the exercise of powers of immediate termination upon payment in lieu of notice count as emoluments of employment for income tax purposes. Perhaps that divergence is explicable in terms of policy considerations which are specific to those two sets of legislative provisions. On the one hand, the Law Lords who decided the former case seem to have shared an intuition that the legislation protecting workers from uncovenanted deductions from wages was not intended to provide a remedial mechanism for failure to make payments due in respect of the termination of employment. On the other hand, the Court of Appeal which decided the latter case seems to have been of the view that, unless payments in lieu of notice were regarded as emoluments of employment, an inappropriate avoidance of income tax would have been permitted. This demonstrates very clearly the problems of maintaining a single account of the law of personal work or employment contracts in diverse interpretative contexts where the pressures towards particular analytical outcomes may be very divergent.

Behind those particular interpretative divergences lies a more general failure, on the part of the law of personal work or employment contracts, to provide a comprehensive or clear analysis of the power of termination by payment in lieu of notice, or to resolve the question of how far such a power is part of the inherent or default pattern of personal work or employment contracts. The reason for that lack of focus is to be found in the primacy or centrality of the 'notice rule'. In the law of personal work or employment contracts, the power to terminate by notice is, as we have argued, the central organizing feature of the whole treatment of contractual termination. The power of termination by payment in lieu of notice has really been treated as a secondary or derived power, a rather ill-defined consequence of the 'notice rule'. As we develop a fuller understanding, in the succeeding sections and chapters, of the full nature and ramifications of the 'notice rule', so the extent and character of the power of termination by payment in lieu of notice will also become somewhat clearer. It will, for example, emerge how far, if at all, we should regard such a power as qualified by the implied obligation of mutual trust and confidence. First, however, we need to consider the power of summary termination which the law of personal work or employment contracts confers upon the employing entity.

SECTION 3: THE POWER OF SUMMARY TERMINATION BY THE EMPLOYING ENTITY

In order to understand the way in which the law of termination of personal work or employment contracts operates and is structured, it is important at

---

[35] [1999] IRLR 630.

this stage of the argument, having previously considered the powers or modes of termination by notice or by expiry or non-renewal of a fixed period of employment, now to consider the power of summary termination by the employing entity in response to major misconduct or repudiatory breach of contract on the part of the worker. Later in this work we shall consider the power of summary termination, which the worker also possesses, and we have referred in the previous section of this chapter to the fact that the employing entity will often also be regarded as having a different kind of power of summary termination, namely a power to end the contractual employment in question by means of a payment in lieu of notice. However, those other powers of summary termination are not our present concern; in this section we focus on what Hugh Collins, Keith Ewing and Aileen McColgan have usefully styled as 'justified summary dismissal'.[36]

The reason for focusing upon justified summary termination by the employing entity, at this stage of our discussion of lawful termination of personal work or employment contracts, is that a study of the evolution of the law upon this particular topic tells us a very great deal about the way that the whole set of issues about the powers of termination by the employing entity is currently regarded and treated within the law of personal work or employment contracts. The argument will proceed by identifying two different, indeed contrasting, approaches to justified summary dismissal in the modern case law, and by considering whether one of those two approaches seems to be predominant over the other. First, however, we should identify the sense in which and the extent to which this power of summary termination is conferred upon employing entities by and within the law of personal work or employment contracts. As often in this work, our discussion is based upon cases decided upon contracts of employment, but we assert that it can be regarded as applicable to personal work or employment contracts in general unless it is stated to the contrary.

We suggest that, while it is correct to assert that the law of personal work or employment contracts confers a power of justified summary termination upon the employing entity, it is important to examine and question the particular sense in which it does so. In the course of this work, we have often depicted the law of personal work or employment contracts as imposing obligations or conferring entitlements or powers upon the respective parties to those contracts. Often, that imposition or conferment takes the form of the implying of terms into contracts as a matter of law. Sometimes, however, this imposition or conferment takes place at an even more fundamental or inherent level, in the sense that it follows from the basic structure or functioning which is accorded to the contract by the law of personal work or employment contracts.

The conferment of the power of justified summary termination upon the employing entity is usually explained or rationalized as being of the latter

---

[36] Collins, Ewing & McColgan 2001 at 487.

kind. It is generally regarded as being an application of a right, which contract law envisages as one which is generally possessed by a party to a bilateral contract, of termination of the contract in response to a major or very serious breach of the contract by the other party. There are two main versions or forms of that right, one which concentrates on the fundamentality of the term which is breached and the other which looks to the repudiatory character of the breach; the power of justified termination is sometimes seen as arising on one basis, sometimes on the other. These function as alternative rationales for what is normally understood to be the employer's power of summary dismissal.

From a long historical perspective, these concepts drawn from general contract principles can probably be seen as rationalizations of a set of disciplinary sanctions which were seen to inhere in the employment relationship even before that relationship was set into a contractual frame. However, by the beginning of the modern era of employment law, which we are locating in the early 1960s, the employing entity's power of summary dismissal was firmly founded upon general contract doctrine; and as such it had an effectively unquestioned status in contracts of employment at large. Particular personal work or employment contracts might accord the employing entity more extensive or more limited powers of summary termination, and we shall revert later to the question of how willing the courts and tribunals have been to recognize those formulations, but the conception of the power of summary dismissal as an intrinsic right of response to a major breach of contract was very strongly presumed or applied as the default model.

This might suggest that the power of summary dismissal was, by the 1960s, being maintained as a static perpetuation of a nineteenth-century stereotype of the master and servant relationship in the guise of general contract principles. There is some truth in that view, but it conceals a set of tensions and emerging divergences in the approach to summary dismissal at that period, which have continued to make themselves felt. Thus, a consideration of the (very sporadic) case law of summary dismissal around that time suggests the elements of two divergent approaches. Some of the cases seem to adhere to a notion that, if the workers have committed any one of a long-accepted category of disciplinary offences, they have straightforwardly rendered themselves liable to summary dismissal for major or repudiatory breach of contract. We might wish to regard in that light the decision in *Sinclair v Neighbour*[37] that the employer of a manager of a betting shop had been entitled to dismiss him summarily for borrowing money from the till without permission, or the decision in *Pepper v Webb*[38] that Major Webb had been justified in summarily dismissing his head gardener for insolence and disobedience, and in particular in regarding an outburst of anger and insults on the gardener's part as the repudiation of his contractual obligations.

---

[37] [1967] 2 QB 279 (CA).   [38] [1969] 1 WLR 514 (CA).

We could therefore think of such decisions as representing an offence-based approach to summary dismissal which concentrates, unilaterally, upon the conduct of the worker. However, even in those decisions, although they manifest a strict view of the behavioural obligations of the workers concerned, there are indications that the judges were not looking solely at the question of whether the worker had committed a disciplinary offence, but were to some extent evaluating the way that the employment relationship had been conducted over a period of time and were inquiring whether the worker or the employing entity was more at fault in causing the breakdown of the relationship, given the particular location of the worker within the organization of the employing entity. Thus in *Sinclair v Neighbour* the judges felt that, although the worker's conduct did not fit straightforwardly into the category of dishonesty, it was incompatible with his duty as the manager of the business concerned, responsible for supervising the conduct of other workers within that business. In *Pepper v Webb*, the judges attached importance to the fact that the worker had been 'acting in a very unsatisfactory way' over a period of months; and they also evaluated the behaviour of the employer, who, although he might have been 'an irritating employer', had not in their view made unreasonable demands upon the employee.

There were the signs here of what we might think of as a bilateral, and relative fault-based, approach to the right or power of summary termination. These signs were more marked in other more or less contemporary cases. One such case was *Laws v London Chronicle (Indicator Newspapers) Ltd*,[39] where it was held that the summary dismissal of an advertisement salesperson was not justified where she had left the room with her immediate superior in the course of a quarrel between that manager and the managing director of the company. The argument, that the worker had been guilty of an act of disobedience which *ipso facto* justified summary dismissal, was rejected on the ground that the conduct of her superiors had presented her with an embarrassing and unpleasant conflict of loyalty, so that her conduct should not be regarded as 'wilful disobedience'. Another such case was *Wilson v Racher*,[40] where, on facts not dissimilar from those of *Pepper v Webb*, Mr Racher was held not to have been justified in summarily dismissing his head gardener for insolence and the use of obscene language during a quarrel, because he the employer had been determined to get rid of the worker and had provoked the quarrel. Edmund Davies LJ stressed that judicial attitudes towards the employment relation had changed from what was 'almost an attitude of Czar-serf' displayed in some nineteenth-century cases, so that:

we have now come to realise that a contract of service imposes upon the parties a duty of *mutual* respect.[41]

---

[39] [1959] 1 WLR 698 (CA).   [40] [1974] ICR 428 (CA).
[41] Ibid at 430 (emphasis added).

It may be useful to attempt to assess which of these two approaches has subsequently been the prevailing one in relation to the power of summary dismissal. It should be explained that, despite a general, marked increase in the volume of litigation relating to personal work or employment contracts since the 1960s, the case law on the common law of summary dismissal has remained sporadic. That is because many of the disputes about summary dismissal, in relation to which the only legal claim formerly available was at common law for wrongful dismissal, have since 1972 tended to be the subject of claims of unfair dismissal,[42] where the common law of summary dismissal has not been part of the issue. A good example is the unfair dismissal claim brought by Mr Mathewson to complain of his summary dismissal following his being arrested outside the workplace for possession of cannabis, which was the subject of the decision of the Employment Appeal Tribunal[43] treated by Hugh Collins as the point of departure for his study of the modern law of termination of employment.[44] In the relatively small number of post-1972 common law actions for wrongful dismissal to have reached the higher courts, the claimants have tended to be highly remunerated professional or managerial workers whose claims for wrongful dismissal have exceeded the compensation limits upon claims for unfair dismissal.

Although recent decisions in this area are therefore not numerous, they do provide a basis for a cautious evaluation of the current approach to the power of summary dismissal. Somewhat different trajectories of case law development can be discerned as between summary dismissal which is effected, on the one hand, on the grounds of dishonest or improper conduct, and, on the other hand, on the grounds of insubordinate, unco-operative, or conflictual conduct. In both those situations, there is a tendency to move from the unilateral, offence-based approach towards the bilateral relative fault-based approach; but that movement seems to be more marked in the latter situation than in the former one. We shall consider each of those two situations in turn.

In the common law of summary dismissal, in those cases where the conduct of the worker is viewed as amounting to dishonesty or financial impropriety, the generally growing willingness of the courts and tribunals to engage in critical evaluation of the conduct of the management of the employing entity tends to be outweighed by the perceived importance of a punitive, exemplary, or deterrent treatment of the offending behaviour of the worker. That tendency, already evident in the modern law of summary dismissal from the case of *Sinclair v Neighbour*, is manifested in more recent

---

[42] Although decided by the Court of Appeal in 1974, *Wilson v Racher* concerned a termination of employment which had occurred in June 1972 just before the unfair dismissal legislation came into force.

[43] *Mathewson v RB Wilson Dental Laboratories* [1988] IRLR 512.

[44] See Collins 1992, chapter 1, 'Harsh but Fair'.

cases, such as that of *Denco Ltd v Joinson*.[45] This was an unfair dismissal claim, but one where a purely contractual issue presented itself of whether the conduct of the worker had come within the meaning of 'gross misconduct' justifying summary dismissal, and where it was held that the use of an improperly obtained password to gain unauthorized access to computer data was gross misconduct although motivated by idle curiosity rather than by an illegitimate purpose, and although it was not demonstrated that the employing entity was damaged or that the employee profited from his actions in any way.

More rounded adjudications, but to similar general effect, took place in the cases of *Neary v Dean of Westminster*[46] and *Wheatley v Control Techniques plc*.[47] In the former case, Lord Jauncey decided that Dr Neary and Mrs Neary as, respectively, Organist of Westminster Abbey, and part-time secretary of its music department, had, in the way they made profits from the musical activities of the Abbey, acted in breach of fiduciary obligations sufficiently seriously as to warrant their summary dismissal. The gravity of that offending conduct seemed to outweigh a degree of laxness on the part of the senior clerical managers of the Abbey in the regulation of the Nearys' conduct of its musical activities. In the latter case, which concerned the summary dismissal of the founder and chairman of the employing company as the result of conflict between him and senior executives within the group of companies concerned, the employing company was allowed to rely upon the doctrine derived from the case of *Boston Deep Sea Fishing v Ansell*[48] to justify the dismissal. That doctrine allows the employing entity to invoke misconduct on the worker's part as a defence to a claim of wrongful dismissal even though that misconduct was not relied upon as the reason for the summary dismissal when that dismissal took place. It is typically, as in this case, invoked in relation to misconduct in the nature of dishonest or improper dealing which comes to the notice of the employing entity after the dismissal has taken place. It may not be confined to such conduct, but seems to be specially applicable to such conduct because an effective sanction is regarded as especially appropriate.

Where the conduct of the worker is not regarded as being in the nature of dishonest or improper dealing, a much more relativistic approach seems to manifest itself, in which the conduct of the management of the employing entity comes into the inquiry to a far greater extent. This tendency could be observed in those aspects of the *Wheatley* decision which did not turn upon the employee's private pursuit of his own business interests. It is

---

[45] [1991] ICR 172 (EAT).

[46] [1999] IRLR 288 (Special Commissioner). In this case, Lord Jauncey of Tulichettle was exercising the jurisdiction of the Queen as Visitor to Westminster Abbey, but applying the common law of personal work or employment contracts.

[47] Unreported—Ebsworth J, 30 September 1999 (QBD).

[48] (1888) 39 ChD 339 (CA).

also evidenced by the very interesting decision of the Inner House of the Court of Session in the case of *Macari v Celtic Football and Athletic Co Ltd*.[49] That is, of course, a decision taken under the Scottish law of contract, but in an area where Scottish and English laws are not fundamentally different. There it was held that the summary dismissal of the manager of a football club had been a lawful one following various refusals on his part to comply with instructions to him from the new managing director of the club; the conclusion in favour of the employing entity was the outcome of close evaluation of the conduct of the managing director as well as of the claimant employee.

It is useful to consider what was the precise basis of that evaluation and how searching it was. Both the leading judgments in the case, those of the Lord President and of Lord Caplan, asserted the requirement that the orders or instruction, upon the disobedience to which the employing entity relied to justify summary dismissal, must comply with an objective standard not just of lawfulness in the most elementary sense but also of reasonableness and legitimacy in the context of the contract as a whole.[50] Beyond that point, the judges appear to diverge in a way that is interesting. The Lord President seems to insist firstly that, if the employer has issued a lawful and legitimate instruction, the motive for doing so is irrelevant to the employee's breach of contract in refusing to follow that instruction. Moreover, if the employee continues in employment he or she cannot claim to treat the employer's conduct as freeing him or her from obeying the employer's lawful and legitimate instructions. Lord Caplan, on the other hand, seems to accord greater effect, in principle, to bad faith or other inappropriate motivation on the part of the employer when issuing instructions which are on the face of them lawful and legitimate, and also seems readier to regard breach of the implied obligation of trust and confidence on the part of the employer as releasing the employee from the obligation to obey those instructions.

One could take the view that it was nuances of expression rather than real points of substance which differentiated the two judgments. Thus the Lord President's point about the irrelevance of motivation was made against the background of his stated view that the employer had not on the facts acted in bad faith. On the other hand, Lord Caplan's theoretical willingness to allow the breach of the implied obligation of trust and confidence to release the employee from subsequent obligations of obedience was not really brought into issue, since he took the view that the employing entity was not in fact issuing instructions which involved breach of those obligations. These might be regarded, moreover, as fine points about the operation of a distinctively Scottish body of case law doctrine

---

[49] [1999] IRLR 787.
[50] See ibid, the Lord President at 791 para 17 and Lord Caplan at 797–798 para 74, both endorsing the approach of the Lord Ordinary at first instance.

about the mutuality or interdependence of particular obligations within a continuing contract.

However, even if those divergences were somewhat esoteric ones and were more apparent than real on the facts of the particular case before the court, they nevertheless represent potential differences of approach to the employer's powers of management, discipline, and termination of the personal work or employment contract. They point towards different views about the pervasiveness and impact of the employer's implied obligation of mutual trust and confidence in relation to the termination of contracts of employment. We shall pursue those possible alternative approaches to the control of powers of termination in the next section of this chapter.

SECTION 4: CONTROLS UPON POWERS OF TERMINATION BY THE EMPLOYING ENTITY

In this section, we explore the crucial question of whether and how far the law of personal work or employment contracts treats the powers of contractual termination which are assigned to the employing entity as limited or controlled ones. In the first subsection, it will be shown how the whole body of law of termination of personal work or employment contracts appears to have been constructed around the notion that the power of termination by notice is an essentially uncontrolled one. In the second and third subsections, it will be shown how challenges to that notion from public law and from the law of unfair dismissal have been rejected. In the final subsection, it will be considered whether there might nevertheless be a more fundamental challenge to that notion, which might be based upon the principles of interpretation of personal work or employment contracts articulated in earlier chapters of this work, as supplemented by the statutory dispute resolution procedures introduced by the Employment Act 2002.

A. The Unlimited Power of Termination by Notice

In an extremely insightful commentary piece written in 1998,[51] Michael Ford called for a 're-thinking of the notice rule'. Although he identified the 'notice rule' as, primarily, a proposition that damages for wrongful dismissal are restricted to the notice period, he also observed that it was 'based on the assumption that the employer could lawfully terminate the contract in that period', and, indeed, that it included the view that:

In a normal contract of employment the notice clause can be relied upon in any and all circumstances, regardless of the other terms of the contract; it confers an unfettered discretion.[52]

---

[51] Ford 1998.   [52] Ford 1998 at 220.

330 Lawful Termination by the Employing Entity

He also drew attention to the way in which 'the rule is taken to be so obvious that it is usually repeated without authorities or analysis to support it'.[53] We shall return in due course to the question of the close association which Ford makes between the restriction of damages to the notice period and the underlying assumption which he styles as the 'unfettered approach' to notice; in this subsection our purpose is to consider what authorities and analysis do in fact support that underlying assumption.

We shall use the terminology of the 'unrestricted notice power' to refer to that assumption which Ford has so correctly identified. Our suggestion is that this assumption amounts to a foundational proposition for the whole of the law of the termination of personal work or employment contracts. It is foundational in two senses. Firstly, it is located in common law thinking about the very basic structure of the personal work or employment contract. Secondly, it forms a conceptual platform upon which a whole superstructure of thinking about the termination of personal work or employment contracts is grounded. We shall develop those two points in that order.

The notion of the unrestricted notice power was part and parcel of the common law view of the very structure of the contract of employment at the outset of the present era of employment law (that is to say in the early 1960s) and has largely remained so. It was structurally integral to the core conception of the contract of employment in the following sense. Earlier in this chapter, we sought to show how the archetypal contract of employment came to be regarded as one which was of indefinite duration but terminable by notice. The key feature of this archetypal contract, the characteristic which defined its duration, was its terminability by notice. Inherent to that understanding of the 'notice rule' is the idea that the power of termination by notice which it confers upon the employing entity (and for that matter upon the employee, but that is a somewhat secondary feature) is an unrestricted one.

There are various ways in which we can explain the treatment of the unrestricted notice rule, at the outset of the period we are discussing, as a self-evident or unquestioned proposition. It might be seen as the product simply of general thinking about freedom of contract, or as a product of the 'collective *laissez-faire*' approach to industrial relations whereby *de facto* joint regulation by collective bargaining was not closely integrated into the legal norms. Perhaps the best explanation lies in the fact that this vision of the archetypal contract of employment simply did not seem to be a matter of controversy in the common law courts; it hardly ever came into question before the higher or appellate courts. The courts could and did accept a received orthodoxy which treated the unrestricted notice rule as an axiomatic feature of the legal contract of employment even if that orthodoxy was sometimes out of accord with the social and economic reality of employment relationships by the early 1960s. (We shall revert to the question

---

[53] Ford 1998 at 220.

of whether and how far the unrestricted notice rule was and is regarded as applicable to non-employee personal work or employment contracts.)

At the outset of the current era of employment law, the unrestricted notice rule had two key manifestations in decisions of the House of Lords, both of which deceptively concealed their defining implications for the archetypal contract of employment. They were the two exceptions which in their different ways proved the rule as to the unrestricted power of termination by notice of the ordinary contract of employment. The case of *McClelland v Northern Ireland General Services Board*[54] is often presented as one which raised the rather esoteric or marginal question of what was meant by a contract for 'permanent' employment. In fact, it raised the much more fundamental and frequently occurring question of whether, when a contract of employment expressly conferred upon the employing entity a power of termination on specified grounds such as that of serious misconduct, that excluded the normally implied unrestricted power of termination by notice on any ground which the employing entity might choose.

By a majority of three to two the House of Lords held that this was the case; but the minority thought that the general presumption in favour of the unrestricted notice rule should prevail even in such circumstances, and the majority regarded themselves as identifying the contract of employment in question as being a wholly exceptional one in not being subject to the unrestricted notice rule. This was all despite the fact that such arrangements were by that time very widespread, perhaps even typical, among established staff of public authorities as well as in the civil service; such workers were normally regarded as dismissible 'for good cause' (in the sense of misconduct or serious incompetence) but not for redundancy.

A comparable sort of marginalization was necessary in order to recognize, in the great administrative law case of *Ridge v Baldwin*,[55] that an employment relationship might be such that the power to terminate by notice was subject to the procedural restriction of an obligation to hear the employed person in his or her own defence. In order to make that recognition, the House of Lords had to identify the employment relationship in question as wholly different in character to, indeed in radical contrast with, the normal contract of employment. As Lord Reid famously expressed it,

The law regarding master and servant is not in doubt....the master can terminate the contract with his servant at any time and for any reason or for none.[56]

We shall see in due course that this is actually a complex proposition which refers in part to the absence of remedies to undo the effects of a wrongful dismissal; but it certainly contains the assertion of a positive unrestricted power of termination by notice as a built-in feature of the standard contract of employment.

---

[54] [1957] 1 WLR 594 (HL).   [55] [1964] AC 40 (HL).   [56] Ibid at 65.

It is hard to say whether, either at that time or subsequently, the unrestricted notice rule should be regarded as equally applicable to semi-dependent workers' contracts. It is informative to assemble the arguments for and against. Against equal applicability is the fact that the rhetoric in which this rule is asserted is very specifically that of the contract of employment, indeed of the 'master and servant' contract; even today, judges seem to find the terminology of 'master and servant' specially appropriate in this particular context. On the other hand, neither the rule nor that surrounding rhetoric is consciously advanced as a point of contrast between the contract of employment and other personal work or employment contracts. Moreover, it is hard to see why contracts of employment should be *more* subject than other personal work or employment contracts to a rule which makes them essentially precarious or readily terminable. Semi-dependent workers' contracts will typically be contracts whose duration is for a fixed term or defined by reference to the completion of a particular task. However, where that is not the case, there seems no good theoretical reason why the courts and tribunals might not be equally ready, perhaps even more ready, to apply the unrestricted notice rule to them as to contracts of employment.

In order to understand the evolution of the unrestricted notice rule since the early 1960s, we should not therefore concentrate on the distinctiveness of contracts of employment from other personal work or employment contracts; it is in any event a general theme of this work that this is a largely illusory distinction so far as the common law is concerned. Instead, we should consider the way in which the law of personal work or employment contracts has responded to some major challenges to the unrestricted notice rule which have arisen since the 1960s, and which have impacted upon contracts of employment as such. Those challenges have come, firstly, from the intrusion of public law, and secondly, from the cultivation of the implied obligation of trust and confidence. The challenges have hitherto been largely rejected; but by charting their impact we can evaluate the present state and future potential of the unrestricted notice rule much better than by relating it to the distinction between contracts of employment and other personal work or employment contracts.

B. THE CHALLENGE FROM PUBLIC LAW PRINCIPLES

For much of the current era of employment law, the unrestricted notice rule has been under some degree of challenge from the principles of public law. Public law developed enormously, and very rapidly, during that period, and has seemed at times to have a major impact upon the law concerning the termination of personal work or employment contracts, significantly confining or modifying the application of the unrestricted notice rule. Latterly, however, that impact has been very greatly reduced, and the unrestricted notice rule has very largely reasserted itself. An examination of that sequence of events tells us a great deal about the nature and current status of the unrestricted notice rule itself.

As we have seen in the previous subsection, from the very outset of the current period there was some degree of encroachment upon the unrestricted notice rule by the body of administrative law principles and remedies which was so dramatically reinvigorated or reinforced by the decision of the House of Lords in the case of *Ridge v Baldwin*.[57] The modern renaissance of administrative law had as its starting point the recognition that the chief constable who challenged the validity of his dismissal was not subject to the unrestricted notice rule but benefited from a more protective regime in which his purported dismissal was to be treated as a nullity if it was not effected in accordance with the principles of natural justice. The question thereafter was whether this was a narrow and sectional encroachment upon the unrestricted notice rule or a wide and pervasive one. Complex twists and turns would take place around that central question.

At the beginning of its development, the new intrusion of administrative or public law into the termination of the employment relationship seemed pervasive in one sense but sectional in another. It seemed pervasive in the sense that the employment relationships which were regarded as subject to the principles of administrative law were treated as being pervaded by those principles, so that it was not in doubt that the termination of those relationships could only be effected by the valid exercise of clearly conferred powers. This was the essential doctrine of *Ridge v Baldwin*, as confirmed in the almost equally significant case of *Malloch v Aberdeen Corporation*,[58] decided by the House of Lords on appeal from the Scottish courts. On the other hand, this doctrine was a highly sectional one in the sense that it applied only to a narrow category of relationships where the employed persons could be regarded as office-holders or as being employed within a statutory framework which conferred a special character upon that employment; again, this is made very clear in the decisions in both the *Ridge* and the *Malloch* cases. Indeed, Lord Reid in each case emphasized the contrast with the 'ordinary' or the 'pure' case of the contractual relationship between master and servant.[59]

In the following years, there were a couple of cases which suggested that the principles of public law were developing so vigorously as to erode that contrast; it began to appear that there might be a wide range of employment relationships in which a contract of employment was subject to public law principles. The decision of the Court of Appeal in the case of *Stevenson v United Road Transport Union*,[60] which concerned the dismissal of a regional officer of a trade union who was employed 'so long as [he]

---

[57] [1964] AC 40 (HL).   [58] [1971] 1 WLR 1571 (HL).
[59] See [1964] AC 40 at 65, [1971] 1 WLR 1571 at 1582.
[60] [1977] ICR 893 (CA).

gave satisfaction to the executive committee', coupled with the decision of Woolf J in the case of *R v British Broadcasting Corporation, ex parte Lavelle*,[61] which concerned the dismissal of a broadcasting worker, suggested that this might be the case for any worker, at least if employed by a body exercising some kind of public function in a broad sense, whose employment was terminable on defined grounds or according to a defined procedure.

However, public law principles have not been destined for such a pervasive impact upon the law of termination of personal work or employment contracts as those cases might have seemed to suggest. From the early 1980s onwards, doctrinal developments in the case law have resulted in a substantial, though not complete, exclusion of public law principles from the law concerning the termination of personal work or employment contracts. The occasion, perhaps even eventually the excuse, for this retrenchment was the creation from 1977 onwards of a distinct and unified procedural and remedial regime for judicial review of administrative action. Judicial review had for a very long time been the main vehicle for the development of public law principles; as the result of these reforms and the interpretation of their effects in the landmark case of *O'Reilly v Mackman*,[62] judicial review was to become, to all intents and purposes, the exclusive domain within which those principles could be applied, and judicial review was to be conducted solely on the basis of public law principles, as distinct from those of private law.

In one sense, the changes wrought by the new Order 53 of the Rules of the Supreme Court[63] were clearly recognized and acted upon by Woolf J in *Ex parte Lavelle*, where he held that the employee could not seek judicial review of her dismissal because her claim was essentially to enforce her private law rights under her contract of employment. On the other hand, Woolf J was ready to accept that those private law rights conferred by the contract of employment were shaped and enhanced by the rights to hearing and appeal in relation to dismissal which the employing entity had conferred upon the employee, which had in his view made her situation much more like that of an office-holder. Her private law contract of employment had to that extent acquired an express content, and perhaps even a further implied content, which resembled or replicated the principles of public law.

A much more fundamental divorce of public law principles from the private law contract of employment was effected by the Court of Appeal in the leading case of *R v East Berkshire Health Authority, ex parte Walsh*,[64] where a senior nursing officer unsuccessfully claimed that his purported dismissal by the employing health authority was vitiated by the improper delegation of the power of dismissal from the authority itself to his line

---

[61] [1983] ICR 99 (QBD).   [62] [1983] 2 AC 237 (HL).
[63] Which was subsequently given statutory force by s 31 of the Supreme Court Act 1981.
[64] [1984] ICR 743 (CA).

manager, a district nursing officer. In this case, the Court of Appeal not only firmly rejected the claim that the dismissal might be susceptible to judicial review because a public law right had been infringed, but also seemed hostile to the idea that the employee's private law contract of employment was in any way imbued with, or even affected by, public law principles. Sir John Donaldson MR asserted firmly that 'employment by a public authority does not per se inject any element of public law', and explained the cases where public law principles had been held to apply to the dismissal of employees of public authorities as ones where the power of dismissal was itself conferred by statute or was directly subject to statutory regulation.[65]

That decision seems effectively to have established the private law of contract as the dominant discourse in the law concerning the termination of personal work or employment contracts, even where the workers concerned are employed by public authorities or are civil servants of the Crown. It was followed and applied by the Court of Appeal to a semi-dependent worker—a doctor employed by a local authority as a deputy police surgeon—in the case of *R v Derbyshire County Council, ex parte Noble*.[66] Although Woolf LJ there reiterated the point he had made in *Ex parte Lavelle* that the unavailability of judicial review to control dismissal does not exclude the possibility that the personal work or employment contract may import the public law principle of natural justice, and although Lord Justices Laws and Sedley have both argued extrajudicially in favour of a general implication of public law principles into contracts of employment,[67] it would seem likely that a strong doctrinal exclusion of those principles from the sphere of termination of personal work or employment contracts will be maintained by the superior courts for the time being.

It is important to seek to identify why the impulse towards exclusion of public law principles from the regulation of dismissal from employment seems to be such a strong one. One possibility is that the senior judiciary, perhaps influenced by a strong tendency in that direction in the development of public policy or governmental policy from the early 1980s onwards, believe that the constraints on the arbitrary or abusive use of powers or discretions, which have been created by the principles of public law in their modern development, should be regarded as truly inapplicable to the regulation of the employment relationships of public sector workers just as

---

[65] Ibid at 751.

[66] [1990] ICR 808 (CA). Compare also *R v Lord Chancellor's Department, ex parte Nangle* [1991] ICR 743 (QBD), where the relationship between a civil servant and the Crown was regarded as taking the legal form of a contract of employment, from which it was deemed to follow that he had no public remedy, but where it was also held that, even had the relationship not been judged to be contractual, there was no sufficient public law element in the dismissal to open the way to judicial review of that dismissal.

[67] See Laws 1997, Sedley 1994.

they are to private sector workers. They might think that both the private law contractual framework, and, more particularly, the unrestricted notice rule and all that follows from it, should apply to employment relationships in general, and that there should be no cadre of public officials which is specially protected in this respect (with the exception of a few clearly non-contractual office-holding relationships of which the only significant category appears to be that of constables[68]).

In support of this view, one might cite the comparable and equally significant rejection of the notion of 'academic tenure' as a doctrine of construction limiting the powers of university authorities to dismiss their academic appointment holders by the Court of Appeal in *R v Hull University, ex parte Page*.[69] In that case, a university lecturer was appointed subject to a power of dismissal for defined good cause under the statutes of the university, but was dismissible upon three months' notice under his letter of appointment, a typical set of arrangements at the time concerned which has since been modified by legislation.[70] The issue was whether there were two independent powers of dismissal, one for good cause and the other upon notice, or whether there was a single power of dismissal both for good cause and upon notice. In adopting the former construction, the Court of Appeal (with the subsequent approval of the House of Lords[71]) was imposing the unrestricted notice rule as the prevailing norm and resolutely resisting encroachments from the doctrines of public law.

Another, and less absolutist, way of identifying recent judicial thinking about this set of issues, is to regard the superior courts as being motivated not so much by a perception that the *principles* of public law should not be applicable to dismissal from employment, but rather that the *procedures and remedies* of public law should not be applicable. For the most part, this will be a difference in style of reasoning rather than a difference with practical substance; and one might wish to regard it as an illustration of the common law method of reasoning from remedies and procedures to rights and duties. On the other hand, it might be significant to the future development of the law in this area to maintain that distinction, and to recognize that the main concern of the courts has been to discourage the development of a habit of seeking judicial review of dismissals from public service, rather than to encourage a view of the power of dismissal as an unrestricted one.

---

[68] As recognized in *R v Secretary of State for the Home Department, ex parte Benwell* [1984] ICR 723 (QBD); see above, 67.   [69] [1992] ICR 67 (CA).

[70] Consisting of the Education Reform Act 1988 and the Commissioners' University Statutes enacted under the powers which that Act conferred.

[71] [1993] ICR 114 (HL). The main issue before the House of Lords was whether the Visitor's decision on construction of the terms of appointment was open to judicial review on the ground of error of law, which it was held not to be.

So the conclusion from this subsection is that possibilities presented themselves, in the 1960s and 1970s, that public sector workers or some significant subset of them might be regarded as employed under personal work or employment contracts, or as being in employment relationships, to which the unrestricted notice rule did not apply. Those possibilities were unrealized and even largely negated in the 1980s and 1990s; but it remains useful to identify those possibilities, not only because of their potential to be realized directly in the future, but also because they identify a public law paradigm for restricted or controlled powers of dismissal which may yet be indirectly realized in other ways within the law of personal work or employment contracts. In the remainder of this chapter we discuss those alternative possibilities; it will be helpful first to elaborate the public law paradigm of controlled powers of dismissal somewhat further.

The paradigm of controlled powers of dismissal, towards which the case law which we reviewed in the previous subsection seemed at one stage to be tending, appeared to have the following features. It seemed to prescribe that powers of dismissal are valid and validly exercised only if they are understood to be limited by requirements of good cause, due process, and reasonableness. Good cause normally consists of some objectively identified set of factors which relate to the conduct or competence of the worker, or to the diminution or cessation of need for the services of the worker (redundancy). Due process normally consists of some combination of the right to be heard and the right of appeal. Reasonableness consists of the notion that dismissal is a suitable and not excessive response to the grounds which exist for dismissal.

At one stage, as we have seen, this paradigm seemed quite likely to be regarded as applicable to a wide category of public sector workers either in the sense that they might seek judicial review of dismissals on the basis of this paradigm, or at least in the alternative sense that this paradigm might be applied to the construction of the contracts under which they were employed. Subsequently there has been a decisive rejection of the first kind of applicability, primarily motivated by the consideration that the judicial review process should not be available to contest dismissal decisions. There seems also to have been a less decisive but nevertheless real rejection of this paradigm as a canon of construction of personal work or employment contracts of public sector workers, mainly because of a basic intuition that the unrestricted notice rule was the more appropriate default model for the construction of personal work or employment contracts in general, but perhaps also because of a perceived difficulty in differentiating between the workers to whom the more protective public law paradigm would and would not apply. We now turn our attention to the question of whether a similar paradigm might be or become applicable, not by way of a sectional application of public law principles, but rather as the result of developments in the private law of personal work or employment contracts.

C. The Challenge from the Law of Unfair Dismissal

Hitherto we have been discussing the evolution since the 1960s of the law concerning the termination of personal work or employment contracts without direct reference to the effects of the introduction of unfair dismissal legislation in 1971 and its maintenance and adaptation since that time. That amounts in one sense to presenting the play of Hamlet without the Prince of Denmark, since that legislation must rank as the most important development in the law of dismissal during the whole recent and current period of its history. However, although the impact of unfair dismissal law upon individual employment law as a whole has been direct and fundamental, its impact upon the law of termination of personal work or employment contracts as such has been much less straightforward. It has generally been complex, and has recently been transformed by the decision of the House of Lords in the leading case of *Johnson v Unisys Ltd*[71a] into a negative impact so far as contractual controls upon powers of dismissal are concerned. This impact, and its implications for the future development of the unrestricted notice rule, are considered and evaluated in the present subsection.

In a real sense, the unfair dismissal legislation envisaged and to quite an extent put in place the set of controls upon powers of dismissal which we described in the previous subsection as constituting the public law paradigm. The legislation itself enacted the requirements of good cause and reasonableness, and the courts and tribunals, rightly understanding the three notions to be interconnected, evolved a requirement of due process around them. Woolf J in *Ex parte Lavelle* recognized the imposition of the public law paradigm onto the contract of employment which the unfair legislation was bringing about:

employment protection legislation has substantially changed the position at common law so far as dismissal is concerned... even the ordinary contract of master and servant now has many of the attributes of an office, and the distinction which previously existed between pure cases of master and servant and cases where a person holds an office are no longer clear.[72]

As we have seen, predictions or aspirations that the public law paradigm would, as such, pervade the interpretation of the personal work or employment contracts of public sector workers have not been realized. The question in this subsection is whether and how far the same paradigm (which we could therefore refer to for this purpose as the unfair dismissal paradigm) has been imposed upon contracts of employment in general by reason of the impact of the unfair dismissal legislation. The short answer is that it has not, but a fuller account of how and why that result has occurred tells us a great deal about the present state and future potential of this area of law.

[71a] [2001] ICR 480 (HL).
[72] [1983] ICR 99 at 111–112.

The crucial question, which seems on the face of it to be an extremely theoretical one but turns out to have the most profound practical implications, is whether the unfair dismissal paradigm can be regarded as having been integrated into the interpretation and construction of contracts of employment as a matter of common law, in which case the unrestricted notice rule will have been fundamentally modified at its common law source, or whether it is, on the other hand, a superficial paradigm, maintained as a legislative superstructure but which has not been built into the infrastructure of the common law. The tribunals and courts entrusted with the administration of the unfair dismissal legislation have for the most part taken the latter view. They have understood, correctly in the view of the present author, that the unfair dismissal legislation was intended to impose a distinct layer of regulatory protection for the worker upon the normative foundations of the common law of the contract of employment, rather than to recast them in an essentially different form. Interestingly, some early decisions of those tribunals and courts tended to fuse unfair dismissal law and the common law of termination of contracts of employment together; but it was soon asserted that two quite separate sets of questions were involved.[73]

Ironically, this very separation of the jurisprudence of dismissal into two separate channels actually led to an enormously significant feedback from the law of unfair dismissal into the common law of the contract of employment. By the mid-1970s, a distinctive unfair dismissal paradigm had evolved in the case law of industrial tribunals and in the specialized courts which heard appeals on points of law from them. The issue arose whether the concept of *constructive* unfair dismissal should be expounded according to the unfair dismissal paradigm, or according to the traditional paradigm of the law concerning the termination of the contract of employment. The former paradigm gave rise to the so-called 'industrial test' of whether the employer had acted so unreasonably towards the employee during the continuance of the employment relationship as to justify the employee in regarding himself or herself as having been in effect dismissed. The latter paradigm gave rise to a more technical question of whether the employer had committed a repudiatory breach of the contract of employment.

In the landmark decision in the case of *Western Excavating (ECC) Ltd v Sharp*,[74] the Court of Appeal established authoritatively that the contract test should be preferred, because it promised a more rigorous or restrictive approach to the question of what constituted constructive dismissal. Intuitively concerned to maintain the integrity of the unfair dismissal

---

[73] Thus, in *Treganowan v Robert Knee & Co Ltd* [1975] IRLR 247 (QBD), Phillips J condemned as incorrect the treatment by an Industrial Tribunal of the contractual wrongfulness and the unfairness of summary dismissal as a single issue in *Abercrombie v Alexander Thomson & Co Ltd* [1973] IRLR 326 (IT).   [74] [1978] ICR 221.

paradigm, the tribunals and courts responded by developing the conception of constructive dismissal in a way which made it much more responsive to notions of abuse of power, lack of due process, and unreasonableness than might have been expected if the corresponding development had taken place outside the context of the law of unfair dismissal. The outstanding product and manifestation of this tendency was the evolution, especially in and from the case of *Woods v WM Car Services (Peterborough) Ltd*,[75] of the implied obligation of trust and confidence owed to the employee by the employing entity.

The decision of the Employment Appeal Tribunal which perhaps represents the high point of this approach to constructive unfair dismissal was given in the case of *Goold (Pearmak) Ltd v McConnell*,[76] where it was held that the management of a firm of wholesale jewellers had constructively, and unfairly, dismissed two of their sales staff, by having first changed their sales methods so as substantially to reduce the commission which those workers earned, then failing to provide a procedure for the consideration of the workers' grievance about this reduction in earnings. On the obligation to afford a grievance procedure, the reasoning of Morison J as President of the EAT was that, by enacting a requirement upon employers to provide employees with a written statement specifying the procedure by which an employee might pursue a grievance, Parliament had indicated its view that 'good industrial relations requires [*sic*] employers to provide their employees with a method of dealing with grievances in a proper and timeous fashion';[77] and that the industrial tribunal had accordingly been entitled to conclude that:

there was an implied term in the contract of employment that the employers would reasonably and promptly afford a reasonable opportunity to their employees to obtain redress of any grievance they might have.[78]

The significance of the decision consists in the very direct set of links which it made between a worker-protective legislative provision and the implied infrastructure of the contract of employment in an unfair dismissal context.

This approach, which amounted to the imposition of a contractual responsibility upon the managers of employing entities to exercise their managerial powers with due consideration of the interests, concerns, and legitimate expectations of their workers, could develop and flourish in the context of adjudication about unfair dismissal. It could even develop, as we saw in the course of our earlier discussion of the principles of interpretation of the terms of personal work or employment contracts, in the context of actions for contractual damages, or declarations, in respect of managerial decisions about or conduct affecting remuneration or other terms and

---

[75] [1981] ICR 666.   [76] [1995] IRLR 516 (EAT).   [77] Ibid at 517.
[78] Ibid.

conditions of employment. This has occurred in a series of cases such as *Scally v Southern Health Board*,[79] *Johnstone v Bloomsbury Health Authority*,[80] *Clark v Nomura International Ltd*,[81] and *Cantor Fitzgerald International v Bird*.[82]

However, this whole development was destined to confront the unrestricted notice rule; for there was a deeply unresolved issue as to how this approach, which exerted, via the implied obligations of the contract of employment, procedural and/or substantive control over the use of managerial power in general, was to be reconciled with the notion of an unrestricted managerial power of termination by notice. Ironically, the very decision in which the implied obligation of trust and confidence was recognized at the highest level at the same time heightened this conflict. This was, of course, the decision, discussed earlier, in the case of *Malik v BCCI*[83] in which it was held that middle level managers employed by BCCI might in principle have a cause of action in damages, for breach of the implied obligation of trust and confidence which the bank owed to them, in respect of their difficulty in obtaining comparable employment, following the collapse of the employing bank, if it could be shown that this difficulty was causally related to the corrupt conduct of the business of the bank by its higher management. (It was eventually decided by the Court of Appeal in a group of test cases that this causal connection was not strong enough to establish liability.[84])

That decision did not on the face of it confront the unrestricted notice rule; it was accepted on all hands that the claimants' contracts of employment had been lawfully terminated by notice or payment in lieu of notice, and that the cause of action which the claimants sought to establish related to the conduct of the management of the employing entity during the continuance of their contracts of employment rather than to the termination of those contracts. However, in a deeper functional sense this decision did impinge upon the unrestricted notice rule, because it recognized that employing entities might be held liable in damages for impairment of workers' job security and employment prospects caused by the exercise of managerial power in a way which unwarrantably disregarded the workers' interests and reasonable expectations as to their treatment by the employing entity.

It was predictable that employees would in due course advance such a claim in respect of the alleged abuse, whether in a procedural or substantive sense, of the managerial power of dismissal; and this is precisely what occurred in the leading case of *Johnson v Unisys Ltd*, discussed in earlier chapters, where the confrontation between that line of reasoning and the unrestricted notice rule therefore came to a head. It is important to note

---

[79] [1991] ICR 771 (HL).   [80] [1991] ICR 269 (CA).
[81] [2000] IRLR 766 (QBD).   [82] [2002] IRLR 867 (QBD).
[83] [1997] ICR 606 (HL).   [84] *BCCI v Ali (No 2)* [2002] ICR 1258 (CA).

exactly how that confrontation occurred and exactly what outcome it had. The claimant was a director of the defendant multinational software service company, who had been summarily dismissed without a hearing, for alleged misconduct but without sustainable justification, and claimed that the fact and manner of his dismissal had caused him a mental breakdown and had made it impossible for him to find work, for which detriments he claimed damages in excess of £400,000 for breach of the implied obligation of trust and confidence. He had successfully claimed compensation for unfair dismissal, but that compensation was limited by the then prevailing statutory maximum of £11,700.

This claim was struck out as disclosing no cause of action at first instance in the County Court, and that decision was upheld unanimously by the Court of Appeal and by the House of Lords. The various judges who decided this case at those different levels advanced a number of different grounds for their decision. At first instance, it was placed on the ground that it was in substance a claim for unfair dismissal rather than a common law claim. In the Court of Appeal, it was held that this claim, unlike the claim which had been made in the *Malik* case, was defeated by the rule in the *Addis* case, which the Court of Appeal regarded as excluding, from damages for wrongful dismissal, compensation for the manner of dismissal, for injury to feelings, or for impairment of employability resulting from the fact or manner of dismissal.

In the House of Lords, the issue was directly addressed whether the implied obligation of trust and confidence applied to the taking of decisions about dismissal, and the majority held that it did not. (Lord Steyn dissented on that point but concurred in the main decision on the different ground that a causative link between the breach of the obligation and the detriment, sufficiently strong to establish a cause of action in principle, had not been made out.) Within that majority, different reasons were advanced for that view. Lord Hoffmann and Lord Nicholls placed their decision on the ground of compliance with what they regarded as the intention of Parliament that the common law of wrongful dismissal should not reduplicate the statutory right to remedies for unfair dismissal. Lord Millett reasoned that the obligation of mutual trust and confidence applied during the continuance of the contract of employment but not to or after its termination. Lord Bingham expressed himself as agreeing both with Lord Hoffmann and Lord Millett.

It must be said that none of these various grounds of decision seems at all compelling in and of itself. In particular, the reasons advanced by the majority of the Law Lords seem rather contrived, and to be in the nature of rationalizations of a prior decision that it would be undesirable as a matter of policy for a claim of this nature to be allowed to succeed. Thus, if the obligation of mutual trust and confidence is a genuine reading of the implied intentions of the parties to the contract of employment, there seems no special reason why it should be regarded as stopping short of controlling the termination of the contract. If, on the other hand, the adjudication is a genuine attempt to comply with the design of the unfair dismissal legislation, it is rather surprising to have regarded Parliament, when it introduced a set of statutory protections for workers with regard to dismissal, as intending, indeed as enjoining, that the common law should not, in the future, develop parallel protections as part of the implied content of their personal work or employment contracts.

In fact, the grounds for the decision, which were advanced in the successive courts through which this case passed, were rationalizations of a deeper intuition on the part of the judges. That intuition was that the challenge to the unrestricted notice rule from the law of unfair dismissal should be rejected, just as the challenge from public law had earlier been rejected. That is to say, they felt that it was inappropriate that the new genre of interpretation of the implied content of the contract of employment, which had developed especially around the notion of constructive dismissal *in the context of the law of unfair dismissal*, should give rise to a reworking of the basic common law approach to outright dismissal, which is constructed around the unrestricted notice rule.

This perception was so strongly held by some of the Law Lords who decided the case of *Johnson v Unisys* that it not merely halted but actually threw into reverse the trend towards modification of the unrestricted notice rule under the influence of the law of unfair dismissal. Thus, one question which was considered in the House of Lords was whether the employee's claim might not need to depend upon the *implied* content of the contract of employment because it might be founded upon the disciplinary procedures laid down in the employee handbook which applied to the claimant's employment, if that could be regarded as part of the *express* content of his contract.

That question was answered in the negative by Lord Hoffmann; and it is of paramount importance to note what his reasoning was. He took the view that the disciplinary procedure should not be regarded as part of the express content of the contract of employment, particularly not as forming terms the breach of which might be actionable at common law, because the disciplinary procedure had been provided for the purpose of ensuring that dismissals would be in compliance with the unfair dismissal legislation; hence, the dismissal procedures should not be accorded a contractual force which would 'create the means of circumventing the restrictions and limits which Parliament had imposed on compensation for unfair dismissal'. He concluded, therefore, that:

It is, I suppose possible that [the disciplinary procedures] may have contractual effect in determining whether the employer can dismiss summarily in the sense of not having to give four weeks' notice or payment in lieu. *But I do not think that they can have been intended to qualify the employer's common law power to dismiss without cause on giving such notice,* or to create contractual duties which are independently actionable.[85]

So the wheel of interpretation has come full circle; whereas, in cases such as *Goold (Pearmak) Ltd v O'Connell*,[86] the content of the contract of employment was being expanded in order to make the law of unfair dismissal effective, now, in *Johnson v Unisys*, the content of the contract of employment was being restricted in order to contain the consequential expansion of the common law of wrongful dismissal. This is a stark illustration of the difficulties which the courts and tribunals face in maintaining a single cohesive approach to the law of personal work or employment contracts in different interpretative contexts. There is now a crucial unresolved question of whether a single approach remains appropriate or even feasible in the area of dismissal, given the degree of tension which now exists between, on the one hand, the contractual control exerted over managerial action short of dismissal by the implied obligation of mutual trust and confidence, and, on the other hand, the permissive contractual regime for managerial decisions about dismissal which is asserted by the re-vindication of the unrestricted notice rule in the case of *Johnson v Unisys*.[87]

D. THE POSSIBLE IMPACT OF THE DISPUTE RESOLUTION PROVISIONS OF THE EMPLOYMENT ACT 2002[88]

It is possible that, for contracts of employment and potentially also for other personal work contacts, an important contribution to the resolution of this tension has now been made by the provisions of Part 3 of the Employment Act 2002, and in particular by section 30 of that Act. Part 3 of the Act has the purpose of minimizing expensive claim making and litigation before Employment Tribunals by maximizing the requirements and incentives for internal resolution within employing entities of disputes concerning fairness of dismissal, or, more generally, concerning compliance with employment protection legislation and legislation controlling discrimination in employment. To that end, statutory dispute resolution procedures, consisting of disciplinary, dismissal, and grievance procedures, are specified by the Act; and section 30(1) provides that:

Every contract of employment shall have effect to require the employer and employee to comply, in relation to any matter to which a statutory procedure applies, with the requirements of the procedure.

However, it is important to note that section 30(3) provides that the application of the statutory procedures for the purpose of section 30 may

---

[85] [2001] ICR 480 (HL) at 502, para 66 (emphasis added).
[86] [1995] IRLR 516 (EAT).
[87] Compare now *McCabe v Cornwall County Council* [2003] IRLR 87 (CA); see above, 166–167, and below, 362, 472.   [88] See also below, 393–394.

be the subject of secondary legislation, which will crucially affect their impact and significance.[89]

It might be that this statutory imposition of a minimum procedural content upon contracts of employment, and possibly upon other personal work or employment contracts too,[90] will serve to re-present, from a new source, the challenge, to the rule that the employer's power of termination by notice is strongly presumed to be contractually unrestricted, which has been largely or entirely rejected so far as it comes from the sources of public law or of unfair dismissal law. It might even be that courts and tribunals will accept that the statutory minimum procedural content itself imposes some degree of substantive contractual control upon the power of dismissal and of termination by notice, to the extent that the requirement to follow even the simplest of dismissal procedures is soon revealed as an empty one if there is no constraint at all upon the arbitrariness of the decision which is the outcome of the procedure.

On the other hand, it is perfectly possible that the sort of concern which the majority of the House of Lords demonstrated in *Johnson v Unisys* to maintain the integrity of the unrestricted notice rule might militate against anything more than a narrow literal implementation of the statutory minimum procedural requirements. At the moment, the unrestricted notice rule exerts a surprising hegemony in the common law concerning the termination of personal work or employment contracts. It has acquired that hegemony, not because it has any particular moral cogency, nor because there is any special reason to believe that it accurately reflects the perceived rights and obligations of employing entities, but rather because it has become part of a web of legal rules or doctrines, which are mainly about the remedies which the common law (including the law of equity) affords for contractually wrongful dismissal. This web of rules and doctrines has become a self-reinforcing one in which each rule sustains the others. This conceals the fact that many of those rules now lack a clear free-standing justification. In the next chapter, we examine and evaluate, under the heading of wrongful termination by the employing entity, the rest of the body of doctrine which surrounds and protects the unrestricted notice rule. We proceed to draw brief conclusions from the present chapter.

CONCLUSION

This chapter has formed the first of a sequence of the four final chapters of this work which between them present and seek to develop a radical critique

---

[89] Thus, Schedule 2 designates, in Part 1 Chapter 1, a standard dismissal and disciplinary procedure consisting of the three steps of (1) statement of grounds for action and invitation to meeting, (2) meeting, and (3) appeal; the Schedule then designates, in Part 2 Chapter 2, a modified procedure omitting the meeting stage. It has been left to regulations to determine in what circumstances the standard procedure will give way to the modified procedure.

[90] Section 29(2)(b) enables the statutory procedures to be extended by regulations to individuals other than employees.

of the law concerning the termination and transformation of personal work or employment contracts. In this chapter, it has been argued that the starting point for a set of concerns about the coherence of this body of law is to be found in the dominant conception, of the powers of termination possessed by the employing entity, as essentially unfettered ones. It has been suggested that this conception asserts itself as a less than fully reasoned or justified but constant feature of a body of jurisprudence about the termination of contracts of employment, which is torn between two genres of adjudication, one of which arises in the context of claims to common law and equitable remedies, while the other has developed in the very different context of adjudication about statutory employment rights, such as the right to remedies for unfair dismissal. It has then been argued that the conception of the unfettered powers of termination of the employing entity is strongly associated with a rather simplistic division of employment contracts into contracts of indefinite duration terminable by notice and fixed-term contracts; and a scheme of analysis of the duration and intended terminability of employment contracts has been advanced which seeks to escape from that oversimplification and to question the appropriateness of this accepted typology. The argument proceeded to examine the other aspect of the unfettered powers of termination ascribed to the employing entity, which is that of justified summary termination. It was shown how, in that aspect too, the conception of these powers as unrestricted ones has proved sufficiently strongly entrenched to resist challenges from reasoning based on public law and based upon the law of unfair dismissal.

The implication was, and the point is now made, that authoritative restatement would be required to address this set of concerns in an adequate way; this body of law could not be reformulated into a conceptually and practically coherent one by means solely of doctrinal exposition. However, the nature of the authoritative restatement which would be needed was not yet clear, because the discussion of lawful termination by the employing entity turned out to be one which was not at all complete in itself; it was concluded that it was but one part of a complex of ideas, the other crucial element in which was the law concerning wrongful dismissal, or wrongful termination of personal work or employment contracts more generally. So that discussion remains to be rounded off in the next chapter; but it is useful first to identify the extent to which the discussion thus far is one which is applicable to semi-dependent workers' contracts as well as to contracts of employment. In this respect this chapter reiterates the recurring conclusion of this work as to the law of semi-dependent workers' contracts, namely that, so far as common law and equitable doctrine is concerned, there is little cause either in terms of theory or authority to make an abrupt or strong differentiation between the substance of the law which is applicable to the two respective types of contracts; but that, on the other hand, a concrete disharmony between the two bodies of law arises when legislation alters the law of the contract of employment while leaving that of the semi-dependent worker's contract untouched. Such an enactment is the Fixed-term Employees (Prevention of Less Favourable Treatment) Regulations 2002; and the already considerable obscurity which surrounds the law of semi-dependent workers' contracts can only be deepened by the fact that this rather complex transformation of the shape of employment contracts will have to be understood differentially as between the two subcategories of employees and semi-dependent workers. Against that background we turn our attention to the other, and crucial, part of the discussion of termination by the employing entity, namely that of wrongful termination.

7

Wrongful Termination by the Employing Entity

INTRODUCTION

In the previous chapter we considered the way in which the law of personal work contracts accords powers of lawful termination to the employing entity; and it was argued that the central concept, which dictated the whole approach to the construction of those powers, was that of the unrestricted notice rule, which was to the effect that, under contracts of employment, the employing entity should be strongly presumed to possess a power of termination by notice which was not subject to substantive or procedural restrictions as to when and how it was to be exercised. Towards the end of that chapter, it began to emerge that, at least in the case law of the period from the early 1960s onwards, the unrestricted notice rule is not a free-standing one, but rather one which is very strongly associated with the way in which the law of personal work contracts conceives of the notion of wrongful dismissal, and of the remedies for wrongful dismissal.

In this chapter, it will be argued that this association between the unrestricted notice rule and the remedial approach to wrongful dismissal is indeed crucial to the understanding of the whole of the law of termination of personal work contracts. In fact, it will be asserted that the unrestricted notice rule and the remedial approach to wrongful dismissal have formed a nexus or complex of ideas, the combined impact of which upon the law of termination of personal work contracts has been allowed to become and to remain a dominant one. In the course of this chapter, that domination will be scrutinized and will be called into question, in the sense that it will be called into doubt whether a body of law of termination of personal work contracts constructed around that central theoretical complex can adequately meet the various interpretative demands which are currently made upon it.[1]

This argument will be developed in the following stages. Firstly, it will be shown how there is a complex of or nexus between the approaches to (1) the unrestricted notice rule, (2) the conception of wrongful dismissal as

---

[1] The discussion in this chapter takes some of its starting points from two very significant articles by Keith Ewing, 'Job Security and the Contract of Employment' (Ewing 1989) and 'Remedies for Breach of the Contract of Employment' (Ewing 1993).

the denial of notice, and (3) the limits upon remedies, with special reference to (a) damages, (b) the equitable remedies of positive enforcement by specific performance or injunction, and (c) claims to remuneration as contractual debt. Secondly, it will be suggested that these approaches have been allowed mutually to support and validate each other to the point at which sight has been lost of the fact that each of these approaches is both fragile and incomplete when considered in separation from the others. Thirdly, we shall attempt to apply this critique to a rather larger area than that of wrongful dismissal, extending it to issues such as that of the status of payment in lieu of notice, and the question of the *time* of termination of the personal work contract.

The terminology of 'wrongful termination by the employing entity' has been chosen as the general heading for this discussion in preference to that of 'wrongful dismissal', although 'wrongful dismissal' is a more familiar notion. The novel terminology has not been devised for the sake of being different, but because of a conviction that the whole notion of 'wrongful dismissal', far from being a simple descriptive heading for a part of the law of personal work contracts, has come to refer to or embody the highly specific and interdependent body of rules, doctrines, and approaches which was identified in the preceding paragraphs, and which it is the task of this chapter to analyse or deconstruct. In other words, the argument will be that the law of 'wrongful dismissal' represents the currently preferred approach, but not the inevitable or uniquely valid approach, to the subject of wrongful termination of personal work contracts. In the first section of this chapter, we develop this notion of 'wrongful dismissal' as a highly particular or contingent set of ideas.

SECTION 1: THE LAW OF WRONGFUL DISMISSAL AS A NEXUS OF IDEAS

Our system of employment law is structured in such a way that it requires, within and from the law of personal work contracts, clear answers to the following central set of questions about the termination of employment:

(1) What rights or powers do the parties to personal work contracts have to terminate those contracts?
(2) When and in what sense is termination of employment contractually wrongful?
(3) When there is contractual wrongfulness in or associated with the termination of employment, what remedies are afforded?
(4) When there is contractual wrongfulness in or associated with the termination of employment, when and how is the personal work contract deemed to be terminated?

Moreover, there seems to be a real need, an interpretative demand, for each of those questions to be answered in a way which is not only clear but also self-sufficient; each question seems to require a free-standing complete answer if the system of employment law is to be free of inefficient, even crippling, conceptual and practical uncertainties.

However, when the first of those questions was considered, with regard to the entity's powers of termination, in the previous chapter, it started to become apparent that there was no free-standing complete answer to that question. Thus, in the *Johnson v Unisys* case, the analysis of the extent of the entity's right of termination was entirely bound up with the answers to the second and third questions about wrongfulness and remedies. This might be regarded as a natural and unremarkable state of affairs, a normal manifestation of the tendency of the English common law in general, and of the English law of contract in particular, to reason often from wrongs and remedies to rights and the formation and termination of rights, rather than the other way round.

So it might be thought; but, with regard to the law of the termination of personal work contracts, there is a much more singular state of affairs. For each of the four questions posed above is the subject of strong doctrinal or policy perceptions on the part of courts and tribunals as to how that particular question should be answered in particular interpretative and remedial contexts. If we use the terminology of 'dismissal' for convenience, it could be said that there is a distinct body of law, with its own doctrine and policy discourse, about each of the following topics: (1) rights of dismissal; (2) wrongfulness of dismissal; (3) remedies associated with dismissal; and (4) dismissal as termination of the contract. Yet, and this is a crucial point, each of these little bodies of law, although distinct, is nevertheless dependent on the others; they lean on each other for support at the levels both of policy and doctrine. In this sense, there is a nexus of ideas or doctrines which links the treatment of each of those topics together, which we may refer to as the nexus of ideas around wrongful dismissal.

Moreover, and this too is a crucial point, this nexus of ideas around wrongful dismissal, although it is presented or articulated as an essentially technical body of legal doctrine, actually expresses and gives effect to a deep-seated set of policy perceptions as to what the role and approach of the common law should be with regard to termination of employment. Indeed, it is the very fact that this set of ideas locks together into a highly complex body of interlinked legal rules which gives it a deceptive appearance of doctrinal inevitability and policy neutrality.

The appearance is deceptive because it obscures the reality of a common law approach to the wrongful termination of personal employment contracts which systematically minimizes the protection accorded to personally employed workers in a way which is neither doctrinally inevitable nor neutral in policy terms. In this and the succeeding sections, it will be argued that, at the present day, this should be regarded as an eclectic approach rather than as a universally valid one; and other possible approaches will be canvassed to see whether they offer viable alternatives to the existing one, and therefore form the basis of a valid critique of that existing approach. It will be helpful to begin by showing how the current approach has been constructed within the relatively recent history of employment law.

The construction of the nexus of ideas which forms the basis of the common law approach to wrongful dismissal can be understood most clearly if we examine carefully the two classic statements by Lord Reid, the first in *Ridge v Baldwin*[2] and the second in *Malloch v Aberdeen Corporation*,[3] in which he contrasts the law concerning the dismissal of office-holders with the law which applies in the 'ordinary' or 'pure' case of 'master and servant'. In the latter case, which is the case of the standard or default model of the contract of employment, we have observed earlier how Lord Reid appears to assert the existence of an unrestricted right in the employing entity to dismiss without a demonstrated good reason and without a hearing.[4] Thus in *Ridge v Baldwin* we find the assertion that 'the master can terminate the contract with his servant ... for any reason or for none';[5] and in the *Malloch* case it is said that 'at common law a master is not bound to hear his servant before he dismisses him. He can act unreasonably or capriciously if he so chooses ...'.[6]

This appears to assert, in a clear and free-standing way, a presumed unrestricted right of dismissal (by notice) on the part of the employing entity. However, a much more complex reality presents itself if we place those extracts in their context and examine Lord Reid's statements more fully. Thus the full statement in *Ridge v Baldwin* is that:

The law regarding master and servant is not in doubt. There cannot be specific performance of a contract of service, and the master can terminate the contract with his servant at any time and for any reason or for none. But if he does so in a manner not warranted by the contract he must pay damages for breach of contract. So the question in a pure case of master and servant does not at all depend on whether the master has heard the servant in his own defence; it depends on whether the facts emerging at the trial prove breach of contract.[7]

And in the *Malloch* case, the expanded, though still very succinct, statement is that:

At common law a master is not bound to hear his servant before he dismisses him. He can act unreasonably or capriciously if he so chooses but the dismissal is valid. The servant has no remedy unless the dismissal is in breach of contract and then the servant's only remedy is damages for breach of contract.[8]

---

[2] [1964] AC 40.   [3] [1971] 1 WLR 1578.   [4] See above, 333.
[5] [1964] AC 40 at 65.   [6] [1971] 1 WLR 1578 at 1586.   [7] [1964] AC 40 at 65.
[8] [1971] 1 WLR 1578 at 1586.

In their expanded form, these statements, from which one seems at first to be able to distil an unrestricted right or power of dismissal, seem rather to be saying that a dismissal may be contractually wrongful but is nevertheless effective in the sense that the remedies obtainable by the dismissed worker are extremely limited. However, this is an ambiguity which there is no easy way to resolve by means of logical or textual analysis; in the first statement there is a deep equivocation as to what 'the question' is. 'The question' might be whether the dismissal is *wrongful* in the absence of a reason and a hearing, or, on the other hand, 'the question' might be merely whether, in the absence of a reason and a hearing, a *remedy* is available. In the second statement there is a similar equivocation as to what it means to say that the dismissal is 'valid'. These doubts are intrinsic and irresolvable, for in truth these statements each contain a series of propositions, some about rights or powers of dismissal and some about remedies, which are interwoven so that the cumulative effect of the whole statement seems, in each case, greater than the sum of its parts.

That cumulative effect is, in fact, the remarkable one of making the whole statement in each case appear to possess an irrefutable and objective logic. Once the statements are deconstructed, it starts to become apparent that they embody much more contingent approaches to the question of what the law of wrongful dismissal should be, and how it should be applied or presumed to apply in the generality of employment situations. We can best understand this nexus of contingent propositions, and consider possible alternatives to it, if, for the purpose of the discussion, we break the complex of ideas down into two groups. The first group concerns the questions of wrongfulness and damages; the second group concerns the questions of specific remedies and effectiveness of termination. That is to say, in terms of the set of topics which we identified earlier, we shall group topics (1) and (2) together, and, on the other hand, topics (3) and (4) together. In the next two sections, we consider those two groups successively, attempting to bring them together again at the end of the chapter.

SECTION 2: THE WRONGFULNESS/ DAMAGES COMPLEX

A. The Wrongfulness/Damages Complex Explained

In the previous chapter, it was argued that much of the law concerning the powers of the employing entity to terminate the personal employment contract is constructed around the unrestricted notice rule. In the previous section it was suggested that this rule is itself part of a nexus of ideas which links up rights, wrongs, remedies, and termination with regard to the contractual treatment of the termination of employment. In this section it is contended that, right at the core of this linked set of ideas, is a set of notions about the remedies for wrongful termination, and, more particularly, about damages for wrongful dismissal. This set of notions is the real motor of this whole body of law; it drives and orients the whole nexus of ideas. We could think of it as the wrongfulness/damages complex.

The wrongfulness/damages complex seems to express a particular sequence of argument or syllogism which starts from propositions about remedies and takes the reasoning onwards into the articulation of notions of wrongfulness in dismissal, powers of dismissal, and termination by dismissal. It may be useful to refer to this as the argument from remedies. It runs as follows:

(1) Remedies for wrongful dismissal are normally and almost without exception limited to damages, in so far as remedies in the nature of specific enforcement are not available in relation to wrongful dismissal, and claims to remuneration as such are normally and almost without exception not available in respect of any time following a wrongful dismissal (P1).

(2) Damages for wrongful dismissal are normally and almost without exception limited so that they compensate only for lost remuneration in respect of the contractual notice period or unexpired fixed term of employment (and are qualified by the worker's duty to mitigate that loss) (P2).

(3) It follows that if notice is given, just as if the worker is allowed to work out a contractual fixed period of employment, no remedy, and in particular no damages, will normally and almost without exception be available in respect of the dismissal concerned (P3).

(4) It is also seen to follow that, for a personal work contract terminable by notice, if notice is given, the dismissal is *not wrongful* in any sense which is recognized by the law of personal employment contracts, and that if notice is not given the dismissal is *wrongful only in the sense that* it represents a denial of due notice or remuneration and benefits in respect of due notice, and in no other sense (P4).

(5) These propositions are also seen to support a very strong presumption that where a personal work contract is terminable by notice, that power is an unrestricted one in a substantive and procedural sense, in so far as no remediable wrong will normally and almost without exception follow from the exercise of that power (P5).

It will be argued in due course that there are further propositions which are seen as corollaries, for example relating to payment in lieu of notice and to termination of the personal employment contract by wrongful dismissal; but the five propositions set out above are the essential ones, around which the whole wrongful dismissal nexus of ideas revolves. We suggest that it is this set of propositions which have been regarded as characterizing the 'ordinary case of master and servant' or archetypal contract of employment as identified and explicated by Lord Reid in *Ridge v Baldwin* and *Malloch v Aberdeen Corporation.*

If it is accepted, as is strongly contended here, that the logic of the wrongful dismissal nexus of ideas really is built upon a basis of propositions about remedies in general and damages in particular, a crucial question poses itself as to the source of legitimacy or validity of those basic remedial propositions which support the whole construct of ideas. The answer is much more difficult and less obvious than might at first appear. There are three main sets of remedial doctrines or rules which are involved, and which, as usual in this whole complex of rules of doctrines, are tied up with each other. Those three sets of remedial doctrines concern, respectively, (1) specific enforcement, (2) liability for remuneration, and (3) damages. It is those doctrines which underlie, and are generally taken without question to sustain, the two propositions about remedies which figure as P1 and P2 above.

We generally assume that each of these three doctrines is soundly established both in terms of judicial authority and juristic reasoning. Scrutiny, however, reveals that each of these doctrines is more fragile than is normally assumed, in the sense that each one is less than rigorously reasoned in modern case law and turns out to be the subject of unresolved controversies, at least at its margins. Thus, doctrine (1), which proscribes specific enforcement of the contract of employment against the employer, is the subject of very significant modern exceptions, the scope of which are significantly uncertain. We return to that set of questions in a later section of this chapter. Doctrine (2), which confines liability for remuneration to the situation where contractual employment has actually occurred, was considered earlier as a set of issues about the relationship between performance and remuneration, from which it appeared that the possibility of 'constructive performance' is one which is both real and yet of very uncertain scope.

These uncertainties are sufficiently great to cast doubt upon the notion that these doctrines are settled rules of law, or that they are ineluctable deductions from fundamental legal principles. This begins to suggest that they should rather be viewed as default rules, or as presumptions about the meaning and construction of contracts, the strength of which is open to debate and reconsideration according to the context and circumstances of the case. That suggestion has even greater force in relation to doctrine (3), which will now be subjected to detailed scrutiny. This is the doctrine which normally confines damages for wrongful dismissal to compensation for loss of remuneration during notice or an unexpired fixed period of contractual employment; it does this by normally excluding damages on any other basis. We shall refer to it as the limited damages rule.

B. The Sources and Scope of the Limited Damages Rule

Once it has been appreciated that the whole wrongfulness/damages complex of ideas turns very largely upon the limited damages rule, it actually becomes worryingly difficult to find an authentic basis in authority or juristic reason for that rule. The general principles of contract law do not do so. We might look to the propositions, for instance, that the object of contract damages is normally to place the claimant in the situation which would have obtained if the contract had been duly performed, or indeed that the defendant is to be given the benefit of the assumption that he, she, or it had performed the contract in the least costly or disadvantageous way for him, her, or it. However, they do not command the application of the limited damages rule; they would do that only if it was clear that the obligations of the employing entity in respect of termination were entirely confined to that of giving notice or compensating for want of notice; as we have seen, it is deeply controversial whether that is the case, and a rule about *damages* should not be allowed to beg that crucial question. So we return to the problem of why the limited damages rule receives such largely unqualified acceptance.

Over a long period of time, and for the generality of workers during that period of time, the rule would have been substantially unquestioned in practice simply because it replicated the normal expectations of employed persons and employing entities. A worker whose employment was terminable by an hour's, or a day's, or a week's notice would not in practice be regarded as having any claim in damages for wrongful dismissal other than one representing remuneration for that very short period of time, whether that period was regarded as the unexpired term of the contract or the contractual notice period. To hold otherwise would be to subvert the effectively 'at will' nature of the underlying employment arrangement. Before the 1960s at least, when a serious statutory minimum floor of protection of job security began to be introduced, it would have seemed almost pointless to challenge that firmly held set of assumptions so far as the generality of workers were concerned.

To that extent, the limited damages rule was based upon custom and practice, rather than being founded upon articulated legal principles. The situations where the limited damages rule came under challenge, and therefore had to be asserted through reasoned judicial decision making, were the atypical ones where workers were employed for long fixed periods or where their employment was terminable only upon long periods of notice. In the very clearly stratified pre-modern labour market, it was almost exclusively company directors and managerial employees who were employed on such terms. Claims by such workers to have suffered extensive compensable injury from wrongful dismissal, going beyond the loss of remuneration for the notice period or unexpired fixed period, itself a more significant loss for such workers than for the generality of workers, would command some credibility and command serious debate in the courts. This was the battle which was fought out in the great case of *Addis v Gramophone Co*,[9]

[9] [1909] AC 488 (HL).

and that is why this case has an entirely pivotal role, more than is normally recognized, in the development of the law of wrongful dismissal.

The importance, indeed the centrality, of the *Addis* decision to the law of wrongful dismissal has been largely obscured by the apparently unclear and curious terms in which it was expressed. No sooner was it decided and reported than an unending controversy broke out as to what, precisely, it had decided. As *Addis* has recently, in the *Malik v BCCI* and *Johnson v Unisys* cases, moved right to the centre of the stage of the law concerning wrongful termination of personal employment contracts, it is essential to understand the true nature and cause of that controversy. This becomes much easier to do if we consider the *Addis* case in the particular forensic context in which it was decided; as often, that explains almost everything. Although the methodology of the present work is largely to concentrate upon the recent, in the sense of post-1950s, development of case law and statute law, a brief excursus into an earlier period of the history of employment law is justified.

By 1909, the year in which the *Addis* case was decided, the common law action for wrongful dismissal seems to have developed to a point where it displayed a number of features similar to those of the modern statutory claim to compensation for unfair dismissal. In particular, it seems to have become a rather open-ended claim both as to the respects in which a dismissal might be treated as wrongful, as to what might constitute justification for otherwise wrongful dismissal, and as to what damages might be awarded for a successful claim. Moreover, all these issues might be referred to a civil jury operating within a loose framework of legal rules. Anxieties about the inadequacy of the trial judge's control over the jury in respect of justification for dismissal are visible in the decision of the Privy Council in *Clouston & Co Ltd v Corry*;[10] the concern was that the jury had taken too narrow a view of justification, and therefore an unduly wide view of the claim for wrongful dismissal.

This set of concerns about the capacity of civil juries to make generous discretionary awards for wrongful dismissal must have been greatly heightened by the ruling in the case of *Maw v Jones*.[11] This case concerned a draper's apprentice, employed under a deed of apprenticeship for four years but which the master was entitled to cancel at a week's notice if the apprentice 'showed a want of interest in his work'. The apprentice was dismissed without notice for insubordination and sued for wrongful dismissal; the jury found that dismissal with notice would have been justified but that summary dismissal had not been justified. The trial judge directed the jury, as to the measure of damages, that they were not bound to limit the damages to the value of the week's notice which the apprentice had lost; the jury awarded damages of £21 which represented more than ten weeks' wages. In a terse

---

[10] [1906] AC 122 (PC).   [11] (1890) 25 QBD 107 (QBD).

but momentous ruling Lord Coleridge CJ held that there had been no misdirection to the jury; the master could have exercised the power of lawful dismissal upon notice but had not done so, and the apprentice was entitled to recover for all the damage flowing naturally from the wrongful dismissal including 'the difficulty that the plaintiff as a discharged apprentice would have in obtaining employment elsewhere'. The jury had judged that 'the *fair* damages were £21' (emphasis added); the direction had been 'perfectly right' and the verdict 'sensible'.[12]

We can be fairly sure that this dramatic departure from the limited damages rule, this admittance of compensation for damage to the claimant's future employability, would not at that time have been regarded as applicable to ordinary domestic servants or industrial workers. However, when in 1906 Mr Addis, the manager of the business of the Gramophone Company in Calcutta, entitled to six month's notice of termination, brought an action for wrongful dismissal, similarly alleging that his dismissal had damaged his employability because of its wrongfully summary character, the jury awarded damages of £600 in respect of wrongful dismissal, a sum representing more than nine months' basic salary even for this very highly remunerated employee and therefore representing another departure from the limited damages rule. The employing entity successfully appealed to the Court of Appeal against that award of damages, and the House of Lords upheld[13] the Court of Appeal, the Lord Chancellor himself expressing indignation at the way in which litigation 'can breed barren controversies and increase costs in a matter of itself simple enough'.[14]

Much subsequent case law shows that the matter was by no means as simple as Lord Loreburn asserted it to be. The actual disposal of the case consisted of a direct reassertion of the limited damages rule; the plaintiff's damages were limited to six months' salary. However, rather than positively articulating a limited damages rule—something the courts have always hesitated to do, perhaps for the reason that it is hard to justify such a rule in doctrinal terms—the Law Lords deciding the case advanced a number of ambivalent or inconsistent propositions about the bases upon which damages should *not* be awarded. Between the different judgments, and within particular judgments, we find variously expressed rejections of damages which are either (1) in respect of the manner of dismissal rather than the fact of dismissal, or (2) in respect of injury to feelings, or (3) in respect of difficulty in obtaining subsequent employment, rather than for deprivation of the present employment, or (4) which are exemplary damages rather than compensatory ones, or (5) which are for injury to reputation, or (6) which are in the nature of tort damages rather than contract damages.

---

[12] (1890) 25 QBD 107 at 109.
[13] *Addis v Gramophone Company Ltd* [1909] AC 488 (HL).
[14] Ibid at 490 (Lord Loreburn LC).

There has been much subsequent controversy about what is the right formulation of the single overall principle or ratio decidendi of the *Addis* case, and as to whether that was correctly identified in the rather sweeping headnote to the report of the case in the Law Reports. In truth, there is no single overall principle, because neither jointly nor severally do these exclusionary rules represent an outcome which was clearly commanded by previously declared principles. The decision in *Maw v Jones* was not obviously in conflict with strongly established principles; its extension from the case of apprenticeship to that of employment was hard to resist; the Law Lords in *Addis* were in no small difficulties in getting the genie back into the bottle. Lord Collins' dissent, a spirited defence of the importance of the discretion of the judge and jury to respond to arbitrary and oppressive behaviour, makes much more convincing reading as an account of the underlying tendency of the English private law of contract and tort.

However, it must be admitted that the restrictive impulses which determined the outcome of the *Addis* case have proved to be surprisingly persistent in relation especially to claims for damages for the wider injurious effects of wrongful dismissal even if a sound principled basis for them is lacking. Now the restrictive approach of the *Addis* case towards such damages has been reasserted in spirit and in detail in the decision of the House of Lords in *Johnson v Unisys Ltd*;[15] the tendency to generate a common law analogue of the statutory claim to compensation for unfair dismissal has again been thwarted. This return to *Addis* is, as we began to observe in the previous chapter, an extraordinarily significant development in the law of personal employment contracts. It is appropriate to consider at the deepest possible level both what the decision in *Addis* stood for in its time, and, even more important, what it stands for in the present law now that it has been re-validated by the decision in *Johnson v Unisys*.

The true significance of the *Addis* decision, both in its time and for the modern law, is that the House of Lords in that decision, deploying the full weight of its authority in a situation where there was real scope for choice, legitimated and cemented in place the nexus of mutually self-sustaining ideas of (1) the employing entity's unrestricted notice power (which we refer to as the 'unrestricted notice rule'), (2) the limited wrongfulness of wrongful dismissal (the 'limited wrongfulness rule'), and (3) the limits on damages for wrongful dismissal (the 'limited damages rule'). Briefly to recapitulate, the unrestricted notice rule asserts the default proposition that the employing entity's power of termination by notice is subject neither to substantive nor to procedural limitations (except those which prescribe the length of the notice).

The limited wrongfulness rule is to the effect that a dismissal is normally to be regarded as wrongful only to the extent and in the sense that it

---

[15] [2001] ICR 480 (HL).

involves a denial of employment for the due notice period or the unexpired fixed term. The limited damages rule basically confines damages to loss of remuneration and benefits in respect of the notice period or unexpired fixed term. In the *Addis* case, it was the latter rule which was in issue, and which it was resolved upon; but the reasoning both depends upon and affirms the other two rules at the same time, especially and directly the limited wrongfulness rule.

In an immediate sense, as we have already indicated, the motive and driver of the decision in the *Addis* case was the perceived need to curtail the development of litigation leading to large and discretionary awards by civil juries in dismissal cases. Behind that specific impulse stood a concern to impose a firmly free-market transactional approach to the termination of contracts of employment, and to resist the encroachment of, at that time tort-based, relational obligations upon the employing entity which would vindicate the dignity and autonomy of the individual employee. It is an exceedingly interesting historical question why the House of Lords inclined so strongly in that direction in the *Addis* case, especially given that the plaintiff was not a domestic, agricultural, industrial, or clerical rank-and-file worker, towards whom such an approach would have been fully predictable, but a managerial and entrepreneurial employee of whose business reputation and business capacity the courts might have been expected to be more protective—as, indeed the judge had been when directing the jury at first instance.

Much more important, however, to the purpose of this study of the present law of personal employment contracts is the question why the House of Lords saw fit to reassert that approach almost a century later in the *Johnson* case, as well as the further question of what impact that crucial choice has upon the modern law of wrongful dismissal. The Law Lords who decided the *Johnson* case could all see perfectly clearly that the common law of the contract of employment had developed to the point where it certainly permitted, and probably commanded, a more open and inclusive approach both to the notion of wrongful dismissal, and, as a corollary, to the scope of damages for wrongful dismissal than had been taken in the *Addis* decision. Both Lord Hoffmann and Lord Millett, the leading protagonists of the return to *Addis*, are at pains to demonstrate that this was an available approach; indeed, Lord Hoffmann is as forceful in articulating this approach as Lord Steyn, who held that this approach should actually be followed.

In one sense, the rejection of that available approach is not a full return to the *Addis* regime, because of the existence of the statutory claim to compensation for unfair dismissal. There is no reason to doubt that the majority in the House of Lords in *Johnson* accepted that there was a functional need to be able to respond to the claim that was being advanced, but that they believed that this need was fully met by the law of unfair dismissal. Had the law of unfair dismissal not existed, they imply that they would have been prepared to invent it within the law of the contract of employment. As it was, they strongly believed that it was undesirable to reduplicate it in the law of the contract of employment, especially as the reduplicative claim in contract would not be subject to the bounds and limits which had been set upon the statutory claim.

However, in another sense there was a full return to *Addis*, to the extent that all the Law Lords who decided the *Johnson* case recognized that the *Addis* case had established the basic common law approach to the action for wrongful dismissal, and only Lord Steyn took the view that this approach should now be regarded as having been fundamentally modified by subsequent evolution of the common law. For his colleagues, any such modification could at best consist of a tort-like graft onto the sturdy plant of the common law action for wrongful dismissal, a graft which might be rejected and, on grounds of policy, should not in fact be made. For them, the true character of the action for wrongful dismissal had been accurately identified by McLachlin J in the Supreme Court of Canada in *Wallace v United Grain Growers Ltd* in the following terms:

> The action for wrongful dismissal is based on an implied obligation in the employment contract to give reasonable notice of an intention to terminate the relationship (or pay in lieu thereof) in the absence of just cause for dismissal...A 'wrongful dismissal' action is not concerned with the wrongness or rightness of the dismissal itself. Far from making dismissal a wrong, the law entitles both employer and employee to terminate the employment relationship without cause. A wrong arises only if the employer breaches the contract by failing to give the dismissed employee reasonable notice of termination. The remedy for this breach of contract is an award of damages based on the period of notice which should have been given.[16]

This analysis, which had come to be regarded as identifying a self-evident truth about the common law of the contract of employment, is in fact a contingent one, based not upon an inherent logic but upon a choice made, between real alternatives, by the House of Lords in the *Addis* decision. But, although the doctrine is in truth the result of a decision which is highly contingent upon the particular procedural and remedial context in which it was taken, it has proved robust enough to be maintained in the present, a present which is very different in procedural terms if not in terms of judicial attitudes. The view that wrongful dismissal is wrongful, and remediable in damages, only because of its prematurity, its denial of a promised period of notice or fixed term of employment, has been and continues to be the dominant approach of English common law.

Thus, the whole philosophical and practical approach both to the *purpose* and to the *quantification* of damages for wrongful dismissal has been largely dictated by this particular view about limited wrongfulness and limited

---

[16] [1997] 152 DLR (4th) 1 at 39.

damages. This approach has led to the conclusions that the *purpose* of damages for wrongful dismissal is simply to protect the worker's interest in remuneration and benefits expected from the denied period of notice or the unexpired fixed term, and that the *quantification* of the worker's loss from the dismissal is also to be conducted on the assumption that his or her losses are limited to that remuneration and those associated benefits. It may be contrasted with an increasingly open-minded and inclusive approach to the purpose of damages and the understanding of attributable loss in the general law of contract, as manifested, for example, in the decision of the House of Lords in the recent *McAlpine* case.[17]

However, although the limited wrongfulness/limited damages approach has been the dominant one, it has not been the exclusive one. The *Johnson v Unisys* decision represents its prevalence over two particular, and associated, doctrinal possibilities for a very different and much more worker-protective approach. These possibilities were, firstly, that the wrongfulness of dismissal might be expanded by reference to the implied obligation of mutual trust and confidence,[18] and, secondly, that damages for wrongful dismissal might reflect injury to the worker's personality or employability caused by wrongful dismissal in that larger sense. But it would be a grave oversimplification to depict the whole approach to wrongful dismissal and to damages for wrongful dismissal in the stark terms of the *Johnson v Unisys* decision.

A different, more worker-protective, approach has manifested itself in various other ways, and some traces of it still remain present within the law of damages for wrongful dismissal. Its manifestations, and its interplay with the limited wrongfulness/limited damages approach, are highly intricate. We shall seek to show in the course of the next section that they can best be understood in the context of the other part of the nexus of ideas which make up the law of wrongful dismissal, that which relates to specific remedies and to the effectiveness of wrongful dismissal to terminate contractual employment. But before we move on to that next stage of the discussion, it will be useful to identify, somewhat more fully, the place which the limited wrongfulness/limited damages approach has in the theory of damages for wrongful dismissal as a whole.

In order to do that, it will be necessary to draw together some apparently disparate rules or doctrines which relate to various different aspects of damages for wrongful dismissal; in particular, those of (1) damages for injury to feelings, and loss of employability, (2) the duty of mitigation of loss, and (3) damages for loss of predicted benefits. The bodies of law which exist in relation to those three topics are perceived as distinct ones; but they are

---

[17] *Alfred McAlpine Construction Ltd v Panatown Ltd* [2001] 1 AC 518.

[18] For the extreme difficulty in resolving the question in what fact situations the doctrine in *Johnson v Unisys* excludes the implied obligation of mutual trust and confidence compare now *McCabe v Cornwall County Council* [2003] IRLR 187; see above, 166, 344 and below, 472.

linked together by an underlying question, which is that of what set of obligations the law of damages imposes upon the employing entity in relation to wrongful dismissal, or, to put it in another way, what set of expectations for workers under personal employment contracts does the law of damages vindicate and protect?

In order to understand this way in which apparently disparate rules or doctrines about damages for wrongful dismissal operate in conjunction with each other to produce a certain distinctive overall outcome, it will be helpful to develop further the contrast, which we began to observe in the discussion of damages for injury to feelings and loss of employability, between two broad approaches which the law of damages might take in relation to wrongful dismissal. Thus far we have identified, in relation to the first set of issues about (1) damages for injury to feelings, and loss of employability, a contrast between a broad inclusive approach and a narrow exclusive approach to the set of obligations upon employing entities, and of expectations of personal workers, which are recognized and vindicated by the law of damages for wrongful dismissal. That analysis can be further refined by extending it to include the other two sets of rules or doctrines, that is to say those relating to (2) the duty of mitigation of loss, and (3) damages for loss of predicted benefits or chances of benefit.

Thus, in particular, it can be observed that the generally narrow and exclusive approach to damages for wrongful dismissal, which emerges from the rejection in the *Addis* and *Johnson v Unisys* cases of damages for injury to feelings or loss of employability, is considerably reinforced by the application of the duty of mitigation of loss. In the leading modern case on the worker's duty of mitigation of loss resulting from wrongful dismissal, that of *Yetton v Eastwoods Froy Ltd*,[19] it was regarded as uncontroversial to apply to a claim for wrongful dismissal the general principle of contract law which requires the claimant's damages to be reduced by reference to replacement gains which the claimant actually did make or could reasonably have been expected to make following or in consequence of the breach of contract, the issue in the case being that of how exactly this principle was to be applied.

The fact that the application of the duty of mitigation of loss to claims for damages for wrongful dismissal is thus regarded as axiomatic is apt to obscure the crucial transformative effect which it has upon the very nature of those claims. Interest has tended to concentrate upon the rigour of the requirements upon the dismissed personal worker to account for actual replacement earnings or to give credit for replacement earnings which could have been gained if the claimant had displayed a reasonable readiness to accept alternative work offered by the dismissing employing entity, or a

---

[19] [1967] 1 WLR 104 (QBD).

reasonable positivity in seeking and accepting alternative employment with other employing entities. Thus Deakin and Morris draw attention to the fact that, as applied in *Yetton v Eastwood Froy*, the common law duty of mitigation is 'considerably less disciplinary in its effects on the unemployed worker than the law of social security'.[20]

However, even if it is, to that extent, applied with a light touch, the duty to mitigate nevertheless has a fundamental limiting effect upon the extent and indeed the very nature of the claim to damages for wrongful dismissal. We have previously observed how the notice/damages rule, as formulated by the decisions in *Addis* and *Johnson v Unisys*, downgrades that claim, from being a general claim not to have been dismissed other than as provided for by the personal employment contract, and so to be compensated for all the detriments attributable to having been dismissed. Instead, it is reduced to a claim not to have been denied a stipulated fixed period of employment or period of notice, and so to be compensated for the loss of the earnings to which the worker would have been entitled during that period of employment. The application of the duty to mitigate reduces the claim one crucial stage further; it narrows it to a claim for earnings during any period of unavoidable unemployment within that contractually fixed period.

This has profound conceptual as well as practical implications; it means that the protected interest is not the interest in the employing entity's compliance with a primary obligation generally to desist from wrongful dismissal, nor yet the interest in the employing entity's employing and desisting from wrongful dismissal for a fixed period, nor even the interest in the employing entity's fulfilling a primary obligation to remunerate during a fixed period, but merely the interest in the employing entity's meeting an entirely secondary obligation to compensate for the marginal loss of not reasonably replaceable earnings during a fixed period. In conceptual terms, it means that the wrongfully dismissed worker in no sense at all enjoys the benefit of a protected period of job security; he or she is required immediately to re-enter the labour market as an unemployed person. The dismissal, though wrongful, has been effective to prevent the worker from claiming damages based upon a claim to full continuation of employment even for the period of notice or for an unexpired fixed term.

This cumulative set of rules or doctrines tending to restrict the nature and extent of the claim to damages for wrongful dismissal is yet further reinforced by the approach which is taken to the third set of issues about damages for wrongful dismissal which we identified above, namely those relating to (3) damages for loss of predicted benefits or chances of benefit. The approach to this set of issues is restrictive in the following sense. The underlying general principle is that damages are to compensate the claimant for the loss of benefits or chances of benefit which the claimant

---

[20] Deakin and Morris 2001 at 401.

would have been reasonably predicted to receive or enjoy but for the breach of contract in question. This involves a comparison of the actual outcome following the breach of contract with a hypothetical situation which would have occurred but for the breach of contract. Constructing that comparison is not an obvious or simple matter, especially in the case of a relational contract where the relationship in question is wrongfully brought to an end by the breach of contract, and where the hypothesis is therefore that the relationship would have continued but for the breach of contract. Many issues are thereby posed as to the length of time for which the relationship should be assumed to have continued, and as to the benefits which that continuance should be assumed to have conferred upon the injured party.

There are few, if any, instances where that set of issues has been more difficult or controversial than in relation to the wrongful dismissal of workers employed under personal employment contracts. In this context, there has been a strong application of a restrictive principle of the general law of contract damages which limits the hypothetical continuation and the benefits attributed to it by imposing an assumption that the contract breaker would have performed the contract in the least disadvantageous or costly manner available. In other words, an assumption of minimal compliance with specific contractual obligations and maximal use of loss-limiting options is imposed in favour of the contract breaker; this prevails over evidence indicating that the contract breaker would not in the normal course of things have behaved in that particular way.

In the context of assessment of damages for wrongful dismissal, there are two highly significant applications of this principle of assumed least disadvantageous performance. These are (1) the assumed negative exercise of discretions with regard to remuneration and benefits, and (2) the assumed positive use of the power of termination by notice. We proceed to consider these two applications in turn. In each case, but more especially in the second case, the application of the principle of least disadvantageous performance turns out to exert a restrictive effect not merely upon the quantification of damages, as one might expect, but also, by a kind of reverse feedback, upon the way in which the protected interest of the worker is itself constructed and vindicated.

The first of those two applications of the principle of assumed least disadvantageous performance has its modern starting point in the decision of the Court of Appeal in 1966 in the case of *Lavarack v Woods of Colchester Ltd*.[21] In that case, the principle was applied to exclude from the calculation of damages a salary increase which fellow workers of the dismissed employee had received subsequent to his dismissal, and which had been given in lieu of a discretionary bonus which had been customarily received by the dismissed employee and his fellow workers before his dismissal.

[21] [1967] 1 QB 278 (CA).

The dissent of Lord Denning MR on this aspect of the decision indicates that there was a genuinely available alternative view of the common law on this point, namely that damages could have taken account of a real expectation that the dismissed employee would have received the salary increase but for his dismissal even if that expectation was not the product of a clear contractual obligation upon the employing entity.

The decision of the majority of the Court of Appeal in the *Lavarack* case had some restrictive effect upon the way in which workers' entitlements to bonuses and salary increases were construed; for much of the subsequent period, it seems to have been accepted that the decision had successfully vindicated the employing entity's capacity to maintain a continuingly unfettered discretion with regard to bonuses and salary reviews. However, we have seen in an earlier chapter how the courts have recently begun to view those discretions as qualified by implied contractual obligations to exercise such discretions in a consistent and non-arbitrary way. In the cases of *Clark v BET plc*[22] and *Clark v Nomura International plc*[23] this brought discretionary bonuses or salary reviews back into account in the calculation of damages for wrongful dismissal, which made a momentous upward difference to the quantum of damages.

It has been rather a different story with regard to the other application of the principle of least disadvantageous performance, namely the assumption that the employing entity would have exercised a power to terminate by notice at the moment at which the wrongful dismissal took place. In one sense this assumption is entirely intrinsic or inherent to the way in which the claim to damages for wrongful dismissal is conceived of; it is the logical outcome, indeed the very expression, of the notice/damages rule which we have already identified. Thus, in *Hill v CA Parsons & Co Ltd*, Lord Denning MR referred to the servant's remedy in damages for wrongful dismissal as:

> his remedy in damages against the master for breach of the contract to continue the relationship for the contractual period. He gets damages for the time he would have served if he had been given proper notice less, of course, anything he has, or ought to have, earned in alternative employment.[24]

In that sense, the principle of least disadvantageous performance, like the duty to mitigate loss, is seen as self-evidently part of the nature of the claim to damages for wrongful dismissal.

However, in this particular application, the principle of least disadvantageous performance seems to have been taken to the lengths not merely of reasserting the basic notice/damages rule but actually of reinforcing and extending it. In the leading case of *Gunton v Richmond-upon-Thames LBC*,[25] which will be discussed in a different aspect in a later section of this

---

[22] [1997] IRLR 348.   [23] [2000] IRLR 766.   [24] [1972] Ch 305 at 314.
[25] [1980] ICR 755 (CA).

chapter, the principle was applied to limit the damages for wrongful dismissal to which an employee was entitled where he was dismissed in breach of a contractual obligation to afford him the benefit of a dismissal procedure for disciplinary dismissal. The least disadvantageous performance principle was invoked to identify and limit the period of employment which the worker was deemed to have lost by reason of the wrongful dismissal.[26] The period was defined and restricted by reference to the employing entity's underlying entitlement to terminate by notice.

The key point here is that the denial of disciplinary procedure was regarded merely as extending that notional period by the time it would have taken to go through the procedure; the least disadvantageous performance principle thus excluded consideration of the chance that, if the procedure had been followed, the worker might not have been dismissed at that point, and might have remained in employment for some much longer period. Furthermore, this application of the least disadvantageous performance principle seems actually to have encouraged the view of the power to terminate as a generally unrestricted one, certainly as a power which, in particular, should not be regarded as fundamentally constrained by the presence of disciplinary or redundancy procedures, or by the contractual specification of disciplinary or redundancy grounds for dismissal.

That approach has remained a strongly entrenched one, especially in the latter particular respect. Thus perhaps we could regard as a minor relaxation of the general principle the decision in the case of *Raspin v United News Shops Ltd*,[27] where the Employment Appeal Tribunal was not only prepared notionally to extend the period of notice to include a period for carrying out the disciplinary dismissal procedure which should have been followed, but also to allow in damages for the fact that this notional extension would have qualified the dismissed worker to bring an unfair dismissal claim which she might have won. However, the restrictive approach had been vigorously reasserted by that Tribunal when, in the case of *Janciuk v Winerite Ltd*,[28] the claimant had sought to advance the particular argument that, where the employing entity had dismissed in breach of the requirement to follow a contractually agreed disciplinary dismissal procedure, the damages should reflect the chance that the dismissal might not have occurred at all.

That contention was not merely rejected but actually condemned by the President of the Tribunal, Morison J in the terms that:

We regard the attempt to introduce the loss of a chance into the calculation of the damages as a heresy and it represents a misunderstanding of the process involved

---

[26] See, for example, Buckley LJ at 772: 'The date when the contract would have come to an end . . . must be ascertained on the assumption that the employer would have exercised any power he may have had to bring the contract to an end in the way most beneficial to himself; that is to say he would have determined the contract at the earliest date at which he could properly do so.'   [27] [1999] IRLR 9 (EAT).
[28] [1998] IRLR 63 (EAT).

in quantifying a dismissed employee's damages for breach of contract. [Counsel for the claimant] is seeking to overlay contractual questions with concepts of fairness which, in our view, do not apply.[29]

The orthodoxy which is being defended against this heretical introduction of notions of fairness is none other than the principle of least disadvantageous performance, as applied to give the employing entity the benefit of an unrestricted power to terminate by notice:

> The court is concerned to know what would have happened, contractually, if instead of unlawfully dismissing the employee the employer had not broken the contract, bearing in mind the *Lavarack v Woods* principle. For this purpose, the assumption that must be made is that the employer would have dismissed the employee at the first available moment open to him, namely after the procedure had been exhausted.[30]

This reasoning positively insists upon the employing entity's capacity to make entirely opportunistic use of the power of termination by notice, and disregards the possibility that such opportunistic behaviour might in and of itself be regarded as constituting a breach of contract (though Morison J leaves open the possibility that different principles might apply where the employer had been 'accused of acting in bad faith'[31]). This discussion has indicated a specific reluctance on the part of courts and tribunals to engage in anything amounting to the enforcement of an actual or notional continuation of contractual employment upon an employing entity which has effected a *de facto* termination of the employment relationship by wrongful dismissal. In order to understand the basis and extent of that reluctance, it is necessary to widen the scope of our discussion of the law of wrongful dismissal to include its treatment of specific remedies, and of the fundamental question of whether and when wrongful dismissal is effective to terminate contractual employment.

SECTION 3: THE SPECIFIC REMEDIES/TERMINATION COMPLEX

A. THE SPECIFIC REMEDIES/TERMINATION COMPLEX PRESENTED

It is doubtful whether the limited wrongfulness/limited damages complex of ideas, described in the previous section, would be as powerfully self-sustaining as it has proved to be, were it not integrally linked with a further set of doctrines which it is convenient to identify as the specific remedies/termination complex. Spelt out more fully, this is a set of ideas which asserts, as mutually complementing notions, the unavailability of specific remedies against wrongful dismissal and the effectiveness of wrongful dismissal to terminate the contract of employment. To be even more precise,

---

[29] [1998] IRLR (EAT) at 64.   [30] Ibid.   [31] Ibid.

which case law and statute law frequently fail to be, the two notions are that (1) injunctions, orders of specific enforcement, or claims for continuance of remuneration, are not available against an employing entity to reverse, remedy, or undo a *de facto* dismissal, and (2) a *de facto* dismissal is effective to bring contractual employment under a contract of employment to an end even though it is wrongful. Like the two ideas of limited wrongfulness and limited damages, these two doctrines are allowed to sustain and legitimate each other; and all four ideas link up to produce a doctrinal circle of wagons which has been powerfully defensive against hostile incursions.

The whole panoply of ideas is encapsulated in Lord Reid's two famous characterizations, cited earlier, of the 'ordinary case of master and servant', which he offered in the course of his judgments in the cases of *Ridge v Baldwin* and *Malloch v Aberdeen Corporation*. In those dicta, which are foundational for the modern law of the wrongful termination of personal employment contracts, the four threads of ideas are skilfully interwoven to form a material with the qualities of chain mail. However, even that steely textile has some propensity to unravel at the edges. In this section, we explore some of the uncertainties and inconsistencies which have presented themselves, as the specific remedies/termination complex of ideas has confronted other or rival approaches, and has generally though not invariably prevailed, though not without considerable sacrifice of doctrinal and policy coherence. We concentrate in turn upon (1) injunctions and other specific remedies, and (2) automatic versus elective termination theories.

B. INJUNCTIONS AND OTHER SPECIFIC REMEDIES

As we have observed earlier, one of the crucial components of the whole complex of ideas, which forms the limited conception of wrongful dismissal and of the remedies available for wrongful dismissal, is the doctrine denying specific remedies for the enforcement of personal employment contracts against employing entities. We should perhaps speak of the *supposed* doctrine against specific remedies, because, like many elements in this whole complex of ideas, this supposedly firm normative proposition turns out upon examination to consist of a series of contingent and context-specific rules or preferences, scarcely deserving the status of a doctrine well established or consistently maintained in the modern law.

That assertion challenges the clear orthodoxy of the law of the contract of employment as it stood at the outset of the modern period of that body of law. In Lord Reid's foundational analysis in *Ridge v Baldwin*, the leading proposition of law which is advanced to characterize the 'pure case of master and servant' is that 'There cannot be specific performance of a contract of service'.[32] It will be argued in this subsection that we should regard the doctrine against specific remedies as being at

---

[32] [1964] AC 40 at 65.

once more general and more specific than that proposition suggests; more general in that the rule against specific performance is only part of a set of objections to specific enforcement of personal employment contracts, yet more specific in that each of those objections turns out to be fragmented and subject to exceptions.

We suggest, in the first place, that it is necessary to think of specific remedies for wrongful dismissal, or for wrongful termination of personal employment contracts more generally, as being of two broad types, namely (1) remedies which compel continuance of employment, and (2) remedies which compel continuance of remuneration and other benefits. The supposed doctrine against specific remedies seems to be regarded as equally, indeed indifferently, applicable to both those types of remedies. That may be a misconception; there seems to be a distinct line of development of doctrine in relation to each of those two types of remedy, possibly even with different outcomes for the present law. We proceed to consider the whole sequence of development with this important distinction in mind.

Firstly, so far as remedies which compel continuance of employment are concerned, it is clear that in the course of the nineteenth century the Chancery judges formed and expressed a clear inclination against deploying their discretionary remedies in such a way as to enforce the continuance of employment upon unwilling employers. In the leading case of *Johnson v Shrewsbury and Birmingham Railway Company*[33] in 1853, Knight Bruce LJ rationalized the refusal of an order of specific enforcement to contractors to whom the running of a railway had been contracted out for seven years by equating their claim to that of a personal servant seeking specific performance of a contract of service.[34] It is notable that this idiom was used to express a very major public policy concern, with profound modern resonances, to ensure the terminability of arrangements for the contracting-out of functions upon which the safety of the public depended.

In a further demonstration of underlying judicial attitudes, in *Rigby v Connol*[35] in 1881, the example of master and servant was used to demonstrate the existence of a category of relationships viewed as sufficiently domestic or private that Courts of Equity would not contemplate their specific enforcement; indeed, the language used by the Master of the Rolls, Lord Jessel, indicates a doubt whether, in those courts at least, the relationship

---

[33] 3 De GM & G 914 (CA in Ch).
[34] 'A man may have one of the best domestic servants, he may have a valet whose arrangement of clothes is faultless, a coachman whose driving is excellent, a cook whose performances are perfect, and yet he may not have confidence in him; and while on the one hand all that the servant requires or wishes (and that reasonably enough) is money, you are on the other hand to destroy the comfort of a man's existence for a period of years, by compelling him to have constantly about him in a confidential situation one to who he objects.' Ibid at 925.
[35] (1881) 14 ChD 482.

of master and servant was regarded as constituting an enforceable contract in the first place:

The Courts as such have never dreamt of enforcing agreements strictly personal in their nature, whether they are agreements of hiring and service, being the common relation of master and servant, or whether they are agreements for the purposes of pleasure . . . or scientific pursuits . . . or charity or philanthropy—in such cases no Court of Justice can properly interfere so long as there is no property the right to which is taken away from the person complaining.[36]

Neither the complete subjectivity of the discretion thereby accorded to the employer, nor the extension of this reasoning from personal domestic employers to large corporate entities, were subsequently questioned in the courts or in legal writings. On the other hand, they were not strongly confirmed, so that Megarry J, reviewing, in 1971, the status of the doctrine against specific enforcement of contracts for personal service, could comment that:

One day, perhaps, the courts will look again at the so-called rule that contracts for personal services or involving the continuous performance of services will not be specifically enforced. Such a rule is plainly not absolute and without exception, nor do I think that it can be based on any narrow consideration such as difficulties of constant superintendence by the court. . . . I do not think it should be assumed that as soon as any element of personal service or continuous services can be discerned in a contract the court will, without more, refuse specific performance.[37]

One of the exceptions which Megarry J might have had in mind, so far as specific enforcement against employing entities was concerned, consisted in a historical willingness on the parts of Courts of Equity to make orders for the continuance of *remuneration* following a wrongful dismissal, as in the old case of *Ball v Coggs* (1710)[38] where a plaintiff employed as a general manager of a brass-wire works for his life obtained an order requiring the employers to pay him his salary (and requiring him to work for them should they request him to do so). In *Denmark Productions Ltd v Boscobel Productions Ltd*[39] in 1968, it was decided that a claim by the managers of a pop group, for an account for remuneration in respect of the unexpired period of their contract following their wrongful dismissal by the members of the pop group, was misconceived and must fail. That decision was grounded on nineteenth century judicial authority,[40] but the contrary decision could still have been sustained. Megarry J was right to be sceptical about the basis for a dogmatic rejection of specific remedies against wrongful dismissal.

In particular, he could have had it in mind that much of the hardening of position against specific enforcement of contracts involving personal

[36] Ibid at 488.   [37] *CH Giles & Co Ltd v Morris* [1972] 1 WLR 307 at 318 (ChD).
[38] Bro Parl Cas 140.   [39] [1969] 1 QB 699 (CA).
[40] *Goodman v Pocock* (1850) 15 QB 576; *French v Brookes* (1830) 6 Bing 354; *Fewings v Tisdal* (1847) 1 Exch 295.

services which took place from the later nineteenth century onwards occurred in the context of claims for injunctions by employing entities seeking to restrain their workers from establishing or working for rival concerns. This is perfectly instantiated by the leading case, decided in 1891, of *Whitwood Chemical Company v Hardman*,[41] which is often advanced as the basis of the modern supposedly general rule. There would always be an argument that similar restrictions should apply by parity of reasoning or as a matter of mutuality or reciprocity to claims in the nature of specific enforcement against employing entities, but this would be an indirect and to that extent less cogent consideration.

In fact, the development from 1970 onwards of the case law of specific enforcement against employing entities has demonstrated a notable absence of dogmatic commitment to the refusal of such remedies to workers, especially with regard to interim or interlocutory injunctions (and even on occasion permanent injunctions) to restrain certain kinds of action on the part of employing entities amounting to or tending towards wrongful dismissal. Such injunctions have been granted in a series of very important cases: in chronological order, *Hill v CA Parsons & Co Ltd*,[42] *Jones v Lee*,[43] *Irani v Southampton and South-West Hampshire Health Authority*,[44] *Hughes v London Borough of Southwark*,[45] *Powell v London Borough of Brent*,[46] *Wadcock v London Borough of Brent*,[47] *Robb v London Borough of Hammersmith and Fulham*,[48] *Jones v Gwent County Council*,[49] and *Anderson v Pringle of Scotland Ltd*.[50] This list is sufficiently long and impressive to suggest that in the modern law the rule against specific remedies to enforce contracts involving personal services might be 'more honoured in the breach than in the observance'. To use another metaphor, this might seem to amount to an open breach in the defences of the limited wrongfulness/limited remedies approach. In the ensuing paragraphs, we shall argue that these cases probably have not displaced that dominant paradigm; and we shall seek to identify the conceptual sphere within which the exceptional cases have been decided and within which they are, ultimately, contained.

Most of these decisions fall within two, not entirely dissociated, conditions which between them set up a certain particular theoretical framework for overcoming judicial reluctance to grant specific remedies tending to override wrongful dismissal. The two conditions are, firstly, that there is some particular procedural or substantive contractual restriction upon the employing entity's power of dismissal—a condition satisfied in all these cases[51] except

---

[41] [1891] 2 Ch 416 (CA).   [42] [1972] ICR 305 (CA).   [43] [1980] ICR 310 (CA).
[44] [1985] ICR 590 (ChD).   [45] [1988] IRLR 55.   [46] [1988] ICR 176 (CA).
[47] [1990] IRLR 223 (ChD).   [48] [1991] ICR 514 (QBD).
[49] [1992] IRLR 521 (ChD).   [50] [1998] IRLR 64 (CSOH).
[51] Though it should be noted that *Powell* is not straightforwardly concerned with dismissal, but rather with refusal to allow the employee to take up a promotion which she had been promised.

that of *Hill v Parsons*, and secondly, that the employing entity is a public authority, which is satisfied in all these cases except those of *Hill v Parsons* and *Anderson v Pringle*. *Hill v Parsons* was a very special case, in the sense that the purported dismissal on insufficient notice, in restraint of which an interlocutory injunction was granted by the Court of Appeal, was effected by the employing entity not of its own volition but in implementation of a closed shop agreement with a trade union which the plaintiff employee was unwilling to join because he belonged to a rival association of professional engineers.

Moreover the claim for an injunction had the aim of maintaining the plaintiff employee's position until there came into operation a set of restrictions upon such closed shop agreements which had been enacted in the Industrial Relations Act 1971. If the dismissal had been a straightforwardly wrongful exercise of the managerial volition of a private sector employing entity, it is almost inconceivable that the Court of Appeal would have been prepared to grant such a remedy. Lord Denning MR and Sachs LJ could rationalize this case as one in which, by contrast with the typical case of wrongful dismissal, 'mutual confidence between master and servant' was not impaired.[52] But the underlying point was that the employing entity was acting as proxy defendant for the trade union with which it had made a closed shop agreement, and those judges felt that the real defendant was seeking to pre-empt the impending statutory regulation of its oppressive practices.

The case is thus concerned with what the Court of Appeal regarded, though they do not so describe them, as the public or civil rights of the plaintiff employee. It is no accident that, although the employment relationship in question consisted of a purely private law contract of employment, those judges drew upon what would now be regarded as public law principles applied to public law employment relationships to sustain the grant of an injunction which would treat the purported dismissal as invalid and ineffective to terminate the plaintiff's contractual employment.[53] This, we suggest, is the key to most of the subsequent cases where such injunctions were given. They fit into and support a paradigm which is different from the 'ordinary case of master and servant' as Lord Reid had identified it. In this different paradigm, a countervailing set of mutually self-sustaining propositions prevail: (1) there are special express or implied substantive or procedural restrictions upon dismissal; (2) the employed person is in a specially protected situation; (3) the restrictions of the limited wrongfulness/limited remedies approach do not and should not apply.

The great difficulty, which has severely perplexed both judges and theorists, is to provide a coherent account of the case law in which specific remedies have been granted or refused against employing entities, which

[52] [1972] Ch 305 at 313, 320.
[53] Particularly in their reliance upon the authority of *Francis v Kuala Lumpur Councillors* [1962] 1 WLR 1411 (PC); see [1972] Ch 305 at 314, 319.

will identify what are the necessary or sufficient conditions in which this paradigm will apply and will displace the underlying common law paradigm of limited wrongfulness and limited remedies for wrongful dismissal. We shall argue for a way of understanding this body of case law which seeks to address that difficulty; this argument could perhaps be styled as that of the public law paradigm transposed into private law. The first step in this argument asserts that, although these cases are decided as issues of private law, the paradigm is essentially that of public law; it is basically the same public law paradigm as that which we identified in an earlier section as presenting a challenge to the unlimited power of termination by notice.

However, and this is a fundamental point, in this group of cases the public law paradigm presents itself in an unfamiliar and indirect form, because it has been transposed into the private law of equitable remedies. In this transposed form, appearing therefore in the guise of private law, the public law paradigm had a rather greater acceptability or tenacity than it did when it posed a direct challenge, from the discourse of public law, to the unlimited power of termination by notice. Whereas we saw in the earlier discussion that the direct challenge from public law to the unlimited power of termination had only very limited success, the indirect challenge to the doctrine against specific enforcement of contracts involving personal service has proved a more insidious one.

In order to trace this development with precision, it is necessary to refer again[54] to the procedural and substantive separation of public law from private law which occurred after and in consequence of the reforms to the administration of justice which were effected by amendment of the Rules of the Supreme Court in 1977, and confirmed by primary legislation in 1981.[55] Until those reforms had taken effect and their substantive consequences had been worked out, the common law courts perceived little or no difficulty in applying what we have since come to regard as the distinctive principles and approaches of public law to determine the availability of equitable remedies such as that of the interlocutory injunction, although those were, primarily at least, private law remedies. As late as 1979 in its decision in *Jones v Lee*,[56] the Court of Appeal perceived no doctrinal difficulty in following a line of cases granting interlocutory injunctions to teachers or head teachers challenging purported dismissal from their positions which would have been in violation of substantive or procedural restrictions imposed by their conditions of tenure. The essentially private law of equitable remedies still provided a context in which the court was remarkably untroubled by the great distinction between the 'ordinary case of master and servant' and that of tenured public office.

---

[54] See above, 71.

[55] Recasting RSC Order 53 to create a new single consolidated procedure for judicial review of administrative action; s 31 of the Supreme Court Act 1981.

[56] [1980] ICR 310.

Moreover, and this is the remarkable point, that judicial capacity to apply an essentially public law paradigm in granting equitable remedies seemed to survive the post-1980 substantial extrusion of the public law paradigm from the common law of the public sector employment relationship, which we noticed earlier and associated especially with the decision of the Court of Appeal in the case of *R v East Berkshire Health Authority, ex parte Walsh*[57] in 1984. The decisive case in maintaining the capacity to apply the public law paradigm was the *Irani* case also decided in 1984. In the latter case, the argument was advanced on behalf of the defendant health authority that the *Walsh* decision prevented the plaintiff, employed as a part-time ophthalmologist, from claiming an injunction to restrain the employing entity from dismissing him without complying with a dismissal procedure which formed part of his conditions of service. This argument was that the granting of such an injunction would allow the plaintiff to invoke the public law rights which had been held in *Walsh* not to be applicable to the essentially private law contractual relationship judged to exist between an NHS health authority and its employees. In *Irani*, Warner J disposed of that argument, saying of the *Walsh* case that it

decides nothing at all about what remedies such a practitioner [as the plaintiff in the present case] may be entitled to *under the court's normal equitable jurisdiction, which is the jurisdiction that I am exercising.*[58]

This decision represented a breakthrough, an effective importation of the public law paradigm into the private law of equitable remedies despite the general exclusion of public sector employment relationships from access to the public law paradigm via judicial review. Combined with the authority of *Hill v Parsons*, the approach in *Irani* sustained the string of decisions cited earlier in which injunctions have since been granted against employing entities purporting to dismiss workers, or otherwise deny them the employment to which they were contractually entitled, in breach of substantive or procedural protections of their job security which their personal employment contracts conferred upon them. The approach came indeed to be regarded as applicable to purely private sector employing entities (as, of course, it had been in the rather special circumstances of *Hill v Parsons*). Thus, although such an injunction was refused in *Alexander v Standard Telephones & Cables plc*,[59] the private sector status of the employing entity was not the ground for that refusal; and in *Anderson v Pringle*, the Scottish law remedy of interdict was granted against a purely private sector employing entity, in a decision drawing upon this same stream of authority in the English courts.

That series of cases in which interlocutory injunctions have been granted raises two very interesting associated questions which it is difficult to answer.

---

[57] [1985] QB 152; see above, 71–72, 334–335.
[58] [1985] ICR 590 at 601F (emphasis added).
[59] [1990] ICR 291 (ChD).

Firstly, how far will such injunctions be available in future? And, secondly, is the availability of such injunctions sufficient to produce a general displacement of the limited wrongfulness/limited remedies paradigm, in favour of the public law paradigm thus transposed into the private law of personal work contracts? We suggest that a cautious and largely negative answer has to be given to both those questions.

As to the first question, the transposition of the public law paradigm into the private law of equitable remedies exposed it to various controlling mechanisms, especially those which apply to the granting of interlocutory injunctions. The most potent of those, as in *Alexander v Standard Telephones & Cables*, has proved to be the requirement that mutual trust and confidence must continue to subsist between the parties. The decision of the House of Lords in *Johnson v Unisys*, which holds that the employing entity's obligation to maintain mutual trust and confidence does not apply to or survive a wrongful dismissal, makes it easier for the employing entity to argue that the requirement of mutual trust and confidence is normally absent after wrongful dismissal, since it largely relieves the employing entity of the accusation that, by alleging such absence, it is invoking its own wrongful behaviour.

That decision also, as we have previously sought to show, strongly reinforces the limited wrongfulness/limited remedies paradigm in a more general sense, and therefore tends to makes the public law paradigm a more marginal and less influential one. In those circumstances the injunction cases are more apt to seem conceptually isolated, and to present themselves as special exceptions to a general norm. That situation can be better understood by considering another aspect of the law of wrongful dismissal in which the two paradigms have been in contestation, that of the terminatory effectiveness of wrongful dismissal.

C. Terminatory Effectiveness, Elective Theory, and Notional Prolongation

Our discussion of wrongful termination of the personal work contract by the employing entity has revealed a complex of ideas which between them produce a determinedly restrictive approach both to the conception of wrongful dismissal and to the remedies which are available for wrongfulness. Various challenges to that approach have been made and rejected, from within the law of implied terms, the law of damages, and the law of specific remedies. The restrictive approach maintains the power of the employing entity to put an immediate end to the contractual employment of the worker on the footing that the wrongfulness of so doing is clearly contained and limited, and that the remedies against so doing are equally clearly contained and limited.

We have also seen that the challenges to this approach seek, unsuccessfully, to assert to the contrary that the employing entity should not be allowed to act opportunistically in that sense. They proceed on the basis that the law should deny that opportunity by, in effect, notionally prolonging the contractual employment in question and the whole set of obligations which go with it. In this, they replicate or even draw upon a public law paradigm in which administrative action is not only subjected to controls against arbitrariness and opportunism but is also treated as invalid or ineffective where it fails to stay within those controls.

According to this paradigm, the status quo ante will, so far as it is practicable, be restored in the face of unlawful administrative action; a relationship or state of affairs which it has been purported to end by unlawful administrative action will to that extent be notionally continued. In this subsection we consider some further respects in which challenges have been presented, in our view equally unsuccessfully, to the restricted wrongfulness/restricted remedies approach, and where it has been sought to treat wrongful dismissal as ineffective and notionally to prolong contractual employment in the way that the public law paradigm makes it possible to do. The discussion will concern the confrontation between elective and automatic theories of termination by wrongful dismissal, and will also touch upon the treatment of the effective date of termination of contractual employment in the construction of statutory employment rights.

The confrontation between elective and automatic theories of termination by wrongful dismissal, specially associated with the two leading cases of *Gunton v Richmond-upon-Thames LBC*[60] and *Boyo v Lambeth LBC*,[61] constitutes one of the most analytically difficult aspects of the whole of the law concerning the termination of personal work contracts. In those cases the Court of Appeal adopted an elective theory of wrongful dismissal, whereby the worker faced with a purported dismissal in disregard of an obligation to follow a dismissal procedure has an option to treat the purported dismissal as ineffective to terminate the contractual employment in question. Superficially it looks as if these cases have replicated the public law paradigm (in which an *ultra vires* purported dismissal will be treated as invalid, and therefore a nullity) in the private law of the personal work or employment contract.

Therefore it appears that these decisions make significant inroads into the restricted wrongfulness/restricted remedies approach to wrongful dismissal. They seem to effect the very sort of notional prolongation of the personal employment contract after wrongful dismissal which we have seen has been rejected in the law of damages and almost rejected in the law of injunctions. It will, however, be argued here that this appearance is deceptive; so far from replicating the public law paradigm in the private law of wrongful dismissal, these decisions transpose that paradigm into private law in such a closely confined and limited way as almost to negate it.

---

[60] [1980] ICR 755 (CA).   [61] [1994] ICR 727 (CA).

The decisions in *Gunton* and *Boyo*, properly understood, signify not the reinvention of public law in a private law context, but, on the contrary, the *marginalization* of public law thinking in the treatment of the wrongful dismissal of workers employed by public authority employing entities. The two decisions tend to be regarded as enhancing the protection of workers against wrongful dismissal; but, compared with the possibilities which public law thinking offered, they actually contrived to diminish it.

In order to understand this apparent paradox, it is necessary to examine the history of these cases in some detail. Much hinges upon the decision at first instance, in the Chancery Division, in the *Gunton* case. That first instance decision represents the high water mark of the public law paradigm in wrongful dismissal cases. It was rendered in 1978, in the twilight period of integrated public and private law, just before the era of procedural and substantive exclusivity which was ushered in by the new Order 53[62] and the judicial response to it in *O'Reilly v Mackman*.[63] In *Gunton*, the plaintiff, in a way which was soon to become impermissible, claimed, in an action commenced by writ, that is to say by ordinary private law procedure rather than by judicial review, a declaration that the purported termination by the defendants of his appointment as registrar and clerk to the governors of a college of technology was illegal, *ultra vires*, and void and that he had therefore remained in post as registrar and clerk.

The plaintiff was granted a declaration and order which very much followed the contours of that essentially public law claim; the defendant's letter of dismissal was declared ineffective lawfully to terminate the plaintiff's contract of service, and an inquiry into damages was ordered on the basis that 'the plaintiff was entitled to remain in the employment of the defendant council until the normal retirement age for a servant of his standing unless in the meantime he became redundant or liable to be dismissed under the disciplinary procedure incorporated into his contract'. That decision really did represent a direct transposition of the public law paradigm into the private law of personal employment contracts, an extension of the kind of claim which succeeded in *Ridge v Baldwin*[64] and in *Malloch v Aberdeen Corporation*,[65] from office-holders and those in special statutory employment structures, to a public sector worker regarded as having a much more ordinary contract of employment.

It is crucial to realize that, while the majority of the Court of Appeal in the *Gunton* case appeared to endorse this approach to the extent of treating the purported dismissal as ineffective and not automatically terminatory of the worker's contractual employment, they actually reasserted, in large measure, the restrictive approach of the private law of personal work or

---

[62] RSC Order 53, introduced in its new form in 1977, and given statutory force by s 31 of the Supreme Court Act 1981; its current counterpart is CPR part 54; see above, 374 n 55.
[63] [1983] 2 AC 237 (HL).   [64] [1964] AC 40.   [65] [1971] 1 WLR 1578.

employment contracts to the conception of wrongful dismissal and to the remedies which were available in relation to it. The Court of Appeal applied the rule restricting damages to the one month's period of notice to which the plaintiff was entitled, merely adding to it a further period, estimated at two months, representing the time it would reasonably have taken to carry out the disciplinary dismissal procedure which the plaintiff had been denied.

The dissentient member of the Court of Appeal agreed with this outcome and regarded it as lying within the scope of the orthodox restrictive approach to wrongful dismissal; he would have refused a declaration that the purported dismissal had been ineffective to determine the dismissal. The majority of the Court of Appeal, in reality no less concerned to reassert the restrictive orthodoxy of the common law, preferred to do so in a more subtle way. As Brightman LJ put it, there was in his opinion no objection to a declaration 'that the purported termination of [the] contract of employment was *unlawful . . . for what it may be worth*' (emphasis added). His judgment, and that of Buckley LJ, ensured that such a declaration, from which the public law notion of *invalidity* has already been dropped, would be worth very little because of the particularly limited way in which they construed the election to continue the contract which such a declaration conferred upon the worker.

Those two judges in fact imposed two crucial limitations upon the worker's election to continue the contract, or, strictly speaking, the contractual employment, which the employing entity had purported to terminate by wrongful dismissal. Those two limitations can be styled respectively as (1) the deemed acceptance limitation, and (2) the denial of positive prolongatory effects. As so often in this whole discussion, these two notions are associated with each other and mutually support each other. Both are profoundly expressive of fundamental common law thinking about the termination of personal employment contracts.

The deemed acceptance limitation comes about as follows. The whole theory of termination of contracts by or as the result of repudiatory breach is imbued with notions of contractual offer and acceptance. The primary contractual rights of a party faced with a repudiatory breach of contract are protected by the idea that the repudiation gives a contractual choice to the injured party, between sticking with those existing primary contractual rights or, on the other hand, making as it were a new contract whereby those primary rights are reduced to secondary rights to compensation by agreeing to treat the repudiation as terminatory.

In *Gunton*, the majority of the Court of Appeal profess to assert and vindicate the former choice on the part of the wrongfully dismissed worker. But they actually undermined that choice in various ways. Buckley LJ did so by his readiness to deem the worker to have made the latter, ostensibly equally voluntary choice, to treat the wrongful dismissal as terminating the contract.[66] Actually, deeming the worker to have made the latter choice, simply by having brought an action in respect of the wrongful dismissal, deprived of all meaning the former choice which they professed to protect. By deeming the plaintiff to have chosen one contractual option Buckley LJ subverted the elective theory which protected the other.

This was particularly ironical where the very nature of the action which the plaintiff brought in respect of the wrongful dismissal was a claim that it should be treated as a nullity so that his contract of employment would be treated as continuing in force. That irony is further heightened by the fact that the plaintiff's deemed acceptance of the wrongful dismissal as terminatory was, in effect, backdated to the time of the wrongful dismissal itself; the plaintiff was deemed to have accepted, by the time of the trial of his action at the latest, that his contract of employment had been terminated by the wrongful dismissal on the date at which the employing entity had purported to effect that wrongful dismissal.

This brings us to the other, even more profound, limitation which both the majority judges placed upon their elective theory of wrongful dismissal; and it also shows the way in which the two limitations are interconnected. The first, deemed acceptance limitation, is rationalized by reference to the idea that the courts will not grant any remedy or allow any claim which would specifically enforce the continuation of employment after wrongful dismissal. The worker is readily, or even axiomatically, deemed to have accepted the wrongful dismissal as terminatory because that is no more than a recognition that there are no remedies which would enable him or her to do otherwise. The second limitation goes further and closes this circle of argument; it is to the effect that, given this absence of specific remedies to compel continuation, the courts should not and will not engage in a notional prolongation of the contract of employment after wrongful dismissal.

That second limitation was indeed imposed in the *Gunton* case; the only degree of notional prolongation which is brought about by the decision in that case is the extension, *for the purpose of calculating damages*, of the reckonable period of lost employment to include the time it would have taken to go through the disciplinary procedure. But this was notional prolongation of the contractual employment only in a totally nominal sense; it amounted to no more than giving damages for exclusion from ongoing employment rather than for denial of that employment; the damages are no greater on the former basis than on the latter basis. That is why the dissentient judge in the Court of Appeal in *Gunton* was able to concur in the damages calculation which the majority proposed, without

[66] See [1980] ICR 755 at 772: 'In the present case the plaintiff has accepted the repudiation. He did so at the trial, if not earlier.' Interestingly, the other judge in the majority seems not to have shared that view; see Brightman LJ at 778, where he seems to speak of the instant case as one where 'the innocent party has not accepted, and indeed has expressly rejected, the attempted repudiation'.

having even to pretend that it involved the recognition of a real election on the part of the worker for continuation of the contract of employment after a purported wrongful dismissal.

These limitations, and indeed these criticisms of them, are largely acknowledged in the main subsequent authority for the elective theory of wrongful dismissal, that is to say the decision of the Court of Appeal in the *Boyo* case. Thus, while in the first instance decision in the case of *Dietman v London Borough of Brent*[67] the elective approach had been at once adopted and immediately negated by deeming the plaintiff to have accepted the repudiation as terminating her contract of employment, the Court of Appeal in *Boyo* was clearly unhappy about the artificiality both of this kind of deemed acceptance, and indeed of maintaining the elective approach itself when no specific remedies were available to make it meaningful. Their response to these difficulties, however, was not to develop the elective approach into a more meaningful one by rejecting those limitations upon it, but, on the contrary, to admit that they only followed the elective approach reluctantly as a matter of deference to the authority of the earlier Court of Appeal which had decided the *Gunton* case, and that, had they felt it open to them, they would simply have reverted to the orthodox view that wrongful dismissal brings about an automatic termination of the contractual employment in question.

In this, it must be said, they seem to reflect a profound intuition on the part of the judges that the restricted wrongfulness/restricted remedies approach to wrongful dismissal is the correct one, and that the law of personal employment contracts should therefore not engage in prolongation of contractual employment in the face of wrongful dismissal. Apart from the injunction cases which were discussed in the previous subsection, almost the only significant instance where there has been remedial prolongation of contractual employment in the face of outright wrongful repudiation is that of *Thomas Marshall (Exports) Ltd v Guinle*.[68] This, however, is truly the exception which proves the rule, for, although it concerned an outright wrongful repudiation of a contract of employment, this was not a wrongful dismissal by the employing entity, but, on the contrary, a wrongful purported resignation by an employee, in fact the managing director of the plaintiff employing entity.

The defendant employee sought to rely upon his own purported resignation, albeit in breach of contract, to release him from both his express and implied contractual obligations of loyalty and non-disclosure of the confidential information of the company. His express contractual obligations were specified as continuing even after the termination of his contractual employment, but his implied obligations were more onerous during the

---

[67] [1987] ICR 737 (QBD). (Different issues were pursued on appeal—see [1988] ICR 842.)   [68] [1978] ICR 905 (ChD).

currency of his contractual employment than after it. Megarry J held that both sets of obligations subsisted despite the employee's purported but wrongful termination of his service agreement. As to his implied obligations, this therefore involved the imposition of a notional continuation of his contractual employment so that those obligations could be regarded as continuing to apply. The employee could not be allowed to take advantage of his own wrong by treating his contractual employment as terminated by his wrongful resignation from it.

However, courts and tribunals seem almost invariably unwilling to engage in that sort of notional prolongation of contractual employment in favour of wrongfully dismissed workers. One might have imagined that, while the restricted wrongfulness/restricted remedies approach militated against their doing so whenever common law or equitable remedies or declaratory relief were sought, they might be more prepared to do so when adjudicating upon contractual issues in the course of construing statutory employment rights. This indeed was what the Court of Appeal was prepared to do in the very singular circumstances of the *Hill v Parsons* case, where, in effect, the plaintiff's contractual employment was notionally prolonged so as to prevent the employing entity from excluding the employee, by wrongful dismissal, from his prospective rights under the Industrial Relations Act 1971.

Nevertheless, in subsequent decisions the courts went strongly in the opposite direction, and steadfastly carried the restrictive approach right into the field of construction of statutory employment rights. This stance was taken up in two judgments of Lord Browne-Wilkinson in two cases which should be regarded as leading cases in the law of personal employment contracts, though not, it will be argued, for the best of reasons. The first case was that of *Cort & Son Ltd v Charman*[69] where Browne-Wilkinson J as he then was gave the judgment of the Employment Tribunal, of which he was the President. The second case was that of *Octavius Atkinson & Sons Ltd v Morris*[70] where, now as the Vice-Chancellor, he gave the judgment of the Court of Appeal.

In *Cort v Charman* the issue was whether, for an employee who had been summarily dismissed with payment in lieu of notice, the 'effective date of termination' was to be treated as that of the summary dismissal or the later date on which due notice given on that date would have expired. If the latter, the employee would have acquired the necessary statutory period of continuous employment to enable him to claim remedies for unfair dismissal;[71] if the former, he would fall short of that qualification. It was

---

[69] [1981] ICR 816 (EAT).   [70] [1989] ICR 431 (CA).
[71] The corresponding current statutory provisions are those of ERA 1996, s 94 (the right not to be unfairly dismissed), s 108 (qualifying period of employment), and s 97 (effective date of termination).

held that, regarding the dismissal as a wrongful one, it nevertheless 'took effect' immediately and thus constituted an immediate 'effective date of termination'. This writer suggests that it could validly have been decided that there should be a notional prolongation of the contractual employment of this worker so that the 'effective date of termination' was the later one; but the EAT held that, even if the elective view of wrongful dismissal in *Gunton* was correct, the more restrictive approach to the statutory concept was still appropriate.

In the second case that approach was pursued even more rigorously to the disadvantage of the claimant worker. *Atkinson v Morris* was a case where a construction worker was dismissed without notice, and in that sense wrongfully, at two pm on a given day. At that moment, good redundancy grounds for fair dismissal existed. Later in that working day, the employing entity's manager became aware of a new job opportunity, but offered that opportunity to his own sons, both of whom had a lesser entitlement to it than the claimant had under the company's redundancy procedure. The issue was whether the claimant had ceased to be contractually employed at two pm or had remained in his contractual employment until the end of that working day. If the latter, he might be judged to have been unfairly dismissed but, if the former, he would not. The Court of Appeal took the former view, on the footing either that his contract of employment had been immediately and unilaterally terminated by wrongful dismissal or that his counsel had conceded that he had accepted the wrongful repudiation of it by leaving the work site to go home.

That decision takes the restrictive approach to very extreme lengths. It allowed the employing entity to take advantage of its own breach of contract in dismissing without notice. It defeats the purpose of the unfair dismissal legislation of ensuring that the fairness of dismissal is judged in a holistic way. There were several different ways in which the contrary result could have been reached as a matter of pure contract theory or as a matter of construction of the contractual and contract-based concepts in their statutory context. All that was required was the notional prolongation of the claimant's contractual employment for the rest of the working day on which he was dismissed. This could have been achieved, for instance, by insisting that the employee had not accepted the wrongful dismissal as terminating his contract of employment before the end of the day of that dismissal at the earliest; or by applying the statutory provision which, where an employee is denied the statutory minimum period of notice, extends the effective date of termination to the date upon which the statutory minimum period would have expired.[72]

---

[72] The provision is currently contained in the Employment Rights Act 1996 (ERA), s 97(2).

The Vice-Chancellor expressed himself as reaching his conclusion with regret, saying that:

> It seems to me artificial that the employee's right to alternative employment should depend on fine distinctions as to the exact point of time in one day at which his employment terminated.[73]

However, given that a fine distinction had to be made one way or the other, it is hard to see why that necessity justified this particularly restrictive interpretative approach.

Later in this chapter, a possible new approach to problems of this kind will be suggested on the basis of the provisions of the Employment Act 2002 concerning dispute resolution procedures. Before that stage in the discussion is reached, some further complexities in the law concerning wrongful termination by the employing entity need to be investigated.

SECTION 4: TOWARDS A COHERENT APPROACH TO WRONGFUL TERMINATION BY THE EMPLOYING ENTITY

A. THE DIFFICULTIES OF A COHERENT APPROACH

Thus far our discussion of wrongful termination of personal employment contracts by the employing entity has proceeded on the assumption that it is possible to give a single consistent account both of how and when personal employment contracts are wrongfully terminated by the employing entity and of what remedies are available in respect of such wrongful termination. Our main focus has been upon the question of whether that account reveals a body of law which produces or conduces to fair and balanced contractual adjudication between the expectations of workers and the interests of employing entities. It has seemed possible to discuss that set of issues without calling into question the fundamental logical coherence or consistency of the body of law in question.

However, in the course of that discussion doubts have begun to present themselves in the latter more fundamental respect. At least three such doubts can be identified. Firstly, it has started to emerge that there may be no single clear conception of what we mean by the termination of a personal employment contract; does it, for example, mean the termination of all the obligations of the contract, or just the termination of employment under the personal employment contract? Secondly, it has become evident that there is great divergence of views around the question of how far and in what way wrongful dismissal fits into the various conceptions of termination of personal employment contracts. In what, precisely, does the

---

[73] [1989] IRLR 158 at 161.

wrongfulness consist, and how does wrongful dismissal relate to the notion of termination by or as the result of repudiation?

Thirdly, we have begun to encounter difficulties about how certain statutory notions in employment legislation relate to the common law of personal employment contracts. How far, for instance, do statutory conceptions of 'dismissal' or of the 'effective date of termination' of contracts of employment fit into, modify, or depart from the common law theory which we have tried to construct? In this concluding section of the present chapter, we examine some particular aspects of the law of wrongful termination by the employing entity which throw these difficulties into particularly sharp relief; and we consider how far the inconsistencies and anomalies which are revealed might be alleviated by reference to certain of the provisions of the Employment Act 2002 concerning dispute resolution.

B. REPUDIATION, DISMISSAL, AND CONSTRUCTIVE DISMISSAL

A very good illustration of the above-mentioned difficulties consists in the variety of conceptual and remedial responses, which is to be found in the modern law of personal employment contracts, to the situation where the employing entity takes unilateral action in serious breach of contract but without bringing the *de facto* employment relationship in question to an end. It is difficult to reconcile these responses with each other, or with the treatment of outright wrongful dismissal as we have considered it thus far in the present chapter, that is to say with the situation in which the employing entity, in major breach of contract, does bring the *de facto* employment relationship to an end. Let us describe the former situation, the one which is under discussion in this subsection, as repudiation by employing entity not ending *de facto* employment; this is cumbersome, but that is difficult to avoid.

In some remedial or interpretative contexts, repudiation by the employing entity is regarded as having no terminatory effects upon the personal employment contract, in and of itself, and merely as giving the worker the right to accept it as terminating the contract. If the worker does not take up that option the contract simply continues in force and effect on its original terms. In *Howard v Pickford Tool Co Ltd*,[74] the Court of Appeal took that view in a case where a managing director sought a declaration against his employing entity that its conduct of its employment relationship with him, by its chairman, amounted to a repudiation of his, the plaintiff's, contract of employment. The ruling was that the plaintiff could not be allowed such a declaration while he continued in employment; in that situation, the actions complained of were regarded as being of no legal significance; as Asquith LJ famously put it:

An unaccepted repudiation is a thing writ in water and of no value to anybody; it confers no legal rights of any sort or kind.[75]

---

[74] [1951] 1 KB 417 (CA).   [75] Ibid at 421.

That is perhaps an overstatement, to the extent that a claimant might in such a situation be able to claim a declaration of and damages for breach of contract; but it forcefully makes the point that the court regarded the conduct complained of as having no terminatory effect upon the contract of employment.

In a different common law remedial context, a similar approach to the legal effect of repudiation by the employing entity operated, not to defeat the worker's claim as in *Howard v Pickford Tool Co*, but instead to make good a different kind of claim. In *Rigby v Ferodo Ltd*,[76] a lathe operator, upon whom a 5 per cent wage reduction had been imposed but who had continued to work at the reduced rate, successfully reclaimed the reduction of wages on a continuing basis, the House of Lords holding that he was entitled to recover the amount of money in question either as damages or as a money debt, on the footing that he had never accepted the repudiatory reduction in wages either as an agreed variation or termination of his contract, or as a wrongful termination of his contract. In this way, the Law Lords felt that they were ensuring that the employing entity could not take advantage of its own breach of contract in unilaterally reducing the plaintiff's wages.[77]

In yet another interpretative or remedial context, a different analysis has been accorded to repudiation by the employing entity. In two very significant decisions, those of *Marriott v Oxford & District Co-operative Society Ltd (No 2)*[78] and *Hogg v Dover College*,[79] it was held that an employee, upon whom there had been imposed a reduction of remuneration and an inferior job specification, could claim that he had been dismissed within the meaning of the redundancy payments legislation or the unfair dismissal legislation although he had remained in employment after that imposition. In both cases the imposition was regarded as an effective wrongful termination of the existing contract of employment by the employing entity. Although, by the time that the second case was decided, there was an alternative statutory concept of constructive dismissal[80] whereby termination of the contract, though regarded as the action of the employee, could nevertheless be deemed to be a dismissal by the employing entity where the latter's conduct had entitled the employee to terminate, no such provision for constructive dismissal had been made in the legislation which applied at the time of the first case. So in that case, the view that the repudiation by the employing entity had amounted to a termination of the existing contract of

---

[76] [1988] ICR 29 (HL).
[77] See Lord Oliver at 34–35: 'I entirely fail to see how the continuance of the primary contractual obligation can be made to depend upon the subjective desire of the contract-breaker and I do not understand what is meant by the injured party having no alternative but to accept the breach.'   [78] [1970] 1 QB 186 (CA).
[79] [1990] ICR 39 (EAT).
[80] The corresponding provision currently in force is that of ERA 1996, s 95(1)(c).

employment by the employing entity was a *sine qua non* to the conclusion that there had been a dismissal in the statutory sense.

Although each of these decisions is fully sustainable, cumulatively they give rise to serious tensions between different analytical and practical approaches. The *Rigby v Ferodo* decision is out of accord with the steadfast refusal of the courts to give a real election of continuation of the existing personal employment contract to workers who have been subject to wrongful outright dismissal, that is to say to wrongful repudiation which does involve termination of *de facto* employment by the employing entity. *Rigby v Ferodo* pursues the elective approach to wrongful repudiation as in *Gunton*, but without the restrictions upon notional prolongation of employment which we have argued are part and parcel of the approach in *Gunton*. It is of course said that there is a crucial difference between the situations where *de facto* employment is and is not terminated.[81] But in a sense this merely draws attention to the difficulty of allowing the employing entity to invoke its own breach of contract as a legally effective termination of contractual employment in the former case though not in the latter, since both cases equally represent a *de facto* termination of the employment in question on its existing terms.

The line of reasoning in the *Marriott* and *Hogg v Dover College* cases does not present that particular problem; but it is hard to reconcile it with the approach in *Rigby v Ferodo*. In order to do so, it is necessary to apply two very different analyses to the worker's continuance in employment on the inferior terms. On the *Rigby v Ferodo* approach, he or she has to be viewed as continuing to assert that the previously existing contract has remained in force. On the *Marriott* approach, he or she has to be viewed as asserting that the previously existing contract has been wrongfully but effectively terminated by the employing entity. This is rather artificial, since the worker in the latter case is protesting against the ending of his employment on its previous terms just as strongly as in the former case.[82] We might, however, say that, if these analyses are rather convoluted, at least they do not offend against a sense of fair and balanced adjudication upon contractual issues. That confidence starts to be shaken when we turn our attention to the next problematical aspect of the law of wrongful termination of contractual employment by the employing entity.

[81] Compare Lord Oliver in *Rigby v Ferodo* [1988] ICR 29 at 34: 'the instant case is not on any analysis one of wrongful dismissal but is concerned with a very different state of facts, including the actual and intended continuation of the relationship of employer and employee without interruption'.

[82] It is this conflict of analyses which underlies an increasing difficulty in resolving the question whether and in what circumstances the worker is deemed to have 'affirmed' the original contract as continuing, following a wrongful repudiation of it by the employing entity. A survey of the authorities was given by McCombe J in *Cantor Fitzgerald International v Bird* [2002] IRLR 867 (QBD) at paras 106 108.

C. The Situation where the Employing Entity Has an Express
   Power of Termination by Payment in Lieu of Notice

Earlier in this work we have encountered the problem of how a dismissal by
the employing entity with payment in lieu of notice fits into the conceptual
and practical system of analysis of termination of personal work contracts;
and we shall consider those problems further in the final chapter;[83] there
are difficult questions about whether and when a dismissal with payment in
lieu of notice is to be viewed as a lawful dismissal or as a wrongful dismissal
with payment of liquidated damages, and about the time at which such a
dismissal is to be regarded as terminating the contract of employment in
question. A rather different set of issues about payment in lieu of notice has
also begun to present itself in recent case law, which requires consideration
as part of our analysis of wrongful termination. They revolve around the
question of whether, when a worker is dismissed without notice, or payment
in lieu of notice, or justification for summary dismissal, the fact that the
employing entity has an express power of termination by payment in lieu of
notice should affect the way in which that dismissal is analysed and the
remedies which are available in relation to it.

   In the case of *Abrahams v Performing Rights Society*,[84] the Court of Appeal
accepted that the presence of a power of termination by payment in lieu of
notice on the part of the employing entity made a crucial difference in such
a case. It meant that the worker could claim that his dismissal should not
be regarded as a wrongful one for which, as such, his remedy was limited
to a claim for damages for deprivation of notice, subject to mitigation.
Instead, it should be regarded as the *lawful* exercise of the power of
dismissal with payment in lieu of notice, in which all that was lacking was
the actual payment of the payment in lieu of notice, so that the worker
could claim the payment in lieu of notice as a money debt or as liquidated
damages, and did not have to give credit for his earnings in other employment
during the period of notice in question.

   This presented an unexpected threat to the whole restrictive approach to
the analysis of wrongful dismissal and remedies for wrongful dismissal as
we have outlined in the course of this chapter, especially since it had
become very common for personal work contracts to contain express provisions for termination with payment in lieu of notice, and since it was, and
has remained, arguable that such provisions might be implied in an even
wider range of situations. The Court of Appeal has since done much to
reinstate the restrictive approach and to reinforce it in cases where there is
provision for payment in lieu of notice. In *Gregory v Wallace*,[85] they held that
the presence of a power of termination with payment in lieu of notice did
not give rise to a claim of the kind which had been made in the *Abrahams*

---

[83] See above, 318–322 and below, 484–487.   [84] [1995] ICR 1028 (CA).
[85] [1998] IRLR 387 (CA).

case, because the contract of employment in question conferred the power of termination by payment in lieu of notice only where notice to terminate had first been given, which in this case it had not; hence, in their view, they could not proceed as if that power had been exercised.

In the subsequent, and exceedingly important, case of *Cerberus Software Ltd v Rowley*,[86] there was no such restriction upon the power of termination with payment in lieu of notice which was available to the employing entity. Nevertheless, the majority of the Court of Appeal held that the presence of that power of payment in lieu of notice did not enhance the claim which the worker could make in respect of his having been summarily dismissed without justification.[87] This was to be regarded, in the normal way, as a wrongful dismissal for which the remedy was damages for the deprivation of the period of notice to which the worker had been entitled, against which must be counted his actual earnings in other employment during that period. Sedley LJ dissented; he took the view that the employing entity should not be free to maintain that it had dismissed *wrongfully* in order to evade the greater liability to which it would be subject on the footing that it had *lawfully* exercised its power of dismissal with payment in lieu of notice.

The argument in favour of the majority approach is superficially compelling. Provisions for payment in lieu of notice normally give the employing entity an additional option to that of termination by notice; they do not normally, and did not in any of these cases, exclude the employing entity's option of termination by notice. Therefore, the employing entity should be no less than normally able to rely on the rule that a dismissal without notice or justification is treated simply as a denial of notice, for which the remedy is damages for that denial subject to mitigation. However, this reasoning does disguise or disregard the fact that it allows the employing entity to take advantage of its own breach of contract in an opportunistic way, and thus creates incentives to act in breach of contract rather than in compliance with contract. It is open to the criticism that it gives the employing entity an implied 'third choice' of dismissal on payment of damages subject to mitigation, and thus in a certain sense a kind of 'right to dismiss wrongfully'.

The decision of the Court of Session in the Scottish case of *Morran v Glasgow Council of Tenants Associations*[88] further heightens that latter concern. For in that case, the employing entity, which had dismissed a worker, the pursuer, without notice, or payment in lieu of notice, or justification, was allowed to invoke its power of termination with payment in lieu of notice to restrict the damages to which it was liable for wrongful dismissal.

---

[86] [2001] ICR 376 (CA). See Fodder and Freer 2001.

[87] The *Abrahams* case was distinguished as one where payment in lieu of notice was an entitlement of the worker rather than an option of the employing entity. That distinction overlooks the fact that in *Abrahams* the contract of employment entitled the worker to payment in lieu of notice *or to notice*, thus giving the employing entity the usual choice between notice or payment in lieu of notice. [88] [1998] IRLR 67 (CS).

The pursuer claimed damages to reflect the fact that the period of notice to which he was entitled would have completed the period of service which would have qualified him to make a claim of unfair dismissal; we have seen earlier that the Employment Appeal Tribunal allowed damages on that basis in the *Raspin* case. In *Morran*, however, Lord Rodger, the Lord President, reasoned that the employer could have fulfilled its primary obligations equally well by terminating with payment in lieu of notice, and so should not be liable to damages for the loss of the claim to unfair dismissal which could be attributed to its failure to give notice.[89]

Rather than pursuing further the conceptual debate about the effect of provision for termination with payment in lieu of notice, we should perhaps concentrate on its implications for our understanding of wrongful dismissal and the remedies for wrongful dismissal more generally. These cases about the effect of provision for payment in lieu of notice arise because of the restrictedness of the general approach of the common law to the wrongfulness of dismissal and to the remedies for wrongful dismissal. They draw particular attention to the very limited extent to which, in the ordinary case of wrongful dismissal, the worker enjoys contractual protection of security of employment or even security of income. The common law of wrongful dismissal establishes that situation by its approach to the analysis of the cause of action for wrongful dismissal and of the remedies for wrongful dismissal, and it validates and reinforces express contractual provisions which have that effect.

It may be said that there can be no objection to this approach, in the sense that it simply creates a default position which employing entities and workers are at liberty to modify by express contracting, and which may be modified by legislation further protecting workers' interests in job security or income security if Parliament so decides. However, it is nevertheless a matter of concern if the common law of wrongful dismissal functions so as to invite opportunistic breach of contract, or if the default position is one which clearly fails to give effect to the reasonable expectations of one of the parties to the personal employment contract as to the mutual rights and obligations which will obtain in the event of wrongful termination. In the next subsection, we consider another area in which the latter concern at least may be thought to arise.

D. The Effect of Wrongful Dismissal upon Post-Employment Obligations

There is one respect in which, rather strangely, the law of wrongful dismissal diverges from its generally restrictive approach to the conception

---

[89] See [1998] IRLR 67 at 69 para 12: 'It seems to us clear that the contract envisages that in substance the defenders are under an obligation to give four weeks' notice or to make a payment in lieu of notice. Provided they do one or other, they will fulfil their obligation under the contact.'

of wrongful dismissal and to the remedies which it provides for wrongful dismissal, and becomes instead highly protective of the wrongfully dismissed worker. This occurs with regard to the effect of wrongful dismissal upon the post-employment obligations of the worker. It is an oddity which results from the decision of the House of Lords in the leading case of *General Billposting Company Ltd v Atkinson*.[90] In this subsection we consider the causes and implications of this deviation from the approach encountered elsewhere in the law of wrongful dismissal.

The *General Billposting* case concerned the manager of a billposting and advertising enterprise, who was employed on twelve months' notice and who was wrongfully dismissed without notice, for which he recovered damages. He went into business as an advertising agent, and later incorporated that business as a company for which he subsequently acted as manager. The company which had acquired the business of his original employing entity sought to proceed against him for breach of his covenant against competition in his contract of employment with his original employing entity, which was expressed to apply for two years after the end of his engagement, and provided for him, in the event of breach, to pay £250, the equivalent of a year's salary, as liquidated damages, and to be subject to an injunction. It was held that the effect of the wrongful dismissal had been to release him from all those obligations and liabilities, so that the acquiring company could in no way enforce them.

The decision has continued to be regarded as good law; but it is out of accord with the generally restrictive approach to wrongful dismissal and to the remedies for it which the House of Lords took, contemporaneously with *General Billposting*, in the *Addis* case, and which the courts have since generally taken. That generally restrictive approach seems to suggest that the wrongful dismissal might have been regarded simply as a denial of due notice, as such fully remedied by the damages which the worker in question had obtained, and thus as constituting no barrier to the employing entity's enforcement of the worker's post-employment obligations. However, there has in fact been very little perception that the decision in *General Billposting* is out of line with the general approach to wrongful dismissal, though it was the subject of some criticism in the Court of Appeal in the case of *Rock Refrigeration v Jones*,[91] where it was ruled that the doctrine in *General Billposting* should not be regarded as wholly invalidating restrictive covenants solely because they purported to be binding after wrongful dismissal as well as after lawful termination of contractual employment.

The general acceptance of the doctrine in *General Billposting* as being good law, despite its disharmony, in the sense outlined above, with

---

[90] [1909] AC 118 (HL).
[91] [1997] ICR 938 (CA), especially from Phillips LJ at 958–959; compare above, 184.

a generally restrictive approach to wrongful dismissal and its effects, probably comes about in the following way. The doctrine in *General Billposting* has been understood as the straightforward application of a clear principle to the effect that a wrongful dismissal, regarded as the repudiation of the contract of employment, entitles the employee, as the injured party, to rescind the contract in the sense of treating it, or at least all the primary obligations which it imposes on the injured party, as being totally at an end.[92] However, that is probably an overgeneralization and oversimplification of the reasoning and decision in *General Billposting*.

Both in the Court of Appeal and in the House of Lords, the conduct of both the original employing entity and its successor were regarded as particularly wrongful in ways which are not identified, but which gave rise to the conclusion that they had totally repudiated the whole of their contractual obligations so as to entitle the employee to regard himself as liberated from the totality of his obligations. Moreover, the Master of the Rolls had indicated in the Court of Appeal that he regarded the employee's obligation to pay damages of £250 as constituting a penalty rather than liquidated damages. So the case for total abrogation of the employee's obligations was specially strong; there is more than a slight implication that neither the Court of Appeal nor the House of Lords would have regarded any and every wrongful dismissal as having such severe consequences for the employing entity.

In the *Rock Refrigeration* case, Simon Brown LJ gave some indications that it should not necessarily be assumed either that all restrictive covenants necessarily become unenforceable upon the employee's acceptance of the employer's repudiatory breach or that any wrongful termination of the contract by the employer will necessarily involve a repudiatory breach.[93] It is certainly to be hoped that a proportional or discriminating approach might be possible today, rather than the doctrinaire application of a supposedly universal rule against enforcement not only of the worker's employment obligations but also of his or her post-employment obligations. Dogmatism of that kind would be as open to criticism as is the rigidly restrictive approach to wrongful dismissal and the remedies for it which has been encountered in the course of this chapter. But the acquisition of conceptual and practical scope for manoeuvre around or within the established doctrinal approaches would seem to depend upon finding some convincing juridical basis for such departures. In the concluding subsection of this chapter, a suggestion is advanced of a possible rationale for that kind of development.[94]

[92] Compare *Photo Productions Ltd v Securicor Transport Ltd* [1980] AC 827 (HL).
[93] [1997] ICR 938 at 947E–F.
[94] Some encouragement is provided by the decision and comments of the Court of Appeal in *Campbell v Frisbee* [2003] ICR 141. See notes on the decision by Linda Clarke and the present author (Clarke 2003, Freedland 2003), and see above, 177, 184.

E. A MUTUAL DUTY OF EFFICIENT DISPUTE RESOLUTION[95]

At a number of points in this chapter, the conceptualization of wrongful termination by the employing entity, and of the remedies for it, have appeared to be rather rigid in character, in such a way as to restrict the ability of courts and tribunals to respond effectively to the reasonable expectations of workers or employing entities in respect of the termination of employment. In this subsection it will be suggested that a useful conceptual tool with which to craft a more responsive body of law and process or practice of adjudication might be envisaged as the result of the provisions in Part 3 of the Employment Act 2002 for the use of statutory procedures in relation to employment disputes.

By those provisions, a set of statutory dispute resolution procedures is established as between employers and employees;[96] they consist of dismissal and disciplinary procedures,[97] and grievance procedures.[98] Two kinds or levels of procedure are provided, referred to respectively as standard procedure and modified procedure.[99] Standard procedure consists of three steps, a statement of grounds of action or grievance, a meeting, and an appeal; modified procedure consists of an abbreviated process in which the meeting step is not included.[100]

Effect is given to this schedule of procedures subject to governmental powers of amendment and extension by statutory order.[101] The powers of extension would enable the statutory dispute resolution procedures to be applied as between employing entities and non-employee workers if it were decided to do so. Crucially for the purpose of the present argument, it is further provided that the statutory procedures are incorporated into contracts of employment; it is enacted that:

Every contract of employment shall have effect to require the employer and employee to comply, in relation to any matter to which a statutory procedure applies, with the requirements of the procedure.[102]

This provision is to have effect 'notwithstanding any agreement to the contrary' but is not to affect additional and not inconsistent contractual procedural requirements upon employers or employees.[103] It is provided that statutory regulations may 'make provision about the application of the statutory procedures';[104] it is not clear how extensive are the powers of modification which are thereby conferred.

---

[95] See also above, 344–345.
[96] EA 2002, Schedule 2 (not yet in force at time of writing).
[97] Schedule 2 Part 1, Dismissal and Disciplinary Procedures.
[98] Schedule 2 Part 2, Grievance Procedures.
[99] Respectively Schedule 2 Part 1 Chapter 1, Part 2 Chapter 1 (standard procedure) and Part 1 Chapter 2, Part 2 Chapter 2 (modified procedure).   [100] Ibid.
[101] Section 29.   [102] Section 30(1).   [103] Section 30(2).
[104] Section 30(3).

These provisions thus incorporate into contracts of employment, and could if so extended incorporate into all personal employment contracts, a duty on both parties to such contracts to follow statutory dispute resolution procedures, which, we suggest, applies with regard to any proposal or intention on the part of the employing entity to take disciplinary action against or to dismiss the worker, and which might, we equally suggest, apply to the employee or worker whenever he or she has a grievance amounting to an allegation of constructive dismissal. Having this wide actual or potential ambit, these provisions may in and of themselves operate to impose a broad contractual obligation of due process upon both parties to contracts of employment or, if the provisions are so extended, to all personal employment contracts, with regard to all issues arising between them which might lead to termination of the employment in question.

We suggest that such contractual requirements of due process might, because it is in the nature of due process requirements to tend in this direction, also turn out to concentrate attention upon the substantive standards of decision making or conduct applicable to both parties in their approach to and handling of issues relating to or giving rise to the termination of employment. They might thus bring about a degree of scrutiny of the proportionality of proposed action to the reasons for that action, and of the rationality and non-arbitrariness of actual or proposed action more generally.

We also suggest, pursuing this line of reasoning further, that the contractual requirement to observe the statutory procedures as currently prescribed by statutory regulation could be viewed as a specific manifestation of a more general underlying contractual duty, which we might identify as a mutual duty of efficient dispute resolution. Such a duty would, we suggest, be an exact expression of the rationale which underlies the dispute resolution provisions of the Employment Act 2002 in general, and the incorporation of statutory dispute resolution procedures into contracts of employment in particular. It would also be fully consonant with the general approach of courts and tribunals in recent years to the development of the implied terms and general juridical infrastructure of personal employment contracts.

This contractual duty, being a mutual one, might provide the basis for a new response to some of the doctrinal and practical difficulties which have been identified in the course of the present chapter. It might serve as a way both of enlarging and yet refining the contractual conception of wrongfulness of dismissal. It might also have significant implications for the approach to remedies for wrongful dismissal. Thus it might possibly be a ground upon which damages could be awarded where the failure of the employing entity suitably to process a dismissal dispute resulted in predictable and avoidable detriment to the employability of the worker concerned. It could also be the means of achieving a less restrictive approach, than currently prevails, to damages in respect of future loss of employment and the benefits of employment or the chances thereof.

Continuing in the same vein, we could envisage such a duty as also being the basis for a more liberal development of remedies in the nature of notional prolongation of contractual employment, such as injunctions, and the allowance as money debts of claims to remuneration and pecuniary benefits following wrongful dismissal. It could also ground a discriminating approach to the application of the concept of constructive dismissal, and to the question of whether and how far the post-employment obligations of the worker might be enforced after and despite a wrongful dismissal. Its ability to function as a finely-tuned instrument of all these remedial adjudications would consist in the fact that it required due process and efficient dispute resolution, not only on the part of the employing entity, but also of the worker. All this, however, is a matter of suggestion and speculation as to how the law concerning wrongful termination by the employing entity might develop in future. It remains to build upon the discussion of the present law of termination in this and the previous chapter, and to develop it into a comprehensive treatment of the termination of personal work contracts as a whole. We seek to complete that task in the next chapter, and proceed to draw some brief conclusions from the present chapter.

CONCLUSION

It has been in this chapter that our critique of the law of termination of personal work or employment contracts has been strongest, and in that sense the method of restatement is deployed in its most prescriptive form in this chapter. It has essentially been argued that the law of wrongful dismissal forms the hub of a circle of ideas or doctrines about the termination of contracts of employment in particular. This circle of ideas is composed of doctrines about rights of dismissal, wrongs associated with dismissal, remedies for wrongful dismissal, and termination by or as the result of wrongful dismissal. It has been suggested that each of the segments of this circle of ideas is of questionable coherence or validity in and of itself, and relies upon the others for support, with the consequence that the whole structure is deficient in coherence. In the previous chapter, the doctrinal basis for unfettered rights of termination was scrutinized; in this chapter the remaining elements have been similarly questioned.

The results of that questioning were to identify the single most important element, in this mutually self-supporting set of ideas, as that of the essentially limited nature of damages for wrongful dismissal. This, it was suggested, was a much more contingent and much less inevitable body of doctrine than is normally assumed, quite strongly tied to the particular adjudicative context of some leading cases such as that of *Addis v Gramophone Company Ltd*, and, most recently, that of *Johnson v Unisys Ltd*. It was then argued that the body of case law against specific enforcement of obligations of continuation of personal employment contracts was to a considerable extent constructed upon the basis of the unfettered nature of rights to terminate and the restricted nature of damages for wrongful dismissal, and that these ideas in turn are much more fragile and circumstantial than is generally asserted. On the other hand, it was argued that the assertion of an elective theory of termination by wrongful repudiation was an unsatisfactory attempt to work out a different approach, which had continued to be maintained as a matter of abstract theory, but which had as a matter of practical reality been undermined by the essentially limited approach to remedies for wrongful termination.

In the concluding section of the chapter, it was argued that a greater coherence might be achieved by constructing an implied duty of dispute resolution, from the base of the provisions of the Employment Act 2002 concerning dispute resolution. This would be a particular derivative, in the context of termination, of the general notion of fair management and performance which was developed in earlier chapters. However, we suggest that legislative intervention would be necessary to bring a real cohesion to this area of the law; doctrinal restatement other than by legislation could not hope, for example, to resolve the inconsistency between the positive development of the implied duty of trust and confidence in the law of the contract of employment generally and its exclusion from the area of dismissal from employment. For that purpose it might be necessary for consideration to be given to the introduction of a statutory rule authorizing damages where they are currently excluded by the doctrine in *Johnson v Unisys Ltd*, but limiting those damages to the maximum permitted award of compensation for unfair dismissal, thus eliminating the objection to such damages which was operative in the decision of the House of Lords in that case.

There is another respect in which we suggest that legislation would be fully appropriate, perhaps even essential, in order to achieve a functionally effective restatement of the law in this area. This would be in order to bring about a harmonization in the approach to remedies for wrongful termination as between the contract of employment and the semi-dependent worker's contract. As with the arguments in previous chapters, there is little reason to suspect disharmony between the two contract types so far as common law and equitable doctrine is concerned. So far as that doctrine depends upon the personal character of the contract of employment, the semi-dependent worker's contract should be regarded as having a similarly personal character. However, statute law does not display that flexibility; a wedge is driven between the two contract types by the confinement of the dispute resolution provisions of the Employment Act 2002 to employees under contracts of employment. Although it has been argued in this chapter that an underlying duty of dispute resolution might be ascribed to both contract types, legislative reformulation would be necessary before this could be maintained with confidence. In the next chapter, we endeavour to place the discussion of the termination of the personal work or employment contract, as thus far developed, into a larger conceptual scheme which will deal with the termination and transformation of such contracts as a whole.

8

Termination by Other Means

INTRODUCTION

In the preceding five chapters, we have mapped out many of the directions in which the personal employment contract may evolve from its initial formation and the initial establishment of its content (performance, breach, and variation), and some of the destinations or end points at or in which it may culminate or terminate (lawful or wrongful termination by the employing enterprise). This places us in a position to complete, so far as it is possible to do so, a general and comprehensive account of the evolution and termination of personal employment contracts.

In order to do that, we shall need to consider the remaining ways in which personal employment contracts may be terminated. Thus we shall look at topics such as that of resignation by the worker, and the termination of personal work contracts by agreement or as the result of frustration. We shall also refer to ways in which personal employment contracts may be regarded as transformed rather than terminated. That discussion will refer mainly but not solely to the topics of suspension and of transfer of employment under the TUPE legislation. The title of this chapter reflects this perception that the completion of the analysis which has been undertaken in the preceding chapters requires us to look at the transformation of the personal employment contract as well as considering its termination.

The main theme of this discussion will be that the law of personal employment work contracts has developed in such a way and to such a point that it is extremely difficult to provide a clear and logical overall account of the law relating to the evolution, termination, and transformation of those contracts. The case law and legislation, upon which such an account would have to be based, have become intractably complex, to the point where we should probably regard it as impossible to resolve all the intricacies, ambiguities, and inconsistencies to which they give rise. However, the attempt needs to be made; it is only by identifying and addressing those theoretical and practical problems that we can hope to produce an adequate description of this body of law, or to assess the adequacy with which this body of law meets the functional demands which are made upon it and ascertain how it might more fully do so.

In the first part of this chapter, a general theory of termination and transformation will be proposed which will seek, firstly, to explain the causes of those difficulties and, secondly, to present a conceptual scheme which may help to minimize them; it is conceded from the outset that the present author does not claim to be able to eliminate them. In the remainder of the chapter, that general theory will be developed and applied in relation to the specific aspects of termination and transformation which have not been addressed in earlier chapters.

SECTION 1: A GENERAL THEORY OF TERMINATION AND TRANSFORMATION OF PERSONAL WORK CONTRACTS

A. The Difficulties about Formulating a General Theory

Although the preceding chapters might have appeared to be tending towards the construction of a systematic account of the evolution and termination of personal employment contracts, some serious difficulties have been encountered in building up a logical progression of ideas, and some ambiguities and inconsistencies have presented themselves. Those difficulties were faintly visible in the discussion of performance and breach, became more prominent in relation to variation, and were glaringly obvious in relation to some aspects at least of lawful and wrongful termination by the employing enterprise.

It is suggested that these difficulties are of two principal kinds: firstly, there is a problem of the identification of the core concept which is the subject of the whole discussion of termination and transformation of personal work contracts; and secondly there is a set of problems about aligning and reconciling the great multiplicity of particular concepts and terminologies which is to be found in the theoretical and juridical elaboration of and around that core concept. We go on to consider each of those two kinds of difficulty in turn.

Firstly, then, we consider ambiguities about the core concept of termination and transformation of personal work contracts. Often in the discussion of the law of personal work contracts, notions of evolution, termination, or transformation are invoked without it being clear to what they apply, that is to say what their subject matter is. We may speak of general notions such as performance, or variation, or suspension, or termination, or transfer without specifying clearly or at all what it is that is being performed, varied, suspended, terminated, or transferred. Many alternatives start to present themselves. Do we, for example, mean performance of the contract itself or performance of a particular set of obligations under the contract? Does 'variation' mean variation of the contract as a whole or of the terms of the contract? Do suspension, termination, and transfer refer to the contract itself or to employment under the contract? We may also use more particular notions such as 'the effective date of termination' without it being clear what is being referred to. The question 'of what?' is all too frequently evaded.

These ambiguities conceal an even greater theoretical and practical imprecision about the concept which is at the core of this whole discussion. If we attempt to fasten upon the notion of the personal employment contract, or, more narrowly, the contract of employment, as that core concept, we come up against the difficulty, which has begun to become apparent at various points in earlier chapters, that we simply do not have a clear single understanding of what it means to say that such a contract is subsisting. Does it for example subsist when its terms have been fundamentally changed? Does it continue though the worker has ceased to work and be remunerated? Does it matter that the worker has contractual rights in respect of such a fundamental change of terms or cessation of work and remuneration?

The law of personal employment contracts turns out to provide no consistent answer to that set of questions. It follows in general that there is no clear set of reference points, or benchmarks, from which to ascertain whether such a contract has been varied, suspended, or transferred. It follows, in particular, that it is inherently difficult to produce a rigorous and consistent analysis of any one concept of the termination of this type of contract, that is to say to identify the point at which or the sense in which it ceases to subsist.

The second and associated set of difficulties is that, around that rather inchoate core concept, a large number of legal terminologies are used which stand in an uncertain relationship with each other. It is often very difficult to say how they interlock or interrelate. This became particularly evident in the discussion of wrongful termination by the employing entity. What is the relationship between 'wrongful dismissal' and 'repudiation'? What is the 'effective date of termination' when there has been a 'constructive dismissal'? Is 'summary dismissal' a subset of 'lawful dismissal' or does it spill over into the category of 'wrongful dismissal'? In the succeeding subsections an explanation will be advanced for both these associated difficulties, and on the basis of that explanation a general theory of termination and transformation of personal employment contracts will be proposed.

B. MULTIPLE VOCABULARIES OF TERMINATION
AND TRANSFORMATION

Many of the difficulties which have been described above result from the fact that the language or terminology, in which the discussion of termination and transformation of personal employment contracts is couched, comes not from one single normative system or discourse as one might expect it to do, but from several. The law of termination and transformation of personal employment contracts is, in fact, constructed in more than one legal language, though these different languages draw on each other. In this subsection we advance this notion of interactive vocabularies as an explanation of the difficulties of devising a single consistent account of this body of law.

Within the general field of employment law we are familiar with this phenomenon of multiple vocabularies; in particular, we know that the terminology of statutory individual employment protection legislation is divergent from that of the law of personal employment contracts. The vocabulary of redundancy payments legislation or unfair dismissal legislation is consciously different from that of the law of the contract of employment at many crucial points. We realize, for instance, that the core concepts of 'redundancy' and of 'unfairness' do not represent notions existing in the law of the contract of employment. We are, however, much less familiar with the idea of distinct vocabularies *within* the law of personal employment contracts; we understand or assume that body of law to be cast in a single discourse and expressed in a single language. An exercise in deconstruction will seek to demonstrate that this is far from being the case.

We suggest that there are at least four distinct vocabularies or discourses which are interwoven in the law of personal employment contracts. One is the factual or non-technical vocabulary which we use to describe the events which may occur in the course of employment relationships. The others are legal technical vocabularies, in which the terminologies have legal connotations and are therefore 'terms of art'. One might expect that there was just one such legal vocabulary for personal employment contracts, a vocabulary coming from a single legal discourse which is the law of personal employment contracts.

In fact, however, we can distinguish at least three such technical vocabularies, each coming from its own subsystem or distinct normative discourse within the body of law on personal employment contracts. The three which can be clearly identified, though they are interactive with each other, are: (1) that of the general law of contract, (2) that of the common law of the contract of employment, formerly known as the law of master and servant, and (3) that of contract-based or contract-related employment legislation. We go on to explain and elaborate these four vocabularies.

We refer, first, to the factual, as distinct from legal-technical, vocabulary. This obviously includes informal terminology such as that of 'sacking', or 'firing', to mean dismissal; but the divergence between factual and legal-technical vocabulary goes much further than that. Many perfectly formal terminologies are to be found in the parlance of employment relationships which either have no legal-technical meaning at all, or at least none within the scope of the law of personal employment contracts, even if we think of that body of law in a loose and inclusive way. It is, of course, no more than a truism that people often speak about their contractual relationships in language which is not legal-technical; however, it is striking to what an extent some terminologies which form part of the common and formal parlance of employment relationships have remained undefined in legal-technical terms.

A good illustration is to be found in the terminology of 'retirement'. The use of that term is pervasive in the making and administration of personal employment contracts and occupational pension schemes. It even has technical significance within the structure of employment law, for instance because the statutory right not to be unfairly dismissed may cease to apply at the 'normal age of retirement' for the worker in question. Yet the terminology of 'retirement' has not, in the view of the present writer, acquired anything remotely like a precise meaning as a concept within the law of personal employment contracts. It has remained as a factual category which has to be fitted into the legal-technical framework which we use to analyse the termination of those contracts. Another good example of a set of notions, which are much used in the parlance of employment law and employment contracting but which lack precise definition, is that of the 'extension' or 'renewal' of employment contracts. There is a deep set of difficulties here, as has been remarked earlier in this work,[1] which is ultimately attributable to the fact that the law of personal employment contracts has never arrived at a clear, general analysis as to whether and when continuing employment relationships are to be regarded as taking place under a single contract of indeterminate duration, or a rolling contract, or a succession of fixed-term contracts.[2]

Moreover, a given terminology may even have a different significance as a factual category from that which it has as a category within the law of personal employment contracts. A highly significant illustration is to be found in the terminology of 'the employer'. Earlier in this work, attention has been drawn to the fact that the terminology of 'the employer' evokes the notion of a single human being exercising employment functions (very much in the same way as the informal terminology of 'the boss' or the archaic terminology of 'the master' do). Yet, within the law of personal work contracts, 'the employer' means the party to the contract who or which exercises the employment functions, and that party is typically a legal corporate entity rather than a single human being.

There are other, even more striking, ways of identifying this particular divergence between factual categories and the technical categories of the law of personal employment contracts. One way of doing so is to say that people falling within the factual category of 'employer' usually fall within the legal-technical category of 'employee'; the 'bosses' of informal factual parlance are usually themselves 'employees' in technical legal parlance. Another is to point out that the factual category of the person employed within an enterprise but exercising management functions, recognized in terminologies such as 'manager' or 'executive', is, at quite a deep level, undefined or unrecognized within the law of personal employment contracts. We go on to suggest reasons why this might be the case.

It has been relatively easy for such key notions as that of 'retirement' or of 'the employer' to escape technical definition within the law of personal employment contracts, or to remain ambiguous as between factual definition

---

[1] See above, 302.   [2] Compare below, 406.

and technical definition, because of the diversity of the conceptual subsystems which make up or contribute to that body of law. Since any given concept within the law of personal employment contracts may be defined in one or more different subsystems, it can easily pass unnoticed that a particular terminology has not actually been defined within any of those subsystems and has in that sense remained as a basically factual category. We earlier distinguished three such subsystems, and now go on to explain and elaborate them and the way in which they interact with each other.

The first two of these three subsystems which we have identified are squarely part of contract law, but they are nevertheless distinct from each other. For there seem to be two discernibly separate terminologies or vocabularies at the heart of the law of personal employment contracts. One is that of the law of contract or contracts in general. The other is that of the law of the contract of employment, in earlier times known as and conceived of as the law of master and servant. Examples of divergence between them can be found at various points. In the former vocabulary, the formation stage is described as that of 'offer and acceptance'; in the latter it is often referred to as that of 'hiring' or 'engagement'. In the field of termination, some terminologies very clearly come from the former vocabulary, such as 'repudiation', 'anticipatory breach', or 'rescission', others equally clearly from the latter, such as 'summary dismissal' or 'wrongful dismissal'.

This divergence of terminology would be of little significance if the terms of the law of the contract of employment were simply and straightforwardly a specialized version of the terms of general contract law, or if there could be direct translation between the two vocabularies. We suggest that in fact these different vocabularies reflect historically distinct conceptualizations of certain key notions, and that attempts at direct translation between the two are apt to produce misleading results. In particular, we suggest that the whole vocabulary of 'dismissal', with its variants of 'summary dismissal', 'lawful dismissal', and 'wrongful dismissal', evolved, in the context of the action or claim for wrongful dismissal, quite autonomously from that of the general law of contract, so that, for example, an equation of the notion of 'wrongful dismissal' with that of 'repudiation by the employer' is a palpably false one.

When writing the original version of this work, the present author was of the view that a convergence of these two discourses was taking place, and that its theoretical completion should be attempted or encouraged. That enterprise seemed to be both feasible and useful as a modernization of the law of the contract of employment, a distancing of it from the archaic trappings of the law of master and servant. Now the present author takes a different view. In the intervening years, there has been extensive development of the law of personal employment contracts as a specialized discourse in which the two vocabularies interact with each other, and produce something which is different from each of its constituent parts. It would be artificial to present this body of law entirely or even predominantly according to the terms and concepts of the general law of contract, although those terms and concepts remain very influential in its formation.

There is a further reason for taking that view. In the formulation and interpretation of the statute law of employment, there has evolved in recent years an extensive apparatus of terms and concepts which are more or less closely based upon the two vocabularies of the law of personal employment contracts which we have hitherto identified, but are nevertheless distinctive from them. This then is our third legal-technical discourse of the law of the termination and transformation of personal employment contracts, that of contract-based or contract-related employment legislation. It stands in a complex relationship with the other two legal-technical vocabularies; we shall now seek to elucidate that relationship.

In order to do that, we first need to distinguish and set aside the many instances where employment legislation directly changes or indirectly modifies the common law concerning the termination of personal employment contracts. That could be said to occur, for instance, when legislation imports into contracts of employment a minimum period of notice of termination, and certainly seems to occur when legislation converts a fixed-term contract of employment into one which is open-ended but terminable by notice. However, our present concern is not so much with those instances of legislative *reform* of the law of personal work contracts, but with the emergence of legislative concepts and terminologies which to a greater or lesser extent *draw upon* the law of personal employment contracts, but do so in their own distinctive way.

This legislative drawing upon the law of termination of personal employment contracts occurs in many different degrees of closeness and directness. It will often be the case that a legislative concept or terminology will be ambiguous as to how far it is drawn from the law of personal employment contracts. For example, the statute law of unfair dismissal evokes a conception of constructive dismissal consisting of termination of the contract of employment by the employee 'in circumstances in which he is entitled to terminate it without notice by reason of the employer's conduct'.[3] For a time it was debated in the case law whether that entitlement was a specifically *contractual* one, until the Court of Appeal decided that it was, in the leading case of *Western Excavating (ECC) Ltd v Sharp*.[4] It has, on the other hand, remained unclear how far the statutory concept of 'redundancy' is a contract-based one, that is to say how far the employee's job, the disappearance of which constitutes redundancy, is defined in purely contractual terms.[5]

Moreover, even where it is clear that a legislative concept or terminology is squarely contract-based, there may be different degrees of fidelity to the

---

[3] Employment Rights Act 1996, s 95(1)(c).
[4] [1978] ICR 221 (see above, 155, 339).
[5] Compare above, 240 et seq.

common law of personal employment contracts. Sometimes, although it is clear that the statutory concept or terminology in question is based upon the law of personal employment contracts, it may nonetheless be evident that the term in question is being used in a special sense. For example, the concept of dismissal which is used in the redundancy payments legislation and the unfair dismissal legislation is, with the removal of the doubt about constructive dismissal, squarely contract-based. Yet it includes the expiry of a fixed-term contract, whereas the term 'dismissal' as ordinarily used in the common law of personal employment contracts does not include the expiry of a fixed-term contract.

Furthermore, and this is an extremely important point, a term may be used in employment legislation on the assumption that it evokes a concept which is clearly understood in or defined by the common law of personal employment contracts, when that is far from being the case. For example, the terminology of the 'fixed-term contract' was used in redundancy payments and unfair dismissal legislation on that assumption; yet the case law reveals how difficult it is to assign a clear meaning to that term. We can go further; it is entirely arguable that the common law of personal employment contracts affords no clear single notion of what is meant by the 'termination' of a contract of employment—yet employment legislation assumes at a number of points that the use of this terminology is soundly based upon a bedrock of common law.

The existence of this multiplicity of discourses or vocabularies within or around the law of termination of personal employment contracts has profoundly important consequences for those who wish to render a clear and coherent account of that body of law. It means that we have to be alive to the risk of ambiguity as to which one or more of these vocabularies is being used when any given terminology is invoked. It means, above all, that it is unsatisfactory to try to systematize this body of law simply by pulling together all the terminologies which are used into a single list, because actually the terminologies come from diverse systems, four of which we have identified. For example, we cannot satisfactorily make a single category of modes of termination which includes both 'retirement' and 'termination under the doctrine of frustration', because those terminologies come from two different discourses, the former a purely factual one, and the latter from general contract law.

The multiplicity of discourses also has this further effect, that a given terminology may be accorded meaning in more than one discourse, and therefore in different functional contexts where different policy considerations apply. There is, for example, a crucial tension in this respect between the construction of notions of termination of the contract of employment in, on the one hand, the remedial common law of personal employment contracts, and in, on the other hand, the statute law of unfair dismissal. In the former context, notions of contractual termination directly confer or deny rights to remedies; in the latter context, notions of contractual termination have the different function of determining whether an employment tribunal has jurisdiction to consider whether the employing entity has acted unfairly. That particular tension is very evident in the evolution of notions such as that of repudiatory breach of contract or constructive dismissal.

We have thus sought to identify some inherent difficulties in establishing, within the existing law, a clear and coherent set of conceptions or categories of termination and transformation of personal employment contracts; and we have argued that those difficulties are to be explained by reference to the multiplicity of discourses within which the existing terminologies have developed and are currently used. That identification of an underlying set of problems in the law of termination of personal employment contracts, and that explanation for the problem, between them suggest the need for some additional organizing concepts which might effectively cut across those diverse discourses. An attempt to meet that need is made in the remainder of this section.

C. The Existence and Identity of the Personal Employment Contract

The discussion in the previous subsections has shown that the notion of the personal employment contract, or of the contract of employment, which we evoke when we speak of its termination, or its variation or suspension or transfer, is currently an extremely imprecise one. In order to create a composite and coherent analysis of the termination and transformation of personal employment contracts, we need to try to specify as clearly as possible what it is that may be ended or changed. We need, in other words, to establish what is the state of existence, that is to say the *existence and identity*, which may be terminated or may be transformed into a different existence and identity.

We advance the suggestion that it is useful to conceptualize that state of existence around a core notion of *a contractual employment under a single personal employment contract*. The existence and identity of the personal employment contract is in certain respects a larger or looser notion than that of contractual employment under a single personal employment contract; the latter notion constitutes the core of the former one. We suggest that contractual employment under a single personal employment contract can be defined and identified in three dimensions, those of *parties, content, and duration*. It consists of, or exists when there are, current contractual obligations for immediate employment in the sense of exchange of work and remuneration between a particular set of parties on a particular set of terms and conditions for a particular period of time.

Around that core, a personal employment contract may have a more expansively defined existence or identity in each of those dimensions. It may in certain conditions retain its existence and identity despite a change of parties, or of content, or of duration. There is some elasticity in each of these dimensions.[6] A personal employment contract may in certain situations undergo novation, variation, or extension while retaining its original existence or identity. On the other hand, changes of parties, content, or duration may deprive a personal employment contract of its existence and identity, so that although the employment relationship in question may be regarded as continuing, it does not continue under the original personal employment contract. (Normally that means it continues under a different personal employment contract, but there may be situations where that is not the case, so that it continues as a non-contractual employment relationship.)

There is, moreover, a further and crucial sense in which a personal employment contract may have an existence and identity which is larger and more extensive than the core of contractual employment around which it is constructed. We return to the suggestion advanced in an earlier chapter[7] that it is useful to think of personal employment contracts as capable of having existence and identity in a number of different states or *modes*, of which the state or mode of full contractual employment is the central and typical one, but not the only one. This suggestion of diverse modes of existence of the personal employment contract is a complex one which obviously requires further explanation in the context of a theory of termination and transformation of personal work or employment contracts.

The suggestion was that a personal employment contract might be regarded as capable of having an existence and identity not just *during* a period of contractual employment, but also *before such a period, between such periods,* or *after such periods.* However, at each of those times, the personal employment contract functions differently. It imposes obligations which are different from those which it imposes at the other times. In that sense, at each of those times the contract exists in a different mode or phase. Hence we can envisage personal employment contracts existing in four different modes, namely:

(1) pre-employment mode, (2) full employment mode, (3) sub-employment mode, and (4) post-employment mode.

The foregoing analysis of the existence and identity of personal employment contracts may at various points assist our understanding of the various terminologies and concepts which are encountered in the course of discussion of the termination and transformation of those contracts. The analysis suggests that we have to understand termination and transformation as

---

[6] When elasticity of duration is considered, it must be borne in mind that there is a considerable lack of precise specification, in the common law of personal employment contracts, as to whether and when continuing employment relationships are to be regarded as taking place under a single contract of indeterminate duration, or a rolling contract, or a series of fixed-term contracts—compare above, 302, 401.

[7] See above, Chapter 2, Conclusion at 106–108.

occurring in a number of different dimensions—those of (1) parties, (2) content, (3) duration, and (4) mode. It has suggested ways in which we may identify some particular terms or concepts with greater precision. For example, 'suspension' of personal employment contracts means a shift from employment mode to sub-employment mode. It will also be argued that 'termination' of personal employment contracts usually refers to the shift from full employment mode to post-employment mode. Building upon the basis of this analysis, we shall attempt first to present a systematic scheme of the different ways in which personal employment contracts may be transformed or terminated, and then to elaborate upon the way in which the concepts and terminologies which are currently used fit into that scheme, and to explain the nature and operation of those of them which have not previously been discussed.

D. A GENERAL ANALYSIS OF THE TERMINATION AND TRANSFORMATION OF PERSONAL EMPLOYMENT CONTRACTS

We are now in a position to suggest a comprehensive set of categories for all the evolutions, in the sense of changes of state or situation, which personal employment contracts may undergo subsequently to their formation. This set of categories is intended to be superimposed upon the existing terminologies, and to serve as a basis for resolving some of the imprecisions and ambiguities of those existing terminologies as revealed in the preceding subsections. We shall therefore set out the suggested list of categories, and indicate briefly how each of them relates to existing terminologies. In the remainder of the chapter and in the next chapter the categories will be explored more fully, especially those which have not been treated in previous chapters.

We suggest, therefore, that the evolutions which personal employment contracts may undergo can be regarded as falling into the two broad categories of (1) termination, and (2) transformation. Each of those categories can be divided into three subcategories, so that the full list of categories is as follows:

A. Termination
  1. Unilateral
  2. Bilateral
  3. Non-lateral

B. Transformation
  1. Variation
  2. Suspension
  3. Change of party or transfer of contract.

We proceed briefly to explain this set of categories in relation to existing categories, before expanding upon it in greater detail. There are two crucial general points of explanation, which follow from the preceding discussion;

each of these two points is the corollary of the other. Firstly, the categories put forward here are not the same as those currently used, so that even where the terms used are in current usage, a special and different meaning may be attributed to them within this new set of categories. The purpose of this is to seek to address the ambiguities in existing categories which were revealed in the preceding discussion. For example, we attribute a particular meaning to 'termination' which aspires to be a more precise meaning than the term has in its current usage.

Secondly, it is to be emphasized that this new set of categories does not map neatly and directly upon terminologies in current usage. It is quite to the contrary, because the new set of categories aims to reveal imprecisions and inconsistencies in current usage. For example, it will be suggested that it is quite unclear whether or when 'retirement' should be regarded as unilateral, bilateral, or non-lateral termination. We shall develop the exposition of the new set of categories by initially allocating existing terminologies to the category which they fit into best; but this will be a provisional allocation which will often turn out to require modification. Bearing those two points in mind, we begin to develop the categories more fully.

A. Termination. As explained earlier, this category is put forward as normally meaning the transition from the employment mode to the post-employment mode of the existence of the personal employment contract. It may, exceptionally, include the transition from sub-employment mode to post-employment mode. In its existing usage, 'termination' usually has one or other of those meanings, but it sometimes seems to include the ending of some or all of the obligations which would otherwise apply during the post-employment phase, in particular where the 'termination' is by or in response to repudiatory breach of contract.

A1. Unilateral termination. This category is put forward as referring to termination either by the employing entity or by the worker, and our discussion of it will distinguish between those two subcategories. Unilateral termination by the employing entity has been extensively discussed in earlier chapters, but some further analysis will be required to relate that earlier discussion to the present set of categories. The notion of unilateral termination by the employing entity is largely coincident with that of 'dismissal', but there are ambiguities to be resolved and divergences to be recognized. In particular there is a question whether and when the non-renewal by the employing entity of a contract for a fixed term should be regarded as a unilateral termination by the employing entity. Unilateral termination by the worker will require exposition; it is largely coincident with the current notion of 'resignation' but there are some complications to resolve.

A2. Bilateral termination. This category refers to termination which is effected jointly by employing entity and worker. It is largely coincident with the current terminology of 'termination by agreement', but the current terminology is ambiguous as between agreement in the original contract and subsequent agreement. That ambiguity, and the whole notion of bilateral termination, will be explored in detail.

A3. Non-lateral termination. This category refers to termination which is not effected by either party or by both parties. It is largely coincident with the current terminologies of 'frustration' and/or 'termination by operation of law'. Detailed analysis of its scope will be required, in particular of the question whether events such as the death of the worker or the insolvency of the employing entity should be regarded as coming within this category.

B. Transformation. This is a new category intended to cover all the changes in state or situation which a personal employment contract may undergo, except that of termination. As a new general category it does not present problems of reconciliation with existing terminologies, but there are a number of such problems in relation to its various subcategories.

B1. Variation. We use this subcategory to refer to change of the content of a personal employment contract which is sufficiently significant to amount to an alteration in the state of the contract but which is not such as to consist of or bring about a termination of the contract and its replacement by another contract. In current usage that distinction is not sharply made or maintained, and considerable exposition in Chapter five was directed towards clarifying that distinction.

We also use the subcategory of variation to include a change in the stipulated *duration* of the personal employment contract which nevertheless does not amount to a termination of the contract and its replacement with another contract. Such change in duration may take the form either of (1) unilateral or bilateral extension, sometimes referred to as 'renewal', or (2) conversion from fixed-term to indefinite duration under the Fixed-term Employees Regulations as described in Chapter six.

B2. Suspension. Rather similarly to that of variation, we use this subcategory to refer to an interruption in employment which is sufficient to bring about a change in the state of the contract from employment mode to sub-employment mode, but which is not sufficient to consist of or bring about a termination of the contract. Some recapitulation and new exposition will be needed to reconcile this subcategory with the current terminology of 'suspension', which is much less precisely used.

B3. Change of party or transfer of contract. The new category of change of party or transfer of contract is, again, somewhat analogous with that of change of duration. It refers to a change of state which does not involve termination of the existing personal employment contract; it has two subcategories, one of which corresponds to an existing rather imprecise terminology, and the other of which refers to a legislative innovation. Those subcategories are, respectively, those of (1) unilateral or bilateral change of party, and (2) TUPE transfer. Rather as with the subcategory of variation, some exposition will be required to relate the terminology of change of party to the existing notion of 'novation', and quite a lot of exposition will be needed to explain how the very radical new conception of TUPE transfer fits into and affects the existing law.

In the succeeding sections these categories are all explored in greater detail. There will be seen to be extremely difficult but interesting issues as to how these categories relate to each other, and how factual occurrences in the course of or at the end of employment relationships are allocated to these different categories. It is hoped that the establishment of the foregoing set of categories will, by breaking away from the existing terminologies, have enabled us to reveal and explore questions about what constitutes coherent law-making and fair functional adjudication with regard to the termination and transformation of personal employment contracts.

SECTION 2: UNILATERAL TERMINATION

At the end of the previous section, a general set of issues was identified in relation to the termination and transformation of personal employment contracts, for which it was hoped that the system of categories which had been established would prove to be a useful tool of analysis. The category of unilateral termination is a good one to which to begin to apply that method of analysis, for it presents particularly acute questions about coherent law-making and fair functional adjudication. We proceed to depict what those questions are and how they arise.

The category of unilateral termination divides straight away into two subcategories, that of unilateral termination by the employing entity and unilateral termination by the worker. For each of those two subcategories, there is an important body of law determining, firstly, what powers of unilateral termination are conferred by or under personal employment contracts, and, secondly, what scope and treatment is accorded to terminatory conduct which is outside those powers. Viewing the unilateral termination by the employing entity as being the central focus of the whole of the law of termination of personal employment contracts, we devoted a chapter to each of those questions, under the respective headings of lawful termination by the employing entity and wrongful termination by the employing entity. Those chapters raised a number of central issues about coherent law-making and fair functional adjudication which it will be useful to recapitulate in the present general analytical framework. These questions are considered in subsection A below.

Unilateral termination by the employing entity assumes this central focal position in the law of termination of personal employment contracts because most (though by no means all) of the legal issues and claims concerning termination of those contracts arise from situations where workers have grievances about the ending of their employment by the enterprises in or by which they are employed. Nevertheless, there is also an independently important set of issues and a corresponding body of law about unilateral termination by the worker, both lawful and wrongful in the sense in which those terms were used with regard to unilateral termination by the employing entity. These issues are addressed in subsection B below.

Moreover, there is a further set of questions, which to some extent informs each of the two bodies of law about unilateral termination, as to whether they are fairly and suitably related to and balanced against each other. This will to some extent have emerged in the course of discussion of unilateral termination by each of the two parties, in the form of issues such as whether the enforcement of post-employment obligations following wrongful termination by the employing entity fairly matches the enforcement of them following wrongful termination by the worker.

However, there is another very complex but important sense in which we have to consider the balance and relation between the law of unilateral termination by the employing entity and the law of unilateral termination by the worker. One of the main functions of the latter body of law is to delimit the former body of law. Since the two subcategories are mutually exclusive, by identifying a given situation as being in one category, we thereby locate it outside the other category. The main importance of unilateral termination by the worker is that it is not unilateral termination by the employing entity. In the current, though at times as we shall see misleading, usage, the importance of resignation by the worker is that it does not constitute dismissal by the employer. It follows that by enlarging either category, we may diminish the other. There is a sensitive frontier between the two categories. These issues of balance and allocation are brought together and explored in subsection C below.

A. Unilateral Termination by the Employing Entity

In this subsection, the law concerning unilateral termination of personal employment contracts by the employing entity, as discussed in the two previous chapters, will be briefly recapitulated, but also represented within the framework of the general theory of termination and transformation which was set out in the first section of this chapter. That general theory seeks both to expose and to escape from some of the ambiguities and misconceptions which are embodied in the current parlance of termination of personal employment contracts. Thus the general theory has argued for an understanding of the very notion of termination of the personal employment contract which is both different from and more complex than the way in which it is currently understood. It will be sought to develop that set of arguments slightly further in this subsection.

The extended presentation of the topic of unilateral termination of personal employment contracts by the employing entity in the previous two chapters proceeded on the basis of a crucial distinction between 'lawful' and 'wrongful' termination, devoting one chapter to each of those two aspects. Continuing with the process of shedding some of the excess baggage of current usage, we suggest thinking of those two aspects as the subcategories of, respectively, contract-compliant termination and non-contract-compliant termination. Our general theory of termination and transformation may help to give a clear account of each of these subcategories, and more especially to resolve some difficulties in the current understanding of the latter one.

We begin therefore with the category of contract-compliant termination by the employing entity. The account of this category in Chapter six showed how the law of personal employment contracts concedes or imputes wide powers of unilateral termination to the employing entity. Such powers may be expressly limited in any one or more of three ways, and could in theory be impliedly limited in any one or more of those three ways, namely: (1) by required duration of warning of exercise, ie by a requirement of notice, and/or (2) by reference to substantive grounds of exercise (for example by reason of misconduct or of redundancy), and/or (3) by requirements of procedure (for example of a hearing as to whether to exercise the power, or an appeal from exercise of the power).

In Chapter six we saw that the common law of personal employment contracts has in fact strongly imputed, at least in the case of contracts of employment, two wide powers of unilateral termination, the one a power limited only by a requirement of notice, and the other a power limited only by reference to widely defined disciplinary grounds, or significant breach of contract on the part of the worker, known as a power of summary dismissal. Legislation has, in the case of contracts of employment, imposed minimum periods of notice in the case of the first power, and has, in 2002, introduced (though not implemented) certain requirements of procedure upon the exercise of both kinds of power.

In Chapter six it was argued that we should also regard the employing entity as having exercised a power of termination where a personal employment contract for a fixed-term is not renewed on the expiry of that term. The terminology of unilateral termination assists in understanding that situation in that way. It is difficult to regard that situation as a 'dismissal'. There can be little doubt that this situation would not be construed as being within the statutory notion of 'dismissal' if the legislation, for example on redundancy payments or unfair dismissal, had not expressly included it, and that is an inclusion which is often felt to be counter-intuitive. It is much less difficult to regard that situation as one of 'unilateral termination by the employing entity', since the employing entity has chosen that the contract should terminate, rather than choosing to extend it.

Where the employing entity does exercise a contract-compliant power of termination in the above sense, it would seem that the termination has what we have argued is its normal meaning of a change from the employment state to the post-employment state of the contract in question. It may be that, in the case where the employing entity is terminating the contract in response to a serious or repudiatory breach by the worker, the termination could be regarded as a 'rescission' and therefore as having the further effect of relieving the employing entity of some or all of its post-employment obligations. However, there do not seem to be significant instances where that conception of 'termination' has been invoked in relation to what is normally known as 'summary dismissal', and express stipulation to that effect might be regarded as being contrary to public policy, as imposing an excessive penalty upon the worker.[8]

When we try to integrate the law concerning wrongful or non-contract-compliant termination by the employing entity into our general analysis of termination and transformation, we find that significant illogicalities or anomalies are revealed. We shall encounter some of these when we come to discuss the issues of balance and allocation between unilateral termination by the employing entity and unilateral termination by the worker, but it will be useful to refer to two of them at this point. Both anomalies seem to stem from rather inflexible approaches to the meaning of 'termination of contract'. The first of these anomalies concerns the dogmatic insistence that 'wrongful dismissal is effective to terminate the contract of employment', which, it was argued in the previous chapter, is pervasive and even operates to undermine the professed doctrine that wrongful repudiation by the employing entity has an elective rather than an automatic effect.

This notion of the effectiveness of wrongful dismissal to terminate the contract seems to stem from a perception that the contract *must* in principle, or at least in practice, be regarded as 'terminated' in the absence of specific remedies to require the employing entity to continue the employment of the worker. Our analysis of the possible alternative meanings of termination of the personal employment contract helps to reveal that this is not a necessary logic. It suggests that there is already an established set of alternative modes of existence of such contracts, so that a contract may be said to be terminated in one sense though not in every possible sense. There is no theoretical objection to denying or limiting the terminatory effect of action by the employing entity which purports to end the employment or modify it to the worker's detriment, nor to the devising of remedial solutions which accept a terminatory effect in some respects but not in others.

In another respect, on the other hand, our discussion in Chapter seven revealed that the law concerning non-contract-compliant action by the employing entity may accord *excessive* terminatory effect to that action. We advanced that criticism of the doctrine in *General Billposting v Atkinson*,[9] which dictates that the worker who accepts wrongful repudiation of the

---

[8] Compare Freedland 1976 at 231, also above at 183.
[9] *General Billposting Co Ltd v Atkinson* [1909] AC 118; see above, 391–392.

contract on the employing entity's part as terminating the contract is thereby freed of express obligations against competition after employment. Again, our general analysis of termination helps to show why that is anomalous, since our analysis suggests that termination of personal employment contracts does not normally involve the ending of post-employment obligations. There is no necessary logic which suggests that termination by or in response to wrongful repudiation has to bring an end to all obligations including post-employment ones. We proceed to consider whether the law concerning unilateral termination by the worker may be clarified by the application of a corresponding analysis.

B. Unilateral Termination by the Worker

In fact we shall find that the law concerning the unilateral termination of the personal employment contract by the worker, although less fully and clearly articulated than that concerning unilateral termination by the employing entity, has nevertheless come to mirror the latter reasonably closely, subject to one or two important divergences, somewhat to the detriment of the worker, which are thrown into relief by the method of general analysis of termination and transformation which is being pursued in this chapter. The terminology of 'resignation' is often used to refer to unilateral termination by the worker, or employee at least. That terminology is not an altogether clear one. It conceals the same divisions between contract-compliant termination and non-contract-compliant terminatory conduct, and between spontaneous termination and responsive termination, as we encountered in relation to unilateral termination by the employing entity; our discussion will seek to go behind the opaque façade of 'resignation' and to develop those distinctions.

The powers of termination which the law of personal employment contracts confers upon the worker, or at least the employee, or which it presumes to have been intended by the contracting parties, were historically much more limited than those of the employing entity, but have latterly converged much more closely upon them. The worker's powers of unilateral termination are of the same two broad types as those of the employing entity, that is to say there is normally regarded as being a power to terminate by notice, and a power of termination in response to serious breach or repudiation on the part of the employing entity.

Taking these two types of power of termination in turn, and starting with the power of termination by notice, we may note that the worker has on the whole been presumed to have such a power on the same terms as those which apply to the employing entity; in particular, the duration of notice regarded as reasonable from the employee has probably been equated to that regarded as reasonable in the case of the employing entity. The Contracts of Employment legislation created a differential from 1963 onwards by requiring a fixed one week's notice of the employee while requiring an increasing length of notice of the employing entity according to the number of years of continuous employment[10] which the employee has achieved, reckoning being taken of up to twelve such years. It is hard to say whether there is now a corresponding differential between the reasonable notice impliedly required of the employee and that impliedly required of the employing entity, because the length of notice required of each party is required to be specified in the statutory particulars of terms and conditions of employment, and so resort rarely needs to be had to the implied or default requirement of notice of reasonable length.

The worker also has a power or right of responsive termination, that is to say a right to leave employment and claim damages, in response to serious or repudiatory breach. Before the introduction of the modern body of employment protection legislation in the 1960s, that power or right was not clearly recognized or articulated, and would probably have been regarded as a very limited one. With the introduction of that employment protection legislation, focused as it was upon the rights of employees arising from dismissal by employing entities, that power or right became of crucial significance because it became the basis upon which an employee who had ended his or her employment could claim to have been constructively dismissed by his or her employing entity.[11]

In other words, the special subcategory of *justified responsive* termination by the employee now assumed a crucial importance as deemed or constructive dismissal. The decision in *Western Excavating v Sharp*[12] that the justification, or entitlement to terminate, which was the basis of the statutory notion of constructive dismissal, was to be assessed strictly on *contractual* terms, made it necessary to articulate this contractual entitlement more fully than was previously the case. The judges in the Court of Appeal which decided that case insisted on a contractual assessment because they believed that the contractual entitlement was both fixed and limited. Ironically, the rapid development of the employing entity's implied obligation of trust and confidence which followed upon that decision defined the employee's entitlement to terminate in as flexible and expansive a way as an extra-contractual approach was expected to do; that development has been discussed earlier in the present work.[13]

Thus far, the law concerning unilateral termination by the worker has seemed to match that applying to the employing entity. However, if we turn to the question of wrongful or non-contract-compliant termination by the worker, we find that there are some significant variations as between worker and employing entity. Initially, the similarities seem to persist. If the worker

---

[10] With the employing entity in question or an 'associated employer' as statutorily defined—see, currently, ERA 1996, ss 210–218.

[11] The current provisions to that effect are made by ERA 1996, ss 95(1)(c) and 136(1)(c).

[12] *Western Excavating (ECC) Ltd v Sharp* [1978] ICR 221 (CA).

[13] See above, 155 et seq.

ends his or her employment, that is to say resigns or leaves the employment, in a way which is not contract-compliant, this will be effective to end the contractual employment, or to move the contract from employment mode to post-employment mode, to the extent that no specific remedy will be available to compel the worker to continue to work. In the case of employees, a statutory provision was made in 1974, in the context of the legal regulation of industrial action, that no court should by way of an order of specific performance of a contract of employment or an injunction restraining the breach or threatened breach of such a contract compel an employee to do any work or attend at any place for the doing of any work.[14]

It is the view of this writer that even in the absence of such a provision the courts would refuse an order of specific performance or an injunction to override a wrongful leaving in the case of an employee, and that the same would almost certainly be true in the case of a semi-dependent worker. Both these conclusions would follow from the doctrine against the specific enforcement of obligations of personal service, which is well established by decisions such as that of *De Francesco v Barnum*.[15] Those conclusions are reinforced by decisions such as that of *Warner Brother Pictures Incorporated v Nelson*,[16] which extend the doctrine to encompass the refusal of negative injunctions against working for other employing entities which would, if granted, have the indirect effect of practically compelling the worker to work for the original employing entity. Neither the decisions establishing the narrower doctrine, nor those establishing its broader corollary, seem to confine themselves to employees as opposed to semi-dependent workers.

Thus far, the treatment of the wrongful leaving by the worker seems to match that of the wrongful dismissal by the employing entity. There, however, the similarities seem to end, for, outside the immediate confines of those two doctrines, the courts have in the modern period of the law of personal employment contracts taken a much narrower view of the effectiveness of wrongful resignation, or wrongful leaving by the worker, to end the contract, than of the effectiveness of wrongful dismissal by the employing entity to end the contract. This is a highly significant development, and it has become the basis on which 'garden leave' arrangements are validated by the courts.

Two crucial decisions in the modern period have moved the law in this direction. The first was that of Sir Robert Megarry as Vice-Chancellor in the case of *Thomas Marshall (Exports) Ltd v Guinle*,[17] where a managing director under a ten-year service agreement resigned from the employing company after five years and claimed thereafter to be free from express and

---

[14] The provision is currently contained in s 236 of the Trade Union and Labour Relations (Consolidation) Act 1992, 'No compulsion to work'.
[15] (1890) 43 ChD 165 (ChD); reiterated on this point by Fry LJ, (1891) 45 ChD 430 at 438.   [16] [1937] 1 KB 209 (KBD).
[17] [1978] ICR 905 (ChD); see also above, 381.

implied obligations of fidelity and confidentiality, and hence free to carry on business in competition with the company. An injunction was granted to enforce those obligations on the footing that the employee managing director should not be allowed to terminate his contract by his wrongful action of leaving his employment in breach of contract. It is absolutely clear that when the Vice-Chancellor referred to termination of contract, he meant it in the sense which we have specified in our theory of termination, that is to say in the sense of moving from employment mode to post-employment mode. The employee was held to be still subject not merely to his post-employment obligations but also to the more stringent obligations which applied during the continuance of his employment.[18]

In that case, the objection that this amounted to an indirect compulsion upon the worker to work for the employing entity, or a 'perform or starve' order, was not specifically discussed, though the Vice-Chancellor noted that the company was willing to continue to pay the worker if he would resume his duties, and moreover that it was not sought to require the worker to refrain from all other work or business activity, merely from solicitation of the company's customers and disclosure of its confidential information.[19] In the not dissimilar case of *Evening Standard Co Ltd v Henderson*,[20] where the employing entity, a newspaper publishing company, did seek to prevent its production manager, who had left his employment without the stipulated year's notice, from working for any rival newspaper during the remainder of that year, the 'perform or starve' objection to an injunction was raised. Although, rather surprisingly, the *Marshall v Guinle* case seems not to have been referred to, a similar outcome was reached, and the 'perform or starve' objection was specifically regarded, in the judgment of Lawton LJ, as outweighed by the importance of preventing employees from breaking their contracts in opportunistic reliance upon the absence of effective remedies against them. Importance was clearly also attached to the employing entity's willingness to continue to provide the employee's salary and benefits, and indeed to allow him to work for the company if he wished to do so.[21]

The courts have since on more than one occasion issued such injunctions to enforce 'garden leave' arrangements whereby the worker is sent on leave though in receipt of remuneration during a period of contractual notice,[22] thus further institutionalizing the view that a worker cannot escape from the exclusivity requirements of the contractual employment period by

---

[18] See [1978] ICR 905 at 921G—enforcement of the implied duty of fidelity and good faith which 'depends on whether the service agreement is, as I have held, still in being and binding upon the defendant'.   [19] Ibid paras 912B and 922G.
[20] [1987] ICR 64 (CA).   [21] See [1987] ICR 588 at 594D–E.
[22] *GFI Group Inc v Eaglestone* [1994] IRLR 119 (QBD), *Euro Brokers Ltd v Rabey* [1995] IRLR 206 (QBD).

departing in breach of contract. In the very recent decision in the case of *White v Bristol Rugby Ltd*,[23] that approach was even extended so far as to produce a finding that the personal employment contract of a professional rugby player was valid and subsisting where he had refused in breach of contract even initially to take up his engagement with the rugby club concerned. The employing entity was judged to have a sufficient legitimate interest in maintaining the contractual relationship with the player[24] although it was not prepared to pay him salary unless and until he actually began to work for them.

C. ISSUES OF BALANCE AND ALLOCATION

The foregoing discussion of the law concerning the unilateral termination of personal employment contracts by employing entities, on the one hand, and workers, on the other, has revealed some very pressing issues of adjudicative balance between the interests of employing entities and those of workers. In their approach to the enforcement of continuation of the obligations of contractual employment in the face of wrongful ending of employment, the courts and tribunals do not seem to have been directly troubled by the disparity between their reluctant approach to such enforcement against employing entities, and their more ready approach to such enforcement against workers.

However, perhaps some unease in this respect is manifested by decisions which place limits on the enforcement of 'garden leave' arrangements. Such decisions were those in *Provident Financial Group plc v Hayward*,[25] where the Court of Appeal denied enforcement of such an arrangement because the employing entity had not shown a real business need for enforcement, *GFI Group Inc v Eaglestone*,[26] where enforcement was granted but for less than the full period of contractual notice, and *William Hill Organisation Ltd v Tucker*,[27] where the Court of Appeal refused enforcement in the absence of an express provision enabling the employing entity to deny the worker the opportunity to work and maintain his skills in the field of spread betting, and where the importance was stressed of ensuring that garden leave arrangements were not enforced where an express covenant against post-employment competition of comparable impact would be judged to be in unlawful restraint of trade.[28]

An extremely interesting and important body of case law has evolved to conduct another kind of adjudicative balancing operation in the law concerning unilateral termination; this concerns the allocation or attribution of

---

[23] [2002] IRLR 204 (QBD).
[24] As it was expressed in the judgment of Judge Havelock-Allan QC, 'if only to secure the payment of a transfer fee when he seeks to move to another club' (at 213).
[25] [1989] ICR 160 (CA).   [26] [1994] IRLR 119 (QBD).
[27] [1999] ICR 291 (CA).   [28] Morritt LJ at 301G; compare below, 487–488.

unilateral termination as between the two parties to personal employment contracts. To put the matter simply, we are speaking of decisions as to whether and when it is the employing entity or the worker that or who is to be regarded as having unilaterally terminated a personal employment contract. The need for this particular kind of adjudication is largely created by the statute law of employment protection, particularly the redundancy payments and unfair dismissal legislation, because that legislation makes rights or claims dependent upon dismissal; that is to say, upon the unilateral termination of contracts of employment by employing entities. So that concept is a jurisdictional gateway to claims under that legislation, and therefore it becomes a key question whether terminations of contracts of employment can be allocated to that category. Since, as we explained earlier, unilateral termination by the worker is definitively contrasted with unilateral termination by the employing entity, so that the former concept limits the latter one, the allocation of particular terminations of employment to one or other of the two categories becomes a crucial matter.

This might appear on the face of it to be an unremarkable proposition, because we might easily assume that this particular kind of allocation was an entirely straightforward matter, requiring neither complex legal rules nor difficult allocative judgments. Such an impression would be entirely mistaken; the matter is one of great difficulty, and an intricate body of law has evolved in an, as yet incompletely successful, attempt to resolve the difficulties. The difficulty can be described thus; it is often very hard to say, upon the ending of employment, which party should be regarded as responsible for that termination either in a descriptive sense or in a normative sense. Two kinds of legal principles (or rules) have evolved to address that difficulty: (1) principles of factual and procedural assessment, (2) principles defining and governing the common law notion of termination of the personal employment contract and the statutory concept of dismissal. We proceed to consider each in turn, and also the question of how these two kinds of principles should work in relation to each other.

The starting point for a legal approach to that difficulty is to ask, after the ending of an employment, which party, as a simple matter of description, took the step of ending the employment in question. However, even at that descriptive level the question is often extremely difficult. If a worker utters words seeming to indicate an intention to leave his or her employment, the utterance may nevertheless be unclear, the product of uncertainty, or it might be a manifestation of anger or bad temper rather than the expression of a definite intention to end the employment in question, or it might signify that the worker regarded himself or herself as having been pushed out by the employing entity; but the employing entity may treat the employment as having been ended unilaterally by the worker. In those circumstances, moreover, normative questions present themselves, as to which party *ought* to be regarded as having terminated the employment.

So principles of assessment evolve to guide and systematize these difficult adjudications. Courts and tribunals will tend to deny that they are formulating such principles, preferring to depict the process of adjudication as one of the application of common sense in a purely factual way; but nevertheless they are doing so. The main principle to emerge is that where a worker has apparently decided to end or leave his or her employment of his or her own volition, the genuineness of that volition must be scrutinized with care, to see whether, on the one hand, the worker's action is the result of pressure from the employing entity, or, on the other hand, the employing entity has been over-ready to treat an impulsive or tentative decision on the worker's part as a settled and firm one. A good example of this kind of principle formation is to be found in the decision of the Court of Appeal in the case of *Sothern v Franks Charlesly & Co*,[29] where the office manager of a firm of solicitors said that she was resigning after a conflictual meeting with the senior partner. The firm treated her as having terminated her own employment; she alleged that she had in reality been dismissed; the Court of Appeal rejected the contention that the words she had used were too ambiguous to support the conclusion that she had terminated her employment.

The usual protestations were made that the attribution of termination as between the employing entity and the worker was a matter of simple common sense; Dame Elizabeth Lane said that:

There is something to be said for the view of the man on the Clapham omnibus, particularly on a topic such as this, and if he were asked 'who terminated this contract?' surely he would say, 'Why, Mrs Sothern, of course, she resigned'.[30]

However, this understated the evaluativeness of the adjudication which was involved. In fact, the Court of Appeal had subjected the conduct of both parties to a critical assessment to test whether the worker should be regarded as having ended her employment of her own free will, and had concluded that she should, on the basis that she was a mature person not acting under overwhelming pressure from the employing entity.

Adjudications of that kind tend to become rather unsatisfactory where they in fact turn upon relative substantive and procedural assessment of the conduct of the two parties, while claiming to be entirely factual in character. In the later case of *Kwik-fit (GB) Ltd v Lineham*,[31] the Employment Appeal Tribunal, while denying that there was anything amounting to a formal onus upon the employing entity to investigate the intentions of an employee who resigns 'in the heat of the moment' (that is to say, in a situation of immediate conflict), nevertheless in effect formulated principles of procedural verification for such situations.

The importance of ensuring the coherence and rigour of these evaluative adjudications is very great. The attribution of unilateral termination to one

---

[29] [1981] IRLR 278 (CA).   [30] Ibid at 279.   [31] [1992] IRLR 156 (EAT).

or other party frequently represents a conclusion that party has, without necessarily failing to comply with the personal employment contract, failed to respect the legitimate substantive or procedural expectations associated with the contract. These attributions therefore embody notions of contractual fault or demerit falling short of breach of contract. The point is well illustrated by the decision in the case of *Caledonian Mining Co Ltd v Bassett*,[32] where the employing entity, a construction contractor, had warned of impending redundancy at the site in question and had in effect persuaded the workers employed there to resign and take work elsewhere. Its argument that the workers had resigned rather than been dismissed was rejected on the ground that the workers had been 'falsely inveigled' into resigning by the prospect of other work with the employing entity, so that the termination had been caused by the employing entity and should be attributed to it.

In that case, Popplewell J perfectly encapsulated the idea of an act which does not amount to a repudiation of contract, possibly not even a breach, but which is nevertheless a contractual offence against good practice in his comment that:

The question whether termination of a contract is dismissal or constructive dismissal is not resolved simply by looking at the label put upon it. It is not enough... to say there has been a resignation, therefore the employer could not have terminated the contract save by way of constructive dismissal.[33]

The point was that the employing entity's conduct, while not amounting to repudiatory breach of contract, was regarded as sufficiently reprehensible to justify the attribution of termination to the employing entity and away from the worker who had taken the factual action of ending the employment.

It might be that the coherence and rigour of such adjudications could henceforth be improved by considering how fully each party has complied with the contractual duty of dispute resolution, which, we argued in an earlier chapter, could now be regarded as having been concretized by the provisions of the Employment Act 2002.[34] It should, on the other hand, be emphasized that an employing entity may be judged to have effected a unilateral termination, although the ending of the employment was, in an immediate sense, carried out by the worker, *without* necessarily any connotation of fault, and merely on the basis of purely factual causation. However, since the *effect* of such adjudications is to place the facts in question either inside or outside a statutory claim based upon dismissal, it could be argued that the adjudications would be more coherent if they were placed on some such overtly normative basis.

If principles of that kind are evolving to differentiate between unilateral termination, by the worker on the one hand and the employing entity on the other, at a supposedly factual, or procedural level, there is, apparently

---

[32] [1987] ICR 425 (EAT).   [33] Ibid at 431.   [34] See above, 344–345.

at the other extreme of legal technicality, an evolution of principles or rules which address or bear upon this question in terms of the conceptual definition of contractual termination or dismissal. A good example is to be found in the debate between automatic and elective theory of termination by or as the result of repudiation. The theory which views wrongful dismissal as bringing about an automatic termination of the personal employment contract seems to point unequivocally to the employing entity as the terminating party.

On the other hand, the countervailing theory, which views wrongful dismissal as giving the worker an election whether to accept the wrongful repudiation as terminatory of the contract, seems to identify the worker as the terminating party when he or she does so elect. Moreover, when the employing entity's repudiatory conduct does not amount to outright ending of the employment, so that the repudiation is regarded as having legal effect only if and when the worker takes terminatory action in response to it, legal logic seems positively to compel us to regard the worker as having terminated the contract. The same set of arguments could be reversed as between the employing entity and the worker, and applied to wrongful resignation or other repudiatory conduct on the part of the worker.

In the context of employment protection legislation, legal rules have been enacted, and legal principles have been propounded, which have the effect of altering some of those attributions of unilateral termination to one or other party. Sometimes that is done by way of exegesis of principles directly concerned with the termination of personal employment contracts, some-times by way of the formulation of a conceptually distinct statutory con-ception of dismissal; and often those two modes of law-making become intertwined or confused with each other. Two examples will be given, the one being the actual law of 'constructive dismissal', and the other being the possible law of 'self-dismissal'.

The law or doctrine of constructive dismissal consists of a principle or a rule which attributes the ending of employment, apparently or in an imme-diate sense effected by the worker, to the employing entity as a 'dismissal' such as may be the basis of a claim to statutory rights contingent upon there having been a 'dismissal' by the employing entity. A statutory rule of constructive dismissal re-attributes what would otherwise count as a ter-mination of the contract of employment by the employee, to the employing entity as a dismissal by the employing entity, where the employee was entitled so to terminate by reason of the conduct of the employing entity.[35] As we have seen, the Court of Appeal in *Western Excavating v Sharp*[36] looped that statutory notion of constructive dismissal back into the law of the contract of employment by deciding that the employee's entitlement to

---

[35] The enactment is currently contained in ERA, ss 95(1)(c) and 136(1)(c).
[36] *Western Excavating (ECC) Ltd v Sharp* [1978] ICR 221; see above, 155–156.

terminate must be judged by deciding whether the employing entity had acted in repudiatory breach of contract.

Moreover, the doctrine of constructive dismissal is linked back into, indeed integrated into, the law which deals directly with the termination of personal employment contracts as such, and which dictates whether and when such a termination is to be attributed to the employing entity, on the one hand, or to the worker, on the other. Thus, as was understood by the Court of Appeal in the case of *Marriott v Oxford & District Co-operative Society (No 2)*,[37] and by the Employment Appeal Tribunal in the case of *Hogg v Dover College*,[38] a repudiatory withdrawal by the employing entity of the existing terms and conditions of employment can be (constructively in a sense, since the employing entity has not ended the employment relationship outright) regarded as a termination of the contract by the employing entity, and hence as a dismissal, *as a matter of pure contract law*,[39] and not solely by reference to a special statutory notion of dismissal, particularly if automatic termination theory can be applied.

The second area of development of re-allocatory rules, which shift the attribution of unilateral termination between the parties to the personal employment contract, has been the one which is associated with the idea of 'self-dismissal'. This is the counterpart notion to that of 'constructive dismissal'; it is the idea that, in a case where a worker is in repudiatory breach of the personal employment contract, then, even where it is the employing entity which effects the definitive ending of employment in response to that repudiatory breach, the employing entity may nevertheless be said not to have dismissed the worker, because instead the worker should be regarded as having dismissed himself or herself; in other words, the situation is constructed as one of unilateral termination by the worker rather than by the employing entity.

It is an approach which, for reasons given earlier, is supported by the automatic termination theory of wrongful repudiation, but which is more difficult (though not impossible) to pursue as a matter of pure contract law if elective termination theory is preferred. It was a line of reasoning which was favoured by the Employment Appeal Tribunal in the early years of judicial interpretation of the unfair dismissal legislation; it reached its high

---

[37] [1970] 1 QB 186 (CA).   [38] [1990] ICR 39 (EAT).

[39] Though at the cost of some sense of artificiality; Lord Denning MR subsequently, in *Western Excavating v Sharp*, said of the *Marriott* decision that: 'we had to stretch it a bit. It was not the employer who terminated the employment. It was the employee: and he was entitled to do so by reason of the employer's conduct.' [1978] ICR 221 at 227. The point of that comment was to draw attention to the fact that the Court of Appeal in the earlier case had been prepared to recognize constructive dismissal at common law only because the statutory category of constructive dismissal which was then applicable was a narrow one, being confined to the case where the employee had left his employment *without notice*, being entitled so to do by the employing entity's conduct.

watermark in the cases of *Gannon v JC Firth Ltd* (1976),[40] and *Kallinos v London Electric Wire Ltd* (1979).[41] In the former case, where a group of workers took sudden strike action, were locked out of work on the next day, and were then told that they had lost their jobs, they were held by the EAT to be ineligible to claim unfair dismissal on the basis that they had brought their own contracts to an end by wrongful repudiation and so were not to be regarded as having been dismissed by their employing entity. In the latter case, the same analysis was applied to a situation where a charge hand was discovered asleep in the rest room when he should have been on duty; it was held that he had broken his contract to such an extent as to bring it to an end.

The scope for this approach was considerably, though not definitively, curtailed by the decision in the case of *London Transport Executive v Clarke* (1981),[42] where the same argument was advanced in relation to a bus mechanic who had been absent from work (in Jamaica) for an extended period without leave, and indeed despite refusal of his earlier application for leave of absence. It was held by a majority of the Court of Appeal that this worker had been dismissed by the employing entity when it notified him of his permanent removal from its books, and that he had not previously terminated his own contract of employment (though they ruled that the dismissal had been a fair one). It is hard to say that 'self-dismissal' was *definitively* curtailed by this decision, because the judges in the majority of the Court of Appeal did not really establish any satisfactory theoretical basis for rejecting it.

Thus, both Templeman and Dunn LJJ profess to reject 'self-dismissal' on the basis that it is elective theory rather than automatic theory of termination by repudiation which should be preferred, so that we should regard the contract as terminated only when the employing entity accepts the worker's repudiation, which then constitutes a dismissal.[43] However, we discovered in an earlier chapter that elective theory has not really been effectively or consistently sustained in the case law more generally;[44] and, as Deakin & Morris usefully point out, Templeman LJ was himself reluctant to apply elective theory to the situation where 'a worker walks out of his job and does not thereafter claim to be entitled to resume work'.[45] Moreover, the application of elective theory to sustain the rejection of self-dismissal is hard to square, conceptually, with the fact that the statutory definition of dismissal clearly assumes that a wrongful ending of employment by the employing entity should be regarded as terminating the contract of employment in and of itself, that is to say automatically, and as qualifying as a dismissal on that basis.

---

[40] [1976] IRLR 415 (EAT).   [41] [1980] IRLR 11 (EAT).
[42] [1981] ICR 355 (CA).   [43] See [1981] ICR 355, at 368C–E and 373C–D.
[44] See above, 376–384.
[45] See Templeman LJ at 368C, Deakin & Morris 2001 at 449–450.

However, if the theoretical basis for the decision of the majority of the Court of Appeal in that case is a somewhat fragile one, the basis for it in practical policy terms is more robust; and this perhaps explains why the decision in that case has on the whole been accepted and sustained, to the extent that there has been little or no subsequent development of the notion of self-dismissal as an exception from or limiting concept of the statutory concept of dismissal. That policy basis consisted in the perception that the unfair dismissal legislation in particular was intended to embody a comprehensive and inclusive approach to the notion of dismissal, so that the question of the fairness of the conduct of the employing entity in relation to the ending of an employment would not be sidetracked into highly complex technical jurisdictional issues as to whether that ending should be ruled out of contention, as a dismissal, because it was properly to be regarded as a termination by the worker.[46]

The assertion of that policy basis for the rejection of the idea of self-dismissal brings us to a concluding reflection for this subsection, and in a larger sense for this section as a whole. The law which delineates the unilateral termination of personal employment contracts, and attributes that unilateral termination either to the employing entity or to the worker, has been revealed to be strongly influenced by normative evaluations of the relative legitimacy of the conduct of employing entities and workers in the ending of employment, and by perceptions of the intended scope of legislation which regulates that conduct, relying upon a technical apparatus of contract law in order to do so. It might be thought that a body of specialized technical law which is thus tailored to that particular set of normative purposes has little claim to be regarded as coherent or rigorous contract law.

It is argued, to the contrary, that this does represent a proper role for a body of law which is authentically contractual but functionally adjusted to the complex remedial, interpretative, and to a significant extent statutory, context in which it is called upon to operate. It will be sought to develop that view, in the succeeding sections, by reference to the other categories of termination and transformation of personal employment contracts which have been identified in our general analysis of those broad topics.

SECTION 3: BILATERAL TERMINATION

In the previous section it was shown how unilateral termination constitutes the main category of the whole conceptual system of termination and transformation of personal employment contracts, and how, in particular, unilateral termination by the employing entity is the focal centre of that

---

[46] Hence Templeman LJ's difficulty (at 367F) with the 'argument of a special category of determination of a contract by self dismissal' in the particular context of unfair dismissal legislation.

category, and the basis of the key statutory concept of dismissal. This meant that unilateral termination by the worker was in a sense itself a marginal concept, the main importance of which was to constitute a limiting alternative to unilateral termination by the employing entity.

The same can be said of bilateral termination of the personal employment contract; its main function, too, in modern employment law, is to identify an alternative explanation for certain kinds of termination of contractual employment which, explained in those alternative terms, do not therefore count as unilateral termination by the employing entity or dismissal in a common law or statutory sense. In this section, the notion of bilateral termination is firstly developed and explained, and subcategories are identified (subsection A). Those subcategories are each more fully explored in the two succeeding subsections B and C. This leads on to an inquiry, which begins by considering bilateral termination as a means of limiting or excluding statutory provisions, but continues, more broadly, as a discussion about the way in which, through the law of bilateral termination, the personal employment contract is connected to the statutory rights and obligations which are constructed upon and around it (subsection D).

A. The Category of Bilateral Termination Explained and Subdivided

In order to arrive at an exact understanding of the way in which the category of bilateral termination functions as a notion which delimits the scope of unilateral termination, and particularly that of unilateral termination by the employing entity, it is necessary to define and analyse the bilateral category with some care. In doing so, it will be important to bear in mind what are the critical operative aspects of that definition or analysis, that is to say the aspects in which it affects or determines legal outcomes, therefore its contentious edge or edges. It follows from what has been said in the introduction to this section that the crucial aspect or contentious edge of the notion of bilateral termination consists of its interface with the notion of unilateral termination by the employing entity.

By contrast, other aspects of the definition or analysis may be no less theoretically interesting or difficult, but they are of lesser practical or operative importance. We can therefore expect that the law will be patchy in its exegesis of bilateral termination. For example, there is little discussion of how to distinguish between, on the one hand, bilateral termination, and, on the other hand, unilateral termination by the worker because both concepts equally exclude that of unilateral termination by the employing entity or dismissal, which is the critical one in practice. However, our analysis, in order to be rigorous and comprehensive, needs to take into account the non-contentious aspects as well as the contentious ones.

We can discern three different kinds of agreement which relate to the termination of personal employment contracts (as to the termination of many if not all other types of contract). Of those three types, one can be regarded as definitely amounting to bilateral termination, another can be regarded as sometimes amounting to or giving rise to bilateral termination, and the third should be regarded as not amounting to or giving rise to bilateral termination. It is difficult to devise completely satisfactory short titles for these three types, but we suggest, (1) pre-termination agreements, (2) *ad hoc* termination agreements, and (3) post-termination agreements. We proceed to explain these three concepts somewhat more fully, and to identify why each of them should or should not be regarded as amounting to or giving rise to bilateral termination.

We begin with the second type, that of *ad hoc* termination agreements, because that is the one of the three which it is easiest to identify in relation to the notion of bilateral termination. In fact, the *ad hoc* agreement represents a straightforward form, we might say the classical form, of bilateral termination; it is an agreement for the ending of a contractual employment which is *ad hoc* in the sense of being a self-contained and unconditional agreement for termination on a stated calendar date, but an agreement which is distinct and separate from the creation of the contractual employment or from the definition of its duration. It may be difficult in certain ways to separate this category from the other two, or to know when to assign some actual transactions to this category, but it is not in doubt that it constitutes bilateral termination.

We continue with the third type, that of post-termination agreements, because that type is again fairly easy to locate in relation to the notion of bilateral termination. This time, however, the location is a negative one; although post-termination agreements are bilateral and relate to termination, they do not *constitute* bilateral termination. For this category refers to agreements, made typically after, and in any event independently of, the termination of contractual employment, which have the function of settling and resolving claims outstanding on the termination of the contractual employment in question, and/or ending or otherwise disposing of outstanding obligations. It may be difficult in practice to say whether an agreement should be regarded as an *ad hoc* termination agreement or a post-termination agreement, but the two categories are strongly conceptually distinct, as witness the fact that a post-termination agreement does not have to be associated with a specifically bilateral termination; it will, more typically, follow on after a *unilateral* termination of contractual employment, with the purpose of resolving disputes arising out of that unilateral termination.

The third category of agreement, that of pre-termination agreements, is, by contrast with the other two, extremely hard to locate as within or outside the notion of bilateral termination. Nevertheless, it is a category which is very important to the understanding of the theory of termination of personal employment contracts, and of some of the difficulties and obscurities which beset the case law concerning that termination. Spelt out more fully, the category is that of agreements for termination but which precede termination. That is to say, they are agreements which provide for termination, but which are prior to, or logically precede, termination in the sense that they form an integral part of the inherently specified duration. Such agreements may be integrated into the specified duration when the personal employment contract is first made, or by subsequent agreed variation of that specified duration.

The articulation of this third category, that of pre-termination agreements, seems at first to present a great logical and practical difficulty in understanding and operating our whole system of categories of termination of personal employment contracts. For it means that, logically, any and every lawful or contract-compliant termination of a personal employment contract can be said to be the result of a pre-termination agreement, and this seems to imply that all such terminations should be viewed as bilateral rather than unilateral, that is to say as terminations by the agreement of both parties, rather than by the unilateral action of one or other party.

The trouble with that logic is that it seems to dissolve out of existence the whole category of contract-compliant unilateral termination by the employing entity (or for that matter by the worker). Yet this is logically difficult, to the extent that this category seems to be very well recognized, under the title of lawful dismissal, in the common law of the contract of employment. It is also practically difficult in the sense that this category is assumed and postulated in most or all of the employment protection legislation which associates statutory rights or claims with dismissal, that being defined so as to include lawful dismissal. Thus, the whole painstaking construction of a conception of *unfair dismissal* which is more extensive than that of *contractually wrongful dismissal* seems to be crucially undermined by the apparent logic of pre-termination agreements.

There is a truly interesting set of underlying issues here, to which we shall return when considering bilateral termination as an exclusion or limitation of statutory rights. However, at this juncture it suffices to say that the apparent logic, which seems to suggest that all terminations which can be traced back to pre-termination agreements must be regarded as bilateral rather than unilateral ones, has not been pressed through to that possible conclusion. It is generally, indeed unquestioningly, accepted that a termination may be regarded as unilateral—by the employing entity or by the worker— although it can be related to a pre-termination agreement.

Nevertheless, *some* terminations are regarded as bilateral rather than unilateral because they can be attributed to pre-termination agreements. There are *some* situations which will be treated as not being dismissal *because* they are viewed as the automatic and bilateral working out of pre-termination agreements—as, in short, termination by prior agreement. We thus arrive at a position in which bilateral termination may be brought about *either* by *ad hoc* termination agreements, *or sometimes* by pre-termination agreements, though not by *all* pre-termination agreements.

We shall seek to delineate those cases more precisely in the following subsections devoted respectively to those two kinds of bilateral termination, and in a further subsection which considers those kinds of terminations as exclusions or limitations upon statutory rights or claims. In the course of doing so, we shall seek to clarify the meaning, or at least pin down the ambiguity, of various terminologies which turn out to be loosely used as between bilateral termination and unilateral termination—such as 'retirement', 'early retirement', 'voluntary redundancy', and 'agreed resignation', or which are loosely used as between our three kinds of agreement relating to termination, such as 'severance agreement' and 'compromise agreement'.

B. BILATERAL TERMINATION BY AD HOC AGREEMENT

We have now explained how it may be held that a personal employment contract has been terminated, not by the unilateral action of the employing entity (or, for that matter, of the worker), but bilaterally by reason of an *ad hoc* termination agreement; and we have shown how that possibility operates as a limiting condition upon claims which have to assert a dismissal on the part of the employing entity. This development of bilateral termination by *ad hoc* agreement as a limiting concept upon dismissal is comparable to the development, described in the previous section, of unilateral termination by the worker as, equally, a limiting concept upon dismissal.

However, the notion of bilateral termination by *ad hoc* agreement potentially encroaches, even more than does the notion of unilateral termination by the worker, upon the core idea of unilateral termination by the employing entity, for it means that a terminatory transaction, even if fully and directly initiated by the employing entity, may nevertheless not count as a termination by the employing entity if it can be regarded as having ended up as a joint transaction in which the worker has participated. In this subsection we consider more fully the conditions in which that has been held to have occurred.

The determining of those conditions has involved an extremely significant evolution in judicial doctrine, which is very interesting both for its conceptual implications and because of the policy considerations which inform it. The issues at stake can best be identified by focusing on terminatory transactions which are described in non-legal-technical language by terminologies such as that of 'early retirement' or 'agreed resignation' or 'voluntary redundancy'. Those terminologies imply that the termination of employment to which they refer is premature, in the sense of being earlier than was expected or stipulated; they also, on the one hand, imply a primary attribution of termination to one or other party—to the worker in the case of early retirement or agreed resignation, and to the employing entity in the case of voluntary redundancy—but, at the same time, imply that the transaction is a consensual one.

Indeed, the notions of voluntary redundancy and early retirement focus most precisely on our key problem area, that of the terminatory transaction initiated by one party but effected with the volition or participation of the other. The notions of voluntary redundancy and agreed resignation are fundamentally equivocal as between unilateral termination by the employing entity, unilateral termination by the worker, or bilateral termination; in this subsection we concentrate on the question of when and on what basis they are allocated to the last of those three categories. Again it is emphasized that the contentious edge of that question is between bilateral termination and unilateral termination by the employing entity, since the contentious issue is normally that of whether the transaction counts as dismissal or not.

We suggest that the case law which has addressed this question has undergone a shift from a causational approach to a contractual one. In the early days of judicial interpretation of unfair dismissal legislation, the courts seem to have approached the issue as one of assigning descriptive or normative responsibility for the termination as between the two parties, with joint responsibility as a possible intermediate alternative between assignment of responsibility to either party, but which would have the effect of negating dismissal just as surely as would the attribution of responsibility to the worker. This approach is well illustrated by the decision in *Burton Allton & Johnson Ltd v Peck*,[47] where the employing entity had arranged for the worker to return to work after long-term sickness in order that he might forthwith be made redundant, and thereby qualify for a statutory redundancy payment, at that time partly reimbursable to the employing entity from state funding. It was held that this was in substance a dismissal for redundancy, and the fact that the employee had agreed to the transaction did not deprive it of that character.

In subsequent cases, however, the question of whether the terminatory transaction should be regarded as unilateral by the employing entity or bilateral came to be tested by the rather different approach of inquiring whether the parties were to be regarded as having made a valid contract for the termination of their personal employment contract. This, therefore, is the contractual approach; it was ushered in by the decision of the Employment Appeal Tribunal in *Sheffield v Oxford Controls Company Ltd*,[48] where a director with a service agreement who had been threatened with dismissal if he did not resign was held not to have been dismissed because he had made an agreement about the terms on which he would resign; that is to say, an agreed resignation was treated as a bilateral termination and hence not a dismissal.

In the leading case of *Birch v University of Liverpool*,[49] the same approach was applied, with the same outcome, to a termination of employment which took place under the employing entity university's 'premature

---

[47] [1975] ICR 87 (QBD). (At that period the QBD functioned as the appellate court from industrial tribunals on unfair dismissal issues; previously that had been a function of the National Industrial Relations Court, subsequently it became a function of the Employment Appeal Tribunal.)   [48] [1979] ICR 396 (EAT).
[49] [1985] ICR 470 (CA).

retirement compensation scheme' whereby employees were invited to apply for early retirement on the basis that they would receive special compensation if the employing entity certified that it was 'in the managerial interest' for them to retire under that scheme. Such terminations are frequently described as 'voluntary redundancy', and may be regarded as ones where, in an underlying sense at least, the termination is initiated by the employing entity. Subsequent case law has broadly maintained this contractual approach, concentrating on the question of whether contractual consent to termination was vitiated or negated by duress.[50] The emergent distinction between 'agreed resignation' and 'forced resignation'[51] seems to lie squarely within that approach.

The policy implications of this shift from a causational approach to a contractual one are of very great interest. Essentially, the contractual approach is more conducive than the causational approach towards the recognition of termination as bilateral rather than unilateral by the employing entity. That is because it is in the form of a contract that the conception of bilateral termination seems real, acceptable, and convincing; the contract is the very embodiment and expression of a joint arrangement voluntarily undertaken by both parties. The fact that the terminatory transaction fulfils the requirements for a contract seems to legitimate and validate its analysis as bilateral termination, and the negation of unilateral termination by the employing entity.

However, if the contractual analysis is to be allowed that legitimating effect, it is important to consider whether it exerts a suitably stringent control upon the notion of bilateral termination. There are reasons for doubting whether it does so. The test of consideration is a purely formal one, as any agreement for the termination of an existing contract under which obligations are outstanding on both sides can in and of itself be regarded as a mutual discharge of those obligations for good consideration on both sides; this is the essence of the common law notion of the termination of a contract by 'accord and satisfaction'. The termination of a personal employment contract fits very readily into that construction even if the worker receives no compensation for the loss of expectations of job security. Moreover, the theoretical requirement of genuineness of consent may not be a very stringent one; the common law approach to negation of consent on the ground of duress or undue influence or inequality of bargaining power is a cautious one.

The foregoing argument might appear to suggest that the courts have found it expedient to adopt a formalistic rationale for what is in reality a simple preference for a narrow view of what should count as dismissal by the employing entity. However, that would be a superficial conclusion.

---

[50] For example, *Logan Salton v Durham County Council* [1989] IRLR 99 (EAT).
[51] As drawn, for example, in *Jones v Mid-Glamorgan County Council* [1997] IRLR 685 (CA).

Something more profound is involved here. Janet Gaymer has perceptively observed that the courts seem, sometimes at least, to view themselves as dealing with workers who should be regarded as having, to an extent which is novel and not allowed for in the received wisdom of the law of the contract of employment, a genuine freedom of contract with regard to the termination of their employment. These are workers who are:

demanding, mobile and self-reliant. They are high on human capital and low on loyalty. These types of workers are well able to understand and cope with the type of mutuality and free consent to the agreement by which employment is terminated and to which all three judges in *Birch v University of Liverpool* referred.[52]

There are major questions as to how far this should be allowed to become the dominant paradigm for the analysis of the termination of personal employment contracts, and as to how far that paradigm should apply to contracting about statutory rights associated with the termination of personal employment contracts. These questions will be carried through into the remaining aspects of the discussion of bilateral termination in the next two subsections.

C. BILATERAL TERMINATION UNDER A PRE-TERMINATION AGREEMENT

It was suggested earlier in this section that the system of analysis of termination which we have put forward indicated the theoretical possibility of a surprisingly large category of cases where the termination of contractual employment might be regarded as the bilateral result of a pre-termination agreement, rather than as the unilateral action either of the worker or, even more significantly in practice, of the employing entity. In other words, we identified a potentially large category of automatic bilateral termination as the result of prior agreement. It was noted, however, that, although this analysis could in theory be extended to all instances of contract-compliant or lawful termination, it was in practice regarded as inapplicable to a wide range of contract-compliant terminations, so that it was not in practice suggested, for example, that termination by notice or termination in response to repudiatory breach or to a defined offence should be regarded as bilateral merely because provision was made for it integrally within the personal employment contract in question.

That left, and leaves, the problem of how the law of personal employment contracts distinguishes between, on the one hand, bilateral termination under a pre-termination agreement, and, on the other hand, unilateral but contract-compliant termination by either party. Despite the fundamental theoretical importance of this problem, and its not inconsiderable practical significance, it is a problem which remains to a surprising extent unresolved.

---

[52] Gaymer, 2001, para 14–051.

In this subsection, we suggest a principle which serves to explain most of the legislation and case law which bears upon this issue; but we also expose and explore the difficulties which undoubtedly remain.

Most of the legislation and case law can be explained in terms of a principle which asserts that contract-compliant termination is to be regarded as *unilateral* if it requires an action or determination by one of the parties which is distinct from the stipulation for duration which is integrally part of the personal employment contract, but that otherwise, in other words *if no such distinct action or determination by one of the parties is required,* a contract-compliant termination is to be regarded as *bilateral,* in that it results from a pre-termination agreement. This principle quite easily explains and resolves why the major forms of contract-compliant termination are regarded as unilateral rather than bilateral; termination by notice, or termination in response to repudiatory breach or a defined offence require a distinct action or determination by one or other party; one or other party has to fix the date of termination, and that actual calendar date cannot be regarded as having been previously specified by the personal employment contract in question.

However, this principle is less precise and easy to apply than it might at first appear to be; and even to the extent that it is precise and easy to apply, it leaves open a surprisingly large terrain for bilateral termination by pre-termination agreement. Our suggested principle has, by elimination, identified this area of bilateral termination by prior agreement as that in which termination can be regarded as the *automatic* or *self-executing* outcome of provision for termination which is integrally part of the personal employment contract, whether by inclusion in its original formation or as the result of subsequent variation. We proceed to consider the main situations which might be so regarded, in order to see how far they have in fact been so regarded.

We can distinguish, not always easily, between two forms of automatic or self-executing provision for automatic termination in the above sense; these are (1) the form in which termination is pre-specified as an actual calendar date (the date-specific form), and (2) the form in which termination is pre-specified as an event which identifies itself as occurring on an actual calendar date without the need for action or decision on the part of either party to make that identification (the event-specific form). The first form would usually be referred to as that of the fixed-term contract, though it is important to realize that the two concepts or terminologies do not necessarily completely coincide. It is useful to consider the application of each of those two categories to actual situations.

There are many terminations of personal employment contracts which might be regarded as the bilateral result of the application of pre-termination agreements in date-specific form. This might include many or all the occurrences which would ordinarily be described as the expiry of a fixed-term contract or of the fixed term of a contract. It might also include 'retirement' under the common, though far from universal, form of contractual provision for 'retirement' as an event stipulated to occur on the worker reaching a certain age. It is useful to concentrate the discussion upon the occurrences usually described as expiry of a fixed-term contract.

In earlier chapters, the expiry of fixed-term contracts has been presented as a form of unilateral termination by the employing entity; but it is important to realize that it can equally well, or perhaps even better, be regarded as a form of bilateral termination. The perception that it *ought* to be regarded in that way is expressed, as we have observed, in the commonly held view or intuition that expiry of a fixed-term contract does not constitute dismissal by the employing entity. This tension between these two ways of categorizing the expiry of fixed-term contracts would cause enormous practical difficulty, had it not been addressed by legislation in the main area of practical contention. That is to say, the main statutory definitions of dismissal for the purpose of employment protection at once recognize that the expiry of fixed-term contracts would probably not be regarded as dismissal as a matter of common law, and at the same time expressly include it within the statutory definition of dismissal.

So far so good, except for some problems about whether a contract with a date-specific termination provision counts as a 'fixed-term contract' for statutory purposes when there is also provision for prior termination by notice.[53] The matter becomes far more difficult when we turn to provisions for termination in the event-specific form. For here we find that such terminations may fall outside both the common law notion of unilateral termination, and also the statutory notion of dismissal, in that they do not count as expiry of a fixed-term contract in the statutory sense. It is this area which, we suggest, is of surprising potential width and whose boundaries are surpassingly ill-defined.

It is, nevertheless, a difficult area, because it seems to constitute a conceptual space within which the employing entity may so arrange an engagement for employment that a termination of employment which would normally be regarded as within the constraints which the law places upon dismissal may be free of those constraints. In *Ryan v Shipboard Maintenance Ltd*,[54] it was held, in relation to a worker in the trade of ship repairing who was engaged on a 'job-by-job basis', to work on the execution of ship repairing contracts undertaken by the employing entity which lasted for varying periods from one to eleven weeks, that the termination of his personal employment contract on the conclusion of each such contract did not constitute a dismissal, either at common law or by counting as the

---

[53] In *Dixon v BBC* [1979] ICR 281 (CA) it was held that a contract might count as being 'for a fixed term' within the meaning of the unfair dismissal legislation if it was to end on a stated date although it was terminable by notice before that date. (Contrast *BBC v Ioannou* [1975] ICR 262 (CA).) See above, 302.   [54] [1980] ICR 88 (EAT).

expiry of a fixed-term contract in the statutory sense. The Employment Appeal Tribunal accepted that there had been, in the terminology used by Lord Denning MR in the earlier decision of *Wiltshire County Council v NATFHE*,[55] a 'discharge by performance' rather than a dismissal; the 'discharge by performance' corresponds to the notion of bilateral termination by prior agreement in the system of analysis which we have adopted.

The same analysis was held, in the case of *Ironmonger v Movefield Ltd*,[56] to apply to the rather similar[57] case of a clerk of works engaged by an employment agency for the duration of a building project which was being carried out by a corporate client of the agency. In each of these cases, which were regarded as self-terminating task contract cases, it may be questioned whether the termination was genuinely automatic, to the extent that in each case the employing entity presumably had to determine or agree to a determination that the job or project in question had been completed and that the worker would therefore not be further needed, and had to communicate that decision to the worker. It might be argued that, in each of those two cases, the completion of the task was judged not by the employing entity but by its contractual client, so that the same analysis might not be applicable where the employing entity engaged the worker for a project of its own, of the completion of which it was the sole judge; the ending of contractual employment in that event might still be treated as a unilateral dismissal by the employing entity.

Even more difficult in the foregoing sense, because taken on facts even more resembling the ordinary case where the employing entity is viewed as unilaterally fixing or determining the date of ending of employment, was the decision in the 'soft-funding-dependent' case of *Brown v Knowsley Borough Council*.[58] This concerned the employment of a teacher, whose contract of employment stipulated that the appointment would last 'only as long as sufficient funds are provided either by the Manpower Services Commission or by other firms/sponsors to fund it'. It was held that the ending of this employment, on the basis that no funding was available to support it, was to be regarded as having occurred automatically when the MSC ceased to make payments, rather than as a dismissal by the employing entity. Yet it was clearly the case that this supposedly automatic effect would occur only as and when the employing entity decided that there was no funding available to be allocated to this employment after a given date.

---

[55] [1980] ICR 455 (CA). In that case, the termination was held to count as the expiry of a fixed-term contract in the statutory sense, because the duration of the contract in question was judged to be specified by date—the end of the academic year—rather than by event—the completion of the courses which the worker was teaching, the date of which was not predetermined.   [56] [1988] IRLR 461 (EAT).

[57] Though different to the extent that, by reason of the triangular nature of the arrangement between the agency worker and client company, the worker was held not to have a contract of employment with the agency (or the client company). See above, 44.

[58] [1986] IRLR 102 (EAT).

Most difficult of all in the foregoing sense is the kind of case where the
personal employment contract purports to provide in advance for its own
demise in the event of a stated non-performance or shortcoming in
performance on the part of the worker, thus attempting to ensure that the
employing entity's disciplinary sanction of termination of employment will
take effect in a self-executing manner and that the employing entity will not
be regarded as having effected a dismissal, but rather that termination will
be regarded as the bilateral outcome of the originally agreed terminatory
provision. Striking off down a different track from that of 'self-dismissal',
counsel for the employing entity successfully contended for this analysis in
the case of *British Leyland (UK) Ltd v Ashraf*,[59] where employment was
ended in reliance on a self-executing termination provision upon the
worker's failure to return to work at the end of a period of leave of absence.

The subsequent decision of the Court of Appeal in the leading case of
Igbo v Johnson Matthey Chemicals Ltd[60] is sometimes regarded as having
decided that a termination of employment on such a basis should be
construed as a unilateral termination, and therefore a dismissal, rather than
as a bilateral termination under the pre-termination agreement. Yet the
Court of Appeal arrived at that result only by the conceptually indirect
route of applying the statutory provision against contractual exclusion of
unfair dismissal rights so as to render the pre-termination agreement void
and of no effect. Had it not been for that statutory provision, the pre-
termination agreement would have been valid, and we suggest that the
Court of Appeal might have regarded the termination as a bilateral one by
reason of that pre-termination agreement. Their decision does not preclude
that approach. On that view, the category of bilateral termination as the
result of pre-termination agreements remains a conceptually open one. In
the concluding subsection, we consider more generally the complex relation
between bilateral termination and the statutory anti-exclusion provisions.

D. BILATERAL TERMINATION AND THE EXCLUSION OF
    STATUTORY RIGHTS

The decision of the Court of Appeal in the *Igbo* case seemed on the face of
it to provide an elegant and workable solution to the problem of whether
self-executing or automatic pre-termination agreements were to be regarded
as negating statutory claims arising upon dismissal. It seemed straightforward to say that, whether or not such an agreement actually meant that the
ending of employment did not amount to dismissal, the agreement would
in any case not stand in the way of a claim of unfair dismissal, because it
could be regarded as an attempt to contract out of the statutory obligations
which are consequent upon dismissal, and such purported contracting out
is rendered void by the provisions which the legislation makes against its

[59] [1978] ICR 979 (EAT).   [60] [1986] ICR 505 (CA).

own exclusion. That solution seemed particularly compelling when, as in the *Igbo* case itself, the agreement for automatic termination had been engrafted onto the contract of employment subsequently to the original formation of that contract.

However, this apparently elegant solution was an evasive one. It left difficulties unresolved both at a logical and at a practical level. In this subsection, it will be sought to address those logical and practical difficulties, and also to suggest that those difficulties raise questions at a general level about the proper role of the law of personal employment contracts and the proper task of those engaged in fashioning it. Those issues arise in relation both to pre-termination agreements and *ad hoc* termination agreements. We proceed to consider them in relation to both kinds of agreement in turn.

The logical difficulty about the approach taken in the *Igbo* case to pre-termination agreements for automatic termination is that if the agreement is taken seriously, that is to say accorded its intended effect, it gives rise to bilateral termination and there is no dismissal. Therefore, the pre-termination agreement, viewed as such, does not amount to an exclusion or limitation on the operation of the statutory provisions which confer rights upon workers who are dismissed; for it is instead an agreement which ensures that the statutory provisions have no application at all to the termination of employment which results from such an agreement. It follows that the only logically satisfactory basis for applying the anti-exclusion provisions to such agreements is that such agreements attempt to present what are really unilateral terminations by the employing entity as if they were bilateral terminations. The *Igbo* decision logically amounts to treating the pre-termination agreement as giving rise to a dismissal rather than to a bilateral termination, without admitting that this is the conclusion of its own reasoning.

The practical difficulty about the approach thus taken in the *Igbo* case is that it therefore accords unilateral effect to a pre-termination agreement without spelling out why that particular pre-termination agreement has been singled out for that treatment. In other cases, such as those of the 'task contracts' which were the subjects of the decisions in the *Ryan* case and the *Ironmonger* case, the pre-termination agreement was accorded bilateral effect, and was not seen as being subject to the anti-exclusion provisions of the legislation; the court in those cases simply took the view that there was no dismissal in the statutory sense. At the moment we lack any way of knowing in which of those two ways an event-specific automatic pre-termination agreement should be treated. Suppose that a personal employment contract provided for its automatic termination in the event that the worker failed to meet a stated performance target. The ending of that employment in the event of that failure would probably be regarded as a dismissal by the employing entity, as in *Igbo*, rather than as a bilateral termination, as in *Ryan* or *Ironmonger*; but the reasoning in *Igbo* has sidestepped the difficulty of making that crucial distinction.

A very comparable set of difficulties presents itself, under the *Igbo* approach, in the treatment of *ad hoc* termination agreements. Again, there are two conflicting alternative analyses of the effect of *ad hoc* termination agreements upon statutory claims based upon dismissal, and the *Igbo* approach leaves it uncertain which of them applies in any given case. In order to understand this problem it is useful to consider the way in which the statutory anti-exclusion provisions are framed.[61] They render any provisions in an agreement void so far as they purport to exclude or limit the operation of a relevant statutory provision or to preclude a person from bringing employment tribunal proceedings under a relevant statutory provision; but they allow exceptions for agreements to refrain from instituting or continuing proceedings either where, in effect, the agreement has been made under the ACAS conciliation procedure or where it satisfies the conditions for a statutory compromise agreement, conditions designed primarily to protect the worker from ill-advised action. That whole set of requirements is clearly intended to apply and does apply to post-termination agreements where, *ex hypothesi*, the agreement relates to a termination which has taken place and so is independent of the termination itself.

The position is much more difficult in relation to *ad hoc* termination agreements, that is to say to agreements which themselves provide for termination of a contractual employment (which has not previously been brought about by a pre-termination agreement). Here, as with pre-termination agreements, strict logic suggests that it is necessary to decide, before we know whether the statutory anti-exclusion requirements are applicable, whether the agreement has succeeded in effecting a bilateral termination. If it has, then the employment has terminated without dismissal and the statutory anti-exclusion requirements should be seen as logically inapplicable. If the agreement has not brought about a bilateral termination, there must have been a dismissal, and then the question is whether the agreement has fulfilled the statutory requirements for valid post-termination agreements. However, in at least one case, that of *Sutherland v Network Appliance Ltd*,[62] the Employment Appeal Tribunal seems, rather as was done in the *Igbo* case for pre-termination agreements, to have regarded the statutory anti-exclusion provisions and conditions as applying to a termination agreement, without deciding whether that agreement had given rise, on the one hand, to bilateral termination or, on the other hand, to dismissal.

On the other hand, we have seen that there are a whole succession of cases, culminating in *Birch v University of Liverpool*, in which the courts have accepted *ad hoc* termination agreements as bringing about bilateral termination, and as therefore ending the employment in question without

---

[61] The provisions are currently contained in the Employment Rights Act 1996, s 203 (as subsequently amended).
[62] [2001] IRLR 12 (EAT).

dismissal; and in those cases it does not seem to have been suggested that the statutory anti-exclusion provisions come into play. Indeed, in the *Logan Salton*[63] case the Employment Appeal Tribunal expressly distinguished *Igbo* and ruled that the statutory anti-exclusion provisions did not apply to the termination agreement which was under consideration in the case before them, because that was freely entered into by the worker without duress.

Hence, rather as with pre-termination agreements, we have an emergent conflict between 'true' *ad hoc* termination agreements to which the anti-exclusion provisions do not apply, and 'false' *ad hoc* termination agreements to which the anti-exclusion provisions do apply. However, because of the way in which the *Igbo* approach sidesteps the problem of classification of the contractual termination as either bilateral or unilateral, we have, equally as in the case of pre-termination agreements, no clear way of distinguishing between 'true' and 'false' termination agreements. Yet this is a matter of the utmost consequence; it may be that the policy underlying the anti-exclusion provisions is fully respected only if those provisions are applied to *all* termination agreements, or it may be that the policy of the legislation is fully implemented even if *some* termination agreements are not subjected to the anti-exclusion requirements. It is vital to have an answer to that question, and, if it is the latter answer, a way of making the distinction which it evokes.

Underlying this very difficult technical discussion is a more profound question about the relation between the law of personal employment contracts and the body of employment legislation which is constructed around or upon it. The question may be put as one of the technology of employment legislation; does it make for good legislation when the framers of the legislation rely upon the law of personal employment contracts to resolve technical and policy difficulties? Or the question may be put, the other way round, as one of whether it is the role of those fashioning the law of personal employment contracts to ensure that it can bear the burden of statutory functionality? And if so, is it possible to maintain a coherent law of personal employment contracts when those demands are so diverse and complex? The foregoing discussion seeks to encourage a positive response, despite all the evident difficulties, at least to the latter two questions and perhaps to the first one. Further discussion of the remaining categories of termination and transformation will indicate whether that is over-optimistic.

SECTION 4: NON-LATERAL TERMINATION

In this section, the establishment of a systematic set of categories for the termination of personal employment contracts is completed by describing

---

[63] *Logan Salton v Durham County Council* [1989] IRLR 99 (EAT); see above, 431.

a category of non-lateral termination, that is to say termination which is not attributable to either party. The main constituent of that category is termination by or as the result of frustration. Termination by frustration has had an important role in the modern law of personal employment contracts, and its development in case law is particularly important to the understanding of the role of the law of personal employment contracts *vis-à-vis* the statute law of employment protection. That topic and that set of issues are considered in a first subsection (A); and in a further subsection (B) it is then considered whether there are other kinds or instances of non-lateral termination which might be described as termination by operation of law.

A. Termination by or as the Result of Frustration

In the previous section, it was seen that the category of bilateral termination of personal employment contracts has a crucial instrumental function in the interpretation of employment protection legislation which attaches rights or claims to dismissal by the employing entity; this function is that of negating the characterization of a termination as a dismissal by providing an explanation of the termination as not being the unilateral action of the employing entity, but instead the joint or bilateral action of both parties. That same instrumental role is also played by a body of law, mainly consisting of the law of termination by or as the result of frustration, but also perhaps comprising a further distinct notion of termination by operation of law, which treats personal employment contracts as having been automatically terminated by occurrences which are not regarded as the fault of either party, or which are regarded as in some sense quite external to the contract or to the volition of the parties to the contract.

It is terminations coming from that body of law which are designated, in the system of categories of termination of personal employment contracts which is being put forward in this work, as non-lateral terminations, that is to say ones which are attributable to neither party acting either jointly or severally. Within the law of personal employment contracts, there have been a number of significant instances, especially in the modern or recent period of the development of this body of law, where occurrences such as the long-term illness or incapacitation of the worker, or the imprisonment of the worker under a custodial sentence, or the calling up of the worker for, or absence of the worker on, military service, have been regarded as constituting or giving rise to this kind of termination. It is possible that we could regard other occurrences as giving rise to termination on the same basis, such as the death of the worker, or the death of the employing entity if that consists of a human being, or the dissolution or liquidation of a corporate or quasi-corporate employing entity.

As with the category of bilateral termination, the practical importance of the category of non-lateral termination is its difference from that of unilateral termination by the employing entity; its contentious edge is with that latter category. The distinction between bilateral termination and non-lateral termination is not of great contentious significance, and indeed it could well be argued that it is not a very important or robust theoretical distinction. It could be doubted whether regarding an automatic termination as the work of *neither* party is different in a theoretically important way from regarding it as the work of *both parties* acting jointly. On either footing, the termination is in some sense the outcome of the contract which both parties have made. In other words, in one sense, we could possibly explain any non-unilateral termination as the bilateral result of a pre-termination agreement, in the way that some forms of automatic termination were explained in the previous section.

However, it still seems useful to recognize non-lateral termination as a category which is distinct from that of bilateral termination. Even if it is not conceptually absolutely necessary to do so, even if, indeed, the distinction is an elusive and at times a flimsy one, nevertheless it has important explanatory force in accounting for the way in which the law of termination of personal employment contracts has in fact developed, particularly in its modern period. For the perception on the part of the judges that a body of doctrine, the law of frustration in particular, identifies a mode of termination which is genuinely exogenous to the contract and to the volition of the parties, has encouraged them to account for the ending of employment as not involving dismissal, much more readily and extensively than they might otherwise have done. We proceed to examine the case law in which that kind of development has occurred; its main locations have been in the areas of absence of the worker as the result of illness or of imprisonment. Both those topics are prominent in the post-1965 case law concerning the issue of dismissal in the context of the redundancy payments and unfair dismissal legislation. We consider illness first, beginning with the pre-1965 case law in which the issue, of whether and in what way a personal employment contract was terminated by or as the result of the illness of the worker, arose almost entirely in a straightforwardly common law remedial context.

In the original version of the present work, the present author was disposed to regard some post-1965 cases, decided in the context of employment protection legislation, which had held contracts of employment to have been terminated by frustration resulting from the illness or incapacitation of the employee, as being in a direct line of descent from a number of much earlier decisions which seemed to articulate a notion of frustration of contract by reason of illness or incapacity. A different view is now suggested; from longer hindsight it is now argued that the post-1965 cases are highly specific to the context of employment protection legislation, and should be regarded differently from the pre-1965 case law.

There are indeed many pre-1965 decisions in which it is held or opined that the employing entity may be entitled to treat a personal work contract as ended by reason of the incapacitating illness of the worker, although that involves no fault or breach of contract on the part of the worker.[64] Those decisions and opinions relate both to employees and to semi-dependent workers without any self-conscious distinction between those two categories.[65] It is true that in *Jackson v Union Marine Insurance Co*[66] Bramwell B spoke of a master as free to hire a fresh servant if the original servant's illness 'would put an end, in a business sense, to their business engagement and would frustrate the object of that engagement'—and that this dictum was one of the foundations of the development of the doctrine of frustration.

However, in those cases the concern was generally with whether or not the employing entity had dismissed the worker *wrongfully* by reason of incapacitating illness, rather than with the question of whether the employing entity had dismissed the worker *at all*. The decisions and opinions which held that the worker had not been wrongfully dismissed generally seemed to reflect the view that the employing entity had a right of dismissal by reason of incapacity, or that the contract was impliedly constructed so as to come to an end by reason of incapacity. It is perfectly within the orthodoxy of the law of personal employment contracts to regard the contract as conferring upon the employing entity a right to terminate in the event of incapacitating illness, or even to regard the contract as providing for its own automatic termination in that event, without that event having to involve fault or breach of contract on the part of the worker.[67]

By the mid-1960s, it is probably the case that some such right of dismissal by reason of incapacity, or some such provision for the employing entity to invoke automatic termination in the event of incapacity, was implied into some personal employment contracts. Nevertheless, the case law also suggested that the courts were cautious about implying such terms. If the engagement was for a substantial fixed term, it might well be held that the risk of incapacity of the worker was to be borne by the employing entity;[68] if, on the other hand, the employment was for an indefinite period terminable upon notice, it might well be held that the employing entity's risk was sufficiently limited by the capacity to give notice.[69] The implication of such provisions for immediate dismissal or automatic termination by reason of incapacity seems even less likely at the present day, especially when employing entities are required by statute to give employees particulars of any terms and conditions relating to incapacity for

---

[64] See Freedland 1976 at 303–307.

[65] Thus the key decision in *Poussard v Speirs* (1876) 1 QBD 410 concerned the engagement of an opera singer, whom it would be hard to classify as between an employee or a semi-dependent worker—compare Freedland 1976 at 305.   [66] (1874) LR 10 CP 125 at 145.

[67] It is, we suggest, precisely in that latter sense that Lord Denning MR in *London Transport Executive v Clarke* speaks of *Poussard v Speirs* as an example of 'discharge by incapacity'—see [1981] ICR 355 at 362D.

[68] As in *Loates v Maple* (1903) 88 LT 288 (KBD) (engagement of a jockey for three years) and *Storey v Fulham Steel Works* (1907) 23 TLR 306 (KBD), 24 TLR 89 (CA) (engagement of a works manager for five years).   [69] As in *Carr v Hadrill* (1875) 39 JP 246 (QBD).

work due to sickness or injury[70] and so would normally be unable to claim such an implication if such a provision had not been specified in statutory particulars.

However, from the mid-1960s onwards, the courts hearing appeals from industrial tribunals began, when adjudicating upon whether there had been dismissal for the purpose of claims to statutory employment rights associated with dismissal, to deploy a rather different notion of genuinely non-lateral termination, to the effect that a worker on prolonged sickness absence whose employment was formally ended by the employing entity and who claimed to have been dismissed by the employing entity might be met by the argument that there was no dismissal because the contractual employment had been ended by frustration at some prior point.[71]

In the latest such case to date, that of *Sharp & Co Ltd v McMillan*,[72] the Employment Appeal Tribunal expressly recognized that the notion of frustration which was being invoked in such cases was the modern one, identified by Lord Radcliffe in *Davis Contractors Ltd v Fareham Urban District Council*,[73] which was not dependent on the imposition of a term upon the contract but instead a direct judicial construction to the effect that an extraneous event had rendered the contract impossible of performance as originally contemplated. In the view of the Employment Appeal Tribunal, if this gave rise to an implied term in any sense, it was a term implied by law rather than a term agreed by the parties, so that the frustration could not be attributed to a 'provision in an agreement' which might be rendered void by the anti-exclusion provisions of the employment protection legislation.[74] That is to say, because of its juridical nature as non-lateral termination, termination by frustration was seen as being beyond the reach of the approach taken in the *Igbo* case, as we saw in the previous section,[75] whereby the statutory anti-exclusion provisions were viewed as applicable to *express* arrangements for automatic termination in the event of prolonged absence of the worker without leave.

It is indeed in relation to statutory but contract-based employment protection rights that the modern case law on frustration by incapacitating illness needs to be understood. On the one hand, the decisions in which incapacitating illness is seen as having given rise to frustration seem to be cases where the court has strongly felt that it would be inappropriate for a worker who has been on long-term sickness absence to enjoy statutory

---

[70] ERA 1996, s 1(4)(d)(ii).

[71] Thus the Divisional Court in *Jones v Wagon Repairs Ltd* (1968) 3 ITR 361, the EAT in *Egg Stores (Stamford Hill) Ltd v Leibovici* [1977] ICR 260, and, similarly, the Court of Appeal on appeal from the County Court in *Notcutt v Universal Equipment Co (London) Ltd* [1986] ICR 414.

[72] [1998] IRLR 632 (EAT—sitting in Scotland, but expressly basing its decision on law common to England and Scotland).   [73] [1956] AC 696 (HL) at 729.

[74] Lord Johnston, [1998] IRLR 632 at 634 para 18.   [75] See above, 436.

employment rights intended for those who are fully contractually employed in the ordinary sense, such as the right to statutory redundancy payment,[76] or to payment during a statutory minimum period of notice.[77]

On the other hand, a number of cases, in which the doctrine of termination by frustration has been regarded as inapplicable, on the facts, to actually or potentially incapacitating illness, can be seen as reflecting a concern that the doctrine should not be allowed to provide employing entities with an artificial escape route from statutory obligations or claims intended to apply where, in substance and reality, it is the employing entity which brings the contractual employment to an end. The decisions in *Marshall v Harland & Wolff Ltd*,[78] *Harman v Flexible Lamps Ltd*,[79] *Converform (Darwen) Ltd v Bell*,[80] and *Williams v Watsons Luxury Coaches Ltd*[81] all seem in varying degrees to be designed to ensure a suitable sphere of application for employment protection legislation in that sense.

In the face of those conflicting instrumentalities, it is not surprising that it has proved difficult for the courts and tribunals to articulate a consistent body of principles to decide whether and when the doctrine of frustration will apply to pre-empt and negate dismissal in cases of incapacitating illness on the part of the worker. For example, the attempt in *Harman v Flexible Lamps*, in response to one set of policy perceptions about statutory employment protection rights, to confine frustration to long fixed-term contracts not terminable by notice, broke down under a contrary policy perception about statutory employment protection rights in the *Notcutt* case, where the Court of Appeal saw no reason why frustration should not apply to contracts of employment determinable by short or relatively short notice.[82]

In fact, it is suggested that there are systemic reasons why this case law is, and is likely to remain, incoherent. In general, the law of personal employment contracts tends to lose its practical and theoretical coherence if it is pushed and pulled hither and yon by the instrumentalities of adjudication upon employment protection legislation. More particularly, there are both conceptual and practical difficulties about trying to systematize the application of the doctrine of frustration to a frequently recurring fact situation such as the incapacitation of the worker by illness. For it becomes an exercise in regularising the application of a legal mechanism which is in its nature conceived of as irregular, or trying to predict that which is meant by definition to be unpredictable.

[76] As in the *Jones v Wagon Repairs* and *Egg Stores v Leibovici* cases.
[77] As in the *Notcutt* and *McMillan* cases; see n 71 and n 72 above.
[78] [1972] ICR 101 (NIRC).   [79] [1980] IRLR 418 (EAT).
[80] [1981] IRLR 195 (EAT).   [81] [1990] ICR 536 (EAT).
[82] [1986] IRLR 414 (CA) at 420B. (The introduction by Dillon LJ of a distinctive notion of 'periodic' contracts is, it is suggested, misleading; the significant distinction is between, on the one hand, contracts for a short or medium fixed term and/or terminable by short or medium-length notice, and, on the other hand, contracts for a long fixed term and/or terminable only on long notice; compare above, 313.)

There is every reason why the law of personal employment contracts should be called upon to provide a clear account of the implied contractual rights and obligations which apply when a worker is incapacitated by illness, and to define the situation of the worker who is, by reason of illness, in the sort of contractual limbo which we have discussed earlier in this work as a question of 'suspension', or in terms of the transition from the employment state or mode of personal employment contracts to the sub-employment mode or the post-employment mode. We could be optimistic about the capacity of the law of personal employment contracts satisfactorily to fulfil those functions, even if it does not at the moment fully do so. However, for the reasons just given, it is unlikely that the doctrine of frustration would provide the means of doing so, especially when its development in the context of personal employment contracts has been a somewhat artificial one, driven by the policy pressures of adjudication in the context of employment protection legislation.

The law of frustration has proved to be at least equally problematical in the case law arising in the context of employment protection legislation which has been concerned with the terminatory effects upon personal employment contracts of a sentence of imprisonment (or other custodial sentence) affecting the worker. From the coming into effect of unfair dismissal legislation in 1972, an issue has frequently presented itself of whether, when an employing entity treats a contractual employment as being at an end by reason of the imprisonment of the worker, that counts as a dismissal, or whether, on the other hand, the employing entity may claim that there has been no dismissal but instead a termination by or as the result of frustration. Initially the law seemed straightforward, but subsequently great practical and theoretical problems have presented themselves.

The role and extent of frustration has been even more problematical in this area than in relation to the incapacitating illness of the worker, largely because, whereas incapacitating illness cannot normally be attributed to the fault of the worker, the imprisonment of the worker can normally be regarded as the result of fault on his or her part, even if that fault is not in and of itself a breach of contract—for example, because the offence attracting the custodial sentence was not in any way work-related. Once there is an element of fault involved, the operation of the doctrine of frustration becomes essentially problematical.

In the early days of unfair dismissal litigation, the position was perceived as being straightforward. In *Hare v Murphy Brothers Ltd*,[83] the Court of Appeal held that the passing of a sentence of twelve months' imprisonment upon an employee had in and of itself brought his contract of employment to an end so that the employing entity's refusal to allow him to resume employment after his release did not count as a dismissal. Lord Denning

---

[83] [1974] ICR 603 (CA).

MR held that being sentenced to imprisonment did not involve a breach or repudiation of contract on the part of the worker, but was instead a frustrating event, even if that could be said to be self-induced on the part of the worker. Stephenson and Lawton LJJ preferred the terminology of termination by or as the result of impossibility of performance; all were agreed that the sentence had brought about an automatic termination.

In subsequent unfair dismissal cases, such as *Harrington v Kent County Council*[84] and *Chakki v United Yeast Co Ltd*,[85] the Employment Appeal Tribunal began to find it difficult both in principle and as a matter of practical adjudication to decide whether and at what point of time it was appropriate to treat a custodial sentence as having a frustrating effect. Should that, for example, depend on the length of the sentence, or on whether there was the prospect of a successful appeal against conviction or sentence? However, a much more deep-seated theoretical difficulty began to present itself. As it became clear, in the early 1980s, that termination by the employing entity in response to the worker's repudiatory breach of contract would be regarded as a dismissal by the employing entity, and would not be regarded as an automatic bilateral termination or a self-dismissal or unilateral termination by the worker,[86] there was seen to be a perverse divergence, in the unfair dismissal context in particular, between the effect of a custodial sentence regarded as a repudiation of the personal employment contract by the worker, and the same event regarded as a frustration of contract. If it was the former, the employing entity's ending of the employment counted as a dismissal; whereas if it was the latter there was no dismissal.

In the context of common law remedies alone that distinction did not matter very much, indeed was not very evident, for if the matter was viewed as dismissal, that dismissal would certainly have been regarded as a lawful or contract-compliant one. However, in the very different context of unfair dismissal law it made the vital difference between whether an industrial tribunal had jurisdiction to consider unfair dismissal or not. In *Norris v Southampton City Council*[87] the Employment Appeal Tribunal ruled that attracting a custodial sentence must be regarded as repudiatory conduct on the part of the worker rather than as an external frustrating occurrence, so that the ending of the contractual employment which was consequent upon it must be regarded as dismissal (albeit fair dismissal) rather than as automatic termination not effected by the employing entity. However, in *Shepherd & Co Ltd v Jerrom*,[88] where a trainee worker after 21 months of a four-year apprenticeship received a custodial sentence for offences of violence and the employing entity decided to treat the apprenticeship as

---

[84] [1980] IRLR 353 (EAT).   [85] [1982] ICR 140 (EAT).

[86] This emerged, in particular, from the decision of the Court of Appeal in *London Transport Executive v Clarke* [1981] ICR 355.   [87] [1982] ICR 177 (EAT).

[88] [1986] ICR 802 (CA).

ended, the Court of Appeal, on the basis of extremely elaborate theoretical reasoning, decided that the contract had been terminated by frustration brought about by the imposition of the custodial sentence, so that the employing entity's decision to treat the apprenticeship as at an end was not to be regarded as a dismissal. In particular, it was decided that the theoretical objection to 'self-induced frustration' did not amount to the proposition that an occurrence attributable to the fault of a party could not amount to frustration at all, but only to the lesser proposition that such an occurrence could not be invoked as frustration by the party at fault—in this case the apprentice, so that the other party, the employing entity, could invoke frustration to negate dismissal.

However formidably justified by theoretical reasoning, this decision suffers from the defects which are apt to attend upon a particular kind of instrumental reasoning in the law of personal employment contracts. As Mustill LJ acknowledged, indeed asserted:

The problem in this case arises from the co-existence in employment law of two barely consistent regimes: the general principles of contract developed by the common law, and the superimposed system created by the statutory law of unfair dismissal. The result has been that the parties have advanced in argument propositions founded on the common law from standpoints diametrically opposed to those which would have been taken up if this had been an action for wrongful dismissal in the County Court.[89]

In a real sense this decision seems designed to cure that inconsistency by ensuring that the unfair dismissal litigation has the same outcome as the wrongful dismissal litigation would have had, namely the rejection of a claim for compensation on the part of the worker. Suitable though that outcome might be, it would perhaps be preferable for the adjudication of it to take place within the law about fairness of dismissal and remedies for unfair dismissal, rather than in this form of contractual pre-emption.

However, despite that evaluation it remains the case that the doctrine of frustration is to be regarded as having a significant, albeit somewhat uncertain, role in bringing about or explaining the automatic non-lateral termination of personal employment contracts by reason of incapacitating illness or the passing of a custodial sentence upon the worker. The doctrine of frustration seems, according to earlier case law, also to apply (perhaps in the form of an implied term as to impossibility of performance) to situations in which the worker goes or is conscripted into military service in wartime, as in *Marshall v Glanvill*,[90] or is interned, as in *Unger v Preston Corporation*.[91] It also merges into a possibly larger notion of automatic termination by operation of law, which will be considered in the next subsection. The existence of a potentially large and certainly rather

---

[89] Ibid at para 32.   [90] [1917] 2 KB 87 (KBD).   [91] [1942] All ER 200 (KBD).

open-ended notion of automatic termination by reason of frustration makes it important to consider how, precisely, this mode of termination works and how it impacts upon the mutual obligations of employing entities and workers.

The mode of operation and the effect of termination by frustration have not been perceived as particularly controversial. In all such situations where the doctrine of frustration does so operate, it seems to effect a termination of the personal employment contract in the sense which our theory of termination of such contracts identifies as the standard one, that is to say it involves the transition of the contract from its employment mode to its post-employment mode in which employment obligations have ceased to apply but in which post-employment obligations such as those of confidentiality may survive. The analysis offered in the original edition of this work[92] asserting the entitlement of the worker to remuneration in respect of service rendered before frustration, whether as a matter of common law[93] or under the provisions of the Law Reform (Frustrated Contracts) Act 1943,[94] seems still to hold good.

If that understanding of the mode of operation and effects of termination by frustration seems a relatively straightforward one, that may reflect an underestimate of the complexities and interdependency of the obligations, both substantive and procedural, of the modern personal employment contract. Thus, at the substantive level, there are very important issues as to how far termination by frustration may deprive the worker of benefits under work-related benefit or insurance schemes which predicate those benefits upon a continuation of contractual employment. In *Villella v MFI Furniture Centres Ltd*,[95] there was an issue as to whether the employing entity could plead the termination of the claimant's contract of employment by frustration, on the ground of incapacitating illness, as a basis for eventually ceasing to pay benefits under the permanent health insurance scheme which the employing entity provided. It was held that the existence of the scheme connoted, in and of itself, a foresight of and provision for long-term incapacity which precluded the application of the doctrine of frustration to that event; but the issue would be a very real one if the frustration occurred on some other, less obviously foreseen, ground.

Moreover, there is a major issue as to whether termination by frustration does and should deprive the worker of the procedural protections which the personal employment contract would otherwise attach to the termination

---

[92] See Freedland 1976 at 326–328.

[93] Where the law seems to be as laid down in *Stubbs v Holywell Railway Co* (1867) LR 2 Ex 311 in the case of the death of the worker in the course of a fixed-term service contract.

[94] Under which remuneration for service rendered before frustration but which has not accrued due by the time of the frustrating event may be the subject of a statutory *quantum meruit* claim under s 1(3) of the 1943 Act; the agreed rate of remuneration would seem to be the primary determinant of the amount of such a claim but might not be the definitive determinant.   [95] [1999] IRLR 468 (QBD).

of contractual employment. That becomes a more significant issue with the recent statutory attachment of general procedural obligations to the termination of contracts of employment by the provisions of the Employment Act 2002, which, it was argued in an earlier chapter, could be seen as the instantiation of an underlying contractual duty of dispute resolution on the termination of employment.[96] Termination by frustration does present the possibility of a sidestepping of those obligations. This is an issue upon which we may focus more clearly by proceeding to consider, in the next subsection, whether termination by frustration should be regarded as part of a larger category of non-lateral termination consisting of termination by operation of law.

B. TERMINATION BY OPERATION OF LAW AS THE RESULT OF WORKER-RELATED OCCURRENCES

As indicated in the previous subsection, in order to establish the full scope and extent of the category of non-lateral termination of personal employment contracts, it is necessary to recognize that it extends beyond the category of frustration in a narrow or strict sense into a wider area of termination by operation of law in which the notion of frustration merges into and is extended by related but distinguishable notions such as that of supervening illegality, thus giving rise to a more general idea of non-lateral or automatic termination by or as the result of legal or factual impossibility of performance as originally contemplated by the contract. That category is of regrettably uncertain scope and effect; in considering its extensions beyond the category of frustration it is useful to distinguish between occurrences primarily relating to the worker (worker-related occurrences) and occurrences primarily related to the employing entity (employing-entity-related occurrences).

We begin by referring to worker-related occurrences, and by considering the particular ways in which the larger notion of termination by operation of law may extend into worker-related occurrences not clearly or satisfactorily regarded as amounting to frustration. If the outline conception of frustration is that of impossibility of performance of the contract as originally contemplated, we saw in the previous subsection that this conception is further limited, though to a rather uncertain extent, by the requirements that the occurrence in question be unforeseen in, or unprovided for by, the contract, and that it should not be attributable to or consisting in the fault or default of a party to the contract. The wider looser notion of termination by operation of law seems to permit a relaxation of some or all of those requirements. It will be useful to consider, as instantiations of that wider notion, the occurrences of the loss of requisite legal basis for the employment of the particular worker, and the death of the worker.

---

[96] See above, 344–345.

A class or group of situations can be clearly discerned where a personal employment contract will be held to have been automatically terminated by operation of law upon the disappearance of the statutory or other regulatory basis, or essential conditions, for the employment of the worker in question, although that disappearance would not easily or naturally be regarded as a frustrating event. We might regard in that light the automatic termination of an employment which may be held to occur upon the abolition of the statutory or other public office on which the employment was based, as for instance in the case of *Reilly v R.*[97] However, such situations are more usefully considered as raising issues about the special nature of the particular employment relationship than as raising issues about termination.

A situation falling squarely within the ambit of discussion of this particular mode of termination, and also as perfectly illustrating the importance of that discussion, is that of the disappearance of the essential regulatory conditions for the continuation of the employment in question occurring when the particular worker is personally deprived of a regulatory licence to work in the occupation in question. Just such an automatic termination was held by the House of Lords to have occurred in the highly significant case of *Tarnesby v Kensington Chelsea and Westminster Area Health Authority*[98] upon the suspension of a hospital doctor's registration for disciplinary reasons, where, and because, the applicable legislation provided that no unregistered doctor should hold an appointment as a hospital medical officer.

The case demonstrates the potential width of the category of termination by operation of law, and also, and by the same token, its capacity to cut across the whole structure of provision made by the personal employment contract for the procedural and substantive protection of the job security of the worker in question. This may be appreciated by reference to the fact that, while it had apparently been uncontroversial for a very long time that a doctor's contract of employment would be terminated by his or her being struck off the medical register, ie permanently de-registered, it had been supposed that the introduction of the lesser penalty of suspension from the register was not necessarily destructive of the doctor's contract of employment. The decision, that the suspension from the register, although temporary, did completely destroy the basis for the continuation of contractual employment, cut right across express contractual provision for the doctor suspended from the register to be suspended from duty without pay but to continue in contractual employment. Lord Bridge accepted or asserted that the inexorable logic of termination by operation of law was to render that provision void,[99] not least by reason of the supervening illegality of continuing the contractual employment. This is a broader and deeper cut

---

[97] [1934] AC 176 (PC).   [98] [1981] ICR 615 (HL).
[99] [1981] ICR 615 at 621F–G.

into express provision than could be made under the doctrine of frustration in its narrow sense.

It is useful to include, in the discussion of the category of termination by operation of law arising out of worker-related occurrences, some consideration of the topic of the death of the worker, not because it is a complicated topic but rather because of an extremely significant set of theoretical contrasts between that topic and the apparently symmetrical one of the death of the employing entity where that is a human being. There is no indication that it has at any stage been regarded as controversial in the history of the law of personal employment contracts that such a contract is automatically terminated by or upon the death of the worker. Given that the contract is regarded as personal to the worker, and given the ordinary sense of termination of the contract as the ending of the employment state or mode of the contract, it could not logically be otherwise—though it is quite consistent with that to say that there are real issues about the extent to which remuneration has accrued due, the subject of controversy at least from the great case of *Cutter v Powell*[100] onwards.

We can therefore say that the death of the worker during the currency of employment under a personal employment contract results in a termination by operation of law in a clear and strict sense. There is a non-lateral termination in the sense that the mutual obligations of employment automatically come to an end (though post-employment obligations[101] may survive as between the personal representatives of the worker and the employing entity); that termination is based upon factual and legal impossibility because the contract is personal to the worker. We go on to suggest that the analysis may not be precisely symmetrical in the case of the death of a human employing entity, and that this possible asymmetry of legal analysis is of great theoretical and practical importance in understanding the effect upon personal employment contracts of certain occurrences relating to the corporate or quasi-corporate employing entity, such as the winding-up of a company or the dissolution of a partnership.

C. Termination by Operation of Law Resulting from Occurrences Related to the Employing Entity

In this subsection it will be considered whether and when personal employment contracts can be regarded as terminated by operation of law by or as the result of a series of occurrences relating to the employing entity which remove or otherwise seriously entrench upon the capacity of the employing entity to maintain or continue the contractual employment as previously constituted. These occurrences range from the case of the death

---

[100] (1795) 6 TR 320; see above, 201–202.

[101] For example obligations of pension maintenance on the part of the employing entity, and quite conceivably obligations of confidentiality on the part of the personal representatives.

of a single human employing entity to the winding-up of a company or the dissolution of a partnership, or a personal bankruptcy or corporate insolvency; and there is even a sense in which the sale or other transfer of the business or the relevant part of the business of the employing entity might be regarded as part of this set of occurrences.

In relation to this set of employing-entity-related occurrences, an argument will be presented to the effect that, although there might appear to be a clear notion of termination by operation of law resulting from some at least of those occurrences, the notion of termination by operation of law actually has very little bearing upon those occurrences. It will be argued that in fact, apart from the death of a single human employing entity or a member of a partnership, this set of occurrences is approached in quite a different set of ways which relate back to earlier discussion about unilateral termination of personal employment contracts, and which also relate forward to discussion later in this work about the personal transformation and transfer of those contracts.

This argument takes its starting point from the occurrence which, of all of these, appears to be the most straightforward and compelling one for the application of termination by operation of law, namely that of the death of the human employing entity. The absence of a clear and systematic doctrine of termination by operation of law resulting from employing-entity-related occurrences starts to reveal itself even in the apparently straightforward case of the death of the single human employing entity. It is generally held that the death of the single human employing entity does result in an automatic termination of the personal employment contract, which is seen as involving no default or breach of contract. That view can indeed be based upon early authority in which that conclusion is seen to follow logically from the personal nature of the contract, as much on the side of the employing entity as on that of the worker. Thus the pronouncement of Willes J in *Farrow v Wilson* (1869) that:

Generally speaking contracts bind the executor or administrator, although not named. Where, however, personal considerations are the foundation of the contract, as in cases of principal and agent and master and servant, the death of either party puts an end to the relation.[102]

However, it has not always been uncontroversial whether personal considerations are the foundation of the contract in the requisite sense. We can say that this is systematically the case so far as the worker is concerned, since we have defined the personal employment contract as having that identifying attribute.[103] But it is of the greatest importance to recall that this is not necessarily or axiomatically the case so far as the employing entity is concerned. It is very much the exception today that the employing entity

---

[102] (1869) LR 4 CP 744 (CP) at 746.   [103] See above, 28.

consists of a single human being actually carrying out the functions of employing in person. Where that is not the case, we suggest that the personality of the employing entity should not necessarily be viewed as foundational to the contract.[104]

Thus, in the very significant case of *Graves v Cohen*,[105] Wright J clearly regarded it as *arguable* that the contractual employment of a jockey had *not* been automatically terminated by the death of the racehorse owner by whom he was employed. It was held that the contractual employment was in fact so terminated, because the personality of the owner was material to the employment, despite the fact that the business of running the racehorses was left to a trainer, in that the choice of horses and of races was a matter for the owner. This leaves open the possibility that a contractual employment where there was continuity of management before and after the death of the human employing entity might be regarded as continuing, on the footing that the personal representatives have assumed the contractual role of employing entity.

In a sense that possibility of continuation was actually realized, though on a rather different footing, in the important though rather curious decision in the case of *Phillips v Alhambra Palace Co.*[106] Here, where the issue was whether the surviving members of a partnership which owned and ran a theatre could plead the death of an inactive or 'sleeping' partner[106a] as a basis for avoiding liability under a personal employment contract with a troupe of actors, the no-fault constituent for termination by operation of law on the death of the partner was clearly present, but the impossibility constituent was regarded as not being present; the contract was simply regarded as continuing to bind the surviving partners, so that the shortly subsequent (and partly at least consequential) ending of the contractual employment in question by closing down the theatre was viewed as wrongful on their part.[107]

So in that case, the personality of the deceased partner was not regarded as in any way essential to the contract. If it were so regarded, which we should assume it typically would be, we might expect the contract to be treated as automatically terminated by operation of law upon that death, without breach of contract, as, normally, upon the death of a single human employing entity. We might also expect that, in the normal case where the personality of the human employing entity or member of an employing

---

[104] This view is advanced subject to discussion of the doctrine in *Nokes v Doncaster Amalgamated Collieries* which does tend to identify the personality of the employing entity as systematically foundational to the contract, even where the employing entity is a legal corporation rather than a human being. For that discussion, see below at 493.

[105] (1930) 46 TLR 121 (KBD).   [106] [1901] 1 QB 59.

[106a] In the sense that he did not have day-to-day employment functions (though he was a significant investor in and guarantor of the financial stability of the enterprise).

[107] And, unusually, also as *ineffective*, so that the actors seem to have recovered remuneration for projected performances on the basis that they had presented themselves as ready and willing to perform.

partnership was regarded as essential to the contract, the complete incapacitation of the person concerned might be expected to have the same automatically terminatory effect on a non-lateral basis.

However, the decision in *Phillips v Alhambra Palace*, although it is an exceptional one in viewing the personality of a human constituent of the employing entity as non-essential, reinforces the realization that, even in the case of the death of a human employer or member of an employing partnership, the analysis of an employing-entity-related occurrence, of the kinds listed earlier, in terms of *impossibility* of continuance of contractual employment, is not necessarily a compelling one. That is because, upon these occurrences, there is usually if not invariably a surrogate employing entity which can *possibly* be regarded as in some sense continuing the contractual employment—in the case of a single human employer, that person's personal representatives, and in the case of the death of a member of an employing partnership, the surviving partners. We suggest that, outside the particular category of death of a human employer or member of an employing partnership, the two general conditions for termination by operation of law, those of impossibility and lack of fault or default, are rarely if ever perceived as fulfilled by the employing-entity-related occurrences which we have listed, so that those occurrences are rarely if ever analysed as giving rise to that kind of termination. The law of personal employment contracts does not seem to have a doctrine of non-lateral, non-fault termination by corporate or quasi-corporate demise or incapacitation, in the way that it does have for the death or incapacitation of the human employer. In the sense in which we are using it, there is a theory of termination by operation of law for human death and illness, but there does not seem to be a corresponding doctrine for corporate or quasi-corporate death or illness.

This is a matter of the greatest theoretical and practical importance, not only in itself, but because it implies that some different analysis of the effect of those occurrences upon personal employment contracts is applicable. The matter is a highly complex one, but the following general analysis is tentatively advanced as the best way of understanding an intricate body of law. Apart from the case of the death of a human employer, or, probably, of a member of an employing partnership, the employing-entity-related occurrences which we have listed are normally and primarily seen as constituting or threatening an actual or imminent cessation of or radical alteration in the contractual employment in question. This is normally and primarily regarded as an immediate or anticipatory repudiation of the personal employment contract on the part of the employing entity, and as resulting in a unilateral and wrongful termination of the personal employment contract by the employing entity.

This analysis works quite well as an account of the underlying effect which is accorded to the employing-entity-related occurrences which we have listed.[108] It is very clearly instantiated by the treatment which was accorded to the compulsory winding-up of the employing company in *Measures Bros Ltd v Measures*,[109] and, much more recently, to the dissolution of an employing partnership in *Briggs v Oates*.[110] In each case, the contractual employment was regarded as wrongfully terminated by the employing entity with the particular consequence, under the doctrine in *General Billposting v Atkinson*,[111] that the wrongful repudiation by the employing entity freed the workers of their obligations under express covenants against post-employment competitive activity.

However, the matter does not end there; the analysis is by no means as simple as that, as a consideration of the case law and statute law concerning the effect upon personal employment contracts of occurrences such as the voluntary winding-up of the employing company, or the appointment of a receiver to the company, quickly reveals. That is because the primary analysis of the occurrence in question as both wrongful repudiation and wrongful unilateral termination by the employing entity may be altered or negated by reference to the fact that the employment in question continues after and despite the occurrence, in a way which might be able to be regarded as a continuation of the *contractual* employment under the original personal employment contract, albeit in a changed situation or circumstance. Thus, there is judicial authority holding that the continuation of employment by a liquidator following a resolution for the voluntary winding-up of the employing entity company,[112] or by a receiver and manager appointed out of court by secured creditors,[113] may count as continuation of existing personal employment contracts, thus denying any terminatory effect, wrongful or otherwise, to the resolution for voluntary winding-up or the appointment of the receiver and manager.

The analysis of when and in what circumstances, and upon what precise conceptual basis, contractual employment may be treated as continuing, so as to negate the primary terminatory effect of the listed occurrences, is a very difficult one, in both theoretical and practical terms. However, that set of questions is rather separate from our present inquiry about whether and when the listed occurrences bring about a termination by operation of law. Whether the occurrences result in a unilateral termination of the personal

---

[108] The present writer expressed the view, in the original work, that a different underlying effect, that of lawful termination by notice, might be accorded to an order for the compulsory winding-up of a company, on the authority of the decision of Chitty J in *MacDowall's Case (Re Oriental Bank Corporation Ltd)* (1886) 32 Ch 366 (ChD). The present writer is now of the view that this may not be the right reading of that decision, and that in any event the decision may be specific to a different treatment of compulsory winding-up in the company law of that time. Compare below, 502.   [109] [1910] 2 ChD 248 (CA).

[110] [1990] ICR 473 (ChD).   [111] [1909] AC 118 (HL)—see above, 391–392.

[112] *Gerard v Worth of Paris Ltd* [1936] 2 All ER 905, Slesser LJ at 907–909.

[113] *Re Foster Clark Ltd's Indenture Trusts* [1966] 1 WLR 125 (ChD) at 123B–G, Plowman J; *Re Mack Trucks (Great Britain) Ltd* [1967] 1 WLR 780 at 786C E, Pennycuick J.

employment contract, or whether the contractual employment is treated as continuing, it remains the case that the listed occurrences are not in general treated as bringing about a non-lateral termination by operation of law.

That proposition at once concludes the present stage and introduces the next stage of our general analysis of the termination and transformation of personal employment contracts. It concludes the present stage because our analysis of the termination of personal employment contracts is, in and of itself, complete. It introduces the next stage because the questions which it opens up, about the conditions in which personal employment contracts will be treated as continuing despite the employing-entity-related occurrences under discussion, can be answered only by developing a more exact account of the law concerning the transformation and transfer of personal employment contracts. The next chapter seeks to provide that account. Meanwhile we draw some brief conclusions from the present chapter.

CONCLUSION

This chapter has been one in which it has been possible to deploy the method of restatement more in the form of doctrinal clarification than in the form of prescriptive reformulation. Its main aim was to propose a general theory of termination and transformation which would constitute a systematic treatment of all the different outcomes or destinations which a personal work or employment contract might have. It was explained that a number of different or competing discourses or vocabularies obscured the formulation of a clear and comprehensive account of termination and transformation, and it was suggested that a single theoretical scheme of termination and transformation was needed to override those divergences and inconsistencies. Quite a lot of the ground had been covered by the discussion in earlier chapters of the areas of variation and termination by the employing enterprise, but it was important to place those outcomes in the larger context of termination and transformation as a whole. Thus, variation was identified as one of a number of possible transformations of which the others were suspension and change of parties (partial or total). Termination by the employing enterprise was located within the area of unilateral termination, which might be effected either by the employing enterprise or by the worker, and it was established that termination might otherwise be bilateral or non-lateral. In order to sustain this schematic treatment, a notion of the existence and identity of personal work or employment contracts was explored which related back to the discussion of contractual continuity of employment in an earlier chapter.

The main claim for this treatment of termination and transformation was that it provided a comprehensive and systematic overview of the whole area; but it also provided the basis or context for some theoretical explorations of certain particular areas or themes which seemed to merit fuller treatment than they usually receive. Thus, for example, it was suggested that there was an important somewhat under-explored question of allocation between unilateral termination by the employing entity, on the one hand, and by the worker, on the other, the analysis of which could help to explain the role and significance of conceptions such as those of 'constructive dismissal' and 'self-dismissal' which have been prominent, in varying degrees, in the history of interpretation of legislation providing contract-based employment rights and obligations. Thus also, by way of further example, it seemed useful to develop quite fully a notion of the distinction between bilateral termination by *ad hoc* agreement and by prior or pre-termination agreement. Finally, by way of yet further example, it seemed important, with regard to non-lateral termination, to try somewhat to resolve the difficult distinction between termination under the doctrine of frustration and termination by operation of law more generally.

Another incidental claim for this schematic treatment of termination and transformation was its capacity to establish a common discourse for the termination and transformation of personal work or employment contracts of all sorts, semi-dependent workers' contracts as well as contracts of employment. That was because it presented a set of categories or concepts which were neutral or non-specific as between those two contract types, unlike terminologies such as those of 'dismissal' or 'retirement' which are strongly associated with the narrower category of the contract of employment as such. That kind of terminological harmonization across the whole area of personal work or employment contracts is of no small significance and utility. However, it is also important not to exaggerate the possibilities of ironing out all the difficulties and inconsistencies in the law of termination and transformation of those contracts. Some major and troublesome issues concerning various kinds of transformation remain to be discussed in the next chapter, the final one in this sequence of five which are concerned with termination and transformation.

9

Transformation and Transfer

INTRODUCTION

In the previous chapter, a general theory of the evolution of personal employment contracts was presented which depicted all the evolutionary developments in personal employment contracts after their initial formation as falling either into the category of termination or into that of transformation. The discussion of the category of termination was completed by recapitulating upon the subcategories previously considered and surveying those not previously considered. In this chapter, the substantive part of this book is completed by carrying out the same exercise for the category of transformation.

The first section considers the topic of transformation, and its relation to those of formation and termination, in terms of an underlying notion of the elasticity of the personal employment contract. That discussion elaborates upon the idea of a set of different types or dimensions of transformation which was introduced in the previous chapter. Subsequent sections provide extended discussion of the particular dimensions of transformation not previously considered in this work, namely those of (1) change of mode, or suspension, and (2) change of parties to the personal employment contract. That discussion concludes by considering the specially complex and interesting topic of transfer of contracts under the TUPE Regulations. Themes of general interest emerge which contribute to the Conclusion of the present work.

SECTION 1: TRANSFORMATION, TERMINATION, AND THE ELASTICITY OF THE PERSONAL EMPLOYMENT CONTRACT

In this section we elaborate further upon the notion of the transformation of personal employment contracts as presented in the previous chapter. We relate the notion of transformation to that of termination, by reference to a general idea of the *elasticity* of the personal employment contract, which also bears upon the topics of the definition and content of the personal employment contract as discussed in the earlier parts of this book.

The purpose and design of this chapter, as indicated above, is to complete a survey, which attempts to be a systematic one, of the ways in which personal employment contracts may evolve from their initial formation, by considering those developments in the state of the contract which may be regarded as transformations rather than as termination. We saw in the previous chapter that the contrast between transformation and termination is in many ways a difficult one, even at a basic conceptual level. For example, the termination of the personal employment contract, in the sense in which we identified the normal usage of that term, is itself a particular kind of transformation, that is to say from the employment state or mode to the post-employment state or mode.

However, we managed to establish a meaningful and important contrast between termination and transformation; and, at some significant points in our account of the law and theory of termination of personal employment contracts, it became apparent that the termination of the contract could best be understood, perhaps could only really be understood, in relation to or in contradistinction from its transformation. For example, that became very evident in the course of the discussion of whether employing-entity-related occurrences such as the winding-up of the employing company terminated the personal employment contract. It was necessary to adjourn that discussion so that it could be completed by considering whether those occurrences should be regarded as transforming the contract rather than as terminating it. So the discussion of transformation of personal employment contracts assumes an importance, not simply for its own intrinsic interest, but because of the light it throws upon another major aspect of the law of personal employment contracts, namely that of termination.

We also suggest that the discussion of transformation of personal employment contracts has further ramifications, and in particular that it has interconnections with other aspects of the law of personal employment contracts, in fact ultimately with many or all of the aspects of definition, formation, structure, and content considered in the early part of this work. Those interconnections, and hence the significance of the topic of transformation as a completion of the theory of personal employment contracts, can better be understood in terms of a notion of the *elasticity* of personal employment contracts, which we proceed to set forth and explain.

There have been very many points in the course of this work where we have sought to specify aspects of the law of personal employment contracts by considering the elasticity or accommodatingness of its key concepts. We have in other words sought to understand those concepts by considering how much room for manoeuvre they provide or how far they can be stretched. Questions were often posed in this form in the course of establishing the identifying attributes of personal employment contracts. This would sometimes be in order to distinguish between different types of personal employment contract, for example to distinguish between the contract of employment and the semi-dependent worker's contract, though that distinction has been argued in this work to be an unsatisfactory one to the point of being illusory. Much more important, therefore, was the posing of questions about the elasticity or accommodatingness of key concepts in order to establish whether and when a personal employment *relationship* qualified as a personal employment *contract*.

A good example is to be found in the notion of a minimum degree of mutuality of obligation, which we have seen constitutes an identifying attribute and fundamental requirement of a valid personal employment contract (with the complicating factor that a *higher* minimum degree of mutuality of obligation seems, in some respects at least, to be requisite for a contract of employment than for a semi-dependent worker's contract). We have seen that the notion of mutuality of obligation includes among other things the idea of a degree of commitment on the worker's part to carrying out the work in question personally rather than by substituting other people or subcontracting with other people.

Yet *some* degree of substitutability is treated as compatible with the existence of a personal employment contract (and apparently a greater degree of substitutability is compatible with the existence of a semi-dependent worker's contract than with that of a contract of employment). So we have to assess the elasticity or accommodatingness of the notion of mutual obligation, in the aspect of substitutability, in order to know when a valid personal employment contract exists (and if so what type of personal employment contract it is).

An arrangement which would stretch that concept beyond its breaking point would not count as a personal employment contract at all. It might count as some other kind of contract entirely—a contract for services which was not a personal employment contract.[1] Or it might simply constitute a sub-contractual relationship, in the form perhaps of an understanding between an employing entity and a group of workers that the employing entity might enter into a personal employment contract with the particular worker put forward by the group on a particular occasion.

We have also treated many issues concerning the *content* of personal employment contracts as questions of the elasticity of the key concepts which govern or prescribe that content, and therefore enable us to distinguish between what counts as performance of the personal employment contract, or contract-compliant conduct, and what counts as non-contract-compliant conduct or breach of contract or repudiation of the obligations of the contract. Thus we often have to establish the precise content of a particular personal employment contract by testing the elasticity of some of its key implied obligations such as that of co-operation, or of loyalty or of trust and confidence. Moreover, because those key implied obligations are defining attributes of personal employment contracts (or particular types of personal

---

[1] Such is the case, for example, of the contract between the Post Office and the sub-postmaster or sub-postmistress, if deemed not to be a personal employment contract as in *Sheehan v Post Office Counters Ltd* [1999] ICR 734. See above, 26.

employment contract), there is a real sense in which such discussions are establishing the elasticity, not just of particular terms of the contract, but of the contract itself as a whole concept.

When we pose such questions about the elasticity of the personal employment contract in terms of its definition, or its formation, or its content, we are in a certain sense considering the contract in the abstract as a bundle of norms or the undertaking of a bundle of obligations. We may equally, on the other hand, find ourselves testing the elasticity of the personal contract of employment, that is to say the accommodatingness of its key defining concepts, not in that way, but rather by assessing the effect of events occurring during the evolution of the contractual employment concerned. In particular, we frequently do this by differentiating between the effect of such events, as constituting either, on the one hand, a termination or, on the other hand, a transformation of the personal employment contract in question.

This point may be illustrated or instantiated by looking at any of the various dimensions of transformation which we identified in the previous chapter, that is to say those of (1) change of content, (2) change of mode, (3) change of duration, and (4) change of parties—though in some of those cases the point will be much less obvious or easily understood than in other cases. A clear case is that of change of content. In the earlier discussion of variation of the terms of personal employment contracts, we confronted the questions, on the one hand, of whether and when imposed unilateral variation amounted to wrongful terminatory repudiation of the contract, and, on the other hand, of whether and when bilaterally agreed variation amounted to the termination of one contract and its replacement by another. In each case, there is a question whether to regard the personal employment contract as, on the one hand, *terminated* or as, on the other hand, merely *transformed* by the actual or attempted variation in its content.

The answer to that question depends, to some extent at least, upon what the identifying basic or foundational content of the contract is judged to be, such that actual or attempted change to that basic content constitutes a termination or threatened termination of the contract as a whole. So the issue of whether the occurrence in question—the agreed or imposed change of content—amounts to termination or transformation is resolved by considering how elastic we regard the core identifying content of the contract as being. The more elastic it is, in other words the more scope there is held to be for variation of content *within the contract*, the less it will be the case that the occurrence is seen as terminating the contract.

Moreover, and this is a critical point, the reasoning may well, and often does, go in the reverse direction. By deciding upon the effect of the occurrence in question, and in particular whether it is terminatory of the contract or merely transformative of it, courts or tribunals often define, by implication, some crucial aspect of their conception of the personal employment contract, or identify, in some crucial dimension, what elasticity they judge the personal employment contract to possess. A very major instance of this consists in the development of the notion of constructive dismissal, that is to say of a conception of conduct on the part of the employing entity amounting to wrongful repudiation and wrongful termination, although it does not consist of a direct or outright ending of the contractual employment. By identifying such a category of terminatory conduct, the courts and tribunals are, in effect, deciding what they judge the foundational content of the personal employment contract to be, and how much elasticity they attribute to that foundational content.

In a variety of complex ways, this kind of interplay of ideas goes on throughout the development of the law concerning the termination and transformation of personal employment contracts. In developing a series of notions of transformative rather than terminatory occurrences in the evolution of personal employment contracts, courts and tribunals (and occasionally legislators) at once draw upon and contribute to a developing conception of the nature and definition of the personal employment contract and of the degree of elasticity which it possesses in its various dimensions. In relation to some of those dimensions, those of change of content, and change of duration, sufficient discussion has taken place in earlier chapters.[2] However, with regard to two of those dimensions, that of change of mode, or suspension, and that of change of party, or transfer, further extended discussion is needed. In the next section of this chapter, the analysis of transformative occurrences which has been offered above will be applied to various situations which are or might suitably be regarded as situations of change of mode, or suspension. Most though not all of that application of transformation theory to situations of suspension will follow from discussion which has taken place in earlier chapters.

With regard to the dimension of change of or to the parties to the contract, the matter is more complex, and there is extensive new ground remaining to be covered. It is, however, in this dimension that the discussion of the transformation of the personal employment contract, and of the elasticity which that connotes, becomes most interesting of all. For here we come across ways in which, by treating some employing-entity-related occurrences, such as for instance the appointment of a receiver and manager to the employing company, as merely transformative of the personal employment contract rather than as terminatory of it, the courts and legislators actually impart a high degree of elasticity to their conception of the employing entity party to the contract. This is a development of the utmost theoretical and practical significance, with which the third section of the chapter is concerned.

---

[2] Compare above, as to content, Chapter 5, as to duration, 400, 405.

That discussion leads on to a yet more complex kind of transformation which the personal employment contract may undergo. This is the transformation which takes place when a contract of employment is transferred, under the TUPE Regulations, from the employing entity transferor to the employing entity transferee of a business or undertaking. When this occurs, it brings about a transformation of the contract of employment which may take place in more than one dimension. Thus, the contract is transformed in the obvious, though nonetheless extremely important, respect that one employing entity is replaced by another.

Moreover, because of the effect which the courts have accorded to the legislation, the contract as transferred may differ in *further* respects from the contract as it was before the transfer. Its elasticity, especially the elasticity of its content, may have been crucially altered; this may also have changed the rules for its eventual termination. This is a phenomenon of daunting complexity, but also of transcendent interest for the theory of the law of personal employment contracts more generally. The concluding section of the chapter seeks to analyse those complexities and to identify their larger implications for this work as a whole.

SECTION 2: SUSPENSION

A. THE IDEA OF CONTRACTUAL SUSPENSION

In this section we consider a centrally important transformation which personal employment contracts may undergo, namely that of change of mode, or suspension. In an initial subsection we seek to define or specify this notion of contractual suspension as precisely as possible, and to identify the exact contractual status of suspension and the mechanisms by which it may be effected. In subsequent subsections that notion is applied to a number of situations or events which may occur during the evolution of personal employment contracts and which are or could be regarded as involving contractual suspension.

The notion of contractual suspension often seems a highly obscure one. All kinds of terminologies are used in the ordinary discourse of employment relations, and in the technical discourse of employment law which refer in different ways to the notion of suspension. Sometimes it is said that a personal employment contract is suspended, sometimes that employment is suspended, and sometimes that the worker is suspended. There may be said to be suspension with pay or without pay. During periods of time regarded as periods of suspension, sometimes the personal employment contract will be regarded as being in force, sometimes it will be regarded as having terminated. Terminologies which hint at the idea of suspension may nevertheless be equivocal as to whether contractual employment continues or whether it has ended, such as 'lay-off' or 'being on strike'.

It is of the greatest importance that the law of personal employment contracts should provide a clear analysis of the meaning of contractual suspension, and a clear account of when it is lawful, in the sense of being in compliance with the personal employment contract, or wrongful in the sense of being out of compliance, and indeed of how it relates to notions such as that of repudiatory breach of contract. It is important for several reasons: firstly because many of the contractual rights and obligations of workers and employing entities crucially turn upon the notion of contractual suspension; secondly because many statutory rights and obligations are constructed around notions or conceptions of contractual suspension; and thirdly because a clear notion of contractual suspension is an essential building block, one of the keystones indeed, in the construction of a rigorous and robust analysis of the law of personal employment contracts as a whole.

It should be acknowledged from the outset that the attempt to provide that clear analysis cannot hope to be wholly successful. The phenomena or materials which form the subject of that analysis, that is to say the legal judgments and legal enactments which make up the law concerning contractual suspension, are too complex, too much extended over diverse historical, social, and economic contexts, and too internally inconsistent, to be fashioned into a fully logical system. It is another case where we offer something which tries to be the 'best fit', knowing that it will not be a complete fit. Nevertheless, the general theory of termination and transformation of personal employment contracts which was presented in the previous chapter does turn out to be of some real assistance in defining and understanding contractual suspension. This is the case in two main respects.

Firstly, the basic definition or conception of contractual suspension which formed part of that general theory operates quite well to explain or clarify the legal treatment of many situations normally described or regarded as constituting suspension. That is to say, most of those situations can be successfully analysed according to an idea of contractual suspension, as the transformation of the personal employment contract from the mode or state of contractual employment into the mode of being between periods of contractual employment, or sub-employment mode. Essential to this idea is the notion that the personal employment contract is transformed but not terminated when it moves into this sub-employment mode. Termination occurs only when there is a further or different move into post-employment mode, at which stage the personal employment contract is regarded as being at an end although it may still give rise to certain post-employment obligations.

The defining feature of contractual suspension, according to that idea, is that, while that situation obtains, there is, on the one hand, no current set of obligations for the exchanging of work and remuneration, such as would denote that the contract is in full employment mode, but there is, on the other hand, some degree of obligation of future resumption of contractual employment so that the personal employment contract has not terminated. So the notion of contractual suspension has two quite different boundaries or contentious edges. On one side, it has an interface with the situation when the contract is in full employment mode, when the state of full or current contractual employment obtains; we are often called upon to distinguish between those two situations, and it is often contentious as to which of them is regarded as obtaining. On the other side, contractual suspension has a quite different interface with the situation where the personal employment contract is regarded as having terminated (that is, as having gone into post-employment mode). Here again, it is often at least as difficult as on the other interface to decide which situation obtains.

To that extent, and in a way which it is hoped will become clear when we turn to consider particular instances of contractual suspension, the general theory of termination and transformation produces a way of understanding what is meant by contractual suspension. That general theory is also helpful in analysing when and in what sense contractual suspension should be regarded as lawful or wrongful, contract-compliant or non-contract compliant. That is to say, it is useful to think of contractual suspension as being effected in a set of ways, or by a set of legal mechanisms, which are similar to or parallel with the ways and mechanisms by which contractual termination is effected.

This means to say as follows. Our general theory of termination and transformation argues that termination of the personal employment contract may be effected either unilaterally, bilaterally, or non-laterally. If it is effected unilaterally, that may be attributed either to the employing entity or to the worker; and it may either be lawful in the sense of being contract-compliant or wrongful in the sense of being non-contract-compliant. If it is effected bilaterally, that may be by prior agreement integrated into the personal employment contract or it may be by *ad hoc* agreement. It is useful to regard contractual suspension as being effected according to the same set of alternatives, and as also being either lawful or wrongful in the above sense.

We can therefore use our general theory of termination to examine the main instances where employment is or might be regarded as suspended, firstly, in order to ascertain whether those situations are really ones of contractual suspension as we have defined and understood that notion, and, secondly, to ascertain whether that suspension is lawful or wrongful, that is to say whether it is contract-compliant or not. It would be possible to split these situations into groups, according, for example, as to whether they are more employing-entity-related or worker-related, but that might be misleading, and offers no great analytical advantage, so we simply list them as (1) disciplinary, precautionary, or appellate suspension, (2) lay-off without pay or suspension for managerial reasons, (3) suspension in the context of industrial action, (4) suspension during sickness or incapacity, and (5) suspension with pay and 'garden leave'. We proceed to consider them in that order, seeking in the course of so doing both to analyse each situation and if possible to produce refinements and clarifications of the idea of contractual suspension as we have so far outlined it.

B. Disciplinary, Precautionary, or Appellate Suspension

In this subsection we group together three situations which may arise in the course of disciplinary action or dismissal proceedings on the part of the employing entity, and which are, or should be regarded as being, in the nature of suspension. The first situation, normally known as that of disciplinary suspension, is that in which the employment of the worker is discontinued for a specified period, normally but not necessarily without pay, as a disciplinary sanction against the worker, on the basis that employment will be resumed at the end of that period. The second situation, also regarded as suspension and not always clearly distinguished from the first situation, is that in which the employment of the worker is discontinued, normally though not necessarily with pay, pending the investigation of a complaint against the worker or of a concern about the worker, on the basis that employment will be resumed after due investigation unless other action is decided to be necessary. We have styled this as precautionary suspension. The third situation is that in which it has been decided to dismiss a worker but an appeal is pending against that dismissal which, if successful, will or may entitle the worker to a resumption of employment. That situation seems to lack a name, but we suggest that it should be regarded as a form of suspension, though not necessarily of *contractual* suspension. We have accordingly styled it as appellate suspension. The contractual analysis of each situation will be considered in turn.

1. Disciplinary Suspension

Despite the extensive occurrence of this situation in practice, and the fact that it is the subject of a certain amount of case law, the contractual analysis of disciplinary suspension is not wholly clear. We suggest that the most coherent analysis of such suspension, and the one which probably best fits the case law, is that disciplinary suspension is normally a true form of contractual suspension as we have defined it, that is to say one in which the personal employment contract subsists in sub-employment mode during the suspension. That view is supported by some older case law, such as the decision in *Hanley v Pease & Partners Ltd* where Lush J spoke of 'suspending' as meaning refusing to pay the employee for a given day without dismissing him, and electing to treat the contract as a continuing one (something which they had no right to do in this case).[3] Rowlatt J referred to 'the implied power to punish the workman by suspending him for a certain period of his employment, the contract subsisting all the time',[4] and Atkin J spoke of the 'power to

---

[3] [1915] 1 KB 698 at 704, 705.   [4] Ibid at 706.

suspend the contract in the sense which really means the fining of the employee in the sum of one day's wages for his previous default'.[5]

Similarly, in *Wallwork v Fielding*, Lord Sterndale MR ruled that a power of disciplinary suspension had the result that the contract was suspended with regard to its performance by both sides,[6] and Warrington LJ commented that 'suspension suspends for the time being the contractual relation between the parties on both sides'[7] without, apparently, terminating the contract itself. The same result seems to follow from the analysis by Scott LJ in *Bird v British Celanese Ltd*,[8] of the operation of a clause in a contract of employment which provided for disciplinary suspension. He remarked that 'the clause operates in accordance with its terms; the whole contract is suspended, in the sense that the operation of the mutual obligations of both parties is suspended; the workman ceases to be under any present duty to work, and the employer ceases to be under any consequential duty to pay'; and that in this case the operation of the clause 'enabled the workman, when the suspension ended, to claim as of right to continue in his old job'.[9]

One other leading case on disciplinary suspension is less clear on this point. In *Marshall v English Electric Co Ltd*,[10] Lord Goddard appeared to take the view that suspension of this kind involved a termination of the personal employment contract. He said, 'In my opinion what is called suspension is in truth dismissal with an intimation that at the end of so many days, or it may be hours, the man will be re-employed if he chooses to apply for reinstatement', and later he described the practice as one of 'dismissal mitigated at the discretion of the employer by a promise to re-employ'.[11] Nor was Du Parcq LJ convinced that there was any meaningful distinction between this type of suspension and summary dismissal with an offer of new employment.[12]

Therefore this case provides no clear-cut answer to the question whether a suspension of this kind results in a severance of the contractual nexus. For if the employing entity 'dismisses with a promise to re-employ' and if the worker can be treated as having made a corresponding promise to return to work, then the contract should be seen as being in force (in sub-employment mode) during the suspension. If, on the other hand, the employing entity dismisses with a mere intimation of intention to re-employ or leaves open an offer to re-employ, then there is no standing contract in the suspension period. The decision concerned factory workers who at that period were liable to be dismissed at very short notice, and its reasoning should be

[5] [1915] 1KB 698 at 706.   [6] [1922] 2 KB 66 at 72.   [7] Ibid at 75.
[8] [1945] 1 KB 336. The contractual term in question was one whereby the employers were entitled 'temporarily to suspend the workman from his employment', the wording of the recognized practice being 'if he was guilty of misconduct or breach of duty or breach of an order'.   [9] Ibid at 341.
[10] [1945] 1 All ER 653.   [11] Ibid at 658E–F.   [12] Ibid at 655E–F, F–G.

viewed as less applicable in an environment in which there are statutory minimum periods of notice applicable to contracts of employment terminable by notice.

If it is accepted that disciplinary suspension normally amounts to contractual suspension in the true sense, the questions arise by what mechanism it is effected, and whether it is effected on a lawful, that is to say contract-compliant, basis. The older cases cited above generally support the view that disciplinary suspension is to be seen as effected by the unilateral action of the employing entity, under the authority of an express or implied power conferred by the personal employment contract. A possible alternative view is that contractual suspension should be regarded as having been effected by *ad hoc* agreement. There was a diversity of view on that point in *Marshall v English Electric Ltd*, where the issue was whether the practice of suspension was a 'condition of service'; McKinnon LJ held that it was, because it took place under an implied term in the original contract which provided for suspension.[13] Du Parcq LJ dissented on the ground that the practice was for suspension by *ad hoc* agreement, and that as such it could not be described as a condition of service because that term connotes only that which is a right or obligation under the original contract and not that which is lawful only by reason of subsequent agreement.[14] The former view would be more likely to be taken today.

That leaves open the question of when such a power of disciplinary suspension would be implied into a personal employment contract if it is not the subject of express provision. Deakin and Morris rightly identify the decision in *Hanley v Pease & Partners Ltd*[15] in 1915 as one of the landmark cases in the development of modern employment law for its denial of an unrestricted implied right of disciplinary suspension to the employing entity.[16] It seems very unlikely that any such general implied power of disciplinary suspension would be recognized at the present day. The disciplinary rules applicable to employees are required to be specified in a note included in the statutory particulars of terms and conditions of employment.[17] To that extent, it is unlikely that the availability of the disciplinary sanction of suspension would be held to have been tacitly agreed in the absence of express provision for it.

This question involves, moreover, a fundamental point of definition of the nature and elasticity of the employing entity's core contractual obligations. In *Hanley v Pease & Partners*, a worker in a coke yard was suspended from work on Monday for having failed to present himself for work on the preceding Sunday.[18] On behalf of the employing entity, it was argued that

---

[13] Ibid at 656F–657B.   [14] Ibid at 658A.   [15] [1915] 1 KB 698 (KBD).

[16] Deakin & Morris 2001 at 356.

[17] Employment Rights Act 1996 (ERA), s 3(2)(a).

[18] The reason given was that the worker had overslept, but there was a background of collective dispute about the working of Sunday shifts.

there was a power of summary dismissal for failure to attend for work, and that the suspension for a day could either be regarded as an exercise of that power, a 'dismissal for a day', or could be justified as the exercise of a lesser power of suspension which was a logical corollary of the greater power of summary dismissal. The Divisional Court refused to accept those arguments, essentially because they recognized that there was a crucial difference between terminating a contract and suspending it, and that to concede to the employing entity a power of suspension derived from the power of termination, would, given the width of the power of summary dismissal (at that period, at least), mean a largely unfettered disciplinary power of suspension. The employing entity's power of *exit from* the contractual employment by summary dismissal would be supplemented by a power of *control within* the contractual employment relationship.

Moreover, and this is a crucial point, the power of control within the contractual employment relationship, which was claimed as a 'merciful substitute' for dismissal, becomes in a real sense more of an unfettered discretionary power than that of dismissal, if the employing entity is completely free to determine the length of the period of suspension, that is to say if there is no limit of proportionality upon that period. The exercise of any such power, whether express or implied, would be most likely to be held to be subject to the employing entity's underlying obligation of mutual trust and confidence, as discussed in an earlier chapter;[19] and furthermore the exercise of such a power (whether express or implied) would, in the case of the contract of employment at least, be subject to the statutory, and possibly also the broader underlying common law, duty of dispute resolution which was also discussed in an earlier chapter.[20] It follows from all this that the specification of the power of suspension turns out to be a way of defining the very nature of the continuing contractual obligation of employment; this is a point to which we revert shortly in connection with the topic of lay-off.

Finally there is the question whether, if the employing entity purports to impose contractual suspension in a way which is wrongful or not contract-compliant, that suspension will be regarded as nevertheless having been effective. The older authorities seem to treat wrongful suspension as ineffective to the extent that they allowed wages to be recovered as such in respect of the period of wrongful suspension. Thus in *Warburton v Taff Vale Railway Co*[21] it was held, where the employee had been subjected to a wrongful disciplinary suspension, that he could recover his wages as such for the period of two weeks which was concerned. And in *Hanley v Pease & Partners Ltd*, where the employee claimed a sum equal to the wages for the day during which he had been wrongfully suspended, Lush J commented that it was unnecessary to determine whether it was a claim for wages or for damages.[22]

---

[19] See above, especially at 161.   [20] See above, 393–394.   [21] (1902) 18 TLR 420.
[22] [1915] 1 KB 698 at 705.

Such a claim would be less likely to be upheld today; but on the other hand the worker might well in such circumstances be able to succeed in a statutory claim of *unlawful deduction* from wages, which we might regard as rendering the wrongful suspension ineffective. We turn to the question of whether different analyses should be regarded as applicable to precautionary suspension.

2. Precautionary Suspension

We referred above to the growing proceduralization of employment practice with regard to the use of employing entities' sanctions, such as disciplinary suspension without pay. That development in employment practice has almost certainly brought with it an enhanced use of precautionary suspension, that is to say the suspension of workers from work, normally on full pay or at least basic pay, while allegations or evidence of misbehaviour are under investigation or while the process of deciding whether they are to be disciplined or dismissed is taking place. Questions arise as to whether the status of precautionary suspension in the law of personal work contracts is different from that of disciplinary suspension.

The first such question is whether precautionary suspension should be regarded as true contractual suspension. Here, the issue is a rather different one from that which arose in relation to disciplinary suspension, because of the fact that precautionary suspension is normally accompanied by full or basic pay, whereas disciplinary suspension is normally without pay. The problem here is not whether the contract has been terminated; the continuance of pay indicates clearly that it has not been terminated. The problem is, on the contrary, whether it has been suspended at all, or whether, on the other hand, it remains in full employment mode, with the worker merely stood down, temporarily, from his or her normal work or duties. The question is conceptually difficult and does not yet seem to be the subject of direct discussion in the courts or tribunals. We suggest that the fact that the worker remains on full pay is not inconsistent with the view that the contract has been suspended. Such a situation should be viewed as not being one in which there are current obligations for exchange of work and remuneration, but rather as one in which the worker's income security is being protected while the question of resumption of contractual employment is being considered.

Precautionary suspension, like disciplinary suspension, should normally be regarded as effected unilaterally by the employing entity; but the next question is whether the contractual right or power of precautionary suspension is more extensive or less extensive than that of disciplinary suspension. Essentially, precautionary suspension, if not authorized by the express terms of the personal work contract, is more likely to be regarded as within the implied contractual powers of the employing entity than is disciplinary suspension. That is to say, the possession of such a power by the employing entity is more likely to be accepted as being within what both parties would have regarded as the implicit content of the personal work contract, because the exercise of such a power is more likely to represent a proportional response on the part of the employing entity to problems posed by the alleged or suspected misbehaviour of the worker. Thus, it seems that tribunals or courts will readily regard employing entities as having dismissed unfairly in terminating employment summarily rather than using a contractual power of precautionary suspension.[23] In the leading case of *Dietman v London Borough of Barnet*,[24] a social worker's contract of employment was construed to the effect that the employing entity had dismissed in breach of contract by viewing it as unnecessary to exercise a contractual power of precautionary suspension in a case which its management viewed as one of gross misconduct. It would seem likely to follow that a power of precautionary suspension would readily be implied.

In a sense this argument is strengthened by the very important decision in *Gogay v Hertfordshire County Council*[25] where, as we saw in an earlier chapter,[26] it was held that an express power of precautionary suspension could be exercised only if and to the extent that its exercise did not involve breach of the employing entity's implied obligations of trust and confidence.[27] The same constraint would apply to the exercise of an *implied* power of precautionary suspension. Therefore the courts could imply such a power, confident that they were doing so within a doctrinal framework which would ensure that it was not an arbitrary power which was being so implied. This may be expected to increase their readiness to make this construction.[28] We turn our attention to the theoretically highly complex situation of appellate suspension.

3. Appellate Suspension

In the situation where a worker has been the subject of a decision in favour of dismissal, but where the outcome of an appeal against that decision is still awaited, the question of the worker's contractual status, and in particular whether there is a state of contractual suspension, has seemed to be one of enormous difficulty, and despite extensive case law on the matter it is not yet fully or satisfactorily resolved. It will be argued that a successful resolution of this problem might be more attainable by resort to the notion of contractual suspension which has been presented here, namely that the personal employment contract may be regarded as suspended in the sense that it may validly subsist in sub-employment mode.

The problem of the contractual status of appellate suspension has presented itself in the form of a hard choice between, on the one hand,

---

[23] Cf *Securicor Guarding Ltd v R* [1994] IRLR 633 (EAT).
[24] [1988] ICR 842 (CA).   [25] [2000] IRLR 703 (CA).   [26] See above, 159–160.
[27] Note, however, the limitation imposed by the decision of the House of Lords in *Johnson v Unisys Ltd* [2001] ICR 480; compare *McCabe v Cornwall County Council* [2003] IRLR 87 (CA); see above, 166–167, 362.
[28] Compare also above, 393–395 (duty of efficient dispute resolution).

regarding the personal employment contract as fully subsisting during appellate suspension, or, on the other hand, regarding it as having terminated when the decision to dismiss was made known to the worker. This has been a crucial question in a series of cases where the availability of a statutory right or claim has depended upon the conclusion that the effective date of termination of the personal employment contract was the later date when the appeal was dismissed rather than the earlier date when the worker was said to be dismissed subject to appeal. For a long time it seemed that the decision of the Court of Appeal in *Savage v J Sainsbury Ltd*[29] in 1980 had ensured that the personal employment contract would normally be regarded as having terminated on the earlier of those two dates. The recent decision of the Court of Appeal in *Drage v Governors of Greenford High School*[30] suggests that the personal employment may sometimes be regarded as subsisting until the later date. However, it does not seem as if a fully satisfactory theoretical basis has yet been established for either view or for distinguishing between the two views.

That difficulty comes about as follows. The Court of Appeal in the *Drage* case could regard the facts before them as constituting a purely provisional decision in favour of dismissal, which would not become a final decision unless and until confirmed on appeal. In the meantime, the worker, who continued to be paid, could be regarded as still being in full contractual employment though stood down from his duties. The judges in that case regarded this as a different situation from the normal one pending appeal, when the worker is not being paid. They seem to have accepted the view of the Court of Appeal in *Savage v J Sainsbury Ltd*, expressed by Brightman LJ, that:

[I]f an employee is dismissed on 1 January, on the terms that he then ceases to have the right to work under the contract of employment, and that the employer ceases likewise to be under an obligation to pay the employee, the contract of employment is at an end . . . If he has had no right to work after 1 January and no right to be paid after 1 January, the contract of employment must have been determined as from 1 January.[31]

However, this in a sense treats the difference between appellate suspension with pay and without pay as decisive when it should not be decisive. Both decisions, the later one as much as the earlier one, demonstrate a reluctance to accept the explanation of appellate suspension as true contractual suspension, in the sense in which we have argued for it. That is to say, the Court of Appeal on both occasions seemed unwilling to regard the personal employment contract as still subsisting unless there were current rights and obligations for the immediate exchange of work and remuneration. The later case could in a loose sense be regarded as meeting that condition, in a way that the earlier case could not.

---

[29] [1981] ICR 1 (CA).   [30] [2000] ICR 899 (CA).   [31] [1981] ICR 1 at 7C–E.

Nevertheless, it should have been possible to regard both cases as ones where the personal employment contract had subsisted in sub-employment mode. The clear recognition of that as being at least a possible analysis, if not the preferable analysis, of the situation of appellate suspension becomes especially important now that the Employment Act 2002 has framed the duty of dispute resolution so as to discourage employees from asserting statutory rights or claims based upon dismissal until after the hearing of an appeal against dismissal has been completed.[31a] In the next subsection we turn our attention to a situation of suspension where the theoretical and practical difficulties of contractual analysis, though very different, are no less considerable, that of lay-off or suspension for managerial reasons.

C. Lay-off Without Pay or Unpaid Suspension for Managerial Reasons

In this subsection we consider the contractual analysis of the situation, or range of situations, in which the worker would be described as having been laid off work without pay, which situation we consider it useful to identify as that of unpaid suspension for managerial reasons. It is the situation in which the employing entity ends the ordinary exchange of work and remuneration on a temporary basis, by reason of managerial considerations such as the unavailability of plant or materials or the lack of demand or outlet for the product of the enterprise. Another situation which might be regarded as one of lay-off, that in which work has been suspended but the worker has been placed on guaranteed minimum remuneration or guarantee pay, is discussed in a later subsection.[32]

The analysis of that situation in terms of contractual suspension, that is to say the consideration of whether and in what sense that situation amounts to one of contractual suspension, is one of the most difficult and important questions in the whole of the law of personal employment contracts. It is a crucial determinant both of the contractual rights and obligations of employing entities and workers, and of the operation of statutory rights and obligations constructed upon personal employment contracts. The analysis of the employing entity's power of managerial suspension, to an even greater extent than that of the employing entity's power of disciplinary or precautionary suspension, raises and is bound up with basic questions about the nature and elasticity of the contractual bond or contractual relationship which is embodied in the personal employment contract. The questions about managerial suspension relate back to, indeed become inseparable from, the questions about the nature, structure, and

---

[31a] See Employment Act 2002 s 31 (not in force at time of writing).

[32] See below, 485–486. An associated situation, that of short-time working where the hours of work and the remuneration of the worker are reduced on a temporary basis (compare ERA s 147(2)), is better regarded as one of *variation* than as one of *suspension*.

content of the personal employment contract which were discussed in earlier chapters of this work.

It is helpful to identify the reason why that is especially true of managerial suspension as compared with other kinds of suspension. The recognition of a right or power on the part of the employing entity to suspend the personal employment contract, in the sense in which we have identified and defined contractual suspension, accords the employing entity the power to avoid the costs and risks of the normal exchange of work and remuneration while still maintaining the contractual relationship in being. If such a right or power of contractual suspension may be exercised for a broad or open-ended category of managerial reasons, the basic contractual obligation of employment becomes a discretionary one. The issue becomes one of whether that degree of elasticity is compatible with the basic definitional concept of the personal employment contract. As we have remarked earlier in this work, the question of whether the personal employment contract subsists (in a suspended mode or state) becomes part and parcel of the question of what the nature of the personal employment contract is.

Because this issue about the contractual status of managerial suspension is thus such a fundamental and far-reaching one, it presents itself in a number of different legal forms and contexts, and is addressed in different ways according to the context. That makes it difficult to derive a consistent body of doctrine from the case law. The best way to do so is by looking successively at a body of mainly older case law directly concerned with the construction and enforcement of personal employment contracts, and a body of more recent case law concerned with contractual status in the context of statutory employment rights.

The older case law directly concerned with the construction and enforcement of personal employment contracts displays two conflicting trends. One trend, emerging from the case of *Devonald v Rosser & Sons*[33] was towards a restricted contractual power of managerial suspension, and the other, emerging from the case of *Browning v Crumlin Valley Collieries Ltd*,[34] was towards a broader contractual power of managerial suspension. Those two trends have never fully been resolved, though the modern case law indirectly favours the former of those trends over the latter. Deakin and Morris rightly identify the leading case of *Devonald v Rosser* as forming a pair with *Hanley v Pease & Partners*[35] because a similar pattern of reasoning was followed. The issue in the *Devonald* case was whether, when the employing tinplate manufacturer shut down its works without notice by reason of adverse conditions of trade, it was liable to continue to pay wages to piece-rate workers, employed upon twenty-eight days' notice on both sides, for the duration of the period of notice. The employing entity asserted that there

---

[33] [1906] 2 KB 728 (CA).   [34] [1926] 1 KB 522 (KBD).
[35] [1915] 1 KB 698 (KBD); see above, 469.

was no obligation to find work for a piece worker 'if they had none for him to do', or alternatively relied upon an alleged customary term of the tinplate trade authorizing the closure of the works, resulting in the immediate suspension of the workers without pay, 'in the event of lack of orders or specifications for orders at remunerative prices'. The Court of Appeal upheld the refusal of Jelf J at first instance to accept such a right of suspension on either basis.

The view was taken that the acceptance of such a term would identify the employing entity's basic obligation to employ as a wholly dispensable one, so that there would be no mutuality between the worker's obligation to give notice to leave employment and the employing entity's obligation to give notice of dismissal. By holding the employing entity to be obliged to provide the worker with 'a reasonable amount of work so long as the employment lasted', and by taking the agreed average earnings of the worker in the period preceding the stoppage as the measure of that reasonable amount, the courts concerned ensured that there was no underlying power of suspension which simply followed from the fact that the worker was paid on a piece-rate basis.

By finding that the requirements for a customary term to be shown to be 'reasonable certain and notorious' had not been fulfilled, the courts ensured that the employing entity could not assert a general open-ended power to suspend on *economic* grounds—rather as, in *Hanley v Pease & Partners*, the Court of Appeal had rejected an alleged open-ended power to suspend on *disciplinary* grounds. A similarly restrictive approach to an alleged general right at common law or by custom for suspension without pay was taken more recently in *Bond v CAV Ltd*.[36] In all these cases the real issue at stake was whether the employing entity had a power to depart from the income security guarantees provided by the terms of collective agreements. The decision in *Devonald v Rosser* recognized that a power to lay workers off on economic grounds, the ascertainment of which was entirely within the assessment of the employing entity, would completely negate the income security guarantee which formed the core of the employing entity's contractual obligation.

The decision in *Browning v Crumlin Valley Collieries Ltd* took a contrary view in the situation where the employing coal mining company refused payment of wages to miners during a closure of the mine in which they worked, which was necessary in order to restore the mine to a safe condition for work.[37] The decision that the employing entity did have the right to withhold wages during the period of closure—and thus in effect to suspend the contractual employment of the workers during that period—was taken on the basis that this was a situation where the continuation of work

---

[36] [1983] IRLR 360 (QBD).

[37] A necessity recognized by the employing entity only as the result of a prolonged dispute in which the workers alleged lack of safety and the employing entity denied it.

had become impossible or impracticable *without any fault on the part of the employing entity*. It was in effect the acceptance of an idea of the temporary frustration of the personal employment contract.

It is suggested that the principle upon which that case was decided would not now be regarded as applicable in a case where a stoppage of work takes place on safety grounds, since current legislation more clearly places a general statutory duty upon the employing entity to provide a safe system and environment for work than the legislation in force at the time of that decision was regarded as doing; and the following of the approach taken in *Browning v Crumlin Valley Collieries* would probably be viewed as conflicting with that duty. However, it may be that a doctrine allowing the employing entity an implied power of suspension, or validating an express power of suspension, by reason of impossibility or impracticability of continuation of work, survives in other respects.

In *Johnson v Cross*,[38] Kilner Brown J indicated such a view, and indeed that his notion of 'inevitable cutting-off of work' from extraneous causes could extend as far as 'a temporary cutting-off of liquidity' from outside sources.[39] The difficulty with such an approach is that, because the arrangement and assessment of liquidity is entirely within the control of the employing entity, a power of contractual suspension conditioned upon it becomes in effect the open-ended discretionary power which was denied in the *Devonald* case. In the earlier case of *Minnevitch v Café de Paris (Londres) Ltd*,[40] where cabaret musicians paid by the performance were laid off for a six-day closure of the club in which they were employed, by reason of national mourning upon the death of King George V, it was held that the employing entity had been entitled to withhold pay for a reasonable two days but not for the further four days. That decision endorses the notion of an implied power of suspension by reason of external impossibility or impracticability, but at the same time imposes what would now be regarded as a test of proportionality upon the exercise of the power.

Those decisions therefore leave some doubt as to whether and when an express or clearly implied power of contractual suspension on managerial grounds will be rejected for incompatibility with the personal employment contract, on the ground that it is so open-ended as to undermine the basic mutuality of the contract. A body of more recent case law addresses the question indirectly, in the context of adjudicating upon statutory claims which are contingent upon the claimant's being judged to be employed under a continually subsisting contract of employment. In those cases, the problem presents itself as one of whether and when the casual or 'as required' worker has a continuing contract of employment which subsists between periods of contractual employment. It has sometimes been regarded as the issue of whether casual or intermittent workers can be said

---

[38] [1977] ICR 872 (EAT).   [39] Ibid at 876.   [40] [1936] 1 All ER 884.

478 Transformation and Transfer

to have 'global' contracts of employment; it was discussed in Chapter two
in those and similar terms. That is, in effect, looking from the other way
round at the problem of whether an unlimited power of managerial suspension is compatible with the continuing existence of the contract of
employment; it is starting from the premise that the employing entity has
an effectively free discretion when to offer contractual working, rather than
asking whether the employing entity may be allowed a free discretion to
discontinue contractual working—but the underlying issue is essentially the
same one.

In that context, and no doubt in order to protect the statutory employment
rights of the employee, the National Industrial Relations Court in the important case of *Puttick v John Wright & Sons Ltd*[41] went against the logic of
Devonald v Rosser and rejected[42] the suggestion of incompatibility between
the casual or 'as required' work arrangement and the continuing subsistence
of the contract of employment, with the result that the casual worker in question was held to have a continuing contract of employment (upon which
basis he could invoke the statutory provision entitling the employee to give
notice to treat lay-off for four consecutive weeks as equivalent to dismissal for
the purpose of claiming statutory redundancy payment).

However, in recent cases[43] culminating in the decision of the House of
Lords in *Carmichael v National Power plc*,[44] the courts have in effect accepted
the logic of *Devonald v Rosser* and have applied it to the effect that a casual
or 'as required' worker cannot be regarded as having a continuing contract of
employment which subsists through periods off work as well as through
periods at work. Several key questions present themselves. One is whether the
courts might yet see fit to accept in such cases that there is either some
minimal obligational constraint upon suspension, or some limited duty to
consider continuation or resumption, which would then itself be reinforced
by the implied obligation of trust and confidence so as to operate as the foundation of contractual continuity. In that respect, it is very important to
remember that the mutual obligations of the parties during a period when
the contract is in sub-employment mode may not necessarily be as exacting,
and may not *need to be* as exacting to make good contractual continuity, as
when the contract is in full employment mode—though it should be stressed
that the case law does not really address that point.

[41] [1972] ICR 457 (NIRC).
[42] Lord Thomson at 461–462: 'In such an arrangement between A and B [whereby A
undertakes to do such work of a particular kind as B provides for him, while B undertakes to
make available to A such work of that particular kind as from time to time comes to hand] A
in effect agrees to be "temporarily suspended" or "laid off" for such periods as no work is
available.... We are unable to find anything in any of the quoted cases to suggest that such an
arrangement does not amount to a contract of employment binding in its terms.'
[43] Also *Clark v Oxfordshire Health Authority* [1998] IRLR 125 (CA)—nurses working on 'as
required' basis in 'nurse bank'; and *O'Kelly v Trusthouse Forte Ltd* [1983] ICR 728 is comparable. Compare above, 103, 140.   [44] [1999] ICR 1226 (HL).

A further and equally fundamental question remains unresolved. Although much of the case law of personal employment contracts does not differentiate strongly between contracts of employment and other, or non-employee, personal employment contracts, and although the older case law is not directed at that distinction, the recent case law in the context of employment protection legislation is either directed precisely at that distinction, or at least decided with that distinction perceived as a significant one. It is thus left as a possibility that the courts might be willing to construct a continuing semi-dependent workers' contract for the casual or freely suspendable worker on a looser basis, one which was more permissive of an extremely wide power of managerial suspension, than that which the recent cases insist upon for the contract of employment as such.[44a]

There is a final important question with regard to the content of the personal employment contract during managerial suspension without pay, that is to say while the contract is in sub-employment mode. For it is clear that, whatever the doubts about whether an unlimited or open-ended power of managerial suspension is compatible with the subsistence of the personal employment contract, those contracts, including contracts of employment as such, are often viewed as conferring some powers of managerial lay-off without pay upon employing entities, for example in the event of bad weather preventing work from taking place on construction sites; and it appears that such suspension may be contract-compliant although the worker is not in receipt of guaranteed pay of any kind, whether statutory or purely contractual.

The question arises, but is not answered by case law, as to what are the mutual obligations of the parties during such periods of contractual suspension. By definition the normal obligations of exchange of work and remuneration have ceased (temporarily) to apply; but what of the broader implied obligations as to mutual trust and confidence, and the requirement on the worker not to engage in competitive activity? We consider that question later with regard to some situations of suspension with pay, where it would seem that those broader obligations are regarded as remaining applicable; but, so far as suspension without pay is concerned, the matter seems open to argument. Given that the situation is by definition one in which the contract has not been terminated, but which is not in full employment mode, are the obligations more like those which obtain in employment mode or in post-employment mode (ie after termination of the contract)? The former view is tentatively suggested, but the matter is very far from clear. We proceed to consider whether any of these rather fundamental uncertainties may be better resolved in the context of other possible or actual forms of contractual suspension, and turn to the question of whether and when contractual suspension may take place by way of or by reason of industrial action.

[44a] Compare above, 99–105, especially at 105.

D. Suspension and Industrial Action

The questions of whether industrial action involves suspension of the personal employment contract, and if so whether that is lawful (contract-compliant) or wrongful (non-contract-compliant) have been crucial ones in the formulation and development of the law concerning industrial action generally. As a result some aspects of those questions have been very fully addressed; but others have not, and it is difficult to resolve the case law into a logical pattern. As various aspects of these questions have been touched upon in the course of this work, a succinct synthesis will be attempted which will attempt to restate those earlier discussions specifically in terms of contractual suspension. That therefore focuses attention upon the question of whether and when industrial action involves either (1) a transformation of the personal employment contract from employment mode to suspended or sub-employment mode, or (2) a termination of the personal employment contract (in the sense of a change to post-employment mode); and if so whether that change is lawful or wrongful on the part of the employing entity or the worker.

We begin by considering those questions in relation to strike action, that is to say complete concerted cessation of work on the part of workers. In the major economic tort cases of the early to mid-1960s, it was essentially decided that strike action, even when preceded by notice of the length required to terminate the contract, should not be regarded as lawful contractual termination on the part of the workers, because it was not intended to be terminatory at all, but rather intended to be a discontinuation of work which nevertheless kept the contract in being.[45] Although it was not particularly expressed in those terms, that placed strike action squarely in the analytical category of wrongful suspension on the part of the workers. This was clearly regarded as repudiatory conduct which entitled the employing entity to respond by lawful termination; but it was not regarded as wrongful termination by the worker in and of itself.[46]

A different view of the effect of strike action, at least where accompanied by notice of the length required for termination, was taken by Lord Denning MR, with the probable but somewhat ambiguous agreement of Davies LJ, in the important economic tort case of *Morgan v Fry*.[47] Lord Denning in that case identified such strike action as the exercise of an

---

[45] *Rookes v Barnard* [1963] 1 QB 623, 676 (Donovan LJ); [1964] AC 1129, 1204 (Lord Devlin); *Stratford & Sons Ltd v Lindley* [1965] AC 269 at 285 (Lord Denning).

[46] A point recognized by the National Industrial Relations Court in *E & J Davis Transport Ltd v Chattaway* [1972] ICR 267—Brightman J at 271: 'Just as a strike does not of itself amount to a repudiation of a contract of employment, with the result that a worker taking part in a strike puts an end there and then to his contract, so also a lock-out does not amount to a like repudiation and determination on the part of the employer.' The first comma in that sentence is misleading; Brightman J means that the strike is repudiatory but nevertheless not a termination in and of itself.

[47] [1968] 2 QB 710 (CA) at 728 (Lord Denning MR); compare Davies LJ at 731, 733.

implied right of suspension on the part of the worker. This was at a time when the legislative articulation of such a right of suspension, for the purpose of limiting the scope of economic torts in relation to industrial action, was a matter of active policy discussion, and just such a legislative measure was taken by the Industrial Relations Act 1971 (section 147), which was repealed in totality in 1974.

In 1976 the previously dominant view was reasserted by the Employment Appeal Tribunal, in the context of statutory employment rights dependent on contractual status, in the highly important case of *Simmons v Hoover Ltd*.[48] The judgment of Phillips J treats Lord Denning's analysis as one which was not clearly shared by the other members of the Court of Appeal, and as an attempt to 'revolutionize the law' which should not be regarded as representing the law as it stood after the subsequent enactment and repeal of the Industrial Relations Act.[49] That restoration of the analysis of strike action as the *unlawful* suspension of the personal employment contract has not since been departed from in case law and that analysis must be regarded as the prevailing one.

That analysis involves the conclusion that it is not the role of the courts to construe the implied terms of the personal employment contract so as to give effect to a socially or politically perceived right to strike; and it must be regarded as unlikely that the enactment and implementation of the Human Rights Act 1998 or the promulgation of the EU Charter of Fundamental Rights will have altered that conclusion.[50] At a more immediately technical level, we can observe that the approach taken in *Simmons v Hoover Ltd* also seems to involve the rejection of another alternative analysis which might be thought applicable to some instances of strike action. The rejected alternative arises where the strike action is taken in response to action on the part of the employing entity which is itself in breach of contract or repudiatory of the contract, but falls short of outright dismissal—the paradigm cases being those where the employing entity fails to provide the contractually required safe work environment or seeks to impose a non-contract-compliant adverse variation of terms and conditions. The strike action might be regarded on that basis as lawful suspension of the contract by the worker. However, although the judgment of Phillips J in *Simmons v Hoover Ltd* left open the possibility that a strike in those circumstances might not be regarded as *repudiatory* of the contract,[51] it still seems to assert that it is *in breach* of contract.

This means that, although the action of the employing entity might be treated by the worker as constructive dismissal, and might even be treated

---

[48] [1977] ICR 61 (EAT).   [49] Ibid at 77.

[50] Compare Deakin & Morris 2001 at 890; Hepple 2001 at 227–229.

[51] [1977] ICR 61 (EAT) at 76: 'We should not be taken to be saying that all strikes are necessarily repudiatory, though usually they will be. For example, it could hardly be said that a strike of employees in opposition to demands by an employer in breach of contract by him would be repudiatory. But what might be called a "real strike" in our judgment always will be.'

for some purposes, under the doctrine in *Hogg v Dover College*, as amounting directly to dismissal,[52] nevertheless there is no power of concerted lawful contractual suspension by the worker in response to it. This further rejection, not just of the idea of a general implied right of suspension by way of strike action, but also of the more limited idea of a *contractually justified* right of suspension by way of strike action, although generally unremarked, is of great theoretical and practical significance. Although there is no reason to think that this is a conscious view on the part of modern courts, it is redolent of the particularly extreme lack of sympathy for the notion of a right to strike, even to protect perceived existing contractual rights, which, in an earlier era, was expressed in the decision in *Parkin v South Hetton Coal Co Ltd.*[53]

Furthermore, and again on a more technical level, it is out of accord with the treatment of the corresponding action on the part of the employing entity by way of or in connection with industrial action, often referred to as the lockout. On the one hand, the National Industrial Relations Court accepted in *Davis Transport Ltd v Chattaway* that a lockout by the employing entity which was 'in order to compel [the employees] to accept terms and conditions of employment differing from the terms of their existing contracts' was an *unlawful suspension* of the contract of employment.[54] This corresponds to the general analysis of the strike as unlawful contractual suspension.

However, a succession of cases in the 1980s which concerned the employing entity's response to industrial action short of a strike clearly conferred upon the employing entity a fully developed right lawfully to suspend the personal employment contract in response to serious or repudiatory breach of contract by the worker.[55] In *British Telecommunications plc v Ticehurst*,[56] the Court of Appeal held that this entitlement enabled the employing entity to suspend the contractual employment pre-emptively for as long as the workers remained in a situation of 'withdrawal of goodwill', which meant for as long as they maintained the threat of sporadic industrial action in the near future. We suggest that this disparity of approach to lawful suspension in the context of industrial action as between the employing entity and the worker remains obtrusively unresolved.

E. SUSPENSION DURING SICKNESS OF WORKER

In this subsection we consider how the analysis of suspension as a non-terminatory transformation of the personal employment contract applies to

[52] See above, 260.
[53] (1907) 97 LT 98; thus AT Lawrence J at 102: 'An extraordinary contention, and not in the least parallel to the right of employers to stop work when circumstances require it.'
[54] [1972] ICR 267 at 271.
[55] See above, 221 et seq; especially *Miles v Wakefield Metropolitan District Council* [1987] ICR 493 (HL) and *Wiluszynski v Tower Hamlets London Borough Council* [1989] ICR 493 (CA).
[56] [1992] ICR 383 (CA).

the worker's absence as the result of sickness or incapacity, short term or long term. This is a matter largely of reconsidering, in terms of suspension, case law which has been discussed earlier in this work in terms either of the implication of terms about sick pay,[57] or of the relationship between performance and remuneration as determining the entitlement to sick pay,[58] or as a question of whether and when the contract is terminated by or as the result of long-term incapacity.[59] The case law in question has not been constructed around the notion of suspension in the way that the case law about lay-off or strike action has been, so the analysis in terms of suspension is not an easy one; nevertheless, some insights are to be gained from such an analysis.

It makes sense to identify contractual suspension in the case of sickness or incapacity as the situation in which the personal employment contract is regarded as subsisting, but in which the worker has ceased to be employed in his or her contractual employment, so that the contractual expectation upon return from absence is reduced to re-employment within the enterprise upon return. In those latter circumstances the contract has been transformed into sub-employment mode as we have defined it. The two key issues then become those of:

(1) When does sickness absence result in termination of the contract rather than suspension of it in the above sense?
(2) When does sickness absence result in the worker's moving from being in full contractual employment (but absent from work), into the situation of suspension due to sickness or incapacity?

Neither question can be clearly answered from the case law, but the first is much more directly addressed by the case law than the second. The rapid development from the 1960s onwards of statutory employment rights premised upon dismissal from a subsisting contract of employment made it crucial to decide whether employees on long-term sickness absence, in a situation where their entitlement to sick pay had ceased but where there was some expectation of resumption of work with the employing entity, were still employed under subsisting (though suspended) contracts of employment. The cases are unclear about this; they recognize the possibility of automatic or non-lateral termination by reason of frustration, but it is difficult to derive from them a consistent view of the circumstances in which that will be held to have occurred.

The second question, that of distinguishing between the situation of being in full contractual employment but absent due to sickness, and, on the other hand, that of contractual suspension due to sickness absence, has become more obscure rather than less in the recent case law. The older case law about sick pay, particularly when it seemed to give rise to a presumption

---

[57] See above, 137–138.   [58] See above, 216–218.   [59] See above, 442–445.

of entitlement to ordinary contractual remuneration during sickness absence as long as the contract of employment subsisted,[60] seemed to exclude the possibility of contractual suspension due to sickness, unless it was expressly provided for by the contract. More recent case law has separated the two issues; in *Howman & Son v Blyth*,[61] the judgment of Browne-Wilkinson J made it clear that sick pay was not to be equated with the continuance of ordinary contractual remuneration.[62] This means that the continuation or cessation of sick pay gives little or no indication whether the personal employment contract is in full employment mode or is suspended.

The difficulty of distinguishing between full employment mode and suspension mode during long term sickness absence is further increased by two very important recent cases, *Aspden v Webbs Poultry Ltd*,[63] and *Hill v General Accident Corporation plc*,[64] which both held that obligations in the nature of mutual trust and confidence remained applicable to workers who were on prolonged sickness absence but in receipt of sick pay under contractual long-term health insurance schemes provided as part of their personal employment contracts.[65] That makes it doubly difficult to say whether and when the contracts of workers in that situation are to be regarded as remaining in full employment mode or as having gone into the mode of suspension. In that particular situation, the very fact that the courts concerned were willing to imply those obligations, regardless of which mode the contracts were in, meant that the distinction between modes did not affect the outcome. So for the time being, although analysis of sickness absence in terms of suspension theory is of potential utility, it is rather difficult to apply that theory to this topic. We proceed to consider a final set of situations in the nature of suspension where that distinction is still very difficult to draw, but may be determinative of outcomes and is of real analytical importance.

F. MANAGERIAL SUSPENSION WITH PAY AND 'GARDEN LEAVE'

In this subsection we gather together a number of situations, not previously discussed, of discontinuation of ordinary or full employment by the employing entity but with continuation of pay. They may be loosely described as a set of situations in which the worker is placed by the employing entity in a situation of idleness but on the footing that the personal employment

---

[60] A presumption last asserted in *Orman v Saville Sportswear Ltd* [1960] 1 WLR 1055 (QBD); see above, 218.   [61] [1983] ICR 416 (EAT).

[62] Ibid at 421.

[63] [1996] IRLR 521 (QBD). Compare now *Jenvey v Australian Broadcasting Corporation* [2003] ICR 79 (QBD).

[64] [1998] IRLR 641 (Ct of Sess—therefore decided under Scottish law, but that does not differ from English law on the point concerned).

[65] The decisions, so far as they involve the application of such obligations to limit the power of the employing entity to *dismiss* where that would render such insurance schemes nugatory, may well have been overtaken by the decision of the House of Lords in *Johnson v Unisys*—see above, 341 et seq—but that does not affect the point made here.

contract subsists and that the worker continues to receive pay during the period concerned. A very important example of that kind of situation is that of 'garden leave', where the worker is placed by the employing entity in that position during the period of notice of termination of employment or during a period of employment leading down to the expiry date of a fixed term of employment (normally with the purpose of, or akin to that of, ensuring that the worker will not be legally free to engage in competitive economic activity during that period).

It will be argued of such situations that it is appropriate, and indeed extremely helpful to a clear legal analysis, to consider these situations as, sometimes at least, constituting a form of contractual suspension in the sense in which we have identified that notion, and, because they are situations in which the discontinuation of ordinary or full employment is imposed by the employing entity for managerial reasons (such as unavailability of work), as amounting to a category of managerial suspension with pay. In order to make out that argument it is first necessary to show that it is conceptually possible to regard such situations as contractual suspension.

It is also necessary to show that it is conceptually and practically possible to distinguish them, regarded as contractual suspension, from, on the one hand, (1) situations where full contractual employment is regarded as continuing despite discontinuation of ordinary working, and, on the other hand, from (2) situations where the personal employment contract is regarded as having terminated despite the continuation of pay. Having sought to do that, we shall consider to what extent and in what conditions the employing entity has a contractual right of managerial suspension with pay, that is to say a right to transform the personal employment contract in this particular way without terminating the contract. That will turn out to be a very revealing way of analysing an otherwise rather impenetrable body of case law normally regarded as being about the 'right to work'.

The initial step in the argument, that of showing that it is conceptually possible to think of a category of managerial suspension despite the continuation of pay, becomes easier if we consider the way in which the same problem arose and was addressed in connection with some of the more specific situations of suspension addressed in previous subsections. Thus it was shown that we readily in practice recognize the idea of precautionary suspension though pay continues, and it was argued that both that situation and some situations of sickness absence may be regarded as true contractual suspension although pay continues. That is because they are situations which meet our conceptual definition of the sub-employment or suspended state of the personal employment contract despite the continuation of pay. They are situations in which the normal obligations of exchange of work and remuneration have ceased to apply; the pay which continues is not remuneration for working in the normal sense of the contract.

That also explains why we may be prepared to regard situations of layoff as ones of true contractual suspension even where the worker receives

guaranteed pay during periods of lay-off. It is sometimes felt that such situations *cannot* be regarded as ones of contractual suspension because of the
continuation of pay. That seems to miss the point that the ordinary
contractual employment may in a meaningful sense have come to a (temporary) end although pay continues. The pay is not remuneration in the
ordinary contractual sense which applies during the full employment mode
of the contract. The difficulty should be regarded as one of how to distinguish between full employment mode and sub-employment mode when
pay continues, rather than as a matter of the conceptual impossibility of
separating the two modes when pay continues.

Admittedly that distinction becomes very hard to draw when we envisage the possibility of a power of contractual suspension with pay on general
managerial grounds. For such a power becomes hard to separate from the
powers which personal employment contracts accord to the employing
entity to stand the worker down from work or duty, or simply indeed to
determine when the worker is required for work or duty, when the worker
is on normal pay and the contract is in full ordinary employment mode. In
order to make that distinction, we have to develop a difficult concept of the
normality of full employment mode; but we argue that such a concept can
be developed and that it is useful to do so.

Equally the distinction between contractual suspension with pay on
managerial grounds, and contractual termination on managerial grounds,
is sometimes difficult but, we argue, conceptually defensible. That difficulty
sometimes presents itself as quite an acute one of the interpretation of the
transaction of termination with pay in lieu of notice, in the form of the
question whether that should be regarded as immediate contractual termination with pay in lieu of remuneration, or as termination to take effect at
the end of a period of notional suspension or 'garden leave'—one of the possible constructions of pay in lieu of notice identified by Lord Browne-
Wilkinson in his authoritative analysis in *Delaney v Staples*.[66] Nevertheless,
it is a distinction which is eventually made and is a meaningful one, since we
can identify contractual obligations when the contract is in sub-employment
mode which are different from those which may apply after the contract has
been terminated. That is to say, when the contract is in sub-employment
mode, the employing entity remains under obligations either of income
replacement or resumption or both, while the worker remains under
obligations either of loyalty or resumption or both.

If that succeeds in identifying and justifying a conceptual category of
managerial suspension with pay, it then becomes useful and important to
consider what powers or rights of managerial suspension with pay are
regarded as being conferred by the personal employment contract. There
are various ways in which that issue might be discussed. We might ask

[66] [1992] ICR 483 (HL); see above, 320.

whether there is an implied power of managerial suspension with pay in particular types of situation. For example, we might ask whether there is a particular implied power to impose garden leave, that is to say suspension with pay on managerial grounds as part of the process of termination of the contract of employment. (That would enable us, incidentally, to identify a functional terminology for 'garden leave'—we could ask whether there is a power of 'terminatory suspension with pay on managerial grounds'.) We might alternatively consider whether there is a general implied power of managerial suspension with pay, or a set of such powers in particular types of situation, but whether that power or those powers are qualified by conditions as how they may be exercised—for example, whether only on reasonable grounds or only in accordance with an underlying obligation of trust and confidence.

The courts, however, have approached the issue in an altogether different way, not in terms of suspension at all, but rather in the form of a question about the type of personal employment contract which the worker has; is it a type of personal employment contract which entitles the worker to be provided with work as well as with remuneration? This approach seems to have originated, or at least to have taken concrete shape, in the highly significant decision of the Court of Appeal in *Turner v Sawdon & Co*[67] in 1901, where it was held that the employing entity of a worker employed as a 'representative salesman' was under no obligation to provide him with work to do as long as it continued to pay the contractually promised remuneration. That approach has been pursued in a succession of cases in the intervening century; the cases are generally regarded as having established a category of workers whose contracts do give them a right to be provided with work as well as with remuneration, either because the contract recognizes their special interest in maintaining their professional reputation or skills by working,[68] or because the contract entitles them to work in a particular post.[69]

The approach was recently applied in the highly significant case of *William Hill Organisation Ltd v Tucker*[70] to the effect that a worker employed by an employing entity in the business of bookmaking, who was a 'senior dealer in the specialized business of spread betting', was entitled to be provided with work to do as well as with remuneration. That case marks out that approach as the primary way of determining whether the employing entity has the right or power to impose 'garden leave'; as Morritt LJ explained it, if the worker is not entitled to be provided with work as well as remuneration, then it follows that no special power to impose garden

---

[67] [1901] 2 KB 653 (CA).
[68] As, particularly, actors or musicians as in *Herbert Clayton and Jack Waller Ltd v Oliver* [1930] AC 209 (HL).
[69] As in the situation of the chief sub-editor of a newspaper in *Collier v Sunday Referee Publishing Company Ltd* [1940] 2 KB 647 (KBD).   [70] [1999] ICR 291 (CA).

leave is required; the contract inherently confers such a power upon the employing entity 'because there is no contractual obligation to prevent him'. If, on the other hand, the worker is entitled to be provided with work as well as remuneration, a power to impose garden leave will normally arise only from express provision and is unlikely to be implied because it would be seen as being in conflict with the general obligation to provide work.[71]

It is important to observe the particular slant which that approach gives to the contractual evaluation of actions on the part of the employing entity which are really in the nature of managerial suspension with pay. This approach has the effect—and probably in *Turner v Sawdon & Co* the aim and intention—of identifying the normal or standard personal employment contract as conferring upon the employing entity a very wide or even unlimited power of managerial suspension with pay. That this is seen as the default or presumed position is made very clear in that case, for example by the statement of Vaughan Williams J that:

> We have to consider in the present case whether there is anything in this agreement to engage and employ the plaintiff which places on the defendants a wider obligation than that which a master ordinarily incurs towards his servant.[72]

This underlying presumption was confirmed by the famous dictum of Asquith J in *Collier v Sunday Referee Publishing Co* that:

> a contract of employment does not necessarily, or perhaps *normally*, oblige the master to provide the servant with work. Provided I pay my cook her wages regularly she cannot complain if I choose to take any or all of meals out. In some *exceptional* cases there is an obligation to provide work.[73]

It is worth reflecting how that approach justifies a broad or unlimited power of managerial suspension with pay, and how, within that approach, the exceptional contrary situations are explained and justified. Asquith J's example of the cook is highly significant. At one level, it is an apparently uncontroversial and innocuous description of a perceived day-to-day managerial power of regulation of working time; the domestic employer may determine on a daily basis whether the cook is required to cook meals on a particular day. However, if asserted as a general paradigm, it translates into a power wholly to transform the situation of the worker, for example by announcing a decision not to take any meals for the next six months. It must be questioned whether it is consonant with a respect for the autonomy and dignity of the worker to assert such a power on the basis merely that the worker continues to be paid, during what is, in that example, clearly a suspension of employment in a very real sense.

It is equally important to consider the implications of the way in which the courts have defined the limiting or countervailing category of contracts

---

[71] [1999] ICR 291 (CA) at 301D–F.   [72] [1901] 2 KB 653 at 658.
[73] [1940] 2 KB 647 at 650 (emphasis added); see also above, 135.

which do entitle the worker to be provided with work as well as with remuneration, and particularly the notions that this is dependent upon whether the worker can be regarded, either as having been appointed to a particular position in which he or she has a particular entitlement to be allowed to work, or as having a special interest in maintaining reputation or skills. Again these notions sound innocuous and uncontroversial. But they readily lend themselves to particular kinds of implicit social and economic stratification which need to be scrutinized, a set of ways of differentiating between a superior and an inferior class of workers.

Thus in *Collier v Sunday Referee Publishing Co*, where the notion of the appointment to a particular position is first fully articulated, it emerges in a form which echoes the idea of the office-holder as a superior order of worker holding a tenure which deserves special protection. Thus, as Asquith J put it:

I do hold that the very foundation of the contract was the appointment of the plaintiff, during the contract period, to a specific *office*. The defendants engaged the plaintiff, not to perform at large the sort of work commonly performed by *any* chief sub-editor. They engaged him to fill the *office* of chief sub-editor of a specific Sunday newspaper.[74]

The notion of a worker specially needing to maintain his or her skills may also imply some similar economic or social value judgements, as witness the reasoning of Sir John Donaldson in *Langston v AUEW (No 2)* upon the question of whether a factory worker came within the protected category:

The complainant's work as a spot welder may have been in the 'skilled' category, but we do not think that he needs practice in order to maintain his skills.[75]

It is suggested that a far more satisfactorily functional analysis of whether the employing entity is acting lawfully (ie in compliance with the contract) or wrongfully (ie out of compliance with the contract) would be achieved by considering the situations concerned as particular assertions of an implied power of managerial suspension with pay, rather than by seeking to classify them according to this rather suspect typology of contracts and of workers. This would permit an assessment of whether the employing entity was asserting or exercising that power in a way which was reasonable, and in accordance with general underlying contractual notions such as the implied obligation of trust and confidence. This was precisely how the asserted use of an express power of precautionary suspension with pay was approached in the leading case of *Gogay v Hertfordshire County Council*,[76] and there is every good reason to apply the same approach to what is, in reality, a potentially even more open-ended implied power.

---

[74] Ibid at 651 (emphasis added).   [75] [1974] ICR 510 at 522B.
[76] [2000] IRLR 703 (CA)—see above, 159–160.

If the leading cases on the 'right to work' are re-examined from this perspective, they come into much clearer focus. Thus, for example, *Turner v Sawdon & Co* was a case where the employing entity was using an asserted power of suspension with pay as an indirect way of dismissing the worker from his employment, apparently because of dissatisfaction with him. *Herbert Clayton and Jack Waller Ltd v Oliver*[76a] was, rather similarly, a case where the asserted power of suspension with pay was presented as a rationale for having refused an actor the major part in a comedy musical for which he had been engaged and for offering him a part which he regarded as a minor one instead.

Equally, *Collier v Sunday Referee Publishing Co* presents itself, under that spotlight, as a case where the employing company had sold its main newspaper business, and had therefore ceased to employ the worker in any meaningful sense, and were, in effect, claiming a power of suspension with pay in the hope that the worker might resign before the expiry of his fixed-term contract, which after a few months of paid inactivity he duly did. In each of these cases the real choice was between regarding the situation as one of lawful suspension with pay, or as actual or constructive dismissal with pay tendered as compensation. In each case, a more appropriate question, than the one of whether the worker had a right to work, might have been the one of whether the assertion of a right of suspension with pay was an abusive one in the particular circumstances.

In fact this latter mode of analysis would produce a more directly functional scrutiny of the claim to managerial suspension with pay than occurred in most of the 'right to work' cases. In *Langston v AUEW (No 2)* it would have focused attention upon the highly important and difficult question of whether the employing entity was to be regarded as having an implied right to suspend the worker with pay, on the ground that his fellow workers threatened industrial action in enforcement of a closed shop arrangement while he was allowed to continue at work though refusing trade union membership. In *William Hill Organisation Ltd v Tucker*, we suggest that it would strengthen the employing entity's case; examined in this way, the case is revealed as one in which the employing entity was asserting a right to maintain the worker on terminatory suspension where the worker was purporting to end his contract of employment in breach of a contractual obligation to give six months' notice.

The employing entity's assertion of such a right, with the purpose of retaining the employee's obligation of loyalty during the subsistence of the contract of employment, had in effect been accepted as a legitimate and non-abusive one in the substantially similar cases of *Thomas Marshall (Exports) Ltd v Guinle*[76b] and *Evening Standard Co Ltd v Henderson*,[76c] a similarity which was masked by the presentation of the argument in terms

---

[76a] [1930] AC 209 (HL).   [76b] [1978] ICR 905 (ChD).   [76c] [1987] ICR 588 (CA).

of the 'right to work' in the *William Hill* case. So the analysis of these situations as transformations of the personal employment contract provides important insights about the law concerning the termination of those contracts. In the succeeding sections of this chapter, we consider how similar insights may be obtained by considering, in terms of transformation theory, a number of situations of change in the identity of the parties to the contract.

SECTION 3: TRANSFORMATION OF PARTIES (1)—PARTIAL TRANSFORMATION

In this section and the next we consider what is probably the most conceptually and practically difficult but at the same time important kind of transformation which personal employment contracts may undergo, namely that of transformation of parties. In subsection A we outline a notion of transformation of parties; we explain that it is important to distinguish between total and partial transformation of parties, and we relate the notion of transformation of parties to the general idea of contractual elasticity as set out at the beginning of the chapter. In the succeeding subsections that framework of ideas is applied successively to changes in the composition of employing partnerships (subsection B), and to various situations of corporate dissolution and insolvency (subsection C). That leads on to a discussion of total transformation of parties or transfer of undertaking in the next section.

A. Transformation of Parties and Contractual Elasticity

In the course of considering the topic of the termination of the personal employment contract by operation of law, an underlying notion began to emerge of the termination of contractual employment by the permanent cessation of existence or activity on the part of the employing entity or the worker. In the case of the worker, this would occur if he or she died or was permanently incapacitated; in the case of the employing entity we listed a set of occurrences which might be so regarded, and which extended from the death of a human employer or member of an employing partnership, to the dissolution of an employing partnership and to various occurrences in the nature of corporate dissolution or insolvency. We should also include in this whole category the cessation by the employing entity from carrying on the activity or undertaking within which the contractual employment takes place, using that notion in a broad sense. It was a category amounting to termination by ceasing to be the employing entity party or the worker party to the personal employment contract.

It was, however, made clear that this was not, in and of itself, a category of termination which formed part of the system of categories of termination which we had identified. It was a looser, more general, category which had to be related to the more precise bases of termination of the personal employment contract which our general theory of termination had sought to identify. It was concluded that some of the occurrences coming within this loose category might give rise to termination by operation of law without fault on either part, such as the death or permanent incapacitation of the worker, or the death of a human employer or member of an employing partnership. However, it was emphasized that these occurrences by no means systematically brought about termination by operation of law without fault; on the contrary, the basic category into which they fell was that of unilateral wrongful, or non-contract-compliant, termination.

On the other hand, it was equally emphasized that these occurrences might be redeemed from that category, or that this category might be negated, not just by reference to the alternative notion of termination by operation of law, but also by reference to other alternatives. This is where the notion of the elasticity of the personal employment contract comes into play, because the most important of those alternatives are the ones which envisage those occurrences, not as terminating the contract at all, but rather as transforming it in some way which lies within the elasticity or area of accommodation of change which the contract inherently possesses. In this section and the next, it will be argued that this area of accommodation, in other words this contractual elasticity, is large enough to provide room for a number of highly significant transformations of or in the parties to the personal employment contract.

It should be said at the outset that this is really a discussion about the elasticity of the concept of the employing entity rather than of the concept of the worker. As has been made clear earlier in this work,[77] there is very little scope for the employee to offer substitute performance of his or her contractual obligations, and probably not a great deal more scope for semi-dependent workers to do so, for otherwise even their contracts would not qualify as 'personal' ones and so would fall outside the whole category. Equally, and for similar reasons, the scope for employees to contract as partnerships is very small—just possibly arising in job-sharing arrangements—though the scope for non-employee workers to contract as partnerships is rather greater—pop groups are an example. But to the extent that partnership contracting by workers is possible, the capacity for transformation of the contract by change of members of the partnership would seem to be very slight.

So far as the employing entity is concerned, the matter is very different. The contractual concept of the employing entity, as we began to indicate in an earlier chapter[78] and will now argue in greater detail, has a much greater elasticity. The orthodox view, it should be said, is to the contrary. The personality, in the sense of the personal uniqueness, of the personal employment contract is seen to attach as much to the employing entity as to the worker.

---

[77] See above, 25–26, 461.   [78] See above, 36–40.

This is seen as very greatly limiting, if not excluding, any scope for transformation of the employing entity compatibly with the continued subsistence of the single personal employment contract. We go on to elaborate the orthodox view and then to explain the way in which it is in reality deeply qualified or modified.

The orthodox view asserts, therefore, that the personal employment contract, or the contract of employment at least, is as much identified by the personality of the employing entity as by that of the worker, and therefore no more susceptible to change of employing entity than to change of worker. The paradigm is that of the employing entity as a particular human being whose identity is fundamental to the contract, and that paradigm is extended to a partnership, arguably to an unincorporated association, and, in particular, to a company incorporated under the succession of Companies Acts which have been in force from the mid-nineteenth century onwards. Thus the classical statement of this orthodoxy consists in the decision of the House of Lords in *Nokes v Doncaster Amalgamated Collieries Ltd.*[79] This concerned the effect upon contracts of employment of the procedure for reconstruction or amalgamation of companies which had been introduced by the Companies Act 1929, whereby a court could make an order for the transfer of a company's undertaking to a transferee. The issue was whether the novation of contracts normally effected by such an order, that is to say the substitution of the transferee company for the transferor company as a party to the contracts in which the transferor company was engaged, would apply to contracts of employment.

In the context of proceedings for damages, for breach of the contract of employment consisting of wrongful absence from work, by the transferee company against a coal miner formerly employed by the transferor company and transferred into the *de facto* employment of the transferee company by or since the amalgamation order, the House of Lords held that the amalgamation order had not resulted in the transfer of the contract of employment to the transferee company, because the personality of the transferor company was so foundational to the contract that there could be no novation of the contract without the agreement of the worker, which had not been sought; the worker had been quite unaware of the purported change of contractual employing entity.

Although this decision was a famous vindication of the autonomy of the worker, an assertion of freedom from serfdom in times of war and tyranny,[80]

---

[79] [1940] AC 1014 (HL). See above, 38, 453.

[80] An assertion stirringly expressed by Lord Atkin at 1026: 'I confess it appears to me astonishing that apart from overriding questions of public welfare power should be given to a court or anyone else to transfer a man without his knowledge and possibly against his will from the service of one person to the service of another. I had fancied that ingrained in the personal status of a citizen under our laws was the right to choose for himself whom he would serve: and that this right of choice constituted the main difference between a servant and a serf.'

it produced a major conceptual and practical problem of seeming to leave the worker without a personal employment contract with any employing entity at all. Although it was a decision which was protective of the worker in the context of the particular proceedings, it propounded a doctrine which would operate against the worker in the more usual situation in which the worker had an interest in maintaining the legal continuity of his or her contractual employment upon the transfer of an employing entity's undertaking to another employing entity. Those issues were in due course addressed by legislation, to be discussed in the next section.

More immediately relevant at this stage of our argument, however, is the fact that the doctrine in *Nokes v Doncaster Amalgamated Collieries* seriously understates or plays down the elasticity or capacity for transformation which the law accorded at that time, and continues to accord, to its conception of the contractual employing entity. The Law Lords who propounded the doctrine in *Nokes* were well aware of one aspect of this elasticity; they perceived it as a problem for their proposed doctrine which they had to address if the doctrine was to appear a coherent one. However, we shall argue that they overlooked or barely touched upon other aspects of this elasticity, the full implications of which it is important to consider.

The Law Lords in *Nokes* realized that their reasoning had to acknowledge and address the complete elasticity in the concept of the contractual employing entity which was, and continues to be, conferred by the approach of company law to the whole issue of corporate ownership and control. That is to say, they had to reconcile their proposed denial of a capacity for transfer of the personal employment contract from one corporate employing entity to another, upon the transfer of the corporate undertaking, with the capacity which undoubtedly existed to achieve the same effect by means of a change in the ownership or control of the corporate employing entity itself: this could be accomplished by acquisition of its shares without any change in the legal identity of the company and hence without any perceived change of or to the contractual employing entity. If this inconsistency was not addressed, their proposed decision could be regarded as Canute-like, quixotic, or, in a more modern idiom, a moving of the deckchairs on the Titanic.

Again Lord Atkin displayed the most beguiling eloquence in relation to this problem:

But it is said how unreasonable this is [ie the objection to the amalgamation of small trading concerns over the heads of their workers or tenants]: for the big company can buy the majority of the shares in the old company: replace the directors and managers: change the policy and produce the same result. Be it so: but the result is not the same: *the identity of the company is preserved*: and in any case the individual concerned, while he must be prepared to run the one risk, is entitled to say that he is not obliged to run the other.[81]

---

[81]   [1940] AC 1014 at 1030 (emphasis added).

But this argument, while seeming to defend the doctrine in *Nokes v Doncaster*, actually exposes its most fundamental weakness. In the case of a takeover by acquisition of shares, the 'identity of the company' can be said to be preserved; but that is only because the 'identity of the company' is an extremely malleable or elastic concept in the first place.

It is well known and well understood that the commercial company has an extremely flexible identity when regarded as a legal corporate vehicle for investment and commercial activity; we know that companies can be 'bought off the peg' and transformed according to the proprietors' requirements. We suggest that this is just as true of the company *as a contractual employing entity*, though perhaps in a slightly different sense. The key to this point lies in Lord Atkin's passing reference to the replacement not just of directors, but also of *managers*. The importance of this cannot be too strongly emphasized. A corporate employing entity has a very broad capacity indeed to delegate or entrust the management of its undertaking to particular directors and/or other managers, and to change the structure and personnel of its management, without thereby bringing about any change in its legal identity in general or its identity as a contractual employing entity in particular. There is an inbuilt power of managerial delegation and transformation of managerial structure and personnel which means that the contractual identity which the company presents to its workers is an essentially mutable one, behind an apparently static institutional and contractual facade.

It is also extremely important to realize that this delegability and flexibility of management in general and the management of employment in particular is by no means confined to the corporate employing entity. It is possessed in much the same way by the employing partnership, or by the employing unincorporated association, or even by a single human employing entity. All of those types of individual employing entities or joint employing entities have the same capacity of delegation of management, in the sense that they may appoint managers to conduct their business; and that capacity extends to the carrying out of the functions of employment. In some sense the corporate employing entity necessarily conducts its business, and carries out its employment functions, via the agency of human beings, whereas a human employing entity can conduct his or her business and carry out his or her employment functions in person; but both types of employing entity are free to operate and carry out their employment functions through the agency of others, and indeed typically do so. The farmer may conduct his or her farming business, and manage his or her farm workers, through the agency of a farm manager in just the same way as a bank may conduct its business and manage its workers through the agency of branch managers.

Despite the importance which we have thus accorded to it, this delegability and flexibility of the management of contractual employment has not seemed to present itself as a significant feature in the analysis of the working of the personal employment contract, and certainly has not been perceived to present any fundamental challenge to the doctrine against imposed change of employing entity which was propounded in *Nokes v Doncaster Amalgamated Collieries*. As we have seen, Lord Atkin could dismiss it as a separate phenomenon, not encroaching upon the identity of the corporate employing entity, so that even a radical change in managerial structure and personnel, consequent upon a takeover by acquisition of a majority shareholding, would leave the identity of the employing entity company intact. Such changes in management structure and personnel have been perceived as taking place behind a façade which is not exactly a corporate veil, but rather the cloak of personality of the contractual employing entity, whether that is a single human being, a legal corporation, or a partnership, or even, possibly, an unincorporated association.

However, if these changes in the management structure and management personnel of the employing entity have been largely invisible so far as the law of personal employment contracts is concerned, that has actually been due to the fact that those changes have normally occurred in a particular limited set of conditions. That limited set of conditions has consisted in the fact that the delegation of management of the business of the employing entity, and of the employment functions of that business, has normally been a purely internal one to the directors and/or employees of the employing entity. In those circumstances, the delegation of the functions of managing the employing entity's business, and of managing its contractual relationships with its workers, has not seemed to involve any change or addition to the employing party to the contracts of those workers, because the managers are purely internal agents of the employing entity.

That analysis starts to break down once the delegation of management of the business of the employing entity, and of the employing entity functions of the employing entity, ceases to take the form of a purely internal agency. For the delegation of management and of employment functions does not have to be a purely internal one. An employing entity might validly make such a delegation of functions to an external agent, such as for example a firm of management consultants. In such a case, the question arises whether that human or legal person should be regarded as an additional or substituted employing entity party to the personal employment contracts of the workers concerned. The doctrine in *Nokes v Doncaster Amalgamated Collieries* seems to preclude such changes in the identity of the employing entity without the express agreement of the workers concerned. Yet we shall find that some situations which occur in the course of proceedings relating to corporate insolvency do seem to involve such changes, and hence imply some relaxation of the *Nokes* doctrine.

The foregoing argument introduces the idea that, despite the orthodoxy of *Nokes v Doncaster*, there may be situations which amount to genuine transformation of the employing party to the personal employment contract, that is to say which involve the kind of imposed novation of such contracts which seems to be precluded by the doctrine propounded in *Nokes*. In order to understand how and when these departures from *Nokes* may arise, it will be helpful to make and use a distinction between the total and the partial transformation of the employing entity as party to the personal employment contract. This will involve a brief recapitulation of discussion earlier in this work[82] of the question of how the employing party to the personal employment contract may be constituted.

In the course of that earlier discussion, it emerged that the employing party does not, as is frequently assumed, have to consist of a single human or legal person; it may consist of a combination of human and/or legal persons operating as a joint party. This occurs routinely when a worker is employed by a firm of partners which has not been incorporated. It may also occur sometimes where a worker is employed by an unincorporated association, though in that case it may well be that an officer of the association acts as the contractual employing party. We have suggested that it may also occur when corporations as well as individual human beings combine to employ workers. It seems, for example, that actors and musicians are frequently employed in this way by combinations of theatre or concert hall proprietors and agents, or impresarios; those proprietors, agents, or impresarios may well be incorporated as commercial companies; if so it seems to be accepted that the employing party may consist of a combination or partnership of companies as well as of individuals.[83] So we have the possibility, and indeed the frequent occurrence, of joint employment by a complex or multi-personal employing party to the personal employment contract.

That possibility of joint employment opens up in turn the possibility of partial rather than total transformation of the employing party. If the employing party had to consist of a single human or legal person, then any change of the person constituting the employing party would have to be a complete one, a complete change from person A to person B. Any novation of the contract, that is to say any replacement of a party by a different party, would have to be a total one so far as the employing party is concerned. It may be different, however, if the employing party can be a complex multi-personal one. For that means that there might be a partial replacement from A plus B to A plus C; or there might be an addition of B to A, or a subtraction of B from A and B. This poses the question, can there be partial transformation of the contractual employing party, and if so in what conditions will it be held to have occurred?

---

[82] See Chapter 1, Section 3B, 40–45.

[83] As in *Harold Fielding Ltd v Mansi* [1974] ICR 347 (NIRC); thus Sir John Donaldson at 349: 'In the case of "The Great Waltz" Mr Mansi was employed by Harold Fielding Ltd and Bernard Delfont Organisation Ltd jointly, these two companies having formed an *ad hoc* partnership for this specific venture, and having agreed that Harold Fielding Ltd would act as managers on behalf of the partnership.' See above, 42.

This is a curiously difficult theoretical and practical problem. Employing parties to personal employment contracts frequently are complex multi-personal ones; many workers are contractually employed by partnerships of one kind or another, and those partnerships frequently undergo changes of membership. Two contrasting approaches are possible. One is to follow a draconian logic, similar to that of *Nokes v Doncaster Amalgamated Collieries*, and to regard any such change of membership as a wrongful termination of personal employment contracts coupled with the actual or attempted forma-tion of a different contract with a differently constituted employing party. Another is to regard the personal employment contracts as capable of par-tial novation corresponding to the sort of partial replacement which we have identified above. This could be regarded as compatible with the logic of *Nokes v Doncaster* because that logic might be regarded as excluding total novation but permitting partial novation.

We shall argue that, in the analysis and treatment of some of the occur-rences affecting the employing entity which were discussed in the previous chapter, both of these approaches are encountered, and indeed that they coexist in a state of unresolved tension. This argument will be primarily developed in relation to occurrences consisting of the change in member-ship in employing partnerships, but it will also turn out to have a bearing upon the way in which some events, occurring in the course of corporate insolvency and restructuring, are regarded as impacting upon personal employment contracts. Moreover, it will be argued that in some of those situ-ations, either of change in membership in employing partnerships, or of corporate insolvency or restructuring, the line between total and partial replacement may become blurred, so that there may possibly be what is in substance a total transformation or transfer contrary to the received doctrine which excludes that possibility.

We are now in a position to sum up this set of arguments, and to indicate how its different strands are interwoven. Firstly, it was observed that the basic orthodoxy or starting position of the common law concerning the scope for transformation of the contractual employing party is a negative one. The approach which assumed its most stringent form in *Nokes v Doncaster* denied the possibility of such transformation save possibly by express *ad hoc* agreement with the worker, which might even so not amount to an agreement for novation of the existing contract but rather to the formation of a new and different contract.

Secondly, however, it was argued that there is a very significant capacity for internal transformation of the management of the employing party in the sense that the management, of the undertaking within which the personal employment contract is situated, may be freely delegated and restructured or allocated to different persons. Normally that sort of delegation and restruc-turing of management remains internal to the employing party in the sense that it takes place within and among the directors and/or employees of the employing party and hence involves no change to the employing party in a contractual sense. However, there is some scope for conceptual slippage, because this capacity for delegation and restructuring of management seems to extend beyond the directors and employees of the employing party so that it may involve a delegation of managerial power and authority to an outside person, human or corporate. In that case we argue that an actual or external transformation of the employing party itself will be regarded as having taken place, or should be regarded as having taken place; but the legal analysis of such occurrences is sometimes inexact and obscure.

Thirdly, it was argued that there may be perceived to be scope in some situations for actual transformation of employing parties which is consistent with the approach which generally excludes such transformation, because that negative approach may apply only to complete transformation rather than to partial transformation. The possibility of partial transformation arises from the fact that the employing party may consist of a multiplicity of persons, human or legal, and in that sense need not consist of one single human or legal person, human or legal. Because that is so, there may be partial change of employing entities in a factual sense which may be treated as having brought about a partial transformation of the employing party in a legal contractual sense. Here again, however, the legal analysis of factual change in combinations of employing entities is not always clear, and conceptual slippage may occur whereby *complete* transformation of the contractual employing party is allowed to take place, slipping under the wire of the negative approach typified by *Nokes v Doncaster*.

These two sets, admittedly less than perfectly defined, of actual or possible exceptions to the doctrine against implied or imposed novation of personal employment contracts, may overlap with each other and interact with each other. Thus an actual transformation of the employing party may be permitted, contrary to general doctrine, partly on the basis that it seems to be similar to, or little more than, an internal change of management, and partly on the basis that it seems to be similar to, or little more than, a partial transformation rather than a complete one. In the ensuing subsections those possibilities will be explored in the areas of change in the composition of employing partnerships, and corporate restructuring and insolvency.

In the course of that discussion, it will be seen that at certain points, whether as the result of judicial reasoning or legislative change or the combination of both, developments have occurred which recognize in minor and obscure respects the possibility of transformation of the employing party, within a framework of continuity of the undertaking in which the contractual employment is situated. That will lead on to a consideration of the way in which the principle and approach of *Nokes v Doncaster* was ultimately reversed by legislation, for contracts of employment, and a direct mechanism of transfer of those contracts upon the transfer of the undertaking was introduced.

B. Transformation of the Employing Party and Change in
   Composition of Employing Partnerships

In this subsection we investigate one of the possibilities which were identified in the preceding subsection for transformation of the employing party
by imposition or on the basis of provision implied in the original personal
employment contract, namely the possibility that this transformation may
occur upon the change in composition of an employing partnership, or
multi-personal employing party. It follows from the argument in the preceding subsection that, to the extent that this possibility exists, it represents
a departure from the basic approach of the law of personal employment
contracts, which is opposed to such transformations.

It seems very clear that the above-mentioned general approach is
strongly maintained with regard to changes between employment by a sole
employing entity and by a partnership of employing entities, and indeed
that it represents the default or presumed approach to changes in composition of an employing partnership. All those occurrences are therefore primarily regarded as effecting a wrongful termination of personal
employment contracts. This was established by the decision of the Court of
Appeal in *Brace v Calder*,[84] subject to the qualification that, although the
death of a partner would equally terminate such contracts, that would be a
lawful termination rather than a wrongful one.[85] This was also assumed in
a succession of decisions about whether statutory continuity of employment
is maintained when employment continues with the new employing entity
after such an occurrence, for the issue of statutory continuity would not
arise if the personal employment contract was regarded as continuing.[86] It
was reaffirmed in the important case of *Briggs v Oates*.[87]

However, there have always been indications of a possible area of exception, within which the personal employment contract would be deemed to
continue despite a change in the composition of the employing partnership.
There is the rather isolated decision in *Phillips v Alhambra Palace Company*[88]
to the effect that the death of a 'sleeping' partner did not put an end to the
personal employment contracts of a troupe of music hall performers. More
significantly, it was made clear by the Court of Appeal in *Brace v Calder* that
there might be instances where a personal employment contract might be
construed as a contract for employment with the partners *for the time being*
in the firm concerned. Scott J reaffirmed that possibility in *Briggs v Oates*:

> In a larger firm than Owen & Briggs the sheer common sense of a construction
> which allowed continuity of employment notwithstanding departures from and
> additions to the body of partners might sway the balance.[89]

---

[84] [1895] 2 QB 253 (CA).   [85] See above, 455.
[86] *Harold Fielding Ltd v Mansi* [1974] ICR 347 (NIRC); *Wynne v Hair Control* [1978]
ICR 870 (EAT); *Tunstall v Condon* [1980] ICR 786 (EAT); *Allen & Son v Coventry* [1980]
ICR 9 (EAT); *Jeetle v Elster* [1985] ICR 389 (EAT).   [87] [1990] ICR 473 (ChD).
[88] [1901] 1 QB 59 (QBD); see above, 453–454.   [89] [1990] ICR 473 at 482.

It is unfortunate that the case law provides no clear guidance as to the scope of this very important area of exception, within which the personal employment contract is regarded as providing for automatic partial trans-formation of the contractual employing party upon change in the compo-sition of the firm. We suggest that the principle underlying this area of exception, which should be regarded as defining the area, is that a personal employment contract with a multi-personal employing party may be con-strued as continuing where a partial change of composition in the employ-ing party does not disrupt the continuity of the undertaking in which the worker is employed or of the management of that undertaking.

It would seem to be on that basis that the death or retirement of a partner in a large firm, or of a partner in a small firm but who is inactive in its management, may be regarded as consistent with the continuation of the personal employment contract. Hence we have here an important case of the judicial construction of an area in which the personal employment con-tract is continuous with the undertaking in which the worker is employed, despite a partial change in the persons conducting that undertaking. We proceed to consider, as a possibly analogous construction, the treatment of certain situations arising in the course of proceedings concerning corporate insolvency and reconstruction.

C. Transformation of the Employing Party during Corporate Insolvency or Restructuring

In this subsection we investigate another of the possibilities which were identified in the first subsection for transformation of the employing party by imposition or on the basis of provision implied in the original personal employment contract, namely the possibility that this transformation may occur in the course of proceedings concerning corporate insolvency and reconstruction. As in the situation of change of composition in an employ-ing partnership, it follows from the argument in the first subsection that, to the extent that this possibility exists, it represents a departure from the basic approach of the law of personal employment contracts, which is opposed to such transformations. It will be argued that there are certain stages in certain corporate insolvency and reconstruction proceedings which probably should be regarded as constituting such exceptions. The proceedings to be considered are those of compulsory winding-up, voluntary winding-up, and the appointment of an administrator or receiver.

In the course of the discussion of termination by operation of law, we argued that all those proceedings should be understood as underlyingly constituting or giving rise to wrongful repudiation and termination by the employing company, save to the extent that such an analysis is negated because there is deemed to be a continuation of the personal employment contracts in question. It was suggested that such a continuation might either be on the basis that the company continues to be the sole employing entity, or on the basis that the employing party has become a multi-personal one involving an additional employing entity. In the latter event, the employing party will thus have undergone a partial transformation of the kind which encroaches upon the orthodoxy of *Nokes v Doncaster*. In this subsection we investigate when such continuations may occur, and upon which of those two alternative bases they may be deemed to occur.

This is a matter about which it is extremely difficult to be precise, mainly because the case law should be regarded as highly dependent on the particular statutory provisions concerning corporate insolvency and reconstruction, in the context of which each case is decided. Assertions are often made as if those provisions had remained unchanged since the mid-nineteenth century, whereas in fact they have undergone crucial changes since that time, and indeed within the last twenty years. Many errors can result from attempting to read across from one statutory context to another. The only one of these situations which is capable of being the subject of a clear statement of the modern law is that of the appointment of a receiver or administrator, and even there the matter is far from straightforward.

Thus, in the situation of compulsory winding-up, the case law is generally seen as deciding that there is no continuation of the personal employment contracts of the company even if the workers continue to be employed by the liquidator, because the liquidator, being appointed by the court, does not act as the agent of the company in continuing the employment.[90] This may have represented a misreading of early decisions such as that in *MacDowall's Case*,[90a] which might have been seen as consistent with the liquidator being regarded as the agent of the company in continuing the employment of the company's workers; but in any event the statutory regime concerning the situation of liquidators has since changed in crucial respects. In the situation of voluntary winding-up, the decision in *Gerard v Worth of Paris Ltd*[91] did indicate clearly enough that the liquidator might continue personal employment contracts as agent of the company, but, again, we cannot be confident that this analysis is applicable in the current statutory regime.[92] In any event, the Insolvency Act 1986 has since ensured that any continuation of the company's business by the liquidator will be very short-lived, making different kinds of provision for the continuation of the business of insolvent companies for rescue purposes.[93]

The 1986 Act essentially built upon, but greatly modified the legal effects of, the practice of continuation of the business of insolvent companies, and

[90] A highly influential article by C Boughen Graham on 'The Effect of Liquidation on Contracts of Service', published in 1952, put forward this view, mainly on the basis of 19th-century cases and dicta in *Reigate v Union Manufacturing Company Ltd* [1918] 1 KB 592 (CA); see Graham 1952.   [90a] (1886) 32 Ch 366 (ChD).

[91] [1936] 2 All ER 905 (CA).

[92] The latest decision to touch upon the point was far from clear about this: *Fox Brothers (Clothes) Ltd v Bryant* [1979] ICR 64 (EAT).

[93] See Insolvency Act 1986, s 87; Davies 1994 at 141.

the continuation of the employment of their workers, by receivers appointed by the debenture holders to enforce and protect their security (thereafter styled 'administrative receivers'). Where previously there had been a strong contrast between the situation of such receivers and receivers appointed (more exceptionally) by the court, there would now be, much more routinely, appointment of administrators by the court, appointable at the instance of the directors or any creditors, with powers and obligations very similar to those of administrative receivers.[94] This means that the pre-1986 case law concerning continuation of employment by a receiver appointed by the court[95] ceases to be of practical significance, and that our attention should now focus upon the administrative receiver or court-appointed administrator, regarded as being in a very similar situation to each other so far as the continuation of employment of employees of the company is concerned.

That situation, as further reformed by the Insolvency Act 1994 and as construed by the House of Lords in the leading case of *Powdrill v Watson*,[96] would seem to be as follows. Continuation of employment of the employees of the company by receivers or administrators has to be considered in two phases, the contract-continuation phase and the contract-adoption phase. The contract-continuation phase begins upon the appointment of the receiver and administrator and continues for fourteen days unless the receiver or administrator ends the employment during that time. After fourteen days the administrator or receiver is deemed to have 'adopted' the contracts of employment, with the result that he or she becomes personally liable upon certain of the obligations of the contract. The 1986 Act ensured that this personal liability would be a comprehensive one, and that it would become a specially prioritized liability of the insolvent company. Because that was perceived to reduce the viability of rescuing the business of insolvent companies, the 1994 Act restricted the scope of those personal and specially prioritized liabilities for subsequent 'adoptions'. We proceed to consider the status of continued employment in the contract-continuation and contract-adoption phases.

It follows from the analysis in the preceding paragraph that the contract-continuation phase is a short and interim one. We suggest that, during that phase, the contract of employment will be regarded as quite unaffected by the appointment of the receiver or administrator, and that in particular the employing party will not be regarded as having undergone any transformation. The situation during the subsequent adoption phase is much more difficult to clarify; it presents the most interesting conceptual problems. Decisions before 1986 suggest that where employment continued after the

---

[94] See Davies 1994 at 142.

[95] The most significant decision was that in *Reid v Explosives Company Ltd* (1887) 19 QBD 264 (CA), suggesting that continuation of employment by a receiver and manager appointed by the court took place on the footing that the receiver was not acting as the agent of the company.

[96] [1995] ICR 1100 (HL). (Further reforms to the machinery of corporate insolvency may be involved when the Enterprise Act 2002 is implemented.)

appointment of a receiver out of court, that is to say by the debenture holders, the receiver was regarded as continuing the employment 'as agent of the company';[97] but it was very far from clear either what effect that had upon personal employment contracts, or how the employing party was regarded as being constituted in those circumstances.

Was it that the contracts had continued to subsist with the company as the sole employing party, or with the receiver as the sole employing party, or with the company and the receiver as joint employing entities making up a multi-personal employing party? Or had new contracts been made on any of those three possible bases? We suggest that it is impossible to resolve those questions under the pre-1986 law of corporate insolvency, and that, even if it were possible, that would not provide any sure guide to the situation under and after the 1986 Act, because there was nothing corresponding precisely to the concept of 'adoption' of contracts of employment by the administrative receiver or administrator which that Act ushered in. We therefore suggest that the situation of the adopted contract of employment has to be analysed afresh, with all the pre-1986 possibilities in mind, and on the assumption that there is no determinative case law from before 1986.

It is suggested that a safe first step in this analysis consists in accepting that the legislative concept of adoption means the continuation of subsisting contracts rather than the ending of subsisting contracts and the making of new ones. That is not incontrovertible, but it seems to be implicit in the language and reasoning of the House of Lords in *Powdrill v Watson*.[98] The whole thrust of their decision is that the receiver or administrator is deemed after fourteen days from appointment to become personally liable, in the sense and with the consequences assigned by the legislation, upon contracts which have subsisted until that point and continue to subsist thereafter as 'adopted contracts'.

That being so, the interesting question then becomes that of how the employing party to those contracts is then constituted. This is very unclear indeed, but a fairly safe step seems to be to conclude that the original employing entity company has not ceased be a constituent of the employing party. There does not, in other words, seem to be a complete transformation of the employing party or complete transfer of the contract from the original employing entity company as sole employing party to the receiver or administrator as sole employing party. Again, that is not incontrovertible, but seems to be implicit in the analysis of 'adoption' in *Powdrill v Watson*, and part of the notion of what it means to regard the contract as a continuing one, in the way that our first step assumes it is intended to be.

---

[97] *In re Mack Trucks (Britain) Ltd* [1967] 1 WLR 780 (ChD); *Deaway Trading Ltd v Calverley* [1973] ICR 546 (NIRC), with some support from a dictum of Plowman J in *In re Foster Clark's Indenture Trusts* [1966] 1 WLR 125 at 132.

[98] See Lord Browne-Wilkinson [1995] ICR 1100 at 1146–1149, 1154–1157.

That leaves two possibilities: (1) that the contract continues with the company as the sole employing party, or (2) that the contract is partially transformed by the addition of the receiver or administrator as the other of two employing entities, between them making up a joint multi-personal employing party. Neither the 1986 legislation nor the case law deciding upon its effect seems to make or imply any choice between those possibilities.[99] The first analysis would be open to the objection that it strains the capacity for internal transformation of the employing entity beyond its logical breaking point, by treating the employing entity as retaining its sole identity although its management is wholly in the hands of an external person, neither a director of the company nor a worker for the company.

It is therefore suggested that the second view would be the more logically coherent one. Admittedly that involves an acceptance of the fact that the statutory notion of adoption connotes a partial transformation of the employing party, and hence an encroachment upon the principle of *Nokes v Doncaster*. However, there is every good reason to regard this as faithful to the intentions with which the Insolvency Act 1986 was devised, namely to ensure that the undertaking of the insolvent company could be maintained in being by the addition of an insolvency practitioner to take over its management. By 1986, it was far from being a startling proposition that legislation might effect this kind of partial statutory transfer of the contract of employment to a differently constituted employing party, since legislation in the shape of the TUPE Regulations had made provision for total transfer of the contract of employment from 1981 onwards in the case of the transfer of the undertaking or part of an undertaking within which the employee in question was employed. In the next and concluding section of this chapter we consider the implications of that radical revision, indeed reversal of direction, of the law concerning the transformation of the personal employment contract.

SECTION 4: TRANSFORMATION OF PARTIES (2)—TOTAL TRANSFER UNDER THE TUPE REGULATIONS

In this concluding section, we consider the way in which the law concerning the transformation of parties to the personal employment contract has been crucially changed by legislation, the TUPE Regulations 1981 as subsequently amended, which, upon the transfer of an undertaking or part of

---

[99]   In *Litster v Forth Dry Dock Ltd* [1989] ICR 341 (HL), where the issue was how the TUPE Regulations operated upon a dismissal effected by a receiver immediately before the transfer of the undertaking to an acquiring company, it seems to have been assumed that the employees had remained in the contractual employment solely of the company in receivership; but the point was not directly in issue, and it cannot in any case be assumed that Scottish law is the same on this point.

an undertaking in the defined sense, effects a total transfer of the employees employed within that undertaking or part of an undertaking, so that their contracts of employment subsist with a complete change of the employing party from the transferor employing entity to the transferee employing entity. The exact contractual nature of such transfers is a complex question which is of the greatest theoretical and practical interest. The first subsection investigates that question in terms of the general relationship between the relevant legislation and the law of personal employment contracts, and the second subsection then pursues that question towards a more precise understanding of the detailed impact of the legislation as interpreted in judicial decisions upon the law of personal employment contracts. Specially interesting notions of contractual sub-transfer and contractual super-transfer will begin to emerge.

A. THE TUPE REGULATIONS, THE ACQUIRED RIGHTS DIRECTIVE, AND
     THE LAW CONCERNING CONTRACTS OF EMPLOYMENT

In the previous section of this chapter, the set of issues about transformation of the parties to the personal employment contract was presented initially as a relatively simple and straightforward one of whether and in what circumstances the law of personal employment allowed or provided for the total or partial transformation or replacement of the parties to the contract. It was suggested that there was very little, if any, scope for this in relation to the worker; in relation to the employing party, a general doctrine against such transformation or replacement was identified, but so were certain actual or possible partial exceptions, such as those of certain changes in the composition of firms of employing partners, and the adoption of contracts of employment by receivers or administrators.

Despite the initial apparent straightforwardness of that analysis, the latter possible exception started to introduce an altogether more complex possibility. This was that a set of legislative provisions, those of the Insolvency Act 1986, had, in order to achieve the particular aims of that legislation, introduced a new form of contractual transformation, that of the 'adoption' of contracts of employment by the receiver or administrator. This turned out to alter the previously existing structure of those contracts of employment in an unfamiliar way, involving intricate consequences of personal liability upon the receiver or administrator coupled with priorities in claims upon the assets of the original employing company, so that it was difficult to relate the idea of 'adoption' to our general analysis of the transformation of contractual parties.

There is a similar but even greater complexity, and a similar but even greater interestingness, in the particular kind of contractual transformation which is brought about by the provisions of the TUPE Regulations. The brief summary of their effect, in the concluding paragraph of the previous section and the introductory paragraph to this section, suggested that they might represent a straightforward reversal of the doctrine in *Nokes v Doncaster*, a simple imposition of total transformation of the employing party upon the transfer of the undertaking. In order to show in what respects the matter is more complicated, it is important to develop a theory to explain the nature of the impact of this legislation upon contracts of employment.

The theory which we advance for that purpose is one which tries to account for the impact of the TUPE Regulations upon contracts of employment as a complex interaction between different normative systems. In effect we began to develop such a theory when accounting for the effect of the adoption of contracts of employment by receivers or administrators. We explored the way in which a conception devised and introduced in one normative system—the conception of adoption in the system of corporate insolvency law—was constructed or interpreted within the law of personal employment contracts. That involved looking at a particular interaction between two normative systems which are generally independent of each other; it was moderately difficult but nevertheless manageable to disentangle the two normative systems and identify the impact of the one upon the other.

So far as the impact of the TUPE Regulations upon contracts of employment is concerned, the matter is similar but very much more complicated. On this occasion, an interaction is involved between four normative systems instead of two; and they are, moreover, normative systems which, far from being generally independent of each other, are entirely interdependent and interactive ones. The four normative systems in question are: (1) The EC Acquired Rights Directive;[100] (2) the TUPE Regulations;[101] (3) statutory unfair dismissal law;[102] and (4) the common law of the contract of employment. The analysis required to disentangle them and understand their impact one upon the other is extremely difficult but of transcendental importance towards the understanding of the working of the law of personal employment contracts as a whole.

Simplifying the matter as much as possible in order to focus upon the impact upon contracts of employment, we could understand these four normative systems as being linked together, in the context of the transfer of undertakings, in the following way. The Acquired Rights Directive established a number of norms for the purpose of safeguarding employees' rights upon the transfer of an undertaking; there are two basic ones which impact most significantly upon contracts of employment. One is the provision[103] that the transferor's rights and obligations arising from a contract of employment or from an employment relationship existing on the date of

---

[100] Originally Directive 77/87/EEC as since amended by Directive 98/50/EC, both being now consolidated into Directive 2001/23/EC.

[101] Transfer of Undertakings (Protection of Employment) Regulations 1981, SI 1981/1794 as since amended.

[102] Currently contained in Part 10 of the Employment Rights Act 1996.

[103] Of Article 3.1.

a transfer shall, by reason of such transfer, be transferred to the transferee ('the transfer rule'); the other is the provision[104] that the transfer of the undertaking shall not in itself constitute grounds for dismissal by the transferor or the transferee, but that this shall not stand in the way of dismissal for economic, technical, or organizational reasons entailing changes in the workforce (the 'no-dismissal-save-for-ETO rule').

The TUPE Regulations are intended to implement the Acquired Rights Directive in the United Kingdom. Much elaboration is required to transpose those two rules into the complex context of the common law of the contract of employment and the statute law of unfair dismissal. The transfer rule is implemented by regulation 5, which deals with the effect of the transfer of an undertaking upon contracts of employment and upon rights and liabilities arising under or in connection with those contracts. The no-dismissal-save-for-ETO rule is implemented by regulation 8 which modifies unfair dismissal law in order to give effect to that rule.

That description might thus far suggest that the whole matter of assessing the impact of the transfer of undertakings legislation upon contracts of employment is a relatively straightforward one; it suggests that the matter consists of the application to contracts of employment of a self-contained transfer rule in TUPE regulation 5. However, the links between the four systems are in reality much more complex. The transfer rule and the no-dismissal-save-for-ETO rule are two parts of a composite strategy which the Acquired Rights Directive requires members states to implement; neither can be viewed in isolation from the other. This means that TUPE regulation 5 and regulation 8 cannot be understood in isolation from each other. Moreover, unfair dismissal law draws on the law of the contract of employment for its concept of dismissal. So the Acquired Rights Directive, the TUPE Regulations, the law of unfair dismissal, and the common law of the contract of employment all become interlinked to that extent.

That interlocking of the normative systems becomes even more intense as the meaning and effect of the legislative provisions are interpreted through judicial decisions. On the one hand, many of the concepts which are used or invoked by the TUPE Regulations have to be interpreted by reference to the common law of the contract of employment and the unfair dismissal legislation. On the other hand, the TUPE Regulations have to be construed so as to give effect to the Acquired Rights Directive. But it has to be decided to what extent the Acquired Rights Directive is deferring to or basing its concepts upon the national employment laws, including the common law of the contract of employment. Then again, the TUPE Regulations provide[105] that provisions in contracts of employment shall be void so far as they purport to exclude or limit the operation of regulations 5 or 8.

---

[104] Of Article 4.1.   [105] In reg 12.

It becomes very hard to identify which are the fixed points and which are the moving parts of this interlinked structure.

In the next subsection, we shall try to deploy this theory to show precisely how the TUPE Regulations have impacted upon contracts of employment, and why that particular impact has occurred. It will be attempted to show that the TUPE Regulations, as interpreted by the courts, have done both more and less than bring about a simple reversal of the doctrine in *Nokes v Doncaster*. It will be suggested that the ways in which they have been interpreted to do more, and the ways in which they have been interpreted to do less, are not easily or satisfactorily reconcilable, and that this manifests an incoherence in the law of personal employment contracts.

B. THE INCIDENCE AND EFFECTS OF CONTRACTUAL TRANSFER
   UNDER THE TUPE REGULATIONS

In this subsection, we seek to use the theoretical scheme developed in the previous subsection in order to make a precise and critical assessment of the impact of the TUPE Regulations upon contracts of employment. In order to do that, it is useful to consider successively (1) when the contractual transfer effect of the TUPE Regulations occurs, and (2) precisely of what it consists. A useful way to focus upon that set of issues is to ask whether the TUPE Regulations amount to an exact reversal of the rule or doctrine in *Nokes v Doncaster*, so that, upon the transfer of an undertaking as defined, they impose a transfer of contract, or complete substitution of the transferee of the undertaking for the transferor of the undertaking, as the employing party to the contract of employment, completely and solely the subject of the rights and obligations arising under or from the contract both as to the past, present, and future.

That is the basic design of the transfer rule as laid down in the Acquired Rights Directive and implemented by regulation 5 in its original form. That design has been refined by subsequent legislation; we will argue that it has also been the subject of interpretation which claims to give effect to that design but which significantly limits or modifies it. We begin with the legislative refinement. As the result of interpretation of the Directive in the European Court of Justice[106] as not being intended to impose a transfer upon the employee against his or her will, regulation 5 was amended[107] so that contractual transfer does not occur if the employee informs the transferor or the transferee that he or she objects to becoming employed by the transferee. In that event the Regulations, as interpreted in the British courts,[108] have the effect that the contract of employment is terminated upon the transfer of the undertaking, and that the employee has the right

---

[106] In *Katsikas v Konstadinidis*, Cases C–132, 138, 139/91 [1993] IRLR 179 (ECJ).

[107] By the insertion of reg 5(4A) by TURERA 1993, s 33.

[108] reg 5 (4A), (4B), and (5) as interpreted in *University of Oxford v Humphreys* [2000] IRLR 183.

to treat that termination as a wrongful dismissal where, but only where, the transfer would have involved a substantial change in his or her working conditions, or the change of identity of the employing entity would be a significant and detrimental one. This partially restores the worker-protective effect of the doctrine in *Nokes v Doncaster*.

That brings us to the limits or modifications which have been placed upon the contractual transfer rule by judicial interpretation. These are of the utmost theoretical and practical significance, especially with regard to the question of whether the content or terms and conditions of the contract of employment can be changed at the time of transfer. The issue is whether contractual transfer takes place when the transferor purports to dismiss the employee at or shortly before the time of transfer. It will be argued that, in the two leading cases of *Litster v Forth Dry Dock Ltd*[109] and *Wilson v St Helens Borough Council*,[110] the courts have interpreted the legislation so that, in that situation, there is an incomplete or partial contractual transfer whereby only secondary liabilities or past obligations are transferred. This amounts to a notion of contractual sub-transfer, which, it may be argued, fails fully to implement the design of the Acquired Rights Directive, and possibly also that of the TUPE Regulations themselves.

This kind of contractual sub-transfer first seems to present itself in *Litster v Forth Dry Dock*, where, however, the difference between sub-transfer and complete transfer is not critical to the outcome and is not decisively addressed. In *Wilson v St Helen's Borough Council*, it represents itself as the critical determinant of the outcome, and the notion of contractual sub-transfer is decisively adopted. In the *Litster* case, the issue was whether the transfer effect could be avoided by pre-emptive dismissal of the workers in question shortly before the transfer of undertaking took place, so that the transferee would be free of liability for unfair dismissal, in respect of employees of the transferor to whom employment was not offered or was refused by the transferor. It was held that the employees could invoke regulation 8 (the no-dismissal-without-ETO rule) to claim unfair dismissal rights against the transferee. The basis for that decision was that regulation 5, which applied the transfer effect to persons employed by the transferor, in the undertaking concerned, immediately before the transfer, could be interpreted sufficiently broadly to include those who would have been so employed had they not been unfairly dismissed in connection with the transfer, ie contrary to the no-dismissal-without-ETO rule of regulation 8.

This was a fully effective response to the problem of avoidance of the transfer effect by pre-emptive dismissal, so far as the unfair dismissal rights of the employee were concerned. However, the terms of the judgments,

---

[109] [1989] ICR 341 (HL).   [110] [1998] ICR 1141 (HL).

in particular that of Lord Oliver, have since been regarded[111] as indicating that the House of Lords baulked at the idea that, in the event of pre-emptive dismissal, the contract of employment could be regarded as having remained in full force and effect until the transfer of the undertaking, so that the full ordinary contractual transfer effect would thereupon occur. Despite the fact that the pre-emptive dismissal seems to have been a contractually wrongful one, effected without contractual good cause or notice, it seems to have been regarded as effective to bring the contractual employment to an end. In the terms of our general analysis, the contract had gone into post-employment mode, giving rise only to post-employment obligations if any, and liabilities for wrongful dismissal or earlier breaches of contract. The transfer of the undertaking operated to transfer the contract of employment to the transferee of the undertaking only in that limited sense. We suggest this can appropriately be analysed as contractual sub-transfer rather than as contractual full transfer.

As we have said, the distinction between contractual sub-transfer and full transfer did not affect the outcome in *Litster*; but it became entirely crucial in *Wilson v St Helen's*. Here, the issue was whether a variation of terms and conditions which was or could be regarded as an adverse one for the employees could be imposed upon the transfer of the undertaking. In other words, the issue was whether the contractual transfer carried with it the whole set of contractual terms and conditions upon which the employee had been employed by the transferor, so that the transferee would be in breach of contract in seeking to impose different terms upon the transfer.

In the *Wilson* case, the House of Lords held that if, as in the cases before them, the dealings with the employees of the transferor were to be regarded as dismissals by the transferor followed by the offer of employment on different terms by the transferee, then those dismissals were to be regarded as effective to terminate the contracts of employment, so that no full contractual transfer would occur upon the transfer of the undertaking. All that would occur would be the kind of contractual sub-transfer which the House of Lords was regarded as having envisaged in *Litster*. In this situation, the distinction between sub-transfer and full transfer made all the difference; it meant that the employees had no right against the transferee to a continuation of the terms and conditions upon which they had previously been employed by the transferor.

It is argued that this evolution of a notion of contractual sub-transfer does less than justice to the notion of transfer of contractual rights and obligations which is embodied in the Acquired Rights Directive and implemented by the TUPE Regulations. It is an intrusion of the notions, which

---

[111] Especially and crucially by the House of Lords in *Wilson v St Helen's Borough Council*: see Lord Slynn [1998] ICR 1141 at 1069.

loomed so large in our earlier discussion of termination of the personal employment contract, that the employing entity has an untrammelled right or power to terminate the contract by notice or on the expiry of a fixed term,[112] and that a dismissal is to be regarded as effective to terminate the contract even if it is contractually wrongful. It elevates those notions to the status of absolute and overriding norms, which precede or trump the construction or conception of the full transfer of the contractual rights and obligations of the contract of employment as they stood when the transfer of the undertaking took place.[113]

This brings us to the second, closely connected, question of what full contractual transfer under the TUPE Regulations consists of when it does occur. A key question in this respect, and one that obviously relates back to the set of issues in the *Wilson* case, is that of whether the right to the continuation of previous terms and conditions of employment after transfer, which is conferred by full contractual transfer, is regarded as susceptible to modification of those terms and conditions by express or implied agreement on the part of the employee. The doctrine has evolved in cases decided in the British courts, that such an agreement might be ineffective under the TUPE Regulations, as being a purported exclusion or limitation of the operation of the transfer rule of regulation 5, as such rendered void by the restrictions on contracting-out which are imposed by regulation 12. The working of that doctrine is well illustrated by the decision in *Credit Suisse First Boston (Europe) Ltd v Lister*,[114] where it operated to deny effect to a covenant restricting post-employment competitive activity on the part of the employee which was more extensive than that which was in force before the transfer, although the employee had expressly agreed to that variation upon the transfer.

The judgment of Lord Slynn in *Wilson v St Helen's Borough Council* seemed to endorse that doctrine, and indeed to endorse the view that it might extend to variations which were agreed *after* the transfer, as well as upon the transfer, though the thrust of that judgment was to restrict the doctrine by insisting strongly that the variation must be sufficiently closely connected with the transfer.[115] It remains controversial how close that

---

[112] A further illustration of the point is provided in *Ralton v Havering College of Further and Higher Education* [2001] IRLR 738 (EAT), where the EAT held that the employing entity's right to rely on the expiry of the contractual fixed term limited the employees' right under Article 3 of the Acquired Rights Directive (directly applicable to this employing entity as an emanation of the State) to the continuation of the terms of a collective agreement applicable to their pre-transfer employment.

[113] In *Wilson v St Helen's Borough Council* [1998] ICR 1141 at 1160B–E, Lord Slynn acknowledges that this involves an assertion that the Acquired Rights Directive significantly defers to national divergence in conception of what is meant by the rights of the employee arising from the contract of employment.   [114] [1999] ICR 794 (CA).

[115] See Lord Slynn [1998] ICR 1141 at 1165D–E, 1166D–F.

connection has to be, and for how long such a connection may be held to exist after the transfer;[116] but, whatever its scope,[117] the doctrine is of great theoretical and practical interest.

For it is clear that, where it applies, agreed variations are ineffective upon or after transfer although the same agreed variations would be fully effective if they had occurred during the ordinary subsistence of a contract of employment. To that extent, the transfer of the employee's right to continuance of existing contractual terms and conditions which is effected under the TUPE Regulations leaves that right more robustly protected, that is to say less derogable by agreement, for a certain length of time, than it was before the transfer. In that sense, the TUPE Regulations bring about not just transfer of existing contractual rights, but an effect which we could regard as contractual super-transfer, in which more is transferred than existed before.

That approach contrasts strongly with the approach which has reduced the effect of TUPE regulation 5 to that of contractual sub-transfer in a wide range of situations; indeed, the effect of the decision in *Wilson* is that super-transfer will rarely come into play to protect variations occurring at the time of transfer of an undertaking, because the situations in which those variations do occur may be treated as ones in which only sub-transfer of the contract of employment has taken place.

In fact, the decision of the House of Lords in *Wilson* strongly suggests that the judiciary may intuitively tend towards giving primacy to the common law of the contract of employment over legislative conceptions of contract-based rights—as sub-transfer does—rather than accepting that the legislation has remoulded the common law—as super-transfer does. This means that the courts are more likely, where choices present themselves, to shape the legislative conception around the common law of the personal employment contract than vice versa. The common law conception of the contract of employment, perhaps of the personal employment contract at large, envisages that contract as essentially identified with its original employing party and limited by that party's powers of termination. That common law conception is not readily susceptible to a notion that the contract may be identified with a looser, less person-specific, conception of an employing undertaking which has a continuity in the hands of different employing entities.

It would be interesting to explore in detail the enormous body of case law which defines the scope of that looser, less person-specific, conception of the

---

[116] See *Ralton v Havering College of Further and Higher Education* [2001] IRLR 738 (EAT).

[117] In *Rossiter v Pendragon plc* [2002] ICR 1063 (CA), the Court of Appeal refused to endorse the view that it might apply even to variations of content which are within the employing entity's contractual power of variation of content, or that it might give rise to a specially extended notion of contractual repudiation, or a specially extended definition of constructive dismissal within the law of unfair dismissal.

employing party, by specifying what may count as the 'transfer of an undertaking' for the purposes of this legislation. Indeed, on the view that has been taken in this chapter, that conception should be regarded as being embedded in and forming part of the law of the personal employment contract, just as the transfer rule of TUPE regulation 5 should be so regarded. However, that would divert attention from the profound significance of the relationship which the foregoing discussion has sought to establish between the legislative innovation which TUPE transfer represents and the underlying common law contractual approach which it has to confront. It is the discussion of that kind of confrontation which leads to and forms the basis of the conclusions to this work as a whole. Before proceeding to that general conclusion, some brief conclusions are drawn from the present chapter.

CONCLUSION

This was a chapter in which the method of restatement was applied in the direction of somewhat adverse criticism of the present law. At the outset, it was attempted to establish a sound theoretical basis for the discussion of the remaining forms of transformation of personal work or employment contracts, that is to say suspension and change of parties. That theoretical basis consisted of a general notion of the elasticity of those contracts, against which the scope for suspension or change of parties within the existing contract might be understood and measured. This seemed to be a coherent notion, which made useful links with discussions in earlier chapters, such as that which dealt with the internal structure and continuity of personal work or employment contracts; but its application to the current law of suspension and change of parties proved rather problematical.

With regard to suspension it turned out to be extremely difficult to arrive at a consistent view, across the full range of relevant factual situations, of what contractual suspension meant and in what circumstances it was deemed to occur. The effort was made to establish a common theory of contractual suspension across areas such as those of disciplinary suspension, economic suspension, suspension during industrial action, sickness, and 'garden leave', but there seemed to be a deep-seated lack of reconciliation between the understanding and application of the notion of suspension in these different areas. Great uncertainties and possible inconsistences were revealed with regard to the crucial notions of contractual mutuality and continuity. This suggests a real need for authoritative reformulation of the law in those various areas.

Comparable difficulties presented themselves with regard to partial or total change of parties. The trenchant simplicity of the common law doctrine against imposed change of the employing enterprise, associated with the decision in *Nokes v Doncaster Amalgamated Collieries Ltd*, proved hard to square with the complexities of the law concerning changes in the composition of employing partnerships, and even more so with those of the law concerning corporate insolvency and restructuring, where, in addition to other difficulties, there was a problem that apparent propositions about the effect of such occurrences upon employment contracts often turned out to be based upon antiquated states of company law. All those problems fade into insignificance by comparison with the new set of issues of contractual doctrine and construction which are presented by the very different approach to change of parties which is taken by the TUPE Regulations in implementation of European Community legislation concerning the acquired rights of workers upon the transfer of undertakings.

Moreover those Regulations, by confining themselves to employees under contracts of employment, provide another of those statutory wedges driven firmly between the two subcategories of personal work or employment contracts, that is to say between contracts of employment and semi-dependent workers' contracts. Such is the sensitivity in policy terms of the application of the TUPE Regulations that it is hard to foresee their extension to semi-dependent workers, but it nevertheless seems appropriate to draw attention to the problems of theoretical disharmony which that confinement of their personal scope seems to present. This is, perhaps, a rather unduly negative note upon which to conclude our primary discussion of the present state of the law of personal work or employment contracts; we turn to consider the overall outcome of that analysis in the general conclusion to this work.

Conclusion: Towards a Codification of Personal Work Contracts—Relation and Contract in Employment Law

In the Introduction to this work, we undertook to conclude with an assessment of how feasible and useful the project of expansion and restatement of the law of the contract of employment had proved to be. In this Conclusion it will be suggested that the project is a feasible and useful one, but that this work has turned out to be a preliminary part of it rather than the complete execution of it. We suggest that the complete execution of it would consist of an authoritative codification of the law of personal work or employment contracts. If that larger project were to be undertaken in the future, as a public exercise in law revision and law reform, that would involve a heavy investment of creative energy on the part of those concerned with the theoretical and practical development of employment law. We proceed to consider whether the preliminary work has indicated that this would be a sound investment both in practical and in theoretical terms.

We begin with a very brief assessment of how the project of expansion and restatement has developed through the work and in what directions it has tended. The initial and crucial step was that of establishing the personal work or employment contract as a clear and coherent definitional category for a composite analysis in contractual terms of semi-dependent as well as fully dependent work or employment relations. It seemed feasible and useful to do this in a way which was aligned with the statutory conceptions of the employed person and the worker which are increasingly being used to designate the personal scope of employment legislation. We suggest that this proves to be a good way of establishing the outline of the territory of contractual employment relations, in the sense that the employment relationships which fall within that boundary display far more similarities than they do differences. The case for a contractual analysis which brings them together seemed to be a very strong one in theoretical terms.

Within the definitional category which was thus established, it seemed feasible, using the method of restatement, to give a reasonably clear composite account of the law concerning the formation, structure, content, termination, and transformation of the contracts concerned, and to propose general theoretical analyses of the approaches taken to judicial interpretation and construction of the law of personal employment

contracts under those various headings. Thus a general theory of interpretation of content and a general theory of termination and transformation
were sketched out for personal employment contracts as a composite category, and reasoning of that kind did not seem to be artificial or distorting of
the law as it is. It seemed possible to make quite extensive use of the method
of restatement in a descriptive way, and to offer reformulations of the existing law which were simply articulations or clarifications of existing doctrine.

However, at many points the analysis which resulted from applying the
method of restatement to the extended category of personal employment
contracts was a critical and prescriptive one, which directed attention at
areas of considerable conceptual and practical uncertainty or lack of coherence. This might be because analysis from the perspective of personal
employment contracts as a whole threw into even more stark relief some
problems previously considered within the narrower context of the law of
the contract of employment, such as the extreme resistance to the construction of employment relations as multilateral contracts. On other occasions, critical and prescriptive points were directed at gaps and at deep
uncertainties in the common law account of semi-dependent workers' contracts, where the law was often found to be extremely sketchy or tenuous,
as for example with regard to the application of the obligation of mutual
trust and confidence to those contracts.

On yet other occasions, critical and prescriptive argument was directed
at situations where the application of statutory provisions directly inform-
ing the content or operation of employment contracts seemed to create
serious anomalies or uncertainties. This might occur where statutory provisions applied only to contracts of employment, when there would seem to
be a strong functional case for applying them across the whole spectrum of
personal employment contracts. Such an argument was advanced with
regard to the provisions concerning statutory particulars of terms of
employment. Moreover, there might be deep difficulties of integration or
reconciliation where statutory conceptions were imposed directly upon
those of the common law, as was observed with regard to the TUPE
Regulations and the newly enacted Fixed-term Employees Regulations.

In the course of the development of the successive chapters of the present work, it became apparent to the author that the project of restatement
was assuming such a prescriptive form that it could not be concluded as a
free-standing or self-sufficient exercise in doctrinal exposition and clarification. Whereas it had been left as an open question at the outset as to
how far effective restatement would have to consist of authoritative reformulation through case law or by legislative pronouncement, by the end it
was clear that extensive reformulation in that positive law sense would be
required if the underlying aim of the present work was to be achieved.
Furthermore, if this reformulation were to be systematic with regard to the
problems and anomalies which had been revealed, and were to resolve the

policy questions which had arisen, it would need to be effected by legislative authority rather than judicial authority.

So, not without a good deal of diffidence, the author acknowledges that his argument tends towards, and ends up by advocating, a legislative codification of the law of personal work or employment contracts. The present work should be seen as doing no more than making out a case for such a codification and presenting some indications as to the form which it might in detail take. It is a signpost pointing down a road which may never be followed. However, as a decision to follow this road would involve the allocation of many intellectual and practical resources on the part of those concerned with the development of employment law, it is important to consider carefully whether it would be the best direction for that development to take. At the outset of this work, we advanced arguments which seemed to justify embarking upon what turns out to be the preliminary phase of a larger enterprise. It is appropriate to revisit those arguments in retrospect, to see whether the arguments developed during the work might support further investment.

It will be recalled that the starting point of the present work was the acceptance of a set of doubts about the adequacy or suitability of the contract of employment to serve or function as the foundational conception or institution of employment law. The analysis which has been conducted has reinforced those doubts, but has tended inexorably towards presenting the expanded category of the personal work or employment contract to take the place of the contract of employment as that foundational conception or institution. This is therefore an exercise in re-validating the central role of contract law in employment law; the claim is that it is possible and desirable to do that by refocusing on this different and enlarged contract type, the personal employment contract. The question is whether or how far that claim has been sustained.

That question may be focused more precisely. It will further be recalled that the challenge to the contract of employment as the foundational conception of employment law has frequently, and powerfully, taken the form of argument that employment law should focus directly upon a conception of the employment relationship or relation as its foundational or definitional institution. That line of argument away from the contract of employment has now been developed further, and on a European scale, by Alain Supiot and his colleagues in the report which they made to the European Commission in 1999, recently published in English under the title of 'Beyond Employment: Changes in Work and the Future of Labour Law in Europe'.[1] That report urges a radical shift towards a new foundational conception consisting of a 'labour force membership status for individuals'.[2]

---

[1] Supiot 2001.
[2] Ibid at 50–52. The concept in the language of the original report is 'statut professionnel' or 'état professionnel des personnes'. See Deakin 2002 at 189 and especially at footnote 42

At the domestic level, Hugh Collins, Paul Davies and Roger Rideout used the notion of 'legal regulation of the employment relation' to provide the title and organizing conception for a recent workshop and symposium of papers about 'the regulation of the contract of employment and the institutional framework within which it operates'.[3] Janet Gaymer has, equally, represented the law of employment contracts around a central organizing conception of the 'employment relationship'.[4]

In view of this weighty body of academic and practitioner opinion renewing the earlier calls for a non-contractual and directly relational conception at the institutional heart of employment law, we therefore have to question specially carefully a proposal to develop employment law within a framework which remains an essentially contractual one. We have to ask whether the extension of the central contractual category of employment law from that of the contract of employment to that of the personal work or employment contract, and the analysis according to the method of restatement, represent a positive advance upon the existing law or an uneasy compromise with it. We endeavour to tease out some premises upon which such doubts might be based, and then, as far as possible, to address those doubts head on.

The push towards a relational notion as a central organizing institution for employment law implies a rejection of the contract of employment as an organizing concept at several levels. At one level, it merely rejects the contract of employment as an excessively narrow contractual category. At other levels, it involves a deeper scepticism about a contractual formulation of any kind, a doubt about the suitability of developing employment law in the whole domain of contract law. Expanding the central contractual category from that of the contract of employment to that of the personal work or employment contract may hope to address the doubts at the first level, but will not meet the ones which arise at those deeper levels. So it is important to identify what those are or might be.

They seem to be of two kinds, which are divergent and perhaps even ultimately conflicting. The first kind could be described as concerns about the dead hand of master and servant law. The second kind could be described as concerns about the poverty of general contract law in an employment context. The concern about the dead hand of master and servant law is the perception that the law of employment contracts is inevitably imbued with the values and approaches of social and economic subordination which were transferred from the old law of master and servant to the modern law of the contract of employment, and that the expansion of the central organizing

for perceptive comments on the nature of this concept and how the original language would best be translated; he suggests 'labour market status'.

[3] Collins, Davies & Rideout 2000, see Preface at v.
[4] See Gaymer 2001, Chapter 1, 'Introduction to the Employment Relationship'.

category to include semi-dependent workers merely effects a further transfer of the same values and approaches.

The concern about the poverty of general contract law in an employment context, on the other hand, represents the different idea that contract law outside or beyond the sphere of employment is in its nature commercialistic or mercantilist, essentially committed to the values and techniques of private law in a narrow sense. From the perspective of those concerns, the kind of expansion and restatement of the law of the contract of employment in which the present work has engaged, and the codification for which it argues, might seem to be not so much an advance towards a better kind of employment law as a leap from the frying pan into the fire.

Both sets of concerns are very real ones with regard to the project of the present work, and we do not suggest that they can be disposed of merely by distinguishing between them. Nevertheless, it does seem to be useful to consider them one by one, and therefore to look first at the problem of pervasiveness or persistence of the values and approaches of master and servant law. At the risk of seeming over-optimistic, we suggest that this is rather less of an issue than it was at the time when the original work, from which the present one is derived, was written. The influence of employment protection legislation, both direct and indirect, upon the law of employment contracts has not been inconsiderable. The development of the mutual obligation of trust and confidence in favour of the worker has been of major significance.

There is, not least because of that latter development, more continuity of approach between the case law concerning the employment of directors and senior managers and that concerning workers elsewhere in institutional hierarchies than there was at that earlier time. Moreover, although not profoundly reflexive of the importance of collective bargaining to the individual employment relationship, the law of employment contracts no longer seems oblivious to it.[5] Important areas remain in which the earlier approaches are still manifest; the unrestricted notice/restricted remedies approach to unilateral termination by the employing entity is a major instance. But such thinking is not ubiquitous throughout the law of employment contracts in the way it formerly was.

Turning to the concern about the poverty of general contract law in an employment context, we suggest that it is possible to be bolder in meeting this concern, indeed to the point of asserting that general contract law in its current state of development provides in some respects a positively suitable conceptual apparatus for the development of the law of the

---

[5] Though the author remains of the view that the decision in *Associated Newspapers Ltd v Wilson* [1995] ICR 406 (HL) was an important lapse; see above, 49. Compare now the decision of the European Court of Human Rights, arising out of the same proceedings, in *Wilson and NUJ v United Kingdom* [2002] IRLR 128; see above, 49.

employment relationship. That is because of the way that, both in theoretical terms and in terms of positive law, general contract law is evolving from an apparatus primarily for the construction and enforcement of voluntary agreements into a body of law for the regulating of contracting[6] in a wider sense. This is the long-term evolution portrayed by Patrick Atiyah in his study of 'The Rise and Fall of Freedom of Contract';[7] it has if anything accelerated since that work was written.

There are two particular respects in which we suggest that this broad trend in the theoretical and practical development of the general law of contract has created a positive environment for the development of employment law in contractual terms. Firstly, it has involved, both conceptually and in positive law, an enhanced recognition of the relational dimension of contracting, and an associated heightening of concern with notions of good faith and the implementation of implicit contracts. The evolution of the implied obligation of mutual trust and confidence in the employment contract does not seem isolated in that larger analytical context.

Secondly, and even more significantly, we suggest that the exponential growth, latterly under the influence of EC Law, of legislative regulation of the fairness of contracting, in the field of contracting with individual consumers of goods and services, has brought about a revolution in the normative structure of general contract law. That is to say, it has to a considerable extent refocused contract law on the intensely difficult task of interrelating statutory norms with those of the standard-form contracts which providers of goods and services offer to the consumers of them. This involves, at a profoundly difficult and complex level, a re-conceptualization in general and in detail of the relation between *jus dispositivum* and *jus cogens*, that is to say the aspects in which the shape and content of economic or social relations are open to be settled by individual agreement or are mandated by external norms such as those of statute law or of self-regulating associations.

Our suggestion is that this set of preoccupations of general contract law corresponds very closely to the regulatory tasks of employment law.[8] The demand for a central institutional focus on the employment relationship rather than upon the contract of employment is in large measure the result of a perceived rigidity of the law of the contract of employment in tempering the unilateral power of the employing entity to make and change the norms of employment by reference to the norms of employment protection legislation and of collective bargaining. It is at least arguable that modern contract law provides the best available conceptual apparatus and environment within which to carry out that set of tasks.

---

[6] This alludes directly to the set of ideas propounded by Hugh Collins in his recent treatise on 'Regulating Contracts'—Collins 2001.   [7] Atiyah 1983.

[8] The present author has advanced a similar suggestion in a recent essay about '*Jus cogens* and *jus dispositivum* in the law of personal work contracts' (Freedland 2002).

If the foregoing arguments succeed in making out a case for investment in the development of the law of the employment relation by means of restatement or codification of the law of personal employment contracts, they also give some indication both of the nature and of the magnitude of the effort which that task requires. The analyses in the foregoing chapters constitute no more than preliminary *travaux preparatoires*. Theorists in the field have provided important pieces of groundwork. At the risk of being invidious, we point again, as earlier in this work, to Douglas Brodie's study of 'Legal Coherence and the Employment Revolution',[9] to Simon Deakin's study of 'The Many Futures of the Contract of Employment',[10] and to Gillian Morris' discussion of 'The Exclusion of Fundamental Rights by Agreement'.[11] The present author hopes both to have made out a case for the codification of the law of personal work or employment contracts, to have encouraged others to pursue that task, and to have provided some initial pointers towards the paths which might be followed in so doing.

[9] Brodie 2001a.   [10] Deakin 2002.   [11] Morris 2001.

Bibliography

Anderman, S. D., 'The Interpretation of Protective Employment Statutes and Contracts of Employment' (2000) 29 ILJ 223

Atiyah, P. S., *The Rise and Fall of Freedom of Contract* (Oxford: Clarendon Press, 1979)

Barrett, B., 'Clarification of Employers' Liability for Work-Related Stress' (2002) 31 ILJ 285

Beatson, J., 'The Role of Statute in the Development of Common Law Doctrine' (2001) 117 LQR 247

Beatson, J., and Friedmann, D., *Good Faith and Fault in Contract Law* (Oxford: Clarendon Press, 1995)

Brodie, D., 'The Heart of the Matter: Mutual Trust and Confidence' (1996) 25 ILJ 121

Brodie, D., 'Beyond Exchange: the New Contract of Employment' (1998) 27 ILJ 79

Brodie, D., 'Legal Coherence and the Employment Revolution' (2001) 117 LQR 604 (Brodie 2001a)

Brodie, D., 'Mutual Trust and the Values of the Employment Contract' (2001) 30 ILJ 84 (Brodie 2001b)

Brodie, D., 'Fair Dealing and the Disciplinary Process' (2002) 31 ILJ 294

Brown, W., 'A Consideration of "Custom and Practice"' (1972) 10 BJIR 42

Burchell, B., Deakin, S., and Honey, S., *The Employment Status of Individuals in Non-standard Employment*, EMAR Research Series 6 (Department of Trade and Industry, London, 1999)

Burrows, J. F., 'Contractual Cooperation & the Implied Term' (1968) 31 MLR 390

Caiger, A., and O'Leary, J., 'The Re-Regulation of Football and its Impact on Employment Contracts', Chapter 16 of Collins, H., Davies, P., and Rideout, R. (eds), *Legal Regulation of the Employment Relation* (London: Kluwer Law International, 2000)

Clarke, L., 'Repudiation of Contract and Breach of Confidence' (2003) 33 ILJ 43

Coase, R. H., 'The Nature of the Firm' (1937) *Economica* NS 4 386

Collins, H., 'Market Power, Bureaucratic Power and the Contract of Employment' (1986) 15 ILJ 1

Collins, H., 'Independent Contracts and the Challenge of Vertical Disintegration to Employment Protection Laws' (1990) 10 OJLS 353

Collins, H., *Justice in Dismissal: The Law of Termination of Employment* (Oxford: Clarendon Press, 1992)

Collins, H., *The Law of Contract*, 3rd edn (London: Butterworths, 1997)

Collins, H., *Regulating Contracts* (Oxford: Oxford University Press, 1999)

Collins, H., 'Employment Rights of Casual Workers' (2000) 29 ILJ 73

Collins, H., 'Regulating the Employment Relation for Competitiveness' (2001) 30 ILJ 17

Collins, H., Davies, P. L., and Rideout, R. W., *Legal Regulation of the Employment Relation* (London: Kluwer Law International, 2000)

Collins, H., Ewing, K., and McColgan, A., *Labour Law: Text and Materials* (Oxford: Hart Publishing, 2001)

Crouch, C., *Social Change in Western Europe* (Oxford: Oxford University Press, 1999)

Davies, P. L., 'Employee Claims in Insolvency: Corporate Rescues and Preferential Claims' (1994) 23 ILJ 141

Davies, P. L., and Freedland, M. R., *Labour Law: Text and Materials*, 2nd edn. (London: Weidenfield and Nicolson, 1984)

Davies, P. L., and Freedland, M. R., *Labour Legislation and Public Policy: A Contemporary History* (Oxford: Clarendon Press, 1993)

Davies, P. L., and Freedland, M. R., 'The Impact of Public Law on Labour Law, 1972–1997' (1997) 26 ILJ 311

Deakin, S. F., 'Logical Deductions? Wages Law before and after Delaney v Staples' (1992) 55 MLR 848

Deakin, S. F., 'The Evolution of the Contract of Employment, 1900 to 1950—the Influence of the Welfare State', Chapter 11 of Whiteside, N., and Salais, R., (eds), *Governance, Industry and Labour Markets in Britain and France—The Modernising State in the Mid-Twentieth Century* (London: Routledge, 1998)

Deakin, S. F., 'Organisational Change, Labour Flexibility and the Contract of Employment in Great Britain', in Derry, S., and Mitchell, R. (eds), *Employment Relations, Individualisation and Union Exclusion, An International Study* (Annandale NSW: Federation Press, 1999)

Deakin, S. F., 'Legal Origins of Wage Labour: the Evolution of the Contract of Employment from Industrialisation to Welfare State' in Clarke, L., de Gijsel, P., and Janssen, J. (eds), *The Dynamics of Wage Relations in the New Europe* (Deventer: Kluwer Law International, 2000)

Deakin, S. F., 'The Changing Concept of the "Employer" in Labour Law' (2001) 30 ILJ 72

Deakin, S. F., 'The Many Futures of the Contract of Employment', in Conaghan, J., Fischl, R. M., and Klare, K. (eds), *Labour Law in an Era of Globalisation—Transformative Practices and Possibilities* (Oxford: Oxford University Press, 2002)

Deakin, S. F., and Morris, G. S., *Labour Law*, 3rd edn (London: Butterworths, 2001)

Druker, J., and White, G., *Reward Management: A Critical Text* (London: Routledge, 2000)

Eisenberg, M. A., 'Relational Contracts', Chapter 11 of Beatson, J., and Friedmann, D. (eds), *Good Faith and Fault in Contract Law* (Oxford: Clarendon Press, 1995)

Fodder, M., and Freer, G., 'The Effect of Contractual Provision for Payment in Lieu of Notice' (2001) 30 ILJ 215

Ford, M., 'Rethinking the Notice Rule' (1998) 27 ILJ 220

Foster, K., 'Strikes and Employment Contracts' (1971) 34 MLR 275

Foster, K., 'Strike Notice and Section 147' (1973) 2 ILJ 28

Foster, K., 'The Legal Form of Work in the Nineteenth Century: The Myth of Contract?', Paper presented to conference on The History of Law, Labour and Crime, University of Warwick (1983)

Fox, A., *Beyond Contract: Work, Power and Trust Relations* (London: Faber, 1974)

Fredman, S. F., 'Contractual and Public Law Remedies in Respect of Unilateral Alteration' (1984) 13 ILJ 174

Freedland, M. R., 'The Meaning of "Dismissal" in the Redundancy Payments Act 1965' (1970) 33 MLR 93

Freedland, M. R., *The Contract of Employment* (Oxford: Clarendon Press, 1976)

Freedland, M. R., 'The Crown and the Changing Nature of Government', in Sunkin, M., and Payne, S. (eds), *The Nature of the Crown* (Oxford: Oxford University Press, 1999) (Freedland 1999a)

Freedland, M. R., 'Deductions, Red Herrings, and the Wage–Work Bargain' (1999) 28 ILJ 255 (Freedland 1999b)

Freedland, M. R., 'The Claim for Unfair Dismissal' (2001) 30 ILJ 309

Freedland, M. R., *'Jus cogens* and *jus dispositivum* in the Law of Personal Work Contracts', Chapter XII of Birks, P., and Pretto, A. (eds), *Themes in Comparative Law* (Oxford: Oxford University Press, 2002)

Freedland, M. R., 'Repudiation of Contract and Breach of Confidence' (2003) 32 ILJ 48

Freedman, J., *Employed or Self-employed? Tax Classification of Workers and the Changing Labour Market—Tax Law Review Committee Discussion Paper No. 1* (London: The Institute for Fiscal Studies, 2001)

Gaymer, J., *The Employment Relationship* (London: Sweet & Maxwell, 2001)

Graham, C. B., 'The Effect of Liquidation on Contracts of Service' (1952) 15 MLR 48

Hepple, B. A., 'A Right to Work?' (1981) 10 ILJ 65

Hepple, B. A., 'Restructuring Employment Rights' (1986) 15 ILJ 69

Hepple, B. A., 'Human Rights and the Contract of Employment' (1998) 8 *Amicus Curia* 19

Hepple, B. A., 'The EU Charter of Fundamental Rights' (2001) 30 ILJ 225

Hepple, B. A., and O'Higgins P., *Individual Employment Law: an Introduction* (London; Sweet & Maxwell, 1971)

Kahn-Freund, O., Chapter II of Flanders, A., and Clegg, H. (eds), *The System of Industrial Relations in Great Britain* (Oxford: Blackwell, 1954)

Kahn-Freund, O., 'Binding Effect of a Collective Agreement—Measure of Damages for Breach of Contract of Employment' (1958) 21 MLR 194

Kahn-Freund, O., *Selected Writings* (London: Stevens (published under the auspices of the Modern Law Review), 1978)

Kenner, J., 'Statement or Contract?—Some Reflections on the EC Employee Information (Contract or Employment Relationship) Directive after *Kampelmann*' (1999) 28 ILJ 205

Laws, J., 'Public Law and Employment Law: Abuse of Power' (1997) PL 455

Leighton, P., 'Problems Continue for Zero-Hours Workers' (2002) 31 ILJ 71

Lindsay, J., 'The Implied Term of Trust and Confidence' (2001) 30 ILJ 1

Morris, D., 'Volunteering and Employment Status' (1999) 28 ILJ 249

Morris, G., 'Fundamental Rights: Exclusion by Agreement?' (2001) 30 ILJ 49

Nobles, R., *Pensions, Employment, and the Law* (Oxford: Clarendon Press, 1993)

Palfreyman, D., and Warner, D. (eds), *Higher Education Law*, 2nd edn (Bristol: Jordans, 2002)

Pollard, D., 'Employers' Powers in Pension Schemes: the Implied Duty of Trust and Confidence' (1997) 11(4) Trusts Law International 93

Oliver, D., *Common Values and the Public—Private Divide* (London: Butterworths, 1999)

O'Higgins, P., 'Strike Notices: Another Approach' (1973) 2 ILJ 152

Rideout, R. W., 'The Contract of Employment' (1966) 19 CLP 111

Schwarzer, W. W., 'Wages During Temporary Disability—Partial Impossibility in Employment Contracts' (1952) 5 Stanford LR 30; republished in (1953) 8 Industrial Law Review 12

Sedley, S., 'Public Law and Contractual Employment' (1994) 23 ILJ 201

Skidmore, P., 'Whose Risk is it Anyway? Allocation of Entrepreneurial Risk in Employment Contracts', in Baldwin, R. (ed), *Law and Uncertainty: Risks and Legal Processes* (London: Kluwer Law International, 1997)

Stoljar, S., 'Prevention and Cooperation in the Law of Contract' (1953) 31 Canadian Bar Review 231

Stoljar, S., 'The Great Case of *Cutter v Powell*' (1956) 34 Canadian Bar Review 288

Supiot, A., *Beyond Employment: Changes in Work and the Future of Labour Law in Europe* (Oxford: Oxford University Press, 2001)

Treitel, G. H., *The Law of Contract*, 10th edn (London: Sweet & Maxwell, 1999)

Veneziani, B., 'The Evolution of the Contract of Employment', Chapter 1 of Hepple, B. A. (ed), *The Making of Labour Law in Europe—A Comparative Study of Nine Countries up to 1945* (London: Mansell Publishing Limited, 1986)

Watson, L., 'Employees and the Unfair Contract Terms Act' (1995) 24 ILJ 323

Wedderburn, K. W., and Clark, J., 'Modern Law: Problems, Functions and Policies', Chapter 6 of Wedderburn, K. W., Lewis, R., and Clark, J. (eds), *Labour Law and Industrial Relations* (Oxford: Clarendon Press, 1983)

Index

534   Index

536   Index